THE OFFICIAL PRICE GUIDE

COLLECTOR KNIVES

TENTH EDITION

THE OFFICIAL PRICE GUIDE

COLLECTOR KNIVES

C. HOUSTON PRICE

TENTH EDITION

HOUSE OF COLLECTIBLES • NEW YORK

© 1991 by C. Houston Price

℔ This is a registered trademark of Random House, Inc.

All rights reserved under International and Pan-American Copyright Conventions.

Published by: House of Collectibles
201 East 50th Street
New York, New York 10022

Distributed by Ballantine Books, a division of Random House, Inc., New York, and simultaneously in Canada by Random House of Canada Limited, Toronto.

Manufactured in the United States of America

Library of Congress Catalog Card Number: 84-644082

ISBN: 0-876-37812-2

Tenth Edition: February 1991

10 9 8 7 6 5

TABLE OF CONTENTS

Acknowledgments   vii

1. *Overview of Knife Collecting*   1

Knives and Man   3
History of Knife Collecting   5
Collecting for Pleasure and Profit   9
Specialization   12
Trend Knives   19
Counterfeit Knives   21
Starting and Building a Collection   27

2. *Learning More about Knives*   35

Bowie Knives   37
Custom Knives   48
Silver Folding Fruit Knives   99
Knife Nomenclature   106
Knife Brands of the World   114
Useful Information for Knife Collectors   189
Factors Affecting Knife Values   193
What's Ahead for the 1990s?   196

3. *Knife Manufacturers*   199

Histories and Listings of Knife Manufacturers   201

4. *Commemorative and Limited-Edition Knives*   647

Listings of Commemorative and Limited-Edition Knives   649

5. *Resources*   705
   Knife Collectors' Clubs   707
   Bibliography   712
   Index   719

ACKNOWLEDGMENTS

I especially appreciate the advice and assistance given by Bob Cargill, Craig Henry, Bill Karsten, Steve Koontz, John Parker, Kevin Pipes, Clarence Risner, Cindy Taylor, and Herman Williams in helping to determine values of specific knife brands.

The way has been paved and made much smoother by earlier reference works by Jim Parker and Bruce Voyles, Jim Sargent, Bernard Levine, Ron Stewart and Roy Ritchie, Dewey Ferguson, and several others. Having read and relied on some of these for quite some time, I perhaps took them too much for granted. This task has reminded me of the progress made during the past dozen or so years and has stimulated a greater appreciation for all who have worked so hard in providing information for collectors. Without these and other researchers, such as Dennis Ellingsen, John Goins, Bill Karsten, Phillip Krumholz, Kurt Moe, Philip Pankiewicz, Allen Swayne, and Cindy and Jim Taylor, as well as numerous other knife collectors who share their knowledge, knife collecting would not have progressed nearly so far.

Wherever I've turned, there has been help as well as encouragement. John Parker and Kevin Pipes of Smoky Mountain Knifeworks have been especially helpful by sharing information and photographs. Jim Weyer has shared the use of some of his exceptional photographs of custom knives. Bernard Levine's exhaustive research within the cutlery field has been an inspiration to me for a number of years; his friendship has been especially meaningful as I labored with this first effort.

There are others. Their names may not be as well known to those who pursue our hobby, but without them this manuscript would never have been completed. My special thanks to Anita Dodson, who spent countless hours typing facts and figures that must have been terribly boring to her, and to Kim Knott, who not only shared the workload of typing and proofing but who offered helpful comments along the way.

My greatest debt of gratitude is to Betty, my wife of thirty-five years. She has supported this effort with tangible and direct contributions such as typing, proofing, and advising; but she has provided the greatest support through countless indirect contributions. As I've worked long into the nights during the past several months, she has allowed me the freedom to do so by taking care of many chores around our home that I should have been doing. She has survived short tempers (mine), frustrations (mine), complaints (mine), faltering confidence and commitment (mine), and crashed computers. I doubt that there has been another period of our lives together when I have leaned on her more or for such a long period. This book is dedicated to her. Without her dedication and commitment, this project would not have been possible.

PART

◁ **1** ▷

Overview of Knife Collecting

KNIVES AND MAN

Wherever on this planet archeologists find evidence of human existence, there also will be found knives in some form. Knives represent one of the first and most useful tools of survival because, without the knife and its development over the ages, there would be no civilization today.

The precursor of the knife was a flake of broken stone, created not by man but by nature. As many as a million years ago, its utility of adding a cutting edge to the hand was recognized, and the edged tool would help assure human dominance over lower animals. Some fifty thousand years ago, man learned to improve on nature by flaking both sides of the stone into beveled edges, and the first knife was created. The Stone Age left us with cutting, scraping, and stabbing tools made of flint, obsidian, slate, or other stones, such as quartz or hard limestone. Although stone was most often used for early knives, it was sometimes supplemented by bone, teeth, stag horn, or other animal-origin materials. As we view these cutlery artifacts today, they may seem crude, but our existence should be a reminder that they served and served well.

The cave dwellers who used them understood the importance of good cutting tools to their survival. One has only to examine a Stone Age flint knife closely to gain respect for the attention paid to the quality of raw materials (stone) and the care dedicated to shaping it into a tool designed for a specific purpose. Wherever it was available, flintstone was recognized as the desirable cutlery material, and it was often used in preference to most other minerals. There is even evidence that flintstone was traded and transported from areas of abundance to other areas lacking in the desirable stone. As a tool, as a weapon, and as the working implement most personal to humans, knives meant survival. Nothing else could have been so important to the carvers of our modern civilization.

With the passage of thousands of years, knives made from stones such as flint, obsidian, or slate were replaced with knives and other cutting instruments made of metals. People had already learned that chipping these stones into certain shapes made them more useful for specific purposes. Stone knives for defense against predators and for taking game as food were usually shaped differently from those that were used in other ways. The discovery and development of bronze and iron, copper and tin, and eventually, steel, allowed people greater freedom to shape and design their cutting or stabbing instruments. The knife could be made much longer and become a sword. It could be shaped into a long curved knife and become a scythe. It could be given greater weight and a special new shape to become an ax. Whatever shape it took, the knife as a tool was becoming more and more useful.

The making of edged tools became so important that an industry of sorts began to develop. Man had learned not only how to best shape metals for knives of his purpose, but, as early as 1000 B.C., he learned to harden metals to make knives of better quality. The cutler's trade, as we would understand it today, began to take shape in the Middle Ages. Production of steel had started to develop in England and Germany during the 10th and 11th centuries. It was only natural that cutlery crafting would follow.

Cutlery centers developed in several parts of the world, so when we think of swords, the names Samurai (Japan) or Toledo (Spain) or Damascus (Syria) come to mind. Likewise, when we think of pocketknives, the names Sheffield and Solingen remind us that England and Germany have had the greatest influence on America's cutlery industry. Not only did a large percentage of our earlier knives come from those countries, but our own manufacturing processes most closely followed theirs. Many of the founders of and workers in the early American cutlery industry had emigrated from England and Germany. The knowledge and skills brought with them helped assure the success of an infant industry in a young country, an industry that would produce the knives we so highly value today.

For thousands of years, the knife has remained the tool that has been most personal to man. Whether it's of flint or steel, an old knife is a material piece of history. It is a personal tool that has survived its maker and original owner. It is our connection to the past, our tangible proof that the old times did exist. Therein lies its romance as a collectible.

HISTORY OF KNIFE COLLECTING

▽

Welcome to a knife renaissance. Although not exactly new, the interest in knives as collectibles is still in its infancy throughout the United States and in several other countries. We are in an era in which there seems to be an almost boundless interest in knives as history, knives as examples of hand craftsmanship, and knives as art objects to be accumulated and passed on to succeeding generations. Collectors have come not only to realize a fascination to knives but also to recognize their value.

Each year, knife shows held throughout the nation attract more and more collectors, dealers, and custom knife makers. Knife clubs, both national and local in scope, can boast of record-setting membership. Publishers have printed dozens of books as well as a growing number of regularly published magazines about knives. It's natural to wonder just where and how it all began.

Since it's impossible to separate knife collecting from knife trading, the genesis of our hobby is probably in the earliest days of our country. Because the knife was a very personal tool and one that was often the object of personal pride, people have always been persuaded to continually seek something perceived as better. "Trading up" to a knife, a gun, or a horse of better quality was a normal event during the pioneering days.

In our own century, knife trading is often attributed to the "courthouse whittlers," who whittled and whiled the time away as they praised the virtues of their pocketknives. Before long, that special knife was traded and would become the pride and joy of another whittler; that is, until it was traded again, often within hours of the earlier trade.

"First Monday Trade Days" were monthly highlights in the lives of many rural folk. That day, especially for the men, was not for work, unless farm-raised products were to be taken for sale or trade. Instead, it was a day to take horses and mules, guns and knives, and whatever else one might want to "swap on" to town to the "bone yard." It was not unusual for a man to spend the entire day "horse trading" on dozens of objects, only to trade again for whatever he brought that morning. After all, that item was too popular as a trade item to let it go. The spirit of "trade days" still lives today, although much more modernized, in garage sales and flea markets.

Some say that knife trading began in the southeast, and there are many who would still allude to that part of the country as "the knife collecting capital of the world." Knife trading and, as a consequence, knife accumulating has been a part of our nation's history from its earliest days. Regardless of whether we hail from north, south, east, west, or somewhere in between, most of us can recall swapping knives. Knife trading, knife accumulating, and ultimately, knife collecting have always been and will continue to be a national avocation.

So the evolution of knife collecting and trading may have taken centuries or even millennia—perhaps even the cavemen swapped their flintstone knives and spears. But the revolution began about two or three decades ago.

There have been several factors contributing to the growing interest in knives as collectibles and as investment pieces. One catalyst was the Gun Control Act of 1968, which made selling and trading guns much more difficult. Since gun shows were already quite popular, the transfer of interest and trading activities from guns to knives was a rather natural course. Through the gun show circuits, antique Bowie knives and military cutlery items had already found their fanciers; antique pocketknives and modern custom knives would soon follow.

A little earlier, in 1965, new government regulations had required every piece of cutlery sold in the United States to be stamped with country of origin. W. R. Case & Sons Cutlery, one of the nation's leading knife manufacturers, revamped its marking system. The trademark, Case XX, was changed to Case XX USA. The change had drawn very little attention until the 1968 act curtailed the gun collectors' interstate trading and many of them decided to switch to knives.

Because Case already enjoyed an excellent reputation for quality and their system made it easy to understand dates of manufacture, their knives quickly captured the lead in the demand for older knives. Before long, growing numbers of bargain hunters and knife traders made their rounds to practically every country store, buying complete dealer displays of Case knives as well as other knives that had been in the dealer's stock for a few years. As these backroad-riding entrepreneurs began gathering for their own buy, swap, and sell events, the knife show came into its own.

Several of these knife traders and seekers of opportunity began to make collectible knives their business. They had the foresight to expand their activities into areas that were nearly impossible to reach by personal travel. The answer was advertisements seeking knives to buy and offering knives for sale in the gun traders' standby, *Shotgun News,* and other magazines such as *Antique Trader.* And before long, they began to mail lists of old knives for sale or trade to collectors or other dealers who would subscribe.

With the arrival of the 1970s, collectors and dealers saw Case change its tang stamping, this time adding ten dots under the Case XX USA marking. The announced intent was to remove a dot each year until 1980, at which time the marking would again change. The dealers and collectors who had chased after the Case XX dealer display boards were now joined by newcomers as they competed in the search for those containing knives stamped USA. Even as they searched, these knife enthusiasts were aided by a new reference book, *Romance of Collecting Case Knives* by Dewey Ferguson.

The only knife publication at that time was *The Blue Mill Blade,* edited by Roy Scott of Del Rio, Tennessee. At Scott's suggestion, a small group of dealers and collectors met on June 9, 1972, and formed the National Knife Collectors and Dealers Association (NKC&DA). This organization, whose members were primarily concerned with antique factory-made knives, would be a positive force in the growing interest of collecting. Meanwhile, another organization, The Knife Collectors Club, was founded by A. G. Russell; its primary emphasis was on custom knives.

The NKC&DA began to sponsor knife shows in a number of cities, promoting trading, buying, and selling of pocketknives. Promotion of custom knives was spearheaded by a new magazine, *The American Blade,* whose premier issue was published in Atlanta in 1973—just as the new knife shows were becoming a reality. Other publications soon followed. In 1975, a classified trade paper named *Knife World* was first published in St. Louis. Two years later, under new ownership, it was relocated to Knoxville, Tennessee, and the format changed to include editorial coverage of collectible knives. NKC&DA introduced its newsletter in 1976 and built it into the *National Knife Collector* magazine in 1977. Reference books and regularly published resource materials were sorely needed by collectors during these early years. Those published during the 1970s can be credited with not only providing information but also with increasing public awareness of a new hobby.

Another major undertaking was begun in 1978, when the National Knife Collectors Association vowed to build a knife museum. Three years later, the National Knife Collectors Museum's grand opening was held.

Continued growth in numbers of collectors went hand in hand during the 1980s with a substantial increase in published works relating to knives. The cause-and-effect relationship has been good for the hobby. Knife collecting interest grew at a rather rapid pace into and through the 1980s as more and more collectors came to recognize the fascination of old knives as pieces of Americana to which most of them could personally relate. And they came to recognize their increasing value. Coincidentally, this period also saw the number of established custom knife makers increase from a few dozen to hundreds. Their customers were people with the desire to own a very special knife and willing to pay a relatively high price for it. The common denominator was recognition of the value of knives, whether antique or newly made one-of-a-kind pieces.

Collectors are still learning that there is something in the knife-collecting field for every budget; and with their investment, regardless of whether it is in knives valued at $5 each or knives that cost several hundred dollars, comes the satisfaction of building a meaningful collection, one that should pay dividends if and when the decision is made to sell.

If you have been a part of the hobby during these years, take a little bow for the part you've played in its growth. If you're a newcomer, welcome—and enjoy!

COLLECTING FOR
PLEASURE AND PROFIT

▽

Every collector, regardless of the collecting field, has decided to become involved for specific and personal reasons. They may be many or few, and the incentives for one may not necessarily be so important to another; they are often very different. The two primary inducements for most collectors, however, are pleasure and profit. The differences usually come in the emphasis one places on each of these motivating factors. Knife collecting can and will fulfill either or both of these goals; the degree of gratification depends on the goals set and steps taken to achieve those goals.

Whether or not pleasure is the primary motivating factor, no one should be involved in knife collecting unless some degree of personal pleasure is derived from the hobby. Regardless of the priority, pleasure in collecting must have its place on the bottom line. To the person who likes knives, collecting them will reap rewards and bring few disappointments. On the other hand, the person who has little fondness or appreciation for knives and is simply seeking profit may do just as well—perhaps better—in a different field.

But make no mistake: there is definitely the potential for profit to the knife collector who defines his goals and invests wisely. Knives, both new and old, have an excellent track record for value increase. As with other types of collectibles, the rate of increase will vary with overall economic conditions. During periods of low to moderate inflation rates, the value increase tends to be substantially less than in higher inflationary periods. At these times, overall value gains of 10 percent per annum are generally considered good. But when the inflation rate is high, as it was during the early part of the last decade, collectibles tend to outpace many other investments in their value increase. For instance, near the turn into the 1980s, knives joined other collectibles in value gains of up to three times the inflation rate.

One may wonder why inflation has such an effect on the prices of knives and other collectibles. Since they are basically resale items, the cost of manufacturing, advertising, and marketing was borne years ago. Although some people consider collectibles as secondhand junk, the collector knows that they are in demand, and demand affects selling price, which establishes value. Collectible knives are certainly valuable, but they are also tangible items that can be held, admired, and put away as hedges against inflation. Whenever a soaring inflation rate exceeds returns on traditional investments such as stocks, bonds, and other securities, investors look for so-called hard assets. Precious gems and metals are joined by collectibles, and in the realm of collectibles, knives have performed extremely well.

A great number of knives purchased a few short years ago are now selling for considerably more than their purchase prices. Although potential profit is recognized by their owners, it may not be realized for a long while because many of these knives are owned by collectors and knife enthusiasts who refuse to sell. And one must always remember that profit or loss does not occur without a sales transaction. As long as demand exceeds supply, prices will continue to rise. For years, comments have been made that the older and more respectable collector knives were getting very hard to find. These comments were often interpreted as a sales pitch to the novice collector. But the time has arrived when practically every collector recognizes the continually increasing demand for those choice collectibles that can be found in the marketplace.

The prices paid for more desirable antique knives continue to rise, and one can only guess when and at what level the peak will come. But there is one foreseeable aspect to the inflation of knife values, and that is the increasing demand for collectible knives in less than mint condition. Although there was a time when the collector was advised to purchase only mint condition knives, that advice is less sound with passing years. Today's astute collector may well be found purchasing knives that, a few years ago, would have been passed by in the search for a mint specimen. There are now a number of collectors who will reconcile themselves to adding these "good" condition knives to their collections, hoping to use them as hedges to increasing knife values and waiting for the opportunity to trade up to an even better specimen. Meanwhile, the pleasure of the search, the gratification of the find, and the pride of owning the new addition to the collection is there.

No one can tell you when to buy—whenever that is, it will have been too late. No one can tell you when to sell—whenever that is, it will have been too early. Will Rogers has been credited with advising a prospective investor, "If it goes up, sell; if it don't go up, don't buy." The decision to buy or to sell must be a personal one but should always be based on the best information at hand. A major factor in the decision should always be one's personal feelings about the knife being bought or sold—keep pleasure and profit in their proper perspective. The what-if's, the I-wish-I-had's, and the I-shouldn't-have's will haunt every stock investor, every land speculator, and, yes, every knife collector who has profit as the primary inducement. If pleasure has played its role, the profits will be sweet; if there are losses, they will not be nearly so bitter.

It is not the purpose of this book to tell one when to buy or when to sell or at what price. Its purpose is to offer information and resources that will help in making those decisions. Only through learning more about knives can the serious collector reap the harvests of pleasure and profit. Assimilation of information should go hand in hand with the acquisition of knives. For collectors who know knives and know the market, profits can be earned on any given day. But those who combine their knowledge with a fondness for knives will profit every day in the pleasure derived from this hobby.

SPECIALIZATION

The majority of knife collectors began their involvement in the hobby as accumulators, and there is nothing at all wrong with that approach. It is, after all, a normal occurrence for the person who likes knives and likes them well enough to buy more than can be carried or used at any one time. The foundation for many of today's highly regarded collections was laid by the purchase of knives that especially appealed to the budding collector. They were carried, used, and eventually put alongside others in a dresser drawer or box, where they became part of the accumulation. Usually, the growth in interest goes hand in hand with the increase in number of knives, and a decision is made to specialize.

Specialization in knife collecting is heartily recommended for several reasons. It makes a collection even more meaningful when specific goals are pursued. A sense of rhyme, reason, and direction adds to the pleasure of acquiring more knives. With a goal comes challenge, and with challenge comes the satisfaction of achieving that goal. Specialization allows one to tailor his collecting to best suit the budget while conscientiously building a collection that is likely to appreciate in value.

Further, specialization allows for a high level of expertise in the chosen area. With the thousands of different knives available to collectors, it is practically impossible to learn a great deal about the majority of them. On the other hand, it is not only possible but entirely feasible for a collector to become an expert in one or a few knife-collecting specialties.

Knife collecting is certainly one of today's most versatile hobbies and there is a special area suited for most anyone. Choosing a specialty is in no way making a permanent commitment, and one should recognize that a change or further refinement is often in store at some future date when the collection becomes more "mature." The search for a greater challenge almost always reveals another specialty—another opportunity—just around the corner.

Perhaps you have already selected one or a few areas for concentrating your efforts and funds as your collection grows, or you may have specialized in an area and determined that further refinement is in order. If a newcomer to the hobby, you may be now at the point of refining an accumulation of knives into a more meaningful collection. Whatever the situation, one should be aware of the choices available in order to determine which best fits a particular interest, the goals in collecting, and the financial means to pursue those goals. Some general areas to consider in choosing a collecting specialty are factory-made (or production) knives, custom knives, antique Bowie knives, military knives, and commemorative or limited-edition knives. Each area has its challenges and rewards; each has its pros and cons. The following discussions may be helpful in determining which is best for you.

FACTORY (PRODUCTION) KNIVES

Those who elect to collect factory-made knives represent the majority of knife collectors. But that is appropriate because the greatest share of knives produced were and still are those made by cutlery manufacturers. The collector who determines that the knives he likes best are those made in industrial settings still has an almost endless number of choices available. The most distinct line for division of collectible factory knives is that of antique or old knives and those of modern or current manufacture.

To the average factory-knife collector, "old knives" is a relative term and one subject to individual interpretation. Old may not necessarily mean antique, although antique always signifies old. Either category almost always means collectible and valuable. A case in point (pun not intended) are those knives made by W. R. Case & Sons Cutlery twenty to twenty-five years ago and stamped Case XX USA. They would not technically qualify as antiques but still are highly desirable to collectors. As a consequence, their current market value is several times their retail price when originally marketed. The fact of collector demand for and value of old and antique knives has been well established over a period of several years. Names such as Case, Remington, Winchester, and Cattaraugus join with a host of others in singing magic to the ears of collectors. Their worth has been proved, and their values continue to climb, making them a specialty that generally requires a higher "entry fee." But the established market allows one to determine which brand, pattern, era of manufacture, and so on best suits his collecting interest and his pocketbook.

Somewhat to the contrary, knives of modern or current manufacture offer greater speculative latitude. This is not to imply that knives in this category are not in demand and valued quite highly by collectors—far from it. Perhaps the area presenting the greatest opportunity to the greatest number of collectors during the decade of the 1990s is new knives. Several brand names, although relatively new, still have a high degree of visibility in the knife-collecting world. Rather than being obscure or of little collector interest, knives stamped with names such as Fight'n Rooster, Cripple Creek, Bulldog, Parker, Frost, or several others can be dominant at some knife shows and in other trading circles. These brands are examples of new knives that are well entrenched within the knife world. Unlike the antique knives that were designed, manufactured, and sold to be used, these knives were born of the recent collecting renaissance. Their popularity as collectibles was and is a major purpose of their manufacture. A very respectable number of these knives have proved or are currently proving their worth as collectibles, especially in certain regions of the country. However, their recognition and acceptance on a national basis is yet to come. Therein lies their speculative nature. Building a collection of current knives will require a lower cash outlay but still will offer rewards such as pride of ownership and potential value appreciation.

Once a collector determines whether to collect old knives or current knives, he still has further opportunities for refinement. It may be specialization by manufacturer's brand, especially if that manufacturer has produced or is producing a rather limited number of patterns or models. Whenever the numbers become too large, further specialization is in order. Specialties may be in the form of patterns and/or handle materials, or they may relate to knives with a particular tang stamping. For example, it is not unusual to find a Case collector specializing in bone-handled Muskrat pattern knives made prior to the 1960s or to find a collector of Remington knives specializing in the famed Remington "Bullets." Likewise, a collector of new brands, such as Fight'n Rooster, may elect to build a collection of pearl-handled beauties of varied patterns.

Specialization may take the form of knife types and be totally unrelated to manufacturer or handle material. Examples of this would be collections of plier and wrench knives made by various manufacturers during the early quarter of this century, picture-handle knives made about the same time, or whittler patterns made either a century ago or last month.

To see specialization first hand, one need only visit a local knife show and spend an enjoyable hour or so studying the collector displays. Since the major portion of this book features factory-made knives, its listings of notable manufacturers, patterns, handle materials, and dates of manufacture will also be of value in selecting a specialty.

CUSTOM KNIVES

The collector who leans toward knives made one at a time by individual makers also has several avenues available in choosing a specialty. Similar to the choice in factory knives, one may elect to concentrate on knives made by twentieth-century pioneer makers such as Scagel, Richtig, Ruana, and Randall—all now deceased. Many collectors of custom knives have an appreciation for the fact that, in buying a knife, they are also buying a piece of the maker's life. It is not unusual, therefore, that these people wish to collect the knives of makers they can get to know—either personally, by telephone conversation, or through correspondence.

Some elect to collect knives of only one maker. That maker may be one who is well established and whose knives have proved desirable. Usually, these knives require either a rather long waiting period or, if found on the secondary market, a higher price. Other, more speculative collectors may like the work of one or a few makers and be willing to invest money, hoping that the knives bought at relatively low prices, while the maker and his work are relatively unknown, will someday bring high prices because that maker's knives are in demand.

Custom-knife collectors usually concentrate on fixed-blade knives or folders. Similar to factory knives, a host of possibilities lie within either of these areas. The fixed blade fancier may choose further refinement into designs such as Bowies, fighters, survival knives, hunters, and skinners. One who prefers the handmade folder may also make further choices in design, locking mechanisms, blade styles, and the like.

Another choice in custom knives is between those made by bladesmiths who hand-forge their blades and those made by makers using the stock removal method. And as if the above avenues aren't enough, there's the choice between the knife that is without decorations such as engraving, file work, and scrimshaw and those embellished with one or more of these art forms. Some art knives seem to practically reach into a knife world of their very own, offering a truly unique specialty for a few collectors.

For additional ideas regarding collecting customs as a specialty and sources of custom knives, refer to page 48.

COMMEMORATIVE OR LIMITED-EDITION KNIVES

The rapidly increasing interest in knives as collectibles, experienced during the past couple of decades, has led to countless numbers of commemorative and/or limited-edition knives being made and sold within the collector market. Although some of these have been handmade or custom knives, by far the majority have been factory knives. The collector who chooses this type of knife as a specialty has fewer alternatives than those described above, but still, choices do exist.

One distinct and viable specialty would be knives that are handmade by custom makers or knives that are factory-made but feature decorative work done individually by recognized artists. These knives are most always limited to relatively small quantities and are truly unique. The advantages of this specialty are pride of ownership and potential value appreciation. After all, not many collectors can own one of Randall's 50th Anniversary limited-edition knives, Gil Hibben's handmade Rambo III's, or a Puma Game Warden. Most collectors would not limit their collecting to this specialty because the total number of knives owned would be quite small and the investment would be quite large.

Club knives are limited editions that have proved to be meaningful as well as valuable collectibles. Clubs such as the National Knife Collectors Association, as well as regional clubs, usually have limited numbers of knives made each year for their membership. Not only are these knives in demand by the clubs' members, but many of them are subject to growing demand and value appreciation outside that membership circle. Club knives, if produced for a regional club, are usually limited in number from 50 to 300, rarely more. National club knives have varied from 1,200 to as many as 10,000 pieces in production and are usually sold out to the membership before production is complete.

Factory-made commemorative knives may be issued by the manufacturer or, as is usually the case, by individual entrepreneurs. They may celebrate an event of national importance or they may commemorate something or someone of significance to a very small percentage of our population. Usually, those that are privately issued are based on a popular-pattern knife that is in full-scale production. That rather ordinary knife is made into something not so common by special blade etching, boxing, and serial numbering. Collectors to whom these knives appeal will likely decide to collect around a theme because there are such a large number available that meaningful parameters would need to be defined.

A complete section on limited-edition and commemorative knives is included on page 649 so that collectors interested in these knives may learn more about this specialty.

ANTIQUE BOWIE KNIVES

Because of the rarity and relative value of most of the knives in this area, collectors may not elect to specialize further. Even a so-called accumulation of antique Bowies would be so difficult to garner that further refinement would be pointless.

Included in this book is a separate discussion of these knives. For further information, refer to page 37.

MILITARY KNIVES

Collecting military knives represents a rather dynamic area of cutlery collecting and one that is already quite specialized, much like antique Bowie knives. Their range, however, is quite broad—from antique swords to weapons used during the Vietnam conflict. These cutlery items of warfare are collected not only by knife enthusiasts but by military history buffs and antique collectors as well. Military knives are so closely related to other items of warfare that their collecting theme often follows specific wars and/or the several branches of the military establishments fighting in those wars. Other choices include special fighting or commando knives, bayonets, machetes, and bolos, as well as general utility knives used in the military. Although condition has a direct effect on the value of military knives, they are often desirable even in worn condition, especially if their use was by recognized "heroes" or in significant battles. Entire books have been written on the several subjects pertaining to this specialty, and for those desiring to become further involved, additional reading and research is recommended.

SILVER FRUIT KNIVES

Folding fruit knives, many of them made during the eighteenth and nineteenth centuries, offer a rewarding specialty. These knives appeal to both men and women alike, but they seem to be special favorites of female collectors. Although they may be found in knife trading circles, they are often encountered at estate sales and in antique shops. Their hallmark stampings allow for accurate cataloging, and learning the system can be a hobby in itself. For further information, refer to page 99.

TREND KNIVES

Trends and fads have long been and will continue to be an important part of buying, selling, and trading of almost any product. Knives are no exception. One has only to look back to the mid-1800s to recognize one important trend in knives—that started by Colonel James Bowie—or, within many of our lifetimes, to recall the popularity of a knife pattern named for the English cutler Barlow and popularized by an American author's stories about two youngsters named Sawyer and Finn.

But there probably has been no period in cutlery history that has produced so many trendy knives as have the past two decades. Knife designers, custom knife makers, and large-scale knife producers alike have created designs that captured the imaginations, the fantasies, and the pocketbooks of knife buyers—at least for a while.

There have been "survival knives"—distinctive fixed-blade knives that capitalized on saw-teeth backs, compass butt caps, and a hollow handle filled with useless gadgets as well as items of practical use for surviving in the wild. They were popularized by moviemakers who introduced us to superheroes wielding superknives. Custom makers made them by the thousands; factories made and sold them by the millions. Now, less than ten years after their heyday, it is difficult to find collectors with interest in any survival knife except those made by already famous custom makers.

Designs known as tantos were also made popular by the silver screen martial artists, and, in theory, they were fashioned after some of the blades of the Samurai warriors. During the early 1980s, practically every custom knife maker who wanted to sell knives sold at least one knife designed in accordance with his interpretation of the tanto. Several makers of production knives built businesses based on their versions of the tanto. With rare exceptions, neither the custom nor the factory knives are in favor today.

A similar story could be told about the Bali-Song, or "butterfly knife," of Philippine origin. The fad came and flourished for a short while before the butterfly knives fluttered into near obscurity.

At the end of the 1980s and beginning of this decade, the trend has been to big knives: Bowie and/or Bowie/machete types. Custom knife makers had continued to make and sell these large utility knives over the years, but the fad has now swept through much of the factory-knife industry—again with much of the credit to hero images.

Currently, within the field of custom folders, the liner lock mechanism is very much in favor. In spite of the fact that several custom makers claim credit, the mechanism is nearly identical to that of utility pocketknives made years ago by the factory-knife producers.

Although most of these examples originated with custom knives, the rage for specific knife designs is not limited to them. The pattern popularly known as a trapper has been a standard production knife for practically all knife manufacturers for decades. At the present time, it could be considered the king of pocketknife collectible patterns. Its popularity is not so much because of the pattern itself as its use for scores of limited editions and commemorative series. In reading and referring to this book's section on those special production knives, you will become increasingly aware of the impact of the trapper pattern on today's and tomorrow's collectors.

There's little doubt that the trapper pattern will still be popular when most of today's collectors are history. Likewise, the Bowie has long been a part of Americana and will undoubtedly remain in favor. Whether the other "hero knives" will someday be valuable collectibles can only be speculated, but there are collectors of Lone Ranger knives and Batman memorabilia. It's not unreasonable to anticipate a future demand for knives representing heroes of the late twentieth century. Most of the knives were first purchased because of their vogue status and with little concern about their future value. And anyone who would dare say that short-lived popularity will not create a collectible knife can be brought back to reality when reminded of the unique and valuable collections built around knives such as plier knives, cotton samplers, fleam knives, timber scribes, and picture-handled knives.

As knife buyers did in earlier times—if you like them, buy and enjoy them.

COUNTERFEIT KNIVES

Those of us who enjoy the hobby of knife collecting view it, for many good and valid reasons, as a wholesome one. Consequently, it's sometimes uncomfortable to acknowledge that counterfeits are found in the knife marketplace. But fakes are an unfortunate fact of life, and perhaps it is a backhanded compliment about the value of knives as collectibles that we must be concerned with them. Whether the area of collecting is stamps, coins, antique furniture, paintings, or an endless list of others, as long as there are objects of value being sold or traded, there will be those who choose to profit by trickery; and refusal to discuss counterfeit knives is certainly not the answer. One hopes that a general awareness of the practice and the practitioners will make it more difficult for counterfeit knives to be sold and traded.

Although no single specialty of knife collecting is immune, primary targets for the counterfeiters' forgeries are antique Bowies and medium-priced factory pocketknives. As a rule, pocketknives selling in the $100 to $200 range are most subject to deceptive practices. Knives selling for less would hardly be worth the counterfeiter's time, effort, and risk; knives selling for higher amounts would normally be subject to greater scrutiny by the prospective buyer.

Guarding against buying counterfeit knives is not unlike caution used with other collectibles. The best rule is, first, know your knives and, whenever possible, know the seller. The collector who has done his homework well should be able to spot inconsistencies either in the piece or in the story behind it, perhaps in both. If the knife and/or its bargain price are too good to be true, that's quite often the case.

One should learn as much as possible about the tricks of the counterfeiter as well as the craft of knife restoration. There is a difference between a knife that has been restored and is represented as such and one that has been altered with an intent to deceive. Properly restored knives or knives that have been taken apart for cleaning, although valued at less than a true mint piece, are certainly acceptable in the marketplace. Counterfeits are not.

RESTORATION

It is not unusual to find knives that have been heavily cleaned, repaired, or restored by replacement of a part or parts as originally used in that specific knife at the time of its manufacture. Knife repair and partial restoration are generally viewed as acceptable as long as the knife is represented as such and there is no deception in intent or practice. Still, no matter how it appears, it is not a mint knife; it may, however, be a very valuable one. Restored knives are acceptable and in demand, but one has to be a little bewildered when advertisements for antique knives are found that state "can be restored to mint." That's a contradiction in and of itself and evidence that many collectors, whether novice or seasoned, need to better understand the real meaning of the words "mint," "original," and "restored."

There are competent knife repairers who disassemble, completely clean, and reassemble a knife, maintaining its integrity of original parts throughout the process. That knife should be represented and offered for sale as such, and the collector who adds it to his collection can usually be proud to own it. Similarly, the competent craftsperson can repair or restore an old knife by interchange of a part such as a handle or a blade. As long as the substituted part is original to the pattern and period of the knife to which it has been added, it may correctly be sold or traded as a restored knife, and the buyer can have pride in ownership. There are many knives that may be found in excellent and original condition with the exception of a cracked handle. In these and similar cases, the repaired knife will most always be preferred to its unrepaired condition, similar to repairing the dented fender of an antique automobile.

The bottom line is one of semantics, and they boil down to honesty. Reworking a knife with the intent to make it appear to be something it is not or misrepresenting it will qualify for Webster's definition of counterfeit. So, when considering an antique knife to purchase, determine if the knife has been taken apart. If it has, ask what work was done to determine if all of its parts are original; if they are not, find out which were replaced. Don't be shy about asking questions, and in most cases you will receive an honest answer. If in doubt, ask. Don't assume the information will be freely offered.

Although restoration is an accepted practice, one should recognize that there are collectors who would prefer that the old piece of history reflect its age and use. Very few would want a rusty piece of junk, but their preference is often the finely made piece seasoned with patina, mild pitting, or signs of handle wear instead of a shiny piece that has had the flavor buffed away or removed by an overly enthusiastic "cleaner-upper." It becomes a matter of individual and personal taste but one that deserves consideration before committing a rare old antique for restoration.

COUNTERFEITING

In one sentence above, a fine-line distinction was made (intent) between a restored knife and a counterfeit. But what about the outright counterfeit, the imitation of an old Remington, Case, or Winchester represented as a genuine valuable knife? Fortunately, there are very few counterfeiters who possess sufficient skill and the necessary equipment to make a foolproof counterfeit knife. But there are those who are able to deceive the inexperienced or naive collector, and even the expert can be fooled on occasion.

In discussing counterfeit knives, we should recognize that there are three classes, or grades, of counterfeits. The first consists of those that have been so poorly reworked that they would deceive only the most naive or truly neophyte collector. One would think that such poorly constructed counterfeits would never find their way into the trading circles, but that is far from the truth. Their presence is not unusual at flea markets, occasional auctions, and, yes, even at knife shows. By reasonably close observation and comparison with other knives, these knives are relatively easy to spot.

The second classification of counterfeits are those that are more difficult to detect. They will usually deceive the novice and occasionally the experienced collector as well. The workmanship used in remaking the knife is of sufficiently high quality that collectors who are considered experts often disagree as to whether the knife is in fact a counterfeit and just what is correct or incorrect about it. Still, the seasoned collector's evaluation and advice should be sought whenever there is any reason to doubt a knife's authenticity. It is not unusual for the experienced collector to ask for the opinion of his peers, and no one should be ashamed to seek help.

Although it's possible that the third classification is purely hypothetical, it likely exists in actuality, even if in small numbers. These are the counterfeit knives that are so masterfully done that they can deceive even a group of experts; only the craftsman who masterminded and created the deception knows for sure.

There are several methods or combinations of methods that an unscrupulous person may use to counterfeit a knife. The more common tricks that a counterfeiter is likely to try include, but certainly are not limited to, the following:

Grinding off the original tang stamp and restamping the blade tang with one that was used on a knife of much greater value.

Removing the master blade and/or other blades and replacing them with blades from an older, more valuable knife.

Replacing the handles of a knife with a different type, such as would have been used on more expensive knives of the same frame pattern and blade design.

Using a knife with blades that are badly worn but with good-quality tangs and welding on new blades to replace those that are worn.

Taking old knife parts and making them into a complete knife that has collector appeal and value.

Replacing or adding a shield to the knife handle, thereby making the knife appear to be older or of greater value than it actually is.

Re-etching blades that have been cleaned and/or refinished, thereby making them appear to have had much less use and wear.

Artificially aging a knife to make it appear to be older than it really is.

Taking knives, old or new, that were not stamped and stamping the mark of a rare knife.

To guard against the counterfeit, there are several precautions to take or areas to watch closely. A key one is to know your knives. Learn as much as possible about materials used, methods of manufacture, patterns, stampings, dates that particular features were commonly used, and so on. Since it's impossible to know all, don't be too shy or too proud to ask the opinion of a reputable and knowledgeable collector.

Look for signs of work on the knife. A nearly new blade or handle on a knife that is otherwise well worn should arouse suspicion, as should marks on the inside of the knife, which may indicate it has been taken apart. Do the handles match, and are they correct for the knife in question? A large percentage of the old Remington, Winchester, Case, Queen, and most other popular brands have their own distinct jigging pattern on their bone or bone stag handles. Check also to see if the handles have been glued onto the liners or if the shield has been glued into the handle rather than pinned or riveted on.

Are blades and backsprings in similar condition and of the same thickness? Does the thickness of the blade tang indicate that it may have been ground down for restamping? Use your magnifying glass to examine the stampings closely, and, if suspicious, compare them with those on other knives you know to be correct.

Do the rivets look original in form, color, and fit? Do the parts seem to belong together as units of the whole knife? Not only should they physically fit one with the other, but they should be in keeping one with another. If the liners are brass, usually the pins and rivets are brass; if one is nickel silver, chances are good that the other should be also.

In short, you must be able to spot inconsistencies, either in the piece or in the story behind it—or in both. Use intelligence and common sense to evaluate what your eyes see, what your hands feel, and what your ears hear. Above all, listen to your intuition.

There are times when intuition may be the deciding factor, and the decision may be to buy the knife. After all, there are knives that are extremely unusual but are not counterfeit. Knives in this category may be salesman or customer samples or prototypes that were never put into production and aren't found listed in catalogs or perhaps in any company records. On occasion, knife company executives may have asked for a few special knives to be used as gifts. Because there was no thought at the time they were done—fifty, seventy-five, or a hundred years ago—that someday these knives would be prized collectibles, no one gave thought to cataloging or maintaining records. New finds are not so unusual, and one of them might be your own.

Any discussion of counterfeiting is sure to concoct negative thoughts about knives and knife collecting. But let's finish this chapter by putting things into proper perspective within the overall market. There are thousands of collectible knives bought, sold, and traded each month. Although no one knows the percentage that is counterfeit, practically all experienced collectors would agree that it is very, very small. Yes, even one counterfeit is too many, but there are large collections of antique knives that are totally genuine. Yours can be, too. At the beginning of this chapter, knife collecting was referred to as a wholesome hobby. It was, it is, and it will continue to be. Enjoy!

STARTING AND BUILDING
A COLLECTION

$\triangledown$

Getting started as a knife collector is extremely easy. The chances are good that most people have the beginnings of a collection tucked away in dresser drawers, trunks, closets, attics, basements, and even shoe boxes. Those are favorite places for storing items handed down from prior generations or from our own past, and after all, every collection began with a first knife.

A knife collection does not have to be large in numbers to be worthwhile. It is true that some collections contain hundreds or even thousands of knives, but others contain less than a dozen. Each offers rewards to the collector. There are so many opportunities that anyone interested in knives can get involved in the hobby.

Knife collecting doesn't necessarily require one to spend large amounts of money, so anyone interested in knives should not be deterred by the high prices of rare knives. A collection can be started with a modest budget and built in the same manner. Even if there are no knives stored away at home, there are numerous opportunities for starting a collection at whatever investment level one finds feasible.

KNIVES ARE WHERE YOU FIND THEM

There are a number of places where collectible knives may be found and purchased; most of them represent good marketplaces for selling knives as well. In practically every town and on most weekends, one can find flea markets, garage sales, and estate sales to visit. They may be as close as a few blocks away from home or as far away as the other side of town, but they are convenient. Auctions and knife shows are most often less convenient, but they are almost always worth the time and expense of travel.

And whether buying or selling, the collector should never overlook the market that is as close as the mailbox or telephone. Quite a large volume of collector knife sales are consummated from the home with professional knife dealers and with other collectors. Very few collectors will pass up the advertisements in the knife publications as they seek new contacts for buying and selling collectible knives.

None of these should be overlooked because each has an important place within the boundaries of the knife world. There are still excellent bargains to be found and choice pieces traded at reasonable prices. Knife collecting is no different from other endeavors in that the harder and smarter one works at the hobby, the luckier one becomes. Yes, luck still plays its important part, especially when it is supported by knowledge. The following discussion about these various sources for knives may help to determine areas in which to use your own expertise and to try your own luck in making that rare find. Good hunting!

GARAGE AND ESTATE SALES

Garage and estate sales can offer opportunities for buying knives, especially to collectors who already enjoy chasing after bargains at these weekend affairs. With the minimal amount of travel and time required, they should never be overlooked. One very important point to remember is to ask about knives. Since they usually find their way into dresser drawers, trunks, and boxes, knives may be forgotten or assumed by the seller to be of little interest and value.

Expect to sift through a lot of junk and expect to find many sales with no collectible knives, but expect also that persistence can pay off. After all, at some point in time, a large number of the knives found at knife shows and through dealers entered the collector market by way of a well-informed and fortunate garage sale shopper.

FLEA MARKETS

Although many good knives exchange owners through flea markets, the percentage is small when compared to the practically worthless ones to be found on these trading grounds. Their abundance and close proximity are the greatest advantages of flea markets. There are disadvantages to be considered also, especially by the novice collector. The average flea market is usually lacking knowledgeable fellow collectors or dealers, leaving the untrained collector much on his own. Knowing knives and their values is essential to successful flea market buying. Most flea market dealers acknowledge that some knives are valuable. Recognizing this fact but often knowing little else about collectible knives, these dealers are usually inclined to overprice their knives for fear of selling them for too little.

Because a large portion of the knives found at flea markets have come out of attics, garages, and basements, their appearance is likely to be less impressive than those found at shows or on the professional dealers' tables. But ordinary dirt and grime can be cleaned off and should be no deterrent to buying a knife that is considered a bargain. And their source often means that the flea market dealer has very little investment in the knife; his interest in it could be even less. The collector who looks earnestly and evaluates wisely may find himself a genuine bargain.

AUCTIONS

Concurrent with the growing interest in knives as collectibles, there has been an increasing number of auctions specializing in them. These auctions are among the best places to buy knives. If the sale is from a well-established collection, the knives offered may be quite rare and difficult to find elsewhere. If the knives are from an estate, a quick sale may take priority over selling price. Even though some prices paid at auctions offer surprises on both extremes—unquestionable bargains to ridiculously high prices—most are good indications of the true collector values of the knives represented.

Some auctions are highly publicized, draw collectors from distant areas, and often welcome absentee bids. Others may be publicized only by direct mail notification or local newspaper advertising. They can offer opportunities to purchase desirable knives at very reasonable prices, or they may be routes used for disposing of junk. If the auction is well publicized, if the knives are listed well in advance of the sale, and if they are available for inspection prior to the actual sale, these auctions are an excellent means for learning the real value of knives.

In addition to the more commonly recognized type of auction, informal and sometimes spontaneous auctions are held at knife show locations. These are often light-hearted gatherings that offer collectors and dealers the opportunity to bid on one another's knives and to swap stories as well. Sitting in on one of these informal affairs of the knife-collecting hobby can often be a special treat.

CLUB SWAP MEETS

Most knife clubs meet on a regular basis, and the major portion of the time is spent in buying, selling, and trading knives. Some meetings are followed by a mini-show, with dealers and collectors spreading out their wares on tables and welcoming offers to buy, sell, or trade. Newcomers to these events not only bring new faces and personalities but they bring "new" (different) knives into the relatively small circle—visitors and new members are usually very much welcomed.

MAIL ORDER

An avenue for buying and selling knives that is available to almost everyone is personal contact with other collectors and dealers via mail and telephone. In most instances, the initial contact between buyer and seller will have been made as the result of an advertisement in a regular knife publication. Shopping the "for sale" and "wanted" columns of classified ad pages is a high-priority activity for many knife collectors.

There are numerous dealers who conduct a large share of their business in this manner. Most of them regularly distribute lists of knives they have for sale and knives they seek, either for their personal collection or for those of regular customers. Collectors wishing either to sell or to buy a number of knives may be well advised to compile a similar listing to be sent to other collectors or to dealers.

Newcomers to the hobby may be surprised to learn that so much knife trading is conducted in this manner and with relatively few problems. As long as both the prospective buyer and the seller accurately represent the knives to be traded and agree to reasonable return privileges, there will be few grievous mail order trades.

DEALERS

Knife dealers are businessmen much like those in other fields. Their goals are to purchase and to market their goods at prices that allow sufficient margin to pay operating expenses plus a reasonable profit. As in any business, there are a very few dealers who may seek excessive profits or conduct their business dealings unfairly. The vast majority of knife dealers deal very fairly with their customers. They are well aware that their own business health is based on good customer relations, and most knife dealers recognize that the same collector who buys knives from him on one occasion may be selling him knives on another. Because knife dealers are both buyers and sellers, their services can usually be beneficial to collectors at almost any time.

The professional dealer is most often an expert in a wide variety of collectible knives and usually has a large number of contacts who may be helpful. Through these contacts, the dealer is often able to sift through the national knife market, not just the local area. The knowledgeable dealer usually has the expertise to detect and reject counterfeits so that his customers can buy with a greater degree of confidence. He offers convenience and often saves the knife buyer or the seller money in travel and other expenses required to buy or sell a knife. There are no special secrets to the dealer's supply source; it's the same knife market that the individual collector works within. The primary difference is in the volume of knives and the size of the investment. Although many dealers are also collectors, their primary goal in buying and selling knives is turning over their inventory as quickly and as profitably as possible. Although the primary goal of most collectors is building a respectable collection, profit—usually long-term—also plays a role in their activities. It is not unusual that many collectors become dealers, since they buy, trade, and sell while seeking to collect.

KNIFE SHOWS

Knife shows have, or at least should have, an entirely different atmosphere from that of flea markets. This does not mean one cannot find bargains at a show. On the contrary, the knife show is perhaps the best single source of good knives at fair prices. Shows are gathering places for the leading dealers and active collectors, and as such, they are ideal forums for building a collection (buying) or refining one (selling).

Table renters at a knife show are not always full-time dealers. Often they are collectors who are refining their collection by selling duplicates or knives that are less desirable to them at the time because their collecting interest has changed. These collectors are usually excellent sources for good knives, often at prices below their current value. In addition, they may be able to offer the bonus of rather extensive information about the specific knife being transferred from one collector to another.

Knife shows offer collectors an opportunity to get personally acquainted with dealers, often the beginning of a long-term relationship. Visiting a dealer's tables can also supply firsthand information about the type and quality of his knives.

Expect a large percentage of knife show visitors to be reasonably well informed and experienced. This means tough competition for the best bargains, and the astute collector seeking knives will arrive as early as possible to survey the offerings. But it also means that knife shows can offer a wealth of firsthand information. In this author's opinion, a good show will feature a number of "exhibit only" tables, used by collectors who proudly display their knives for the education of others. These displays offer opportunities for collectors to see many rare and valuable knives, often accumulated through years of searching and substantial financial investment. One can most always expect these collectors to freely offer the benefit of their hard-earned wisdom.

Knife shows can be impressive events, especially to the novice collector. Just as they can leave the visitor with good or with bad impressions, shows also offer the foundation on which the visitor can build a reputation—good or not so good. Although there are no posted rules of etiquette, there are rules of courtesy that one should keep in mind. Doing so will make the experience more enjoyable for everyone concerned. Here are several suggestions.

Ask permission before handling a knife. This courtesy is especially important if the knife is for display only and not for sale. The collector who is displaying his or her collection is doing so without compensation. These collectors have invested considerable expense and effort to show their knives and to share their knowledge with other collectors and show visitors. Cleaning fingerprints off knives after they have been handled by visitors is certainly no reward for their selfless efforts.

Do not handle the blade or its edge. If invited to examine a knife, open it carefully by the nail nick and avoid touching the blade itself. Not only could you leave it with a blemish, but a sharp blade carelessly handled can return the favor.

Do not open more than one blade of a folding knife at any one time. Doing so can weaken the springs and will not be appreciated by the dealer or collector who has both pride and money invested in the knife. Once you've opened a blade, resist the temptation to hear the resounding snap of its closing. If the knife "walks and talks," your sense of touch will find its quality as evident as will your sense of hearing.

Do not participate uninvited nor interfere with other persons' knife trading business. Whatever transpires is their personal affair, and even though you may be very interested in the knife being discussed, wait your turn. If their transaction is not completed, then and only then feel free to enter into your own.

Do not block a dealer's table from his prospective customers if you are just browsing. Most dealers invite casual lookers, but they have traveled to the show and paid their table fees in order to sell knives. Preventing them from doing so is unfair to both the dealer and the prospective buyer.

Unless invited to do so, do not use the table of another collector or dealer to sell or trade knives you may have brought to the show. The effect of this discourteous act should require no explanation.

Attendance and participation in a knife show can and should be a very rewarding experience, an experience that the serious collector can ill afford to miss. Listings of show dates and locations for most shows can be found in regular knife publications such as *Knife World, National Knife Magazine,* and *The Blade.*

PART
◁ 2 ▷

Learning More about Knives

BOWIE KNIVES

There has been no knife style that has been linked with and the subject of so much adventure, fantasy, conjecture, and controversy as the one named for James Bowie. There are so many legends about Jim Bowie and his knife that drawing distinct lines between fact and fiction have long been almost impossible for historians and collectors alike.

Even his place and year of birth, generally conceded to be Tennessee, 1795, are in debate. But we know that Bowie's family moved—from wherever—to Louisiana, where he later became a planter, a land speculator, and in the meantime, a legend, even before his unforgettable death at the Alamo in 1836. His stature, in the minds and imaginations of many, became bigger than life, and the knife made famous by those legends grew in renown even beyond the man himself. Although he may have had some local reputation, Jim Bowie's fame was set afire on September 19, 1827. That's the date that an "affair of honor" took place on a Mississippi River sandbar near the town of Natchez. The duel that nearly became a free-for-all for the dozen or so men present came to be called the Vidalia Sandbar Duel. The knife Bowie carried and used to save his own life, at the expense of the life of one Major Norris Wright, carved its image into history.

Through the telling and retelling of the story, the excellent qualities of the knife Bowie used became almost magical in the minds of those who read and heard it. Even in the absence of television, radio, satellite news transmission, and the wide-screen cinema, Jim Bowie was quickly fashioned into an early nineteenth-century "Rambo." It seems that practically everyone wanted a knife "just like Bowie's." This country's knife makers obliged, but their efforts were dwarfed by those of cutlers from other parts of the world, especially the highly regarded Sheffield, England, cutlery center.

Although he is often credited with invention, Jim Bowie most likely did not design the knife named for him. The knife used at the duel had been lent to him by his brother Rezin. The knife's basic design was by no means new in 1827, and this specific knife had been made for Rezin Bowie by a plantation blacksmith. Even if Jim Bowie did later develop or suggest a knife design, he certainly had no input into the innumerable variations that were made, many of which are still sold today as "the original Bowie knife." Just like the legends about Bowie, the styles of what became known as the Bowie knife were created by colorful journalism and vivid imaginations.

But this is not to say that the knife design was and is without merit. Far from it! It was not unlike an improvement, with specific purposes in mind, on the butcher knife or chef's knife. The primary purpose of the Bowie knife, as well as of the variations made before and after 1827, was fighting. Whether in defense or offense, it was a knife designed to save a life by taking a life. The cap-and-ball pistol had superseded the sword as a primary weapon, but it had its shortcomings. Consequently, even if two small pistols were carried, there needed to be a backup weapon. Knives of the dagger type had been used for centuries, and after its ballooning reputation, the so called "Bowie" knife was envisioned as the ideal complement to the single-shot and not-so-trustworthy pistol.

Students of the Bowie knife, along with students of close combat, will verify that "a knife like Bowie's" could often have made the difference in a life-and-death encounter. The fact that the knives that became so popular after Bowie's well-publicized duel may or may not have been just like the one used on the sandbar does not detract from the utility of the knives that would become known as Bowies. Regardless of knives marked and/or marketed as reproductions of the original Bowie knife, there is still an absence of documentation that would tell or show us the exact design of the knife Jim Bowie used either in 1827 or in 1836 at the Alamo. Bowie knives of both nineteenth-century and twentieth-century origins are variations, limited only by the imagination, of a very sensible piece of combat cutlery. Those that were made and sold in the 1800s as Bowies had blades that could be considered relatively short or relatively long for a fighting knife. The blades were both double- and single-edged, and they had either spear or clip points or variations of the two. The fact that the thousands upon thousands made and sold were not in fact "exactly like Bowie's" made little difference. They were formidable knives; they still are.

As the nineteenth century drew to a close, there was less need—either imagined or real—for such a weapon. In fact, the knife earned such a reputation that several states had prohibited its wearing, sale, or ownership. Some of these laws are still on the books. The primary factor, however, in the diminishing demand for the Bowie knife was developed by a man named Samuel Colt. And as the revolver became more reliable, the perception of the need for a large backup knife diminished. The "Iron Mistress" became not quite so necessary, but today it is often considered the king of cutlery collectibles.

MAKERS AND MARKINGS

Although it is impossible to know every maker of Bowie knives, the following list includes the major nineteenth-century makers whose knives one may encounter. Bear in mind that knives were often made in those days by craftsmen bearing titles other than knifemaker or cutler. The blacksmith, the gun maker, the surgical instrument maker, the silversmith, and numerous other tradesmen were called on to make knives along with the established cutlers. The knives they made during the 1800s are, in the majority, highly desirable as collectibles. It should be no surprise, therefore, that their prices are normally quite high. The majority of Bowie knives a collector will encounter came from Sheffield, England, and only a small percentage were made in this country. Of the markings, the Wostenholm IXL will be encountered more than all of the rest. Whether of U.S. or other origin, top-grade Bowie knives command prices into the thousands of dollars. The quality pieces are held in such high regard that price often takes second place to ownership—whether it's the prospective buyer or seller who wants most to call the piece his own.

An antique Bowie knife must be evaluated on its own specific merits. Period, style, condition, and especially maker are determining factors in value. Because their prices will vary greatly based on those and other factors, no attempt is made to offer specific values. After all, most antique Bowies one will encounter are one-of-a-kind pieces and deserve individual evaluation. Some very generalized guidelines are offered, however, so that one may conclude ranges of values.

For instance, Bowies made in this country during the first quarter to first half of the nineteenth century may demand prices into five figures if made by well-known and respected makers and if their condition is extremely good. Don't expect that every Bowie made about 1825 would be valued at $10,000, but it would not be unusual to learn that quite a few, if in excellent condition, would be worth $2,000 to $3,000. Those made in the latter half of the 1800s by individual makers or even some made by cutlery manufacturers could be valued from $500 up.

Although not generally valued as highly, Bowies imported from other countries during the same periods may range in value from $200 to several thousand dollars, depending again on the period, maker, materials, decoration, and—as always—condition.

Our suggestion is that the list be used to help identify a Bowie's time and place of origin as well as to determine its maker. From that point, a great deal of research into the specific knife may be in order. Whether or not the knife in question has a value in the five-figure area, using the Bowie as a vehicle for a trip back into history makes the world of antique Bowie knives worthy of considerable collector interest.

Please note that the listing is printed in alphabetical order as most of the knives would be marked, rather than in order of makers' last names.

BOWIE MAKERS

A. H. DUFILHO, New Orleans, c. 1855–1867.
A surgical instrument maker whose knives were of exceptional quality. He later made swords for the Confederate army.

A. LEON, 10 Solly Str., Sheffield, c. 1850.

ALEXANDER, Sheffield.

ALEXANDER McKINSTRY, Alabama, c. 1861.
This company made many Civil War–era knives, most having blades 8″ or less in length.

ALFRED HUNTER, New York and New Jersey, c. 1830–1865.

AMOS BELKNAP, St. Johnsbury, Vermont, c. 1839–1883.

ANDREW C. HICKS, Cleveland, Ohio, c. 1830–1859.
Working through the Allegheny arsenal, he is credited with making the first official military knives for the U.S. government.

AUGUST EICKHOFF, New York, c. 1848–1900.

BELL & DAVIS, Atlanta, c. 1861.

BENJAMIN JONES, Tredyffrine, Pennsylvania, c. 1875–1881.

BEST ENGLISH CUTLERY, c. 1849–1850.
Some will be found with cast-metal handles and etched "The Gold Seekers Protection."

BOWN & TETLEY, Pittsburgh, Pennsylvania, c. 1848–1862.

BOYLE, GAMBLE & MACFEE, Richmond, Virginia, c. 1866–1875.

BROOMHEAD & THOMAS, Sheffield, c. 1835.
Massive-style knives with pearl handles, sheaths sometimes marked "The Celebrated Arkansas Toothpick."

BUCK BROTHERS, Worcester, Massachusetts, c. 1853–1864.

BUNTING & SONS, Sheffield, c. 1837–1868.

BURGER & BROS., Richmond, Virginia, c. 1861.

C. J. BLITTERDORF, Philadelphia, c. 1849.

C. WESTER ROBY, Chelmsford, Massachusetts, c. 1860.

CHARLES C. REINHARDT, Baltimore, c. 1840–1845.

CHARLES C. REINHARDT JR., Baltimore, c. 1868.

CLARENBACH & HERDER, Philadelphia, c. 1849–1872.

CLEMENT CUTLERY CO., Northampton, Massachusetts, c. 1855.

CONGREVE, Sheffield, c. 1835.
Early massive-style knives.

COOK & BROS., New Orleans, c. 1860.

DANIEL C. HODGKINS & SON, Macon, Georgia, c. 1860.

DANIEL CLARKE, Philadelphia, c. 1850.

EDW. K. TRYON, Philadelphia, c. 1811.
Later became Edw. K. Tryon & Co. The company ceased manufacturing in 1872 but continued in business until 1952, when it was purchased by Simmons Hardware.

EDWARD BARNES & SON, Sheffield, c. 1856–1865.
Blades up to 12″, usually with patriotic mottos and sometimes "American Hunting Knife" etched on the blades.

ENOCH DRABBLE, Sheffield, c. 1838.
Usually stamped with name and "Celebrated Cutlery." Massive style with horsehead pommels were a specialty.

ETOWAH IRON WORKS, Georgia, c. 1861.

F. ALLDEON, Memphis, Tennessee.

F. M. HAIL, Georgia, c. 1862.

FENTON & SHORE, Sheffield, c. 1850–1870.
Made horsehead pommels.

FRED WATSON, San Francisco, c. 1890.

FREDERICK KESMODEL, San Francisco, c. 1856–1868.
One of the most colorful Bowie makers, Kesmodel trained dogs to power his machines. His knives were made to order. He hired Frederick Will in 1861, and, after going out of business in 1868, Kesmodel was employed by Will & Finck.

G. STEWART, Norwich, Connecticut, c. 1857–1860.

G. W. TAYLOR, California, c. 1860–1875.

GEO. WOSTENHOLM & SONS, Sheffield, c. 1832–1890s.
Markings include Geo. Wostenholm & Sons Rockingham Works (1832–1848), I*XL V(crown)R Geo. Wostenholm & Sons Celebrated Cast Steel Bowie Knife (1837–1890), Geo. Wostenholm & Sons Washington Works (1848–1890), and Geo. Wostenholm & Son Celebrated California Knife (1848–1890). Wostenholm's I*XL trademark is the most common found on Bowies because so many were sold in the U.S.

GITTER & MOSS, Beal St., Memphis, Tennessee, c. 1860s.
Civil War Bowie makers.

GRAVELY & WREAKS, New York, c. 1835.
This company was an importer of Sheffield knives, but their names will be marked on the knives.

H. GILLELAND, Georgia, c. 1862.

H. W. WILKINSON & CO., c. 1855.

H. WILKINSON, Hartford, Connecticut, c. 1860–1880.

HARTENSTEIN, San Francisco, c. 1870.
Began working in 1868 for Michael Price. Operated his own shop from 1870 until 1876.

HASSAM, Boston, c. 1860s.

HAWKSWORTH & ELLISON, Sheffield, c. 1840s.
Ellison was a New York agent for English Bowies.

HENRY HARRINGTON, Worcester, Massachusetts, c. 1819.

HENRY SHIVELY, Philadelphia, c. 1831.

HIRAM PEABODY, Richmond, Virginia, c. 1850.

HUGH McCONNELL, San Francisco, c. 1852–1863.

I. LONGARD, Sheffield.

I*XL, Sheffield.
See Geo. Wostenholm.

IBBOTSON PEACE & CO., Sheffield, c. 1847–1864.
They made some Bowies with horsehead pommels.

J. ENGLISH & HUBERS, Philadelphia, c. 1840s.

J. H. SCHINTZ, San Francisco.
Started his own knife-making company in 1860 after working for McConnell. In 1866 he went to work for Frederick Will but left to work for Michael Price in 1867. In 1874 he resumed making his own knives.

J. J. FORD, Georgia, c. 1862.

J. M. SCHMID & SON, Providence, Rhode Island, c. 1857–1879.

J. P. SNOW & COMPANY, Hartford, Connecticut, c. 1860s.
Made folding dirks and other knives.

J. W. & L. L. MOORE, Georgia, c. 1862.

JACKSON, Baltimore.

JAMES RODGERS, Sheffield, c. 1850.
Many of their knives were marked "Cast Steel Bowie knife."

JAMES WALTERS & CO., Sheffield, c. 1850s.

JAMES WESTA, Sheffield, c. 1860.

JOHN BAKER, Georgia, c. 1862.

JOHN C. NIXON & SONS, New York, c. 1840–1865.

JOHN D. CHEVALIER, New York, c. 1835–1871.
Considered among the best Bowie makers, his knives usually featured wood, pearl, or stag handles.

JOHN D. GRAY, c. 1862.
Made Bowies for the state of Georgia.

JOHN HENDRICK, Philadelphia, c. 1783–1790.

JOHN L. STATON, Scotsville, Virginia, c. 1861.

JOHN P. MURRAY, Columbus, Georgia, c. 1862.

JOHN TODD, New Orleans, c. 1833.

JOHN YEOMANS, c. 1850.

JONATHAN CROOKS & SON, Sheffield, c. 1837–1925.

JOSEPH ALLEN & SONS, Sheffield, c. 1864–1947.

JPH. HOLMES, c. 1830s.
Made knives marked "Arkansas Toothpick" with half horse and half alligator pommels.

L. OPPLEMAN, Lynchburg, Virginia, c. 1860s.

L. W. BABBITT, Cleveland, Ohio, c. 1832–1838.

LAMONTHE, New Orleans.

LAMPHREY.
Made knives with a small horsehead pommel of carved ivory.

LAN & SHERMAN, Richmond, Virginia, c. 1861.

LOUIS BAUER, San Francisco, c. 1872–1879.
From 1879 until 1887 operated Bauer Bros.

M. H. HANES, San Francisco, c. 1880s.
He worked for Michael Price until 1887. His knives are very similar to the M. Price knives.

M. J. HAYES & SON, San Francisco.

M. PRICE, San Francisco, c. 1850–1889.
Michael Price emigrated from Ireland, where he had been a cutler, to San Francisco in 1850 because of Ireland's potato famine. His knives are among the most prized in the world. He died in 1889.

MANSON, Sheffield, c. 1865.
Made a large quantity of spear-pointed plain dirks for Civil War use.

MAPPIN BROS, Sheffield, c. 1860s.

MARKS & REES, Cincinnati, Ohio, c. 1845.

McCONNELL, San Francisco, c. 1852–1856.
John McConnell did not stamp his knives but sold them under others' brand names. He worked for all of the area's top-name makers in the 1850s.

MURDOCH MORRISON, Rockingham County, North Carolina, c. 1862.

N. P. AMES, Springfield, Massachusetts, c. 1834–1841.

NASH SHELDON, Cincinnati, Ohio, c. 1853.

NATHAN JOSEPH, San Francisco, c. 1873.
A dealer, his knives were made by "Queens Own Co. Sheffield."

NATHAN P. AMES, Chicopee Falls, Massachusetts, c. 1829.

NATHANIEL HUNT, Boston, c. 1840–1853.

NOAH SMITHWICK, San Felipe, Texas, c. 1835.

O. S. HAYNES, Georgia, c. 1862.

OTTO & KOEHLER, New York, c. 1845.

PETER K. KRAFT, Columbia, South Carolina, c. 1860.

PETER W. KRAFT, Columbia, South Carolina, c. 1801.

R. ALLDEON, Memphis, Tennessee, c. 1860.

R. BUNTING & SONS, Sheffield, pre-1840.
This company also made folding dirks and is best known for its horsehead pommels.

R. HEINISH, Newark, New Jersey, c. 1830s.

REES FITZPATRICK, Natchez, Louisiana, 1830–1861.
One of the several makers credited by some as making Jim Bowie's original knife.

REINHARDT, Baltimore, c. 1840–1868.
Started in 1840 by a surgical instrument maker, it became Reinhardt & Bro. in 1865. Charles Reinhardt, Jr., assumed management in 1868 but stayed only one year before closing the business.

REINHOLD HOPPE, San Francisco.
Went to work for Will & Finck in 1876, started his own business in 1877, and retired in 1906.

RICHARD COLLISHAW, Sheffield, c. 1850–1863.

RICHARDS UPSON & CO., New York, c. 1808–1816.
Makers of naval dirks, later became Richard & Raylor in 1817.

ROSE, New York, c. 1833–1855.
Top of the line in quality and demand by collectors. Beware of counterfeits.

RUDOLPH HUG, Cincinnati, Ohio, c. 1853–1882.
Instrument maker.

S. TAFT, Millbury, Massachusetts, c. 1860.

SAMUEL BELL, Knoxville, Tennessee, c. 1830–1840.
Beware of fakes marked "The Gamblers Companion." Bell moved from Pennsylvania to Knoxville in the 1830s. A well-known silversmith, he made the spurs that fellow East Tennessean Sam Houston would later wear at the battle of San Jacinto. Bell became mayor of Knoxville but left Tennessee for San Antonio, Texas, in the 1840s; there he again started a successful silver business and later ran a jewelry business.

SAMUEL C. WRAGG, Sheffield, c. 1846–1857.
Wragg made Bowie knives under a variety of names and locations, including Wragg & Sons.

SAMUEL JACKSON, Baltimore, c. 1833–1851.

SAMUEL SUTHERLAND, Richmond, Virginia, c. 1850–1881.

SCHIVLEY, Philadelphia, late 1700s–mid-1800s.
Top-grade knives. Schivley made one knife that was presented by Jim Bowie's brother Rezin to a friend.

SEARLES, Baton Rouge, Louisiana, c. 1830s.
Daniel Searles made a presentation knife for Rezin P. Bowie.

SHIRLEY'S CELEBRATED OIO CUTLERY, Sheffield, c. 1850.

SILAS WALKER, Bennington, Vermont.

SIMON F. DODGE, Winchester, Virginia, c. 1863.
Civil War Bowie maker.

SOMMIS, Providence, Rhode Island, c. 1850.

STENTON, c. 1847–1867.

T. A. POTTS, New Orleans, c. 1840.

THOMAS LAMB, Washington, DC, c. 1846–1850.

THOMAS SHORT, JR., Sheffield, c. 1850.

UNION CAR WORKS, Portsmouth, Virginia, c. 1860s.

UNWIN & RODGERS, Sheffield, c. 1830s.
Early makers of high-quality Bowies.

W. & H. WHITEHEAD, Sheffield, c. 1860.
Many are found etched with patriotic mottos.

W. BUTCHER, Sheffield, c. 1836.
One of the most common names, but good-condition knives by
this name are hard to find. Commonly counterfeited.

W. C. REAVES, Sheffield.
Made knives with horsehead pommels.

W. F. JACKSON, Sheffield, c. 1850s.
Their most famous knife was marked "Rio Grande Camp
Knife" and used by John Wilkes Booth to stab Major Rathbone
in the President's Box at Ford Theater after shooting Abraham
Lincoln.

W. GREAVES & BUNTING & SONS, c. 1835.
Greaves was the New York agent for Bunting.

W. J. McELROY, Macon, Georgia, c. 1860s.

W. M. COTTON, Leominster, Massachusetts, c. 1860s.

W. R. GOULDING, New York, c. 1837–1841.
Surgical instrument maker. Most of his knives date from
1837–1840s. In 1841 his company became William R. Goulding
Co.

W. T. CLEMENT, Northampton, Massachusetts, c. 1857.
Later bought Bay State Tool Co., also recognized as Clement
Hawks Mfg. Co. in 1866 and as Clement Cutlery Co. in 1882.
He was a former employee of Lamson & Goodnow.

W. W. AYER BROS.

WILL & FINCK, San Francisco.
Frederick Will began work for McConnell 1859 and later took over McConnell's business. In 1863, he merged with Julius Finck. Will retired in 1883. The company incorporated in 1896 but went bankrupt in 1904. Others continued the name, but when the 1906 earthquake hit San Francisco, they reopened in a poor location. By 1930 their main trade was barber supplies. The company went completely out of business in 1932.

WILL BERRY, c. 1862.
Made knives for the state of Georgia.

WILLIAM BACON, New York, c. 1843.

WILLIAM WALKER, Salt Lake City, Utah, c. 1851.

WOLFE & CLARK.
Large-style knives.

WOODHEAD & HARTLEY, Sheffield, c. 1840–1849.
Top-of-the-line knives, particularly those with horsehead pommels.

ZEITZ & CO., Boston, c. 1830–1850.

CUSTOM KNIVES

▽

Although the major portion of this book is devoted to manufactured, or factory-made, knives, the field of handmade, or custom, knives will not be overlooked. Collecting of custom knives is an exciting and dynamic part of the overall knife-collecting hobby.

Collector as well as user interest in these knives, made one at a time by an ever increasing number of knife crafters, has grown at a very rapid pace. Handmade or, as most knife fanciers prefer, custom-made knives are far from a passing fad. Nor is the custom blade merely a status symbol or a statement of affluence. Whether the knife is purchased to use or to add to a collection, the demand is real and it is here to stay.

Some estimates indicate that approximately 25,000 custom knives are now being made each year. When compared to the millions of commercial factory knives made annually, those numbers may seem small. But when one considers the relative infancy of the custom-knife industry as compared to the manufactured-knife industry, they are impressive indeed.

No less than twenty years ago, one could practically count the number of nationally known custom makers on one's fingers. Their numbers steadily grew for a decade and then, during the 1980s, increased in almost geometric proportions. The list of custom makers included in this section is evidence of that phenomenal growth.

Some of the finest knives to be found in the world today come from the workshops of custom makers. Not only are they excellent examples of quality utilitarian cutlery, many of them surpass the simple name of knife and become real works of art. Like fruits of the labors of a fine painter, sculptor, or composer, these knives are recognized and appreciated as creations of another type of artist—the knife maker. One only has to see maker Buster Warinski's "King Tut Dagger," a re-creation (including 20 ounces of gold plus numerous precious stones) of the dagger found in the ancient Egyptian tomb, or Gil Hibben's "Saint George's Axe" to be convinced that knife crafters are indeed artists. Numerous examples are deserving of mention, but no words can compare with pictures. Anyone interested in the art of custom knives would be well advised to obtain a copy of *Points of Interest*, a wonderland of custom-knife photography by Jim Weyer.

Just as several knife makers are truly artists working in the medium of steel, there are many others whose artistic capabilities are evident in their decoration of pieces that might otherwise be only cutting tools. Hand engraving, exquisite file work, or scrimshawed handles are a few of the several ways that knife makers have gone beyond the craft to the art. But whether a specific handmade knife can or should be called a work of art is perhaps secondary to the fact that it almost always is a finely crafted piece of cutlery.

The term "custom knife" has become widely accepted as applying to practically all of the products of "custom knife makers." Some knife fanciers will differ on terminology as to whether these knives should be referred to as handmade, benchmade, or custom made. Although it is important for the collector to understand the fine-line difference in the terminology of handmade, benchmade and custom made, the net effect on the values of these knives is negligible. Therefore, except for the following brief explanation, the term "custom" will be used in this discussion.

The true custom-made knife is made exclusively for a specific customer and usually to his specifications, with slight artistic license offered to the maker. In the real world of the 1990s, most are not truly custom made. The majority are variations of fairly standard designs preferred by a particular maker, often combined with the customer's choice of handle material, decoration, and so on. So, although it is reasonable to assume that any true custom knife is a handmade knife, the majority of handmade knives one will find on the collector market are not custom knives in the true sense of the word. Whether the knife is a true custom or one of the maker's standard selections with special options, it is a one-of-a-kind knife made one at a time, usually in a home shop.

Today's custom knives indeed take numerous shapes and forms, and they deal with the cold, hard facts of fine using cutlery or with artistic fantasy. They are made by crafters and artists working with bar stock steel and skillfully changing that rather ordinary commodity into a special knife. They are also made by bladesmiths who use heat and hammers to alter the steel's nature along the way to make it into that fine piece of cutlery. Fixed-blade knives now take many blade forms to become hunters or skinners, fighters or survival knives, tantos or Bowies; and folding knives now feature unique locking or opening mechanisms that work so smoothly that they could come only from a knife maker's shop. After the revival of the ancient art, hand-forged Damascus blades have become quite popular with collectors. Because there is so much available in the custom knife area, the collector who chooses to specialize is making a wise decision.

The custom-knife collector has several routes to satisfaction in his collecting hobby and, he hopes, to profitable investing. One is to buy from a relatively unknown knife maker who produces a superior knife but has not achieved the fame of other, better-known makers. If his knives are truly superior, they will soon be sought by custom-knife fanciers and collectors. As demand for this maker's knives rise, so will their prices, and knives purchased earlier will appreciate in value. This method can be a rather speculative route to follow. If the maker loses interest or if his sales do not justify his staying in business long enough to establish a favorable reputation (read demand), the collector may have knives of excellent quality but of lowered resale value. If the maker and his work earn the sought-after fame, the collector will realize considerable appreciation in the value of his knives.

Another method is to buy only knives made by well-known and established makers. An obvious advantage is that of an easier market if and when you decide to sell. Remember that each custom knife is unique, but makers' names either sell knives or open the door for their sale. If one offers for sale a knife made by Moran, Frank, Henry, Lake, Loveless, or any of a few dozen other makers, collectors will recognize it as a desirable piece to own, and the only matter to be resolved is its price. The disadvantage to this method is that many of these makers are years behind in fulfilling their orders. A long wait may be in store, or if waiting is a problem, the alternative is to pay an appreciated price to another collector for one of the maker's creations. Either way, owning one of their knives will require a relatively high investment. It can also offer a relatively high return.

Another system is to seek knives of deceased makers, and, to many collectors, owning a creation of a knife-making pioneer has its own special meaning. Often, when compared to those of modern-day makers, the knife may be crude, and very seldom is it decorated.

But numerous collectors are willing to part with a few thousand dollars to own a knife made by William Scagel or Michael Price. Advertising a Richtig, a Draper, a Cooper, or a Ruana for several hundred dollars will bring buyers to your doorstep. Most of these knives are far from easy to find and, as should be expected, not inexpensive to buy. Knowledge of the custom market is especially important in this method. One should not assume that just because a maker is no longer living his knives are valuable.

Whichever route he determines to take, the collector should endeavor to buy the very best examples he can afford and ones he will enjoy owning. Whether or not there are financial returns on the investment, an almost certain return in custom knives is pride of ownership.

Prices for custom knives will range from about $70 to several thousand dollars. Their price depends not only on style, age, quality of workmanship, and amount of decoration but on the maker as well. There have been several hundred thousand knives made by hand, and many of these are available to the collector market. Since no two are exactly alike, it would be virtually impossible to offer meaningful pricing within the scope of this book. Instead, we offer suggestions for sources of information on specific knives.

Custom knives have their specialty dealers, just as do the collectible factory knives. These purveyors of the knife-makers' craft and art have studied their field and have developed a high level of expertise. They are not only excellent sources for knives, most are quite helpful in providing information. The novice collector of custom knives would be well advised to use them as key contact persons.

Attendance at knife shows will usually be quite helpful in learning more about knives and their makers. Unlike factory knives that were produced in large quantities and meet specifications of style, handles, and so forth, custom knives can best be evaluated when personally examined. The show can offer this opportunity. If your interest is primarily in custom knives, choose your show rather carefully before traveling a great distance. Be sure that it is one normally attended by makers, collectors, or purveyors of custom knives.

Other marketing channels present opportunities for learning more specifically the value of a custom knife or knives. Advertisements, especially within the classified sections of knife publications, often reveal contacts for trading of either knives or information.

As with other collecting specialities, your own reading and research will be of key importance. Fortunately, there has been much written about custom knives, and the few dollars spent on reference materials can pay dividends when high-dollar knives are involved.

The final and very important suggestion has been made easier for you by this book. If you seek information about a knife that is marked with the maker's last name or initials—and the majority are—the best source is usually the maker. The listing of custom makers that follows is the most extensive one included in any publication. Although some are former knife makers, most are known to be currently active. Addresses given are the last known, and the majority were current as of this writing. Compare the knife's marking with the knife-maker list and you're most likely well on your way to learning more about your knife from the person who knows it best—its maker.

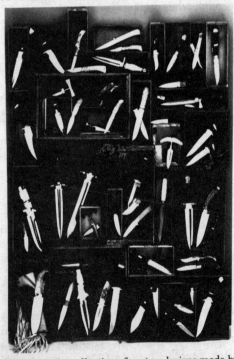

"Knives, Points of Interest," a collection of custom knives made by a variety of craftsmen and owned by Jim Weyer. The collection was displayed at a number of knife shows and used as the subject of a poster-size color print.   *(Courtesy of Jim Weyer. Photo by Weyer)*

High-density Ladder-pattern Damascus folder by Wayne Valachovic. Handle is also of Damascus steel with pearl inlay.   *(Photo by Weyer)*

Randall Model 1 knife surrounded by miniature models handmade by Earl Witsaman.   *(Photo by Weyer)*

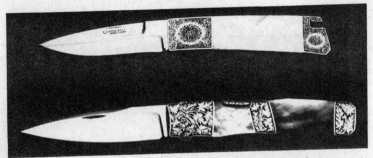

Handmade folders with pearl handles made by Frank Centofante. *(Photo by Weyer)*

Samurai sword made by Phil Hartsfield with black-and-white cord handle wrapping. Overall length is 36". *(Photo by Weyer)*

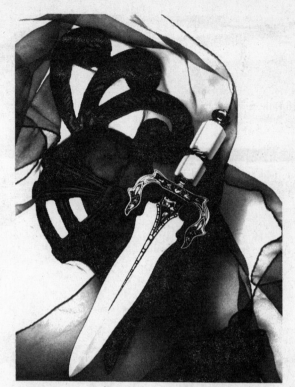

Art dagger by Rick Eaton.   *(Photo by Weyer)*

Hunter with ivory and Micarta handle made by Gil Hibben.   *(Photo by Weyer)*

George Cousino made this 12″-overall-length Fighter-pattern knife.   *(Photo by Weyer)*

Tensinch Hunter with stag handle made by Jimmy Lile.   *(Photo by Weyer)*

Model AB Survival Knife made by Jim Siska.   *(Photo by Weyer)*

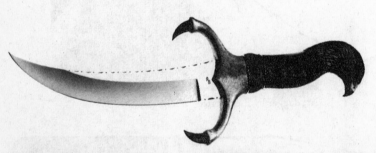

Made by Ray Beers, this 14″ knife features a handle of brass, buffalo horn, jade, and wood, with carving by the maker.   *(Photo by Weyer)*

Rear-lock-release Folder with stag handle inlay, made by Ron Lake.   *(Photo by Weyer)*

Sub-Hilt Fighter model made by Colin Cox features blade engraving and stag handle. *(Photo by Weyer)*

W. F. "Bill" Moran forged this Cinquededa Dagger in the early 1960s. It is stamped with his "Lime Kiln" marking.

Stamped "Scagel Handmade," this knife was made by pioneer knifemaker William W. Scagel during the first half of this century.

CUSTOM KNIFE MAKERS OF
THE UNITED STATES

Abbott, William, Rt. 2 Box 102A, Chandlerville, IL 62627

Abdulky, Al, 2630 Michaelangelo Dr., Stockton, CA 95207

Abdulky, Jamin, 2630 Michaelangelo Dr., Stockton, CA 95207

Adair, Earl, 4714 44th St., Dickenson, TX 77539

Addison, Ed, 325 E. Pritchard St., Asheboro, NC 27203

Albach, Larry, 7537 Del Mar Ln., La Palma, CA 90623

Alexander, Darrel, P.O. 745, Big Piney, WY 83113

Allen, Joe, Rt. 3 Box 182, Princeton, IN 47670

Allen, Mike, Rt. 1 Box 1080, Malakoff, TX 75148

Allen, Steve, 200 Forbes St., Riverside, RI 02915

Alverson, Tim, P.O. Box 92, Keno, OR 97627

Amero, Tony, 21920 Piedra Dr., Tehachapi, CA 93561

Amick, Ron, Rt. 7 Box 668-B, Sylacauga, AL 35150

Amoureux, A. W., 3210 Woodland Pk., Anchorage, AK 99517

Amspoker, Kirk, 3161 Claudia Dr., Concord, CA 94521

Anderson, Charles, West Shore, Polson, MT 59860

Anderson, Charles B., 5260 S. Landings Dr., Ft. Myers, FL 33919

Anderson, Chuck, P.O. Box 508, Estes Park, CO 80517

Anderson, Edwin, 189 Forrest Ave., Glen Cove, NY 11542

Anderson, Marvin, 7745 N.W. Cardwell Hill, Corvallis, OR 97330

Anderson, Virgil, 16318 S.E. Taggart, Portland, OR 97236

Andrews, Don, 5155 Ezy St., Coeur D'Alene, ID 83814

Andrews, E. R., P.O. Box 126, Harrisonville, MO 64701

Ankrom, W. E., 14 Marquette Dr., Cody, WY 82414

Anselmo, Victor, 11100 Cumpston St., North Hollywood, CA 91601

Antonio, William, Jr., P.O. Box 186 Rt 299, Warwick, MD 21912

Appleton, Ray, P.O. Box 321, Byers, CO 80103

Archer, Bent E., P.O. Box 128, Steilacoom, WA 98388

Atkinson, Dick, General Delivery, Warsaw, FL 32463

Bagwell, Bill, P.O. Box 265, Marietta, TX 75566

Baker, Ray, P.O. Box 303, Sapulpa, OK 74067

Baldwin, Phillip, P.O. Box 563, Snohomish, WA 98290

Balzar, John, 925 L St., Apt 680, Sacramento, CA 95814

Barbee, Jim, P.O. Box 1173, Ft. Stockton, TX 79753

Barber, Robert E., 1828 Franklin Dr., Charlottesville, VA 22901

Barber, Will, Rt. 2, Shiloh, OH 44878

Bardsley, Norman P., 197 Cottage St., Pawtucket, RI 02860

Barefoot, Joe W., P.O. Box 1248, Easley, SC 29641

Barlow, Ken, 3800 Rohner St., Fortuna, CA 95540

Barminski, Tom, 809 S. Del Norte Ave., Loveland, CO 80537

Barnes, Gary L., 305 Church St., New Windsor, MD 21776

Barnett, Jack, 1496 East Caley Ave., Littleton, CO 80121

Barney, Richard, P.O. Box 375, Mt. Shasta, CA 96067

Barr, A. T., 54 Fox Circle, Denton, TX 76205

Barret, Cecil T., 2514 Linda Lane, Colorado Springs, CO 80909

Barrett, Jack, 2133 Peach Orchard Rd., Augusta, GA 30906

Barron, David, Rt. 13 Box 415, Hendersonville, NC 28739

Barron, Jay L., 1910 Jerome S.W., Grand Rapids, MI 49507

Barry, James J., P.O. Box 1571, West Palm Beach, FL 33401

Barry, Scott, P.O. Box 354, Laramie, WY 82070

Bartlow, John, 111 Orchard Rd., Box 568, Norris, TN 37828

Bartrug, Hugh E., 505 Rhodes St., Elizabeth, PA 15037

Baskett, Gene, 240 Oakwood Dr., Elizabethtown, KY 42701

Bass, Bill, 690 Lincoln Rd. East, Vallejo, CA 94590

Bassney, John, Rt. 3 Box 277-A, Lodi, WI 53555

Bates, Ken, 3051 Henrietta Ave., La Crescenta, CA 91208

Batson, James, 171 Brentwood Lane, Madison, AL 35758

Bauchop, Peter, P.O. Box 68, Hunt Valley, MD 21030

Baylis, Brian R., P.O. Box 1771, San Marcos, CA 92069

Bear, Charles, 4042 Bones Rd., Sebastopol, CA 95472

Beatty, Gordon H., Rt. 1 Box 79, Seneca, SC 29678

Beauchamp, Dan, 467 8th Ave., Menlo Park, CA 94025

Beaver, Devon, P.O. Box 3067, Phoenix, AZ 85027

Beck, P. F., 1504 Hagood Ave., Barnwell, SC 29812

Beck, Wayne, Rt. 2 Ridgecrest Dr., High Point, NC 27260

Beckwith, Michael R., 48282 Donahue Dr., New Baltimore, MI 48047

Beers, Ray, 8 Manorbrook Rd., Monkton, MD 21111

Behnke, William, 3936 Wolcott Terrace, West Bloomfield, MI 48033

Belk, Jack, 5321 Country Rd. 3, Marble, Co 81623

Bell, Frank, 409 Town and Country Dr., Huntsville, AL 35806

Bell, Michael, Rt. 1 Box 1220, Coquille, OR 97423

Benitez, David, P.O. Box 584, Guerneville, CA 95446

Benjamin, George, Jr., 3001 Foxey Lane, Kissimmee, FL 32741

Benson, Don, 2505 Jackson St. #112, Escalon, CA 95320

Benton, Dale, Rt. 1 Box 395, Ingleside, TX 78362

Benton, W. F., 104 Lapine Dr., Eufaula, AL 36207

Ber, Dave, P.O. Box 203, Nooksack, WA 98276

Berendt, Andrew G., 2803 South 48th St., Milwaukee, WI 53219

Berland, Mrs. Ed, 309 Decker St., Santa Rosa, CA 95401

Bernhardt, J., P.O. Box 28066, Dallas, TX 75228

Berryman, Les, 39885 San Moreno Ct., Fremont, CA 94538

Berzas, Larry, 208 W. 26th St., Cut Off, LA 70345

Besic, Leroy, 40881 Johnston Ave., Hemet, CA 92344

Beubendorf, Bobby, 221 Summit St., Bridgeport, CT 06606

Beverly, Larry H., P.O. Box 6, Hartwood, VA 22471

Biggs, H. L., 3816 Via Selva, Palos Verdes, CA 92266

Bill, Wild, Rt. 9 Box 170, West Monroe, LA 71291

Birch, Robert F., P.O. Box 1901, Huntsville, TX 77340

Birt, Sid, Rt. 3 Box 269A, Nashville, IN 47448

Bizal, Paul W., P.O. Box 19834, Raytown, MO 64133

Black, Earl, 3466 South 700 East, Salt Lake City, UT 84106

Black, J. C., 3218 Castle Rock, Garland, TX 75042

Black, Tom, 921 Grecian NW, Albuquerque, NM 87107

Blackton, Andrew E., 12521 Fifth Isle, Bayonet Point, FL 33667

Blackwood, Edward W., 235 Montgomery St., San Francisco, CA 94104

Blade, Joe, P.O. Box 526, Port Townsend, WA 98368

Blakley, William E., Rt. 4 Box 106B, Fredericksburg, VA 22405

Blalock, Keith W., Jr., 1611 The Lane, Pleasanton, TX 78064

Blaum, Roy, 319 N. Columbia St., Covington, LA 70433

Bledsoe, Orville, Rt. 3 Box 280, Dobson, NC 27017

Blomberg, Gregg, Rt. 1 Box 1762, Lopez, WA 98261

Bloomer, Alan T., P.O. Box 134, Maquon, IL 61458

Bloomfield, L. H., P.O. Box 3588, Kingman, AZ 86402

Blum, Chuck, 743 S. Brea Blvd. #10, Brea, CA 92621

Blum, Ronald A., 28712 Colina Vista, Agoura Hills, CA 91301

Bochman, Bruce, P.O. Box 693, El Granada, CA 94018

Bodewitz, Dennis, P.O. Box 77, Davenport, CA 95017

Boeckman, R. Von, P.O. Box 40506, Memphis, TN 38174

Boguszewski, Phil, P.O. Box 99329, Tacoma, WA 98499

Bohannon, Mike, 19755 S.W. Marlin Dr., Beaverton, OR 97007

Bohrmann, Bruce, 29 Portland St., Yarmouth, ME 04096

Bolton, Charles B., P.O. Box 6, Jonesburg, MO 63351

Bone Knife Company, 4009 Avenue A, Lubbock, TX 79404

Bonner, Jeremy, Rt. 5 Box 427A, Asheville, NC 28803

Booth, Lew, 16 Cypress Terrace, Boonton, NJ 07005

Borgman, Leon, 2526 Park Ave., Laramie, WY 80701

Boultinghouse, David, Rt. 6 Box 265, Leander, TX 78641

Bowen, James, Rt. 1 Box 225A, Baker, WV 26801

Boyd, Francis, 2128 Market St., San Francisco, CA 94114

Boye, David, P.O. Box 187, Davenport, CA 95017

Brack, Douglas D., 5274 Teton Lane, Ventura, CA 93003

Bradley, Dennis, Rt. 3 Box 3815, Blairsville, GA 30512

Bradley, John, P.O. Box 37, Ponomo Park, FL 32081

Bragg, Jerry, P.O. Box 4289, Visalia, CA 93278

Brandsey, Edward P., 406 St. Joseph Circle, Edgerton, WI 53534

Brandstetter, Larry, 827 N. 25th, Paducah, KY 42001

Brandt, J. H., P.O. Box 5493, Irving, TX 75062

Brannan, Ralph, Rt. 1 Box 342, West Frankfort, IL 62896

Branton, Robert, 4976 Seewee Rd., Awendaw, SC 29429

Brayton, Jim, 713 Park St., Burkburnett, TX 76354

Brdlik, Dan, 166 Campbell St. South, Prescott, WI 54021

Breeze, Oran E., Star Rt. 1 Box 266-C, Blue Eyes, MT 65611

Brend, Walter J., 109 Grove St., Walterboro, SC 29488

Breshears, Clint, 2219 Belmont Lane, Redondo Beach, CA 90278

Brewer, Jack, 2415 Brandy Lane, Lafayette, IN 47905

Brewer, Lonnie, 880 Dekwood, Wesilla, AK 99687

Bridwell, Richard A., Rt. 1 Milford Ch. Rd., Taylors, SC 29687

Brightwell, Mark, 21104 Creekside Dr., Leander, TX 78641

Brignardello, Ed, Rt. 2 Box 152A, Beecher, IL 60401

Britton, G. M. "Tim," Rt. 1 Box 141, Kingston, NC 28501

Broadwell, David, P.O. Box 4314, Wichita Falls, TX 76308

Brock, Kenneth L., P.O. Box 375, Allenspark, CO 80510

Brooker, Dennis, Rt. 1 Box 12A, Derby, IA 50068

Brooks, Michael, 1108 W. 6th, Littlefield, TX 79339

Brooks, Steve R., P.O. Box 105, Big Timber, MT 59011

Broome, Thomas A., P.O. Box 4294, Kenai, AK 99611

Brower, Max, 2016 Story St., Boone, IA 50036

Brown, Bud, 306 West Rialto, Clovis, CA 93612

Brown, D. L., 1803 Birdie Dr., Toledo, OH 43615

Brown, David, P.O. Box 112, Doniphan, NE 68832

Brown, David B., 922 D St., Fairbury, NE 68352

Brown, E. H., P.O. Box 1906, Eustis, FL 32727

Brown, Floyd E., 1940 S.W. 83rd Ave., Miami, FL 33155

Brown, Harold E., Rt. 7 Box 335, Arcadia, FL 33821

Brown, L. E., 9533 Cedar St., Bellflower, CA 90706

Brown, Ted, 7603 E. Firestone Blvd., Downey, CA 90241

Browne, Rick, 1464 Gertrudita Ct., Upland, CA 91786

Brunckhorst, C. Lyle, P.O. Box 476, White Sulphur Springs, MT 59645

Bryan, Jack, 724 Highland Ave., Gardendale, AL 35071

Bryner, Barry, 448 N. 1st Ave., Price, UT 84501

Buchman, Bill, 63312 South Rd., Bend, OR 97701

Buchner, Bill, HC60 Box 35B, Idleyld Park, OR 97447

Bucholz, Mark A., 9197 W. Parkview Terrace, Eagle River, AK 99567

Buck, Bob, 582 Laurel St., Eagle Point, OR 97524

Buckbee, Donald M., 8704 Forest Ct., Warren, MI 48093

Buckner, Jimmie H., P.O. Box 162, Putney, GA 31782

Bugden, John, Rt. #6 Box 7, Murray, KY 42071

Bullard, Bill, Rt. 5 Box 33D, Andalusia, AL 36420

Bumpus, Steve, 106 Bridle Ridge, Collinsville, IL 62234

Bundick, Jim, P.O. Box 34875, Houston, TX 77234

Burkhart, Dan, 262 Mesa Dr., Camarillo, CA 93010

Burnette, Skip, 14 Wildwood Ct., Spartanburg, SC 29301

Burns, Dave, 2825 S.W. 5th St., Boynton Beach, FL 33435

Burnstead, Dave, 1929 Burnstead No. 4, Billings, MT 59101

Burton, Bryan, 6218 Everglades Dr., Alexandria, VA 22312

Busch, Ray, 418 Depre St., Mandeville, LA 70448

Busfield, John, 153 Devonshire Circle, Roanoke Rapids, NC 27870

Busse, Jerry, 11651 Co. Road 12, Wauseon, OH 43567

Butler, D. L., 25 Mallard Lane, Wilmington, IL 60481

Bybee, Barry, Rt. 1 Box 312-A, Almo, KY 42020

Caldwell, Bill, 255 Rebecca, West Monroe, LA 71292

Callahan, Errett, 2 Fredonia, Lynchburg, VA 24503

Callan, Peter, 7813 River Rd., Wagerman, LA 70094

Campbell, Dick, 20000 Silver Ranch Rd., Conifer, CO 80433

Campbell, Don, P.O. Box 82, Jerome, AZ 86331

Campbell, Irvin, Mile 20 Star Rt., Seward, AK 99664

Candrella, Joe, 1219 Barness Dr., Warminster, PA 18974

Cannady, Daniel, P.O. Box 301, Allendale, SC 29810

Cannon, Raymond W., P.O. Box 871009, Wasilla, AK 99687

Canter, Ronald E., 96 Bon Air Circle, Jackson, TN 38305

Cantini, Don, 3933 Claremont Pl., Weirton, WV 26062

Cargill, Bob, Rt. 1 Box 501-B, Oldfort, Tn 37362

Carlson, Rudy, Rt. 1 Box 163, Moscow, ID 83843

Carnes, Wendel, P.O. Box 18, Whiteberg, GA 30185

Carothers, Harley, 17473 Via Susana, San Lorenzo, CA 94580

Carson, Harold J., 559 Congress Dr., Radcliff, KY 40160

Carter, Fred, 5219 Deer Creek Rd., Wichita Falls, TX 76302

Carver, R. K., P.O. Box 29096, Atlanta, GA 30329

Casey, Dennis E., 2758 Devonshire, Redwood City, CA 94063

Casteel, Douglas, P.O. Box 72, Hillsboro, TN 37342

Cellum, Tom S., 9 Cude Cemetary Rd., Willis, TX 77378

Centofante, Frank, P.O. Box 17587, Tampa, FL 33682

Chamberlain, Paul, Rt. 2 Inverness Acres Unit, Inverness, FL 32650

Chamberlin, John A., 11535 Our Rd., Anchorage, AK 99516

Champion, Robert, 3710 Harmony, Amarillo, TX 79109

Channel, Tom, 7370 Peacock Way, Sacramento, CA 95624

Chapman, Gene, 27449 Baywood Dr., Kingston, WA 98346

Chapman, Mike, 826 East 14th St., Houston, TX 77009

Chappel, Rod, 410 Walnut, Edmonds, WA 98020

Chard, Gordon R., 104 S. Holiday Lane, Iola, KS 66749

Chase, John E., P.O. Drawer H, Aledo, TX 76008

Cheatham, Bill, 2930 W. Marlette, Phoenix, AZ 85017

Cheatham, Don E., 22 East 61st, Savannah, GA 31405

Chelquist, Cliff, P.O. Box 91, Arroyo Grande, CA 93420

Childress, D. W., Rt. 1 Box 240X, Clinton, SC 29325

Childs, C. D., 1307 Bing St., Olympia, WA 98502

Christian, Bennie, Rt. 3 Box 1925, Odessa, TX 79763

Clark, D. E., 314 Woodlawn St., Mineral Point, PA 15942

Clark, Howard, Rt. 1 Box 74, Runnells, IA 50237

Clark, Roger, 13415-74th St. N.E., Lake Stevens, WA 98258

Clay, J. D., Rt. 1 Box 1655, Greenup, KY 41144

Clay, Wayne, P.O. Box 474B, Pelham, TN 37366

Click, Gerald, 2410 N. Townleyn Ct., Santa Ana, CA 92706

Cobb, Lowell, 823 Julia St., Daytona Beach, FL 32114

Coberly, Ken, P.O. Box 1031, Petaluma, CA 94952

Cochran, Foy, 41924 N. River Dr., Sweet Home, OR 97386

Cockrell, Dan, 7235 Baldy Vista, Glendora, CA 91740

Cohen, Terry A., 114 Barson St., Santa Cruz, CA 95060

Coleman, Keith E., 107 Jardin Rd., Los Lunas, NM 87031

Coleman, Ken, 45 Grand St., Brooklyn, NY 11211

Coleman, Vernon W., 141 Lakeside Park Dr., Hendersonville, TN 37075

Collins, A. J., 1834 W. Burbank Rd., Burbank, CA 91506

Collins, Lynn M., 138 Berkley Dr., Elyria, OH 44035

Collins, Michael, 3075 Batesville Rd., Woodstock, GA 30188

Collins, Walter "Blackie," P.O. Box 100, North, SC 29112

Combs, Ralph, Jr., P.O. Box 1371, Naples, FL 33940

Compton, Paul E., 108 Overbrook Rd., Goldsboro, NC 27530

Conley, Bob, Rt. 14 Box 467, Jonesboro, TN 37659

Conn, C. T., Jr., 206 Highland Ave., Attalia, AL 35954

Connolly, Jim, 273 Kirk Ave., San Jose, CA 95127

Connor, Michael, P.O. Box 502, Winters, TX 79567

Conti, Jeffery, 2495 John Carlson Rd. N.E., Bremerton, WA 98310

Coogan, Robert, Rt. 3 Box 430, Smithville, TN 37166

Cook, James Ray, Rt. 5 Box 2188, Nashville, AR 71825

Cook, R. C., 604 Phyllis, Conroe, TX 77303

Cook, Ron, Rt. 2 Box 5800, Superior, MT 59872

Cooper, George J., 1834 West Burbank Blvd., Burbank, CA 91506

Cooper, J. N., Rt. 8 Box 653, Lufkin, TX 75901

Copeland, George S., Star Rt. Box 36, Alpine, TN 38543

Corby, Harold, 1714 Brandonwood Dr., Johnson City, TN 38604

Cordova, Joseph G., 1450 Lillie Dr., Bosque Farms, NM 87068

Corlee, Leonard, P.O. Box 143, Georgetown, GA 31754

Corrado, Jim, 2915 Cavitt Creek Rd., Glide, OR 97443

Corwin, Don, 5064 Eber Rd., Monclove, OH 43542

Cosgrove, Charles, 7105 Jameson Rd., Amarillo, TX 79106

Costa, Scott, Rt. 2 Box 503, Spicewood, TX 78669

Cottrill, James, 1776 Ransburg Ave., Columbus, OH 43223

Couchman, Don, Rt. 1 Box 283-A, La Mesa, NM 88044

Courtney, Danny, Jr., Rt. 8 Box 237, Martinsville, VA 24112

Courtney, Eldon, 2718 Bullinger, Wichita, KS 67204

Cousino, George, 22386 Beechwood Ct., Woodhaven, MI 48183

Cover, Raymond A., Rt. 1 Box 194, Mineral Point, MO 63660

Cox, Colin J., 1609 Votaw Rd., Apopka, FL 32703

Cox, James O., 1203 Evergreen Dr., Smackover, AR 71762

Cox, Mike, Rt. 1 Box 69, Cowiche, WA 98923

Crabtree, H. W., Rt. 1, Ruby, AR 72952

Craft, Richard C., 3045 Longwood Dr., Jackson, MS 39212

Craig, James H., 334 Novara, Manchester, MO 63021

Crain, Jack, 400 Walden Rd., Weatherford, TX 76087

Crane, Arnold H., 134 North La Salle, Chicago, IL 60602

Crawford, Larry, 1602 Brooks St., Rosenberg, TX 77471

Crawford, Pat, 205 N. Center, West Memphis, AR 72301

Crawford, Stewart, 504½ Front St., Morgan City, LA 70380

Crisp, Harold, 3885 Bow St. N.E., Cleveland, TN 37312

Crockford, Jack, 1859 Harts Mill Rd., Chamblee, GA 30341

Cross, Stuart, P.O. Box 1519, Alpine, TX 79831

Cross, Tim, 743 Loma Vista Dr., Long Beach, CA 90813

Crowder, Robert, P.O. Box 1374, Thompson Falls, MT 59873

Crowell, James L., HC 74 Box 368, Mountain View, AR 72560

Cruze, Dan, 14406 Winterset Dr., Orlando, FL 32812

Cullity, W. Daniel, Old Country Rd. East, Sandwich, MA 02537

Culpepper, John, 2102 Spencer Ave., Monroe, LA 71201

Cumming, Bob, American Embassy, FPO New York, NY 09170

Cunningham, Jim, 1911 Madison, Memphis, TN 38104

Cute, Thomas, Road 4, Rt. 90, Cortland, NY 13045

D'Elia, Frank, 2050 Hillside Ave., New Hyde Park, NY 11040

Dabbs, Bill, 18330 Wards Ferry Rd., Sonora, CA 95370

Dachtler, Orville, 35182 Cabral Dr., Fremont, CA 94536

Dade, C. M., 19759 Chef Mentour Hwy., New Orleans, LA 70129

Dagget, Dan, 1961 Meteor, Flagstaff, AZ 86001

Dahl, Cris W., Rt. 4 Box 558, Lake Geneva, WI 53147

Dailey, G. E., 577 Lincoln St., Seekonk, MA 02771

Daniels, Alex, 1410 Colorado Ave., Lynn Haven, FL 32444

Daniels, Travis E., 5531 Pinebrook Ln., Winston Salem, NC 27105

Darakis, Art A., 18181 Quarry Rd., Wellington, OH 44090

Darby, Rick, 4026 Shelbourne, Youngstown, OH 44511

Davenport, Jack, 1304 W. Center Ave., Dade City, FL 32525

Davenport, Steve, 15 Roman Lane, Alvin, TX 77511

Davidson, Edmund, Rt. 1 Box 319, Goshen, VA 24439

Davidson, Rob, 2419 25th St., Lubbock, TX 79411

Davis, Barry, 1365 Van Antwerp Rd., Schenectady, NY 12309

Davis, Barry L., 1871 Pittsfield Rd., Castleton, NY 12033

Davis Brothers, 1209 Woodlawn Dr., Camden, SC 29020

Davis, Dixie, Rt. 3, Clinton, SC 29325

Davis, Don, 3918 Ash Ave., Loveland, CO 80538

Davis, Gerald, P.O. Box 793, Camden, SC 29020

Davis, Jesse W., 5810 Hwy. 301, Walls, MS 38680

Davis, K. M., P.O. Box 267, Monroe, WA 98272

Davis, Larry, 411 Cedar Dr., Pierce, ID 83456

Davis, Syd, 1220 Courtney Dr., Richmond, TX 77469

Davis, Terry, P.O. Box 111, Sumpter, OR 97877

Davis, Vernon M., 1226 LaClede, Waco, TX 76705

Davis, W. C., 2010 S. Madison, Raymore, MO 64083

Dawson, Dane and Barry, P.O. Box 10, Marvel, CO 81329

Day, Phillip, Rt. 1 Box 464 T Bay, Minetta, AL 35607

De Intinnis, Ed, 107 Summit Ave., Staten Island, NY 10306

Dean, Harvey J., Rt. 2 Box 137, Rockdale, TX 76567

Dearhart, Richard, Rt. 1, Lula, GA 30554

Defeo, Robert A., 12 Morningside Dr., Mays Landing, NJ 08330

Defreest, William G., P.O. Box 573, Barnwell, SC 29812

Degraeve, Richard, 329 Valencia St., Sebastian, FL 32958

Del Pinto, Paul, 5901 Warner Ave., Apt. 3, Huntington Beach, CA 92649

Delong, Dick, 17561 E. Ohio Circle, Aurora, CO 80017

Demers, Roy, Rt. 1 Box 104 A, Wever, IA 52658

Dempsey, Gordon S., P.O. Box 7497, N. Kenai, AK 99635

Dennard, J. R., 907 Greenwood Pl., Dalton, GA 30720

Dennehy, Dan, 13321 Hwy. 160, Del Norte, CO 81132

Dent, Douglas M., 1208 Chestnut St. S., Charleston, WV 25309

Detloff, Larry, 130 Oxford Way, Santa Cruz, CA 95060

Detmer, Phillip, Rt. 1 Box 149A, Breese, IL 62230

Dew, Norman, 742 Hobhollow, Channel View, TX 77530

Deyong, Clarence, 5211 Maryland Ave., Racine, WI 53406

Diana, Julius S., P.O. Box 152, Carmichaels, PA 15320

Dias, Jack, P.O. Box 223, Palermo, CA 95968

Dickey, Charles, 803 N.E. A St., Bentonville, AR 72712

Dickson, Jim, 2349 Eastway Rd., Decatur, GA 30033

Dietz, Bill, 501 S.W. 18th St., Ft. Lauderdale, FL 33315

Digangi, Joseph M., P.O. Box 225, Santa Cruz, NM 87567

Dill, Dave, 2609 N.W. 33rd, Oklahoma City, OK 73112

Dillon, Earl E., 8908 Stanwin Ave., Arleta, CA 91331

Dilluvio, Frank, 13611 Joyce, Warren, MI 48093

Dingman, Scott, HCO 5 Box 134, Park Rapids, MN 56470

Dion, Greg, 3032 S. Jackson St., Oxnard, CA 93033

Dion, Malcolm, 820 N. Fairview Ave., Goleta, CA 93117

Doak, Charles A., P.O. Box 143, Saddle River, TN 37458

Dodge, Robert O., 1515 Braley St., Saginaw, MI 48602

Dodson, Dr. Frank, Jr., Rt. 3 Box 372, Little Rock, AR 72211

Dolan, Robert L., 220-B Naalae Rd., Kula, HI 96790

Donaghey, John, P.O. Box 402021, Garland, TX 75046

Donovan, Patrick, 1770 Hudson Dr., San Jose, CA 95124

Doolittle, Mike, 13 Denise Ct., Novato, CA 94947

Dorough, Dick, Rt. 1 Box 210, Gadsden, AL 35901

Douglas, Dale, 361 Mike Cooper Rd., Ponchatoula, LA 70454

Dow, Thomas G., 195 River Rd., Grandview, NY 10960

Dowell, T. M., 139 N.W. St. Helen's Pl., Bend, OR 97701

Downing, Larry, Rt. 1 Box 387, Bremen, KY 42325

Downing, Tom, 129 S. Bank St., Cortland, OH 44410

Downs, Jim, 35 Sunset Rd., Londonderry, OH 45647

Draper, Kent, 323 E. Romona, Salt Lake City, UT 84115

Drew, Frank, 729 Main St., Klamath Falls, OR 97601

Driskill, Beryl, P.O. Box 187, Braggadocio, MO 63826

Duff, Bill, P.O. Box 694, Virginia City, NV 89440

Dufour, Arthur J., 8120 Dearmoun Rd., Anchorage, AK 99516

Dugan, Brad, P.O. Box 693, Milford, DE 19963

Dugger, Dave, 2504 West 51, Westwood, KS 66205

Duke, R. D., 7160 Belgium Circle, Pensacola, FL 32506

Dumatrait, Gene, P.O. 3071, Beaumont, TX 77704

Dungy, Lawrence, 10 Southmont Dr., Little Rock, AR 72209

Dunkerley, Rick, P.O. 114, Cameron, MT 59720

Dunn, James E., 1560 Brookhollow, Santa Ana, CA 92705

Dunn, Melvin T., 5830 N.W. Carlson Rd., Rossville, KS 66533

Duran, Jerry T., 442 Montclaire S.E., Albuquerque, NM 87108

Durio, Fred, 289 Gulino St., Opelousas, LA 70570

Duvall, Fred, Rt. 8 Box 677, Benton, AR 72015

Duvall, Larry E., Rt. 3, Gallatin, MO 64640

Eagan, Tim, 118 Las Ondas Ct., Santa Cruz, CA 95060

Easler, Russell O., P.O. Box 301, Woodruff, SC 29388

Eaton, Al, P.O. Box 43, Clayton, CA 94517

Eaton, Rick, 1847 Walnut Grove Ct., Oakley, CA 94561

Ecker, Dave, 110 Bleecker St., 22 A, New York, NY 10012

Edwards, Fain E., 209 E. Mountain Ave., Jacksonville, AL 36265

Edwards, Homer W., 6429 Camelback Rd., Phoenix, AZ 85033

Edwards, Thomas W., 6429 Camelback Rd., Phoenix, AZ 85033

Elder, Ray, 121 E. 11th St., Colorado City, TX 79512

Elkins, R. Van, P.O. Box 156, Bonita, LA 71223

Ellefson, Joel, 1233 Storymill Rd., Bozeman, MT 59715

Ellerbe, W. B., 3871 Osceola Rd., Geneva, FL 32732

Ellis, David, P.O. Box 487, Reseda, CA 91335

Ellison, Don, 670 Browning, Ypsilanti, MI 48197

Elmore, Clarence, 4944 Angeles Crest Hwy., La Canada, CA 91011

Embry, Brad, P.O. Box 11931, Tampa, FL 33680

Emerson, Ernest R., 4166 W. 172nd St., Torrance, CA 90504

Emery, Roger, 3514 South Central Ave., Phoenix, AZ 85041

Ence, Jim, 145 S. 200 East, Richfield, UT 84701

Enders, Robert, 3028 White Rd., Cement City, MI 49233

England, Mike, 608 West 4th, Cordell, OK 73632

England, Virgil, 629 W. 15th Ave., Anchorage, AK 99501

Englebretson, George, 1209 N.W. 49th St., Oklahoma City, OK 73118

Engnath, Bob, 1217 B Crescent Dr., Glendale, CA 91205

Ennard, J. R., 907 Greenwood Pl., Dalton, GA 30720

Enos, Thomas M., 12302 State Road 535, Orlando, FL 32819

Enton, W. F., 104 Lapine Dr., Eufaula, AL 36207

Erickson, Curt, 449 Washington Blvd., Ogden, UT 84404

Erickson, L. M., P.O. Box 132, Liberty, UT 84310

Erickson, Walter E., 23883 Ada St., Warren, MI 48091

Eriksen, James T., 3702 Dividend Dr., Garland, TX 75042

Essegian, Richard, 4219 E. Shields Ave., Fresno, CA 93726

Etienne, Serge, 14875 Esters Rd., Valley Ford, CA 94972

Evans, John D., 5414 Grissom Dr., Arlington, TX 76016

Evans, Vincent K., 556-B Kamani St., Honolulu, HI 96813

Ewing, John H., Rt. 2 Box 301, Clinton, TN 37716

Ewing, William S., 2724 Northcrest, Plano, TX 75075

Falconer, Ralph, P.O. Box 1021, Frederick, OK 73542

Fassio, Melvin G., 2012 Rattlesnake Dr., Missoula, MT 59802

Faucheaux, Howard J., P.O. Box 206, Loreauville, LA 70552

Faulkner, Allan, 6103 Park Ave., Marysville, CA 95901

Fawcett, Alexander R., 3241 Kerner Blvd., San Rafael, CA 94901

Fecas, Stephen, 1312 Shadow Lane, Anderson, SC 29625

Feccia, Ron, 1600 Holloway Ave., San Francisco, CA 94132

Feragotti, Vince, Rt. 1 Beechwood Dr., Industry, PA 15052

Ferdinand, Don, P.O. Box 2790, San Rafael, CA 94941

Ferguson, Jim, P.O. Box 764, San Angelo, TX 76902

Ferguson, Lee, Rt. 2 Box 109, Hindsville, AR 72738

Ferguson, Lewis, 1200 Pico Blvd., Santa Monica, CA 90405

Ferguson, Roy, P.O. Box 224, Wedderburn, OR 97491

Ferry, Thomas, 4208 Canoga Dr., Woodland Hills, CA 91364

Fielder, William V., 2715 Salem Bottom Rd., Westminster, MD 21157

Fikes, Jimmy L., 93 Farley Rd., Wendell, MA 03179

Filbrun, Robert, 3843 Beckwith Rd., Modesto, CA 95351

Finger, L. C., 1001 113th N., Weatherford, TX 76086

Finley, C. H., 4176 St. Patrick Ave., Redding, CA 96001

Fiorini, Bill, 1590 Hwy. 16, La Cresent, NM 55974

Fischer, Clyde E., P.O. Box 310, Nixon, TX 78140

Fisher, Mike, Rt. 3, Beatrice, NE 68310

Fisher, Theo, 8115 Modoc Lane, Montague, CA 96064

Fisk, Jerry, Rt. 1 Box 41, Lockesburg, AR 71846

Fister, Jim, Rt. 1, Finchville, KY 40022

Fitch, C. S., 1755 Laurel St., Baton Rouge, LA 70802

Fitzgerald, Dennis, P.O. Box 12847, Fort Wayne, IN 46866

Flemming, Jim, Yonna Valley Forge, Bonanza, OR 97623

Flournoy, Joe, Rt. 6 Box 233, El Dorado, AR 71730

Flynn, Bruce, Rt. 1 Box 234A, Middletown, IN 47356

Fogg, Don, P.O. Box 335, Littleton, NH 03561

Ford, Allen, 3927 Plumcrest Rd., Smyrna, GA 30080

Foreman, Bill, 1200 Catherine St., Metropolis, IL 62960

Forester, Del W., 7355 Sanborn Lane, Sacramento, CA 95823

Forge, H. B., Rt. 2 Box 24, Shiloh, OH 44878

Forthofer, Pete, 711 Spokane Ave., Whitefish, MT 59937

Foster, Al, Rt. HC 73 Box 117, Dogpatch, AR 72648

Foust, Roger, 1925 Vernon Ave., Modesto, CA 95351

Fowler, Ed, Willow Bow Ranch, Box 1519, Riverton, WY 82501

Fowler, Jerry, P.O. Box 85, Thorndale, TX 76577

Fox, Paul, Rt. 3 Box 208F, Claremont, NC 28610

Fox, Wendell, 4080 South 39th, Springfield, OR 97477

Frank, Heinrich H., P.O. Box 984, Whitefish, MT 59937

Franklin, Mike, 71 Marketplace, Aberdeen, OH 45101

Franks, Joel, 6610 Quaker, Lubbock, TX 79413

Frazier, Ron, 2107 Urbine Rd., Powhatan, VA 23139

Freeman, Art F., P.O. Box 2545, Citrus Heights, CA 95611

Freeman, Douglas J., 4154 Dellwood, Macon, GA 31204

Freiling, Albert J., 3700 Niner Rd., Finksburg, MD 21048

Frese, William R., 5374 Fern Beach, St. Louis, MO 63128

Frey, W. Frederick, 305 Walnut St., Milton, PA 17847

Friedly, Dennis, 12 Cottontail Lane, Cody, WY 82414

Frizzell, Ted, Rt. 2, Box 326, West Fork, AR 72774

Froehlick, R., 740 North California, Lodi, CA 95240

Fronefield, Mike, P.O. Box 9764, Truckee, CA 95737

Fuegen, Larry, Rt. 1 Box 279, Wiscasset, ME 04578

Fujisaka, Stanley, 45-004 Holowai St., Kaneohe, HI 96744

Fukuta, Tak, 1495 Brummel Ave., Elk Grove Village, IL 60007

Fuller, Burt, P.O. Box 734, Livingston, AL 35470

Fuller, Jack, 7103 Stretch Ct., Mt. Airy, MD 21771

Fuller, Jim, P.O. Box 51, Burnwell, AL 35038

Fuller, John W., 6156 Ridge Way, Douglasville, GA 30135

Fuller, W. T., 400 S. 8th St., East Gadsden, AL 35903

Fulton, Mickey, P.O. Box 1062, Willows, CA 95988

Funderburg, Joe, 1255 Bay Oaks Dr., Los Osos, CA 93402

Gallop, Bob, 44021 White Oak Ct., Rocklin, CA 95677

Gamble, Frank, P.O. Box 2243, Gilroy, CA 95021

Gardner, Mark, 11585 Lincoln St., Grand Haven, MI 49417

Garlits, Chuck, P.O. Box 577, Rosman, NC 28772

Garner, William, 2803 East Desoto St., Pensacola, FL 32503

Gartman, M. D., Rt. 3 Box 13, Gatesville, TX 76528

Gaston, Ron, 330 Gaston Dr., Woodruff, SC 29388

Gaudette, Linden L., 5 Hitchcock Rd., Wilbraham, MA 01095

Gault, Clay, Rt. 1 Box 287, Lexington, TX 78947

Geisler, Gary R., P.O. Box 294, Clarksville, OH 45113

Genge, Roy E., P.O. Box 57, Eastlake, CO 80614

Genovese, Rick, 3722 Surry Lane, Colorado Springs, CO 80918

George, Harry, 3137 Old Camp Long Rd., Aiken, SC 29801

George, Tom, P.O. Box 1298, Magalia, CA 95954

Gilbreath, Randall W., P.O. Box 195, Dora, AL 35062

Gillenwater, E. E. "Dick," 921 Dougherty Rd., Aiken, SC 29801

Gilmore, Jon, 849 University Pl., St. Louis, MO 63132

Giovannetti, Jim, 2710 Denison St., San Pedro, CA 90731

Gladius, Terra, 1802 5th S.E., Olympia, WA 98501

Glaser, Ken, Rt. 1 Box 148, Purdy, MO 65734

Gleason, Roger, 13518 Grover St., Omaha, NE 68144

Glover, Ron, P.O. Box 44132, Cincinnati, OH 45244

Goddard, Wayne, 473 Durham Ave., Eugene, OR 97404

Goertz, Paul S., 201 Union Ave., S.E., #207, Renton, WA 98056

Goff, Darrel W., 5725 Newholme Ave., Baltimore, MD 21206

Gofourth, Jim, 3776 Alisco Canyon Rd., Santa Paula, CA 93060

Goldenberg, T. S., P.O. Box 963, Herndon, VA 22070

Golding, Robin, 14911 E. Hwy. 120, Ripon, CA 95366

Goltz, Warren L., 802 E. 4th Ave., Ada, MN 56510

Gonzalez, Gene, P.O. Box 33, Roma, TX 78584

Goo, Tai, 506 W. First St., Tempe, AZ 85281

Goodwin, Butch, 1345 Foothill Dr., Vista, CA 92084

Gottage, Dante, 21700 Evergreen, St. Clair Shores, MI 48082

Gottage, Judy, 21700 Evergreen, St. Claire Shores, MI 48082

Gottschalk, Gregory, 12 First St., Carnegie, PA 15106

Gouker, Gary B., P.O. Box 955, Sitka, AK 99835

Graber, Cliff C., 315 East 4th St., Ontario, CA 91764

Graham, Charles W., Rt. 1-A Box 11, Eolia, MO 63344

Graham, Robert, 1632 Creighton Ave., Akron, OH 44310

Granquist, William R., 5 Paul St., Bristol, CT 06010

Grant, John B., 59 Wood Lane, Fairfax, CA 94930

Grant, Larry, P.O. Box 404, Auburn, WY 83111

Gravelle, Mike, 4710 Shabbona Rd., Deckerville, MI 48427

Grebe, Gordon S., P.O. Box 116, Ancho Point, AK 99556

Greco, John, Rt. 6 Box 55, Bay St. Louis, MS 39520

Green, Larry, 6911 N.W. 77th Terrace, Kansas City, MO 64152

Green, Roger M., 3412 Co. Road 1022, Joshua, TX 76058

Greenfield, G. O., P.O. Box 2405, Missoula, MT 59806

Gregory, Michael, 211 Calhoun Rd., Belton, SC 29627

Grey, Bruce, 145 West 20th St., Chico, CA 95926

Griffin, Howard, 14299 S.W. 31st Ct., Davie, FL 33330

Griffin, Rendon, 9706 Cedardale, Houston, TX 77055

Grigg, Walt, 1303 Stetson, Orlando, FL 32804

Grigsby, Ben, 80 King George St., Batesville, AR 72501

Grigsby, John D., 5320 Circle Rd., Corryton, TN 37721

Gross, W. W., 325 Sherbrook Dr., High Point, NC 27260

Grossman, Stewart, 747 Main St., #1, Clinton, MA 01510

Grow, Jim, 1712 Carlisle Rd., Oklahoma City, OK 73120

Grubb, Richard E., 2759 Maplewood Dr., Columbus, OH 43231

Guess, Jack, 12 N. Rockford, Tulsa, OK 74120

Gurganus, Melvin H., Star Rt. Box 50A, Colerain, NC 27924

Guth, Kenneth, 8 S. Michigan, 32nd Fl., Chicago, IL 60603

Guthrie, George, Rt. 3 Box 432, Bessemer City, NC 28016

Gwozdz, Bob, 71 Starr Lane, Attleboro, MA 02703

Hagen, Philip, P.O. Box 58, Pelican Rapids, MN 56572

Haggerty, George S., P.O. Box 88, Jacksonville, VT 05342

Hagwood, Kellie, 9231 Ridgetown, San Antonio, TX 78250

Hajovsky, Robert J., P.O. Box 21, Scotland, TX 76379

Halbrook, Gary R., 17564 Arrow Blvd., Fontana, CA 92335

Hall, Douglas A., 1450 Alta Vista Dr., Vista, CA 92083

Hamby, Skip, P.O. Box 447, Portola, CA 96122

Hammock, Mr. and Mrs. Paul, 1433 South Broadway, Santa Maria, CA 93454

Hammond, Jim, P.O. Box 486, Arab, AL 35016

Hancock, Ronald E., P.O. Box 68, Inverness, FL 32651

Hansen, Robert W., Rt. 2 Box 88, Cambridge, MN 55008

Hanson, Burt, 440 N. 21st St., Las Vegas, NV 89901

Hardin, Robert K., 814 Pamela Dr., Dalton, GA 30720

Hargis, Frank, 321 S. Elm St., Flora, IL 62839

Harless, Walt, P.O. Box 5913, Lake Worth, FL 33466

Harley, Larry W., Rt. 3, 348 Deerfield Dr., Bristol, TN 37620

Harmon, Jay, 462 Victoria Rd., Woodstock, GA 30188

Harn, Robert, 228 Pensacola Rd., Venice, FL 33595

Harper, D. J., 2817 W. Glenrosa, Phoenix, AZ 85017

Harrington, Mike, 408 S. Cedar, Abilene, KS 67410

Harris, Ralph Dewey, P.O. Box 597, Grovetown, GA 30813

Harrison, Dan, and Son, P.O. Box 42, Edom, TX 75756

Harrison, Gene, 17731 Redding, Hesperia, CA 92345

Harsey, William W., 82710 N. Howe Lane, Creswell, OR 97426

Hartman, Arlan, 340 Ruddiman, N. Muskegon, MI 49445

Hartsfield, Phill, 13095 Brookhurst St., Garden Grove, CA 92643

Harwood, Oscar, 903 S. Cooper St., Memphis, TN 38104

Hatch, Ken, P.O. Box 82, Jensen, UT 84035

Hawk, Joe, Rt. 1 Box 195, Ceres, VA 24318

Hawkins, Rade, P.O. Box 400, Red Oak, GA 30272

Hayes, Robert, P.O. Box 141, Railroad Flat, CA 95248

Haynes, George, 906 South Wilson, El Reno, OK 73036

Heath, William, P.O. Box 131, Bondville, IL 61815

Hedgecock, Walter F., P.O. Box 175, Glen Daniel, WV 25844

Hedland, Gregory W., 736 Masonic, San Francisco, CA 94117

Hedrick, Don, 131 Beechwood Hills, Newport News, VA 23602

Hegedus, Lou, P.O. Box 441, Cave Spring, GA 30124

Hegwald, J. L., 1106 Charles, Humboldt, KS 66748

Hegwood, Joel, Rt. 4 Box 229, Summerville, GA 30747

Hein, L. T., 3515 4 Mile Rd., Racine, WI 53404

Heller, Henry, 4107 Keeler Ct., Pasedena, TX 77503

Helton, Roy L., P.O. Box 26598, San Diego, CA 92126

Helzer, Elwin, P.O. Box 898, Oracle, AZ 85623

Hembrook, Ron, P.O. Box 153, Neosho, WI 53059

Henderson, Bert, Rt. 1 Box 215, Eddyville, OR 97343

Hendrickson, E. J., 4204 Ballenger Creek Pike, Frederick, MD 21701

Henry, D. E., Star Rt., Old Gulch Rd, Mountain Range, CA 95246

Hensley, Wayne, P.O. Box 904, Conyers, GA 30207

Henson, Russell, P.O. Box 779, Jackson, WY 83001

Herman, R., 4607 Pasadena Ave., Sacramento, CA 95821

Herman, Tim, 7721 Foster, Overland Park, KS 66204

Herndon, William R., 32520 Michigan Ave., Acton, CA 93510

Herron, George, Rt. 1 Box 25A, Springfield, SC 29146

Hethcoat, Don, P.O. 1764, Clovis, NM 88101

Hetmanski, Thomas S., 1107 William St., Trenton, NJ 08610

Hewitt, Ron, P.O. Box 632, Ludowici, GA 31316

Hibben, Daryl, P.O. Box 2287, Pocatello, ID 83206

Hibben, Gil, P.O. Box 24213, Louisville, KY 40224

Hickory, Beau, P.O. Box 34235, San Francisco, CA 94103

Hicks, Vernon W., Rt. 1 Box 387, Bauxite, AR 72011

High, Tom, 5474 S. 112.8 Rd., Alamoso, CO 81101

Hightower, C., Rt. 1, Beauville, TX 75631

Hilker, Tom, 4884 Harmony Lane, Santa Maria, CA 93455

Hill, Howard E., Jette Lake, Polson, MT 59860

Hill, Rick, 576 Clover Dr., Edwardsville, IL 62025

Hill, Steven E., 7814 Toucan Dr., Orlando, FL 32822

Hinderer, R., 5423 Kister Rd., Wooster, OH 44691

Hinkle, John, P.O. Box 1793, Roswell, NM 88201

Hinston, R., & Son, 2419 Edgewood Rd., Columbus, GA 31906

Hitt, Robert, 2111 Livingston Ave., Helena, MT 59601

Hock, Ron, 16650 Mitchell Creek Rd., Fort Bragg, CA 95437

Hodge, J. B., 1100 Woodmont Ave. S.E., Huntsville, AL 35801

Hodge, John, 422 S. 15th St., Palatka, FL 32077

Hodges, Frank, 3710 85th St., Lubbock, TX 79423

Hodgson, Richard J., 9081 Tahoe Lane, Boulder, CO 80301

Hoel, Steve, P.O. Box 283, Pine, AZ 85544

Hoffman, Harold, 7174 Hoffman Rd., San Angelo, TX 76905

Hoffman, Kevin, 6392 Holly Ct., Lisle, IL 60532

Hoffman, Kevin L., P.O. Box 5107, Winter Park, FL 32793

Hoffmann, Donald, P.O. Box 174, San Miguel, CA 93451

Holder, D'Alton, 4412 W. Diana, Glendale, AZ 85302

Holguin, Paul, 2015 Lees Ave., Long Beach, CA 90815

Holland, Dale J., 4561 247th Pl. S.E., Issaquah, WA 98027

Holloway, Paul, 714 Burksdale Rd., Norfolk, VA 32518

Holmes, Robert, 4423 Lake Larto Circle, Baton Rouge, LA 70816

Holstrom, Ron, 615 West Alcott, Fergus Falls, MN 56537

Horn, Jess, 2850 Goodwater Ave., Redding, CA 96002

Hornby, Glen, P.O. Box 444, Glendale, CA 91209

Hover, Richard, 300 East Mineral King, Visalia, CA 93278

Howard, Durvyn M., Rt. 5 Box 77, Gadsden, AL 35903

Howie, David M., P.O. Box 615, Deer Park, TX 77536

Howser, John C., 54 Bell Lane, Frankfort, KY 40601

Hrisoulas, Jim, 15258 Lakeside, Sylmar, CA 91342

Hubbard, Arthur J., 574 Cutlers Farm Rd., Monroe, CT 06468

Huddleston, Richard, 2965 E. Fairview, Santa Ana, CA 92704

Hudson, C. Robbin, Rt. 1 Box 128B, Rockhall, MD 21661

Hudson, Robert, 3802 Black Cricket Ct., Humble, TX 77396

Huelskamp, David, Rt. 1 Box 177, Breese, IL 62230

Huertas, Eppy, 1026 Thompson Ave., Apt. 3, Glendale, CA 91201

Hueske, Chubby, 4808 Tamarisk Dr., Bellaire, TX 77401

Huey, Steve, 27645 Snyder Rd. #38, Junction City, OR 97448

Huff, John, 2131 Keatking St., Hillcrest Hts., MD 20013

Hughes, Dan, 13743 Persimmon Blvd., West Palm Beach, FL 33411

Hughes, Daryle, 10979 Leonard, Nunica, MI 49448

Hughes, Ed, 280½ Holly Lane, Grand Junction, CO 81503

Hughes, Lawrence, 207 W. Crestway, Plainview, TX 79072

Hull, Michael, 2118 Obarr Pl., Apt C, Santa Ana, CA 92701

Hull, Michael J., 1330 Hermits Circle, Cottonwood, AZ 86326

Humenick, Roy, P.O. Box 414, Rescue, CA 95672

Hunnicutt, Robert E., 2636 Magnolia Way, Forest Grove, OR 97116

Hunt, Dick, 703 Eratz Brown, Moberly, MO 65270

Hunt, Jerry, 4606 Princeton Dr., Garland, TX 75042

Hunt, Maurice D., 5450 Dan Jones Rd., Plainsfield, IN 46168

Hurst, Jeff, Rt. 1 Box 22A, Rutledge, TN 37861

Hurst, Jim, 4537 South Irvington, Tulsa, OK 74135

Husman, Dennis, P.O. Box 997, Patterson, CA 95363

Hyer, Jack, 4 Worthdale Ct., Winston Salem, NC 27103

Imboden, Howard L., 4216 Barth Lane, Kettering, OH 45429

Imel, Billy Mace, 1616 Bundy Ave., New Castle, IN 47362

Isaacs, Dan, 3701 Eureka #59-A, Anchorage, AK 99503

Jacks, Jim, P.O. Box 2782, Covina, CA 91722

Jackson, Dave, 1914 East Harold Ave., Visalia, CA 93278

Jackson, Mark, 2405 33rd Ave. South, Minneapolis, MN 55406

James, Clifton, Star Route Box 10, Atmore, AL 35611

Janiak, John S., Rt. 2, Park Rd., Colchester, CT 06415

Jean, Gerry, 25B Cliffside Dr., Manchester, CT 06040

Jensen, Carl A., Rt. 3 Box 74, Blair, NE 68008

Jernigan, Steve, 298 Tunnel Rd., Milton, FL 32571

Jirik, Sid, 11301 Patro St., Anchorage, AK 99516

Job, Robert, 1046 Goffle Rd., Hawthorne, NJ 07506

Jobs, S. R., 1513 Martin Chapel Rd., Murray, KY 42071

Johnsen, Steve, P.O. Box 1015, Morro Bay, CA 93442

Johnson, Brad, 3477 Running Deer Dr., El Paso, TX 79936

Johnson, Durrell, P.O. Box 594, Sparr, FL 32690

Johnson, Gene, 5648 Redwood Ave., Portage, IN 46368

Johnson, Gorden W., 5426 Sweetbriar, Houston, TX 77017

Johnson, Harold C., 1014 Lafayette Rd., Chickamauga, GA 30707

Johnson, Herbert, 6515 Irving Ave. South, Richfield, MN 55423

Johnson, Keith L., P.O. Box 382, Lyle, WA 98635

Johnson, Ladow "Doc," 2322 W. Country Club Park, Toledo, OH 43614

Johnson, Ronald B., P.O. Box 11, Clearwater, MN 55320

Johnson, Ruffin, 215 Lafonda Dr., Houston, TX 77060

Johnson, Ryan M., P.O. Box 267, Hixson, TN 37343

Johnson, Steve R., 554 S. 500 East, Manti, UT 84642

Johnson, Wm. C., 2242 N.W. 5th St., Okeechobee, FL 34972

Johnston, Frank, 11435 Ogle Rd. N.E., Poulsbo, WA 98370

Jokerst, Charles, 9312 Spaulding, Omaha, NE 68134

Jones, Bob, 6219 Aztec N.E., Albuquerque, NM 87110

Jones, Curtis J., 39909 176th St. E., Palmdale, CA 93550

Jones, Enoch, 4132 Novar Dr., Chantilly, VA 22021

Jones, Fred, 858 East I St., Ontario, CA 91762

Jones, Gomer G., 13313 E. 13th, Tulsa, OK 74108

Jones, Jolly, 1240 Abbott Ave., Campbell, CA 95008

Juarer, Jacques, 1131 University Blvd., Silver Springs, MD 20902

Kapela, Robert A., 10060 Packard Rd., Temperance, MI 48182

Karlin, Don, P.O. Box 668, Aztec, NM 87410

Keeler, Bob, Sams Lane, Ijamsville, MD 21754

Keene, Harvey, 2135 Golden Gate Blvd., Naples, FL 33999

Keeslar, Joseph F., Rt. 1 Box 252, Almo, KY 42020

Keeton, William, Rt. 2 Box 20, Laconia, IN 47135

Kelley, Gary, 17485 S.W. Pheasant Lane, Aloha, OR 97006

Kellog, Robert, P.O. Box 2006, West Monroe, LA 71291

Kelly, Lance, 1824 Royal Palm Dr., Edgewater, FL 32032

Kelly, Stephen, 819 Flume, Chico, CA 95926

Kelso, Jim, Rt. 1 Box 5300, Worcester, VT 05682

Kemal Knives, P.O. Box 127, Bryant Pond, ME 04219

Kennedy, Bill, P.O. Box 850431, Yukon, OK 73085

Kennelley, J. C., P.O. Box 145, Leon, KS 67074

Kersh, Todd, 1805 Highview, Joplin, MO 64801

Kessler, Ralph A., P.O. Box 202, Elgin, SC 29045

Keyes, Dan, 6688 King St., Chino, CA 91710

Keys, Bill, 1398 Whitsett Dr., El Cajon, CA 92020

Khalsa, Jot Singh, 368 Village St., Millis, MA 02054

Ki, Shiva, 5222 Ritterman Ave., Baton Rouge, LA 70805

Kilby, Keith, Foxwood Route 4, Jefferson, GA 30549

Kimble, Robert, 1100 East Main St., Visalia, CA 93278

King, Bill, 14830 Shaw Rd., Tampa, FL 33625

Kinney, R. W., 313 North 2nd Ave., Hailey, ID 83333

Kious, Joe, Rt. 2 Box 232, Alamo, TX 78516

Kirk, Jon W., 800 North Olive St., Fayetteville, AR 72701

Kirtley, George, Salina Star Route, Boulder, CO 80302

Kitsmiller, Jerry, 62435 Gerry Rd., Montrose, CO 81401

Knipschield, Terry, 808 12th Ave. N.E., Rochester, MN 55904

Knipstein, Joe, 731 N. Fielder, Arlington, TX 76012

Kolitz, Robert, 9342 Canary Rd., Beaver Dam, WI 53916

Kormanik, Chris, 510 Highland Ave., Athens, GA 30606

Koustopoulos, George, 312 W. 9th St., Marysville, OH 43040

Koval, Michael T., 822 Busch Ct., Columbus, OH 43229

Kovar, Eugene, 2626 W. 98th St., Evergreen Park, IL 60642

Kraft, Steve, 315 S.E. 6th, Abilene, KS 67410

Kranning, Terry L., 1900 West Quinn, #153, Pocatello, ID 83202

Krause, Roy W., 22412 Corteville, St. Clair Shores, MI 48081

Kray, John S., 22451 Tula Dr., Saugus, CA 91350

Kreibich, Donald L., 6082 Boyd Ct., San Jose, CA 95123

Kreiger, G. J., and Son, P.O. Box 346, New Milford, NJ 07646

Kreimer, James J., Rt. 2 Box 280, Milan, IN 47031

Kremzner, Raymond L., P.O. Box 31, Stevenson, MD 21153

Kretsinger, Philip W., 17536 Bakersfield Rd., Boonsboro, MD 21713

Krouse, Al, 1903 Treble Drive #4A, Humble, TX 77338

Kruse, Martin, P.O. Box 487, Reseda, CA 91335

Kubaiko, Hank, HCO1 Box 6910, Palmer, AK 99645

Kuykendall, Jim, P.O. Box 539, Tulare, CA 93275

Kvitka, Dan, 17600 Superior St., Northridge, CA 91324

Ladd, Jim, 1120 Helen, Deer Park, TX 77536

Laduke, Ken, 1038 Pearl St., Santa Monica, CA 90405

Lainson, Tony, 114 Park Ave., Council Bluffs, IA 51503

Lake, Ron, 3360 Bendix Ave., Eugene, OR 97401

Lam, Brian, 1803 N. 38th St., Phoenix, AZ 85008

Lampson, Frank G., 2052 I Rd., Fruita, CO 81521

Land, John, Dr., P.O. Box 917, Wadesboro, NC 28170

Landers, Steve, 3817 N.W. 125th St., Oklahoma City, OK 73120

Lane, Don, Rt. 4 Box 291, Blackfoot, ID 83221

Lane, Ed, 440 N. Topping, Kansas City, MO 64123

Lane, Jerry, 1529 Stafford, Carbondale, IL 62901

Lang, Kurt, 4908 S. Wildwood Dr., McHenry, IL 60050

Langbein, Jerry, 1670 River Dr., Fountain, CO 80817

Lange, Donald, Rt. 1, Pelican Rapids, MN 56572

Lange, Kurt, Rt. 1 Box 1317, Trego, WI 54888

Langley, Gary, 1001 Powell, Dumas, TX 79029

Langley, Gene H., Rt. 1 Box 426, Florence, SC 29501

Lankton, Scott, 8065 Jackson Rd., Ann Arbor, MI 48103

Lapen, Charles, Box 529, W. Brookfield, MA 01585

Laplante, Brett, 301 Coral Circle, Richardson, TX 75081

Largin, Ken, 110 W. Pearl, Batesville, IN 47006

Lary, Ed, 651 Rangeline Rd., Mosinee, WI 54455

Lattimer, R. E., P.O. Box 3393, Glendale, CA 91201

Laughlin, Don, 190 Laughlin Dr., Vidor, TX 77662

Lawless, Ed, P.O. Box 277, 58611 Grand Rd., New Hudson, MI 48165

Lawson, Stephen M., 2638 Baker Rd., Placerville, CA 95667

Lay, L. J., 602 Mimosa Dr., Burkburnett, TX 76354

Leach, Mike J., 5377 W. Grand Blanc, Swartz Creek, MI 48473

Leavitt, Earl F., Jr., Pleasant Cove Rd., Boothbay, ME 04544

Lebatard, Paul, 14700 Old River Rd., Vancleave, MS 39564

Leblanc, John, P.O. Box 81, Sulphur, LA 70663

Ledford, Bracy R., 3670 N. Sherman Dr., Indianapolis, IN 46218

Lee, Tommy, Rt. 2 Box 392, Gaffney, SC 29340

Leet, Larry W., 1120 Radcliffe Ave., Bakersfield, CA 93305

Lemery, Howard, P.O. Box 98, Knoxboro, NY 13362

Lenaze, Emmett, 4449 Metaire, Metaire, LA 70001

Lenderman, Cliff, Rt. 8 Box 653, Lufkin, TX 75901

Leone, Nick, 9 Georgetown, Pontoon Beach, IL 62040

Lepore, Michael J., 66 Woodcutters Dr., Bethany, CT 06525

Leppert, A. R., 17718 Rhoda St., Encino, CA 91316

Levengood, Bill, 15011 Otto Rd., Tampa, FL 33624

Levine, Bob, 3201 Iowa Dr., Anchorage, AK 99517

Levine, Norman, 34582 Farm Rd., Lake Elsinore, CA 92330

Lewis, Ron, P.O. Box S 365, Edgewood, NM 87015

Lewis, Tom R., 1613 Standpipe Rd., Carlsbad, NM 88220

Lieneman, L. B., 625 Grand Ave., Billings, MT 59101

Likarich, Steve, 2780 Randolph Ave., Carmichael, CA 95608

Lile, Jimmy, Rt. 6 Box 27, Russellville, AR 72801

Lindsay, Chris, 16237 Dyke Rd., Lapine, OR 97739

Little, Gary M., HC84 Box 10301, Broadbent, OR 97414

Little, Jimmy L., P.O. Box 871652, Wasilla, AK 99687

Livingston, Robert C., P.O. Box 6, Murphy, NC 28906

Lloyd, Richard, 520 South 500 West, Salt Lake City, UT 84101

Lockett, Sterling, 527 Amherst Dr., Burbank, CA 91504

Lofgreen, Bob, P.O. Box LOF, Lakeside, AZ 85929

Loflin, Bob, Rt. 7 Box 199A, Fayetteville, AR 72701

Lokmor, Kevin, 2253 Lynbrook Ct., Pittsburgh, CA 94565

Longworth, Dave, 151 McMurchy, Bethel, OH 45106

Loomis, Lewis A., 7120 South E. Cavalier St., Milwaukie, OR 97222

Lorditch, Charles R., 7 Tollgate Rd., Johnstown, PA 15906

Louchard, Ed, 311 Jackson Point Hudson, Port Townsend, WA 98368

Louis, Tony, Jr., 7310 Stonemill Ct., Louisville, KY 40291

Love, Ed, 125 Carriage Trace Dr., Stockbridge, GA 30281

Loveless, R. W., P.O. Box 7836, Riverside, CA 92503

Lovestrand, Schuyler, 319 Rolfe Dr., Apopka, FL 32703

Lovett, Mike, 3219 E. Rancier, Killeen, TX 76543

Lozito, Joseph F., P.O. Box 511, Forest Hills, NY 11375

Luchak, Bob, 15705 Woodforest Blvd., Channelview, TX 77530

Luchini, Richard M., 6909 Pacific Ave., Stockton, CA 95207

Lucie, Jim, 3125 South St., Fruitport, MI 49415

Luck, Greg, P.O. Box 536, LaPorte, CO 80535

Luckett, Bill, 10 Amantes Lane, Weatherford, TX 76086

Lui, Ronald, 4042 Harding Ave., Honolulu, HI 96816

Lum, Robert W., 901 Travis Ave., Eugene, OR 97404

Lutes, Robert, 24878 U.S. 6 Route 1, Nappanee, IN 46550

Luttrell, Jay, 26255 Walker Rd., Bend, OR 97701

Lyle, Ernest L., 4501 Meadowbrook Ave., Orlando, FL 32808

Lyle, Mac, 813 Evergreen Lane, Rockhill, SC 29750

Lynds, Norman W., 1142 Marianas Lane, Alameda, CA 94501

Macbain, Kenneth C., 30 Briarwood Ave., Norwood, NJ 07648

Maddox, J. M "Mickey," 63 Spring Circle, Ringgold, GA 30736

Madison, Wes, 390 Crest Dr., Eugene, OR 97405

Madsen, Jack, 3311 Northwest Dr., Wichita Falls, TX 76306

Maestri, Peter A., Rt. 1 Box 111, Spring Green, WI 53588

Mahon, Charles, 243 Millbrook Way, Vacaville, GA 95688

Malitzke, Jeffrey G., 4804 Lovers Lane, Wichita Falls, TX 76310

Malloy, Joe, P.O. Box 156, Freeland, PA 18224

Manley, Cliff, 186 River St., Glenview, WV 26351

Manley, Clinton J., P.O. Box 326, Zolfo Springs, FL 33890

Manrow, Mike, 6093 Saddlewood, Toledo, OH 43613

Mansfield, Dale, 1010 Woodleaf Dr., Forbestown, CA 95941

Manx, Ralph, 811 F St., San Diego, CA 92101

Maragni, Dan, Rt. 1 Box 106, Georgetown, NY 13072

Marchant, Larry, 2005 N. Park Ave., Tifton, GA 31794

Maringer, Tom, 2306 S. Powell St., Springdale, AR 72764

Marks, Chris, Rt. 2 Box 879-R, Breaux Bridge, LA 70517

Marlowe, Donald, 2554 Oakland Rd., Dover, PA 17315

Marshall, Glenn, P.O. Box 1099, Mason, TX 76856

Martin, Bruce E., Rt. 6 Box 164-B, Prescott, AZ 71857

Martin, Joe, P.O. Box 6552, Lubbock, TX 79413

Martin, Randall, 184 Gravel St., #40, Meriden, CT 06450

Marx, Dave, 40 Erie St., Tonawanda, NY 14150

Mase, Bill, 1740 West Orange Grove Rd., Tucson, AZ 85704

Masek, Dick, Rt. 3 Box 41, David City, NE 68632

Mason, Bill, 1114 St. Louis, #33, Excelsior Springs, MO 64024

Massey, Ronald J., 61638 El Reposo St., Joshua Tree, CA 92252

Maxfield, Lynn, 382 Colonial Ave., Layton, UT 84041

Maxwell, Gypsy, Rt. 2 Box 63 Gypsy Lane, Beech Bluff, TN 38313

Maxwell, Lindsay, 4301 Main, Springfield, OR 97477

May, Henry J., 1216 Odell, Thermopolis, WY 82443

May, James E., Rt. 2 Box 191, Auxvasse, MO 65231

Maynard, Larry Joe, P.O. Box 85, Helen, WV 25853

Mayo, Tom, 67-177 Kanoulu St., Waialua, HI 96791

Mayville, Oscar L., 5660 Cooper Rd., Indianapolis, IN 46208

McAlpin, Jerry, P.O. Box 71, Bullard, TX 75757

McBurnette, Harvey, P.O. Box 227, Eagle Nest, NM 87718

McCarley, John, 1710 Keysville Road S., Keymar, MD 21757

McCarty, Harry, 1121 Brough Ave., Hamilton, OH 45015

McCarty, Zollan, 101½ Ave. E., Thomaston, GA 30286

McClung, C. O. "Mac," 800 North Janeway, Moore, OK 73160

McConnell, Charles R., 158 Gentell Ridge, Wellsburg, WV 26070

McConnell, Loyd A., P.O. Box 7162, Odessa, TX 79760

McCormick, John, 9632 E. 26th St., Tulsa, OK 74129

McCoy, Fred, 9937 Moss Ave., Silver Springs, MD 20901

McCrackin, V. J., 3720 Hess Rd., House Springs, MO 63051

McCray, James F., P.O. Box 137, Loami, IL 62661

McCullough, Larry E., Rt. 4 Box 556, Mocksville, NC 27028

McDearmont, Dave, 1618 Parkside Trail, Lewisville, TX 75067

McEvoy, Harry K., 2155 Tremont Blvd. N.W., Grand Rapids, MI 49504

McFall, Ken, P.O. Box 458, Lakeside, AZ 85929

McFarland, Les, P.O. Box 2732, Opelika, AL 36801

McFarlin, Eric E., 319 W. Manor, Anchorage, AK 99501

McGill, John, P.O. Box 302, Blairsville, GA 30512

McGovern, Jim, 31 Scenic Dr., Oak Ridge, NJ 07438

McGowan, Frank E., 12629 Howard Lodge Dr., Sykesville, MD 21784

McKendrick, Bob, P.O. Box F, Sausalito, CA 94965

McKissack, Tommy, P.O. Box 991, Sonora, TX 76950

McLane, Thomas, 7 Tucson Terrace, Tucson, AZ 83745

McLeod, James, 941 Thermalito Ave., Oroville, CA 95965

McWilliams, Sean, 4334 CR 509, Bayfield, CO 81122

Mead, Herbert, Star Rt. 2 Box 171, Bonners Ferry, ID 83805

Mecchi, Richard, 6504 Fair Ave., North Hollywood, CA 91606

Meeks, John, Rt. 9 Box 392-M, Glencoe, AL 35905

Meier, Daryl, Rt. 4, Carbondale, IL 62901

Mendenhall, Harry E., 1848 Everglades Dr., Milpitas, CA 95035

Mercer, Mike, 14 N. Waynesville Rd., Lebanon, OH 45036

Merchant, Ted, 7 Oldgarrett Ct., Whitehall, MD 21161

Merritt, Jim, 3630 Poppy St., Long Beach, CA 90805

Merz, Robert L., 20219 Prince Creek Dr., Katy, TX 77450

Messer, Glen David, Rt. E-1, Sumrall, MS 39482

Mettler, J. Banjo, 129 S. Second St., North Baltimore, OH 45872

Meyers, Max, 418 Jolee, Richardson, TX 75080

Miller, Bill, P.O. Box 434, Ashford, AL 36312

Miller, Chris, 3959 U.S. 27 South, Sebring, FL 33870

Miller, Hanford, J., 5105 S. Lemaster Rd., Evergreen, CO 80439

Miller, James P., 9024 Goeller Rd., Fairbank, IA 50629

Miller, R. D., 10526 Estate Lane, Dallas, TX 75238

Miller, Robert, P.O. Box 144, Sonora, KY 42776

Miller, Ronald T., 12922 127th Ave. N., Largo, FL 33544

Miller, Ted, P.O. Box 6328, Santa Fe, NM 87502

Miller, Terry, 450 S. 1st, Seward, NE 68434

Mills, Andy, 414 E. Schubert, Fredericksburg, TX 78624

Mills, Louis G., 9450 Water Rd., Ann Arbor, MI 48103

Minnick, Jim, 144 North 7th St., Middletown, IN 47356

Mitchell, Bobby, 511 Ave. B, South Houston, TX 77587

Mitchell, James A., P.O. Box 4646, Columbus, GA 31904

Mitchell, Max, 997 VFW Rd., Leesville, LA 71446

Mitchell, R. W., P.O. Box 1444, Walnut, CA 91786

Miyakawa, Johnny, P.O. Box 43, Knippa, TX 78870

Montegna, Delmar R., P.O. Box 6261, Sheridan, WY 82801

Montjoy, Claude, Rt. 2 Box 470C, Clinton, SC 29325

Moore, Ed, 6829 North River Dr., Baltimore, MD 21220

Moore, James B., 1707 N. Gillis, Ft. Stockton, TX 79735

Moore, Richard, 5413 Maple St., Rialto, CA 92335

Moore, Tom W., Rt. 7 Reece Church Rd., Columbia, TN 38401

Moran, William F., P.O. Box 68, Braddock Heights, MD 21714

More, Keith B., P.O. Box 164, Charlotte, MI 48813

Morgan, Emil, 2690 Calle Limonero, Thousand Oaks, CA 91360

Morgan, Jeff, 9200 Arnaz Way, Santee, CA 92071

Morgan, Justin, 2690 Calle Limonero, Thousand Oaks, CA 91360

Morgan, Tom, 14689 Ellett Rd., Beloit, OH 44609

Morlan, Tom, 30635 S. Palm, Hemet, CA 92343

Morris, C. H., 828 Meadow Dr., Atmore, AL 36502

Morseth, Steve, 131 E. Naches Ave., Selah, WA 98942

Moser, James W., 17432 Marken Lane, Huntington Beach, CA 92647

Mosser, Gary E., 15605 204th Ave. S.E., Renton, WA 98056

Moyer, Russ, 227 71st Ave. N.W., Havre, MT 59501

Mulholland, Gary, P.O. Box 93, Davenport, CA 95017

Mullins, Steve, 500 W. Center Valley Rd., Sandpoint, ID 83864

Mumford, Peter, P.O. Box 3, Farasita, CO 81037

Munro, Paul, Rt. 1 Box 32, Franklin, ME 04634

Murphy, Dave, P.O. Box 256, Gresham, OR 97030

Myers, Mel, 611 Elmwood Dr., Spencer, IA 51301

Myers, Paul, 128 12th St., Wood River, IL 62095

Myers, Ron, 100 Shady Acre Rd., Packwood, WA 98361

Naifeh, Woody, Rt. 13 Box 380, Tulsa, OK 74107

Nativo, George, 15011 Florwood Ave., Hawthorne, CA 90250

Neal, Jerry C., P.O. Box 1092, Banner Elk, NC 28604

Nealey, Ivan F., Anderson Dam Rd., Mt. Home, ID 83647

Nealy, Bud, 822 Thomas St., Stroudsburg, PA 18360

Neeley, Vaughn, 666 Grand Ave., Mancos, CO 81328

Neil, W. D., 579 White Ave., Chico, CA 95926

Neilson, Larry, 9520 S. Emerald Dr., Port Orchard, WA 98366

Nelson, Keith, 18D Chughole Ln., Los Lunas, NM 87031

Nelson, Roger S., P.O. Box 294, Central Village, CT 06332

Newcomb, Corbin, 628 Woodland Ave., Moberly, MO 65270

Nibarger, Charlie, 4908 E. 15th St., Tulsa, OK 74112

Nicholson, R. Kent, 615 Hollen Rd., Baltimore, MD 21212

Nishiuchi, Melvin S., 6121 Forest Park Dr., Las Vegas, NV 89115

Nolen Bros., R. D. and George, P.O. Box 2895, Estes Park, CO 80517

Norris, Mike, 2115 Charlotte Rd., Albermarle, NC 28001

Norton, Don, 3206 Aspen Dr., Farmington, NM 87401

Nymeyer, Earl, 2802 N. Fowler, Hobbs, NM 88240

O'Leary, Gordon, 2566 Hearthside Dr., Ypsilanti, MI 48198

O'Neill, H. C., 9252 Deering Ave., Chatsworth, CA 91311

Ochs, Charles, 124 Emerald Lane, Largo, FL 34641

Oda, Kuzan, P.O. Box 2632, Palmer, AK 99645

Ogg, Robert G., Rt. 1 Box 345, Paris, AR 72855

Oliver, Milford, 3832 W. Desert Park Ln., Phoenix, AZ 85021

Olson, Wayne C., 11655 W. 35th Ave., Wheath Ridge, CO 80033

Ortiz, Ron, 854 West B St., Ontario, CA 91762

Osborne, Don, 5840 North McCall, Clovis, CA 93612

Osborne, Warren, 215 Edgefield, Waxahachie, TX 75165

Ottmar, Maurice, P.O. Box 657, Coulee City, WA 99115

Outlaw, Anthony, 1131 E. 24th Plaza, Panama City, FL 32405

Overeynder, T. R., 1800 S. Davis Dr., Arlington, TX 76013

Overholser, W. C., 235 N.E. 11th St., Newport, OR 97365

Owens, Dan, P.O. Box 284, Blacksburg, SC 29702

Owens, John, 8755 S.W. 96th St., Miami, FL 33176

Owens, John, 6513 E. Lookout Dr., Parker, CO 80134

Oyster, Lowell R., Rt. 1 Box 432, Kenduskeag, ME 04450

Page, Larry, 165 Rolling Rock Rd., Aiken, SC 29801

Palmer, Howard, 2031 Tronjo Rd., Pensacola, FL 32503

Pankiewicz, Philip R., Rt. 1 Waterman Rd., Lebanon, CT 06249

Papp, Robert, P.O. Box 246, Elyria, OH 44036

Pardue, Melvin M., Rt. 1 Box 130, Waxahachie, TX 75165

Parrish, Dwayne, P.O. Box 181, Palestine, TX 75801

Parrish, Robert, 1922 Spartanburg Hwy., Hendersonville, NC 28739

Parsons, Michael R., 1600 S. 11th St., Terre Haute, IN 477802

Pate, Lloyd D., 219 Cottontail Lane, Georgetown, TX 78626

Patrick, Chuck, Rt. 1, Brasstown, NC 28902

Pearce, Hill Everett, P.O. Box 72, Gurley, AL 35748

Pease, W. D., Rt. 2 Box 13, Ewing, KY 41039

Peel, W. K., 570 O'Farrell St., Apt. 204, San Francisco, CA 94102

Pendleton, Lloyd, 2116 Broadmore Ave., San Pablo, CA 94806

Pendray, Alfred H., Rt. 2 Box 1950, Williston, FL 32696

Peters, Owen, 9008 Sparrow Dr., Richmond, VA 23233

Petersen, Dan L., 3020 Sowers Ct., Topeka, KS 66604

Peterson, Chris, P.O. Box 62, Aurora, UT 84620

Peterson, Eldon G., 260 Haugen Hts. Rd., Whitefish, MT 59937

Pharris, Glen, 6247 Whitecliff Way, North Highlands, CA 95660

Phelps, Paul S., 1306 Woodlawn Dr., Maryville, TN 37801

Phillipini, Jim, 5448 Highview Lane, Citrus Heights, CA 95610

Phillips, Harold, Rt. 1 Box 37, Waukomis, OK 73773

Phillips, John, 31 Parker Way, Santa Barbara, CA 93101

Phillips, Randy, P.O. Box 792, Bloomington, CA 92316

Phillips, Wayne, P.O. Box 78, Olancha, CA 93560

Pickens, Andrew, 8229 C.R. 334, Ignacio, CO 81137

Pickens, Selbert, Rt. #1 Box 216, Liberty, WV 25124

Pickering, Larry, 440 Belle Alliance, Laplace, LA 70008

Pierce, Bruce M., 49 Laguna Way, Hot Springs, AR 71909

Pierce, Harold L., 7150 Bronner Circle, #10, Louisville, KY 40218

Pierce, Jack L., 15945 S.W. Lake Forrest Blvd., Lake Oswego, OR 97034

Pitt, David, P.O. Box 7653, Klamath Falls, OR 97602

Pittman, Leon, Rt. 2 Box 2097, Pendergrass, GA 30567

Pixley, Jim, Rt. 1 Box 344, Pelican Rapids, MN 56572

Poag, James, Rt. 1 Box 213, New Harmony, IN 47631

Poehlman, Paul, P.O. Box 487, Stinson Beach, CA 94970

Pogreba, Larry, P.O. Box 861, Lyons, CO 80540

Pohlers, Rick, 4351 Toyon Rd., Riverside, CA 92504

Poletis, Jerry, P.O. Box 1582, Scottsdale, AZ 85252

Polk, Clifton, 3526 Eller St., Ft. Smith, AR 72904

Polk, Rusty, 3225 Albert Pike, Apt. 11, Ft. Smith, AR 72904

Polkowski, Al, 8 Cathy Ct., Chester, NJ 07930

Pomykalski, L. T., 15800 Le Claire, Oak Forest, IL 60452

Poplin, James L., 103 Oak St., Washington, GA 30673

Porter, James E., P.O. Box 2583, Bloomington, IN 47402

Porter, William R., 3403 Orchard Way, Oceanside, CA 92054

Portus, Robert, 130 Ferry Rd., Grants Pass, OR 97526

Poston, Alvin, 1813 Old Colony Rd., Columbia, SC 29209

Poteet, Merle, 4616 W. Cochise Dr., Glendale, AZ 85302

Pou, Ed, 322 Cleveland St., New Albany, MS 38652

Powell, Wesley R., 7211 Tropicana St., Miramar, FL 33023

Prater, North, Rt. 3 Box 1240, Chickamauga, GA 30707

Price, Jerry L., P.O. Box 782, Springdale, AR 72764

Price, Joel H., Rt. 1 Box 3067, Palatka, FL 32077

Prince, Joe, 5406 Reidville Rd., Moore, SC 29369

Pritchard, Ron, 613 Crawford Ave., Dixon, IL 61021

Prouty, Ralph, 5240 S.W. 49th Dr., Portland, OR 97221

Provenzano, Joseph D., 3024 Ivy Pl., Chalmette, LA 70043

Pugh, Jim, P.O. Box 711, Azle, TX 76020

Pullen, Martin, 813 Broken Bow WHH, Granbury, TX 76048

Pulliam, Morris C., Rt. 7 Box 272, Shelbyville, KY 40065

Pursley, Aaron, P.O. Box 1037, Big Sandy, MT 59520

Puterbaugh, Don, 3650 Austin Bluff Pkwy. S., Colorado Springs, CO 80907

Quarton, Barr, P.O. Box 2211, Hailey, ID 83333

Quenton, Warner, P.O. Box 607, Peterstown, WV 24963

Quinn, George, P.O. Box 692, Julian, CA 92036

Racy, Richard Ray, 8820 West Mescal, Peoria, AZ 85345

Rados, Jerry F., Rt. 1 Box 516, Grant Park, IL 60940

Rafferty, Dan, P.O. Box 1415, Apache Junction, AZ 85220

Rainville, Richard, 126 Cockle Hill Rd., Salem, CT 06415

Ramey, Marshall F., P.O. Box 2589, West Helena, AR 72390

Randall Knives, P.O. Box 1988, Orlando, FL 32802

Rapp, Steven J., 3437 Crestfield Dr., Salt Lake City, UT 84119

Rappazzo, Richard, 217 Troy-Schenectady Rd., Latham, NY 12110

Rardon, A. D., Rt. 1 Box 79, Polo, MO 64671

Ratelle, Bill, 470 Raymond Dr., Benicia, CA 94510

Ray, Michael, 533 W. 36th North, Wichita, KS 67204

Read, Bob, 916 Near Top Dr., Nashville, TN 37205

Read, Dick, 4616 North 5th, Fresno, CA 93726

Rece, Charles V., 1305 Bird Rd., Albemarle, NC 28001

Redfearn, Dennis, 2542 Bobwhite, Mesquite, TX 75149

Redmon, Mark, 7946 Modesto Dr., Riverside, CA 92503

Ree, David, 816 Main St., Van Buren, AR 72956

Reed, Dave, P.O. Box 132, Brimfield, MA 01010

Reed, Del, 13765 S.W. Parkway, Beaverton, OR 97005

Reeve, Chris, 6147 Corporal Lane, Boise, ID 83704

Reeves, Winfred M., P.O. Box 300, West Union, SC 29696

Reh, Bill, 2215 Kensington, #1, Missoula, MT 59801

Renner, Terry L., P.O. Box 575, Estes Park, CO 80517

Reno, Lou, P.O. Box 253, Okeechobee, FL 34973

Reynolds, Dave, 4519 26th Loop S.E., Lacey, WA 98503

Reynolds, John C., Box 119 Mica Ct., Gillette, WY 82716

Rhea, David, Rt. 1 Box 272, Lynnville, TN 38472

Rhea, Jerry, 440 Clark, Turlock, CA 95380

Rial, Douglas, Rt. 2 Box 117A, Greenfield, TN 38230

Rice, Adrienne, Rt. 1 Box 1744, Lopez Island, WA 98261

Richard, Ron, 4875 Calaveras Ave., Fremont, CA 94538

Richards, Art, 1725 Bonita Ave., Burbank, CA 91504

Richards, Don T., 170 23rd St., Costa Mesa, CA 92627

Richardson, Charles, P.O. Box 38329, Dallas, TX 75238

Richardson, William J., 1026 W. 1700 S., #1, Syracuse, UT 84041

Ricke, Dave, 1209 Adams, West Bend, WI 53095

Rigney, Willie, Rt. 3 Box 404, Shelbyville, IN 46176

Riker, Tom, 313 S. Raleigh St., Martinsburg, WV 25401

Roath, Dean, 3050 Winnepeg Dr., Baton Rouge, LA 70819

Robbins, Howard P., 875 Rams Head Rd., Estes Park, CO 80517

Roberts, Asa, 1222 Willow Lane, Nampa, ID 83651

Robertson, Ron, 6708 Lunar Dr., Anchorage, AK 99504

Robinson, Michael B., 860 South McClelland St., Salt Lake City, UT 84102

Rocha, Gay, c/o General Delivery, Glide, OR 97443

Rochford, Michael, P.O. Box 607, Dresser, WI 54009

Rodrigues, Joe, 10606 San Gabriel Ave., South Gate, CA 90280

Roe, Fred D., 4005 Granada Dr., Huntsville, AL 35802

Rogers, Robert P., 3979 South Main St., Acworth, GA 30101

Rogers, Rodney, 602 Osceola St., Wildwood, FL 32785

Rohn, Fred, W7615 Clemetson Rd., Coeur D'Alene, ID 83814

Rollert, Steve, P.O. Box 65, Keenesburg, CO 80643

Romano, Richard, 31 Arlington Rd., Windsor Locks, CT 06096

Ronk, W. W., 511 Boyd Ave., Greenfield, IN 46140

Root, George R., P.O. Box 6, Manchester, KY 40962

Root, Jon Paul, P.O. Box 474, Benson, AZ 85602

Roper, Mark H., 206 Plymouth Rd., Martinez, GA 30907

Rose, Alex, 3624 Spring Valley Dr., New Port Richey, FL 34655

Ross, Stephen, P.O. Box 951, Evanston, WY 82930

Ross, Tom, 4962 Sierra Vista, Riverside, CA 92505

Rotella, Richard A., 643 75th St., Niagara Falls, NY 14304

Roy, John, P.O. Box 191, Veneta, OR 97487

Royal, B. M., P.O. Box 934, Helen, GA 30545

Ruana Knifeworks, P.O. Box 520, Bonner, MT 59823

Rubley, James A., Rt. 3 Box 682, Angola, IN 46703

Russell, A. G., 1705 Hwy. 71 North, Springdale, AR 72764

Russell, Roger, P.O. Box 27, Peralta, NM 87042

Russell, Tom, 6500 New Liberty Rd., Jacksonville, AL 36365

Rust, Charles C., P.O. Box 374, Palermo, CA 95968

Salley, John D., 3965 Frederick-Ging Rd., Tipp City, OH 45371

Salpas, Bob, P.O. Box 117, Homewood, CA 95718

Sampogna, Michael, 45 East Argyle St., Valley Stream, NY 11580

Sampson, Lynn, Rt. 2 Box 283, Jonesboro, TN 37659

Sams, Joseph D., 5108 Juliandra Ave., El Paso, TX 79924

Samson, Jody, 1834 W. Burbank Blvd., Burbank, CA 91506

Sanders, Albert, 3850 72 Ave. N.E., Norman, OK 73071

Sanders, Bill, P.O. Box 957, Mancos, CO 81328

Sanders, Michael, P.O. Box 1106, Ponchatoula, LA 70454

Sanders, Sandy, 2358 Taylor Lane, Louisville, KY 40205

Sasser, Jim, 926 Jackson, Pueblo, CO 81004

Sawby, Scott, 500 W. Center Valley Rd., Sand Point, ID 83864

Scarrow, Will, P.O. Box 33, El Cerrito, CA 94804

Schedenhell, Jack, P.O. Box 307, Superior, MT 59872

Scheid, Maggie, P.O. Box 8059, W. Webster, NY 14580

Schenck, Clifton, P.O. Box 1017, Bonners Ferry, ID 83805

Schepers, George B., P.O. Box 83, Chapman, NE 68827

Schiffman, N. H., 963 Malibu, Pocatello, ID 83201

Schiller, Arthur R., 143 Granada, San Clemente, CA 92672

Schmidt, James A., Rt. 3 Eastern Ave., Ballston Lake, NY 12019

Schmidt, Ray, P.O. Box 598, Whitefish, MT 59937

Schmier, Jack, 16787 Mulberry Circle, Fountain Valley, CA 92708

Schneider, Herman J., 24296 Via Aquara, Laguna Niguel, CA 92677

Scholten, Bob, 511 Laguna Honda Blvd., San Francisco, CA 94127

Schrock, Maurice and Al, 1708 South Plum St., Pontiac, IL 61764

Schroder, Jeff, P.O. Box 794, Costa Mesa, CA 92627

Schroen, Karl, 4042 Bones Rd., Sebastopol, CA 95472

Schulds, John, 5711 Melvin, Tarzana, CA 91356

Schulenburg, E. W., 406 Sunset Blvd., Carrollton, GA 30117

Schultz, Bob, 3650 Austin Bluffs Pkwy. S., Colorado Springs, CO 80907

Schwartz, John J., 41 Fifteenth St., Wellsburg, WV 26070

Schwarzer, James, P.O. Box 4, Pomona Park, FL 32181

Schwarzer, Stephen, P.O. Box 4, Pomona Park, FL 32181

Scott, Winston, Rt. 2 Box 62, Huddleston, VA 24104

Seldomridge, John, 221 N. 61st St., Kansas City, KS 66102

Selvey, W. H., 108 S. 11th, Blue Springs, MO 64015

Serven, Jim, 6153 Third St., Mayville, MI 48744

Sharp, Robert G., 17540 St. Francis Blvd., Anoka, NM 55303

Sharpe, Philip, 483 Landmark Way S.W., Austell, GA 30001

Shaw, David L., 2009 North 450 East, Ogden, UT 84404

Shearer, Robert A., 2121 Ave. T, Huntsville, TX 77340

Sheehan, Paul P., P.O. Box 90, Sandwich, MA 02563

Shelor, Ben, Rt. 14 Box 318-B, Richmond, VA 23231

Shelton, Scott, 5230 Pressley Rd., Santa Rosa, CA 95404

Sherrill, Dave, 2905 F½ Rd., Grand Junction, CO 81501

Shirley, Dave, 39723 Plumas Way, Fremont, CA 94538

Shiva, Ki, 5222 Ritterman, Baton Rouge, LA 70805

Shoemaker, Scott, 316 S. Main St., Miamisburg, OH 45342

Shostle, Ben, 1121 Burlington, Muncie, IN 47302

Shuford, Rick, 431 Hillcrest Dr., Statesville, NC 28677

Shulenberger, William E., Rt. 4 Box 312, Newville, PA 17241

Sibrian, Aaron, 4308 Dean Dr., Ventura, CA 93003

Sigman, Corbet, Rt. 1 Box 212A, Liberty, WV 25124

Sigman, James P., 52474 Johnson Rd., Three Rivers, MI 49093

Silva, Joe, 6829 Mayhews Landing, Newark, CA 94560

Silva, Manuel, 829 Pine St., Ramona, CA 92065

Simonich, Rob, P.O. Box 278, Clancy, MT 59634

Simons, Bill, P.O. Box 311, Highland City, FL 33846

Simons, Norman, 12006 Newbrook, Houston, TX 77072

Sims, Bob, P.O. Box 772, Meridian, TX 76665

Sinyard, Cleston, 27522 Burkhardt Dr., Elberta, AL 36530

Siska, Jim, 6 Highland Ave., Westfield, MA 01085

Sites, David, 2665 Atwood Terrace, Columbus, OH 43211

Skirchak, Samuel, Rt. 1 Lisbon Rd., Midland, PA 15059

Skorupa, Larry, Rt. 1 Box 1152, Bridger, MT 59014

Slee, Fred, 9 John St., Morganville, NJ 07751

Sloan, John, P.O. Box 486, Foxboro, MA 02035

Sloan, Shane, Rt. 1 Box 17, Newcastle, TX 76372

Small, Ed, Rt. 1 Box 178A, Keyser, WV 26726

Small, Jim, P.O. Box 67, Madison, GA 30650

Small, Michael, 332 Lindbergh Ave., Frederick, MD 21701

Smith, Cary, 946 Marigny Ave., Mandeville, LA 70448

Smith, D. W., Rt. 1 Box 141, Mars, PA 16046

Smith, Dan, 7334 Clear Creek Rd., Parkdale, OR 97041

Smith, David Lynn, 1773 E. 4500 South, Vernal, UT 84078

Smith, F. L., P.O. Box 817, Fair Oaks, CA 95628

Smith, Glenn L., 630 E. 39 St., Hialeah, FL 33013

Smith, Gregory H., 8607 Coddington Ct., Louisville, KY 40299

Smith, Harry R., 2105 S. 27th Ave., Missoula, MT 59801

Smith, Jack, 1404 Deerfield Lane, Woodbridge, VA 22191

Smith, James B., Rt. 2 Box 199, Morven, GA 31638

Smith, Jim, 1608 Joann, Wichita, KS 67203

Smith, John M., Rt. 6 Box 52, Centralia, IL 62801

Smith, John T., 8404 Cedar Crest Dr., Southhaven, MS 38671

Smith, Newman L., Rt. 1 Box 119A, Glades Rd., Gatlinburg, TN 37738

Smith, Ralph L., P.O. Box 395, Greer, SC 29652

Smith, W. F. "Red," 409 Country Club Blvd., Slidell, LA 70458

Snell, Jerry L., 235 Woodsong Dr., Fayetteville, GA 30214

Soares, John, 3115 Ozark Ave., Port Arthur, TX 77640

Somerville, Jim, P.O. Box 165, Salem, IL 62881

Sonneville, W. J., 1050 Chalet Dr. W., Mobile, AL 36608

Sontheimer, G. Douglas, 3120 S. Florence Terr., Olney, MD 20832

Sornberger, Jim, 25126 Overland Dr., Volcano, CA 95689

Sparks, Bernard, P.O. Box 73, Dingle, ID 83233

Spencer, John E., HC63 Box 267, Harper, TX 78631

Spencer, Velden L., 2664 Salton Vista Dr., Julian, CA 92036

Spendlove, Dale, 211 S. 1000 East, Orem, UT 84057

Spicer, William F., 2213 Inverness, Rawlins, WY 82301

Spinale, Richard, 3415 Oakdale Ave., Lorain, OH 44055

Spivey, Jefferson, P.O. Box 60584, Oklahoma City, OK 73146

Stafford, Richard, 104 Marcia Ct., Warner Robbins, GA 31088

Stahl, John, 2049 Windsor Rd., Baldwin, NY 11510

Stalter, Harry L., 2509 N. Trivoli Rd., Trivoli, IL 61569

Stapel, Chuck, P.O. Box 1671, Glendale, CA 91209

Staples, Richard, 1904 Miflin Rd., Beach Bluff, TN 38313

Stefani, Randy, 2393 Mayfield Ave., Montrose, CA 91020

Stegall, Keith, 3206 Woodland Park Dr., Anchorage, AK 99517

Stegall, Steve, 4588 Woodworth Dr., Mount Hood, OR 97041

Steigerwalt, Ken, 20 Twig Lane, Levittown, PA 19054

Steinberg, Al, 2499 Trenton Dr., San Bruno, CA 94066

Stephani, Randy, 2393 Mayfield Ave., Montrose, CA 91020

Stephens, Kelly Lee, 4235 78th Lane N., St. Petersburg, FL 33709

Stewart, Charles, 2996 Walmsley Circle, Lake Orion, MI 48035

Stice, Douglas, 1901 Elmhurst Dr., Norman, OK 73071

Stites, Kay, 4931 Rands Rd., Bloomfield Hills, MI 48013

Stoddart, W. B., 917 Smiley, Forest Park, OH 45240

Stone, G. W., 610 North Glenville Dr., Richardson, TX 75081

Stout, Johnny, 1514 Devin, Braunfels, TX 78130

Stover, James, 9130 Highway 140, Eagle Point, OR 97524

Straight, Donald B., P.O. Box 501, c/o Nvkc Inc., Falls Church, VA 22046

Stranahan, Dan, 445 North Walch, Porterville, CA 93257

Strong, Bob, 1616 Camino Verdi, Walnut Creek, CA 94596

Strong, Scott, 2138 Oxmoor Dr., Beaver Creek, OH 45431

Stuckey, Fred B., 1227 Baxley Lane, Longview, TX 75604

Stumpff, George, P.O. Box 2, Glorieta, NM 87535

Sturgeon, Jim, 1826 Deleware, West Sacramento, CA 95691

Suedmeier, Harlan, Rt. 2, Nebraska City, NE 68410

Swain, Rod, 1020 Avon Pl., South Pasadena, CA 91030

Swan, Ed, 5107 95 Ave. N.E., Everett, WA 98205

Syslo, Chuck, 3418 South 116 Ave., Omaha, NE 68144

Taglienti, Antonio, P.O. Box 221, Darlington, PA 16115

Tamboli, Michael, 12447 N. 49 Ave., Glendale, AZ 85304

Tausher, Jeff, 9951 Windon, San Ramon, CA 94583

Taylor, C. Gray, 137 Lana View Dr., Kingsport, TN 37664

Tedder, Mickey, Rt. 2 Box 22, Conover, NC 28613

Terrill, Stephen, 21363 Rd. 196, Lindsay, CA 93247

Terzuola, Robert, Rt. 6 Box 83A, Santa Fe, NM 87501

Thayer, Leroy, 15600 Pinto Way, Chino, CA 91710

Thissell, Stiles B., P.O. Box 21, Inverness, CA 94937

Thomas, Jerry, 6302 Holida Dr., Forest Park, GA 30050

Thomason, Bill, 167 Lower Dawnville Rd. N., Dalton, GA 30720

Thompson, Bruce Lee, 4101 W. Union Hills Dr., Glendale, AZ 85308

Thompson, Leon, 1735 Leon Dr., Forest Grove, OR 97116

Thornton, Danny, P.O. Box 334, Fort Mill, SC 29715

Thourot, Michael W., T814 Rt. 1 Rd. 11, Napoleon, OH 43545

Thuesen, Ed, 10649 Haddington, #190, Houston, TX 77043

Timberline Knives, P.O. Box 36, Mancos, CO 81328

Timm, Bob, 655 W. Tomah Rd., Castle Rock, CO 80104

Tinker, Carolyn D., P.O. Box 5123, Whittier, CA 90607

Tison, Robert E., 1844 Bartram Circle East, Jacksonville, FL 32207

Tokar, Daniel, P.O. Box 1776, Shepherdstown, WV 25443

Tomes, Anthony S., 280 Gano Ave., Orange Park, FL 32073

Tomes, P. J., Rt. 1 Box 78, Grottoes, VA 24441

Tompkins, Dan, 310 N. Second St., Peotone, IL 60468

Towell, Dwight L., Rt. 1 Box 66, Midvale, ID 83645

Trabbic, R. W., 4550 N. Haven, Toledo, OH 43612

Tracy, Bud B., 339 Kingman Dr., Nampa, ID 83651

Treijs, Norm, 54 Browns Rd., Huntington, NY 11743

Treutel, Terry A., P.O. Box 187, Hamilton, MT 59840

Trindle, Barry, Rt. 1 Box 63, Earlham, IA 50072

Trujillo, Thomas A., 2905 Arctic Blvd., Anchorage, AK 99503

Tsoulas, Jon, 1 Home St., Peabody, MA 01960

Turecek, Jim, P.O. Box 882, Derby, CT 06418

Turnbull, Ralph A., 5722 Newburg Rd., Rockford, IL 61108

Tye, Virgil Dee, 901 South Chester Ave., Bakersfield, CA 93304

Underhill, Richard W., 1493 Sycamore Canyon Rd., Santa Barbara, CA 93108

Underwood, W. L., 1643 Pennsylvania Ave., East Liverpool, OH 43920

Urstadt, E. W., Rt. 4 Box 296, Deer Park, MD 21550

Valachovic, Wayne, Rt. 1 Box 215B, Hillsboro, NH 03244

Valdes, Albert, 2708 Lakewood Ave., Los Angeles, CA 90039

Valois, A. Daniel, 4299 Hawthorne Rd., Walnutport, PA 18088

Vans, John D., 5414 Grissom Dr., Arlington, TX 76016

Varnum, Fran, 1206 Cobblestone Lane, Santa Maria, CA 93454

Vaughan, Michael, 1610 Lisle St., Oildale, CA 93308

Vaughn, Eddie, 1905 Virginia Dr., Grand Prairie, TX 75050

Veit, Michael, Rt. 1 3070 E. 5th Rd., Lasalle, IL 61301

Viele, H. J., 88 Lexington Ave., Westwood, NJ 07675

Viniard, Billy, P.O. Box 644, Monticello, MS 39654

Voss, Ben, P.O. Box 3654, Davenport, IA 52808

Votaw, David, P.O. Box 327, Pioneer, OH 43554

Vought, Frank, 115 Monticello Dr., Hammond, LA 70401

Vunk, Robert, 4408 Buckeye Ct., Orlando, FL 32804

Waddle, Thomas, 9713 Lower River Rd., Louisville, KY 40272

Wade, James M., Rt. 1 Box 56, Moss Rd., Wade, NC 28395

Wadeson, Joe, Rt. 1 Box 366, Interlachen, FL 32048

Wagaman, John K., 903 Arsenal Ave., Fayetteville, NC 28305

Waggoner, Les, 12542 Loraleen, Garden Grove, CA 92641

Wahlers, Herman F., Star Route Box 1, Austerlitz, NY 12017

Wahlster, Mark D., 1404 N. Second St., Silverton, OR 97381

Waldrop, Mark, P.O. Box 129, Ladylake, FL 32659

Walker, George A., Star Route, Alpine, WY 83128

Walker, John W., Rt. 2 Box 376, Bon Aqua, TN 37025

Walker, Michael L., P.O. Box 2343, Taos, NM 87571

Wallace, Roger L., 4902 Collins Ln., Tampa, FL 33603

Walters, A. F., 609 E. 20th St., Tifton, GA 31794

Walters, Brian, P.O. Box 2124, Des Moines, IA 50310

Ward, A. R., 753 West Main St., Moore, OK 73160

Ward, Ken, 6010 W. Cheyenne St., Las Vegas, NV 89108

Ward, W. C., Rt. 6 Lynn Rd., Box 184B, Clinton, TN 37716

Warden, Roy A., Rt. 2 Box 138-2, Union, MO 63084

Wardman, Dave, 9910 U.S. 23, Ossineke, MI 49766

Ware, D., Rt. 2 Box 2298, Benton City, WA 99320

Ware, J. D., 209 Cutbred St., Philadelphia, PA 19106

Ware, Tommy, Star Rt. Box 79, Blanco, TX 78606

Warenski, Buster, P.O. Box 214, Richfield, UT 84701

Warren, Al, P.O. Box 332, Porterville, CA 93258

Warther, Dale, 331 Karl Ave., Dover, OH 44622

Warzocha, Stanley, 32540 Wareham Dr., Warren, MI 48092

Wasuta, Steve J., 1983 Jefferson, San Francisco, CA 94123

Watson, Daniel, 350 Jennifer Lane, Driftwood, TX 78619

Watson, Thomas J., 1103 Brenau Terrace, Panama City, FL 32405

Watt, Freddie, P.O. Box 1372, Bigspring, TX 79721

Watts, Wally, Rt. 1 Box 81, Gatesville, TX 76528

Weather, Ron, 4775 Memphis St., Dallas, TX 75207

Weber, Fred E., 517 Tappan St., Forked River, NJ 08731

Weddle, Del, P.O. Box 10, Stewartsville, MO 64490

Wehman, E. A., 104 Dr Ave., Summerville, SC 29483

Wehner, Rudy, 2713 Riverbend Dr., Violet, LA 70092

Weiland, J. Reese, 14919 Nebraska Ave., Tampa, FL 33612

Weiler, Donald E., P.O. Box 1576, Yuma, AZ 85364

Weinand, Gerome W., P.O. Box 385, Lolo, MT 59847

Weiss, Charles L., 18847 N. 13th Ave., Phoenix, AZ 85027

Weiss, Martin, 23 Bergwall Way, Vallejo, CA 94590

Weiss, Steven, 1465 Polk St., San Francisco, CA 94109

Welch, William H., 5226 Buell Dr., Fort Wayne, IN 46807

Werth, George W., 9010 Cary Rd., Cary, IL 60013

Wertz, Victor W., 1501 Arizona Ct., Woodbridge, VA 22191

Wescott, Cody, 5610 Hanger Lake Lane, Las Cruces, NM 88001

Wescott, Jim, 4225 Elks Dr., Las Cruces, NM 88005

Wesolowski, Mike, 902A Lohrman Lane, Petaluma, CA 94952

West, Jim, 4504 Del Amo Blvd., Torrance, CA 90503

Westwood, Tom, P.O. Box 177, Newberry, SC 29108

Wheat, Jon S., P.O. Box 323, Lakin, KS 67860

Whitaker, Bob, 4633 Berta Rd., Memphis, TN 38109

White, Gene E., 1015 Cross Dr., Alexandria, VA 22302

White, Robert, Rt. 1, Gilson, IL 61436

Whitehead, James D., P.O. Box 540, Durham, CA 95938

Whitley, Weldon, P.O. Box 746, Jal, NM 88252

Whitman, Jim, HC 80 Box 5387, Chugiak, AK 99567

Whitmarsh, Jay, 19100 Dalton St., Newhall, CA 91321

Whitmire, Earl T., 725 Colonial Dr., Rock Hill, SC 29730

Whittaker, Robert E., P.O. Box 204, Mill Creek, PA 17060

Whitworth, Ken J., 41667 Tetley Ave., Sterling Heights, MI 48078

Wiggins, Horace, 203 Herndon, Mansfield, LA 71502

Wiggins, James C., 1540 W. Pleasant Rd., Hammond, LA 70401

Wilber, W. C., 400 Lucerne Dr., Spartansburg, SC 29302

Wilding, L. R., 1485 Loretta Dr., Pittsburgh, PA 15235

Willey, W. G., Rt. Box 235, Greenwood, DE 19950

Williams, Chip, 3519 Seneca Ave., Aiken, SC 29801

Williams, Jack F., 4317 Boston Ave., La Crescenta, CA 91214

Williams, Jack H., 11803 North East 67th Pl., Kirkland, WA 98033

Williams, Sherman A., 1709 Wallace St., Simi Valley, CA 93065

Williams, W. C., 711 Main St., Atlanta, TX 75551

Williamson, Tony, Rt. 3 Box 503, Siler City, NC 27344

Williamson, Walt, 1935 Hewitt Dr., Billings, MT 59102

Wills, Lowell, P.O. Box 452, Lake Forest, IL 60045

Wilson, Bob, 10116 Holman Rd., S.E., Port Orchard, WA 98366

Wilson, James G., Moraine Rt. UC 2004, Estes Park, CO 80517

Wilson, R. W., P.O. Box 2012, Weirton, WV 26062

Wiman, Art, P.O. Box 92, Plumerville, AR 72107

Wine, Michael, 265 S. Atlantic Ave., Cocoa Beach, FL 32931

Winkler, Daniel, P.O. Box 255, Boone, NC 28607

Winn, Bill, Star Route, Gruver, TX 79040

Winn, Travis A., 558 E. 3065 So., Salt Lake City, UT 84106

Witsaman, Earl, 3957 Redwing Circle, Stow, OH 44224

Wolfe, Jack, P.O. Box 1056, Larkspur, CA 94939

Wood, Barry, 38 S. Venice Blvd., Venice, CA 90291

Wood, Dale, Rt. 1, Seymour, TX 76380

Wood, Larry B., 6945 Fishburg Rd., Huber Heights, OH 45424

Wood, Webster, 4726 Rosedale, Clarkston, MI 48016

Wood, William W., P.O. Box 877, Vera, TX 76388

Woodward, Harold E., Rt. 3 Box 64A, Woodbury, TN 37190

Woodworth, Al, Rt. 1 Box 13, Plainville, IL 62365

Wooldridge, Roy, 3106 Edgewood Dr. S.E., Jefferson, OR 97352

Worel, Joe, 3040 N. Laporte, Melrose Park, IL 60164

Worthen, Richard, 834 Carnation Dr., Sandy, UT 84070

Wright, Harold C., 1710 Bellwood Dr., Centerville, TN 37033

Wright, Kevin, 671 Leland Valley Rd. W., Quilcene, WA 98376

Wright, Ninda, 2643 Appian Way, Pinole, CA 94564

Wright, Timothy, 4100 W. Grand Ave., Chicago, IL 60651

Wright, Tom, P.O. Box 54, Noel, MO 64854

Yancey, T. J., P.O. Box 943, Estes Park, CO 80517

Yates, Pat, P.O. Box 2047, Ridgecrest, CA 93555

Yaun, Christopher, 31240 Hwy. 43, Albany, LA 70711

Yopp, Col. D. C., Rt. 3 Box 63, Old Town, FL 32680

York, David C., P.O. Box 1342, Crested Butte, CO 81224

York, Ray, 815 Dadds Rd., Angels Camp, CA 95222

Young, Charlie, 8252 Auburn Blvd., Citrus Heights, CA 95610

Young, Errol, 4826 Storey Land, Alton, IL 62002

Young, Paul A., Rt. 1 Box 139-A, Vilas, NC 28692

Yunes, Yamil R., P.O. Box 573, Roma, TX 78584

Yurco, Mike, 260 E. Laclede Ave., Youngstown, OH 44507

Zaccagnino, Don, P.O. Box 583, Pahokee, FL 33476

Zahm, Kurt, 488 Rio Casa, Indialantic, FL 32903

Zeanon, Bill, 8612 Waxford Rd., Richmond, VA 23235

Zeleski, W. M., 83 Bradley St., East Hartford, CT 06118

Zeller, Dennis J., 1791 South West Lilyben, Gresham, OR 97030

Zembko, John, III, 228 Spruce Brook Rd., Berlin, CT 06037

Zima, Michael, 732 State St., Ft. Morgan, CO 80701

Zowada, Tim, 14141 P. Drive North, Marshall, MI 49068

Zscherny, Michael, 2512 N Ave. N.W., Cedar Rapids, IA 52405

SILVER FOLDING FRUIT KNIVES
by Bill Karsten

▽

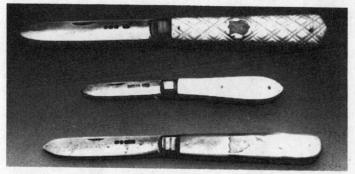

During the seventeenth century, it was fashionable for French gentlemen to present knives featuring one blade of precious metal and one of steel as gifts to their ladies. These folding knives served a dual purpose. Since they were not stained by the acids, the silver or gold blades were used to cut fruit, and the steel blade was used for general cutting purposes.

Some years later, about 1760, the English began to follow suit. After silver assay offices were established at Sheffield and Birmingham in 1773, the manufacture of fruit knives and forks flourished.

Silver hallmarks were first introduced in London during the fourteenth century and eventually there were five. Hallmarks are a very effective means for evaluating fruit knives. The complete series disclosed the city of origin, the maker's initials, the year of assay, the sterling silver content (92.5%), and a duty stamp. After 1890, when Queen Victoria revoked the duty on silver, four marks remained in the hallmark system.

(Photo by Bill Karsten)

During the later Georgian period (1773 to c. 1830) the duty mark, a stamping of the reigning monarch's profile, and the sterling mark, a lion passant, were usually the only marks stamped on the blade. The maker's mark and that of the year of assay have been found on the blade tang, covered by the bolster. Eventually, by making the marks smaller, there was room for all five on the face of the blade.

(Photo by Bill Karsten)

Georgian period knives were elegant, featuring slim lines with handles usually of mother-of-pearl and very often a bright-cut design along the top of the blade. The springs were usually chaised, the earliest being of a diagonal pattern.

(Photo by Bill Karsten)

There came slow but definite changes in fruit knife design during the reign of William IV, which started in 1830. They continued through the reign of Queen Victoria, 1837–1901. More shapely handles, engraved in a variety of pleasing geometric and floral themes were introduced. Possibly the Georgian designs were thought to be too austere. Toward the end of Queen Victoria's reign, the handles were made thick and almost cumbersome.

During the reign of Edward VII (1901–1910), mass production methods resulted in diminished quality.

After World War I fewer fruit knives were made. This was partly because of the introduction of stainless steel. Too, there was a change in the style of English living. One very seldom finds a fruit knife dated 1925 or later.

AMERICAN FOLDING FRUIT KNIVES

(Photo by Bill Karsten)

In America, with the exception of one brief period (1814–1830), there was no hallmark system. Early silversmiths used their initials, names, or marks. Occasionally, pseudo-hallmarks featuring symbols such as a lion passant or a crown were used, probably to lead a buyer to assume he had bought an article of English origin.

A number of American silver firms, particularly those of the New England area, made fruit knives. The collector will find some beautiful examples made and identified by Gorham or Albert Coles, but Rogers Cutlery, Meriden, Brittania, Wallace Bros., Empire Knife Co., Miller Bros., and others also turned out some fine pieces. Some bore marks similar to those of England, and some were not identified or were stamped only "coin" or "Sterling."

Usually, American knives were handled in silver, but other materials such as ivory were used also. Some beautiful pieces were silver-plated. There were no date marks, but one can be fairly certain that these knives were made from the beginning of the nineteenth century for a period of approximately one hundred years.

Price estimates are for knives and forks in excellent condition, as defined elsewhere in this book.

ENGLISH KNIVES AND FORKS

Late Georgian Era (1773–c. 1830)

(Photo by Bill Karsten)

(Photo by Bill Karsten)

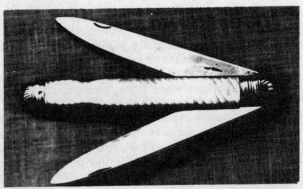

(Photo by Bill Karsten)

(Photo by Bill Karsten)

Single knife or fork	*$90–$125 each*
Matching knife and fork	*$200–$275 pair*
Gold-bladed knives	*$400–$600 each*

Era of William IV (1830–1837) and Victoria (1837–1901)

(Photo by Bill Karsten)

(Photo by Bill Karsten)

(Photo by Bill Karsten)

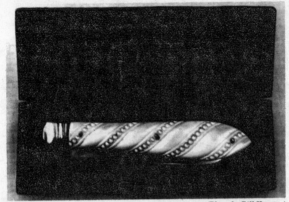

(Photo by Bill Karsten)

(Photo by Bill Karsten)

Single knives and forks	$70–$110
Take-apart knife and fork combination	$175–$230
Knives with a blade and seed pick	$80–$120
Matching knife and fork	$180–$225 pair

Era of Edward VII (1901–1910)
and George V (1910–1936)

Excepting knives of the quality of the previous period, those of this era may be bought for $70 or less.

AMERICAN FRUIT KNIVES

(Photo by Bill Karsten)

(Photo by Bill Karsten)

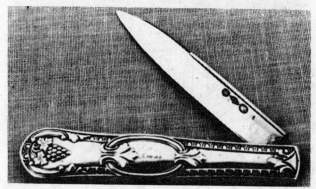

(Photo by Bill Karsten)

Knives by Coles or Gorham	*$80–$110*
Knives by other companies	*$70–$95*
Silver fruit knives marked coin or sterling	*$60–$80*
Silver fruit knives bearing only pseudo-hallmark	*$60–$80*
Plated fruit knives, identified	*$40–$60*
Plated fruit knives, not identified	*$35–$55*
Knives bearing advertising or other odd features	*$25–$45*

Note. W. C. "Bill" Karsten is a collector and researcher of several types of knives. He has written a number of articles that have been published in *Knife World* and other magazines. Recognized in the United States and several other countries as an authority on the subject, he is the author of the book *Silver Folding Fruit Knives.*

KNIFE NOMENCLATURE

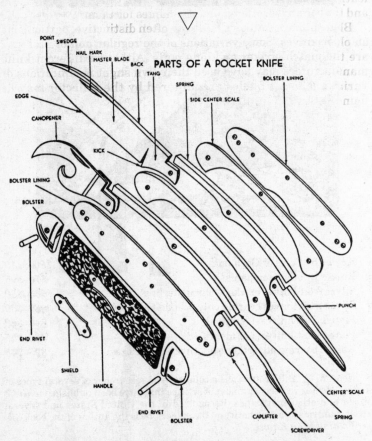

PARTS OF A POCKET KNIFE

POINT
SWEDGE
NAIL MARK
MASTER BLADE
BACK
TANG
SPRING
SIDE CENTER SCALE
BOLSTER LINING
EDGE
CANOPENER
KICK
BOLSTER LINING
BOLSTER
END RIVET
SHIELD
HANDLE
END RIVET
BOLSTER
CAPLIFTER
SCREWDRIVER
CENTER SCALE
SPRING
PUNCH

BLADES, PATTERNS, AND HANDLES

Blade patterns—their shape and size—are influenced by their intended use. Blade names are usually derived from the tasks they were designed to perform or, occasionally, from their shapes. Some blades are quite commonly used in numerous styles of knives and have been for centuries. The pen blade was originally used for trimming quill pens for office work and has been a very popular blade, finding many other uses in modern times. The spear and sheepfoot blades, named for their shapes, are joined by the clip and spey blades as the types most used and widely recognized. The functions of several other blade types, such as nail file, leather punch, screwdriver, cap lifter, spatula, cotton sampler, and timber scribe, offered obvious names for them.

Blade pulls or nail nicks also are often distinctive, particularly on older knives. Some variations of the regular pull or nail nick are the match-striker and long pulls. Although different knife manufacturers may have used their own slight modifications or variations, most blades encountered by the collector may be found in the illustration below.

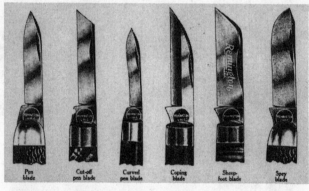

Pen blade   Cut-off pen blade   Curved pen blade   Coping blade   Sheep-foot blade   Spey blade

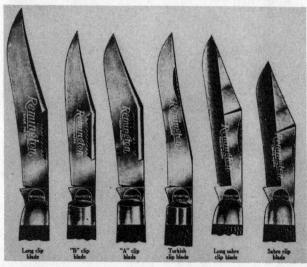

Long clip blade   "B" clip blade   "A" clip blade   Turkish clip blade   Long sabre clip blade   Sabre clip blade

Budding
blade

Wharncliffe
blade

Razor blade

Long spear or
physician's
blade

Cotton sampler's
blade

Pruning blade

Punch
blade

Electrician's
screw-driver
and wire-
scraper

Screw-driver

Screw-driver
cap-lifter

Can-opener

Spatula

Manicure
blade

Corn
blade

Surgical
pen blade

Curved
manicure
blade

Lawton
manicure
blade

Grooved
manicure
blade

Long
curved
spey blade

Long
spey
blade

Spear
blade

Sabre spear
blade

Long
sheep
foot blade

Texas Tickler
clip blade

Pocketknife styles or shapes are derived from handle frame patterns. Their names have most often been derived from overall appearance or their similarity with another object. Whether or not the name is one that would immediately come to mind, most knife enthusiasts find that names fit the patterns they represent. Names such as equal end, swell center, serpentine, teardrop, and dog leg are as appropriate today as when they were first used many decades ago. The illustration that follows will help to identify some of the more common patterns.

In studying the illustrations, keep in mind that several handle dies have been used to make a variety of styles. For instance, equal-end jacks and cattle knives are often the same shape and size, their difference being primarily in selection of blade types. Likewise, swell-center or balloon knives have been used for whittlers, jacks, folding hunters, and a number of other knife types.

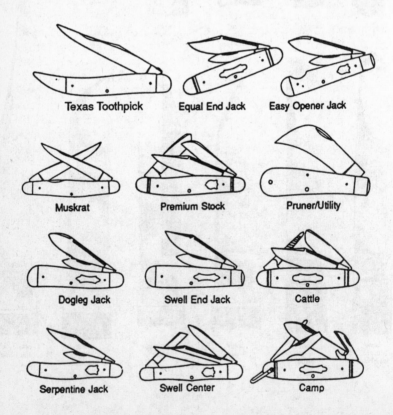

Texas Toothpick   Equal End Jack   Easy Opener Jack

Muskrat   Premium Stock   Pruner/Utility

Dogleg Jack   Swell End Jack   Cattle

Serpentine Jack   Swell Center   Camp

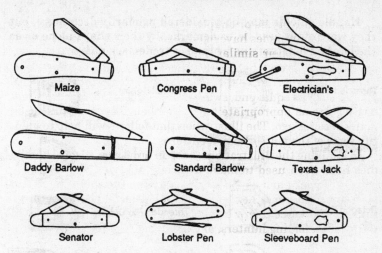

Maize   Congress Pen   Electrician's

Daddy Barlow   Standard Barlow   Texas Jack

Senator   Lobster Pen   Sleeveboard Pen

Pocketknife names are usually derived from the combination of handle frame pattern and the blades used within that frame. Pen knives may take the shapes known as lobster, senator, or sleeveboard, but their primary blade type is pen. An equal-end pattern may be called a jack or, with blades of use to farmers or ranchers, it may be called a cattle knife. Serpentine patterns may have long skinning blades and be called a muskrat, or they may have different blades such as spey, sheepfoot, and clip and be called a stock knife or stockman pattern. Numerous variations will be noted in illustrations contained throughout this book's listings.

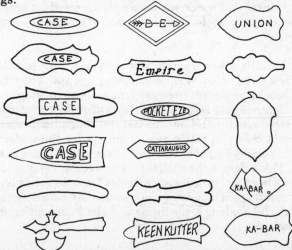

Handle shields may be considered primarily decorative, but they were often used as trademarks, by their shape alone or as the location for stamping a brand or trademark name.

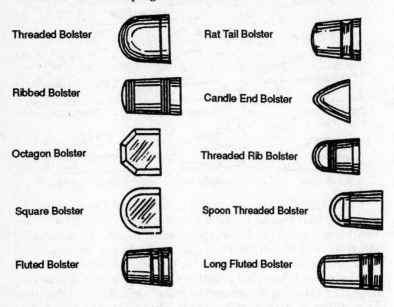

Threaded Bolster

Rat Tail Bolster

Ribbed Bolster

Candle End Bolster

Octagon Bolster

Threaded Rib Bolster

Square Bolster

Spoon Threaded Bolster

Fluted Bolster

Long Fluted Bolster

Bolsters have many names, most of which are descriptive of their appearance. Square, crimped, tip, rat tail, threaded, or fluted are typical bolster types found on pocketknives.

Both natural and manmade materials are used for knife handles. Those most commonly used for pocketknives, however, are listed below.

Bone. Usually taken from the cow shinbone, bone handles are most often dyed with various coloring agents. They can be smooth, scored, or jigged (often referred to as "bone stag").

Stag. Genuine stag is the outside layer of antlers from deer and other related species and has the natural rough texture and appearance. A material called second-cut stag is the underneath layer. It is usually jigged or textured to simulate stag or bone.

Shell. This refers to the shells of reptiles (tortoise) or mollusks. "Pearl," as used for knife handles, comes from the inner lining of mollusk (oyster) shells and is more accurately called mother-of-pearl. Colorful abalone is the lining of shells from a different species of mollusk.

Ivory. Ivory can come from tusks of mammals such as elephant, walrus, or hippopotamus teeth, but elephant ivory is more commonly used. Fossilized ivory, usually from mastodon and walrus, is used more commonly by custom knife makers.

Horn. Buffalo horn was used by older knife companies. Sheep horn, from both wild and domestic sheep and related species, is used primarily on custom knives.

Woods. Nature has provided a nearly endless selection, but those most used on older factory knives are cocobolo, ebony, and walnut. More exotic woods are often found on custom knives.

Celluloid. A durable manmade plastic, it offers many possibilities of colors and patterns.

Other manmade materials such as linen Micarta and Delrin have been prominently used in factory knife production during recent years. Although they are much more durable than their natural lookalikes, neither compares in appeal nor value to the natural materials.

KNIFE BRANDS
OF THE WORLD

▽

The following list includes a major portion of the company names and/or trademarks for pocketknives that will be found in today's collector market. The listing is designed to offer basic information about a large number of brands, and space limitations dictate that such a listing be condensed. It includes brands of both major and lesser importance within the knife-collecting hobby and is intended *only* as a quick reference. Collectors interested in any brand listed are advised to seek further information from within this book or from other reference materials.

The collector value of any knife depends on a number of factors, some of which are discussed elsewhere in this book. The value ranges offered below are general guides to the desirability or collector demand for knives of the brands or specific stampings listed and should not be considered as a value estimation for any specific knife. The ranges are often wide and are for knives in mint condition. One should also be mindful of the fact that knives stamped with one marking may vary substantially in value from knives made by the same manufacturer but stamped with a different marking.

The listing is the most complete ever offered in any edition of this book. In compiling it, the author has relied on the research and knowledge of others to complement his own. Especially noteworthy is research done by John E. Goins and Bernard Levine, as well as that done by James F. Parker and Bruce Voyles in their earlier editions of this guide. Goins's work during the past two decades has revolutionized the knowledge of cutlery brands and trademarks and has become the accepted standard reference work on the subject. Knife researchers will readily admit that there are still knife brands to be found and documented. Information on brands not listed would be welcomed, and readers are invited to write to Houston Price, P.O. Box 3395, Knoxville, TN 37927.

One should note that the listing is in alphabetical order but by first name or initial, *not* by last name—the order that is most often found on a knife trademark stamping. For example, one will find W. R. Case & Sons listed as the knives are stamped rather than as the more awkward Case, W. R. & Sons.

The dates given usually help in determining the age of a knife, but in some instances they indicate the period of years that a company or brand has been in existence, and further research is needed to learn more about the specific date of manufacture for a particular knife. Locations given may be location of manufacture, of the company's headquarters, or both; they are often the same. References are brands or trademarks used by the listed company, the company manufacturing or selling the brand, the importer, or the company ownership.

Brands and Manufacturers (Location)	Reference	Dates	Value Range
20TH CENTURY CUTLERY CO.	A. J. Jordan	c. 1890–1906	$20–70
AARON BURKINSHAW (Pepperell, MA)	Exile, Pain, X-L	1853–1920	75–600
ABERCROMBIE & FITCH (New York, NY)	A. & F. Co.	1892–c. 1978	25–200
ABRAHAM DAVY (Sheffield)		c. 1836–1870	75–600
ABRAM BROOKSBANK (Sheffield)	Defiance	c. 1849–1864	75–600
ACCO (Atlanta, GA)		c. 1970	5–25
ACE (San Francisco, CA)	Bauer Mfg. Co.	c. 1930	5–25
ACE CUTLERY CO. (Fremont, OH)			5–25
ACME (New York, NY)	F. Westpfal	c. 1884–1928	10–30
ADAMS & BROS.			30–100
ADOLPH BLAICH, INC. (San Francisco, CA)	Reno, NV 1954	1915–present	20–180
ADOLPH BLAICH/ J. S. HOLLER (San Francisco, CA)	Arrow Brand	c. 1893–1915	25–175
ADOLPH KASTOR & BROS (Germany)	X.L.N.T., Clover, Morley	c. 1876–1947	20–125
ADOLPHUS BUSCH (St. Louis, MO)	Anheuser Busch	1932–1948	50–400

Brands and Manufacturers (Location)	Reference	Dates	Value Range
ADOLPHUS CUTLERY CO. (England/Germany)	A. J. Jordan	c. 1882–1891	$20–120
AERIAL CUTLERY CO. DULUTH, MN (Duluth, MN)	Jaeger Bros.	1909–1912	20–300
AERIAL CUTLERY CO. MARINETTE, WI (Marinette, WI)		c. 1912–1944	20–300
AERIAL MFG. CO. (Marinette, WI)	Jaeger Bros.	1912–1944	20–300
AKC (Germany)			3–20
AKRON CUTLERY CO. (Akron, OH)		c. 1911–1928	25–140
AL MAR KNIVES (Lake Oswego, OR)	made in Japan	1979–present	20–200
ALAMO (Japan)		c. 1980s	2–10
ALBERTSON CO. (Kane, PA)	formerly Hollingsworth	c. 1930–1938	30–90
ALCOSO (Solingen)	Alexander Coppel	c. 1933–present	5–25
ALEX FRASER & CO. (England)			15–50
ALEXANDER (Sheffield)		c. 1860s	45–350
ALEXANDER COPPEL (Solingen)	Balance, Alcosco, A. C. S. Criterion	1884–1892	15–75
ALFRED FIELD & CO. (England/Germany)		1886–1942	20–150
ALFRED HOBSON & SONS (Sheffield)		c. 1880s	50–300
ALFRED WILLIAMS (Sheffield)	EBRO, imported by Kastor	c. 1890–1920	25–250
ALFRED & SON CELEBRATED CUTLERY			60–200
ALLDIS			45–175
ALLEN CUTLERY CO. (Newburgh, NY)		1917–1925	20–125
ALLENBACH (Germany)			5–20
ALLMAN (Germany)			10–70

Brands and Manufacturers (Location)	Reference	Dates	Value Range
ALOISE (Germany)			$5–20
ALPHA (England)	Harrison Brothers & Howson	c. 1900	15–150
ALTENBACH (Germany)		1920–present	3–20
AMBASSADOR (Providence, RI)	Colonial Knife Co.	1951–present	3–10
AMERICAN ACE (USA)	New Jersey Cutlery Co.	c. 1919–1920	12–25
AMERICAN AUTOMATIC KNIFE CO. (Brooklyn, NY)		c. 1894	25–175
AMERICAN BLADE CUT-LERY CO. (Chattanooga, TN)	Parker Cut-lery Co.	1981–1986	10–65
AMERICAN CUTLERY CO. (Chicago, IL)	pocketknives date before 1900	1879–c. 1923	25–90
AMERICAN HARDWARE & SUPPLY CO. (Pittsburgh, PA)	American Beauty	c. 1911–1935	25–75
AMERICAN IMPORT CO. (Germany)	Arrow Brand	1885–1964	10–25
AMERICAN KNIFE CO./ GERMANY (Germany)		c. 1970	10–40
AMERICAN KNIFE CO./ JAPAN (Japan)			3–15
AMERICAN KNIFE CO./ PLYMOUTH (Plymouth, MA)	Plymouth Hollow	c. 1849–1875	65–350
AMERICAN KNIFE CO./ THOMASTON (Thomaston, CT)	called Plym-outh Hol-low to 1875	1849–1911	30–275
AMERICAN KNIFE CO./ WINSTED CONN (Winsted, CT)		1919–1955	35–125
AMERICAN SHEAR & KNIFE CO. (Hotchkissville, CT)	first pocket-knives 1870	1853–1914	25–200
AMERICA'S BEST (New York)		c. 1930	10–40

Brands and Manufacturers (Location)	Reference	Dates	Value Range
AMES CUTLERY CO. (Chelmsford, MA)		c. 1829–1935	$50–300
ANGLO-PACIFIC (Sheffield)		19th century	25–150
ANHEUSER BUSCH (St. Louis, MO)	by KASTOR, WESTER BROS., CAMILLUS	1880–1922	50–400
ANTELOPE (Germany)			5–50
ANTON WINGEN, JR. (Solingen)	Othello	1888–present	8–30
ANVIL (USA)	Colonial	c. 1932–1948	10–35
ARDOBO CUTLERY CO. (Germany)		c. 1930	10–30
ARGYLE CUTLERY CO. (Germany)	Brown Bros.	c. 1910	20–45
ARKANSAS TRAVELER (Little Rock, AR)	Fones Bros.	c. 1881–1914	25–150
ARMSTRONG CUTLERY CO. (USA)		c. 1901	10–65
ARNEX (Solingen)			4–10
ARROW BRAND KNIFE CO.	American Import Co.	c. 1920	5–35
ART KNIFE CO. (Nicholson, PA)	Made in USA	c. 1920	20–150
ATCO (Japan)		recent	3–10
ATENBACK (Germany)			10–50
ATLANTIC CUTLERY CO. (Germany)		1900–1914	15–45
AUTO KNIFE CO. (Middletown, CT)	Wilizin's patent	c. 1890s	50–175
AUTOMATIC	Eagle Pencil Co.	c. 1883–1945	50–175
AUTOPOINT (Chicago, IL)		c. 1950	5–15
AXEL NIELSSON (Germany)	some imported by Thompson Hdw.	pre–1914	25–95
A-1 NOVELTY CUTLERY (Canton, OH)			20–200

Brands and Manufacturers (Location)	Reference	Dates	Value Range
A. A. A. 1 (St. Louis, MO)	A. J. Jordan, Sheffield made	c. 1886	$25–150
A. A. FISHER CO. (New York)			15–90
A. B. CALDWELL CUTLERY CO. (Indianapolis, IN)	Van Camp Hdw. Co.	c. 1910	35–105
A. CO. (Kane, PA)	Albertson Co.		20–150
A.C. (Nashville, TN)			15–60
A. C. MFG. CO. (Marinette, WI)	Aerial Cutlery Co.	c. 1912–1944	20–300
A. C. M. COMPANY (Marinette, WI)	Aerial Cutlery Mfg. Co.	c. 1912–1944	20–300
A. C. PENN (New York, NY)		c. 1914–1921	20–80
A. C. S. (Solingen)	Alexander Coppel	1884–1892	15–75
A. DINCER (Germany)		c. 1930s	15–125
A. E. MERGOTT & CO. (Newark, NJ)		1888–1950	5–45
A. FEIST & CO. (Solingen)	Omega, Lunawerk, English Steel	c. 1870–1948	25–150
A. FIELD & CO. (Prussia/Germany)	Criterion, Progress	c. 1886–1942	20–125
A. FISHER (Solingen)		c. 1930s	15–90
A. FRIEST & CO. (Solingen)			4–20
A. F. BANNISTER & CO. (New Jersey)		c. 1867–1915	15–100
A. F. SHAPLEIGH HDW. CO. (St. Louis, Mo)	Diamond Edge (after 1888)	1843–1960	20–350
A. G. RUSSELL (Springdale, AR)	Germany, USA, Japan	c. 1974–present	50–500
A. HERMES (Germany)			10–35

Brands and Manufacturers (Location)	Reference	Dates	Value Range
A. J. JORDAN (St. Louis, MO)	AAA1, Adolphus, Old Faithful	c. 1870–1926	$30–175
A. J. JORDAN CUTLERY CO. (St. Louis, MO)	Sheffield & Solingen	c. 1878–1926	20–125
A. J. WESTERSSON (Sweden)		c. 1900	10–60
A. KASTOR & BROS. (New York, NY)	XLNT, EBRO, Clover, Morley, Duane	1876–c. 1947	25–300
A. L. S. N.			5–20
A. M. IMPLEMENT CO. (Germany)			3–15
A. M. LEONARD, INC. (Pigua, OH)	made by Schrade prior 1960	1885–present	10–95
A. P. CO. (New York, NY)			10–25
A. P. S. (Germany)			10–30
A. R. JUSTICE (Philadelphia, PA)	Battle Axe Cutlery Co.	c. 1897–1937	35–150
A. STRAUSS COMPANY (New York, NY)	bought by William Elliot	c. 1907–1918	10–40
A. TILLES & CO. (Philadelphia, PA)			35–75
A. ULMER (Portland, ME)	C. F. Ulmer after 1890	1869–1928	20–60
A. WINGEN (Solingen)		c. 1875–present	5–90
A. W. BRADSHAW & SONS (Germany)			8–30
A. W. FLINT & CO. (Sheffield)		20th century	30–150
A. W. WADSWORTH & SONS (Germany)	XLNT (A. Kastor & Bros. Trademark)	c. 1905–1936	25–150
A. W. WADSWORTH & SONS (Austria)		c. 1905–1936	25–150

Brands and Manufacturers (Location)	*Reference*	*Dates*	*Value Range*
A. W. WADSWORTH & SONS (New York, NY)	part of A. Kastor & Bros.	c. 1905–1922	$20–125
A. W. WALKER & SONS (Austria/Germany)			5–25
A. & A. MFG. CO. (Solingen)			10–125
A. & F. CO. (New York, NY)	Abercrombie & Fitch	c. 1900–1977	25–200
A. & K. (Germany)			10–30
BADGER STATE KNIFE CO. (Germany)			8–20
BAKER (New York, NY)			8–35
BAKER & HAMILTON (San Francisco, CA)	Damascus, Eclipse, Golden Gate	1853–1981	15–150
BAKER, HAMILTON & PACIFIC (San Francisco, CA)	Stiletto	1918–c. 1945	30–350
BALDWIN CUTLERY CO. (Jamestown, NY)		c. 1912–1932	35–150
BANNER KNIFE CO. (Germany)		pre-1915	15–45
BARHEP (Solingen)			3–10
BARLOW (Sheffield)		c. 1667–1798	75–350
BARNSLEY BROS. (Monett, MO)		1898–1906	20–150
BARON (Solingen)			5–25
BARRE TT & SONS (England)			15–55
BARRETT-HICKS CO. (Fresno, CA)		c. 1920s	25–125
BARRY & CO. (Germany)			6–15
BARTON BROS. (Sheffield)			15–95
BASSETT (Derby, CT)			8–25
BASTIAN BROS. CO. (Rochester, NY)		c. 1895–present	25–65

Brands and Manufacturers (Location)	Reference	Dates	Value Range
			$25–150
BATES & BACON (New York)			
BATTLE AXE (Winston-Salem, NC)	made in Germany	1980s	20–175
BATTLE AXE CUTLERY CO. (Philadelphia, PA)	A. R. Justice Co.	c. 1897–1937	35–150
BAUER (Germany)	Ace	c. 1930	5–25
BAY RIDGE WORKS (Solingen)			10–40
BAY STATE MFG. CO. (Worcester, MA)		c. 1890	45–250
BAYONNE KNIFE CO. (Bayonne, NJ)		1888–1898	25–150
BEAVER BROOK KNIFE CO. (Beaver Brook, MA)	B. B. Knife Co.	c. 1880	50–350
BEAVER FALLS CUTLERY CO. (Beaver Falls, PA)	Beaver Brook Knife Company	1866–1886	50–350
BECK & GREGG HDWE. CO. (Atlanta, GA)	Dixie Knife	1890–1894	25–150
BELKNAP HARDWARE CO. (Louisville, KY)	Primble, Blue Grass	c. 1840–1986	20–300
BELMONT KNIFE CO.	E. Morris	c. 1920–1930	15–35
BENCH MARK KNIVES (Portland, OR)	made by Gerber	1984–present	35–125
BENCHMARK KNIVES (Gastonia, NC)	Jenkins Metal Corp.	1970s–1984	25–225
BENEDICT, WARREN DAVIDSON & CO. (Memphis, TN)			20–150
BENNETT CUTLERY WORKS (Canton, NY)			20–200
BERING-CORTES HARD- WARE CO. (Houston, TX)		c. 1905–1947	15–55
BERKSHIRE CUTLERY CO. (Germany)	O-U-NO	c. 1890	20–85
BEST ENGLISH CUTLERY		c. 1800–1860	35–130
BESTEEL WARRANTED		c. 1930s	10–25
BETA BOS'N (Germany)			6–10
BETZ BIFFMAN (Germany)			3–15

Brands and Manufacturers (Location)	Reference	Dates	Value Range
BIDDLE HARDWARE (Philadelphia, PA)	Robbins, Clark & Biddle	c. 1837–1920	$25–350
BIG HORN (Italy)		1971–present	4–10
BIGELOW & DOWSE (Boston, MA)		1872–1954	25–150
BILLINGS & SPENCER (Hartford, CT)	knives c. 1890–1914	1890–1914	25–150
BINGHAM CULTERY CO. (Cleveland, OH)	BBB, XLCR	1841–1930	15–160
BIRMINGHAM KNIFE FACTORY (Birmingham, CT)		c. 1849	50–200
BISON (Japan)			2–5
BLAKE & LAMB (Utica, NY)	made by Utica	c. 1930	20–165
BLANDULA CUTLERY CO. (Germany)			5–20
BLISH-MIZE & SILLIMAN HDWE. CO. (Atchison, KS)	Mohawk	1871–present	20–175
BLITZKNIFE (Charlotte, NC)	W. F. Harwell	c. 1947	10–50
BLUE GRASS (Louisville, KY)	Belknap Hdw. Co.	c. 1898–1986	25–150
BLUE RIBBON (Louisville, KY)	Belknap Hdw. Co.	1910–1950	15–65
BOKER, U.S.A. (Maplewood, NJ)	sold to J. Wiss 1969	1899–present	10–160
BON KNIFE CO.			3–15
BONSA (Solingen)	Boentgen & Sabin	1867–1983	10–50
BONSER INC. (Germany)			6–10
BOOTH BROS./BOONTON N.J. (Boonton, NJ)		1879–1889	25–300
BOOTH BROS./NEWARK N.J. (Newark, NJ)	exhibited at 1867 Paris Exposition	1864–1879	25–300
BOOTH BROS./ STOCKHOLM N.J. (Stockholm, NJ)		1889–1903	25–300
BOOTH BROS./SUSSEX N.J. (Sussex, NJ)		1903–1909	45–375

Brands and Manufacturers (Location)	Reference	Dates	Value Range
			$3–10
BORNEFF (Germany)			
BOSTWICK BRAUN CO. (Toledo, OH)		1873–present	25–175
BOWEN KNIFE CO. (Waycross, GA)	Bullet	1973–present	20–150
BOWER IMPLEMENT CO. (Germany)	F. A. Bower		5–35
BOWMAN CUTLERY CO. (Germany)			15–25
BRACH (Germany)	NCRF		10–25
BRADFORD & ANTHONY (Boston, MA)	became Dame, Stoddard & Kendall	1856–1883	25–200
BRANTFORD CUTLERY CO. (USA)	"Warranted Never Dull," Butler Bros.	c. 1900	20–150
BRIDGE CUTLERY CO. (St. Louis, MO)	sold by Shapleigh Hdw.	c. 1915	65–375
BRIDGEPORT KNIFE CO. (Bridgeport, CT)		c. 1904	40–150
BRIGHTON CUTLERY WORKS (Germany)		c. 1900	15–45
BRISTOL LINE (Germany)		c. 1950s	8–45
BRIT-NIFE (St. Louis, MO)			15–30
BROCH & KOCH			15–65
BROCH & THIEBES CUTLERY CO. (St. Louis, MO)		c. 1882–1892	20–150
BROOKES & CROOKES (Sheffield)	Bell (picture)	c. 1859–1947	20–350
BROOKLYN KNIFE CO. (New York)			15–75
BROWN BROS. KNIFE CO. (Tidioute, PA)	Union Cutlery Co.	prior 1902	50–150
BROWN BROS. KNIFE CO. (Olean, NY)	Union Cutlery Co.	after 1911	50–150
BROWN BROS. MFG. CO. (Tidioute, PA)	became Union Razor Co.	c. 1890–1902	25–150

Brands and Manufacturers (Location)	Reference	Dates	Value Range
BROWN BROS./GERMANY (Germany)	Union Cut	prior 1902	$40–250
BROWN CAMP HARDWARE CO. (Des Moines, IA)	I. O. A.	c. 1907–1959	25–150
BROWN & BIGELOW (St. Paul, MN)	B & B, made by Colonial	1931–1950s	25–75
BROWNING (Germany/USA)		c. 1969–present	10–75
BROWN-CAMP HDWE. CO. (St. Louis, MO)		1907–1959	30–200
BRUNSWICK CUTLERY CO. (San Francisco, CA)	Dunham-Carrigan-Hayden	c. 1897–1907	20–75
BUCK (El Cajon, CA)	started by H. H. Buck c. 1900	1963–present	20–175
BUCK BROS. (Worcester, MA)		c. 1853–1927	25–500
BUCK CREEK (London, KY)	made in Germany	1970–present	10–95
BUD BRAND CUTLERY CO. (Winstead, CT)		c. 1922	25–100
BUFFALO CUTLERY CO. (Germany)		c. 1915	35–160
BUHL & SONS CO. (Detroit, MI)			15–65
BULL BRAND (Germany)	Lauderdale, Castilian Springs, TN	1985–present	15–45
BULLDOG (Solingen)	S & D Products	c. 1980–present	20–250
BURGON & BALL (Sheffield)	Sound	c. 1873–1917	15–75
BURKINSHAW KNIFE CO. (Pepperell, MA)		c. 1881–1920	35–350
BUSTER BROWN SHOE CO. (St. Louis, MO)	by Camillus via Shapleigh	c. 1930s	15–125
BUTLER BROS. (Chicago, IL)	Warranted Never Dull	1865–1952	25–120
BUTLER & CO. (Sheffield)		1865–1952	15–75
BUTTERICK PATTERN CO.	B. P. Co. Ltd.	c. 1910	10–25
B. ALTMAN & CO. (New York, NY)		c. 1900	10–40

Brands and Manufacturers (Location)	Reference	Dates	Value Range
B. B. KNIFE CO. (Beaverbrook, MA)	Beaver Brook Knife Co.	c. 1880	$50–350
B. H. MORSE (Waterbury, CT)	Waterville Co.	c. 1857	25–125
B. H. SPECIAL (Germany)	Biddle Hardware	c. 1910	15–30
B. J. EYRE CO. (Germany)	Wiebusch trademark	c. 1876–1910	25–75
B. J. EYRE & CO. (Sheffield)	late W. Greaves & Son	1850–c. 1876	25–125
B. K. CUTLERY CO. (Cleveland, OH)			5–20
B. SVOBODA (Montrose, CA)	imported by Liberty	c. 1950–present	10–25
B. T. CO. (New Haven, CT)	Bridgeport Tool Co.		20–100
B. WORTH & SONS (Sheffield)		c. 1874–1919	25–75
B. & A. (Boston, MA)	Bradford & Anthony	c. 1867–1881	10–25
B. & B. (St. Paul, MN)	Brown & Bigelow	c. 1931–1952	5–35
B. & T. IMPLEMENT CUTLERY CO.			30–150
CALDWELL CUTLERY CO. (Indianapolis, IN)	Van Camp Hdwe.	c. 1879–1929	25–100
CALIFORNIA NOTION & TOY CO. (San Francisco, CA)		1894–c. 1930	25–75
CAM III (Vacaville, CA)		1980s	10–65
CAMBRIDGE CUTLERY CO. (Sheffield)	(US Navy contractor)	c. 1865	25–350
CAMCO (Camillus, NY)	Camillus Cutlery Co.	1948–present	5–50
CAMDEN CUTLERY CO. (Germany)			15–90
CAMERON KNIFE CO.		c. 1920s	15–65
CAMILLUS (New York, NY)		c. 1902–present	5–110
CAMILLUS CUTLERY CO. (Camillus, NY)	(mark used through WW II)	1902–present	10–175

Brands and Manufacturers (Location)	*Reference*	*Dates*	*Value Range*
CAMILLUS/NEW YORK/USA (Camillus, NY)	(mark used after WW II)	1902–present	$10–75
CAMP BUDDY (USA)	Camillus Cutlery Co.	1902–present	5–25
CAMP KING (Germany)			5–25
CANASTOTA KNIFE CO. (Canastota, NY)		1875–1895	50–350
CANTON CUTLERY CO. (Canton, OH)	W. S. Carnes	1879–c. 1930	20–175
CANTON HARDWARE CO. (Canton, OH)	Keen Edge	c. 1910	15–150
CAPITOL CUTLERY CO. (Indianapolis, IN)	Van Camp Hdw.	1904–1948	35–300
CAPITOL KNIFE CO. (Winsted, CT)		c. 1920s	15–125
CARL BERTRAM (Solingen)	Hen & Rooster	1864–1983	20–250
CARL KAMMERLING & CO. (Germany)	P. L. Schmidt, Wintgen	1904–present	10–90
CARL KLAUBERG & BROS. (New York, NY)		c. 1883–1940	10–90
CARL LINDER (Solingen)	Rehwappen	1980–present	25–175
CARL SCHLIEPER (Solingen)	Eye Brand, Fan, El Gallo, Jim Bowie	1796–present	10–150
CARL SCHMIDT SOHN (Solingen)		1829–present	20–120
CARL WUSTHOF (Solingen)	Gladiator, Hejo, James	1895–present	20–150
CARRIER CUTLERY CO. (Elmira, NY)	Cronk & Carrier	1900–1921	45–225
CARTER BLADE MASTER (Cleveland, OH)			15–35
CARTERS (Scottsville, KY)	C. Bertram's Hen & Rooster logo	1969–1983	40–200
CAR-VAN S P (Canton, OH)	Canton Cutlery Co.	1911–1930	10–175

Brands and Manufacturers (Location)	Reference	Dates	Value Range
CASE BROS. (Little Valley, NY)		1900–1914	$40–1000
CASE BROS. (Springville, NY)		c. 1912	75–1200
CASE BROTHERS (Little Valley, NY)	Tested XX	1900–1912	50–1650
CASE BROTHERS (Springville, NY)	Tested XX	1912–1915	50–1650
CASE BROTHERS & CO. (Gowanda, NY)	made by C. Platts & Sons	1869–1900	25–1700
CASE CUTLERY COMPANY (Kane, PA)	Case Bros. 1907–1911	1907–1911	50–700
CASE MFG. CO. (Little Valley, NY)		c. 1898–1899	50–850
CASE XX METAL STAMPING LTD. (Bradford, PA)	by Case for Canadian gov't	1940s	15–75
CATSKILL KNIFE CO. (New York)		c. 1930s	15–150
CATTARAUGUS (Springdale, AR)	A. G. Russell	1984–present	15–50
CATTARAUGUS CUTLERY CO. (Little Valley, NY)		1886–1963	25–500
CEB MULLER (Germany)			3–15
CENTAUR CUTLERY (Germany)	Sperry & Alexander	c. 1893–1913	5–25
CENTENNIAL MILLS (Solingen)			15–45
CENTRAL CITY KNIFE CO. (Phoenix, NY)	C. C. Knife Co.	1880–1892	20–200
CENTRAL CUTLERY CO. (Elizabeth, NJ)		c. 1926	40–130
CHALLENGE CUTLERY CO. (Germany)	Wiebusch & Hilger	1877–1891	25–225
CHALLENGE CUTLERY CO. (Sheffield)	B. J. Eyre Co.	1867–1877	20–350
CHALLENGE CUT. CORP. (Bridgeport, CT)		c. 1891–1928	20–150
CHALMERS & MURRAY (New York, NY)		c. 1890s	35–95
CHAMPION (Birmingham, AL)	Moore-Handley Hardware	c. 1925–1932	15–75

Brands and Manufacturers (Location)	Reference	Dates	Value Range
CHAPMAN CUT. CO. (Muncie, IN)	Chapman Hand Forged	1915–1931	$35–60
CHARLES HALL (Sheffield)	C. Hall	c. 1836–1872	25–200
CHARLES LAND (Sheffield)			60–80
CHARLES LANGBEIN (New York)		c. 1880–1890	65–125
CHARLES R. RANDALL (Germany)			15–35
CHERO-COLA CO.			35–70
CHICAGO CUTLERY (Minneapolis, MN)		current	3–20
CHICAGO KNIFE WORKS (Chicago, IL)		c. 1911	25–125
CHICAGO POCKET KNIFE CO. (Chicago, IL)			25–125
CHIPAWAY CUTLERY CO. (England)	for E. C. Simmons Hdw.	c. 1891–1907	35–400
CHRISTOPHER JOHNSON & CO. (Sheffield)	CJ in flag; to I*XL 1955	1865–c. 1977	25–200
CHRISTY (Fremont, OH)	Russ J. Christy Knife Co.	1890-present	5–30
CLARK BROTHERS (Kansas City, MO)	bought Northfield in 1919	1895–1929	25–125
CLARK & CARRIERS MFG. CO. (Montour Falls, NY)			35–75
CLARKS CUTLERY (USA)	Baker & Hamilton, XLT on blade		15–45
CLAUBERG CUTLERY CO. (Germany)		1857–present	10–55
CLAUSS (Freemont, OH)	made by Shatt & Morgan	1887–present	10–75
CLAY CUTLERY CO. (Andover, NY)	probably by Robeson	c. 1930s	30–300
CLAYSEN & SON (Germany)			10–35

Brands and Manufacturers (Location)	Reference	Dates	Value Range
CLEAN CUT (San Francisco, CA)	imp. by Kastor for Dunham	c. 1884–1912	$20–95
CLEARCUT (U.S.A.)	George Worthington	1835–1949	12–30
CLEMENTS (Sheffield)	Hand Forged	20th century	10–60
CLEVELAND CUTLERY CO. (Cleveland, OH)	made in Japan & Germany		3–45
CLIM (Germany)	Schmachtenberg	c. 1887–1939	10–75
CLIPPER CUTLERY CO. (Richmond, VA)	Watkins-Cottrell Co.	c. 1901	10–50
CLOVER BRAND (Syracuse, NY)	Kastor & Camillus	c. 1941–1942	15–35
CLYDE CUTLERY CO. (Clyde, OH)		c. 1929–1949	12–80
COAST CUTLERY CO. (Portland, OR)		1919–present	25–125
COCA COLA (Atlanta, GA)	made by Camillus	1930–1940s	25–200
COHELLE COIN			30–90
COLEMAN CUTLERY CO. (Titusville, PA)			15–60
COLES (New York)	Hand Forged	c. 1960s	8–50
COLLINS BROS. (Atlanta, GA)	made by Camillus	c. 1970–1973	20–75
COLLINS CO. (Collinsville, CT)		c. 1826–1966	25–250
COLONIAL (Providence, RI)	Colonial Cutlery Company	1926–present	10–55
COLT (Germany)		c. 1969–1973	30–45
COLT (Hartford, CT)	by Barry Wood, Venice, CA	1969–1973	50–350
COLUMBIA KNIFE CO. (New York)		c. 1900	45–60
COL. COON (Columbia, TN)	Racoon	c. 1978–1986	25–150
COMMANDER (Little Valley, NY)	Metropolitan Cutlery Co.	c. 1891–1928	65–100

Brands and Manufacturers (Location)	Reference	Dates	Value Range
CONCORD CUTLERY CO.		c. 1880	$25–150
CONN. CUTLERY CO. (Naugatuck, CT)		1867–1883	25–250
CONTINENTAL CUTLERY CO. (Kansas City, MO)	Clark Bros.	1915–1920	25–125
COOK BROTHERS (Sheffield)		c. 1890	55–150
COOPER BROTHERS (Sheffield)			5–25
COOPERATIVE KNIFE CO. (New York)	Walden/ Ellenville, NY, became Ulster	1871–1876	50–375
CORA (Germany)			5–15
CORLISS CUTLERY (Germany)			20–35
CORNING KNIFE CO. (New York, NY)		c. 1930s	10–50
CORNWALL KNIFE CO. (Cornwall, CT)		19th century	25–95
CORSAN DENTON BURDEKIN (Sheffield)		c. 1860	25–300
CRAFTSMAN (Chicago, IL)	by Camillus, Schrade Ulster	1940s–present	5–65
CRANDALL CUTLERY CO. (Bradford, PA)	merged with W. R. Case	1905–1912	75–500
CRESCENT CUTLERY CO. (Fremont, OH)		c. 1917–1950	15–50
CRIPPLE CREEK (Old Fort, TN)		1986–present	40–150
CRIPPLE CREEK (Lockport, IL)	by Bob Cargill	1981–1986	40–500
CRITERION (Sheffield)	Alfred Field	1886–1942	10–200
CRONK & CARRIER MFG. CO. (Elmira, NY)	Carrier Cutlery Co.	1900–1921	45–225
CROSMAN BLADES (Wichita, KS)		1982–present	5–75

Brands and Manufacturers (Location)	Reference	Dates	Value Range
CROWN CUTLERY CO. (New York, NY)		1910s–1920s	$15–65
CRUCIBLE KNIFE CO. (Lynn, MA)	sold by W. T. Grant, NYC	1926–1932	20–80
CULF & KAY (Sheffield)			65–90
CUMBERLAND CUTLERY CO. (Sheffield)	Gray & Dudley, C. M. McClung	c. 1897–1948	15–65
CURLEY BROS. (New York)		c. 1885–1905	10–75
CURTIN & CLARK CUTLERY CO. (St. Joseph, MO)		c. 1898–1910	25–110
CUSSINS & FEARN (USA)		1930s	25–75
CUT SURE	Kruse & Bahlman	c. 1889–1962	20–150
CUTINO CUTLERY CO. (Kansas City, MO)	some made by Challenge	c. 1914–1935	20–50
CUTWELL CUTLERY CO. (Germany)	A. Kastor & Bros.	c. 1886–1945	20–200
C. BERTRAM (Solingen)	Hen & Rooster	c. 1872–present	40–250
C. B. BARKER & CO. (New York, NY)	Howard Cutlery Co.	c. 1880–1905	25–150
C.B.S. (Solingen)			15–25
C. CONGREVE (Sheffield)		1829–1843	50–350
C. C. KNIFE CO. (Phoenix, NY)	Central City Knife Co.	c. 1880–1892	20–400
C. FRIEDR. ERN & CO. (Germany)		1874–1926	10–25
C. F. KAYSER (Germany)			8–125
C. F. SIMON (Solingen)			5–20
C. F. WOLFERTZ & CO. (Allentown, PA)	(Mfr. 1862– c. 1920)	1862–c. 1944	25–200
C. JUL HERIETZ (Germany)			10–35
C. J. & CO. (Sheffield)			40–65

Brands and Manufacturers (Location)	Reference	Dates	Value Range
C. K. CO. (Germany)	Colonial Knife Co.		$10–35
C. LUTTERS & CO. (Solingen)	reclining lion trademark	1840–present	10–100
C. M. McCLUNG & CO. (Knoxville, TN)	Cranberry, Keener Edge	1882–c. 1960	25–125
C. PLATTS & SONS (Gowanda, NY)	in old S. & M. plant	1896–1900	50–700
C. PLATTS & SONS (Elred, PA)	became C. Platts' Sons	1897–1900	50–600
C. PLATTS' SONS (Elred, PA)	merged with W. R. Case 1905	1900–1905	50–600
C. PRADEL	1er Choix (first choice)		15–60
C. SARRY (Thiers, France)			10–50
C. T. ERVIN CO. (Germany)			15–50
C. & R. LINDER (Solingen)	crown/ pruning knife	1842–1971	25–175
C. & X. (Sheffield)			12–25
DAHLIA (Germany)			5–15
DAMASCUS STEEL PRODUCTS CORP. (Rockford, IL)	DASCO	1922–1962	10–150
DAME STODDARD & CO. (Boston, MA)	D S & C	c. 1901–1930	10–150
DAME STODDARD & KENDALL (Boston, MA)	(DS&K, Hub) was Bradford & Anthony	c. 1881–1901	10–150
DANCE CUTLERY CO. (Germany)			10–25
DANIEL PERES & CO. (Solingen)	Ale Barrel	1792–present	15–175
DART (USA)			3–20
DASCO (Rockford, IL)	Damascus Steel Products	c. 1922–1962	5–35

Brands and Manufacturers (Location)	Reference	Dates	Value Range
DAWES & BALL (Sheffield)		1925–1962	$65–125
DECORA (Germany)			5–15
DEERSLAYER BRAND	Precise		10–40
DEFENDER	.22 cal. knife-pistol	c. 1912	200–600
DEHERD (Solingen)			5–15
DELMAR CUTLERY CO.		c. 1910	25–95
DELTA (Germany)	Hugo Linder	1878–1953	5–20
DELUXE (Torrence, CA)	Salm	1918–1925	5–20
DEPEND-ON-ME CUTLERY CO. (New York, NY)		c. 1945	10–75
DIAMOND EDGE (St. Louis, MO)	Shapleigh Hardware	1864–1960	25–250
DIAMOND EDGE VAL-TEST (Chicago, IL)	Schrade trademark	1960–1967	5–50
DIAMOND EDGE (IMPERIAL) (Providence, RI)	Imperial Knife Co. trademark	c. 1967–present	5–15
DICTATOR		c. 1930s	10–25
DISSTON STEEL (Philadelphia, PA)	commemorative knife	1940	10–50
DIXIE KNIFE (Atlanta, GA)	Beck & Gregg Hdw.	c. 1890–1894	30–60
DIXON CUTLERY CO. (Germany)		c. 1920s	10–55
DODSON MFG. CO. (Chicago, IL)		c. 1937	25–125
DOLLAR KNIFE CO. (Atlanta, GA)		c. 1922	15–150
DOLLAR KNIFE CO. (Titusville, PA)	Schatt & Morgan	c. 1927	15–150
DOLMETACH (Zurich, Switzerland)			5–20
DOLPHIN CUTLERY CO. (New York, NY)		1918–1920s	20–95
DOMAR CUTLERY CO. (Oklahoma City, OK)	Theodore M. Green Co.	c. 1916–1920	15–85
DOUBLE COLA (USA)			3–20

Brands and Manufacturers (Location)	Reference	Dates	Value Range
DOUBLE SHARP (Sheffield)	G. Ibberson	c. 1932–1942	$10–40
DOUGLAS (Brockton, MA)			15–35
DRAKE HARDWARE CO. (USA)		c. 1890	10–50
DREITIUM (Germany)			5–15
DRESDEN (Germany)			4–12
DRIEZACK (Germany)			4–12
DRITTES (Germany)			10–35
DUANE CUTLERY CO. (Germany)	A. Kastor	c. 1910	5–20
DUKE PETERSON HDW. CO.		c. 1920s	25–125
DUKES	"Father of Barlows" on bolster		35–65
DUNHAM CARRIGAN & HAYDEN (San Francisco, CA)	Clean Cut, Springbrooke, Volka	1848–1927	25–200
DUNLAP (USA)		c. 1877–1930	25–150
DUNN BROS. (Providence, RI)		1927–present	6–25
DURO-EDGE (Utica, NY)	Montgomery Ward	c. 1928–1930	5–10
DWIGHT DIVINE & SONS (Ellenville, NY)	Ulster Knife Co., Kingston	1876–1941	35–175
D. C. & H. (San Francisco, CA)	Dunham Carrigan & Hayden	c. 1849–1964	25–125
D. PERES (Germany)		c. 1885–present	5–14
D. S. & CO. (Boston, MA)	Dame Stoddard & Co.	c. 1901–1930	10–150
D. S. & K. (Boston, MA)	Dame Stoddard & Kendall	c. 1881–1901	10–150
EAGLE BRAND (Japan)	Parker Cutlery	c. 1974–present	10–900
EAGLE CUTLERY CO.	Eagle Pencil Co.	c. 1883–1945	10–150

Brands and Manufacturers (Location)	Reference	Dates	Value Range
EAGLE KNIFE CO. (New Haven, CT)	Hemming Pat. 10/1/1918	1916–1919	$20–100
EAGLE PENCIL CO. (New York, NY)		c. 1883–1945	5–25
EAGLETON KNIFE CO. (Germany)	Wester & Butz	c. 1890	20–125
EAGLE/PHIL'A (Philadelphia, PA)	Creutzberg	c. 1883–1945	20–70
EAL K. CO. (Germany)			15–50
ECLIPSE CUTLERY CO. (San Francisco, CA)	Baker & Hamilton, by Boker	c. 1897–1918	25–125
EDER & CO. (Germany)			25–65
EDGAR CUTLERY CO. (Germany)			5–25
EDGE MARK (Japan & Germany)	for Gutmann Cutlery, Inc.	c. 1950–present	3–15
EDGEMASTER (USA)	Switchblade knife	c. 1940s	10–45
EDIRLAM (Solingen)			5–15
EDITHWERKS (Solingen)			15–35
EDUARD WUSTHOF (Solingen)	Dreizack (Trident)	1814–present	25–200
EDULON (Solingen)			5–15
EDWARD BARNES (USA)	made in Sheffield	c. 1900	50–750
EDWARD BARNES & SONS (Sheffield)		c. 1856–1865	65–400
EDWARD K. TRYON (Philadelphia, PA)	3/T. Some by Utica.	c. 1811–1952	45–300
EDWARD PARKER & SONS (New York)	Germania Cutlery Works	c. 1900	25–95
EDWARD WECK (New York, NY)	also Pauls Bros.	1893–1943	15–75
EDWARD WECK & SONS (New York, NY)	New York, NY	c. 1893–1943	25–85
EDWARD ZINN (New York, NY)	made in Germany	c. 1920	5–15

Brands and Manufacturers (Location)	*Reference*	*Dates*	*Value Range*
EL GALLO (Germany)	Eye Brand, Carl Schlieper	c. 1968–1970	$5–12
ELBERFIELD CUTLERY CO. (Germany)	made by Wester & Butz	c. 1866–1891	20–150
ELBERON CUTTING WORKS (Germany)			5–15
ELDER & CO. (Germany)			10–25
ELECTRIC (Germany)	Friedmann & Lauterjung	c. 1873–1901	25–250
ELECTRIC CUTLERY CO./ NEWARK N.J. (New York, NY)	Friedmann & Lauterjung	1873–c. 1901	45–140
ELECTRIC CUTLERY CO./ WALDEN N.Y. (New York, NY)	Friedmann & Lauterjung	after 1901	55–350
ELGIN A M MFG. CO. (USA)			6–25
ELIKSCH KADISON (Germany)			3–7
ELLENVILLE KNIFE CO. (Ellenville, NY)	Dwight Divine & Sons	1876–1920	45–350
ELLIOTT CUTLERY CORP. (Germany)			5–25
ELOISE (Germany)			5–35
ELYRIA CUTLERY CO. (Elyria, OH)	became Clauss Cutlery Co.	1878–1887	25–150
ELYTE			3–15
EMHAWCO (Huntington, WV)	Emmons-Hawkins Hardware	1899–1969	15–100
EMPIRE KNIFE CO. (Winsted, CT)	in West Winsted post-1880	1856–1930	40–350
EMROD CO. (Germany)			4–15
ENDERSES (Albert Lea, MN)		c. 1918	30–125

Brands and Manufacturers (Location)	Reference	Dates	Value Range
ENDMON			$4–25
ENDURE	J. Beal	1870–1890	10–75
(Sheffield)			
ENGELSWERK			3–20
(Germany)			
ENGLISH CUTLERY CO.			15–65
(Sheffield)			
ENTERPRISE CUTLERY CO.	Kastor,	c. 1920s	25–85
(St. Louis, MO)	Camillus		
ERBER		c. 1890	5–15
(Austria)			
ERMA		c. 1950s	5–50
(Germany)			
ERN		1916–1926	5–15
(Solingen)			
ERNEST BRUECKMANN	Bridge	1891–c. 1956	25–125
(Solingen)	(picture)		
ERNEST G. AHRENS		1930s	15–65
(Solingen)			
ERNEST WARTHER		1920s–1940s	30–350
(Dover, OH)			
ERNST GERLEREG			15–50
(Germany)			
ESEMCO	Shiman Mfg. Co.	1921–1949	5–8
ESSEM CO.		1921–1949	10–20
ESSEX CUTLERY CO.			20–110
EUREKA CUTLERY CO.	became Lackawanna	1911–1915	25–175
(Nicholson, PA)			
EVERKEEN			15–65
EVER -SHARP	American Wholesale Co.	1923–1925	25–250
(Baltimore, MD)			
EXCELSIOR KNIFE CO.	sold to Northfield c. 1884	1880–1884	55–150
(Torrington, CT)			
EXECUTIVE	Colonial Knife Co.		5–35
(USA)			
EXPLORER	Gutmann Cutlery Co.		5–20
(Germany)			
EYE BRAND	Carl Schlieper	c. 1769–present	10–75
(Germany)			
EYRE WARD & CO.	Sheaf Works	c. 1840–1869	25–150
(Sheffield)			
E. BARNES & SONS		c. 1856–1865	25–200
(Sheffield)			

Brands and Manufacturers (Location)	Reference	Dates	Value Range
E. BRUCKMANN (Solingen)		c. 1920–1956	$15–175
E. B. EXTRA (Germany)	Hartford Cutlery Company	c. 1914	25–75
E. C. SIMMONS HDW. CO. (St. Louis, MO)	Keen Kutter/ Shapleigh after 1940	1868–1960	25–300
E. DIRLAM (Solingen)			15–35
E. DULON (Solingen)			4–25
E. FABER (Germany)			5–25
E. FELSENHELD (New York)			35–65
E. MOULIN (Greenville, IL)			15–65
E. M. DICKINSON (Sheffield)		c. 1870–1912	25–95
E. T. ALLEN (San Francisco, CA)	The Club	1878–1899	25–300
E. WILD & SONS (Germany)			15–50
E.A.A. (Solingen)			5–10
E.F. & S. (England)	Furness	c. 1870–1915	65–200
E.K.A. (Eskilstuna, Sweden)		1885–present	20–75
FABICO (Germany/Japan)	by Bower		2–10
FABYAN KNIFE CO. (Germany)	Q. E. D.	c. 1890	25–110
FAIRMONT CUTLERY CO. (Camillus, NY)	Camillus brand	1930s	20–65
FAIRPLAY BROS.			5–100
FALCON KNIFE CO.			15–35
FALL RIVER KNIFE CO. (Fall River, MA)	Germany made	c. 1900	15–75
FARWELL OZMUN KIRK & CO. (St. Paul, MN)		1881–1959	35–110
FAULKHINER & CO. (Germany)			10–20

Brands and Manufacturers (Location)	Reference	Dates	Value Range
FAVORITE KNIFE CO. (Germany)			$4–25
FAYETTEVILLE KNIFE CO. (Fayetteville, NY)	F. K. Co.	c. 1911	30–90
FEDERAL KNIFE CO. (Syracuse, NY)	by Camillus (?)	c. 1920s	20–75
FIDELITY KNIFE CO. (New York)			5–35
FIFE CUTLERY CO. (Mount Sterling, KY)	made by C. Bertram	1968–1974	40–150
FILLMORE CUTLERY CO. (Germany)			10–60
FINEDGE CUTLERY CO. (New York, NY)	Ostiso	c. 1921–1923	15–125
FLENEF (USA)			5–100
FLETCHER KNIFE CO. (Detroit, MI)	Fletcher Hardware Co.	c. 1863–1913	25–175
FLORAWORKS CUTLERY CO. (Germany)			5–15
FLOSA (Germany)			25–65
FLOYD & BOHR CO. (Louisville, KY)			35–125
FLYLOCK KNIFE CO. (Bridgeport, CT)	by Challenge Cutlery	1918–1928	40–225
FONES BROTHERS (Little Rock, AR)	Arkansas Traveler	c. 1881–1914	25–150
FORD & MEDLEY (Sheffield)		1872–c. 1930	20–95
FOREST MASTER (Providence, RI)	Colonial	1934–present	10–25
FOSTER BROS. & CHATILLON CO. (Fulton, NY)		c. 1930–1937	15–65
FOX CUTLERY (Milwaukee, WI)	Koeller & Schmidt	c. 1884–1955	35–85
FRANCE & RUSSIE			10–15
FRANCIS NEWTON & SONS (Sheffield)	J. & R. Dodge	c. 1838–present	10–500
FRANK BUSTER CELEBRATED CUTLERY (Solingen)	Fight'n Rooster logo	c. 1973–present	15–1500
FRANK BUSTER CUTLERY CO. (Lebanon, TN)	Fight'n Rooster logo	1977–present	15–1000

Brands and Manufacturers (Location)	Reference	Dates	Value Range
FRANK MILLS & CO. (England)		c. 1860	$8–85
FRANK OWEN HDWE. CO.			15–35
FRANKFURTH HDWE. CO. (Milwaukee, WI)		c. 1862–present	30–50
FRARY CUTLERY CO. (Bridgeport, CT)	A-1 Warranted	1876–1884	25–350
FRARY & SON (Bridgeport, CT)		c. 1876–1884	25–350
FRED BIFFAR (Chicago, IL)	Dixie Switch	1917–1922	20–75
FRED KRONER HDWE. (Germany)			10–50
FREDERICK FENNEY (Sheffield)	Fox, Tally-Ho	1824–1852	25–100
FREDERICK REYNOLDS (Sheffield)		18??–1920s	25–275
FREDERICK WESTPFAL (New York, NY)	Acme	c. 1884–1940	25–125
FRITZ ERN & CO. (Solingen)			15–50
FRONTIER (Providence, RI)	Imperial	current	10–25
FROST CUTLERY CO. (Chattanooga, TN)	made in Japan	1978–present	5–60
FRYE PHIPPS & CO. (Boston, MA)		1860–19??	20–85
FULTON CUTLERY CO. (New York, NY)		c. 1910	35–125
F. A. KOCH & CO. (New York, NY)		c. 1880–1933	25–175
F. SEM CO.			5–15
F. STERLING (Germany)			5–25
F. WARD & CO. (Sheffield)	B 4 * ANY (regis. 1867)	c. 1850s–1979	25–300
F. WIEBUSCH (New York, NY)	Challenge, Wester, Monum'l	c. 1874–1928	25–400
F. W. JORDAN (New York)	probably by Krusius Bros.	c. 1920s	10–125
F. W. SHELDON & CO. (Germany)			4–25
F. & K. (Solingen)			6–15

Brands and Manufacturers (Location)	Reference	Dates	Value Range
F. & L. (New York, NY)	Friedmann & Lauterjang	c. 1866–1920	$45–195
F. & L. CELEBRATED CUTLERY (Germany)	Friedmann & Lauterjung	c. 1873–1881	75–125
GAMBLE STORES (Minneapolis, MN)	made by Camillus	c. 1930s–1950s	10–45
GARDEN CITY CUTLERY			25–60
GARLAND CUTLERY CO. (Germany)		c. 1913	10–25
GATEWAY CUTLERY CO.			5–25
GEBRUDER CHRISTIANS (Solingen)	Fork (picture), Christians Bros.	1824–present	20–150
GEBRUDER KRUSIUS (Solingen)	Krusius Bros.	1856–1983	10–150
GEBRUDER RICHARTZ & SOEHNE (Solingen)	Whale	1900–present	15–75
GELBROS. CO. (Germany)			12–40
GELLMAN BROS. (Minneapolis, MN)		c. 1920	15–60
GENERAL (Chicago, IL)			15–30
GENEVA CUTLERY CO. (Geneva, NY)	became Geneva Forge 1934	1902–1934	30–60
GENEVA FORGE, INC. (Geneva, NY)	div. of E. Katzinger (EKCO)	1934–c. 1948	25–75
GEORGE BARNSLEY & SONS (Sheffield)	Wide Awake	c. 1839–1938	25–350
GEORGE DOBSON (Sheffield)		c. 1880s	25–250
GEORGE F. CREUTZBERG (Philadelphia, PA)	Eagle/Phil'a	c. 1875–1943	10–100
GEORGE HANCOCK & SONS			25–115
GEORGE IBBERSON & CO. (Sheffield)	Violin (after 1880)	1700–present	15–175
GEORGE JOHNSON & CO. (Sheffield)	Seven stars (picture)	1810–1855	25–250

Brands and Manufacturers (Location)	Reference	Dates	Value Range
GEORGE SAVAGE & SONS (Sheffield)		c. 1855	$25–150
GEORGE SCHRADE KNIFE CO. (Bridgeport, CT)	Presto [H], Commando	c. 1925–1945	20–200
GEORGE TRITCH HDW. CO. (Denver, CO)	made by Ulster	c. 1910	25–85
GEORGE WOLSTENHOLME (Sheffield)		c. 1745–1775	40–1000
GEORGE WOODHEAD & SON (Sheffield)	G. W.*I.	c. 1845–1870s	25–350
GEORGE WOSTENHOLM (Sheffield)	I*XL, Oil The Joints	c. 1930s–1977	25–300
GEORGE WOSTENHOLM (Sheffield)	Rockingham Works	1815–1848	40–900
GEORGE WOSTENHOLM (Sheffield)	I*XL, ENGLAND on blade	c. 1891–1971	40–900
GEORGE WOSTENHOLM (Sheffield)	I*XL Celebrated	c. 1860s–1890s	40–900
GEORGE WOSTENHOLM (Sheffield)	I*XL Washington Works	1848–1870s	25–300
GEORGE WOSTENHOLM (Sheffield)	I*XL (see other listings)	1745–c. 1971	40–1000
GEORGE WOSTENHOLM IMPROVED CUTLERY (Sheffield)		c. 1832–1837	50–1000
GEORGE WOSTENHOLM & SON CUTLERY CO. (Sheffield)		c. 1815–1971	20–1000
GEORGE WOSTENHOLM & SONS (RKS)	Washington Works	c. 1848–1890	50–1000
GEORGE W. KORN (New York, NY)		c. 1880–1925	25–2000
GEO. SCHRADE KNIFE CO. (Bridgeport, CT)	Wire Jack knives	c. 1940–1956	20–350
GERBER (Portland, OR)	Legendary Blades	1939–present	20–150
GERBR HOPRE (Germany)	Hopre Bros.		10–15
GERLACH (Poland)			8–20

Brands and Manufacturers (Location)	Reference	Dates	Value Range
GERMANIA CUTLERY CO. (Germany)	O.N.B. on bolster		$10–25
GERMO MFG. CO. (Germany)			5–18
GERSON CO. (Germany)			6–18
GESCO (Japan/Ireland)			2–5
GIANT GRIP			15–65
GIESEN & FORSTHOFF (Solingen)	G(man)F. Timor	1920–present	10–75
GILBERT (Sheffield)	Saville Works	c. 1900	60–150
GITZ RAZOR NIFE (Chicago, IL)	by Gits Molding Co.	c. 1938	5–25
GLADSTONE			15–50
GLASNER & BARZEN (Germany)			10–30
GLEN FALL CUTLERY CO. (England)		c. 1898	15–60
GLOBE CUTLERY CO. (New York, NY)	Pat. 4-25-05	c. 1922	20–55
GLOBRISMEN (Germany)			8–15
GOLD SEAL	F. M. O'Brian	c. 1927–1948	18–40
GOLD TOP (N. Attlebury, MA)	P. J. Cummings	c. 1924–1948	10–30
GOLDEN GATE CUTLERY CO. (San Francisco, CA)	Baker & Hamilton	c. 1890s	20–75
GOLDEN RULE CUTLERY CO. (Chicago, IL)	G. R. C. Co.	1911–c. 1924	35–150
GOODELL CO. (Antrim, NH)		1913–1948	60–90
GRACE BROS. (Germany)	Graef & Schmidt		25–75
GRAEF & SCHMIDT (New York, NY)	agency for J. A. Henckels	1883–c. 1948	20–200
GRAHAMSVILLE CUTLERY (Grahamsville, NY)			40–100
GRAND LEADER (Germany)			15–30
GRIFFON (New York, NY)	Griffon XX. Carbomagnetic	c. 1918–1966	30–125

Brands and Manufacturers (Location)	Reference	Dates	Value Range
GRIFFON XX (Worchester, MA)	Griffon Cutlery Works	c. 1918–1966	$25–200
GROVE MFG. CO. (Chicago, IL)			25–75
GISTAV FELIX (Solingen)	Gloria-Werke	1850–present	10–20
GUTTMAN CUTLERY CO. (Mount Vernon, NY)	Explorer; Edge; G. C. Co.	1947–present	15–75
G. C. KNAUTH (Spring Valley, NY)		c. 1900–1941	20–45
G. DUNBAR (Germany)		c. 1901	5–25
G. GREGORY			10–20
G. HANNES FAHR			3–10
G. H. LAWRENCE (Sheffield)	Laurel	c. 1919–1952	10–50
G. OR H. CROOKES & CO. (Sheffield)		c. 1836–1867	25–500
G. R. C. CO. (Chicago, IL)	Golden Rule Cutlery Co.	c. 1911–1924	20–175
G. R. SPRINGER (Kansas City, MO)		c. 1894–1906	25–175
G. TIEMAN (New York)			15–65
G. WOODHEAD WARRANTED (Sheffield)		1850–1876	100–2500
G. W. & H. HDWE CO. (St. Louis, MO)	Geller-Ward-Hosner Hardware Co.	c. 1903–1937	15–150
HACKET-WALTER GATES			65–125
HALE BROTHERS (Sheffield)		c. 1871–1907	25–150
HALL			15–35
HAMMER-BRAND (Walden, NY)	New York Knife Co.	c. 1878–1932	40–500
HAMMER BRAND (Providence, RI)	Imperial	c. 1936–present	3–40
HARGREAVES SMITH & CO. (Sheffield)		c. 1866–1920	25–300
HARRIS BROS. SHEFFIELD (Chicago, IL)			25–150
HARRISON BROTHERS & HOWSON (Sheffield)	Alpha	c. 1853–1919	35–250

Brands and Manufacturers (Location)	Reference	Dates	Value Range
HART CUTLERY CO. (New York, NY)	probably by Camillus	c. 1920s	$20–200
HART KOPT & CO. (Solingen)			15–65
HARTFORD CUTLERY CO. (Duluth, MN)		c. 1928	15–100
HARTFORD CUTLERY CO. (Tariffville, CT)		c. 1880	150–410
HARVEY BROS. (Germany)			5–15
HASSAM BROTHERS (Boston, MA)	formerly N. Hunt & Co.	c. 1853–1872	25–350
HATCH CUTLERY CO. (Bridgeport, CT)	moved to Wisconsin	1892–1898	40–200
HAWTHORNE CUTLERY CO. (Germany)			25–60
HAY MARKET			20–60
HAYNES STELLITE (Kokomo, IN)		1911–1919	100–500
HAYWARD			15–45
HAYWARD KEY KNIFE	Empire		15–50
HEATHCOTE (England)			25–60
HEINRICH KAUFMANN & SOHNE (Solingen)	Mercator, K55K, Indiawerk	1856–present	25–150
HEINZ (Germany)			3–15
HELLER BROS. CO. (Newark, NH)		1900–1930	25–75
HEN & ROOSTER (Solingen)	Carl Bertram	1872–present	15–1000
HENCKELS INTERNATIONAL (Solingen)	Half Twin with halberd	c. 1970s	10–45
HENDINGTAN & SONS ESKILSTUNA (Sweden)			3–15
HENKLE & JOYCE HDW. CO. (Lincoln, NE)		c. 1900–1934	35–115
HENRICH BOKER (Solingen)	Tree Brand, Arbolito	1868–present	25–400
HENRY BARGE (Sheffield)		c. 1850	25–200
HENRY HARRINGTON (Southbridge, MA)	Cutler to the People	1818–1876	25–400

Brands and Manufacturers (Location)	Reference	Dates	Value Range
HENRY HOBSON & SONS (Sheffield)	Express	c. 1860s	$25–350
HENRY MASON (Sheffield)			10–35
HENRY SEARS 1865 (St. Paul, MN)	Farwell-Ozmun-Kirk	c. 1897–1959	30–250
HENRY SEARS CO. (Prussia)			25–100
HENRY SEARS & CO. (Chicago, IL)		1865–1878	15–300
HENRY SEARS & SON (Chicago, IL)	(1865) Farwell Ozmun Kirk	1878–c. 1959	40–225
HENRY TAYLOR (Sheffield)	Acorn	c. 1858–1927	25–300
HERBERT M. SLATER (Sheffield)	Venture, Bee Hive, H. G. Long)	1853–present	15–300
HERBERT ROBINSON (Sheffield)	Grinder (picture)	c. 1873	15–275
HERDER & CO. (Germany)		c. 1872–present	10–125
HERDER'S (Philadelphia, PA)		1847–present	25–150
HERMITAGE CUTLERY (Nashville, TN)	Gray & Dudley Hdwe	c. 1895–1927	8–25
HERMS (Germany)			10–35
HIBBARD (Chicago, IL)	Hibbard, Spencer, Bartlett	c. 1913–1927	20–250
HIBBARD SPENCER BARTLETT & CO. (Chicago, IL)	O.V.B. (Our Very Best)	1855–c. 1950	20–350
HICKORY (Duluth, MN)	Kelly How Thomson	c. 1902–1947	5–200
HIGH CARBON STEEL (Camillus, NY)	Camillus brand	1930s	20–150
HIKE CUTLERY CO. (Solingen)		c. 1923	10–45
HILL BROS.			20–60
HILLARD & CHAPMAN (Glasgow, Scotland)		c. 1850	25–300
HINDNBURG SEHNEID (Solingen)			15–60

Brands and Manufacturers (Location)	Reference	Dates	Value Range
HIT (USA)			$20–60
HOFFRITZ (New York, NY)	some made by Schrade	c. 1930–present	5–95
HOLLEY (Lakeville, CT)		c. 1854–1930s	25–450
HOLLEY MFG. CO. (Lakeville, CT)		c. 1854–1930s	25–450
HOLLEY & CO. (Lakeville, CT)		1844–1846	50–750
HOLLINGER (Fremont, OH)			15–150
HOLLINGSWORTH KNIFE CO. (Kane, PA)	formerly Kane Cutlery	c. 1916–1930	25–200
HOLUB (Sycamore, IL)			15–35
HOME			15–35
HONK FALLS KNIFE CO. (Napanoch, NY)	old Napanoch factory	1921–1929	50–900
HORIZONT (Germany)			14–28
HORNET (St. Louis, MO)			20–150
HORNIS CUTLERY CO.			20–60
HOWARD BROS. (Germany)			15–75
HOWARD CUTLERY CO. (New York, NY)	C. B. Barker Co.	c. 1890	45–200
HOWARD W. SHIPLEY (Philadelphia, PA)	Coquanoc Works	c. 1876	25–275
HOWES CUTLERY CO. (Germany)		c. 1900	25–135
HUBERTUS (Solingen)	Kuno Ritter, owner	1932–present	20–100
HUDSON KNIFE CO. (Germany)		c. 1927	20–65
HUDSON VALLEY CUTLERY CO. (New York)		c. 1890s	25–200
HUDSON'S BAY COMPANY (Winnipeg, MB)	pocketknives date to c. 1880	1670–present	25–200
HUGAL 7 WORKS (Germany)			10–50

Brands and Manufacturers *(Location)*	*Reference*	*Dates*	*Value Range*
HUGO KOLLER (Solingen)	Eagle	1861–1980s	$15–65
HUGO LINDER (Solingen)	Deltawerk	1878–1957	25–200
HUMASON & BECKLEY (New Britain, CT)	H. & B.	1852–1914	20–275
HUMASON & BECKLEY MFG. CO. (New Britain, CT)	H. & B., sold to L. F. & C. 1912	1852–1916	20–275
HUNKILL HUNTER (Pittsburgh, PA)			65–90
HUNTER CUTLERY CO. (Germany)	Radigan-Rich	1905–1907	15–75
H'VILLE KNIFE CO. (Hotchkissville, CT)	Hotchkissville Knife Co.	c. 1870s	15–90
H. A. DREER (Philadelphia, PA)			35–75
H. BOKER'S IMPROVED CUTLERY (Newark, NJ)	merged into Broker U.S.A.	1837–1917	25–400
H. C. PRICE CO. (Solingen)			20–75
H. G. LIPSCOMB & CO. (Nashville, TN)	Watauga	1891–1913	25–95
H. G. LONG & CO. (Sheffield)	currently owned by H. M. Slater	c. 1846–present	20–85
H. G. LONG & CO. (Sheffield)		c. 1846–present	65–175
H. HOWSEN & SONS			60–110
H. H. TAYLOR & BRO. (Sheffield)	(US Navy contractor)	c. 1855–1890	25–250
H. KESCHNER (Germany)	Diamond	c. 1920s	25–45
H. K. CO. (Kane, PA)	Hollingsworth Knife Co.	c. 1916–1930	25–200
H. M. SLATER, LTD (Sheffield)		c. 1853–present	15–120
H. SEARS MFG. CO. (Chicago, IL)		c. 1865–1883	25–250
H. SEYMOUR CUTLERY CO.		c. 1865–1917	15–55
H. S. B. & CO. (Chicago, IL)	Hibbard Spencer Bartlett	1855–1960	15–250

Brands and Manufacturers (Location)	Reference	Dates	Value Range
H. S. C. CO.			$25–75
H. UNDERWOOD (London, England)	56 Haymarket	c. 1820–19??	15–200
H. & B. MFG. (New Britain, CT)	Humason & Beckley	c. 1852–1914	25–275
H. & J. W. KIND			15–50
H. & L. MFG. CO. (Bridgeport, CT)			15–75
IBBOTSON BROTHERS & CO. (Sheffield)	Globe	1841–c. 1925	25–400
IBBOTSON PEACE & CO. (Sheffield)	became W. K. Peace & Co.	c. 1847–1864	25–400
IBBOTSON & SONS (Sheffield)			25–200
IBBOTSON, CHARLES, & CO. (Sheffield)		c. 1868–1896	25–400
IDEAL (Louisville, KY)	I-D-L, Belknap Hdw. Co.	1890s	15–25
IDEAL KNIFE CO. (Providence, RI)	IDEAL/ U.S.A.	1924–present	25–175
IKCO (USA)	Imperial Knife Co.		2–10
ILLINOIS CUTLERY CO. (Chicago, IL)	probably made by Golden Rule	c. 1911–1912	15–150
ILLO CUTLERY CO. (Germany)			3–15
IMPERIAL (Germany)			5–15
IMPERIAL (Mexico)		recent	3–10
IMPERIAL KNIFE CO. (Providence, RI)	IKCO, Crown, Hammer	1917–present	10–100
INDIA STEEL WORKS (Louisville, KY)	Belknap Hdw. Co.	1890–1940	25–300
INDIANA CUTLERY CO. (Terre Haute, IN)	Wabash Cutlery Co.	c. 1932	45–95
INDUSTRY NOVELTY CO. (Chicago, IL)		1908–1917	10–75

Brands and Manufacturers (Location)	Reference	Dates	Value Range
INTER (Italy)			$3–10
INTERNATI ONAL CUTLERY CO. (Freemont, OH)		c. 1920s	20–200
INTRINSIC JOHN MILNER & CO. (Sheffield)			15–55
IROQUOIS CUTLERY CO. (Utica, NY)	Utica Cutlery Co.	c. 1930–1940	3–25
IROS (Keen, NY)			5–45
IRVING CUTLERY CO. (Germany)			4–15
ISAAC BARNES (Sheffield)		c. 1837–1870	25–400
ISAAC MILNER (Sheffield)			25–60
IVER JOHNSON S. G. CO. (Boston, MA)	by Russell, N. Y. K. Co., etc.	c. 1912	25–150
IVY (Germany)	S. Hecht & Son	c. 1901	5–20
I*XL (Sheffield)	George Wostenholm	1890–1971	20–2000
I-KUT (Louisville, KY)	Belknap	c. 1898–1907	15–75
I. ELLIS & SONS LTD. (England)			125–200
I. E. HARUKSWORT			10–25
I. H. S. ROSE & CO. (Sheffield)			15–60
I. K. CO. OR IKCO (Providence, RI)	Imperial Knife co.	1920s–1940s	3–10
I. MANSON (Sheffield)		19th century	20–55
I. N. C. CO. (Cedar Rapids, IA)	Iowan Novely Cutlery Co.	c. 1910s	40–110
I. & J. MFG. CO. (Plainfield, NJ)	Shur-Lock	c. 1950	10–50
I.B.Y. (Germany)			55–15

Brands and Manufacturers (Location)	Reference	Dates	Value Range
JACK KNIFE BEN (Chicago, IL)		1887–1940s	$45–250
JACK KNIFE SHOP (Chicago, IL)	Union Stock-yards	c. 1900s	25–300
JACKMASTER (Providence, RI)	Imperial Knife Co.	1938–present	10–60
JACKSON KNIFE & SHEAR CO. (Fremont, OH)		c. 1900–1914	25–85
JACK-O-MATIC (Providence, RI)	made by Imperial Knife	1943–1958	10–50
JACOBY & WESTER (New York)		c. 1891–1904	40–250
JAEGER BROS. (Marinette, WI)	Aerial Cutlery Co.	c. 1912–1944	10–125
JAMES BARLOW & SON (Sheffield)		c. 1828–1856	25–200
JAMES BODEN (Sheffield)		c. 1860	15–200
JAMES BURNAND & SONS (Sheffield)	Indian (picture), Self Defense	c. 1865–1970s	25–200
JAMES CRANSHAW	successor to Nowill & Kippax	c. 1826	25–200
JAMES JOHNSON (Sheffield)		c. 1818–1853	25–200
JAMES NILLWARD & CO.			5–15
JAMES RODGERS (Sheffield)		c. 1830s–1950s	25–300
JAMES W. PRICE	Pine Knott, Belknap Hardware		45–400
JANKER WORKS			8–35
JEAN CASE (Little Valley, NY)			40–400
JEFFREY (Germany)	made by C. Bertram	c. 1971	25–95
JENSEN-KING BYRD CO. (Spokane, WA)			50–110
JET KNIFE CORP. (USA)			10–40
JETTER & SCHEERER (Germany)		c. 1880–1932	10–150

Brands and Manufacturers (Location)	Reference	Dates	Value Range
JET-AIRE CORP. (Paterson, NJ)	G-96	current	$3–25
JIM BOWIE (Solingen)	Carl Schlieper		4–45
JIM DANDY			20–150
JOHN BARBER (Sheffield)		1810–1834	25–250
JOHN BARBER & SON (Sheffield)		1834–c. 1852	25–250
JOHN BLYDE (Sheffield)	Genius	c. 1875	25–300
JOHN BROWN (Sheffield)		c. 1830–1880s	25–400
JOHN CHATILLION & SONS (New York, NY)		c. 1894–1937	50–300
JOHN CLARKE & SON (Sheffield)	Wm. Rodgers, John Holmes	1848–present	25–300
JOHN ENGSTROM (Eskilstuna, Sweden)	Wiebusch import	1874–c. 1893	20–45
JOHN FARR (Sheffield)		c. 1821–1852	25–300
JOHN HINCHCLIFFE (Sheffield)		c. 1850	25–300
JOHN HOLMES & CO. (Sheffield)	sold to J. Clarke before 1900	1860–present	50–90
JOHN JOWETT (Sheffield)		c. 1870s	15–250
JOHN KAY (New Haven, CT)		c. 1857	25–250
JOHN KENYON & CO. (Sheffield)	Fulton, Fulltone, IK	c. 1870–1920	15–150
JOHN McLORY & SONS (Sheffield)	Scotia, Thistle (picture)	c. 1870–present	15–100
JOHN NEWTON (Sheffield)	H. Boker, Newark, NJ	c. 1906	25–275
JOHN NOWILL & SONS (Sheffield)	Krosskeys, *D	c. 1848–present	10–1500
JOHN PETTY & SON (SHEFFIELD)			15–125

Brands and Manufacturers (Location)	*Reference*	*Dates*	*Value Range*
JOHN PRIMBLE (Louisville, KY)	Belknap Hdwe. Co.	1940–1986	$30–800
JOHN PRITZIAFF KNIFE CO. (Milwaukee, WI)	Everkeen	c. 1850–1957	15–50
JOHN SALM (Torrance, CA)	DeLuxe	1918–1935	10–50
JOHN SELLERS & SONS (Sheffield)	Signal	1820–c. 1900	25–275
JOHN WALTERS & CO. (Sheffield)	Globe Works	c. 1846–1862	25–300
JOHN WATTS (Sheffield)	"Estb. 1765"	c. 1855–present	15–75
JOHN WEISS & SONS (London, England)		1878–present	25–300
JOHN WILTON (Sheffield)			45–125
JOHN W. HOBSON (Sheffield)		19th century	25–300
JONATHAN CROOKES (Sheffield)	Heart and Pistol	c. 1780–1827	25–250
JONATHAN CROOKES & SON (Sheffield)	sold to H. Slater 1947	1827–present	25–250
JONATHAN HALL (Sheffield)	I. Hall	1795–1830	25–300
JONES & SON (Germany)		c. 1970	5–15
JOSEPH ALLEN & SONS (Sheffield)	NON-XLL	1886–1947	25–350
JOSEPH ELLIOTT & SONS (Sheffield)		1795–present	20–200
JOSEPH FEIST (Germany)		1898–1924	25–65
JOSEPH FENTON & SONS (Sheffield)		c. 1860	25–300
JOSEPH GARDNER (Shelburne Falls, MA)	GARDNER 1876	1876–1883	25–250
JOSEPH HAYWOOD (Sheffield)	Tea kettle (picture) trademark	c. 1850–1869	25–200
JOSEPH JAEGER (Los Angeles, CA)	Palm	c. 1891–1909	25–200
JOSEPH LAW (Sheffield)	LIBERTY on bolster	c. 1820	55–100
JOSEPH LINGARD (Sheffield)	I-Fly Shuttle (picture)	c. 1842–1925	25–300

Brands and Manufacturers (Location)	Reference	Dates	Value Range
JOSEPH RODGERS & SONS (Sheffield)		c. 1837–1901	$25–1000
JOSEPH RODGERS & SONS (Sheffield)	Cutlers to His Majesty	c. 1901–1948	25–250
JOSEPH RODGERS & SONS (Sheffield)	No. 6 Northfolk St.	1682–1971	25–1000
JOSEPH THORPE (Sheffield)		c. 1853–1873	25–250
JOSH. BEAL & SONS (Sheffield)	Endure, Sound, Boar	c. 1870s–1890s	25–350
JUDSON CUTLERY CO. (New York, NY)		c. 1900–1940	20–65
JULANCO (Germany)			5–25
JUSTUS BIERHOLFF (Solingen)			40–80
J. AMBACHER (Sandusky, OH)	Pat. April 27, 1880	c. 1869–1891	40–300
J. A. HENCKELS (Solingen)	Twinworks	1731–present	20–200
J. A. SCHMIDT & SOHNE (Solingen)	Dreiturm (Three Spires)	1829–present	15–200
J. BUNGER & SONS CELEBRATED CUTLERY			30–150
J. COPLEY & SONS (Sheffield)	XX	c. 1876–1924	25–175
J. CURLEY & BRO. (New York, NY)		c. 1880–1925	25–175
J. C. N. CO. (Jersey City, NJ)	made by G. Schrade	c. 1940	25–150
J. DIXON CUTLERY CO. (Germany)	XTRA on blade		8–25
J. DUNLAP (New York, NY)	Schmachtenberg	1916–c. 1939	10–25
J. DUNN (New York, NY)		c. 1879–1922	15–125
J. D. CASE (Little Valley, NY)	Case Mfg. Co.	c. 1898–1899	40–400
J. E. BASSETT & CO. (New Haven, CT)		c. 1784–1897	15–200
J. E. MERGOTT CO. (Newark, NJ)		1888–1950	30–60

Brands and Manufacturers (Location)	Reference	Dates	Value Range
J. HOFFMAN (Germany)			$15–35
J. H. ANDREW & CO., LTD. (Sheffield)		c. 1860	25–300
J. H. SUTCLIFFE & CO. (Louisville, KY)	Hickory Hand Forged	c. 1900	20–125
J. H. THOMPSON CUTLER LTD. (Sheffield)			30–200
J. KOESTER & SONS (Ohligs, Germany)	imported by Kastor	c. 1930s	15–100
J. KOWILL (Sheffield)			50–95
J. LEE (Medway, MA)		c. 1830	25–250
J. M. SCHMID & SON (Providence, RI)		1857–1964	15–175
J. M. SWIFT			15–35
J. M. THOMPSON HDW. CO. (Minneapolis, MN)	Sterling Service	c. 1910–1922	25–150
J. PRITXLAFF HDW. CO. (Milwaukee, WI)	Everkeen	c. 1850–1957	35–95
J. P. SNOW CO. (Chicago, IL)		c. 1861	25–65
J. RUSSELL & CO. GREEN RIVER WKS. (Turner Falls, MA)	R(arrow) 1875–1941	1834–present	25–400
J. RUSSELL & CO. GRW (Turner Falls, MA)		c. 1884–1941	25–400
J. R. TORREY RAZOR CO. (Worcester, MA)		1858–1963	25–150
J. S. HOLLER (New York, NY)	A. Blaich	c. 1867–1906	65–400
J. T. MOUNT & CO. (Newark, NJ)			35–75
J. W. BILLINGS (Sheffield)	X. X. L. Cutlery	c. 1880s	25–200
J. W. HICKEY & SONS (Solingen)		c. 1976–present	20–125
J. W. JAMES (Sheffield)			15–55
KABAR (Cleveland, OH)	Cole National	c. 1966–present	10–200
KAMP CUTLERY CO. (Germany)		c. 1910	8–20

Brands and Manufacturers (Location)	Reference	Dates	Value Range
KAMP HAUSER (Germany)			$15–60
KAMP KING (Providence, RI)	Imperial Knife Co.	1935–present	5–25
KANE CUTLERY CO. (Kane, PA)	became Hollingsworth	c. 1910–1916	65–375
KANE GERMANY (Solingen)	made by C. Bertram	c. 1971	25–65
KAN-DER (Germany)			15–35
KA-BAR (Olean, NY)	Kabar, Union Cutlery Co.	1923–1951	25–600
KA-BAR (Olean, NY)	KA-BAR, KA-BAR/ U.S.A.	1951–c. 1966	25–75
KA-BAR UNION CUTLERY CO. OLEAN (Little Valley, NY)		c. 1923–1951	25–750
KA-BAR/OLEAN N.Y. (Olean, NY)	KA-BAR/ UNION CUT. CO.		25–600
KA-BAR/UNION CUT. CO. (Olean, NY)	Union Cutlery Co.	1923–1951	25–600
KA-BAR/U.S.A. (Olean, NY)	Kabar Cutlery Co.		25–75
KA-BAR/(NUMBER) USA (Olean, NY)	Kabar (Cole National)		25–75
KEEN CUTLERY CO. (New York)	made by Napanoch	c. 1910	25–350
KEEN CUTTER (VALTEST) (Chicago, IL)	Schrade Cutlery Co.	1960–1965	15–75
KEEN EDGE (Nashville, TN)	Keith Simmons & Co.	1901–1927	25–150
KEEN KUTTER (St. Louis, MO)	E. C. Simmons	c. 1870–1940	25–350
KEEN KUTTER (St. Louis, MO)	Shapleigh	c. 1940–1960	25–200
KEENER EDGE (Knoxville, TN)	C. M. McClung Hdw.	c. 1932	10–75
KEENITE (Boston, MA)			15–65
KEENWELL MFG. CO. (Olean, NY)	by Union Cutlery Co.	c. 1910	25–200

Brands and Manufacturers (Location)	Reference	Dates	Value Range
			$5–15
KEINORITTER (Germany)			
KEITH SIMMONS & CO. (Nashville, TN)	Keen Edge	c. 1901–present	25–200
			15–65
KELLIN & CO. (Germany)			
KELLY HOW THOMSON CO. (Duluth, MN)	Hickory	1902–1947	25–150
KENDALL MFG. CO. (Winsted, CT)		c. 1948	5–40
KENT (Camillus, NY)	F. W. Woolworth Co.	c. 1934	10–45
KERSHAW (Portland, OR)	Japan	current	5–125
KEYES CUTLERY CO. (Unionville, CT)		prior to 1893	25–150
KEYSTONE CUTLERY CO. (Milwaukee, WI)		c. 1925–1938	45–200
KHYBER (Cleveland, OH)	Cole National (Kabar)	1980s	3–15
KINFOLKS INC. (Little Valley, NY)	Kinfolks, K. I., Jean Case	1925–c. 1951	45–375
KING CUTLERY CO. (Germany)			15–30
KINGS QUALITY (USA)			4–10
KINGSTON (Ellenville, NY)	Joint venture by Ulster & Imperial	1943–1947	10–65
KINGSTON USA (Ellenville, NY)	D. Divine & Sons & Ulster	c. 1915–1958	15–75
KIPSI KUT (Poughkeepsie, NY)	Pokipsi, N. Y.	c. 1900	25–150
KIRKAN & CO. (Germany)			5–15
KISSING CRANE (Solingen)	Robt. Klass	1896–1988	10–175
KLICKER (St. Louis, MO)	Shapleigh	c. 1958	20–40
KLOSTERMEIER BROS. (Atchison, KS)			35–75
KNAPP & SPENCER (Sioux City, IA)	Regent	c. 1895–1905	15–175

Brands and Manufacturers (Location)	Reference	Dates	Value Range
KNICKERBOCKER CUTLERY			$10–100
KNIFE CRAFTERS	H. C. James	c. 1944–1945	15–50
KOELLER BROS. (Solingen)	F. Koeller & Co.	c. 1905–1927	10–100
KOELLER & SCHMIDT (Milwakee, WI)		c. 1884–1916	30–90
KOESTER & SONS			15–60
KORIEN (Germany)			5–15
KORN'S PATENT	G. W. Korn	1883–1907	15–75
KREMITZ			10–15
KRUSE & BAHLMAN HDW. CO. (Cincinnati, OH)	K. & B., Cut Sure	c. 1896–1962	35–150
KRUSIUS BROTHERS (New York, NY)	K. B. Extra	c. 1888–1927	10–150
KRUSIUS CUTLERY CORP. (Germany)		c. 1856–1983	20–300
KUNDE & CO. (Germany)		current	20–95
KUTMASTER (Utica, NY)	Utica Cutlery Co.	1937–present	3–50
KUTWELL (Olean, NY)	made by Union	c. 1930s	50–300
KWIK CUT (St. Louis, MO)		1921–1926	15–60
K. & B. CUTLERY CO. (Germany)	Kruse & Bahlman Hardware	1884–1962	15–125
K.I.E. (Sweden)			3–15
LABELLE CUTLERY WORKS (Bridgeport, CT)	Smith Sutton & Co., Harry L. Frary	c. 1884–1888	45–120
LACKAWANNA CUTLERY CO. (Nicholson, PA)	L. C. Co.	1917–c. 1930	55–300
LACLIDE SIMMONS (Germany)			5–30
LAFAYETTE CUTLERY CO. (New York)		c. 1910–1920s	5–55
LAKESIDE CUTLERY CO. (Chicago, IL)	Challenge— sold by Montgomery Ward	c. 1922–1928	45–400

Brands and Manufacturers (Location)	Reference	Dates	Value Range
LAKOTA CORP. (Riverton, WY)		current	$20–100
LALLI BROS. CELEBRATED CUTLERY			35–200
LAMSON & GOODNOW (Shelburne Falls, MA)	pocketknives date to c. 1870s	1844–present	25–300
LANDERS FRARY & CLARK (New Britain, CT)	Universal	1863–1954	25–125
LANDIS BROTHERS (Canton, OH)	Pat. Nov. 11, 1879	c. 1879	25–200
LANDWERK (Solingen)			4–10
LANGSTAFF HDWE. CO. (Prussia)			15–60
LATOMA (Italy)			4–8
LAUTERJUNG & CO. (Solingen)	Tiger Brand, Cervo	1813–present	25–300
LAUTERJUNG & SOHN (Solingen)	Puma-Werk		25–300
LAW BROTHERS			5–100
LAWTON CUTLERY CO. (Chicago, IL)		c. 1895	25–75
LAYMAN CAREY CO. (Independence, IN)		c. 1920	25–175
LE BALKANIQUE			3–15
LEADER (USA)			5–20
LEE HARDWARE CO. (Salina, KS)			15–75
LEHENBERG (Solingen)			12–20
LENOX CUTLERY CO. (Germany)		c. 1910	10–25
LEVERING KNIFE CO. (USA)			10–65
LEWIS MURAY			5–15
LIBERTY KNIFE CO. (New Haven, CT)		c. 1920s	25–60
LINCOLN NOVELTY CO.			5–40
LINDER & CO. (Solingen)	Junkerwerk	1887–present	25–200
LINGRIAM MFG. CO. (Chicago, IL)			12–25
LION CUTLERY CO. (Sheffield)			5–20

Brands and Manufacturers (Location)	Reference	Dates	Value Range
LIPSCHULTZ (Solingen)	Bertram Hen & Rooster	c. 1975	$30–90
LISH (Germany)			5–10
LITTLE VALLEY KNIFE ASSOCATION (Little Valley, NY)	L.V.K.C.	1900–1905	75–250
LOCKWOOD BROS. (Sheffield)	C + X, Pampa, Rhea (bird)	c. 1849–present	25–175
LONG (Oxford, England)		c. 1880	25–175
LORD BROS.		c. 1880s	25–175
LOTT & SCHMITT (New York)			25–75
LUBOT CO. (Cincinnati, OH)			5–20
LUGROSSE (Germany)			5–100
LUHDT CO. (Solingen)			4–15
LUKE FIRTH (Sheffield)		c. 1850	25–400
LUNA (Germany)	A. Feist & Co.	1903–1948	15–75
LUSTERN			5–15
LUT OATES			12–75
LUX (Solingen)		c. 1920	5–55
LUXRITE (Hollywood, CA)			15–60
LYON CUTLERY CO. (Bridgeport, CT)		1880s	25–95
L. C. A. HARDWARE (Omaha, NE)			25–60
L. F. & C. CO. (New Britain, CT)	Landers, Frary & Clark	c. 1912–1950	10–150
L. K. CO. (New Britain, CT)	Liberty Knife Co.		5–15
L. L. BEAN (Freeport, ME)		1912–present	20–300
L. L. H. CO. (Cleveland, OH)	Lockwood Luetkemeyer Henry		5–15
L.V.K. ASSN. (Little Valley, NY)	Little Valley Knife Assocation	1900–1905	75–250

Brands and Manufacturers (Location)	Reference	Dates	Value Range
MADDEN & SONS (Sheffield)			$25–95
MADE IN USA	Sears & Roebuck		5–35
MAGNETIC CUTLERY CO. (Philadelphia, PA)	Otto and Frank Maussner	c. 1900–1932	25–95
MAHER & GROSH (Toledo, OH)	to Clyde, OH 1963	1877–present	40–300
MAJESTIC CUTLERY CO. (Germany)	Matthews & Lively	c. 1910	5–225
MANCHESTER (USA)		c. 1920s	5–100
MANHATTAN CUTLERY CO. (Sheffield)	H. Boker's, Newark, NJ	c. 1868–1916	25–300
MANHATTAN KNIFE CO. (USA)			10–20
MAPPIN BROTHERS (Sheffield)	Queen's Cutlery Works, Sun	c. 1840–1872	75–250
MAPPIN & WEBB (Sheffield)	Turstworth, Sun	c. 1835–1964	25–1500
MARBLE'S SAFETY AXE CO. (Gladstone, MI)	knives c. 1900–1942	1898–present	75–2000
MARIEL CO. (New York)			8–15
MARSH BROS. (Sheffield)	W. & T. Marsh	c. 1850–1947	45–400
MARSHALL FIELD & CO. (Germany)		c. 1909–1923	15–60
MARSHALL WELLS HDW. CO. (Duluth, MN)	M. W. H. Co., Zenith (before 1917)	1893–1963	35–700
MARSHES & SHEPHERD (Sheffield)	Pond Works	1818–1850	50–2000
MARTIN BROS. & NAYLOR (Sheffield)		c. 1860	60–100
MARTIN L. BRADFORD & SON (Boston, MA)	became Bradford & Anthony	1845–1856	10–150
MARX & CO.		c. 1800s	50–300
MASON & SONS			5–100
MASSILLON CUTLERY CO. (Massillon, OH)	was Ohio Cutlery Co.	c. 1924	20–200

Brands and Manufacturers (Location)	Reference	Dates	Value Range
MAUSSNER (Germany)		1900–1932	$20–60
MAYER (Germany)			5–15
McINTOSH HDW CO. (Cleveland, OH)	Heather; became L. L. H.	1875–1911	20–150
MCL HDW. CO. (Waco, TX)	some by Schatt & Morgan	c. 1890–1945	25–150
McNITOR KNIFE CO.			5–20
MERCATOR (Solingen)	Heinrich Kauffmann	c. 1856–present	3–15
MERIDAN CUTLERY CO. (Meriden, CT)	made by Southington, Valley Forge	1855–c. 1925	25–150
MERIDEN KNIFE CO. (Meriden, CT)	made for Miller Bros.	1917–c. 1932	25–150
MERRIMAC CUTLERY CO. (Germany)	Knox All on blade		40–70
METROPOLITAN CUTLERY CO. (New York, NY)	Commander	c. 1918–1951	10–35
METROSE CUTLERY CO. (Germany)			35–65
MILL MFG. CO.			35–90
MILLER BROS. CUT. CO. (Meriden, CT)		c. 1872–1926	25–350
MILLER BROTHERS (Yalesville, CT)		c. 1863–1926	35–400
MILLER, SLOSS & SCOTT (San Francisco, CA)	Pacific Hardware & Steel	1891–1901	25–150
MISSOULA MERCANTILE CO. (Missoula, MT)	Buffalo Brand (c. 1917)	1885–c. 1972	25–150
MITCHELL & CO. LTD. (Manchester, England)		c. 1910	10–150
MIZZOO CUTLERY CO. (St. Louis, MO)	Norvell-Shapleigh	c. 1906–1918	25–250
MONROE CUT. CO. (Germany)	Monroe Hdw.	c. 1904–1916	35–60
MONUMENTAL CUTLERY CO. (New York, NY)	F. Wiebusch	c. 1874–1893	20–125

Brands and Manufacturers (Location)	Reference	Dates	Value Range
MOORE HANDLEY HDW. CO. (Birmingham, AL)	made by Camillus	c. 1882–present	$20–150
MORLEY BROS. (Saginaw, MI)	Wedgeway Cutlery Co.	1865–present	15–150
MORRIS CUTLERY CO. (Morris, IL)		1882–c. 1930	35–200
MOSLERY CUTLERY CO.			15–65
MOUNT VERNON CUTLERY CO.		c. 1890	10–50
MSA (Gladstone, MI)	Marbles Safety Axe Co.	c. 1898–1942	50–2000
MUELLER & SCHMIDT (Solingen)	Five arrows around circle	1896–present	10–75
MUMBLEY PEG (Camillus, NY)	Camillus brand	c. 1937–1948	50–95
MURCOTT (Germany)			5–25
MUTUAL CUTLERY CO. (Canton, OH)			15–50
M. B. CO.			25–125
M. F. & S. (England)			60–135
M. KLEIN & SONS (Chicago, IL)		c. 1911–present	5–25
M. MOCAL, INC. (Germany)			8–15
M. PRESSMAN & CO. (New York)			15–150
M. PRICE (San Francisco, CA)		1856–1889	1000–5000
M. S. A. CO. (Gladstone, MI)	Marble's Safety Axe		50–2000
M. S. LTD. XX (Canada)	Case XX Metal Stamping Ltd.	c. 1940s	20–200
M. W. H. CO. (Duluth, MN)	Marshall Wells Hdw.	1893–1963	25–150
M. & C. CO.	Anvil. Meriden Cut.		15–30
NAGLE REBLADE KNIFE CO. (Poughkeepsie, NY)		1912–1916	200–2500

Brands and Manufacturers (Location)	Reference	Dates	Value Range
NAPANOCH KNIFE CO. (Napanoch, NY)	some made by J. Cushner 1931–1939	1900–1919	$50–500
NASH HARDWARE CO. (Fort Worth, TX)		1873–1975	25–150
NATHAN JOSPEH (San Francisco, CA)	Queen's Own Co.	c. 1873–1894	25–250
NATIONAL SILVER CO. (New York)			10–30
NAUGATUCK CUTLERY CO. (Naugatuck, CT)		1872–1888	45–175
NAYLOR & SANDERSON (Sheffield)		c. 1810–1830	25–350
NEEDHAM BROS. (Sheffield)	Repeat (Wiebusch import)	c. 1860–1900	70–300
NEFT SAFETY KNIFE (Newark, NJ)		c. 1920–1930s	65–125
NELSON KNIFE CO.			15–35
NEVER DULL CUT. CO. (Chicago, IL)	Butler Bos.	c. 1896–1940	20–65
NEW BRITAIN KNIFE CO. (New Britain, CT)	The N. B. Knife Co.		10–75
NEW CENTURY CUTLERY CO. (Germany)		c. 1900	20–55
NEW ENGLAND CUTLERY CO. (Wallingford, CT)		1852–1860	10–150
NEW ENGLAND KNIFE CO.		c. 1910	45–125
NEW HAVEN CUTLERY CO. (San Francisco, CA)	Baker & Hamilton, Damascus	c. 1890s	15–90
NEW JERSEY CUTLERY CO. (Newark, NJ)	American Ace	c. 1921	25–300
NEW YORK CUTLERY CO. (Gowanda, NY)	became Schatt & Morgan	1890s	10–150
NEW YORK KNIFE CO. (Matteawan)	moved to Walden 1856	1852–1856	25–500
NEW YORK KNIFE CO. (Walden, NY)	Hammer Brand (post-1880)	1856–1931	25–400

Brands and Manufacturers (Location)	Reference	Dates	Value Range
NEWTON PREMIER (Sheffield)			$10–25
NIFTY (New York, NY)	G. Borgfeldt	c. 1913–1914	4–10
NIPPES & PLUMACHER (Germany)			15–65
NON-XLL (Sheffield)	Joseph Allen	c. 1886–1947	25–500
NORBERIS CUTLERY (Germany)			15–30
NORMARK (Minneapolis, MN)	Mfd. by E. K. A.	1959–present	10–65
NORSHARP			10–35
NORTH AMERICAN KNIFE CO. (Wichita, KS)		c.1920s	15–65
NORTH WEST CUTLERY CO.		c. 1890	10–90
NORTHFIELD KNIFE CO. (Northfield, CT)	UN-X-LD	1858–1919	45–300
NORTHHAMPTON CUTLERY CO. (Northhampton, VT)			25–200
NORVELL'S BEST (St. Louis, MO)	Norvell-Shapleigh	c. 1902–1917	25–300
NORVELL-SHAPLEIGH HDW. CO. (St. Louis, MO)	Shapleigh Hardware Co.	c. 1902–1917	15–300
NORWICH CUTLERY CO.			15–60
NOVELTY CUTLERY CO. (Canton, OH)	Canton Knife Co., A. Vignos	1879–c. 1949	20–500
NOXALL CUTLERY CO. (Germany)	Kastor Bros.	c. 1907	5–100
N. C. CO. (Canton, OH)	Novelty Cutlery Co.	1879–1948	20–500
N. HUNT & CO. (Boston, MA)	sold to Kingman & Hassam	c. 1840–1853	15–200
N. Y. KNIFE CO. (Walden, NY)			25–1000
OAK LEAF (St. Louis, MO)	William Enders, Simmons Hdwe. Co.	c. 1888–1920	20–200
OAKLAND CUTLERY CO.			5–15

Brands and Manufacturers (Location)	Reference	Dates	Value Range
OAKMAN BROS. (New York, NY)		c. 1900	$25–500
OBON (New York)			25–125
OCCIDENT CUTLERY CO. (Seattle, WA)	sold by Seattle Hdw. Co.	c. 1910	25–200
ODELL HDW. CO. (Greensboro, NC)	Southern (cross) Cutlery		25–150
OEHM & CO. (Baltimore, MD)	some made by Miller Bros.	c. 1860–1936	15–275
OHIO CUTLERY CO. (Massillon, OH)	O. C. Mfg. Co. Tru-Temper	1919–1923	40–200
OKLAHOMA CITY HARD-WARE (Oklahoma City, OK)		1911–1951	25–65
OLBOS (Germany)			5–8
OLCUT (Olean, NY)	Olean Cutlery Co.	c. 1911–1914	45–300
OLD AMERICAN KNIFE (USA)			10–35
OLD CUTLER (Providence, RI)	Colonial Knife Co.	c. 1978–present	5–20
OLD TIMER (USA)	Schrade Cutlery Co.		5–50
OLEAN CUTLERY CO. (Olean, NY)	Olcut. Div. of Union Cut.	c. 1911–1914	50–300
OLSEN KNIFE CO. (Howard City, MI)	sheath knives	c. 1960–1983	10–75
OMEGA (Germany)	Joseph Feist	c. 1898–1924	5–15
ONTARIO KNIFE CO. (Franklinville, NY)	Old Hickory (by Queen)	1889–present	20–150
OPINEL (France)	Crowned Hand	c. 1890–present	5–15
ORANGE CUTLERY CO. (Walden, NY)	(ex. Walden Knife employ-ees)	1923	25–200
OSGOOD BRAY & CO.	(Three Stars) made by Burkinshaw	19th century	15–200

Brands and Manufacturers (Location)	Reference	Dates	Value Range
OTHELLO (Solingen)	A. Wingen	c. 1923–present	$10–150
OVAL CUTLERY CO. (Sheffield)			15–75
OVERLAND (Solingen)	Fred Mac Overland	1951–1953	5–100
O'NEILL & THOMPSON (Dublin, Ireland)			6–16
O. BARNETT TOOL CO. (Newark, NJ)	Patent; H. H. H.	1900–c. 1915	50–375
O. D. GRAY & CO.			30–500
O. N. B. (Germany)	A. W. Wadsworth & Sons	c. 1910	25–125
O. S. T. CUTLERY CO. (Newark, NJ)			15–75
O. V. B. (OUR VERY BEST) (Chicago, IL)	Hibbard, Spencer & Bartlett	1884–1960	10–100
PACIFIC HDWE. & STEEL CO. (San Francisco, CA)	Stiletto	1901–1918	45–175
PAL (Germany)		c. 1924–1939	15–90
PAL BLADE CO. (Plattsburg, NY)		c. 1929–1953	15–90
PAL CUTLERY CO. (Holyoke, MA)		c. 1929–1953	15–90
PALACE CUTLERY CO.			25–30
PAPES-THIEBES CUTLERY CO. (St. Louis, MO)	Unitas	c. 1903–1929	40–200
PARIS BEAD (Chicago, IL)		c. 1920s	25–55
PARISIAN NOVELTY CO. (Chicago, IL)		c. 1915	5–20
PARKER BROS. (Chattanooga, TN)	made in Japan	c. 1978–present	5–20
PARKER CUTLERY CO. (Chattanooga, TN)	Eagle, Parker Bros., Amer. Blade	c. 1970–present	5–900
PARKER-EDWARDS CUTLERY CO. (Jacksonville, AL)			20–250

Brands and Manufacturers *(Location)*	*Reference*	*Dates*	*Value Range*
PARKER-FROST CUTLERY CO. (Chattanooga, TN)		1976–1978	$10–200
PASTIAN BROS. CO.			5–18
PAVIAN-ADAMS CUTLERY CO. (St. Paul, MN)	Summit	1906–c. 1920	10–125
PAXTON & GALLAGHER (Omaha, NE)	CutAway	c. 1864–1959	25–75
PEERLESS (Wichita, KS)	G. H. Fralick		5–15
PENNSYLVANIA KNIFE CO. (Tidioute, PA)		c. 1914–1921	45–200
PENN. CUTLERY CO. (Tidioute, PA)		c. 1914–1921	10–150
PEPSI COLA			15–30
PETERS BROS. CELE-BRATED CUTLERY (Solingen)		c. 1876–1886	60–165
PETERS CUTLERY MFG. CO. (Solingen)		c. 1876–1886	10–125
PETERS CUTLERY CO. (Chicago, IL)			25–85
PHOENIX KNIFE CO. (Phoenix, NY)	was Central City Knife Co.	1892–1916	45–175
PINE KNOT JAS. W. PRICE (Louisville, KY)	Belknap Hdw. Co.	1930s	45–300
PLATTS (Northfield, CT)		c. 1920s	25–175
PLATTS BROS. (Union, NY)		1905–1907	80–600
PLATTS BROTHERS CUT-LERY CO. (Andover, NY)		1907–c. 1911	50–800
PLATTS N'FIELD (Northfield, CT)	from parts—by Ray Platts	post-1919	25–175
PLI-R-NIF CO. (San Francisco, CA)		1905–c. 1908	20–400
POCKETEZE (Rochester, NY)	Robeson	1922–1977	25–300
POOR BOY			5–100
POP CUTLERY CO. (Camillus, NY)			5–20

Brands and Manufacturers (Location)	Reference	Dates	Value Range
POTTERY HOY HDWE. CO. (USA)			$35–65
POWELL BROS. (Germany)			15–60
POWER KRAFT (Chicago, IL)	made for Montgomery Ward	c. 1939–present	5–10
PRADEL (France)			15–60
PRATT & CO. (London, England)			70–110
PRECISE (Suffern, NY)	Deerslayer	current	10–125
PREMIER (Germany)			3–10
PREMIER CUTLERY CO. (New York, NY)	Elk, Lifetime	c. 1921–1955	5–15
PRENTISS KNIFE CO. (New York, NY)		c. 1910	25–45
PRESS BUTTON KNIFE CO. (Walden, NY)	Geo. Schrade/ Walden Knife Co.	c. 1892–1923	50–190
PRESTO (Bridgeport, CT)	George Schrade Knife Co.	c. 1925–1945	30–175
PRIBYL BROS. (Chicago, IL)		1880–1905	25–45
PRIMBLE (Louisville, KY)	Belknap Hdwe.		20–75
PRODUX (Sheffield)			10–25
PROGRESS (Sheffield)	Alfred Field	1886–1942	10–150
PRONTO (Providence, RI)	Colonial Knife Co.	c. 1926–1952	5–75
PROVIDENCE CUTLERY CO. (Providence, RI)		c. 1890s–1980s	15–150
PUMA (Solingen)	was Lauterjung & Sohn	1769–present	25–1200
PUTMAN CUTLERY CO. (New Britain, CT)		c. 1886–1909	50–75
P. HOLMBERG (Eskilstuna, Sweden)		c. 1900	10–75
P. KAMPHAUS (Solingen)	Granate	c. 1797–present	10–35

Brands and Manufacturers (Location)	Reference	Dates	Value Range
Q & CROWN (QUEEN) (Titusville, PA)	Queen Cutlery Co.	c. 1932–1955	$7–200
QUEEN (USA)			3–15
QUEEN CITY (Titusville, PA)		c. 1922–1945	20–250
QUEEN CUTLERY CO. (Titusville, PA)	Q/Crown, Queen Steel	1945–present	10–175
QUEEN STEEL (Titusville, PA)			10–110
QUICK POINT (St. Louis, MO)	Remington	c. 1930s	25–75
QUICK-KUT, INC. (Freemont, OH)			10–35
Q. C. C. C. (Titusville, PA)	Queen City Cutlery Co.	c. 1922	12–300
Q. C. MFG. CO. (Massillon, OH)			15–75
Q/CROWN (Titusville, PA)	Queen Cutlery Co.	1932–1955	15–175
RACE BROS. CELEBRATED CUTLERY			50–200
RAINBOW (Providence, RI)	Boker USA	c. 1933–1954	5–15
RAND (Germany)			4–15
RANDAL HALL & CO. (Germany)			5–15
RANGER (Providence, RI)	Colonial	1938–present	5–10
RAOLA CUTLERY	Raola Hardware & Iron		4–10
RAHTER & CO. (Germany)			12–40
RAWSON BROS. (Sheffield)		c.1860	65–150
REC-NOR CO. (Boston, MA)			15–30
RED STAG (Chattanooga, TN)		current	20–125
REGENT (St. Louis, MO)			10–30
REICHERT BROS. (Germany)			45–90

Brands and Manufacturers (Location)	Reference	Dates	Value Range
REMINGTON (Bridgeport, CT)		c. 1920–1940	$25–2500
REV-O-NOV (Chicago, IL)	Hibbard Spencer Bartlett	1905–1960	45–75
RICHARD ABR. HERDER (Solingen)	4-pointed star	1885–present	15–110
RICHARDS (Southbridge, MA)		1862–1908	35–60
RICHARDS BROS. & SONS LTD. (Sheffield)	Imperial Knife Associated Cos.	c. 1980s	5–30
RICHARDS & CONOVER HDW. CO. (Kansas City, MO)	Rich-Con., R. & C.	c. 1894–1956	30–55
RICHMOND CUTLERY CO.		19th century	25–100
RIGID KNIVES (Santee, CA)		c. 1970–present	25–150
RIVERSIDE CUTLERY (New York)			15–130
RIVERSIDE CUT. CO. N.Y. (San Francisco, CA)	by Boker USA	c. 1918	15–50
RIVINGTON WORKS (Sheffield)	Alfred Williams	1900–1946	15–65
ROBBINS CLARK & BIDDLE (Philadelphia, PA)	became Biddle Hdw.	19th century	25–200
ROBERT HARTKOPF & CO. (Solingen)	Winged lions trademark	c. 1855–1957	15–125
ROBERT KERDER (Solingen)	4-leaf clover, Windmill	1872–present	15–175
ROBERT KLAAS (Solingen)	Two Cranes "Kissing"	1834–present	15–250
ROBERT LINGARD (Sheffield)		19th century	25–1500
ROBERT WADE (Sheffield)	Wade	c. 1810–1819	25–275
ROBERTS & JOHNSON & RAND (St. Louis, MO)			15–75
ROBESON (Rochester, NY)		1824–1922	15–400
ROBESON (Germany)		c. 1894–1896	25–75
ROBESON CUTLERY (Rochester, NY)		1894–1922	10–400

Brands and Manufacturers (Location)	Reference	Dates	Value Range
ROBESON CUTLERY CO. (Rochester/Perry, NY)	ShurEdge, PocketEze	c. 1894–1977	$35–470
ROBINSON BROS. & CO. (Louisville, KY)		c. 1880–1925	45–300
RODGERS CUTLERY (Hartford, CT)			15–30
RODGERS CUTLERY (Sheffield)			40–1000
RODGERS WOSTENHOLM LTD. (Sheffield)	Division of Imperial 1977–1982	1971–1984	10–50
RODGERS KNIFE CO. (Germany)			15–50
ROMO (Germany/Japan)		current	3–15
ROYAL CUTLERY CO.		1814–1954	10–25
ROYAL OAK			15–45
ROYCE CUTLERY CO.			15–35
RUNKEL BROS.	made by Wester & Butz	c. 1920s	15–35
RUSSELL USA (CURVED) (Turner Falls, MA)	John Russell Co.	c. 1875–1941	25–1500
RUSSELL & CO. GREEN RIVER WORKS (Turner Falls, MA)	John Russell Co.	c. 1875–1941	25–1500
R. BUNTING & SONS (Sheffield)		c. 1837–1868	90–500
R. C. CO. (Rochester, NY)			25–400
R. C. KRUSCHIL (Duluth, MN)			40–60
R. I. KNIFE CO.			15–35
R. J. RICHTER (Germany)			4–15
R. J. & R. S. CO. (Germany)			14–35
R. KELLEY & SONS (Liverpool, England)	Bulldog on tang		25–75
R. MURPHY (Boston, MA)			15–25
R. & W. BRADFORD (Cork, Ireland)	9 Patricks Road	c. 1850	15–150
SABATIER (France)			15–35
SABRE (Japan)	Cole National	1960–1980	2–8

Brands and Manufacturers (Location)	Reference	Dates	Value Range
SABRE (Germany)		current	$4–12
SALEM			2–5
SALM (Torrence, CA)	Salm Manufacturing Co.	1918–1935	15–60
SAM L. BUCKLEY & SON (Sheffield)			10–35
SAMCO (Nashville, TN)			15–30
SAMUEL BARLOW (Sheffield)	BARLOW Z Scimitar (picture)	c. 1780–1840	25–500
SAMUEL BRADFORD (Ireland)		c. 1850	15–150
SAMUEL BRADLEE (Boston, MA)	sold to M. L. Bradford	1799–1845	25–250
SAMUEL E. BERNSTEIN (New York, NY)	Royal Brand Sharp Cutter	c. 1890–1950s	15–125
SAMUEL HAGUE (Sheffield)		c. 1830s–1950s	25–200
SAMUEL HANCOCK & SONS (Sheffield)	Mazeppa, Zephyr	c. 1836–1924	25–200
SAMUEL NORRIS (Sheffield)	*P Cast Steel	c. 1795–1815	25–300
SAMUEL OSBORN & CO. (Sheffield)	Hand & Heart (picture)	c. 1841–1928	25–300
SAMUEL ROBINSON (Sheffield)		19th century	25–400
SAMUEL WRAGG & SONS (Sheffield)		c. 1930s–1960s	25–175
SANDERS MANUFACTURING CO. (Nashville, TN)	SAMCO	current	35–85
SANDS			10–40
SAVORY CUTLERY CO. (Germany)			5–25
SAXONIA CUTLERY CO. (Germany)			15–35
SAYNOR COOKE & RIDAL (Sheffield)	Saynor, Obtain	c. 1840–1868	45–90
SCEPTRE			5–15
SCHATT & MORGAN (Gowanda, NY)	was N. Y. Cutlery Co.	189?–1896	15–450

Brands and Manufacturers (Location)	Reference	Dates	Value Range
SCHATT & MORGAN (Titusville, PA)	S. & M.; sold to Queen City	1896–1931	$45–300
SCHMACHTENBERG BROS. (Solingen)	Dunlap, Clim (Axe), Anchor/ Swords	1887–c. 1939	20–65
SCHMIDT & ZIEGLER (Solingen)	Bull head shield	c. 1930s	20–95
SCHOLFIELD (Germany)			8–20
SCHRADE (Ellenville, NY)	div. of Imperial-Schrade	c. 1973–present	10–45
SCHRADE CUTLERY CO. (Walden, NY)	Albert & Henry Baer	1904–1946	40–1000
SCHRADE-WALDEN (Walden, NY)	Imperial owned	1946–1973	15–450
SCHWABACHER HARDWARE CO. (Seattle, WA)	Colonial Cutlery Co.	1869–present	15–150
SEABOARD STEEL CO. (France)			5–65
SEARS ROEBUCK & CO. (Chicago, IL)	marking c. 1900	1886–present	10–150
SEATTLE HARDWARE CO. (Seattle, WA)	Occident Cutlery Co.	c. 1908	15–200
SECO WORKS (New Orange, NJ)			15–35
SENECA CUTLERY CO. (Utica, NY)	Utica Cutlery Co.	c. 1932–1942	15–65
SEVERIN R. DROESCHERS (New York, NY)	S.R.D./ Arrow	c. 1891–1924	10–18
SHAPLEIGH HWDE. CO. (St. Louis, MO)	curved	c. 1920–1960	15–400
SHAPLEIGH'S (St. Louis, MO)	curved	c. 1920–1960	15–150
SHARPKUTTER XX CUTLERY CO.			15–55
SHELBURNE FALLS CUTLERY CO. (Shelburne Falls, MA)	by Waterville for L. & G.	c. 1870s–1880s	25–400
SHELDON (Sheffield)			15–35
SHUMATE CUTLERY CORP. (St. Louis, MO)		1901–1928	20–75

Brands and Manufacturers (Location)	Reference	Dates	Value Range
SHUREDGE (Rochester, NY)	Robeson Cutlery Co.	c. 1922–1977	$15–250
SHURGER			8–12
SHUR-SNAP (Providence, RI)	Colonial Knife Co.	c. 1949	20–45
SILBERSTEIN LAPORTE & CO. (Germany)	S.B. & C. Co. Diamond		35–65
SIMMONS BOSS	Simmons Hdwe.	c. 1940–1960	25–50
SIMMONS HARDWARE CO. (St. Louis, MO)		c. 1890–1940	25–400
SIMMONS HDWE. CO. (Germany)		c. 1868–1960	20–300
SIMMONS, WARDEN, WHITE CO. (Dayton, OH)	SWWCo, made by Camillus	1937–1946	20–75
SINGLETON & PRIESTMAN (Sheffield)		c. 1861	50–150
SIX STEEL EDGE CUTLERY CO. (Germany)			5–20
SLASH (Sheffield)	C. Ibbotson & Co.	1868–1896	25–75
SMALL BROS. INC. (Germany)			10–25
SMETHPORT CUTLERY CO. (Smethport, PA)	sold to W. R. Case	1907–1909	45–200
SMITH BROTHERS HDW. CO. (Columbus, OH)	CutEasy	1903–1959	40–85
SMITH & CLARK (Bronxville, NY)		c. 1850	25–250
SMITH & HEMENWAY (Utica, NY)	Red Devil S. & H. Co.	c. 1890–1920	25–175
SMITH & HOPKINS (Naugatuck, CT)		c. 1850	25–500
SMITH & WESSON (Springfield, MA)	S & W	c. 1974–present	20–1200
SMOKY MOUNTAIN KNIFE WORKS (Sevierville, TN)		current	20–200
SOLIDUS			10–20
SOUTHERN & RICHARDSON (Sheffield)	Nest, Cigar, Squatter	1846–present	10–35
SOUTHINGTON CUTLERY CO. (Southington, CT)	dist. by Meriden Cut. Co.	1867–c. 1914	45–200

Brands and Manufacturers (Location)	Reference	Dates	Value Range
SPARTTS (England)			$35–90
SPEAR CUTLERY CO. (Germany)		pre-1915	10–25
SPERRY & ALEXANDER (New York, NY)	S. & A.	1893–1920s	15–200
SPRING CUTLERY CO. (Sheffield)		c. 1890	45–150
SPRINGBROOKE KNIFE CO. (San Francisco, CA)	D. C. & H. made by N. Y. Knife Co.	c. 1849–1927	25–400
SPYDERCO (Golden, CO)	Clipit	current	10–45
STA SHARP (USA)			15–30
STACY BROS. & CO. (Sheffield)		1847–19??	15–200
STAINLESS CUTLERY CO. (Camillus, NY)	Camillus, Kastor	1924–1930s	10–150
STANDARD CUTLERY CO. (Sheffield)			5–25
STANDARD CUTLERY CO. (USA)	Dean & Elliott Case	1901–1903	50–200
STANDARD KNIFE CO. (Little Valley, NY)	owned by two Case Brothers	1901–1903	50–300
STANDARD KNIFE CO. (Bradford, PA)	made by W. R. Case & Sons	1920–1923	50–300
STAR (Knoxville, TN)	Star Sales, Inc. made in Japan	1978–1988	3–20
STA-SHARP (USA)	Sears Roebuck & Co.	c. 1927–1940	20–150
STEELTON CUTLERY WORKS (Germany)			15–25
STELLAR (Japan)			2–5
STELLITE (Kokomo, IN)	Haynes Stellite	1911–1920	125–600
STENTON			5–15
STERCY			3–15
STERLING (New York, NY)	McIlwaine, Linn & Hughes	1896–1914	15–100

Brands and Manufacturers (Location)	Reference	Dates	Value Range
STILETTO (San Francisco, CA)	Miller, Sloss & Scott	c. 1900s	$15–150
STILLETTO CUTLERY CO. (New York)	M. S. & S., later B. H. & P.	1896–1926	15–400
STOCKER & CO. (Solingen)	S. M. F. (after 1933)	1897–1970s	15–45
STRAUSS BROS. & CO. (Germany)			12–25
STREAMLINE (Camillus, NY)	Camillus	c. 1935	15–35
STRINGER (Philadelphia, PA)			35–85
STURDY (USA)			10–35
ST. LAWRENCE CUTLERY CO. (St. Louis, MO)	Schmachten-berg	1886–1916	25–75
SUDAG (USA)			5–23
SUMMIT KNIFE CO. (St. Paul, MN)	Pavian-Adams	c. 1906	10–35
SUPERIOR CUTLERY (Solingen)			15–65
SUPPLEE HDWE. CO. (Philadelphia, PA)		1905–1906	10–35
SWAN WORKS (Germany)	Altenbach		5–35
SWANK			7–15
SWANNER (Fairfield, OH)	made in Japan	1980s	5–50
SWORD BRAND (Camillus, NY)	Kastor and Camillus	c. 1906–present	5–35
SYRACUSE KNIFE CO. (Camillus, NY)	Camillus brand	1930s	15–75
S. B. LUTTRELL & CO. (Knoxville, TN)	Samuel Bell Luttrell Hardware	c. 1880	15–200
S. E. OATES & SONS (Sheffield)	S. E. O. & S.	pre-1915	15–150
S. M. E. (Solingen)			5–10
S. P. CO. (Centaur, NY)			15–30
S. SALEM			25–50

Brands and Manufacturers (Location)	Reference	Dates	Value Range
S. TRAKERT			$5–15
S. & A. (New York)	Sperry & Alexander	1893–1913	12–55
S. & CO.			5–15
S. & C. WARDLOW (Sheffield)	Terrifik	1855–c. 1920	10–200
S. & M. (Gowanda, NY)	Schatt & Morgan	c. 1890–1895	20–300
S. & M. (Titusville, PA)		1895–1928	20–300
TAMMEN (Germany)			5–12
TAMPA HDW. CO. (Tampa, FL)	W. C. T.	c. 1910	15–150
TARRY	Lizard on blade		15–45
TAYLOR CUTLERY CO. (Kingsport, TN)	made in Japan	1978–present	5–45
TAYLOR (EYE) WITNESS (Sheffield)	Needham Veall Tyzack	c. 1836–present	10–35
TELL (Germany)			5–100
TELLIN & CO.			8–40
TERRIER CUTLERY CO. (Rochester, NY)	made by Robeson	c. 1910–1916	45–110
THE RALPH BROWN CO. (San Francisco, CA)		c. 1910	10–75
THEILE & QUACK (Elberfeld, Germany)	by Wester, Wade Bros., Tyler, A*1	c. 1866–1890	25–300
THELCO (Cleveland)	Lockwood Luetkemeyer		15–60
THEO M. GREEN CO. (Oklahoma City, OK)	later named Domar Cutlery	c. 1916–1920	5–60
THOMAS ELLIN (Sheffield)	J. Barber ERA, Vulcan	c. 1840–1970	15–275
THOMAS FENTON			14–20
THOMAS MFG. CO. (Dayton, OH)	sold HHH, American Shear & Knife	1907–1911	40–150

Brands and Manufacturers (Location)	Reference	Dates	Value Range
THOMAS TURNER & CO. (Sheffield)	Encore, Suffolk, Haywood	1830–1932	$25–175
THOMAS WARD & SONS (Sheffield)	Stacey Bros.	c. 1805–present	15–200
THOMAS WILTON (Sheffield)			15–75
THOMASTON KNIFE CO. (Thomaston, CT)		1877–c. 1930	25–85
THOMPSON (Germany)			5–15
THOMPSON & GASCOIGNE (Winsted, CT)	became Empire Knife Co.	1852–1856	25–400
THORNTON (USA)		c. 1950s	5–15
TIC (Italy)			2–8
TIDIOUTE CUTLERY CO. (Tidioute, PA)	sold to Union Razor Co.	1897–1902	25–500
TIGER CUTLERY (Solingen)	Herfarth Bros.	1905–1931	15–35
TILLOTSON & CO. (Sheffield)		c. 1840	15–500
TINA		c. 1890–present	20–95
TINK HDWE. CO. (Quincy, IL)			35–75
TIP TOP (Germany)	A. Kastor Bros.	1904–1941	25–40
TOLEDO CUTLERY CO. (Germany)			15–35
TOM RAY CUTLERY CO. (Kansas City, MO)		c. 1910	45–200
TORREY (Worcester, MA)	J. R. Torrey	c. 1858–1963	25–400
TOWNLEY HDW. CO. (Kansas City, MO)		1884–present	45–95
TRENTON CUTLERY CO. (Sheffield)		1880–1906	15–30
TROUT HARDWARE CO. (Chicago, IL)	Square Deal	c. 1896–1907	40–80
TURTON BROTHERS & MATTHEWS (Sheffield)	T. B. & M. Torpedo	c. 1860–1914	25–150
TWENTY GRAND (USA)			15–40

Brands and Manufacturers (Location)	Reference	Dates	Value Range
TWIG BRAND (New York, NY)	G. Borgfeldt	c. 1911	$15–75
TWITCHELL BROS. (Naugatuck, CT)			25–600
TWO EAGLES			10–45
T. C. BARNSLEY MFG. CO. (Oklahoma City, OK)		c. 1898	15–200
T. E. ROWBOTHAM & SON (Sheffield)		c. 1820	25–400
T. HESSENBRUCH (Philadelphia, PA)	Bear with cane (picture)	1873–1926	25–55
T. RENSHAW & SON (Sheffield)	Stand	c. 1870	75–1500
T. ROSS & SON			30–60
T. T. C. DIAMOND BRAND, N. Y. (Chicago, IL)	sold by Sears Roebuck	c. 1909	10–200
ULERY (New York, NY)	U. J. Ulery Co.	c. 1902–1919	10–45
ULRICH (Germany)			4–15
ULSTER KNIFE CO. (Ellenville, NY)	Dwight Divine & Sons	1876–1941	45–225
ULSTER USA (Ellenville, NY)	Albert and Henry Baer	1941–present	5–50
UNCLE HENRY (Walden, NY)	Schrade-Walden, Imperial-Schrade		12–30
UNION CUTLERY CO. (Olean, NY)	KA-BAR	1911–1951	45–2000
UNION CUTLERY CO. (Tidioute, PA)		1909–1911	25–750
UNION CUTLERY & HDWE. CO. (Unionville, CT)		1877–1925	20–200
UNION KNIFE CO. (Naugatuck, CT)		1851–1885	75–450
UNION KNIFE WORKS (Union, NY)		c. 1911–1913	45–300
UNION RAZOR CO. (Tidioute, PA)	became Union Cutlery	1898–1909	70–800
UNITED (Germany)			3–10

Brands and Manufacturers (Location)	Reference	Dates	Value Range
UNITED CUTLERY (Grand Rapids, MI)			$5–25
UNITED CUTLERY CO. (Germany)	None Better	1908–1920	5–50
UNIVERSAL (New Britain, CT)	L. F. & C.	1898–1950	15–35
UNIVERSAL KNIFE CO. (Germany)	L. T. Snow	c. 1897–1909	10–150
UNWIN & ROGERS (Sheffield)	knife-pistols	c. 1848–1867	25–2500
UN-X-LD	Northfolk Knife Co.		25–500
UTICA CUTLERY CO. (Utica, NY)	Kutmaster, Seneca	1929–present	10–150
UTICA K. & R. CO. (Utica, NY)	Utica Knife & Razor Co.	1910–1929	25–500
U. C. CO. (USA)			15–75
U. D. CO. (USA)			5–15
U. K. CO. (USA)			46–115
U. K. & R. CO. (Germany)	Utica Knife & Razor		75–200
U. S. KNIFE CO. (Terre Haute, IN)		c. 1904	20–85
U. S. SMALL ARMS CO. (Chicago, IL)	small knife-pistol	c. 1914–1923	150–450
VALLEY FALLS CUTLERY CO. (USA)		c. 1915	15–75
VALLEY FORGE CUTLERY CO. (Newark, NJ)		1892–1916	40–300
VALLEY FORGE (VF IN CIRCLE) (Newark, NJ)	owned by Boker	1915–c. 1950	25–500
VALOR (Japan)		c. 1970–present	3–15
VAN CAMP HDWE. CO. (Indianapolis, IN)		c. 1888–1960	25–200
VAN CAMP HDW. & IRON CO. (Indianapolis, IN)	owned Capitol Cut. Co.	c. 1876–1960	35–275

Brands and Manufacturers (Location)	*Reference*	*Dates*	*Value Range*
VANCO (Indianapolis, IN)	Van Camp Hardware		$5–35
VERITABLE PRADEL	Anchor on blade		12–20
VERMONT CUTLERY CO.	made by Wester & Butz	1898	20–60
VERNIDER (St. Paul, MN)			5–25
VICTOR	knife tool kit	c. 1907–1913	5–20
VICTORINOX (Switzerland)	Karl Elsener	c. 1891–present	10–150
VICTORY CUTLERY CO. (New Haven, CT)		c. 1925	35–200
VIGNOS CUTLERY CO. (Canton, OH)	Novelty Cutlery Co.	c. 1879–1948	15–125
VIKING (USA)	Eric Wedemeyer	c. 1931–1934	5–15
VINTERS (Sheffield)			3–8
VOM CLEFF & CO. (New York, NY)	V. C. & Co.	1887–c. 1930	40–135
VOOS CUTLERY CO. (New Haven, CT)	Voos/Arrow	c. 1920s–1981	25–90
VOSS CUTLERY CO. (HEN & ROOSTER) (Solingen)		c. 1968–1975	40–200
VOYLES CUTLERY		c. 1970s	10–40
VULCAN (Sheffield)	T. Ellin & Co.	1886–1944	15–75
VULCAN KNIFE CO. (Germany)	Thomas Ellin		5–30
VULCAN & TELLIN & CO.			10–35
V. K. CUTLERY CO. (Germany)			5–15
WABASH CUTLERY CO. (Terra Haute, IN)	Indiana Cut Co. c. 1932	1921–1935	50–200
WADE BROS. (Germany)	Theile & Quack	1866–1876	15–1000
WADE & BUTCHER (Sheffield)	W. & S. Butcher	c. 1819–1947	20–1000
WADSWORTH (Germany)		1905–1917	5–40
WADSWORTH & SONS (Austria)		1905–1917	10–45

Brands and Manufacturers (Location)	Reference	Dates	Value Range
WAHL WAGNER (Solingen)			$5–15
WAIT CO. (USA)			5–30
WALDEN KNIFE CO. (Walden, NY)	sold to E. C. Simmons 1902	c. 1870–1923	50–400
WALKER CUTLERY WORKS (Germany)			5–35
WALKER & HALL (Sheffield)	W. & H. (in a flag)	1867–c. 1900	15–500
WALKILL RIVER WORKS (Walden, NY)	N. Y. Knife Co.	1928–1931	35–200
WALL BROS. (Sheffield)			35–150
WALLACE BROS. (Wallingford,CT)		c. 1895–1955	35–60
WALSH & LOVETT (Sheffield)			25–150
WALT CO. (USA)			5–16
WALTER BROS. (Germany)	Boy's Own, Dime Knife	1904–1914	15–75
WALTHAM CUTLERY (Germany)			5–15
WANDY (Italy)			4–10
WARD BROS. (Sheffield)			5–35
WARD & CO. (Bronxville, NY)		c. 1860s	10–300
WARDION CUTLERY CO. (Walden, NY)			25–85
WARDS (Chicago, IL)	Montgomery Ward	c. 1935–1950s	10–100
WARREN (Baker, OR)			5–25
WARREN BROS. (England)			35–150
WARWICK KNIFE CO. (Warwick, NY)		c. 1907–1928	35–200
WASHINGTON CUTLERY CO. (Tidioute, PA)	Gray & Dudley Hardware	c. 1885–1927	25–175

Brands and Manufacturers (Location)	Reference	Dates	Value Range
WASHINGTON CUT. CO. (Nashville, TN)	Gray & Dudley Hardware	c. 1885–1927	$15–150
WATAUGA (Nashville, TN)	H. G. Lipscomb & Co.		15–75
WATER BROS. CUTLERY (Germany)			10–30
WATERVILLE MFG. CO. (Waterbury, CT)		1843–c. 1913	40–250
WATKINS COTTRELL CO. (Richmond, VA)	Clipper (after 1901)	c. 1867	25–150
WEBSTER CUTLERY CO. (Germany)			5–15
WEBSTER, SYCAMORE WORKS (USA)			10–35
WEDGEWAY CUTLERY CO. (Saginaw, MI)	for Morley Bros. Hdw. Co.	1887–1933	35–55
WEED & CO. (Buffalo, NY)			35–75
WENGER (Switzerland)	Wengerinox	c. 1908–present	5–100
WESKE CUTLERY CO. (Sandusky, OH)		c. 1946–1952	5–75
WEST VIRGINIA CUTLERY CO.			5–75
WESTER BROS. (New York, NY)	Anchor-Star-Arrow mark	1902–c. 1967	10–200
WESTER & BUTZ (Solingen)	Wester Bros.	1832–1966	10–200
WESTERN (Boulder, CO)		c. 1911–1978	10–500
WESTERN CUTLERY CO. (New York, NY)	imported by Wiebusch & Hilger	c. 1874–1914	20–125
WESTERN CUTLERY CO. (Longmont, CO)	sold to Coleman 1984	1978–present	5–65
WESTERN STATES CUTLERY CO. (Boulder, CO)	Western Cutlery Co.	1911–1951	10–500
WESTMARK (Longmont, CO)	Western Cutlery Co.	1970s–1980s	3–15

Brands and Manufacturers (Location)	Reference	Dates	Value Range
WESTPFAL CUTLERY CO. (New York, NY)	Standpoint	c. 1920–1951	$15–200
WEYHAND (Solingen)			10–15
WHERWOLF CUTLERY WORKS (Germany)			10–120
WHITEHEAD & HOAG CO. (Newark, NJ)	made by Boker USA	1892–1940s	5–100
WILBERT CUTLERY CO. (Chicago, IL)	made by Napanoch, Empire	c. 1909	45–250
WILHEIM CLAUBERG (Solingen)	A. Wingen	1857–present	10–150
WILKINSON SWORD LTD. (London & Sheffield)		c. 1905–present	15–150
WILL ROLL BEARING CO. (Terre Haute, IN)	W. R. B. Co.	c. 1920s	25–200
WILL & FINCK (San Francisco, CA)	also imported	1863–1932	50–1500
WILLIAM ATKINS (Sheffield)	Turtle (picture)	c. 1848–1913	10–175
WILLIAM BAGSHAW (Sheffield)		c. 1830s–1850s	25–300
WILLIAM BROKHAHNE (New York, NY)	W. B. Speed	c. 1875–1881	25–450
WILLIAM ELLIOT (New York, NY)	owned by Adolph Strauss 1907–1918	c. 1880–1918	25–500
WILLIAM J. DONOVAN (Springfield, MA)		c. 1893–1901	25–250
WILLIAM LANGBEIN & BROS. (New York, NY)		c. 1900–1940s	25–300
WILLIAM NICHOLSON (Sheffield)		c. 1846–1864	50–250
WILLIAM RODGERS (Sheffield)	I Cut (Axe) My Way; J. Clarke c. 1855	1830–present	25–500
WILLIAM SHAW (Sheffield)		c. 1847–1871	50–700
WILLIAM THOMAS STANIFORTH (Sheffield)	Ascend	1852–c. 1906	25–400

Brands and Manufacturers (Location)	*Reference*	*Dates*	*Value Range*
WILLIAM W. MARSDEN (Sheffield)		c. 1850–1870	$25–400
WILLIAM & J. R. PARKER (Sheffield)			400
WILLIAMS CUTLERY CO. (San Francisco, CA)		c. 1900–present	10–150
WILSON, HAWKSWORTH & MOSS (Sheffield)		19th century	25–400
WINCHESTER (New Haven, CT)	Winchester Arms Co.	c. 1919–1942	45–1200
WINGFIELD & ROWBOTHAM (Sheffield)		c. 1830–1850s	25–400
WITTE HDW. CO. (St. Louis, MO)		c. 1865–present	10–200
WM. ENDERS (St. Louis, MO)	Oak Leaf, E. C. Simmons	1908–1929	25–125
WM. JACKSON (Sheffield)		c. 1859	50–1250
WOODBURY CUTLERY CO. (Woodbury, CT)		19th century	25–250
WYETH HDW. & METAL CO. (St. Joseph, MO)	Wyeth's Warranted Cutlery	c. 1884–present	15–200
WYETH'S CUTLERY USA (USA)		c. 1884–1934	15–200
W. A. IVES MFG. CO. (Meriden, CT)		19th century	25–500
W. A. TYZACK & CO. (Sheffield)		c. 1850–1953	25–350
W, BINGHAM & CO. (Cleveland, OH)	XLCR, BBB. Ulster's agent	c. 1841–1930	25–250
W. F. FORD (SHEPARDS & DUDLEY) (New York, NY)	Shepards & Dudley		35–125
W. GREAVES WARRANTED (Sheffield)		c. 1780–1816	25–500
W. GREAVES & SONS (Sheffield)		c. 1816–1870	25-500
W. H. MORLEY & SONS (New York, NY)	A. Kastor & Bros.	c. 1913–1927	25–125
W. H. PARKER (Sheffield)			65–135

Brands and Manufacturers (Location)	Reference	Dates	Value Range
W. JNO. BAKER (Sydney, Australia)		1888–present	$15–200
W. K. PEACE & CO. (Sheffield)	Eagle, Ibbotson Peace	c. 1867–present	25–500
W. R. B. CO. (Terre Haute, IN)	Will Roll Bearing Co.		35–75
W. R. CASE & SON CUTLERY CO. (Little Valley, NY)	made by Napanoch & Platts	1902–1905	100–1500
W. R. CASE & SONS (Bradford, PA)	many stampings	1905–present	15–4000
W. R. HUMPHREYS & CO. (Sheffield)	Radiant	c. 1875–present	10–25
W. THORNHILL (England)		19th century	25–500
W. WILKINSON & SON (Sheffield)		c. 1760–1892	25–1500
W. W. BINGHAM (Cleveland, OH)		1841–1930	15–175
W. & A. CO. (Providence, RI)			15–65
W. & H. CO. (Newark, NJ)	Whitehead & Hoag		10–35
W. & S. BUTCHER (Sheffield)	Wade & Butcher, X.C.D.	c. 1819–present	25–300
W. & T. MARSH (Sheffield)		c. 1780–1840	25–500
w. & w. (Sheffield)	Walter Warrington		15–65
X. C. D. (Sheffield)	W. & S. Butcher	1830–present	10–150
X. L. N. T. (Germany)	Adolph Kastor, A. Kastor & Bros.	1876–1947	10–150
YALE CUTLERY CO. (Meriden, CT)	owned by Son Bros. S.F.C.A.	c. 1800s	10–150
YANKEE CUTLERY CO. (New York, NY)	Colonial Knife Co.	c. 1910s	5–75
ZENITH (Duluth, MN)	Marshall Wells Hdwe.	c. 1893–1917	25–150

USEFUL INFORMATION FOR KNIFE COLLECTORS

▽

The astute collector will assimilate knowledge that will be an asset throughout years of buying, trading, and accumulating a collection of valuable knives. Listed in this section are various tidbits of information that will be of assistance in determining country of origin, probable dates of manufacture, and the like.

Some of the terms listed below may occasionally be found as a part of a knife's stamping. They are markings that indicate such information as place of manufacture, patent or trademark protection, and rust-free or stainless steel.

PLACE NAMES—LOCATION OF MANUFACTURE

Albacete (Spain)
Maniago (Italy)
Nogent (France)
Pavlovo (Russia)
Rampur (India)
Sheffield (England)
Solingen (Germany)

Thiers (France)
Toldeo (Spain)
Ohligs (Germany)
Frosolone (Italy)
Eskilstuna (Sweden)
Seki (Japan)

PATENT, TRADEMARKS, STEEL TYPE, ETC.

Arbolito—"Little Tree" (Tree Brand in Spanish)
Colt Riun—cutlers' union (Italian)
D.R.G.M.—patented (German)
D.R.P.—patented (German)
D.R.Pat—patented (German)

Depose—registered (French)

Fein Stahl—fine steel (German)

Gebr.—brothers (German)

Ges. Gesch.—design patent (German)

Guss Stahl—cast steel (German)

Hecho en Mexico—made in Mexico (Spanish)

Inox—stainless (French)

Nachf.—successor (German)

Nirosta—no rust (German)

Rostfrei—stainless (German)

Veritable—genuine (French)

Weidmannshell—good hunting (German)

HELPFUL DATING INFORMATION

Aluminum handles were first used on knives c. 1883.

Cast steel was used from the late 1700s to the first quarter of the 1900s.

Celluloid handles were first used on knives c. 1870.

Etched tang stamps date to c. 1880.

Freeze treatment of stainless blades developed c. 1950.

Frosted etch on blades was first used c. 1940.

Fruit knives were first made in France in the seventeenth century.

Fork/knife combinations were first made in America c. 1860s.

Hard rubber handles were first used on knives c. 1850s.

Integral iron bolsters and liners date from about 1860.

Iron liners were used on Case knives prior to 1920.

Liner lock mechanism dates from early 1900s.

Nickel silver dates from early 1800s.

Official Boy Scout knife was adopted c. 1911.

Pick bone (bone stag) handles date from the nineteenth century.

Prussia, stamped as country of origin, was used prior to 1915.

Rhineland, stamped as country of origin, was used c. 1920–1935.

Stainless steel was first used on knives c. 1916.

Sterling silver fruit knives were rarely made after 1925.

Stellite was first used as blade material c. 1910.

Switchblade knives made in the United States would date from before 1958.

PATENT NUMBERS AND DATES

If a knife bears a patent number, one can determine from this number that the knife cannot have been made earlier than a particular year. The following table shows the beginning invention (not design) patent numbers issued by the U.S. Patent Office for each year from 1836 and through 1990.

Date	Patent No.	Date	Patent No.
1836	1	1866	51,784
1837	110	1867	60,658
1838	546	1868	72,959
1839	1,061	1869	85,503
1840	1,465	1870	98,460
1841	1,923	1871	110,617
1842	2,413	1872	122,304
1843	2,901	1873	134,504
1844	3,395	1874	146,120
1845	3,873	1875	158,350
1846	4,348	1876	171,641
1847	4,914	1877	185,813
1848	5,409	1878	198,733
1849	5,993	1879	211,078
1850	6,981	1880	223,211
1851	7,865	1881	236,137
1852	8,622	1882	251,685
1853	9,512	1883	269,820
1854	10,358	1884	291,016
1855	12,117	1885	310,163
1856	14,009	1886	333,494
1857	16,324	1887	355,291
1858	19,010	1888	275,720
1859	22,477	1889	395,305
1860	26,642	1890	418,665
1861	31,005	1891	443,987
1862	34,045	1892	466,315
1863	37,266	1893	488,976
1864	41,047	1894	511,744
1865	45,685	1895	531,619

Date	Patent No.	Date	Patent No.
1896	552,502	1943	2,307,007
1897	574,369	1944	2,338,081
1898	596,467	1945	2,366,154
1899	616,871	1946	2,391,856
1900	640,167	1947	2,413,675
1901	664,827	1948	2,433,624
1902	690,385	1949	2,292,944
1903	717,521	1950	2,494,944
1904	748,567	1951	2,536,016
1905	778,834	1952	2,580,379
1906	808,618	1953	2,624,046
1907	839,799	1954	2,664,562
1908	875,679	1955	2,698,434
1909	908,436	1956	2,728,913
1910	945,010	1957	2,775,762
1911	980,178	1958	2,818,567
1912	1,013,095	1959	2,866,973
1913	1,049,326	1960	2,919,443
1914	1,083,267	1961	2,966,681
1915	1,123,212	1962	3,015,103
1916	1,166,419	1963	3,070,801
1917	1,210,389	1964	3,116,487
1918	1,251,458	1965	3,163,865
1919	1,290,027	1966	3,226,729
1920	1,326,899	1967	3,295,143
1921	1,364,063	1968	3,350,800
1922	1,401,948	1969	3,419,907
1923	1,440,362	1970	3,487,470
1924	1,478,996	1971	3,551,909
1925	1,521,590	1972	3,633,214
1926	1,568,040	1973	3,707,729
1927	1,612,700	1974	3,781,914
1928	1,654,521	1975	3,858,241
1929	1,696,897	1976	3,930,271
1930	1,742,181	1977	4,000,520
1931	1,787,424	1978	4,065,812
1932	1,839,190	1979	4,131,952
1933	1,892,663	1980	4,180,867
1934	1,941,449	1981	4,242,757
1935	1,985,878	1982	4,308,622
1936	2,026,516	1983	4,366,579
1937	2,066,309	1984	4,423,523
1938	2,104,004	1985	4,490,885
1939	2,142,080	1986	4,562,596
1940	2,185,170	1987	4,633,526
1941	2,227,418	1988	4,716,594
1942	2,268,540	1989	4,794,652
		1990	4,890,335

FACTORS AFFECTING
KNIFE VALUES

▽

The axiom that an item's value is precisely the amount of money or goods that a seller is willing to accept and a buyer is willing to pay is never so true as within the collector market. Value must stand this test and does so numerous times every day and in almost any location. In any situation, the two perceptions of value are those of the prospective seller and the prospective buyer. Whenever a compromise is reached and the knife changes ownership, true value for that knife at that time and that place has been established. It may be different at another time, at another place, and with other prospective trade partners. Still, in spite of the variables, this measurement signifies true value because it directly relates to the willing buyer/seller axiom. Another type of value is mentioned here only because it seems to be so prominent in any collecting field. It is value perceived, and that value may or may not pass the market test. This very personal value is one that a collector often places on knives or other possessions. Knives that are of special significance to their owner may be "valued" at several times the amount that they would bring in the marketplace. If the knife is really not for sale, value is a moot point.

The values presented in this guide are what one can expect to find in a "typical"—if there is in fact such a thing—marketplace. There are numerous factors that affect the value of a knife as a collectible. Primary considerations are, first, with the knife itself; they include things such as age, manufacturer, brand stamping, pattern, number of blades, handle material, shield, rarity, and condition.

A knife's brand, manufacturer, and stamping are fundamental to the collector value of a knife. Although age is usually of importance, it does not always directly relate to value. Just because a knife is 50 or 150 years old doesn't mean that its value is higher than a knife of more recent manufacture. Likewise, relating quality to value can be misleading. Some extremely well made knives are not so highly valued as those of perhaps lesser quality but greater desirability in the marketplace. The importance of brand stamping can be illustrated by considering two old and nearly identical knives made by Camillus, their difference being the brand stamping. Ironically, the contract knife is often valued more highly than the one marketed with the manufacturer's own brand stamping.

Rarity plays a significant role in establishing the value of any collectible. To a degree, the numbers of knives produced contributes to rarity, but this is not always true. For instance, Remington produced unbelievable numbers of some knife patterns, but because they were intended for use—and they were well used—the relatively few found in mint condition are highly valued. On the other hand, there are knives of relatively recent production that were produced in very limited numbers and were seldom used. Rarity can also relate directly to specific patterns, handle materials, stampings, or a variety of other things.

Directly related to rarity (supply and demand) is locality. The collector should be aware that time and place have a significant effect on the buying/selling price of a knife. We're not speaking of the good fortune of "being in the right place at the right time" or the distress sale factor but, instead, the direct relationship of supply and demand within varying locations. To recognize and appreciate these geographical area variations, one need only visit with a few dealers at knife shows in various parts of the country. A dealer from the southeast may have attended a northwestern show and sold very few knives. Still, because he has been able to purchase knives known to return a profit in other areas, participation in the show may be considered very rewarding.

The universally accepted variable affecting value is condition, and it should always be kept in mind when referring to this or other pricing guides. Grading the condition of a knife varies with the individual and is almost always interpreted differently and not impartially by the prospective buyer and the seller. The most widely accepted guidelines, however, are those established by the National Knife Collectors Association and are described below.

Mint: A knife that is absolutely original as it came from the manufacturer. Never used, carried, sharpened, nor heavily cleaned. An unblemished knife.

Near Mint: A new-condition knife that may show very slight signs of carry or shop wear. Blades are not worn and snap perfectly. Handles show no cracks. Most of original finish is obvious.

Excellent: A knife that shows no more than 10 percent blade wear. Handles are sound with no cracks. Blades snap well. Some discoloration of blades or handles is acceptable. May have been heavily cleaned.

Very Good: A knife with up to 25 percent blade wear, slight cracks in handles. No blades nor other parts replaced or repaired. Stamping clearly visible to the naked eye.

Fair: A knife with up to 50 percent blade wear, cracks, or chips in handles. Blades "lazy" (lacking snap) and may have been repaired. Stamping faint but readable with magnifying glass.

Poor: Blades very worn or may have been replaced with ones of same type. Handles bad or missing. Reading of stamping nearly impossible. A knife valued only for its parts.

The value guides offered in this book are for knives in mint condition. A knife that has been sharpened after leaving the factory may still be near mint, but it definitely is not a mint knife and its value is approximately no more than 70 percent of a true mint knife. As the knife's condition grading further diminishes, so does its value. At or near the bottom of the grading scale (Poor to Fair), a knife may bring only 10–20 percent of its mint value.

When using this or any other pricing reference work, one should always be mindful that they are guides and *only* guides. Used as such, to enhance one's knowledge of specific areas of interest or of knife prices in general, pricing guides are valuable aids to buyer and seller alike. When mistakenly used as "gospel," without consideration of other circumstances, the pricing guide loses much of its potential value to both buyer and seller. We hope this book will be a guide not only to prices but to greater pleasures and profits in the knife-collecting hobby.

WHAT'S AHEAD
FOR THE 1990s?

▽

One could not review the progress made during the last few years nor witness the atmosphere of the knife-collecting community without a great deal of optimism. The number of collectors continues to grow, and their collecting interests often diversify into fields that lay dormant a few short years ago. Just as the increasing availability of reference books may be credited with a rise in popularity of knives as collectibles, it will also have a positive effect during this decade. Concurrent with the rise in collector numbers, new opportunities for personal involvement and for self-education come in the form of increasing numbers of collecting clubs, knife shows, and swap meets.

With access to so much information, the knife collector of the 1990s will have a decided advantage over those who had fewer resources available and were necessarily dependent on the trial-and-error method. Still, experience will remain a great teacher—especially for those who leap first and learn later. The astute collector or investor will utilize the many resources, establish goals, and plan collecting activities that will help achieve those goals.

Anticipate prices of desirable antique knives to rise considerably during the coming decade because finding these knives is becoming increasingly difficult, and whenever they can be found, they are already far from inexpensive. Purchasing knives for investment means that one should acquire the very best examples that the budget will allow. Because the pieces in excellent condition are becoming harder to find, one should expect an increasing demand for the value of knives in less than mint or excellent condition. Purchasing a desirable knife rated in good condition is probably the best hedge against future value inflation and useful for the time when a better piece for the collection may become available.

Custom knives will continue to be an exciting and growing area to watch but one that merits a great deal of attention to the information available. Selected handmade knives will represent some of the greatest investment opportunities, but as a rule, don't expect the aftermarket in the average custom knife to be especially strong. The strength of custom knives will, by and large, remain in their appeal to pride of ownership.

Military knives, especially those used by our own country's armed forces, will continue to increase in demand and value. Although this specialty is far from new, the number of collectors specializing in this area is rapidly growing.

Some exciting and perhaps surprising events during the late 1980s indicate that limited-production, commemorative, and reproduction knives may indeed be specialties of opportunity during the 1990s. These knives had most often appealed to the beginning collector, and in many cases they had not represented significant investment opportunities. That has not changed to a great degree, but some of the greatest value increases can be found in a number of knives in this category. Within the constraint of wise choices, collecting special knives in these categories will offer excellent opportunities.

To the majority of pocketknife collectors, Case knives have reigned as king of the collectibles during previous decades. Although there are many other brands worthy of collecting—and their values are proof of that fact—Case has been at the forefront of the early knife-collecting movement. Antique knives by Case continue to be very desirable and valuable, but during the 1980s, the collector charm of their current production knives was diminished. This decade finds the company entering its second century under new ownership and direction. Although the complete significance of these changes may not be realized for several years, it is likely to be positive. The new Case offerings will be knives to watch.

Not unlike other areas of collecting, knives have been and will continue to be subject to cyclic changes—some gradual and reasonably predictable, others relatively rapid and often surprising. At times it appears that the only constant is the variability. But the collector who looks to this century's final decade with optimism tempered by knowledge will find many rewards in the hobby of collectible knives.

PART
◁ 3 ▷

Knife Manufacturers

HISTORIES AND LISTINGS
OF KNIFE MANUFACTURERS

▽

AERIAL CUTLERY COMPANY

The story of Aerial begins with an industrious salesman named Fred Jaeger, who began selling knives and razors to his fellow papermill laborers near the turn of this century. Motivated by his success, Jaeger quit his job and took to the road with his cutlery satchel, seeking business in back-country mills, mines, and lumber camps. Before long, his growing sales exceeded the capability of his supplier, Morris Cutlery Company, to furnish the quantity sold.

In 1910, "Fritz" Jaeger was joined by his brothers Chris and Richard and by Thomas Madden in forming a company to buy the Morris factory. The purchased company was reorganized in Duluth, Minnesota, and was given a new name: Aerial Cutlery Manufacturing Company. It was an unusual name but one that held a great deal of significance for the new owners. The Aerial Bridge, located in Duluth, was the first suspension bridge of its kind in the country. The name and a bridge trademark were selected by the company's owners as a symbol of stamina, hard work, and determination against all odds.

The name Aerial would remain as a part of the company name when it was shortened in 1912 to Aerial Cutlery Company. At that time, a major move of manufacturing facilities was made from Duluth to Marinette, Wisconsin. According to Jaeger family records, the old factory was moved "lock, stock and barrel." Equipment and tools, whether large or small, were loaded onto a train of flat cars for the journey. As late as 1982, some of that old equipment was still in use at Olsen Knife Company.

During the early part of this century, one of the popular types of pocketknives featured pictures within transparent handles.

Although picture knives were made by a few other companies, Aerial was the most prolific producer and the one with the longest history. These picture-handle knives were made in practically all sizes and patterns, from small pen knives to folding hunters and sheath knives. The pictures used in decorating the handles included but were not limited to natural scenes (such as farm animals), lodge and fraternal emblems, bathing beauties, comic strip characters, political slogans, and made-to-order advertising messages. In fact, Aerial's customers could even order their own special knife with a handle displaying their favorite personal picture. The company claimed that the knife handles were practically indestructible, especially when compared to other commonly used materials such as ivory, stag, horn, or wood.

In addition to picture-handle knives, Aerial made a number of other knife types. Some of them were stamped with the Aerial trademark, and some used other Aerial brand names—such as Jaeger Bros. and A.C. Mfg. Co.—as well the tradenames of customers such as Belknap Hardware and Butler Brothers.

One of Aerial's major undertakings was the manufacture of the military trench knife and M-1 bayonet during World War II. But shortly after the war's end, the company's cutlery business began to falter, due in no small part to celluloid's falling into disfavor. In the last-known Aerial cutlery catalog, dating to the latter half of the 1940s, the previously extensive line of knives had been reduced to a few pocketknife patterns with Pyralin handles and fixed-blade knives with leather washer handles. By 1950, the company had ceased knife production but continued in its growing business of barber and beauty shop supplies. Although it has been nearly half a century since Aerial made picture-handle knives, finding one in mint condition is not so unusual. In 1973, well over two thousand mint knives were found in storage and were sold within the collector market.

BAKER & HAMILTON

A product of the California Gold Rush, Baker and Hamilton was formed in 1853 by Livingston L. Baker and Robert M. Hamilton, who had worked together in the mining supply business. During its early years, the company was a supplier of agricultural hardware and supplies. Their knife line was primarily made up of butcher knives, hay knives, and other farm-type utility cutlery.

Later the company became a major hardware wholesaler serving the far western part of the country, and cutlery represented an important part of its business.

Pocketknives were first offered in 1879, but it is doubtful that these products were actually available for sale since an arrangement with an eastern manufacturer failed to materialize. By 1895, the company's full line of cutlery products included pocketknives.

Brands sold by the company near the turn of the century include "Damascus," "New Haven Cutlery Company," and "Eclipse Cutlery Company." These were followed in the early 1900s by knives stamped with the "Baker & Hamilton" name.

In 1917, Baker and Hamilton merged with Pacific Hardware & Steel to form Baker, Hamilton & Pacific. Pacific's established "Stilleto Cutlery Co., New York" brand was added to the company's line of pocketknives and remained along with nationally known brands until the early 1940s.

BELKNAP HARDWARE COMPANY, INC.

In 1840, W. B. Belknap formed a company in Louisville, Kentucky, that was to grow into one of the nation's larger hardware firms. Originally, the company sold items such as carriage supplies, horseshoes, and blacksmith supplies but added cutlery as well. By the late 1800s, pocketknives had been established as one of Belknap's primary lines, and names such as "Blue Grass" and "John Primble" were introduced. Although they would survive to current times, another company trademark stamping of "Pine Knot" and "Pine Knot, Jas. W. Price" would be sold only during the 1930–1934 period.

Pine Knot knives were probably made for Belknap by Robeson, and most were handled in bone, redwood, and celluloid.

Except for the Barlow pattern, the Blue Grass knives were discontinued in the 1950s. Any knife pattern other than the recently made Barlow is considered collectible.

The best known of Belknap's stampings is that of Primble, which, except for the knives stamped Prussia or Germany, has been manufactured under contract by companies such as Camillus, Boker, and Schrade. Primble stampings include the following:

John Primble (c. 1890–present)
John Primble East India Works

John Primble India Steel Works (c. 1890–1940)

John Primble India Steel Works Prussia (c. 1890–1914)

J. Primble Belknap Germany

John Primble Belknap Hdw. & Mfg. Co. (c. 1940–1968)

John Primble Belknap Inc. (c. 1968–present)

Belknap Hardware went out of business in 1986. The Primble India Steel Works trademark was transferred to Blue Grass Cutlery Corporation, which has recently released new knives bearing that marking.

BENCHMARK KNIVES

Originally formed by knife designer and custom maker Walter "Blackie" Collins in the mid-1970s, Benchmark has changed ownership several times. Shortly after the company's founding, it became a division of Jenkins Metal Company of Gastonia, North Carolina. In 1985, the Benchmark business was sold to Gerber Legendary Blades, which continued to market a few of the models. The new Benchmark parent company was, in turn, sold to Fiskars in 1987.

Of interest to collectors are the older (pre-Gerber) Benchmark knives, especially the patented Rolox knife made by Jenkins Metal and those made by both Collins and Jenkins, known as the Ninja and the Com-Belt.

C. BERTRAM—HEN AND ROOSTER

The Hen and Rooster knife was produced by a Solingen, Germany, company established in 1872 by Carl Bertram. Knives were stamped with the words C. BERTRAM/GERMANY plus the logo of a hen and a rooster. The Hen and Rooster name and logo soon became recognized for very high quality knives, a reputation that continues to this day. Early knives were handled in stag and pearl and were primarily congress patterns. The firm also made a considerable number of knives on a contract basis, and these were stamped with the trademark logo plus the importer's name.

The firm, its factory, and trademark were owned by Bertram family members until 1975, when they were sold to A. G. Russell of Springdale, Arkansas. Production ceased in the early 1980s, and the business was liquidated in 1983. Russell was able to obtain a number of knives from the factory's inventory and offered them to his customers. Meanwhile, their value has continually increased.

At that time, the trademark and Bertram name for cutlery was purchased by Tennessee businessmen James Frost and Howard Rabin, operating as Bertram, USA. Knives made since 1983 have been manufactured at other German factories, probably Robert Klaas. Although the Hen and Rooster trademark continued, these knives should not be confused with the earlier knives made by C. Bertram, which are valued much higher within the collector market.

BOKER

The name Boker is one of the oldest in American cutlery, beginning during the early part of the nineteenth century. Hermann and Robert Boker began a cutlery manufacturing operation, located in Remscheid, Germany, in 1829. The brothers came to North America in 1837 to develop a market for knives branded with their name. Hermann Boker established the importing firm H. Boker & Co's., with headquarters in New York City. Robert Boker at first concentrated on the Canadian market and later opened headquarters for his importing firm in Mexico City.

Along with Herman Heuser, Heinrich Boker started Heinrich Boker & Co. in 1869. This Solingen, Germany, manufacturing operation was built to make Boker's "Tree Brand" cutlery products for the companies owned by Heinrich's cousins in the United States and Mexico. Although the Heinrich Boker & Co. manufacturing facilities had large production capacity, the H. Boker company also imported knives made in Sheffield.

When protective tariffs increased the U.S. cost of German and other foreign-made cutlery, H. Boker & Co. began acquiring U.S. manufacturing facilities about 1916. One factory used to produce Boker's knives was the Valley Forge Cutlery Company of Newark, New Jersey. Whether H. Boker & Co. acquired the factory about that time or had owned it earlier is unknown. Valley Forge stampings have been traced to 1892, and Hermann Boker had established a warehouse at that location shortly after his arrival in the states. In either case, knives branded VALLEY FORGE CUTLERY CO. NEWARK N.J. and BOKER USA were both made at the factory.

In 1921 H. Boker & Co. established a manufacturing facility in Maplewood, New Jersey, probably to supplement production of the Newark and German factories. This facility was expanded in 1930, making it one of the largest cutlery manufacturing factories.

Boker stampings used during its long history have included but are not limited to H. BOKER & CO.'S CUTLERY, H. BOKER & CO. IMPROVED CUTLERY, H. BOKER & CO. SOLINGEN GERMANY, HEINR. BOKER & CO., and BOKER USA. Typical handle materials for Boker knives have been bone, stag, celluloid, pearl, hard rubber, and wood.

The Boker U.S.A. business was purchased in 1969 by J. Wiss and Sons, a shears manufacturer since 1847. In 1978, the Boker cutlery business was sold to the tool-manufacturing Cooper Group, headquartered in Apex, North Carolina. Another transfer of the cutlery business came in 1986, when it reverted back to the Heinrich Boker firm in Germany. Boker's U.S. business, Boker USA, is now headquartered in Golden, Colorado.

ERNST BRUCKMAN

Using the MANN trademark, the German firm of E. Bruckman produced a large number of high-quality knives during the 1920 to 1956 era. In the early 1970s, a considerable quantity of fine old knives in mint condition were discovered. For several years they were largely unappreciated by collectors, but that has changed. Now that they are more difficult to find and their excellent quality is recognized, their value has appreciated considerably.

BUCK KNIVES

The first knives made by a member of the family owning Buck Knives were made about 1900 by Hoyt Heath Buck, a blacksmith's apprentice. Young Buck had developed an effective method of tempering and had used it in his work of rebuilding worn-out grub hoes used by local farmers and gardeners. Those for whom he had worked recognized that the rebuilt hoes were superior to new ones. Because of this, one of his customers asked Buck to forge a knife.

Using the same type of worn farrier's files that he used to rebuild the cutting edges of hoes, Buck made his first knife, and personal recommendations led to his making others. As the reputation of his knives spread, he began to custom-make knives on a regular but part-time basis. During the years from 1907 to 1930, Hoyt Buck earned the family's livelihood by working in the logging industry but supplemented his income by making knives during his spare time.

A son, Alfred Charles, was born to Hoyt and Daisy Buck in 1910. After his discharge from the Coast Guard in 1940, Al Buck settled in San Diego, California. Meanwhile, Hoyt Buck had been ordained a minister and had moved to Mountain Home, Idaho, to be pastor of a small church. His forge was set up in the church basement, and he continued to forge knives for local customers. With our nation's involvement in World War II, a growing number of the area's young men left for military service with their own knives made by Buck. For the first time, knives made at the Buck forge gained more than a local reputation for quality as the few fortunate servicemen proudly showed their knives to their comrades-in-arms.

In 1945, Hoyt and Daisy Buck moved to San Diego to join their son. Hoyt began to make knives full-time, and Al made knives part-time whenever he wasn't at his job as a bus driver. The Bucks reasoned that their knives could be sold by mail order via advertisements in outdoor magazines because some of their readers could well have been former servicemen who had already learned of the knives made by H. H. Buck. Continuing in the four-decade tradition, most of the early Buck knives were made from old files or power hacksaw blades. They were usually handled in Lucite plastic of various colors, South American lignum vitae, or local desert ironwood. The Bucks' reasoning was sound, and business during the 1945–1950 period was good.

Hoyt Buck died in 1949, but his son Al continued to make knives at his San Diego shop. In 1959, he was joined in the business by his own son, Charles T. Buck. In 1961, incorporation of the business and sale of stock allowed for expansion of the knife business by moving to a larger workshop and employing three knife makers.

Buck's line was still limited to fixed-blade hunting and filet knives made from files and sawblade steel. Soon, however, a nearby commercial forging company made the blades, which were finished into knives and stamped "Buck" at the company shop. Models produced at this time included:

102—Woodsman	118—Personal
103—Skinner	119—Special
105—Pathfinder	120—General
116—Caper	121—Fisherman

Some general determination of a fixed-blade Buck knife's age may be made by noting tang style. The early production knives followed the system of their handmade predecessors in that their tangs were threaded and a barrel nut was used to hold on the handle and butt cap. Knives produced after 1962 have a flat tang with the butts pressed on and held with a pin.

The knife that would bring fame and fortune to Buck Knives was the Model 110. Although it has become synonymous with the term "folding hunter" and is the most copied knife made today, the basic locking design was not new when Al Buck first made it in 1962. But the phenomenal demand for knives of this type was created through the qualities of the Buck 110, and it remains today as the market leader. The company's success with the 110 led to production, in 1969, of the slightly smaller version, Model 112.

During the 1960s, the company expanded its line of pocket-knives through contracting for their manufacture by Schrade and Camillus. In 1975, the 500 series models were introduced and were made for Buck by Camillus. Production of Buck pocket-knives was moved to the company's own factory in 1979.

When Buck began to market knives in Canada in 1968, the stamping was changed to "Buck/U.S.A." or "Buck, Made in U.S.A." Older Buck fixed-blade knives and Model 110 folding hunters are becoming more popular with collectors, as are several recently marketed limited editions (see this book's section on commemorative and limited-edition knives). The contract-made pocketknives and recent standard production are of little interest to collectors.

BULLDOG KNIVES

In 1980, Charles Dorton introduced the Bulldog brand of quality German-made knives to the collector market. The foundation for the brand had been laid a couple of years earlier when Dorton had a very few special-issue knives made bearing the "Pit Bull" trademark or saluting the Henry repeater rifle.

S & D Enterprises assumed marketing responsibility for the brand a short time later, when Dorton joined with David Scott.

Production of the brand ceased in 1986 when a new company, Blue Grass Cutlery, was formed to reintroduce Winchester knives.

3½″ Gunstock with brown bone handles; two blades; razor master blade; banner shield; "Pit Bull" etching   *$100*

    As above but variations of master blade style   *$100*

3½″ Gunstock with pearl handles; no shield; two blades; variations of master blade styles; "Bulldog Brand" etching   *$125*

3½″ Gunstock with "Butter & Molasses" celluloid handles; three blades; rifle shield; "Henry Repeater" etching   *$150*

3¾″ Gunstock Stockman; three blades; stag handles; heart shield; square bolsters; "Pit Bull etching"   *$75*

    As above with "Saddle Tramp" etching   *$90*

    As above with various celluloid handles; "Pit Bull" etching   *$65*

4″ Gunstock Stockman; three blades; stag handles; square bolsters; spear shield; "Pit Bull" etching   *$90*

    As above with various celluloid handles   *$70*

4″ Stockman; three blades; square bolsters, celluloid handles; spade shield; "Cowboy's Pet" etching   *$70*

    As above except with green bone handles   *$75*

As above except with stag handles $80

As above except with spear shield; "Pit Bull" etching $75

As above with "Quarter Horseman" etching $85

As above with "S & D" etching $80

As above with various celluloid handles; "Pit Bull" etching $65

4″ Moose Stockman; two blades; square bolsters, stag handles; diamond shield; "Lumber Jack" etching $75

As above except with celluloid handles $65

As above except with purple swirl celluloid handles; Peacock shield $200

3¾″ Stockman; three blades; square bolsters; brown bone handles; banner shield; "Pit Bull" etching $80

As above except with stag handles $90

As above except with celluloid handles $75

As above except with "Bulldog Brand" etching $60

As above except with brown bone handles; "Coal Miner" shield and etching $80

As above except with stag handles $75

3¾″ Stockman; three blades; square bolsters; brown bone handles; crest shield; "Pit Bull" etching; Winchester tang stamp; 28 were made in 1978 $500

As above except with "Pit Bull" tang stamp; 138 made in 1979 $300

3¼″ Stockman; three blades; square bolsters, brown bone handles; crest shield; "Pit Bull" etching $95

As above except with tortoise handles; heart shield $150

As above except with celluloid handles $110

3½″ Stockman; three blades; square bolsters; stag handles; heart shield; "Pit Bull" etching $110

As above except with brown bone handles $90

As above except with celluloid handles $90

3⅞″ Stockman; three blades; round bolsters; stag handles; crest shield; "S & D Enterprises" etching $85

As above except with banner shield; "Pit Bull" etching $75

As above except with celluloid handles $65

As above except with "Coal Miner" shield on black celluloid handles; "Pick & Shovel" etching $80

3½″ Stockman; three blades; square bolsters; stag handles; crest shield; "S & D Our Best" etching $80

As above except with spade shield; "Pit Bull" etching $75

As above except with brown bone handles $70

As above except with celluloid handles $65

As above except with pearl handles; no shield; "Bulldog Knife Club" etching $125

4¼″ Stockman; three blades; stag handles; clip master blade; "Cattle King" etching $110

As above except with bone handles   *$80*

As above except with celluloid handles   *$70*

3⅜″ Serpentine Stockman; three blades; round bolsters; stag handles;
horseshoe shield; "Run for the Roses"   *$70*

As above except with celluloid handles   *$60*

As above except with beer stein shield; "Oktoberfest" etching   *$60*

3⅝″ Serpentine Stockman; round bolsters; three blades; stag handles; tobacco leaf shield; etched "Tobacco King" with state names   *$75*

As above except with celluloid handles   *$65*

As above except five blades; stag handles; crest shield; "S & D Our
Best" etching   *$150*

As above except with acorn shield; "Pit Bull" etching   *$125*

3⅞″ Serpentine Stockman; three blades; round bolsters; stag handles;
crest shield; "S & D Our Best" etching   *$125*

As above except with club shield; "Cutting Horse" etching   *$110*

As above except with green bone handles   *$90*

As above except with celluloid handles   *$80*

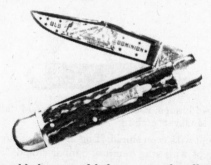

4⅛″ Trapper; two blades; round bolsters; stag handles; OKCA shield;
"Old Dominion" etching   *$90*

As above except with celluloid handles; coon shields; "Dog & Coon" etching $80

As above except mountain man shield; "Trapper Jack" etching $85

As above except with stag handle; banner shield; "S & D Buckeye Special" etching $125

3⅞" Trapper; two blades; round bolsters; stag handles; acorn shield; "Old Reliable" etching $75

As above except with green bone handles $70

As above except with celluloid handles $65

As above except with stag handles; crest shield; "Our Best" etching $90

As above except with "Pit Bull" etching $85

As above except three blades; banner shield $115

As above except two blades; celluloid handles $70

3⅞" Muskrat; two blades; round bolsters; celluloid handles; muskrat shield; "Johnny Muskrat" etching $70

As above except with coon shield; "Dog & Coon" etching $80

As above except with stag handles; banner shield; "S & D Buckeye Special" etching $125

3¾" Copperhead; two blades; round bolsters; celluloid handles; heart shield; "Rabbit Hound" etching   *$70*

    As above except with stag handles   *$80*

    As above except with "S & D Our Best" etching   *$90*

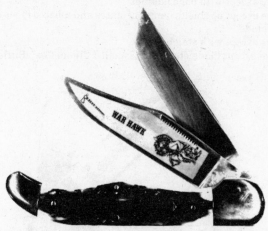

4⅞" folding hunter; two blades; round bolsters; stag handles; spear shield; "War Hawk" etching   *$90*

    As above except with brown bone handles; round tapered bolster; oval shield; "Pit Bull" trademark   *$125*

    As above except with either "Mountain Hunter," "Bull of the Woods," or "Hunter's Pride" etching   *$70*

4⅞" lockback folding hunter; one blade; stag handles; square bolsters; no shield; Bulldog brand   *$200*

3½" *Barlow;* two blades; Fancy Tobacco bolster; stag handles; S & D shield; master blades vary (spear, clip, razor, spey, or sheepfoot); "S & D Our Best" etching $60

As above except with bone handles $55

As above except no shield; names of states and tobacco types etched on master blade $55

As above except with stag handles $60

As above except blade etching misspelled "Tenneffee" Burley (on 96 knives) $110

3⅝" *Canoe;* two blades; round bolsters; stag handle; leaf shield; "Tobacco" etching $75

As above except bone handles $70

As above except red sparkle celluloid handles $100

As above except with stag handles; crest shield; "S & D" etching $85

As above except with three blades $85

As above except with bone handles; "Tobacco" etching $70

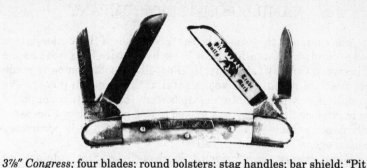

3⅞″ Congress; four blades; round bolsters; stag handles; bar shield; "Pit Bull" etching $110

As above except crest shield; "S & D Enterprises" etching $150

As above except celluloid handles; leaf shield; "Tobacco" etching $85

As above except with pearl handles; no shield $125

3⅞″ Congress; four blades; grooved bolsters; stag handles; bar shield; "Tobacco" etching $100

As above except celluloid handles $75

As above except pearl handles; no shield $115

As above except with heart shield; "Tennessee Walking Horse" etching $110

3⅝″ Congress; four blades; round bolsters; stag handles; crest shield; "S & D Our Best" etching $85

As above except with diamond shield; "Old Chum" etching $70

As above except with celluloid handles $65

As above except with "Fulton Hardware" etching $85

As above except with stag handles; spade shield; "Pit Bull" etching $75

As above except with bone handles $65

As above except with celluloid handles $60

3⅞″ Congress; two blades; grooved bolsters; stag handles; crest shield; "S & D Our Best" etching $90

As above except with bar shield; "Cut Plug" etching $75

As above except with celluloid handles; leaf shield $55

4¼″ Congress; four blades; round bolsters; torched stag handles; leaf shield; "Our Best" etching $135

As above except with "Tobacco" etching $110

As above except with bone handles $100

As above except with tortoise celluloid handles $90

As above except with purple swirl celluloid handles $125

9⅞″ boot knives; stag handles; miscellaneous blade etching $85

As above except with white Micarta handles $70

15½″ Bowie; stag handle; 10″ blade etched "Simon Kenton's Ride 1785" $200

CAMILLUS CUTLERY COMPANY

The company that was to be the forerunner of this cutlery giant was founded in Camillus, New York, by Charles Sherwood as the Sherwood Cutlery Company. In 1894, Sherwood's company made its first shipment of knives, a total of thirty dozen pieces. The small cutlery manufacturing operation lasted only a couple of years before the factory was leased to Robeson Cutlery Company. Sherwood remained as manager during the two-year occupancy and reopened his business in 1901.

Some twenty years prior to Sherwood's venture, Adolph and Nathan Kastor had formed a hardware wholesale and knife importing business known as A. Kastor & Bros. The Kastor business grew to become the country's largest knife importer, but passage of the 1897 Tariff Act caused a substantial increase in the cost of imported knives. Adolph Kastor & Bros. purchased Sherwood's manufacturing facility in 1902 and renamed it Camillus Cutlery Company. In addition to pocketknives, wartime saw the company making military knives for the United States as well as for other allied countries.

After the war, renewed emphasis was placed on the manufacture and sale of pocketknives, and a new Camillus salesman, Albert Baer, was hired in 1922. Within his first year, Baer was successful in landing the large Sears, Roebuck account, and Camillus began manufacturing the Sears STA-SHARP brand. Other large contracts such as KENT knives made for Woolworth, became a major portion of the company's business.

Camillus adopted a number of its own brand names and stampings, and large quantities of knives marked CAMILLUS CUTLERY CO. CAMILLUS NY USA, CAMCO, SWORD BRAND, and MUMBLY PEG have been sold over the years. Although these brands have not become particularly desirable in the collector market, the company has been the major contract manufacturer of dozens of other brands that are in demand. Brand stampings such as O.V.B., KEEN KUTTER, DIAMOND EDGE, VAN CAMP HARDWARE, HENRY SEARS & SONS, and BUCK are but a few that reflect the manufacturing capabilities of this cutlery giant.

Albert Baer remained with the company until 1941 and, in 1963, purchased the firm on behalf of his two daughters. Operational control now comes under the Baer-owned conglomerate Imperial Knife Associated Companies.

CANASTOTA KNIFE COMPANY

This firm was incorporated in the town of Canastota, New York, in 1875. Their knives, which were of high quality, were stamped CANASTOTA KNIFE CO. N.Y. and were marketed by the William Cornwall firm of New York City. Prominent handle materials for the company's knives were bone and wood. In addition to their own brand, the factory produced other brands under contract.

The company went out of business in 1895. Canastota knives are quite rare and are desirable collectibles.

CANTON CUTLERY COMPANY

Knives stamped CCC, CANTON CUTLERY CO., and CARVAN. were made by this company, which was formed c. 1879. W. Stuart Carnes of Canton, Ohio, was one of two local businessmen licensed to make picture-handle knives by their inventors, Henry and Rueben Landis. Recognizing an opportunity, Carnes produced these knives under his own trade names and was successful in their sale for a number of years. Canton Cutlery Co. ceased knife manufacture in the 1930s.

CASE (W. R. CASE & SONS AND RELATED COMPANIES)

The story of knives branded with the name *Case* encompasses dozens of markings and as many members of a family that would make cutlery history. To study the brand that is recognized by most collectors as king of factory knife collectibles, W. R. Case & Sons Cutlery, it is important to include information on other companies, some of which may be discussed in greater detail elsewhere in this book.

Although Job Russell Case was never directly involved with the manufacture or the sale of knives, he is considered by many to be the grandfather of the several knife brands that carried his name. And the name Case is magic to the ears of collectors of factory-made knives. It's a name that is best known, widely respected, and intertwined with the American cutlery industry. Grandpa Job Case was born in 1821 and spent his adult years as a farmer, horse trader, freighter, and lumberman. It is through his descendants that he exerted so much influence on the knives we collect today. These descendants were introduced to the cutlery business by their relatives who were knife makers, and in turn they influenced several other family members to become part of what became a knife manufacturing dynasty.

The story of Case knives begins in the latter part of the nineteenth century and continues through at least a half-dozen significant stages in the history of the knives and the family that created them. To make them more meaningful to collectors, the knife stampings associated with these periods are included.

The Early Years

The Case family was introduced to knife making when Job's daughter Theresa married a cutlery salesman named John Brown Francis Champlin. In 1882, Champlin resigned from the cutlery importing firm of Friedman and Lauterjung to begin his own business as a knife broker. In this capacity, he contracted for knives to be made and then sold them under his own brand name. The brand, J.B.F. Champlin Little Valley New York, was so successful that four of his wife's brothers joined the business in 1886. When Champlin's brothers-in-law, William R., Jean, John D., and Andrew Case, joined his firm, it was renamed Cattaraugus Cutlery Company. The company continued to do well with Champlin and his son Tint directing its manufacturing. For further information about this era and the knife stampings, see the section on Cattaraugus Cutlery Company.

The Case brothers' employment with Cattaraugus was shortlived, but its impact on their lives was not. When they left in 1887, they took with them the desire to be involved in the cutlery industry.

Entering the Knife Brokerage Business

The first cutlery company to use the family name was Case Brothers Cutlery Company, a brokerage firm also located in Little Valley, New York. The company's owners were Jean, John, and Andrew but did not include their brother and former Cattaraugus associate, William Russell Case. The new company contracted with various knife manufacturers to make knives and sold them marked with several tang stampings.

CASE BROS.
LITTLE VALLEY

CASE BROS.
LITTLE VALLEY
N.Y.

JOHN D. CASE
KANE, PA.

CASE BROS.
LITTLE VALLEY

CASE BROTHERS
SPRINGVILLE
N.Y.

XX CO.
KANE, PA.

CASE BROS.
LITTLE VALLEY
N.Y.

CASE BROS.
SPRINGVILLE, N.Y.

J. CASE

CASE BROS
LITTLE VALLEY
N.Y.

J. D. CASE
KANE, PA.

CASE MFG. CO.
SMETHPORT, PA.

CASE BROS. & CO.
LITTLE VALLEY
N.Y.

J. D. C.
KANE, PA.

CASE MFG. CO.
WARREN, PA.

CASE BROTHERS
LITTLE VALLEY, NY

C.J. CASE
KANE PA

(Photo by Allen Swayne)

Beginning the Manufacture of Knives

The Case Brothers' cutlery business was so successful that in 1900 they built their own factory. Sales responsibility belonged to Jean Case, and he apparently did an outstanding job because sales continued to increase along with the number of knife models produced. The brothers' specialty was hand-forged cutlery, and they were justly proud of the company's high-quality products. Desiring to impress their customers with a trademark signifying excellent quality, the brothers began to use the XX mark that is so well known today. Knives of the 1900–1914 period were stamped with the XX mark, usually near the middle of the blade but sometimes on the reverse tang. It would also occasionally appear as Tested XX.

Further expansion came as Case Brothers knives were manufactured briefly in a few other locations, such as the Pennsylvania towns of Kane, Smethport, and Warren. Whether this diversification of manufacturing was the cause or the effect is not known, but there was disagreement between the brothers and Andrew withdrew from the firm in 1911. He retained an interest in the industry, however, as evidenced by his 1940 obituary, which stated that he had held a proprietary interest in Union Cutlery Company—later known as KaBar. It also indicated that he had been a salesman for W. R. Case & Sons Cutlery Company until a few years before his death.

Not only did the Case Brothers factory produce high-quality knives, it also served as a training ground for the family's succeeding generation. When, in 1912, the Little Valley factory burned, a relocation to Springville, New York, was attempted. Within a couple of years, the company had failed, and in 1914 the famous XX trademark was transferred to the competing family firm of W. R. Case & Sons Cutlery Company. During the tenure of the Case Brothers company, a large number of tang marks were used:

CASE BROS.
LITTLE VALLEY

CASE BROS
LITTLE VALLEY
N.Y.

CASE MFG. CO.
LITTLE VALLEY
N.Y.

CASE BROS.
CUT.
CO.

CASE BROS.
LITTLE VALLEY

CASE BROS. & CO.
LITTLE VALLEY
N.Y.

CASE
MANUFACTURING CO.
LITTLE VALLEY, N.Y.

CASE BROS. CUT CO.
LITTLE VALLEY
N.Y.

CASE BROS.
LITTLE VALLEY
N.Y.

CASE BROTHERS
LITTLE VALLEY, NY

CASE BROS.
MFG
CO.

CASE BROS. CUT'L CO.
LITTLE VALLEY
N.Y.

CASE CUT.
MFG. CO.

CASE BROS. & CO.
GOWANDA, N.Y.

(Photo by Allen Swayne)

In the meantime, as Case Brothers Cutlery was getting well established, a new knife brokerage company was started by Case family members. Dean and Elliot, sons of Jean Case, had been involved in the early years of Case Brothers, but they left that company to start their own business in 1901. Upon Elliot's death in 1903, the business closed; the only trademark used was the company name, Standard Knife Company.

STANDARD
KNIFE CO.   Standard Knife Co.

(Photo by Allen Swayne)

W. R. Case & Son Cutlery—the Beginning

As stated earlier, W. R. Case was not involved with his brothers' business, but the Case Brothers company had served to train his son. During the years of 1900 to 1902, John Russell Case had worked for his uncles and earned his indoctrination into the cutlery business. Through the support and financial assistance of his father, "Russ" Case founded a knife brokerage firm in Little Valley, New York, in 1902. In an effort to have customers perceive his new business as well established, he not only used his grandfather's (Job R. Case) picture in the company's advertising but he also used his father's name in naming the company W. R. Case & Son.

Russell Case purchased knives for his brokerage business on contract from Platts Brothers Cutlery Co., Cattaraugus Cutlery Co., and others. Consequently, there were many pattern variations during this 1902–1905 period preceding the establishment of his own factory. Various tang marks were used on the contract knives of this period:

(Photo by Allen Swayne)

W. R. Case & Sons—Knife Manufacturers

Russ Case was an excellent salesman, and flourishing business encouraged him to move to Bradford, Pennsylvania, and build a knife factory there. Another family member, by marriage, would provide the manufacturing expertise needed to complement Case's sales ability. The husband of Russ's sister Debbie had come from a family well established in knife making, so in 1905 H. N. Platts joined his brother-in-law, combining their operations under one company name. Since Platts was a son-in-law of W. R. Case, and since Russ Case had established strong brand recognition, the letter *s* was added to the company name. The new combined company became W. R. Case & Sons Cutlery Company.

Business was excellent, and many new knife patterns were introduced during the 1905–1914 period, but the prestigious XX symbol still belonged to Case Brothers. With the failure of that company in 1914, W. R. Case & Sons was able to acquire the trademark, one that has been a standby for the company to this day.

Because of failing health, H. N. Platts left the company about 1910 and moved to Colorado, where he started a new cutlery company. For further information, see the section on Western Cutlery Company. At about the same time, Russ Case's other brother-in-law, Herbert Crandall, merged his Crandall Cutlery Company with W. R. Case & Sons.

John Russell Case had no children, but for many years his company remained under the ownership and leadership of family members. When he died in 1953, majority ownership of W. R. Case & Sons Cutlery Company passed to his niece. Rhea Crandall was the daughter of Theresa (Case) and Herbert Crandall, Russ Case's early partner. Rhea was first married to Harold Osborne, to whom she bore a son. After Osborne's death, she married John O'Kain. O'Kain led the company as president until his retirement in 1971. At that time, he became chairman of the board, and Rhea's son, Russell B. Osborne, became the company's president.

Ending of Case Family Ownership

In 1972, ownership of the W. R. Case & Sons Cutlery Company was passed from the Case family members to American Brands, Inc., but leadership influence of the Case family remained for a while. Russell Osborne continued as president until his death in 1975, and his son John served as vice-president and new products manager.

American Brands' ownership of the famed cutlery giant continued until the end of 1988. The cutlery business, which the conglomerate had purchased sixteen years earlier, had enjoyed a reputation built over several decades. Although it might not have been recognized by the average consumer, many dedicated knife enthusiasts perceived a dwindling interest by the parent company in maintaining that image. They were, therefore, not surprised when American Brands made public their interest in selling the old company. By the beginning of 1989, W. R. Case & Sons Cutlery Company was under the ownership and leadership of James F. Parker, an enterprising businessman who had already built a thriving cutlery business of his own.

From the above history, it is easy to see that the Case family has made a tremendous impact on the knife industry over a period of one hundred years. Now, at the beginning of the new decade of the 1990s, Case is again guided by cutlery-oriented leadership. For the company and for collectors, it marks a turning point that will likely be significant for generations to come.

W. R. Case & Sons Stampings

During the long history of W. R. Case & Sons, there have been about three dozen different stamps used on their knives. These include but are not limited to the following:

W.R. CASE
& SONS
BRADFORD, PA.

W.R. CASE
&
SONS
MADE IN USA

CASES
STAINLESS

W. R. CASE
& SONS
BRADFORD, PA.

CASE
BRADFORD, PA.

CASE
STAINLESS

W.R. CASE & SONS
BRADFORD
PENNA.

CASE & SONS
BRADFORD
PA.

CASE
PAT.
9-21-26

W. R. CASE & SONS
CUTLERY, CO.
BRADFORD, PA.

Case

R. CASE
BRADFORD
GERMANY

W.R. CASE & SONS
CUTL. CO.
BRADFORD, PA.

Case
25¢

CASE XX

W.R. CASE
& SONS
CUT. CO.

CASE'S
BRADFORD, PA.

CASE
TESTED XX

CASE XX
STAINLESS

CASE
TESTED XX

W. R. CASE
& SONS
BRADFORD, PA.

CASE XX
U.S.A.

CASE

CASE XX
U.S.A.
. . . . . .

CASE
XX
TESTED

CASE
XX

CASE XX
. . . . §§ . . . . .
U.S.A.

(Photo by Allen Swayne)

The "Case XX" stamping was used from 1940 to 1965, with pattern numbers added to the reverse side of the tang in 1949. In 1965, the company began stamping their knives "Case XX U.S.A." In 1970, the logo was again changed, this time to "Case XX U.S.A." but with ten dots under the logo. Each year after that, a dot was removed, so a 1975 knife will have five dots and a 1979 knife will have one dot. In 1980, the stamping was again changed. The dotting system, beginning with ten dots was renewed, but the name stamp was modified to what was to become known as "the Lightning S"—the "S" in the company name was no longer curved; it now resembled a lightning bolt. On the occasion of each logo change, there were large numbers of collectors who bought store displays of the old-logo knives. Some of these displays can still be found intact, but individual knives that were on those boards usually fade on one side and do not bring as much as knives of the same stamping that were not on a board.

Transitions

With each logo change there were some knives, such as the 6488 and the 64052, that had two blades stamped with the logo. Sometimes one blade with the old logo and one blade with the new logo were used in the same knife. These knives with transitory markings can be found in XX to USA, USA to ten dots, and in various combinations of dots, with eight to ten dots being most common for the 6488. The knife in question would be considered a USA, XX, or 10-dot by the tang stamping on the master blade (the blade closest to the shield).

The collector should be aware that minor variations in many of these stampings are not unusual. Whenever a worn-out or broken die was replaced, the replacement die was occasionally not identical to its predecessor. One may see this variation on some Tested XX knives. For instance, the top point of the large *C* often varies in its relative position with the top of the *a*. Most knife collectors choose to ignore these small variations as being of relative insignificance.

How to Use the Case Section of This Price Guide

The collector who specializes in knives made by W. R. Case & Sons or other Case-related companies will be pleased with the extensive listing that follows. Although the listing is much larger than that of any other single brand, it is justified because of

Case's undisputed leadership in collectible pocketknives. More collectors choose Case than any other brand, and the field is so large that most of them further specialize into patterns, stamping variations, handle materials, and so on.

Please note that the value guides to Tested knives are shown along with Case XX, USA, and Dot knives. Under the heading "Stamping," the following criteria should be remembered:

Tested . . . Case Tested XX stamping (prior to 1940)

XX . . . . . . Case XX stamping (1940–1965)

U.S.A. . . . . Case XX U.S.A. stamping (1965–1970)

Dots . . . . . Case XX U.S.A. with dots beneath (1970–1990)

A price guide for knives stamped W. R. Case & Sons, Bradford, PA (last used around 1920) is not included in the master list. Very few knives with this stamping will be encountered, so it is hard to develop a reliable price structure for them; but on most patterns, a W. R. Case- or Bradford-stamped knife will bring 15 to 20 percent more than the same pattern with a Case Tested stamping.

Please note also the pricing structure of Dot knives. By far the majority of collectors of Case "dotted" knives collect the 10-dot only, or they collect the 9, 8, 7, 6, and 5 dots only as a group. A 5-dot knife with bone handles is valued basically the same as a 9-dot of the same handle and pattern.

One should also note that the era of Case dotted stampings also has been one of Delrin handles on quite a few patterns. This handle material, although worthy of hard use, has not been popular with knife collectors. The average collector would value them at less than retail price, although a person seeking a using knife may be happy to purchase the knife at full retail.

All Tested knives are priced as though they are handled in green bone, since that is true for over 90 percent of this era's patterns. The remaining small percentage is handled in red bone and rough black. While red bone-handled knives will sell for only slightly less than green bone, rough black-handled knives will be valued at 20 to 30 percent below green bone tested knives.

Linings on Case Knives

Case used iron liners until the late 1920s, when a change was made to nickel silver. At times, the company would substitute brass for nickel silver. The exception to this note of interest is the

"Big Daddy Barlow," which was lined with iron until 1973, when the pattern was changed to Delrin handles with brass liners.

Pattern Numbers

Case's knife-numbering system offers the collector quite a bit of information about a knife, allowing one to determine whether the knife has the proper handle, number of blades, and so on. These pattern numbers can be relied on, however, only for Case knives made after 1949, when the pattern numbers were stamped on each knife produced.

A Case pattern number usually consists of four digits. The first indicates the handle material, the second represents the number of blades, and the last two are the factory pattern numbers. A zero between the second and third digits represents a variation of an existing pattern.

The First Digit

The handle material numbers and letters are listed below. An asterisk (*) indicates a handle material found only on Case Tested XX knives (1920–1950):

1   Walnut
2   Black Composition
3   Yellow Composition
4   White Composition
5   Genuine Stag
6   Second Cut Stag
7   *Tortoise Shell
    Current usage: see note
8   Genuine Mother-of-Pearl
9   Imitation Pearl
B   *Imitation Onyx
CI Cracked Ice
G   *Green and Red Metal Flake ("Christmas Tree")
    Current usage: Green Bone
GS Gold Stone (Gold Metal Flake)
H   *Mottled Brown and Cream Composition
HA *A bathing beauty under clear celluloid

I Imitation Ivory

M Metal

P Pakkawood

S Silver

R *Red Striped Celluloid ("Candy Stripe")
Current usage: Red Bone

RM Red Mottled

W *Wire

Note. Although "7" denoted imitation tortoise shell during Tested XX days, when Case introduced the "Sharkstooth" knife they originally planned to use Curly Maple and to use the number 7 for its designation. A few blades were already stamped "7" when the company decided to use black-dyed pakkawood instead. Some blades stamped "7" were put into the pakkawood-handled knives and will sometimes be found in the Sharkstooth.

Since Case has used so many handle materials, the following discussion is offered as additional information on the materials, their origin, and usage.

Appaloosa is smooth, mottled-brown bone first used in 1979.

Black composition has a smooth texture and usually a glossy appearance. Its use began before 1940.

Bone stag comes from the shinbone of a cow, and at one time almost every knife manufacturer used this material for its knife handles. With much of the bone used on knives coming from South America, it has become more difficult to get, and shortages sometimes cause Case to resort to Delrin.

Celluloid-based materials have often been impregnated with colors and metal flakes, offering unusual handle designs. Called by names such as Candy Stripe, Christmas Tree, Goldstone, and Metal Flake, these and other celluloid materials were used on Case Tested knives.

Delrin is a manmade material first used by Case in 1967. It looks much like genuine bone. Since 1974, the shield of a genuine bone stag–handled knife has a circle around the word "CASE" on the shield, while a Delrin or laminated-wood handle will not have a circle. Prior to 1974, all shields had the circle around the name.

Genuine mother-of-pearl comes from the shell of an oyster, not from a pearl. Due to shortages of this material, Case has significantly curtailed production of pearl-handled knives except for special issues. The first cutback came in 1967, and the company's 1968 catalog listed no pearl-handled knives. In 1970, they again made the 8261, 8279½, 82053SC SS, and 8364SC SS patterns but then discontinued all pearl-handled knives (except 82079½) in 1975.

Genuine stag has been used since Case's earliest days. It was temporarily discontinued in 1971, but the company still puts stag handles on the Kodiak sheath knife and has issued collector's sets of stag-handled knives.

Green bone is bone stag with a deep green or brown-green tint. It was quite commonly used on Tested knives and is found on the older XX knives. Used between 1940 and 1955, knives with green bone handles are fast becoming one of the more desirable Case collectibles.

High art is a handle type similar to those made famous by Canton Cutlery Co., Aerial Cutlery Co., and others. It features a photo under a transparent plastic cover and is found on extremely old Case knives and on a 1980 limited-issue knife, the HA199½.

Imitation pearl is produced in several variations; the usual one has a flaked appearance and is popularly known as "cracked ice."

Red and green bone in a different shading has been used on some special Case contract knives.

Red bone in its true form is found only on XX or Tested knives, and its color probably comes from a particular dye that Case was using at the time. On a true red bone the front handle should have the same tint as the back handle. Knives that have been displayed in sunlight sometimes fade to a red color but one that is usually dull and does not match the back handle—not a true red bone. Many USA's and Dot knives have red handles that would be the true red bone if they were on a Case XX. These knives are valued slightly higher than knives of the same pattern with regular bone handles.

Red stag is genuine stag with a reddish cast, usually found on pre-1940 Case knives.

Rough black was used as a substitute for bone stag during and shortly after World War II. Called Plastag by W. R. Case & Sons, it has a rubberlike base and no set pattern of jigging.

Second-cut stag is made from the remaining antler after the stag slabs have been removed for use as "genuine stag."

Jigged, as is bone, it will be found on knives stamped both 5 and 6. This type of handle has been used only on patterns 5254, 6254, 5375, 6375, 6488, and 5488.

Smooth bone is a red bone handle that is not jigged, first used by Case in 1979.

Walnut has been used on Case knives since 1920.

White composition was discontinued about 1974. It is white but the same texture as black composition.

Yellow composition may be seen in two variations. One has a deep, glossy, yellow handle with a white line around its outer edge, sometimes referred to as a white liner. This variation, when found, is only on XX or older knives. The other variation lacks the white liner and can be found on knives today.

The Second Digit

The second digit of the Case pattern numbers indicates the number of blades. W. R. Case & Sons made a few patterns with five blades in the Tested XX and Bradford days, but since that time has made only one-, two-, three-, and four-blade knives.

Factory Design Numbers

The remaining digits of a Case pattern number denote the factory designation for that handle pattern. A zero as the first digit denotes a variation from an existing pattern. For example, 06247 is a two-blade variation of the 6347 pattern.

A few Case knives omit the handle material and blade number digits, leaving only the factory pattern number. An example is the 6225½ stamped 25½.

Blade Abbreviations

After many pattern numbers there are abbreviations for the various blades or description of the knife, as follows:

DR	Drilled through bolster for lanyard
EO	Easy open
F	File blade
I	Iron liners

L	Blade locks open
P	Punch blade
PEN	Pen blade
R	Bail in handle
RAZ	One arm man blade or razor blade
SAB	Saber-ground master blade
SH	Sheepfoot blade
S or *SHAD* (shadow)	No bolsters
SC or *SICS*	Scissors
SP	Spey blade
SS	Stainless steel blades and springs
SSP	Stainless steel blades and springs, polished edge
T	Tip bolsters
$1/2$	Clip master blade
$3/4$	Saber-ground like a dagger

Sheath Knives

The collector interested in Case sheath knives should recognize several peculiarities relating to their collector value and stampings. Sheath knives have yet to be in great demand by Case collectors; they are not valued nearly as highly as pocketknives of the same period. For example, when Case issued its collector's sets, there were five stag-handled sheath knives in each set. At the time when many of the pocketknives were selling for $30, the sheath knives sold for about one half that amount. As older pocketknives become more difficult to find and more expensive to buy, sheath knives could be "sleepers." Consequently, it may be wise for collectors to occasionally purchase Case sheath knives that are reasonably priced. Those marked Jean Case Cutlery Co. and the related Kinfolks types are worth noting.

Case did stamp sheath knives with "Case Tested XX," but when the pocketknife stamping was changed to "Case XX" about 1940, the stamping on the sheath knives was changed from "Case XX" to "Case." When the pocketknife stamping was again changed from "Case XX" to "Case XX, U.S.A." in 1965, the sheath knife stamping was changed to "Case XX Made in U.S.A." When pocketknife stamping was changed to the dot system in 1970, sheath knife stamping was not changed. The fact that there is no way to date the manufacture of most sheath knives made during the past twenty-five years is a major factor in their lower collector demand.

W.R.CASE &SONS
BRADFORD,PA.

(Until 1932)

(A)

CASE
BRADFORD, PA.

(Until 1932)

(B)

Case
STAINLESS

(Mid 1930s)

(C)

CASE

(About 1932 - 1940)

(D)

CASE
TESTED XX

(About 1932 - 1940)

(E)

CASE'S
TESTED XX

(About 1932 - 1940)

(F)

CASE

(About 1932 - 1940)

(G)

CASE'S
STAINLESS

(About 1945 - 1955)

(H)

CASE

(About 1940 - 1965)

(I)

CASE

(About 1940 - 1965)

(J)

CASE XX

(About 1940 - 1965)

(K)

CASE XX
U.S.A.

(1965 to Date)

(L)

CASE XX
· · · · · · · · ·
U SA

(1980)

(M)

(Photo by Allen Swayne)

FIXED-BLADE KNIVES

Pattern	Stamping	Years Made	Handle	Variation / Blade	Mint Price
M-15	D	1940–1965			$140
	I	1940–1965			75
	J	1940–1965			125
	K	1940–1965			75

3¾″ Blade

Pattern	Stamping	Years Made	Handle	Variation / Blade	Mint Price
147	D	1937–1940	Walnut	Chrome Plated	90
	E	1937–1940	Walnut	Chrome Plated	90
	F	1937–1940	Walnut	Chrome Plated	90
	G	1937–1940	Walnut	Chrome Plated	90
	H	1945–1955	Walnut	Chrome Plated	65
	I	1940–1965	Walnut	Chrome Plated	65
	J	1940–1965	Walnut	Chrome Plated	65
	K	1940–1965	Walnut	Chrome Plated	65
	L	1965–1975	Walnut	Chrome Plated	50

(Photo by Allen Swayne)

4½″ Blade

Pattern	Stamping	Years Made	Handle	Variation / Blade	Mint Price
161	D	1934–1940	Bone Stag	Chrome Plated	150
	E	1934–1940	Bone Stag	Chrome Plated	150
	F	1934–1940	Bone Stag	Chrome Plated	150
	G	1934–1940	Bone Stag	Chrome Plated	150
	I	1940–1949	Bone Stag	Chrome Plated	125

Pattern	Stamping	Years Made	Handle	Variation/ Blade	Mint Price
	J	1940–1949	Bone Stag	Chrome Plated	$125
	K	1940–1949	Bone Stag	Chrome Plated	125

4½″ Blade

Pattern	Stamping	Years Made	Handle	Variation/ Blade	Mint Price
2FINN	L	1968–present	Black Plastic	Chrome Plated	25
E-22-5	D	1937–1940			150
	E	1937–1940			150

5″ Blade

Pattern	Stamping	Years Made	Handle	Variation/ Blade	Mint Price
E-23-5	D	1937–1940	Pearl/ Black/Red	Chrome Plated	250
	E	1937–1940	Pearl/ Black/Red	Chrome Plated	250
	F	1937–1940	Pearl/ Black/Red	Chrome Plated	250
	G	1937–1940	Pearl/ Black/Red	Chrome Plated	250
	H	1945–1949	Pearl/ Black/Red	Chrome Plated	250
C-23-5	D	1937–1940			175
	E	1932–1942			175
206	I	1940–1949			100
	J	1940–1949			100

5″ Blade

Pattern	Stamping	Years Made	Handle	Variation/ Blade	Mint Price
208-5	E	1934–1940	Black Rubber	Chrome Plated	100

Pattern	Stamping	Years Made	Handle	Variation / Blade	Mint Price
	I	1940–1949	Black Rubber	Chrome Plated	$90

5″ Blade

Pattern	Stamping	Years Made	Handle	Variation / Blade	Mint Price
209	H	1942–1949	Brown & Black Rubber	Chrome Plated/ Saber	100
	J	1942–1949	Brown & Black Rubber	Chrome Plated/ Saber	90

5″ Blade

Pattern	Stamping	Years Made	Handle	Variation / Blade	Mint Price
216-6	L	1972–present	Black Plastic	Chrome Plated	25

5″ Blade

Pattern	Stamping	Years Made	Handle	Variation / Blade	Mint Price
223-5	L	1965–present	Black Plastic	Chrome Plated/ Saber	30

6″ Blade

Pattern	Stamping	Years Made	Handle	Variation / Blade	Mint Price
223-6	L	1968–present	Black Plastic	Chrome Plated/ Saber	30

5″ Knife Blade—4½″ Axe Blade

Pattern	Stamping	Years Made	Handle	Variation / Blade	Mint Price
261-KNI-FAX	E	1934–1940	Walnut	Chrome Plated	400
	F	1934–1940	Walnut		400
	K	1940–1965	Walnut		300
	L	1965–1968	Walnut		240

5″ Blade

Pattern	Stamping	Years Made	Handle	Variation / Blade	Mint Price
261 Deluxe	J	1940–1964	Walnut	Chrome Plated/ Large Axe	375
	K	1960–1964	Walnut	Chrome Plated/ Large Axe	300

4½″ Blade

Pattern	Stamping	Years Made	Handle	Variation / Blade	Mint Price
262	D	1932–1940	Rubber	Chrome Plated/ Skinning	100

Pattern	Stamping	Years Made	Handle	Variation / Blade	Mint Price

Pattern	Stamping	Years Made	Handle	Variation / Blade	Mint Price
			4¼″ Blade		
3-FINN	D	1937–1940	Leather	Chrome Plated/ Saber	$50
	I	1940–1965	Leather	Chrome Plated/ Saber	40
	L	1965–present	Leather	Chrome Plated/ Saber	25
			4¼″ Blade		
013-FINN, CC SS	H	1949–1955	Leather	Carbon Steel	40
			4¼″ Blade		
3-FINN	H	1949–1955	Leather	Carbon Steel	45
			4¼″ Blade		
3-FINN, SSP	L	1966–present	Leather	Carbon Steel	25
			4¼″ Blade		
3-TWIN-FINN	I	1942–1965	Leather	Carbon Steel	75
	L	1965–1977	Leather	Carbon Steel	55
			3″ Blade		
M3-FINN	I	1942–1965	Leather	Chrome Plated/ Saber	35
	L	1965–present	Leather	Chrome Plated/ Saber	20

Pattern	Stamping	Years Made	Handle	Variation / Blade	Mint Price
M3-FINN	H	1949–1955			$35
M3-FINN, SSP	L	1966–present			25
34	D	1937–1949			90
	E	1937–1942			90
	F	1937–1940			90

4¼″ Blade

Pattern	Stamping	Years Made	Handle	Variation / Blade	Mint Price
303	D	1934–1940	Fiber	Chrome Plated	50
	K	1940–present	Fiber	Chrome Plated	35

5″ Blade

Pattern	Stamping	Years Made	Handle	Variation / Blade	Mint Price
309	D	1932–1940	Leather over Aluminum	Chrome Plated/ Saber	150
	G	1937–1949	Leather over Aluminum	Chrome Plated/ Saber	150

4″ Blade

Pattern	Stamping	Years Made	Handle	Variation / Blade	Mint Price
315-4	D	1934–1940	Leather and Fiber	Chrome Plated	75
	K	1940–1965	Leather and Fiber	Chrome Plated	60
	L	1965–1975	Leather and Fiber	Chrome Plated	40

4¼″ Blade

Pattern	Stamping	Years Made	Handle	Variation / Blade	Mint Price
315-4¼	I	1942–1949	Leather and Fiber	Chrome Plated	55
	K	1940–1949	Leather and Fiber	Chrome Plated	55

4½″ Blade

Pattern	Stamping	Years Made	Handle	Variation / Blade	Mint Price
315-4½	I	1955–1965	Leather and Fiber	Chrome Plated	55
	L	1965–present	Leather and Fiber	Chrome Plated	25

5″ Blade

Pattern	Stamping	Years Made	Handle	Variation / Blade	Mint Price
316-5	I	1942–1965	Leather and Fiber	Chrome Plated	45

Pattern	Stamping	Years Made	Handle	Variation / Blade	Mint Price
	J	1940–1965	Leather and Fiber	Chrome Plated	$45
	K	1940–1965	Leather and Fiber	Chrome Plated	25
	L	1965–present	Leather and Fiber	Chrome Plated	20

5″ Blade

Pattern	Stamping	Years Made	Handle	Variation / Blade	Mint Price
316-5SSP	L	1966–present	Leather and Fiber	Stainless Steel	30
317	D	1932–1940			125
	E	1932–1940			125
	F	1932–1940			125
	G	1932–1940			125

5″ Blade

Pattern	Stamping	Years Made	Handle	Variation / Blade	Mint Price
322-5	D	1937–1940	Leather and Fiber	Chrome Plated	150
	E	1937–1940	Leather and Fiber	Chrome Plated	150
	F	1937–1949	Leather and Fiber	Chrome Plated	150
	G	1937–1949	Leather and Fiber	Chrome Plated	150
322-½-5	I	1942–1949			100
	J	1942–1949			100
	K	1942–1949			100

3¼″ Blade

Pattern	Stamping	Years Made	Handle	Variation / Blade	Mint Price
323-3¼	I	1959–1965	Leather		25
	J	1959–1965	Leather		25
	K	1959–1965	Leather		25
	L	1965–present	Leather		18

5″ Blade

Pattern	Stamping	Years Made	Handle	Variation / Blade	Mint Price
323-5	D	1934–1940	Leather		60
	E	1934–1940	Leather		60

Pattern	Stamping	Years Made	Handle	Variation / Blade	Mint Price
	F	1934–1940	Leather		$60
	G	1934–1940	Leather		60
	I	1940–1965	Leather		45
	J	1940–1965	Leather		50
	K	1940–1965	Leather		30
	L	1965–date	Leather		20

6" Blade

Pattern	Stamping	Years Made	Handle	Variation / Blade	Mint Price
323-6	D	1934–1940	Leather and Fiber		70
	E	1934–1940	Leather and Fiber		70
	F	1934–1940	Leather and Fiber		70
	G	1934–1940	Leather and Fiber		70
	I	1940–1965	Leather and Fiber		55
	J	1940–1965	Leather and Fiber		50
	K	1940–1965	Leather and Fiber		50
	L	1965–present	Leather and Fiber		30

4⅝" Blade

Pattern	Stamping	Years Made	Handle	Variation / Blade	Mint Price
324	D	1934–1940	Leather and Fiber	Skinning	70
	E	1934–1940	Leather and Fiber	Skinning	70
	F	1934–1940	Leather and Fiber	Skinning	70
	G	1934–1940	Leather and Fiber	Skinning	70

4" Blade

Pattern	Stamping	Years Made	Handle	Variation / Blade	Mint Price
325-4	D	1934–1940	Leather/ Fiber/Brass	Chrome Plated	75

Pattern	Stamping	Years Made	Handle	Variation / Blade	Mint Price
	E	1934–1940	Leather/ Fiber/Brass	Chrome Plated	$75
	F	1934–1940	Leather/ Fiber/Brass	Chrome Plated	75
	G	1934–1940	Leather/ Fiber/Brass	Chrome Plated	75
	I	1940–1965	Leather/ Fiber/Brass	Chrome Plated	55
	J	1940–1965	Leather/ Fiber/Brass	Chrome Plated	60
	K	1940–1965	Leather/ Fiber/Brass	Chrome Plated	55
	L	1965–1974	Leather/ Fiber/Brass	Chrome Plated	35

5″ Blade

3025-5	C	1932–1938	Leather/ Fiber/ Brass	Chrome Plated	120
	D	1932–1940	Leather/ Fiber/ Brass	Chrome Plated	110
	E	1932–1940	Leather/ Fiber/ Brass	Chrome Plated	110
	F	1932–1940	Leather/ Fiber/ Brass	Chrome Plated	110
	K	1940–1959	Leather/ Fiber/ Brass	Chrome Plated	65

6″ Blade

| 3025-6 | D | 1937–1940 | Leather/ Fiber/ Brass | Chrome Plated | 90 |

Pattern	Stamping	Years Made	Handle	Variation / Blade	Mint Price
	K	1940–1965	Leather/ Fiber/ Brass	Chrome Plated	$70
	L	1965–1966	Leather/ Fiber/ Brass	Chrome Plated	80

4½″ Blade

Pattern	Stamping	Years Made	Handle	Variation / Blade	Mint Price
326	D	1937–1940	Leather/ Fiber/Brass	Chrome Plated	80
	E	1937–1940	Leather/ Fiber/Brass	Chrome Plated	80
	F	1937–1940	Leather/ Fiber/Brass	Chrome Plated	80
	G	1937–1949	Leather/ Fiber/Brass	Chrome Plated	80

5″ Blade

Pattern	Stamping	Years Made	Handle	Variation / Blade	Mint Price
352	D	1934–1940	Cream Composition	Chrome Plated/ Saber	80
	E	1934–1949	Cream Composition	Chrome Plated/ Saber	80
	F	1934–1949	Cream Composition	Chrome Plated/ Saber	80
	G	1934–1939	Cream Composition	Chrome Plated/ Saber	75

4½″ Blade

Pattern	Stamping	Years Made	Handle	Variation / Blade	Mint Price
361	D	1934–1937	Leather and Fiber	Chrome Plated/ Skinning	75
	E	1934–1937	Leather and Fiber	Chrome Plated/ Skinning	75
	F	1934–1937	Leather and Fiber	Chrome Plated/ Skinning	75
	G	1934–1937	Leather and Fiber	Chrome Plated/ Skinning	75

Pattern	Stamping	Years Made	Handle	Variation / Blade	Mint Price

4½" Blade

Pattern	Stamping	Years Made	Handle	Variation / Blade	Mint Price
362	D	1934–1940	Leather/ Fiber/ Brass	Chrome Plated	
	J	1940–1965	Leather/ Fiber/ Brass	Chrome Plated	$150
	L	1965-1974	Leather/ Fiber/ Brass	Chrome Plated	115
					55

4½" Blade

Pattern	Stamping	Years Made	Handle	Variation / Blade	Mint Price
364SAB	D	1934–1940	Leather and Fiber	Chrome Plated/ Saber	55
	I	1940–1965	Leather and Fiber	Chrome Plated/ Saber	45
	L	1965–present	Leather and Fiber	Chrome Plated/ Saber	25

5" Blade

Pattern	Stamping	Years Made	Handle	Variation / Blade	Mint Price
365	D	1934–1940	Leather/ Fiber/ Brass	Chrome Plated	50
	I	1940–1965	Leather/ Fiber/ Brass	Chrome Plated	40
	L	1965–1974	Leather/ Fiber/ Brass	Chrome Plated	25

Pattern	Stamping	Years Made	Handle	Variation / Blade	Mint Price
5" Blade					
365SAB	I	1942–1965	Leather/ Fiber/ Brass	Chrome Plated/ Saber	$40
	J	1942–1965	Leather/ Fiber/ Brass	Chrome Plated/ Saber	40
	L	1965–present	Leather/ Fiber/ Brass	Chrome Plated/ Saber	25
4" Blade					
366	D	1937–1940	Leather/ Fiber/ Brass	Chrome Plated	50
	I	1940–1965	Leather/ Fiber/ Brass	Chrome Plated	40
	L	1965–present	Leather/ Fiber/ Brass	Chrome Plated	22

Pattern	Stamping	Years Made	Handle	Variation / Blade	Mint Price
4½" Blade					
378	D	1934–1940	Leather and Fiber	Chrome Plated	70
	I	1940–1959	Leather and Fiber	Chrome Plated	50
	J	1940–1959	Leather and Fiber	Chrome Plated	55
	K	1940–1959	Leather and Fiber	Chrome Plated	40
4½" Blade					
392	D	1934–1940	Ivory	Chrome Plated/ Skinning	150

Pattern	Stamping	Years Made	Handle	Variation / Blade	Mint Price
	E	1934–1940	Ivory	Chrome Plated/ Skinning	$150
	F	1934–1940	Ivory	Chrome Plated/ Skinning	150
	G	1934–1940	Ivory	Chrome Plated/ Skinning	150
		4½″ Blade			
3361	D	1934–1942	Ivory	Chrome Plated/ Skinning	150
	J	1940–1942		Chrome Plated/ Skinning	150
		3¾″ Blade			
457	D	1934–1940	Ivory Composition	Chrome Plated/ Saber	125
	E	1934–1940	Ivory Composition	Chrome Plated/ Saber	125
		4¼″ Blade			
5-FINN	D	1937–1940	Stag	Chrome Plated/ Saber	130
	I	1940–1965	Stag		75
	L	1965–present	Stag		40
		4¼″ Blade			
5-FINN	I	1962–1975	Second Cut	Chrome Plated/ Saber	150
5-FINN CCSS	H	1949–1955			85
	I	1949–1955			75
5-FINN SS	H	1949–1955			75
	I	1949–1955			65

Pattern	Stamping	Years Made	Handle	Variation / Blade	Mint Price
		5″ Blade			
M-5-FINN	G	1940-	Stag		$65
	I	1940–1965	Stag		55
	L	1965–present	Stag		35
		5″ Blade			
523-5	D	1934–1940	Stag	Chrome Plated	170
	E	1934–1940	Stag	Chrome Plated	170
	I	1940–1965	Stag	Chrome Plated	110
	L	1965–1974	Stag	Chrome Plated	70
		5″ Blade			
M-5-FINN SS	I	1949–1955	Stag	Stainless Steel	65
F52	D	1934–1940			100
	E	1934–1940			100
	F	1934–1940			100
	G	1934–1940			100
501	D	1937–1940			100
	E	1937–1940			100
	F	1937–1949			100
	G	1937–1949			100

Pattern	Stamping	Years Made	Handle	Variation / Blade	Mint Price
		4″ Blade			
515	D	1934–1940	Stag	Chrome Plated	90
	E	1934–1940	Stag	Chrome Plated	90
	F	1934–1940	Stag	Chrome Plated	90

Pattern	Stamping	Years Made	Handle	Variation / Blade	Mint Price
	I	1940–1949	Stag	Chrome Plated/ Saber	$85
	J	1940–1949	Stag	Chrome Plated/ Saber	95
	K	1940–1949	Stag	Chrome Plated/ Saber	85

5″ Blade Knife—4¼″ Blade Axe

Pattern	Stamping	Years Made	Handle	Variation / Blade	Mint Price
561 Deluxe	E	1937–1940	Stag	Large Axe Head	450
	F	1937–1940	Stag	Large Axe Head	450
	K	1940–1965	Stag	Large Axe Head	375
	L	1965–1974	Stag	Large Axe Head	375
578	D	1934–1940	Deer Horn		90
	E	1934–1940	Deer Horn		90
	J	1940–1959	Deer Horn		80
	K	1940–1959	Deer Horn		55

4⅝″ Blade

Pattern	Stamping	Years Made	Handle	Variation / Blade	Mint Price
5324	D	1934–1940	Stag	Skin-ning	140
	E	1934–1940	Stag	Skin-ning	140
	I	1940–1941	Stag	Skin-ning	120
	J	1940–1941	Stag	Skin-ning	120
	K	1940–1941	Stag	Skin-ning	120

5″ Blade

Pattern	Stamping	Years Made	Handle	Variation / Blade	Mint Price
5325-5	D	1934–1940	Stag	Chrome Plated	150
	E	1934–1940	Stag	Chrome Plated	150

Pattern	Stamping	Years Made	Handle	Variation / Blade	Mint Price
	I	1940–1965	Stag	Chrome Plated	$100
	K	1940–1965	Stag	Chrome Plated	100
	L	1965–1966	Stag	Chrome Plated	175

6″ Blade

Pattern	Stamping	Years Made	Handle	Variation / Blade	Mint Price
5325-6	D	1934–1940			180
	E	1934–1940			180
	I	1940–1965			125
	K	1940–1965			125
	L	1965–1968			200

4½″ Blade

Pattern	Stamping	Years Made	Handle	Variation / Blade	Mint Price
5361	D	1934–1940	Deer Horn	Chrome Plated/ Skinning	225
	J	1940–1965	Deer Horn	Chrome Plated/ Skinning	200
	K	1940–1965	Deer Horn	Chrome Plated/ Skinning	160
	L	1965–1975	Deer Horn	Chrome Plated/ Skinning	200

4½″ Blade

Pattern	Stamping	Years Made	Handle	Variation / Blade	Mint Price
5362	D	1934–1940	Deer Horn	Chrome Plated	225
	I	1940–1949	Deer Horn		190
E62	F	1937–1942			220
RE-62	F	1937–1940			175

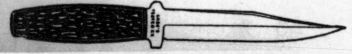

5″ Blade

Pattern	Stamping	Years Made	Handle	Variation / Blade	Mint Price
62-5	F	1934–1949	Bone Stag	Chrome Plated	275

Pattern	Stamping	Years Made	Handle	Variation / Blade	Mint Price
			6" Blade		
62-6	F	1934–1949			$275
			5" Blade		
63-5	D	1934–1940	Bone Stag	Chrome Plated/ Saber	275
	J	1940–1942	Bone Stag	Chrome Plated/ Saber	240
			5" Blade		
63-6	B	1926–1934	Bone Stag	Chrome Plated	300
	D	1934–1940	Bone Stag	Chrome Plated	275
	I	1940–1942	Bone Stag	Chrome Plated	195

Pattern	Stamping	Years Made	Handle	Variation / Blade	Mint Price
			4" Blade		
64	F	1934–1940	Bone Stag	Chrome Plated/ Straight	165
	H	1940–1949	Bone Stag	Chrome Plated/ Straight	165
	K	1940–1949	Bone Stag	Chrome Plated/ Straight	135
E66	F	1934–1940			165
	I	1940–1941			165

Pattern	Stamping	Years Made	Handle	Variation / Blade	Mint Price
			4" Blade		
RE66	F	1934–1940	Pearl and Brown	Chrome Plated	145

Pattern	Stamping	Years Made	Handle	Variation / Blade	Mint Price
	I	1940–1941	Pearl and Brown		$130
67	D	1934–1940	Bone Stag	Chrome Plated/ Skinning	130
	F	1934–1940	Bone Stag	Chrome Plated/ Skinning	130
	I	1940–1949	Bone Stag	Chrome Plated/ Skinning	110
	K	1940–1949	Bone Stag	Chrome Plated/ Skinning	110

5″ Blade

Pattern	Stamping	Years Made	Handle	Variation / Blade	Mint Price
652	D	1934–1940	Bone Stag	Chrome Plated/ Saber	150
	I	1940–1949	Bone Stag	Chrome Plated/ Saber	125
	K	1940–1949	Bone Stag	Chrome Plated/ Saber	125

5″ Blade

Pattern	Stamping	Years Made	Handle	Variation / Blade	Mint Price
652-5	J	1962–1965	Bone Stag	Chrome Plated/ Saber	100
	K	1962–1965	Bone Stag	Chrome Plated/ Saber	100
	L	1965–1968	Bone Stag	Chrome Plated/ Saber	80

Pattern	Stamping	Years Made	Handle	Variation / Blade	Mint Price
F78	E	1934–1937			$140
	G	1934–1937			140
PS78	E	1934–1937			140
	G	1934–1937			140

5″ Blade Knife—4¼″ Axe Blade

661-KNIFAX	D	1934–1942	Bone Stag	Chrome Plated	500
	E	1934–1942	Bone Stag	Chrome Plated	500
	F	1934–1942	Bone Stag	Chrome Plated	500
	G	1934–1942	Bone Stag	Chrome Plated	400

5″ Blade

709	E	1934–1942	Metal	Chrome Plated/ Saber	275
M-8-FINN	I	1940–1949			70
	K	1940–1949			70

Pattern	Stamping	Years Made	Handle	Variation / Blade	Mint Price
		4½" Blade			
9-FINN	F	1934–1940	Pearl	Chrome Plated/ Saber	$90
	K	1940–1955	Pearl		70

Pattern	Stamping	Years Made	Handle	Variation / Blade	Mint Price
		3" Blade			
M-9-FINN	E	1934–1955	Pearl	Chrome Plated/ Saber	90
	K	1940–1955	Pearl	Chrome Plated/ Saber	70

Pattern	Stamping	Years Made	Handle	Variation / Blade	Mint Price
		4½" Blade			
92	D	1934–1940	Leather and Fiber	Chrome Plated	80
	E	1934–1940	Leather and Fiber	Chrome Plated	80
	F	1934–1940	Leather and Fiber	Chrome Plated	80
	G	1934–1940	Leather and Fiber	Chrome Plated	80
	I	1940–1949	Leather and Fiber	Chrome Plated	70
	J	1940–1949	Leather and Fiber	Chrome Plated	80
	K	1940–1949	Leather and Fiber	Chrome Plated	70
PS97	D	1934–1937			135
	E	1934–1937			135

Pattern	Stamping	Years Made	Handle	Variation / Blade	Mint Price
903	E	1934–1937			$125

5″ Blade

Pattern	Stamping	Years Made	Handle	Variation / Blade	Mint Price
923-5	D	1934–1940	Leather		110
	I	1940–1949	Leather		95
	J	1940–1949	Leather		105
	K	1940–1949	Leather		90

6″ Blade

Pattern	Stamping	Years Made	Handle	Variation / Blade	Mint Price
923-6	D	1934–1940	Leather		110
	I	1940–1949	Leather		85
	J	1940–1949	Leather		110
	K	1940–1949	Leather		85
952	D	1934–1940			95
	E	1934–1942			95
	G	1934–1943			95
957	D	1934–1940			110
	E	1934–1940			110
	G	1934–1940			110
	I	1940–1942			95
	J	1940–1942			110
957-SAB	D	1937–1940			95
	E	1937–1940			95
	G	1937–1940			95
	I	1940–1949			85
961	E	1934–1940	Imitation Pearl		450
	F	1934–1940	Imitation Pearl		450
	K	1940–1949	Imitation Pearl		375

5″ Blade

Pattern	Stamping	Years Made	Handle	Variation / Blade	Mint Price
961-Deluxe	E	1932–1940	Imitation Pearl		450
	F	1932–1940	Imitation Pearl		450

Pattern	Stamping	Years Made	Handle	Variation / Blade	Mint Price
		4″ Blade			
964	F	1932–1940	Fancy Composition	Chrome Plated/ Straight	$140
	I	1940–1965	Fancy Composition	Chrome Plated/ Straight	110
	K	1940–1965	Fancy Composition	Chrome Plated/ Saber	110
		4½″ Blade			
978	F	1932–1940	Pearl Composition		115
		5″ Blade			
9235-5	F	1932–1940			150
	I	1940–1965			125
		4½″ Blade			
9362	F	1932–1940	Deer Horn	Chrome Plated/ Straight	125
	I	1940–1965	Deer Horn	Chrome Plated/ Straight	125
		5¼″ Blade			
APACHE 300	L	1966–1980	Stag	Stain- less Steel	35
	M	1981	Stag	Stain- less Steel	30
		11½″ Blade			
BOWIE	L	1967–present	Black		100
	M	1980	Stag		135
		4¼″ Blade			
CHERO- KEE 200	L	1967–1980	Stag	Stain- less Steel	35

Pattern	Stamping	Years Made	Handle	Variation / Blade	Mint Price
			5″ Blade		
CHEY-ENNE	L	1967–1980	Stag	Stain-less Steel	$45
	M	1981	Stag	Stain-less Steel	80
			4⅜″ Blade		
FINN	D	1934–1937	Pearl	Chrome Plated	125
KODIAK	I	1964–1966	XX Model		150
	K	1966–1967	Transi-tional Model		135
	L	1967–1973	No Stars Model		95
	M	1973–present			85
MA-CHETE	K	1942		Mili-tary	150
			2¼″ Blade		
MIDGET	D	1934–1940	Pearl	Chrome Plated	175
	I	1940–1948	Pearl	Chrome Plated	175
			5″ Blade		
TWIN-FINN	D	1940–1949	Stag	Chrome Plated	250
	K	1950–1964	Stag	Chrome Plated	160
	L	1965–1974	Stag	Chrome Plated	125
			5″ Blade		
380 COMBO	L	1968–1974		Axe and Hunter	100

Pattern	Stamping	Years Made	Handle	Variation / Blade	Mint Price
		5″ Blade			
580 COMBO	L	1968–1974	Walnut	Axe and Hunter	$90
		3″ Blade			
M-5-FINN		1977–1980	Stag	Stainless Steel	50
		4¼″ Blade			
5-FINN SSP	L	1972–1982	Stag	Stainless Steel	45
		5″ Blade			
516-5 SSP	L	1972–1982	Stag	Stainless Steel	45
		5″ Blade			
523-5 SSP	L	1972–1988	Stag	Stainless Steel	50
SPORTS-MEN SET	A	1930		5 Piece Set	2200

POCKETKNIVES

Pattern	Stamping	Years Made	Handle	Variation / Blade	Mint Price
		2³⁄₁₆″ Closed			
Watch Fob	Tested	Prior 1940	Pearl		200
		12″ Case Display Knife			
Display	Bradford	Prior 1940	Black Composition		1200
		5½″ Swell Center			
61213	Tested	Prior 1940	Green Bone		600
		5½″ Switchblade			
Zipper	Tested	Prior 1940	Stag		3500
Zipper	Bradford	Prior 1940	Green Bone		4500

Pattern	Stamping	Years Made	Handle	Variation / Blade	Mint Price

3¼" Maize

Pattern	Stamping	Years Made	Handle	Variation / Blade	Mint Price
Maize No. 1	Tested	Prior 1940	Cocobola	3⅝"	$300
Maize No. 2	Tested	Prior 1940	Cocobola	4"	300

4½" Saddle Horn

Pattern	Stamping	Years Made	Handle	Variation / Blade	Mint Price
3100	Tested	Prior 1940	Yellow Composition		600
6100	Tested	Prior 1940	Green Bone		700

3¼" Press Button Slide Blade

Pattern	Stamping	Years Made	Handle	Variation / Blade	Mint Price
M100	Tested	Prior 1940	Cracked Ice		150
	Tested	Prior 1940	Green Bone		200
	Tested	Prior 1940	Royal Blue	Celluloid	150
	XX	1940s	Nickel Plated		140
	XX	1940s	Gold Plated		175

5½" Melon Tester

Pattern	Stamping	Years Made	Handle	Variation / Blade	Mint Price
4100	XX	1960–1965	White Composition		100
	USA	1965–1970			75
	10 Dots	1970–1971			75
	Dots	1971–1974	White Composition		50

2⅞" Press Button Slide Blade

Pattern	Stamping	Years Made	Handle	Variation / Blade	Mint Price
M101	Tested	Prior 1940	Metal		125

Pattern	Stamping	Years Made	Handle	Variation / Blade	Mint Price

3¼″ Budding Knife

Pattern	Stamping	Years Made	Handle	Variation / Blade	Mint Price
4103 B&G	Tested	Prior 1940	White Composition		$175
6103 B&G	Tested	Prior 1940	Bone		250

3⅜″ Jack

Pattern	Stamping	Years Made	Handle	Variation / Blade	Mint Price
6104B	Tested	Prior 1940	Green Bone	3⅜″	250
6104B	XX	1940–1955	Green Bone		200

3¼″ Budding Knife

Pattern	Stamping	Years Made	Handle	Variation / Blade	Mint Price
2109B	Tested	Prior 1950	Black Composition		175
2109B	XX	1950–1965	Black Composition		125
2109B	USA	1965–1968	Black Composition		100
6109B	Tested		Bone		250

3⅛″ Spaying Knife

Pattern	Stamping	Years Made	Handle	Variation / Blade	Mint Price
M110	Tested	Prior 1940	Nickel Silver		150
M110	XX	1940s	Nickel Silver		100

3⅜″ Switchblade

Pattern	Stamping	Years Made	Handle	Variation / Blade	Mint Price
91210½	Tested	Prior 1940	White Onyx		500

Pattern	Stamping	Years Made	Handle	Variation / Blade	Mint Price

4″ Hawkbill

Pattern	Stamping	Years Made	Handle	Variation / Blade	Mint Price
11011	Tested	Prior 1950	Walnut		$100
	XX	1950–1965	Walnut		50
	USA	1965–1970	Walnut		25
	5 Dots	1974	Pakkawood		30
	10 Dots	1970–1971	Walnut		40
	Dots	1970s	Walnut		30
61011	Tested	Prior 1940	Green Bone		150
	XX	1940s	Green Bone		125
	XX	1940s–1965	Bone		50
	XX	1964–1965	Laminated Wood		40
	USA	1965	Bone		100
	USA	1965–1970	Laminated Wood		35
	10 Dots	1970–1971	Laminated Wood		40
	Dots	1970s	Laminated Wood		20
	Lightning S Dots	1980s	Laminated Wood		18

4″ Switchblade

Pattern	Stamping	Years Made	Handle	Variation / Blade	Mint Price
31211½	Tested	Prior 1940	Cream Composition		550

Pattern	Stamping	Years Made	Handle	Variation / Blade	Mint Price
H1211½	Tested	Prior 1940	Brown/ Cream Celluloid		$550

4" Switchblade

Pattern	Stamping	Years Made	Handle	Variation / Blade	Mint Price
31212½	Tested	Prior 1940	Cream Composition		550
R1212½	Tested	Prior 1940	Red/White Celluloid		600

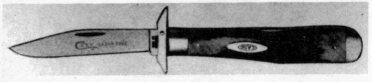

4⅜" Lockback

Pattern	Stamping	Years Made	Handle	Variation / Blade	Mint Price
5111½	8 Dots	1973	Stag	Small Stamp	160
5111½	8 Dots	1973	Stag	Large Stamp	160
5111½	4 Dots	1977	Stag	"Case Razor Edge"	75
5111½	3 Dots	1978	Stag	Blue Scroll	70

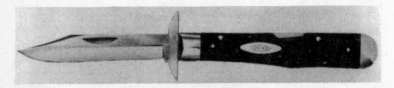

The Cheetahs

Pattern	Stamping	Years Made	Handle	Variation / Blade	Mint Price
3111½	Tested	Prior 1940	Yellow Composition		600
6111½	Tested	Prior 1940	Green Bone		550
6111½	Tested	Prior 1940	Green Bone	Long Pull	600
6111½L	Tested	Prior 1940	Green Bone		550
6111½L	XX	1940–1945	Green Bone		415
6111½L	XX	1955–1965	Bone		110
61111½L	USA	1965	Bone	Pattern No. Factory error	190
6111½I	USA	1965–1970	Bone		70

Pattern	Stamping	Years Made	Handle	Variation / Blade	Mint Price
6111½L	10 Dots	1970–1971	Bone		$70
6111½L	Dots	1970s	Bone		55
6111½L	Dots	1970s	Delrin		45
6111½L	Lightning S 10 Dots	1980	Bone		40

4″ Pruner

61013	Tested	Prior 1940	Green Bone		230

4″ Switchblade

61213½	Tested	Prior 1940	Green Bone		600

4⅛″ Switchblade

61214½	Tested	Prior 1940	Bone		650

Pattern	Stamping	Years Made	Handle	Variation / Blade	Mint Price
61215½	Tested	Prior 1940	Bone	As above except 5" long	$775

5" Switchblade

Pattern	Stamping	Years Made	Handle	Variation / Blade	Mint Price
51215G	Tested	Prior 1940	Bone stag horn		1000
51215½F	Tested	Prior 1940	Bone stag horn	Fish scaler on back	950

3½" Budding Knife

Pattern	Stamping	Years Made	Handle	Variation / Blade	Mint Price
1116SP	XX	1950–1965	Walnut		40
	USA	1965–1970			30
	10 Dots	1970–1971			35
	9 Dots	1971–1972			28

3⅜" Jack

Pattern	Stamping	Years Made	Handle	Variation / Blade	Mint Price
6116½	Tested	Prior 1950	Green Bone		195
6116SP	Tested	Prior 1950	Green Bone		195
6116	Tested		Green Bone		200

3⅛" Wire Jack

Pattern	Stamping	Years Made	Handle	Variation / Blade	Mint Price
W1216	Tested	Prior 1940	Wire	One-piece handle and back	170
W1216K	Tested	Prior 1940	Wire	Cap lifter in blade	170
W1216Pr	Tested	Prior 1940	Wire	Pruner Blade	170
M1217	Tested	Prior 1940	Metal	Pull ball switchblade	185

Pattern	Stamping	Years Made	Handle	Variation / Blade	Mint Price

3″ Pen Knife

Pattern	Stamping	Years Made	Handle	Variation / Blade	Mint Price
M1218K	Tested	Prior 1940		Metal	$150

3″ Jack

Pattern	Stamping	Years Made	Handle	Variation / Blade	Mint Price
3124	Tested	Prior 1950	Yellow Composition		125
6124	Tested	Prior 1950	Green Bone		150
61024	Tested	Prior 1950	Green Bone		170
31024	Tested	Prior 1950	Yellow Composition		135
31024½	XX	1955–1965	Yellow Composition	Also in white-lined yellow	50
61024½	XX	1955–1965	Bone		40
61024½	USA	1965–1967	Bone		40

3¹⁄₁₆″ Jack

Pattern	Stamping	Years Made	Handle	Variation / Blade	Mint Price
11031SH	Tested	Prior 1950	Walnut		125
11031 SH CC	Tested	Prior 1950	Walnut	Concave ground blade	135
11031 SH CC	XX	1950–1952	Walnut	Concave ground blade	50

Pattern	Stamping	Years Made	Handle	Variation / Blade	Mint Price
11031SH	XX	1950–1965	Walnut		$30
	USA	1965–1970	Walnut		25
	10 Dots	1970–1971	Walnut		25
	Dots	1970s	Walnut		18

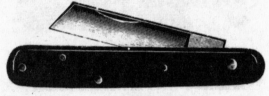

4⅛″ Budding Knife

2136	Tested	Prior 1940	Black Composition	Not made in XX	150

3⅝″ Sodbuster Jr.

2137SS	10 Dots	1970–1971	Black Composition		35
2137SS	Dots	1970s			20
2137SS	Lightning S Dots	1980			18
2137SS	Lightning S Dots	1984			18
2137	10 Dots	1970–1971	Rare		70
2137	Dots	1970s			20
2137	Lightning S Dots	1980			18
2137	Lightning S Dots	1984			18
P137SS		1970s	Pakkawood	Kentucky Bicentennial	35

Pattern	Stamping	Years Made	Handle	Variation / Blade	Mint Price
G137SS		1970s	Green Delrin	Kentucky Bicentennial	$35
5137SS		1970s	Stag	Kentucky Bicentennial	40

5⅝" Sodbuster

Pattern	Stamping	Years Made	Handle	Variation / Blade	Mint Price
2138	USA	1967–1970	Black Composition		30
2138	10 Dots	1970–1971			30
2138	Lightning S 10 Dots	1980			20
2138	Dots	1970s			20
2138	Lightning S Dots				20
2138SS	10 Dots	1970–1971			27
2138SS	Lightning S 10 Dots	1980			20
2138SS	Dots	1970s			20
2138SS	Lightning S Dots				20
2138SSL	10 Dots	1970–1971		Blade locks open	40
2138SL	Dots	1970s		Blade locks open	30
2138LSS	Lightning S 10 Dots	1980			20

Pattern	Stamping	Years Made	Handle	Variation / Blade	Mint Price
2138LSS	Lightning S				$20
P138LSS	Dots	1970s	Alyeska		145

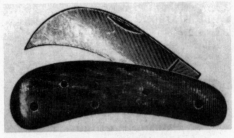

4¼″ Banana Knife

Pattern	Stamping	Years Made	Handle	Variation / Blade	Mint Price
1139	XX	1955–1965	Walnut		150
1139	Tested XX	Prior 1940			185

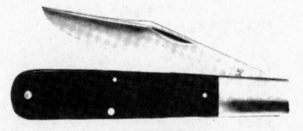

5″ Daddy Barlow

Pattern	Stamping	Years Made	Handle	Variation / Blade	Mint Price
6143	Tested	Prior 1940	Brown Bone		225
6143	XX	1940s	Smooth Black	Iron liners	100
6143	XX	1941s	Green Bone	Iron liners	225
6143	XX	1950–1965	Bone	Iron liners	75
6143	USA	1965–1970	Bone	Iron liners	50
6143	10 Dots	1970–1971	Bone	Iron liners	50
6143	Dots	1970s	Bone	Iron liners	40
6143	Dots	1970s	Delrin	Brass liners	35
6143	Lightning S 10 Dots	1980		Brass liners	32

Pattern	Stamping	Years Made	Handle	Variation / Blade	Mint Price
6143	Lightning S Dots		Delrin		$32

4⅛″ Serpentine Jack

Pattern	Stamping	Years Made	Handle	Variation / Blade	Mint Price
21048LS		1984	Black Composition	Etched	22
31048SHR	XX	1950–1965	Yellow Composition	Florists Knife	55
31048	XX	1950s–1965			45
	USA	1965–1970			40
	10 Dots	1970–1971			25
	Dots	1970s			28
	Lightning S 10 Dots	1980			22
	Lightning S Dots				22
31048SP	XX	1958–1965			50
	USA	1965–1970			40
31048SP	10 Dots	1970–1971			35
	Dot	1971–Oct 1972			25
B1048	Tested XX	Prior 1940	Imitation Onyx		250
61048	Tested	Prior 1940	Green Bone		175
	XX	1940–1955	Green Bone		125
	XX	1950–1965	Red Bone		60
	XX	1950–1965	Bone		40
	USA	1965–1970	Bone		35
	USA	1965–1970	Delrin		30
	10 Dots	1970–1971	Delrin		24
	Dots	1970s	Delrin		15
	Lightning S 10 Dots	1980			20
	Lightning S Dots		Red Bone		45
61048SP	XX	1957–1963	Bone		45

Pattern	Stamping	Years Made	Handle	Variation / Blade	Mint Price
61048SP	XX	1963–1965	Delrin		$35
61048SP	USA	1965–1970	Bone		35
61048SP	USA	1965–1970	Delrin		30
61048SP	10 Dots	1970–1971	Delrin		30
61048SSP	USA	1966–1969	Bone	"Tested XX Stainless"	40
61048SSP	USA	1966–1969	Bone		45
61048SSP	USA	1965–1970	Bone	Blade polished	50
61048SSP	10 Dots	1970–1971	Delrin		25
61048SSP	Dots	1970s	Delrin		20

4 1/16" Serpentine Jack

61049	Tested	Prior 1940	Green Bone		295

5 1/8" Swell Center Hunter

310050	Tested	Prior 1940	Green Composition		450
610050	Tested	Prior 1940	Green Bone Stag		550
B10050	Tested	Prior 1940	Christmas Tree Stripe		850

5 3/8" Swell Center Hunter

C51050-SAB	Tested	Prior 1940	Genuine Stag		1150
C61050-SAB	Tested	Prior 1950	Green Bone		650

Pattern	Stamping	Years Made	Handle	Variation / Blade	Mint Price
C61050-SAB	Tested	Prior 1950	Red Bone		$525
C61050-SAB	XX	1940s	Green Bone		500
C61050-SAB	XX	1950–1965	Red Bone		300
C61050-SAB	XX	1950–1965	Bone		185
C61050-SAB	XX	1964–1965	Laminated Wood		115
C61050-SAB	USA	1965–1970	Laminated Wood		75
C61050-SAB	10 Dots	1970–1971	Laminated Wood		75
C61050-SAB	Dots	1970s	Laminated Wood		55
C61050-SAB	USA		Bone		225

5½" Swell Center Hunter

Pattern	Stamping	Years Made	Handle	Variation / Blade	Mint Price
C61050L	Tested	Prior 1940	Green Bone		2400
C61050L	Dots	1983	Bone	NKCA Club Knife	150

5⅜" Swell Center Hunter

Pattern	Stamping	Years Made	Handle	Variation / Blade	Mint Price
61050	Tested	Prior 1950	Green Bone		500

5⅜" Press Button Slide Blade

Pattern	Stamping	Years Made	Handle	Variation / Blade	Mint Price
PBB1050	Tested	Prior 1940	Imitation Onyx		650
PB31050F	Tested	Prior 1940	Cream Composition	Fish scaler on blade back	550

Pattern	Stamping	Years Made	Handle	Variation/ Blade	Mint Price

5¼" Curved Folding Hunter

Pattern	Stamping	Years Made	Handle	Variation/ Blade	Mint Price
6151	Tested	Prior 1940	Green Bone		$600
6151L	Tested	Prior 1940	Green Bone		600
9151	Tested	Prior 1940	Imitation Pearl		600
8151L	Tested	Prior 1940			1150
6151L-LS	10 Dots	1981	Bone	Case Club Knife	95

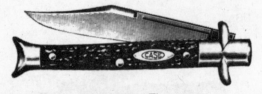

3⅞" Bow Tie

Pattern	Stamping	Years Made	Handle	Variation/ Blade	Mint Price
61051	Tested	Prior 1950	Green Bone		325
B1051	Tested	Prior 1940	Celluloid		300
GS1051	Tested	Prior 1940	Celluloid		300

4⅜" Switchblade

Pattern	Stamping	Years Made	Handle	Variation/ Blade	Mint Price
5161L	Tested	Prior 1940	Stag	4⅜"	1000
6161L	Tested	Prior 1940	Green Bone		1000

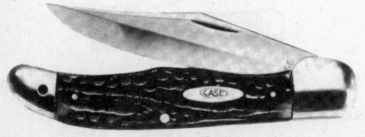

5½" Folding Hunter

Pattern	Stamping	Years Made	Handle	Variation/ Blade	Mint Price
2165		1984	Black Composition	Etched	55

Pattern	Stamping	Years Made	Handle	Variation/Blade	Mint Price
3165	Tested	Prior 1940	Yellow Composition		$450
5165SAB	Tested				375
5165	Tested	Prior 1940	Stag		400
6165	Tested		Green Bone		425
9165	Tested		Imitation Pearl		375
9165SAB	Tested				375
5165	XX	1940s	Stag	Flat Ground Blade	400
5165SAB	XX	1950–1965	Stag	Bolster Drilled	125
5165SAB	XX	1964–1965	Stag	Bolster Not Drilled	125
5165SAB	USA	1965–1968	Stag	Small pattern	325
5165SAB	USA	1965–1966	Stag	Large pattern	325
6165	XX	1940s–1955	Green Bone	Flat Ground Master Blade	325
6165SAB	XX	1940–1955	Green Bone		300
6165SAB	XX	1940s	Rough Black		285
6165SAB	XX	1950–1960	Red Bone		225
6165	XX	1940s	Bone	Flat Ground Master Blade	275
6165SAB	USA		Bone		200
6165SAB	XX	1950–1965	Bone		150
6165SAB	XX	1964–1965	Laminated Wood		100
6165SAB	USA	1965–1966	Laminated Wood	XX Frame Bolster Not Drill	95
	USA	1965–1966	Laminated Wood	XX Frame	75
	USA	1965–1970	Laminated Wood		55

Pattern	Stamping	Years Made	Handle	Variation / Blade	Mint Price
	10 Dots	1970–1971	Laminated Wood		$55
	Dots	1970s	Laminated Wood		45
	Lightning S 10 Dots		Laminated Wood		35
	Lightning Dots	1982	Laminated Wood		35

5½″ Folding Hunter

Pattern	Stamping	Years Made	Handle	Variation / Blade	Mint Price
6165LSSP	2 Dots	1978	Laminated Wood		35
6165LSSP	Lightning S 10 Dots	1982	Laminated Wood		35
6165LSSP	Lightning S Dots				32

5½″ Switchblade

Pattern	Stamping	Years Made	Handle	Variation / Blade	Mint Price
5171L	Tested	Prior 1940	Stag	5⅜″	1250
6171L	Tested	Prior 1940	Green Bone		1250

5½″ Clasp Knife

Pattern	Stamping	Years Made	Handle	Variation / Blade	Mint Price
5172	Tested	Prior 1940	Stag		1500
7172	Tested	Prior 1940	Imitation Tortoise Shell		1200
3172	Tested	Prior 1940	Yellow Composition		1000
6172	Tested	Prior 1940	Green Bone		1500
5172	XX	1950s	Stag	"Hand-made in USA"	250
5172	XX	1957–1965	Stag		225
5172	USA	1965–1970	Stag		200

Pattern	Stamping	Years Made	Handle	Variation / Blade	Mint Price
5172	Transition	1964–1965	Stag		
5172	4 Dots	1978	Stag	Part of	$225
5172	3 Dots	1979	Stag	1978 Set	75
				Blue Scroll	70

5½" Buffalo

Pattern	Stamping	Years Made	Handle	Variation / Blade	Mint Price
P172	USA	1969–1970	Pakkawood		65
	9 Dots	1971–1972	Pakkawood		65
	Dots	1970s			65
	Lightning				
	S 10 Dots				60
M1051L	4 Dots		Metal		15
21051L	4 Dots		Black		
			Composition		15
61051L	4 Dots		Jigged		
			Laminated		
			Wood		15

Mako

Pattern	Stamping	Years Made	Handle	Variation / Blade	Mint Price
P158LSSP	3 Dots	1977	Black Pakkawood		35
5158LSSP	1 Dot	1979	Stag		55
P158LSSP	Lightning S 10 Dots	1980	Pakkawood		55
5158LSSP	Lightning S 10 Dots	1980	Stag		55
5158LSSP	Lightning S 10 Dots	1980s	Stag		40

Hammerhead

Pattern	Stamping	Years Made	Handle	Variation / Blade	Mint Price
2159LSSP	Lightning S 10 Dots				30

Pattern	Stamping	Years Made	Handle	Variation / Blade	Mint Price
5158LSSP	3 Dots	1977	Black Pakkawood		$45
P159LSSP	Lightning S 3 Dots	1977	Black Pakkawood		45
5159LSSP	1 Dot	1979	Stag		75
5159LSSP	Lightning S 10 Dots	1980	Stag		75
5159LSSP			Stag		75

3⅝″ Doctor's Knife

3185	Tested	Prior 1949	Yellow Composition		250
	XX	1950–1965	Yellow Composition		100
	USA	1965–1970	Yellow Composition		75
	10 Dot	1970–1971	Yellow Composition		150
	Dots	1971–1975	Yellow Composition		50
6185	Tested	Prior 1949	Green Bone		290
6185	Tested	Prior 1949	Red Bone		250
	XX	1950–1965	Bone		150
	XX	1950–1965	Bone		95
	USA	1965–1970	Bone		70
	10 Dots	1970–1971	Bone		60
	Dots	1971–1976	Bone		50
	Dots	1971–1976	Delrin		40

Pattern	Stamping	Years Made	Handle	Variation / Blade	Mint Price

5″ Texas Toothpick

Pattern	Stamping	Years Made	Handle	Mint Price
61093	Tested	Prior 1940	Green Bone	$250
R1093	Tested	Prior 1940	Candy Strip Celluloid	325
61093	XX	1940s	Green Bone	200
	XX	1949–1953	Red Bone	125
	XX	1949–1965	Bone	75
31093	XX	1960–1965	Yellow Composition	100
61093	USA	1965–1970	Bone	85
61093	10 Dots	1970–1971	Bone	75
61093	Dots	1970–1975	Bone	55
	Dots	1973–1975	Delrin	45
61093	7 Dots		Bone	85

5″ Texas Toothpick

Pattern	Stamping	Years Made	Handle	Mint Price
31095	Tested	Prior 1940	Yellow Composition	250
R1095	Tested	Prior 1940	Red/White Stripe Celluloid	325
HA1095	Tested	Prior 1940	Picture celluloid	350
61096	Tested			325

4¾″ Sharkstooth

Pattern	Stamping	Years Made	Handle	Mint Price
P197LSS	Dots	1970s	Black Pakkawood	55

Pattern	Stamping	Years Made	Handle	Variation/Blade	Mint Price
P197LSS	Lightning S 10 Dots	1980	Black Pakkawood		$55
P197LSSP	Dots	1980s			55
7197LSS	Dots	1976	Black Pakkawood		65
7197LSSP	8 Dots		Curly Maple		125
7197LSSP	7 Dots		Curly Maple		125
5197LSSP	1 Dot		Stag		85
5197LSSP	Lightning S Dots				85

5½" Texas Toothpick

61098	Tested	Prior 1940	Green Bone		350

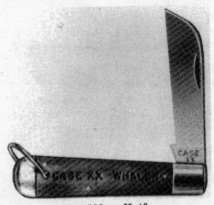

4⅛" Navy Knife

1199 SHRSS	XX	1960–1965	Walnut		30
	USA	1965–1970	Walnut		25
	10 Dots	1970–1971	Walnut		25
	Dots	1970s	Walnut		15
	Lightning S Dots	1980	Walnut		15

Pattern	Stamping	Years Made	Handle	Variation / Blade	Mint Price

5″ Leg Knife

Pattern	Stamping	Years Made	Handle	Variation / Blade	Mint Price
B1097	Tested	Prior 1940	Christmas Tree		$425
RM1097	Tested	Prior 1940	Yellow Composition		350

3⅞″ Muskrat

Pattern	Stamping	Years Made	Handle	Variation / Blade	Mint Price
Musk-rat	Tested	Prior 1940	Green Bone		725
	XX	1940s	Green Bone		325
	XX	1940s	Rough Black		275
	XX	1950s–1965	Red Bone		150
	XX	1950s–1965	Bone		75
	USA	1965–1970	Bone		45
	10 Dots	1970–1971	Bone		45
	Dots	1970s	Bone		40
	2 Dots	1979	Stag	Collector's Set	45
	Lightning S 10 Dots		Bone		35

Pattern	Stamping	Years Made	Handle	Variation / Blade	Mint Price
	Lightning S 10 Dots		Bone		$25

3⅞″ Muskrat Hawbaker Special

Pattern	Stamping	Years Made	Handle	Variation / Blade	Mint Price
	XX	1950–1960s	Bone		350
	USA	1965–1970	Bone		275
	10 Dots	1970–1971	Bone		200
	Dots	1970	Bone		65
	Dots	1970–1973	Delrin		45
	2 to 3 Dots	1978	Bone	1000 made in 1978	45

5½″ Melon Tester

Pattern	Stamping	Years Made	Handle	Variation / Blade	Mint Price
4200SS	XX	1964–1965	White Composition		225
	USA	1965–1970	White Composition		75
	10 Dots	1970–1971	White Composition		75
	Dots	1971–1973	White Composition		65

5½″ Melon Tester Contract Knife

Pattern	Stamping	Years Made	Handle	Variation / Blade	Mint Price
4200SS	USA	Approx. 1965	White Composition	Serrated blades	150

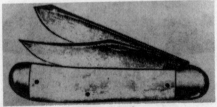

3¹⁵⁄₁₆″ Jack

Pattern	Stamping	Years Made	Handle	Variation / Blade	Mint Price
9200	Tested	Prior 1940	Imitation Pearl		600

Pattern	Stamping	Years Made	Handle	Variation / Blade	Mint Price
5200	Tested	Prior 1940	Genuine Stag		$700
6200	Tested	Prior 1940	Green Bone		700
3200	Tested		Yellow Composition		600

4⅝" Closed

Pattern	Stamping	Years Made	Handle	Variation / Blade	Mint Price
62100	Tested	Prior 1940	Green Bone		750

2⅝" Senator Pen

Pattern	Stamping	Years Made	Handle	Variation / Blade	Mint Price
3201	Tested	Prior 1950	Yellow Composition		100
	XX	1950–1965	Yellow Composition		55
	USA	1965–1970	Yellow Composition		40
	10 Dots	1970–1971	Yellow Composition		40
	Dots	1971–1975	Yellow Composition		22
6201	Tested	Prior 1950	Green Bone		125
	XX	1964–1965	Bone		40
	USA	1965–1970	Bone		30
	10 Dots	1970–1971	Bone		25
	Dots	1970s	Bone		20
		1970s	Delrin		15
9201	Tested	Prior 1950	Cracked Ice		100
	XX	1950–1965	Imitation Pearl		30
	XX	1950–1965	Cracked Ice		35
9201R	XX	1950–1965	Imitation Pearl	Bail in Handle	30
9201R	XX	1950–1965	Cracked Ice	Bail in Handle	35
9201	USA	1965–1970	Imitation Pearl		30

Pattern	Stamping	Years Made	Handle	Variation / Blade	Mint Price
9201	10 Dots	1970–1971	Imitation Pearl		$30
9201	Dots	1970–1975	Imitation Pearl		20

2⅝″ Senator Pen

Pattern	Stamping	Years Made	Handle	Variation / Blade	Mint Price
22001R	Tested	Prior 1940	Black Composition		60
62001	Tested	Prior 1940	Green Bone		125
82001	Tested	Prior 1940	Pearl		150
82001R	Tested	Prior 1940	Pearl		150

2¼″ Lobster Pen

Pattern	Stamping	Years Made	Handle	Variation / Blade	Mint Price
S2	XX	1963–1965	Sterling Silver	Long Pull	150
	XX	1963–1965	Sterling Silver		135
	USA	1965–1968	Sterling Silver		125
S2	Tested				150

2¼″ Sleeveboard Pen

Pattern	Stamping	Years Made	Handle	Variation / Blade	Mint Price
82101R	Tested	Prior 1940	Pearl		150
92101R	Tested	Prior 1940	Imitation Pearl		100

3⅜″ Grafting and Budding Knife

Pattern	Stamping	Years Made	Handle	Variation / Blade	Mint Price
1202 D&B	Tested	Prior 1940	Cocobolo		425

3⅜″ Jack

Pattern	Stamping	Years Made	Handle	Variation / Blade	Mint Price
5202RAZ	Tested	Prior 1940	Stag		400

Pattern	Stamping	Years Made	Handle	Variation / Blade	Mint Price
5202½	Tested	Prior 1940	Stag		$250
6202	Tested	Prior 1940	Green Bone		175
6202½	Tested	Prior 1940	Green Bone		175
6202½XX		1940–1965	Green Bone		100
2202½	XX	1940s	Black Composition		125
6202½	XX	1940–1955	Bone		45
6202½ USA		1965–1970	Bone		35
6202½ 10 Dots		1970–1971	Bone		35
6202½ 10 Dots		1970–1971	Delrin		30
6202½ Dots		1970s	Delrin		18

1¾″ Pen Knife

Pattern	Stamping	Years Made	Handle	Variation / Blade	Mint Price
82103	Tested	Prior 1940	Pearl		150
82103R	Tested	Prior 1940	Pearl		150

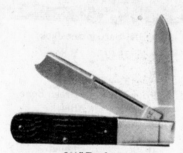

3¾″ Barlow

Pattern	Stamping	Years Made	Handle	Variation / Blade	Mint Price
6205	Tested	Prior 1950	Green Bone		350
5202	Tested	Prior 1950	Stag		350
6205½	Tested	Prior 1950	Green Bone		350
5202½	Tested	Prior 1950	Stag		350
5205RAZ	Tested	Prior 1950	Stag		350
6205RAZ	Tested	Prior 1950	Green Bone		350
6205	XX	1950s	Green Bone		200
6205	XX	1950s	Bone		100
6205RAZ	XX	1950s	Green Bone		225
6205RAZ	XX	1950–1965	Bone		75
6205RAZ	USA	1965–1970	Bone		75
6205RAZ	10 Dots	1970–1971	Bone		75

Pattern	Stamping	Years Made	Handle	Variation / Blade	Mint Price
6205RAZ	Dots	1970s	Bone		$55
6202RAZ	Dots	1970s	Delrin		35

2⅝″ Jack

Pattern	Stamping	Years Made	Handle	Variation / Blade	Mint Price
5206½	Tested	Prior 1940	Green Stag		175
6206½	Tested	Prior 1940	Green Bone		160
6206½	Tested	1940s	Rough Black		125
6206½	XX	Early 1950s	Rough Black		100

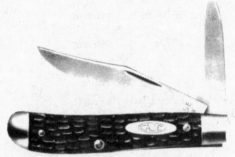

3½″ Serpentine Jack

Pattern	Stamping	Years Made	Handle	Variation / Blade	Mint Price
3207	Tested	Prior 1940	Yellow Composition		325
5207	Tested	Prior 1940	Stag		325
6207	Tested	Prior 1940	Green Bone		300
2207	XX	1940s	Black Composition		300
6207	XX	1940s	Green Bone		265
	XX	1940s	Rough Black		225
	XX	1940–1955	Red Bone		130
	XX	1950–1965	Bone		65
	USA	1965–1970	Bone		45
	10 Dots	1970–1971	Bone		45
	Dots	1970s	Bone		30
	Dots	1970s	Delrin		20
6207SSP	Lightning S 10 Dots	1980	Bone	Mini Trapper	20
6207SSP	Lightning S Dots	1980s	Bone		20

Pattern	Stamping	Years Made	Handle	Variation / Blade	Mint Price

3¼″ Half Whittler

Pattern	Stamping	Years Made	Handle	Variation / Blade	Mint Price
5208	Tested	Prior 1940	Stag		$200
6208	Tested	Prior 1940	Green Bone		150
6208	XX	1950–1953	Green Bone		125
	XX	1950–1955	Rough Black		60
	XX	1950–1965	Bone		40
6208	USA	1965–1970	Bone		35
	10 Dots	1970–1971	Bone		35
	Dots	1970–1979	Bone		30
	Dots	1970–1979	Delrin		15
A6208	1 Dot	1979	Bone		20
A6208	Lightning	1980	Bone		
	S 10 Dots				20

3⅛″ Baby Copperhead

Pattern	Stamping	Years Made	Handle	Variation / Blade	Mint Price
62109	Tested		Green Bone		410
62109X	XX	1940–1951	Rough Black		125
	XX	1940–1965	Green Bone		150
	XX	1950–1955	Bone		65
	USA	1965–1970	Bone		45
	10 Dots	1970	Bone		45
	Dots	1971	Bone		35
	Dots		Delrin		30
	Lightning	1980	Bone		
	S 10 Dots				25

Pattern	Stamping	Years Made	Handle	Variation / Blade	Mint Price

3⁵⁄₁₆″ Barlow

Pattern	Stamping	Years Made	Handle	Variation / Blade	Mint Price
62009SH	Tested	Prior 1940	Brown Bone		$195
62009SH	XX	1940–1945	Black Composition	3⁵⁄₁₆″	125
62009SP	Tested	Prior 1940	Brown Bone		185
62009	Tested	Prior 1940	Brown Bone		165
62009	XX	1940–1945	Black Composition	3⁵⁄₁₆″	100
62009	XX	Early 1950s	Green Bone		125
	XX	1940–1945	Red Bone		75
	XX	1940–1965	Bone		50
	USA	1965–1970	Bone	Master Blade in Front	40
	USA	1965–1970	Bone	Master Blade in Back	40
	10 Dots	1970–1971	Bone		40
	10 Dots	1970–1971	Delrin		40
	Dots	1970–1976	Delrin		20
62009½	Tested	Prior 1940	Green Bone		175
	XX	1940s	Black Composition	3⁵⁄₁₆″	100
	XX	1950–1955	Green Bone		125
	XX	1945–1955	Red Bone		75
	XX	1950–1965	Bone		50

Pattern	Stamping	Years Made	Handle	Variation / Blade	Mint Price
	USA	1965–1970	Bone	Master Blade in Front	40
	USA	1965–1970	Bone	Master Blade in Back	40
	10 Dots	1970–1971	Bone		40
	10 Dots	1970–1971	Delrin	62009½	40
	Dots	1970s	Delrin		20
A62009½	1 Dot	1979	Slick Bone		25
A62009½	Lightning S 10 Dots		Slick Bone		25
A62009½ SS	Lightning S Dots				25
62009RAZ	Tested	Prior 1940	Green Bone		250
	XX	1940–1955	Green Bone		200
	XX	1955–1965	Bone	Long Pull	90
	XX	1955–1965	Bone		75
	USA	1965–1970	Bone	Master Blade in Front	60
	USA	1965–1970	Bone	Master Blade in Back	60
	10 Dots	1970–1971	Bone		60
	10 Dots	1970–1971	Delrin		60
	Dots	1970s	Delrin		20

3⅜″ Switchblade

| 62210 | Tested | Prior 1940 | Green Bone | | 450 |
| 92210 | Tested | Prior 1940 | Imitation Pearl | | 450 |

Pattern	Stamping	Years Made	Handle	Variation / Blade	Mint Price
H2210	Tested	Prior 1940	Brown/ Cream Composition		$450
T2210	Tested	Prior 1940	Tortoise Shell Composition		450

3⅛″ Sleeveboard Jack

5210½	Tested	Prior 1940	Stag		210
6210½	Tested	Prior 1940	Green Bone		200

4⅜″ Slim Jack

5211	Tested	Prior 1940	Genuine Stag		700
6211	Tested	Prior 1940	Green Bone		500
6211½	Tested	Prior 1940	Green		475

3⅝″ Electrician Knife

2212L	Tested	Prior 1940	Walnut		150

4″ Swell Center Jack

6213	Tested	Prior 1940	Green Bone		375

Pattern	Stamping	Years Made	Handle	Variation / Blade	Mint Price

3⅜″ Jack

Pattern	Stamping	Years Made	Handle	Variation / Blade	Mint Price
6214	Tested	Prior 1940	Green Bone		$160
6214	XX	1940–1955	Green Bone		120
	XX	1940s	Rough Black	With Shield	60
	XX	1940s	Rough Black	Without Shield	50
	XX	1950–1965	Bone		35
	USA	1965–1970	Bone		30
	10 Dots	1970–1971	Bone		35
	10 Dots	1970–1971	Delrin		25
	Dots	1970s	Delrin		25
5214½	Tested	Prior 1940	Stag		225
6214½	Tested	Prior 1940	Green Bone		160
	XX	1940–1955	Green Bone		100
	XX	1940s	Rough Black		70
	XX	1955–1965	Bone		35
	USA	1965–1970	Bone		30
	10 Dots	1970–1971	Bone		30
	10 Dots	1970–1971	Delrin		25
	Dots	1970s	Delrin		20

3⅜″ Jack

Pattern	Stamping	Years Made	Handle	Variation / Blade	Mint Price
6216	Tested	Prior 1950	Green Bone		175
6216	XX	1964–1965	Bone		75

Pattern	Stamping	Years Made	Handle	Variation / Blade	Mint Price
6216½	Tested	Prior 1950	Green Bone		$185
6216½	XX	1964–1965	Bone		40
6216½	USA	1965–1967	Bone		35

4″ Curved Jack

Pattern	Stamping	Years Made	Handle	Variation / Blade	Mint Price
2217	Tested	Prior 1940	Black Composition		250
6217	Tested	Prior 1940	Green Bone		250
6217	XX	1940s	Black Composition		225
	XX	1940–1955	Green Bone		175
	XX	1950–1965	Red Bone		100
	XX	1950–1955	Bone		50
	USA	1965–1970	Bone		50
	USA	1965–1970	Wood		50
6217	10 Dots	1970–1971	Laminated Wood		50
	10 Dots	1970–1971	Bone		50
	Dots	1970s	Laminated Wood		30

4⅛″ Slim Jack

Pattern	Stamping	Years Made	Handle	Variation / Blade	Mint Price
62019	Tested	Prior 1940	Green Bone		375

Pattern	Stamping	Years Made	Handle	Variation / Blade	Mint Price

2¾″ Peanut

Pattern	Stamping	Years Made	Handle	Variation / Blade	Mint Price
2220	Tested	Prior 1950	Black Composition		$225
	XX	1950–1965	Black Composition		50
	USA	1965–1970	Black Composition		50
	10 Dots	1970–1971	Black Composition		50
	Dots	1970–1975	Black Composition		35
3220	Tested	Prior 1950	Yellow Composition		225
	XX	1950–1965	Yellow Composition		70
	USA	1965–1970	Yellow Composition		65
	10 Dots	1970–1971	Yellow Composition		65
	Dots	1971–1975	Yellow Composition		35
5220	Tested	Prior 1950	Stag		275
	XX	1950–1965	Stag		75
	USA	1965–1970	Stag		50
	10 Dots	1970–1971	Stag		50
	2 Dots	1979	Red Scroll		35
6220	Tested	Prior 1950	Green Bone	Saber Ground	360
	XX	1950–1965	Green Bone		200
	XX	1940s	Rough Black		150
	XX	1950–1965	Red Bone		100
	XX	1950–1965	Bone		50
	USA	1965–1970	Bone		45

Pattern	Stamping	Years Made	Handle	Variation / Blade	Mint Price
	10 Dots	1970–1971	Bone		$45
	10 Dots	1970–1971	Delrin		75
	9 Dots	1971–1972	Bone		100
	Dots	1970s	Delrin		20
A6620	Dots	1979	Bone "Appaloosa"		35
SR6220	1 Dot	1979	Red Bone "Slick Bone"		30
SR6620	Lightning S 10 Dots				25
8220	Tested	Prior 1950	Pearl		450
9220	Tested	Prior 1950	Imitation Pearl		225
	XX	1950–1965	Cracked Ice		125
	XX	1950–1965	Imitation Pearl		125

3¼" Wharncliffe

Pattern	Stamping	Years Made	Handle	Variation / Blade	Mint Price
0221½	Tested	Prior 1940	Black Composition		200
06221½	Tested	Prior 1940	Green Bone		225

3" Jack

Pattern	Stamping	Years Made	Handle	Variation / Blade	Mint Price
220024SP	XX	1959–1968	Black Composition		875
Without Box					225

3″ Jack

Pattern	Stamping	Years Made	Handle	Variation / Blade	Mint Price
2224SH	Tested	Prior 1940	Black Composition		$200
2224RAZ	Tested	Prior 1940	Black Composition		250
2224SP	XX	1940s	Black Composition		150
2224SH	XX	1940s	Black Composition		150
2224RAZ	XX	1940s	Black Composition		175
3324	Tested	Prior 1940	Yellow Composition		150
3224½	Tested	Prior 1940	Yellow Composition		150
5224½	Tested	Prior 1940	Stag		175
32024½	XX	1957–1965	Yellow Composition		50
32024½	USA	1965–1968	Yellow Composition		40
52024½	Tested	Prior 1940	Stag		200
62024	Tested	Prior 1940	Green Bone		150
62024RAZ	Tested	Prior 1940	Green Bone		225
62024½	Tested	Prior 1940	Green Bone		150
62024½	XX	1950–1965	Green Bone		100
62024½	XX	1955–1965	Bone		40
62024½	USA	1965–1968	Bone		35

3″ Coke Bottle

Pattern	Stamping	Years Made	Handle	Variation / Blade	Mint Price
5225½	Tested	Prior 1940	Stag		235

Pattern	Stamping	Years Made	Handle	Variation / Blade	Mint Price
6225½	Tested	Prior 1940	Green Bone		$210
6225½	XX	1940–1955	Green Bone		175
6225½	XX	1942–1950	Rough Black		140
6225½	XX	1950–1965	Bone		50
6225½	USA	1965–1970	Bone		45
6225½	10 Dots	1970–1971	Bone		45
6225½	Dots	1970s	Bone		30
6225½	Dots	1970s	Delrin		25
SR6225½	1 Dot	1979	S. Bone		25
SR6225½	Lightning S 10 Dots	1980	S. Bone		25
32025½	Tested	Prior 1940	Yellow Composition		225
62025½	Tested	Prior 1940	Green Bone		250

3″ Jack

6226½	Tested	Prior 1940	Green Bone		275
6227	XX	1955–1965	Bone		40
	USA	1965–1970	Bone		30
	10 Dots	1970–1971	Bone		30
	10 Dots	1970–1971	Delrin		30
	Dots	1970s	Delrin		20
62027	Dots	1978–1979	Delrin		18
SR62027	1 Dot	1979	Red Bone		25
SR62027	Lightning S 10 Dots				25

Pattern	Stamping	Years Made	Handle	Variation / Blade	Mint Price

2¾″ Sleeveboard

Pattern	Stamping	Years Made	Handle	Variation / Blade	Mint Price
62027	Tested	Prior 1950	Green Bone		$140
62027½	Tested	Prior 1950	Green Bone		140
62027½	XX	1960–1965	Bone		45
92027	Tested	Prior 1950	Imitation Pearl		130
92027½	Tested	Prior 1950	Imitation Pearl		135
92027½	XX	1950	Cracked Ice		90

3½″ Easy Open Jack

Pattern	Stamping	Years Made	Handle	Variation / Blade	Mint Price
6228EO	Tested	Prior 1950	Green Bone		225
2228EO	Tested	Prior 1950	Black Composition		175
6228EO	XX	Early 1950	Red Bone		160

3½″ Serpentine Jack

Pattern	Stamping	Years Made	Handle	Variation / Blade	Mint Price
22028	Tested	Prior 1940	Black Composition		150

Pattern	Stamping	Years Made	Handle	Variation / Blade	Mint Price
62028	Tested	Prior 1940	Green Bone		$175
62028½	Tested	Prior 1940	Green Bone		175
62028½	XX	1950–1965	Black Composition		100
62028½	XX	1940s	Rough Black		125

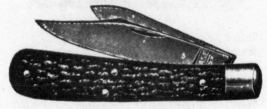

2½″ Curved Jack

Pattern	Stamping	Years Made	Handle	Variation / Blade	Mint Price
6229½	Tested	Prior 1940	Green Bone		135
9229½	Tested	Prior 1940	Imitation Pearl		175
9229½	XX	1940–1955	Imitation Pearl		125
2229½	XX	1958–1965	Black Composition		50
6229½	XX	1960–1965	Bone		45
6229½	USA	1965–1967	Bone		40
8229½	Tested	Prior 1940	Mother-of-Pearl		250
2229½	USA		Black Composition		125
B229½R	Tested	Prior 1940	Waterfall		140

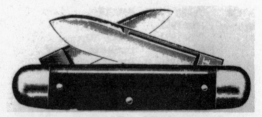

3¼″ Equal End

Pattern	Stamping	Years Made	Handle	Variation / Blade	Mint Price
02230	Tested	Prior 1940	Black Composition		125
2230½	Tested	Prior 1940	Black Composition		125

Pattern	Stamping	Years Made	Handle	Variation / Blade	Mint Price
05230½	Tested	Prior 1940	Stag		$200
06230	Tested	Prior 1940	Green Bone		180
06230½	Tested	Prior 1940	Green Bone		180
06230SP	Tested	Prior 1940	Green Bone		190
06230SH	Tested	Prior 1940	Green Bone		190
09230	Tested	Prior 1940	Cracked Ice		200

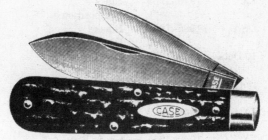

3¾″ Jack

Pattern	Stamping	Years Made	Handle	Variation / Blade	Mint Price
6231	Tested	Prior 1940	Green Bone	Long Pull	150
6231	XX	1940–1955	Green Bone		130
	XX	1940s	Green Bone	Long Pull	145
	XX	1950–1965	Red Bone		95
	XX	1940s	Rough Black		95
	XX	1950–1965	Bone		50
62031	XX	1940–1955	Green Bone		140
	XX	1940s	Green Bone	Long Pull	155
	XX	1950–1965	Red Bone		80
	XX	1940s	Rough Black		95
	XX	1940s	Rough Black	Long Pull	100
22031½	Tested	Prior 1940	Black Composition		150
22031½	XX	Prior 1940	Black Composition		75
52031	Tested	Prior 1940	Stag		225
52031½	Tested	Prior 1940	Stag		235
62031	Tested	Prior 1940	Green Bone		175
62031½	Tested	Prior 1940	Green Bone		175
62031½	XX	1940–1955	Green Bone		160
62031½	XX	1940s	Rough Black		95
62031½	XX	1950–1960	Bone		55

Pattern	Stamping	Years Made	Handle	Variation / Blade	Mint Price
2231½	Tested	Prior 1940	Black Composition		$175
2231½	XX	1940–1954	Black Composition		80
2231½ SAB	Tested	Prior 1940	Black Composition		170
2231½ SAB	XX	1940–1965	Black Composition		75
2231½ SAB	USA	1965–1970	Black Composition		40
2231½ SAB	10 Dots	1970–1971	Black Composition		40
2231½ SAB	Dots	1970s	Black Composition		30
4231½	XX	1948–1949	White Composition		190
6231½	XX	1940–1955	Green Bone		125
	XX	1950–1965	Red Bone		75
	XX	1940s	Rough Black		95
	XX	1950–1965	Bone		50
	USA	1965–1970	Bone		30
	10 Dots	1970–1971	Bone		30
	Dots	1970s	Bone		20
	Lightning	1980			
	S 10 Dots				20

3¹¹⁄₁₆″ Electrician Knife

12031	Tested	Prior 1950	Walnut		100
	XX	1950–1965	Walnut		35

Pattern	Stamping	Years Made	Handle	Variation / Blade	Mint Price
	USA	1965–1970			$30
	10 Dots	1970–1971			30
	Dots	1970s			25
12031LHR	Dots	1978		Hawk-bill blade	20

3⅝″ Canoe

Pattern	Stamping	Years Made	Handle	Variation / Blade	Mint Price
52131	Tested	Prior 1940	Stag		375
52131	XX	1940–1950	Stag	Long Pull	260
52131	XX	1950–1965	Stag		125
52131	USA	1965–1970	Stag		100
52131	10 Dots	1970–1971	Stag		100
52131SS	3 Dots	1978	Genuine Stag	Blue Scroll	50
62131	XX	1966	Bone		200
62131	USA	1966–1970	Bone		50
62131	10 Dots	1970–1971	Bone		50
62131	Dots	1970s	Bone		35
62131	Dots	1970s	Bone	"Canoe" etching	35
	Lightning S	1980	Bone		25

3⅝″ Premium Jack

Pattern	Stamping	Years Made	Handle	Variation / Blade	Mint Price
3232	Tested	Prior 1940	Yellow Composition		150

Pattern	Stamping	Years Made	Handle	Variation / Blade	Mint Price
5232	XX	1960–1965	Stag		$75
	USA	1965–1970	Stag		50
	10 Dots	1970–1971	Stag		50
	9 Dots	1973	Stag	From collector sets	40
5232	2 Dots	1979	Stag	From collector sets	40
6232	Tested	Prior 1940	Green Bone		135
	XX	1940–1955	Green Bone		100
	XX	1950–1965	Red Bone		55
	XX	1940s	Rough Black		90
	XX	1950–1965	Bone		40
	USA	1965–1970	Bone		40
	10 Dots	1970–1971	Bone		35
	Dots	1970s	Bone		30
	Dots	1970s	Delrin		25
	Lightning	1980	Bone		
	S 10 Dots				20

2⅝″ Pen

Pattern	Stamping	Years Made	Handle	Variation / Blade	Mint Price
G5233	Tested	Prior 1950	Gold Metal Flake		300
3233	Tested	Prior 1950	Yellow Composition		150
	XX	1950–1965			45
	USA	1965–1970			35
	10 Dots	1970–1971			35
	Dots	1971–1975			30
5233	XX	1960–1965	Stag		50
	USA	1965–1970	Stag		40
	10 Dots	1970–1971	Stag		40
5233SSP	4 Dots	1977	Stag		35

Pattern	Stamping	Years Made	Handle	Variation / Blade	Mint Price
5233SSP	3 Dots	1978	Stag		$35
52033SSP	3 Dots	1978	Stag		65
6233	Tested	Prior 1940	Rough Black		140
6233	XX	1940s	Rough Black		120
6233	XX	1940s	Rough Black	Long Pull	135
	Tested	Prior 1940	Green Bone		200
	XX	1940–1955	Green Bone		150
	XX	1940–1955	Green Bone	Long Pull	175
	XX	1950–1965	Bone		45
	USA	1965–1970	Bone		35
	10 Dots	1970–1971	Bone		35
	10 Dots	1970–1971	Delrin		70
	Dots	1970s	Delrin		25
62033	Dots	1976	Delrin		18
62033	Dots	1976–1979	Delrin		18
A62033	1 Dot	1979	Smooth Bone		25
A62033	Lightning S 10 Dots		Smooth Bone		25
8233	Tested	Prior 1940	Pearl		240
	XX	1960–1965	Pearl		50
	USA	1965–1970	Pearl		40
	10 Dots	1970–1971	Pearl		40
	Dots	1970–1975	Pearl		35
9233	Tested	Prior 1950	Imitation Pearl		145
	XX	1950–1965	Cracked Ice	Shad, no bolsters	250
	XX	1950–1965	Imitation Pearl		65
	XX	1950–1965	Cracked Ice		50
	XX	1950–1965	Cracked Ice		85
	USA	1965–1970	Imitation Pearl		35
	10 Dots	1970–1971	Imitation Pearl		35
	Dots	1970s	Imitation Pearl		25

Pattern	Stamping	Years Made	Handle	Variation / Blade	Mint Price
92033	Dots	1976	Cracked Ice		$25

3⅝" Premium Stock

Pattern	Stamping	Years Made	Handle	Variation / Blade	Mint Price
5234	Tested	Prior 1940	Stag		500

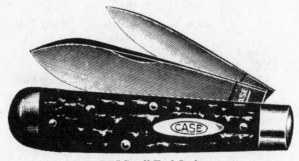

3¼" Swell End Jack

Pattern	Stamping	Years Made	Handle	Variation / Blade	Mint Price
6235EO	Tested	Prior 1940	Green Bone	Easy Open	175
6235EO	XX	1940–1950	Bone	Easy Open	150
6235EO	XX	1940s	Rough Black	Easy Open	150
6235	Tested	Prior 1940	Green Bone		125
	XX	1940–1955	Green Bone		100
	XX	1940s	Rough Black	With Shield	50
	XX	1940s	Rough Black	Without Shield	50
	XX	1950–1965	Bone		40
6235SH	Tested	Prior 1940	Green Bone		150
3235½	Tested	Prior 1940	Yellow Composition		140
5235½	Tested	Prior 1940	Stag		150
6235½P	Tested	Prior 1940	Green Bone		200
6235½	Tested	Prior 1940	Green Bone		125
	XX	1940–1955	Green Bone		100
	XX	1940s	Rough Black	With Shield	50
	XX	1940s	Rough Black	Without Shield	50
	XX	1950–1965	Bone		40
	USA	1965–1970	Bone		30
	10 Dots	1970–1971	Bone		30
	Dots	1970s	Bone		28

Pattern	Stamping	Years Made	Handle	Variation / Blade	Mint Price
62035½	Tested	Prior 1940	Green Bone		$145
A6235½	1 Dot	1979	Smooth Bone		35
A6235½	Lightning S 10 Dots	1980	Smooth Bone		35
A6235½SS	Lightning S 10 Dots	1980	Smooth Bone		35

3¼" Jack Knife

Pattern	Stamping	Years Made	Handle	Variation / Blade	Mint Price
620035	XX	1950–1960	Black Plastic	Standard Long Pull	40
620035½	XX	1950–1960	Black Plastic	Standard Long Pull	40
620035EO	XX	1945–1950	Black Plastic	Standard Long Pull	100

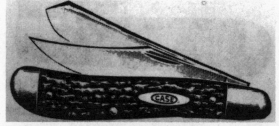

4⁷⁄₁₆" Serpentine Jack

Pattern	Stamping	Years Made	Handle	Variation / Blade	Mint Price
6240	Tested	Prior 1940	Green Bone		500
6240SP	Tested	Prior 1940	Green Bone		600

Pattern	Stamping	Years Made	Handle	Variation / Blade	Mint Price

3″ Pen Knife

Pattern	Stamping	Years Made	Handle	Variation / Blade	Mint Price
6237½	Tested				$300
52042	Tested	Prior 1940	Stag		140
62042	Tested	Prior 1940	Green Bone		125
62042	XX	1940–1955	Green Bone		75
	XX	1940s	Rough Black		50
	XX	1950–1965	Bone		40
	USA	1965–1970	Bone		30
	10 Dots	1970–1971	Bone		30
	Dots	1970s	Bone		25
	Dots	1970s	Delrin		20
62042R	XX	1957–1965	Bone	Bail in Handle	40
	USA	1965–1970	Bone		30
	10 Dots	1970	Bone		30
82042	Tested	Prior 1940	Pearl		250
92042	Tested	Prior 1940	Imitation Pearl		100
92042	XX	1940–1965	Imitation Pearl		35
	XX	1940–1965	Cracked Ice		35
	USA	1965–1970	Imitation Pearl		30
	10 Dots	1970–1971	Imitation Pearl		30
	Dots	1970s	Imitation Pearl		25
92042R	XX	1957–1965	Imitation Pearl	Bail in Handle	40
	XX	1957–1965	Cracked Ice	Bail in Handle	35

Pattern	Stamping	Years Made	Handle	Variation / Blade	Mint Price
	USA	1965–1970	Imitation Pearl	Bail in Handle	$30
	10 Dots	1970	Imitation Pearl		30
A62042	1 Dot	1979	Smooth Bone		28
A62042	Lightning S 10 Dots	1980	Smooth Bone		28
52042R	Lightning S Dots		Stag		35

3¼″ Premium Jack

Pattern	Stamping	Years Made	Handle	Variation / Blade	Mint Price
3244	Tested	Prior 1940	Yellow Composition		125
3244	5 Dots	1976	Acorn Shop		28
5244	Tested	Prior 1940	Stag		150
6244	Tested	Prior 1940	Green Bone		125
9244	Tested	Prior 1940	Imitation Pearl		125
6244	XX	1955–1965	Bone		45
6244	USA	1965–1970	Bone		30
6244	10 Dots	1970–1971	Bone		30
6244	10 Dots	1970–1971	Delrin		28
6244	Dots	1970s	Delrin		25
SR-6244	1 Dot	1979	Smooth Bone		24
SR-6244	Lightning S 10 Dots	1980	Smooth Bone		24
SR-6244SS	Lightning S Dots		Smooth Bone		24

Pattern	Stamping	Years Made	Handle	Variation / Blade	Mint Price

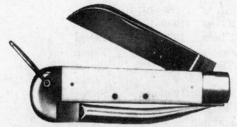

3¼″ Pen

Pattern	Stamping	Years Made	Handle	Variation / Blade	Mint Price
05244	Tested	Prior 1940	Stag		$140
06244	Tested	Prior 1940	Green Bone		125
06244	XX	1940–1955	Green Bone		75
06244	XX	1950–1965	Red Bone		50
06244	XX	1950–1965	Bone		35
06244	USA	1965–1970	Bone		30
06244	10 Dots	1970–1971	Bone		30
	10 Dots	1970–1971	Delrin		25
	9 Dots	1971–1972	Bone		20
	Dots	1970s	Delrin		18

3¼″ Pen

Pattern	Stamping	Years Made	Handle	Variation / Blade	Mint Price
82044	Tested	Prior 1940	Pearl		200

3¼″ Grafting Knife

Pattern	Stamping	Years Made	Handle	Variation / Blade	Mint Price
2245SHSP	XX	1960–1965	Black Composition		100

3⅝″ Equal End

Pattern	Stamping	Years Made	Handle	Variation / Blade	Mint Price
6245DG	Tested	Prior 1940	Green Bone	Dog Grooming Knife	375
06245	Tested	Prior 1940	Green Bone	Long Pull	175
06245	XX	Prior 1940	Green Bone	Long Pull	150
06245½	Tested			Long Pull	250

4⅜″ Riggers Knife

Pattern	Stamping	Years Made	Handle	Variation / Blade	Mint Price
3246	Tested	Prior 1940	Yellow Composition		250

Pattern	Stamping	Years Made	Handle	Variation / Blade	Mint Price
3246R	XX	1940–1952	Yellow Composition		$150
3246SS	XX	1950–1965	Yellow Composition		75
3246SS	USA		Yellow Composition		225
6246SS	Tested	Prior 1940	Green Bone		225
6246SS	XX	1963–1965	Bone		100
6246SS	USA	1965–1970	Bone		50
6246SS	10 Dots	1970–1971	Bone		50
6246SS	Dots	1970s	Bone		40
6246RSS	Lightning S 10 Dots		Delrin		35

4″ Greenskeeper Knife

Pattern	Stamping	Years Made	Handle	Variation / Blade	Mint Price
4247K	Dots	1970	White Composition		300
	10 Dots				300
4247K	USA	1965–1970			300
4247K	XX	Prior 1965			300

3⅞″ Moose

Pattern	Stamping	Years Made	Handle	Variation / Blade	Mint Price
6247J	Tested	Prior 1940	Green Bone		500
5247J	Tested	Prior 1940	Stag		550

Pattern	Stamping	Years Made	Handle	Variation / Blade	Mint Price

3⅞" Premium

Pattern	Stamping	Years Made	Handle	Variation / Blade	Mint Price
04247SP	Tested	Prior 1940	White Composition		$125
05247SP	Tested	Prior 1940	Stag		175
06247SP	Tested	Prior 1940	Green Bone		145
06247PEN	Tested	Prior 1940	Green Bone		145
05247SP	XX	1940–1965	Stag		125
05247SP	USA	1965–1966	Stag		150
04247SP	XX	1940–1965	White Composition		100
04247SP	USA	1965–1966	White Composition		100
06247PEN	XX	1940–1955	Green Bone		125
	XX	1940s	Rough Black		100
	XX	1940–1965	Bone		45
	USA	1965–1970	Bone		40
	10 Dots	1970–1971	Bone		40
	Dots	1970s	Bone		30
	Dots	1970s	Delrin		25
	Lightning	1980	Bone		
	S 10 Dots				25

Pattern	Stamping	Years Made	Handle	Variation / Blade	Mint Price

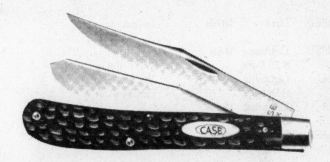

4″ Slim Serpentine Jack

Pattern	Stamping	Years Made	Handle	Variation / Blade	Mint Price
32048SP	XX	1949–1965	Yellow Composition		$50
	USA	1965–1970	Yellow Composition		30
	10 Dots	1970–1971	Yellow Composition		30
	Dots	1970s	Yellow Composition		25
62048	Tested	Prior 1940	Green Bone		160
62048SP	Tested	Prior 1940	Imitation Onyx		275
62048SP	Tested	Prior 1940	Green Bone		200
	XX	1940–1955	Green Bone		140
	XX	1950–1965	Bone		40
	USA	1965–1969	Bone		35
	USA	1969–1970	Delrin		30
	10 Dots	1970–1971	Delrin		30
	Dots	1970s	Delrin		25
62048 SP SSP	USA	1966–1967	Bone	"Tested XX Stainless"	50
62048SP SSP	USA	1967–1969	Bone	"Tested XX Razor Edge"	40
62048SP SSP	USA	1967–1969	Bone	"Tested XX Razor Edge"	50
62048	10 Dots		Bone		75
62048SP SSP	USA	1966–1970	Delrin		28

Pattern	Stamping	Years Made	Handle	Variation / Blade	Mint Price
62048SP SSP	10 Dots	1970–1971	Delrin		$28
62048SP SSP	Dots	1970s	Delrin		20
62048SP SSP	Lightning S 10 Dots	1980	Delrin		20
32048	Lightning S Dots	1980s	Yellow Composition		20
62048	Lightning S Dots	1980s			22
62048SS	Lightning S Dots	1980s			25

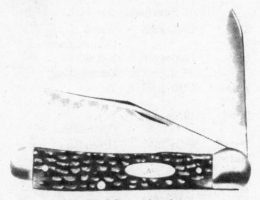

3⁵⁄₁₆″ Copperhead

6249	Tested	Prior 1940	Green Bone		325
	XX	1940–1955	Green Bone		300
	XX	1950s–1965	Bone		75
	USA	1965–1970	Bone		50
	10 Dots	1970–1971	Bone		50
	Dots	1970s	Bone		35
	Dots	1 970s	Delrin		30
	Lightning S		Bone		25
	1 Dot		Stag		40

6¾″ Knife & Fork Combo

6251 CLASP	Tested	Prior 1940	Green Bone	Knife/ Fork	550

Pattern	Stamping	Years Made	Handle	Variation / Blade	Mint Price
9251	Tested	Prior 1940	Imitation Pearl	Knife/ Fork	$600
	Lightning S Dots	1983	Bone	Case Club Knife	95

4⅜″ Sunfish

Pattern	Stamping	Years Made	Handle	Variation / Blade	Mint Price
6250	Tested	Prior 1940	Green Bone		500
	XX	1940–1955	Green Bone		450
	XX	1940–1965	Red Bone		285
	XX	1940–1965	Bone		140
	XX	1964–1965	Laminated Wood		90
	USA	1964–1965	Bone		225
	USA	1965–1970	Laminated Wood		65
	10 Dots	1970–1971	Laminated Wood		65
	Dots	1970s	Laminated Wood		50
	Dots	1970s	Laminated Wood	Elephant etching	50
	1 Dot	1979	Laminated Wood	"Bradford Bonanza"	50
	Lightning S 10 Dots		Laminated Wood		50

3¾″ Hobo

Pattern	Stamping	Years Made	Handle	Variation / Blade	Mint Price
6252	Tested	Prior 1940	Green Bone		350

Pattern	Stamping	Years Made	Handle	Variation / Blade	Mint Price
3252	Tested	Prior 1940	Composition Ivory handles		$350

3½″ Congress

Pattern	Stamping	Years Made	Handle	Variation / Blade	Mint Price
62052	Tested	Prior 1950	Green Bone		135
	XX	1950–1956	Green Bone		100
	XX	1950–1965	Bone		50
	USA	1965–1970	Bone		45
	10 Dots	1970–1971	Bone		45
	Dots	1971–1976	Bone		30
	Dots	1971–1976	Delrin		25

3¼″ Equal End Pen

Pattern	Stamping	Years Made	Handle	Variation / Blade	Mint Price
5253	Tested	Prior 1950	Stag		135
	XX	Approx. 1950	Stag		80
6253	Tested	Prior 1950	Green Bone		100
6253	XX	1940–1950	Green Bone		80
6253	XX	Approx. 1950	Rough Black		65
9253	Tested	Prior 1950	Imitation Pearl		110
9253	XX	Approx. 1950	Imitation Pearl		65

Pattern	Stamping	Years Made	Handle	Variation / Blade	Mint Price

2¹³⁄₁₆″ Equal End Pen

Pattern	Stamping	Years Made	Handle	Variation / Blade	Mint Price
62053SS	XX	1950–1965	Bone		$50
62053SS	USA	1965–1969	Bone		125
82053SR	Tested	Prior 1940	Pearl		125
82053	XX	1950–1964	Pearl		50
82053SS	XX	1949–1964	Pearl	Bolsters	50
82053SRSS	XX	1949–1965	Pearl	Bail, no bolsters	50
	USA	1965–1970	Pearl		40
82053SRSS	Dots	1970s	Pearl		30

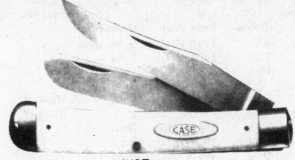

4⅛″ Trapper

Pattern	Stamping	Years Made	Handle	Variation / Blade	Mint Price
3254	Tested XX		Yellow Composition		1500
3254	XX	1950–1965	Yellow Composition		120
	USA	1965–1970	Yellow Composition		75
	USA	1965–1967	Yellow Composition	Muskrat Blade	125
	10 Dots	1970–1971			75
	Dots	1970s			35
3254	Lightning S 10 Dots	1980			20
3254	Lightning S Dots	1980			20
5254	Tested	Prior 1950	Rogers Stag		1650
5254	Tested	Prior 1950	Stag		1600
5254	XX	About 1950	Stag	Tested Frame	375

Pattern	Stamping	Years Made	Handle	Variation / Blade	Mint Price
	XX	1950–1965	Stag		$250
	USA	1965–1970	Stag		95
	USA	1965–1967	Stag	Muskrat Blade	130
	USA	1965–1970	Stag (second cut)		550
	USA	1965–1967	Stag (second cut)	Muskrat Blade	600
	10 Dots	1970–1971	Stag		95
5254SS	4 Dots	1978	Stag	Part of 1976 Set	45
5254SSP	3 Dots	1978	Stag	Part of 1977 Set	45
6254	Tested	Prior 1940	Green Bone		2200
	XX	1941–1953	Green Bone		1800
	XX	1958–1965	Bone		150
	USA	1965–1970	Stag (second cut)		650
	USA	1965–1967	Bone	Muskrat Blade	200
	USA	1965–1970	Bone		75
	10 Dots	1970–1971	Bone		75
	Dots	1970s	Bone		35
	Dots	1970s	Delrin		35
	Lightning S 10 Dots	1980	Bone		25
	Lightning S dots	1980	Bone		25
6254SSP	USA	1965–1966	Bone		200
	USA	1965–1967	Bone		200
	USA	1965–1967	Bone		95
	USA	1965–1970	Bone		75
	10 Dots	1970–1971	Bone		75
	Dots	1970s	Bone		35
	Dots	1970s	Delrin		40
	Lightning S 10 Dots		Bone		25
	Lightning 10 Dots	1980	Bone		25
	Lightning S Dots		Bone		25

Pattern	Stamping	Years Made	Handle	Variation / Blade	Mint Price

3½″ Equal End Jack

Pattern	Stamping	Years Made	Handle	Variation / Blade	Mint Price
32055	Tested	Prior 1940	Yellow Composition		$175
92055	Tested	Prior 1940	Imitation Pearl		180
22055	Tested	Prior 1940	Black Composition		175
22055	XX	1940–1965	Black Composition		50
22055	XX	1940s	Black Composition	Long Pull	100
22055	USA	1965–1967	Black Composition		160
62055	Tested	Prior 1940	Green Bone		170
62055	XX	1940–1955	Green Bone	Long Pull	135
62055	XX	1940–1955	Green Bone		110
62055	XX	1940s	Rough Black	Long Pull	120
62055	XX	1940s	Rough Black		85
62055	XX	1950–1965	Bone		50
62055	USA	1965–1970	Bone		40
62055	10 Dots	1970–1971	Bone		40
62055	Dots	1970s	Bone		28
62055	Dots	1970s	Delrin		20

Pattern	Stamping	Years Made	Handle	Variation / Blade	Mint Price

3⁵⁄₁₆″ Office Knife

Pattern	Stamping	Years Made	Handle	Variation / Blade	Mint Price
92057	Tested	Prior 1940			$100
42057	Tested	Prior 1940			100
4257	Tested	Prior 1940			100
42057	XX	1940–1950	Imitation Ivory		85
42057	XX	1950–1955	Imitation Ivory	Handle not etched	50
4257	XX	1940–1950	Imitation Ivory		85
4257	XX	1950–1960	Imitation Ivory	Handle not etched	50

3¼″ Equal End Pen

Pattern	Stamping	Years Made	Handle	Variation / Blade	Mint Price
92058	Tested	Prior 1940	Imitation Pearl		100

3¼″ Senator Pen

Pattern	Stamping	Years Made	Handle	Variation / Blade	Mint Price
62059	Tested	Prior 1940	Green Bone		110
62059SP	Tested	Prior 1940	Green Bone		110

3⁷⁄₁₆″ Senator Pen

Pattern	Stamping	Years Made	Handle	Variation / Blade	Mint Price
5260	Tested	Prior 1950	Stag		265
5260	XX	1950–1952	Stag		235

Pattern	Stamping	Years Made	Handle	Variation / Blade	Mint Price

2⅞″ Pen

Pattern	Stamping	Years Made	Handle	Variation / Blade	Mint Price
2261	Tested	Prior 1940	Black Composition		$100
6261F	Tested	Prior 1940	Green Bone		100
6261	Tested	Prior 1940	Green Bone		100
8261F	Tested	Prior 1940	Pearl		150
8261	Tested	Prior 1940	Pearl		150
	XX	1950–1965	Pearl		70
	USA	1965–19 70	Pearl		50
	10 Dots	1970–1971	Pearl		50
	Dots	1970–1976	Pearl		35
9261F	Tested	Prior 1940	Imitation Pearl		100
9261	Tested	Prior 1940	Imitation Pearl		100
	XX	1950–1965	Imitation Pearl		40
	XX	1945–1950	Cracked Ice		40
	USA	1965–1970	Imitation Pearl		30
	10 Dots	1970–1971	Imitation Pearl		30
	Dots	1970–1975	Imitation Pearl		20

3⅛″ Equal End Pen

Pattern	Stamping	Years Made	Handle	Variation / Blade	Mint Price
05263	Tested	Prior 1940	Stag		140
05263	XX	1950–1952	Stag		100

Pattern	Stamping	Years Made	Handle	Variation / Blade	Mint Price
05263SS	XX	1940–1965	Stag		$50
05263SS	USA	1965–1970	Stag		40
05263SS	10 Dots	1970–1971	Stag		40
06263	Tested	Prior 1950	Green Bone		125
06263	XX	1945–1950	Green Bone		90
06263SS	XX	1945–1955	Green Bone		75
06263	XX	1945–1955	Bone		55
06263SS	XX	1950–1965	Bone		35
06263SS	USA	1965–1970	Bone		28
06263SS	10 Dots	1970	Bone		28
06263F	XX	1940–1945	Bone		45
06263SS	XX	1950–1965	Bone		35
	USA	1965–1970	Bone		28
	10 Dots	1970–1971	Bone		28
06263SSP	USA	1965–1966	Bone	"Tested XX Stainless"	50
	USA	1965–1970		"Tested XX Razor Edge"	30
	10 Dots	1970–1971			30
	Dots	1970s	Bone		20
	Dots	1970s	Delrin		18
	Lightning		Delrin		
	S 10 Dots				18

3¹⁄₁₆″ Sleeveboard Pen

62063½SS	XX	1950–1960	Bone		30
62063½SS	XX	1950–1955	Green Bone		75
62063½S	XX	1940–1955	Green Bone		90
82063	Tested	Prior 1940	Pearl		
SHAD					150
82063½	Tested	Prior 1940	Pearl		150
82063	Tested	Prior 1940	Pearl		150

Pattern	Stamping	Years Made	Handle	Variation/ Blade	Mint Price
82063 SHAD	XX	1950–1955	Pearl		$75
82063 SHAD SS	XX	1950–1965	Pearl		75
90063½	Tested	Prior 1940	Imitation Pearl		100
	XX	1940–1942	Imitation Pearl		75

3⅛″ Senator Pen

Pattern	Stamping	Years Made	Handle	Variation/ Blade	Mint Price
8264T	Tested	Prior 1940	Pearl		175
9264TF	Tested	Prior 1940	Imitation Pearl		125
6264TG	Tested	Prior 1940	Green Bone		135
6264T	Tested	Prior 1940	Green Bone		135

5¼″ Folding Hunter

Pattern	Stamping	Years Made	Handle	Variation/ Blade	Mint Price
5265	XX	1940–1950	Stag	Flat ground blade	300
5265SAB	Tested	Prior 1940	Stag		400

Pattern	Stamping	Years Made	Handle	Variation / Blade	Mint Price
	XX	1940–1965	Stag		$150
	XX	1964–1965	Stag	Drilled Bolster	150
	USA	1965–1966	Stag	XX frame, not drilled	150
	USA	1965–1966	Stag	XX frame, drilled	145
	USA	1965–1970	Stag	Drilled	85
	10 Dots	1970–1971	Stag		85
5265SS	4 Dots	1978	Stag	From 1978 sets	65
5265SSP	3 Dots	1978	Stag		65
6265	Tested	Prior 1940	Green Bone		400
	XX	1940–1955	Green Bone	Flat ground blade	335
	XX	1940s	Green Bone		325
6265SAB	Tested	Prior 1940	Green Bone		375
	XX	1940–1955	Green Bone		280
	XX	1940s	Rough Black		280
	XX	1950–1965	Red Bone		175
	XX	1950–1965	Bone		150
	XX	1964–1965	Laminated Wood		100
	USA	1965–1966	Bone	XX frame, not drilled	225
	USA	1965–1966	Bone	XX frame, drilled	225
	USA	1965–1966	Laminated Wood	XX frame, not drilled	85
	USA	1965–1970	Laminated Wood		50
	10 Dots	1960–1971	Laminated Wood		50
	Dots	1970s	Laminated Wood		35
6265SAB	Lightning S Dots	1980	Laminated Wood		30
6265SAB SS	Dots	1970s	Laminated Wood		35

Pattern	Stamping	Years Made	Handle	Variation / Blade	Mint Price
6265SAB SS	Lightning S 10 Dots	1980	Laminated Wood		$30
6265SAB DD	Lightning S Dots	1980s	Laminated Wood		30

5¼″ Bill Boatman Special

Pattern	Stamping	Years Made	Handle	Variation / Blade	Mint Price
6265SAB	XX	1960–1965	Bone	Serrated Skinner Blade	275
6265SAB	XX	1964–1965	Laminated Wood	Serrated Skinner Blade	175
	USA	1965–1966	Bone	Serrated Skinner Blade	250
	USA	1965–1970	Laminated Wood		175
	10 Dots				160
	Dots				110

3¼″ Swell Center Balloon

Pattern	Stamping	Years Made	Handle	Variation / Blade	Mint Price
06267	Tested	Prior 1940	Green Bone		175
	XX	1940–1965	Bone	Long Pull	75
	USA	1965–1970	Bone		70

3¼″ Congress

Pattern	Stamping	Years Made	Handle	Variation / Blade	Mint Price
6268	Tested	Prior 1940	Green Bone		375

Pattern	Stamping	Years Made	Handle	Variation / Blade	Mint Price

3″ Congress

Pattern	Stamping	Years Made	Handle	Variation / Blade	Mint Price
6269	Tested	Prior 1940	Green Bone		$135
8269	Tested	Prior 1940	Pearl		275
9269	Tested	Prior 1940	Imitation Pearl		150
6269	XX	1940s	Rough Black		95
	XX	1940–1955	Green Bone		100
	XX	1940–1965	Red Bone		60
	XX	1940–1965	Bone		40
	USA	1965–1970	Bone		35
	10 Dots	1970–1971	Bone		35
	Dots	1970s	Bone		25
	Dots	1970s	Delrin		18

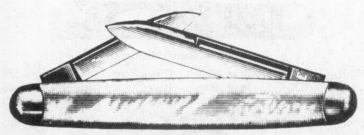

3¼″ Senator Pen

Pattern	Stamping	Years Made	Handle	Variation / Blade	Mint Price
8271	Tested	Prior 1950	Pearl		240
8271F	Tested	Prior 1950	Pearl		240
8271	XX	1950–1958	Pearl	Long Pull	210
8271F	XX	1950–1958	Pearl		175
8271SS	XX	1950–1960	Pearl	Long Pull	195
8271SS	XX	1950–1960	Pearl		175
6271SS	XX	1963–1965	Bone		55

Pattern	Stamping	Years Made	Handle	Variation / Blade	Mint Price

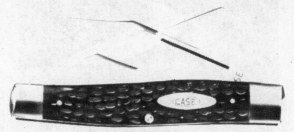

4¼″ Moose

Pattern	Stamping	Years Made	Handle	Variation / Blade	Mint Price
6275SP	Tested	Prior 1940	Green Bone		$295
5275SP	Tested	Prior 1940	Stag		300
6275SP	XX	1940–1955	Green Bone	Long Pull	245
	XX	1940s	Rough Black	Long Pull	250
	XX	1950–1965	Red Bone	Long Pull	225
	XX	1950–1965	Red Bone		120
	XX	1950–1965	Bone		75
	USA	1965–1971	Bone		55
	10 Dots	1970–1971	Bone		55
	Dots	1970s	Bone		35
	Dots	1970s	Delrin		30
	Lightning	1980	Bone		
	S 10 Dots				25
5275SSP	10 Dots	1979	Stag		50
6275SP	Lightning	1980s	Bone		
	S Dots				25

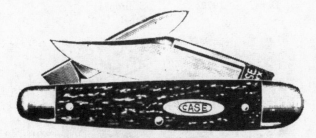

3⅝″ Sleeveboard Pen

Pattern	Stamping	Years Made	Handle	Variation / Blade	Mint Price
5276½	Tested	Prior 1940	Stag		265
6276½	Tested	Prior 1940	Green Bone		225

3⅛″ Senator Pen

Pattern	Stamping	Years Made	Handle	Variation / Blade	Mint Price
M-279	Tested	Prior 1940	Metal		$90
M279R	Tested	Prior 1940	Metal		90
GM279	Tested	Prior 1940	Gun Metal		90
M-279SS	XX	1940–1965	Stainless Steel		35
	USA	1965–1970	Stainless Steel		25
	10 Dots	1970–1971	Stainless Steel		25
	Dots	1970s	Stainless Steel		18
	Lightning S 10 Dots	1980	Stainless Steel		15
M279FSS	XX	1962–1965	Stainless Steel		40
	USA	1965–1970	Stainless Steel		28
	10 Dots	1970–1971	Stainless Steel		28
	Dots	1970s	Stainless Steel		20

3⅛″ Senator Pen

Pattern	Stamping	Years Made	Handle	Variation / Blade	Mint Price
M279SC SS	XX	1958–1964	Stainless Steel	Special Order Knife	55

Pattern	Stamping	Years Made	Handle	Variation / Blade	Mint Price
	USA	1965–1970			$45
	10 Dots	1970–1971			40
	Dots	1970s			28
R279	Tested	Prior 1940	Red Striped Celluloid		175
2279SHAD SS	Tested	Prior 1940	Black Composition	No bolster	110
3279 R	Tested	Prior 1940	Yellow Composition		110
3279	Tested	Prior 1940	Yellow Composition		100
5279	Tested	Prior 1940	Stag		175
5279	XX	1940–1950	Stag		125
5279SS	XX	1950–1965	Stag		90
5279SS	USA	1965–1966	Stag		175
5279SSP	2 Dots	1979	Stag		28
6279	Tested	Prior 1940	Green Bone		120
6279	XX	1940–1955	Green Bone		80
6279	XX	1940s	Rough Black		75
6279SS	XX	1940s	Rough Black		50
6279	XX	1950–1965	Bone		50
6279SS	USA	1965–1970	Bone		35
6279SS	10 Dots	1970–1971	Bone		30
	Dots	1970s	Bone		25
	Dots	1970s	Delrin		22
	Lightning	1980	Delrin		
	S 10 Dots				22
8279	Tested	Prior 1940	Pearl		150
8279	XX	1940s	Pearl		95
8279SS	XX	1950–1960	Pearl		75
9279	XX	1945–1955	Imitation Pearl		75
9279SHAD SS	XX	1962–1963	Cracked Ice	No bolster	45

Senator Pen

M279 CASE Prototypes—Only 12 Sets sent to each CASE salesman 100

Pattern	Stamping	Years Made	Handle	Variation / Blade	Mint Price

3¼″ Sleeveboard Pen

Pattern	Stamping	Years Made	Handle	Variation / Blade	Mint Price
62079½F	Tested	Prior 1940	Green Bone		$140
62079	Tested	Prior 1940	Green Bone		135
92079	Tested	Prior 1940	Imitation Pearl		125
92079½	XX	Late 1940	Imitation Pearl		75
82079½	Tested	Prior 1940	Pearl		200
82079	Tested	Prior 1940	Pearl		195
82079½	XX	1940–1965	Pearl		60
82079½SS	USA	1965–1970	Pearl		45
82079½SS	10 Dots	1970–1971	Pearl		45
82079½	Dots	1970–1971	Pearl		35

2¾″ Square End Jack

Pattern	Stamping	Years Made	Handle	Variation / Blade	Mint Price
6282	Tested	Prior 1940	Green Bone		300

3⅝″ Doctor's Knife

Pattern	Stamping	Years Made	Handle	Variation / Blade	Mint Price
6285	Tested	Prior 1940	Green Bone		375

Pattern	Stamping	Years Made	Handle	Variation / Blade	Mint Price
7285	Tested	Prior 1940	Imitation Tortoise Shell		$550
7285	Tested	Prior 1940	Christmas Tree Handles		550
5285	Tested	Prior 1940	Stag		400

3¼″ Square End Jack

52086	Tested	Prior 1940	Stag		400
62086	Tested	Prior 1940	Green Bone		375
82086	Tested	Prior 1940	Pearl		425

3½″ Gunstock

| 5287 | Tested | Prior 1940 | Stag | | 650 |

3⅜″ Serpentine Stock

22087	Tested	Prior 1940	Black Composition		110
	XX	1940–1955	Black Composition		45
	USA	1965–1970	Black Composition		30

Pattern	Stamping	Years Made	Handle	Variation / Blade	Mint Price
	10 Dots	1970–1971	Black Composition		$28
	Dots	1970s	Black Composition		22
22087	Lightning S 10 Dots	1980	Black Composition		20
22087	Lightning S Dots	1984	Black Composition	Etched	15
42087	Tested	Prior 1940	White Composition		150
52087	XX	1955–1965	Stag		75
	USA	1965–1970	Stag		55
	10 Dots	1970–1971	Stag		55
62087	Tested	Prior 1940	Green Bone		125
	XX	1940–1955	Green Bone		80
	XX	1940s	Rough Black		75
	XX	1940–1955	Red Bone		50
	XX	1950–1965	Bone		35
	USA	1965–1970	Bone		25
	10 Dots	1970–1971	Bone		25
	10 Dots	1970–1971	Delrin		22
	Dots	1970s	Delrin		18
52087SS	4 Dots	1978	Stag	1978 Sets	40
52087SSP	3 Dots	1979	Stag	1979 Sets	35
52087SSP	2 Dots	1979	Stag	1979 Sets	60

4⅛″ Congress

| 5288 | Dots | 1981 | Genuine Stag | ABC Club Knife | 35 |
| 6288 | Tested | Prior 1940 | Green Bone | | 500 |

Pattern	Stamping	Years Made	Handle	Variation / Blade	Mint Price

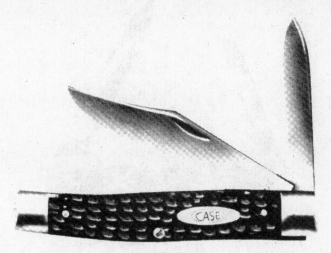

4″ Texas Jack

Pattern	Stamping	Years Made	Handle	Variation / Blade	Mint Price
3292	Tested	Prior 1940	Yellow Composition		$200
6292	Tested	Prior 1940	Green Bone		185
6292	XX	1940–1955	Green Bone		145
6292	XX	1940s	Rough Black		120
	XX	1950–1965	Red Bone		75
	XX	1950–1965	Bone		45
	USA	1965–1970	Bone		30
	10 Dots	1970–1971	Bone		30
	Dots	1970s	Bone		25
	Lightning S 10 Dots	1980	Bone		22
5292SSP	1 Dot	1979	Genuine Stag		48

5″ Texas Toothpick

Pattern	Stamping	Years Made	Handle	Variation / Blade	Mint Price
32093F	Tested	Prior 1940	Yellow Composition		175
62093F	Tested	Prior 1940	Green Bone		210

Pattern	Stamping	Years Made	Handle	Variation / Blade	Mint Price

3⅛″ Toledo Scale

Pattern	Stamping	Years Made	Handle	Variation / Blade	Mint Price
T3105SS	XX	1950–1953	Brass		$150
T3105SS	XX	1973	Brass		75

4¼″ Equal End Moose

| 6294J | Tested | Prior 1950 | Green Bone | | 1050 |

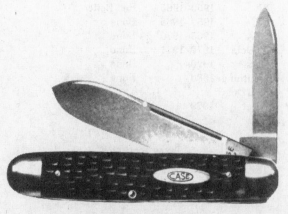

4¼″ Equal End Jack

| 6294 | Tested | Prior 1950 | Green Bone | Long Pull | 425 |

Pattern	Stamping	Years Made	Handle	Variation / Blade	Mint Price
	XX	1950–1955	Green Bone	Long Pull	$350
	XX	1950–1955	Red Bone	Long Pull	375
	XX	1950–1965	Red Bone		225
	XX	1950–1965	Bone	Long Pull	200
	XX	1950–1965	Bone		125

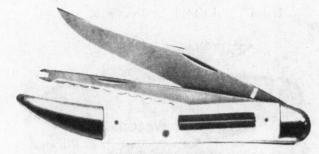

4⅞″ Fisherman Knife

32095FSS	Tested	Prior 1950	Yellow Composition	165
B2095FSS	Tested	Prior 1950	Imitation Onyx	150
32095FSS	XX	1950–1965	Yellow Composition	40
	USA	1965–1970	Yellow Composition	30
	10 Dots	1970–1971	Yellow Composition	25
	Dots	1970s	Yellow Composition	20
	Lightning S 10 Dots	1980	Yellow Composition	18

4¼″ Citrus

6296X	Tested	Prior 1950	Green Bone	550
6296XSS	XX	1950–1955	Green Bone	375
6296XSS	XX	1950–1965	Bone	125
6296XSS	USA	1965	Bone	250

Pattern	Stamping	Years Made	Handle	Variation / Blade	Mint Price
			4½″ Leg Knife		
3297	Tested	Prior 1940	Yellow Composition		$300
			4⅛″ Swell End Jack		
6299 SHOPR	Tested	Prior 1940	Green Bone		275

2⅞″ Oval Lobster

Pattern	Stamping	Years Made	Handle	Variation / Blade	Mint Price
82099R	Tested	Prior 1940	Pearl		155

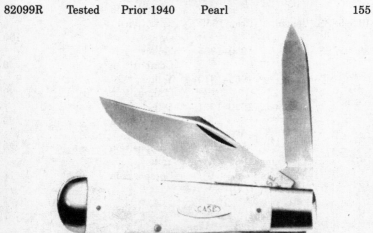

4″ Swell End Jack

Pattern	Stamping	Years Made	Handle	Variation / Blade	Mint Price
2299½	Tested	Prior 1940	Black Composition	"A" Blade	175
3299½	Tested	Prior 1940	Yellow Composition		185
3299½	XX	1950–1965	Yellow Composition	"A" Blade	75

Pattern	Stamping	Years Made	Handle	Variation / Blade	Mint Price
	XX	1950–1965	Yellow Composition		$65
	USA	1965–1970	Yellow Composition		40
	10 Dots	1970–1971	Yellow Composition		40
3299½	Dots	1970s	Yellow Composition		35
5299½	Tested	Prior 1950	Stag		270
	XX	1950–1965	Stag	"A" Blade	140
	XX	1950–1965	Stag		120
	USA	1965–1970	Stag		75
	10 Dots	1970–1971	Stag		75
5299	Tested	Prior 1940	Stag		285
6299½	Tested	Prior 1950	Green Bone		250
6299	Tested	Prior 1950	Green Bone		220
6299	Tested		Rough Black		175
6299	XX	1940s	Rough Black		125
6299	XX	1940s	Green Bone		175

5½" Fish Knife

Pattern	Stamping	Years Made	Handle	Variation / Blade	Mint Price
32098F	Tested	Prior 1940	Yellow Composition		225
62098F	Tested	Prior 1940	Green Bone		275
62100	Tested	Prior 1940	Green Bone		675

3¼" Whittler

2308	Tested	Prior 1940	Black Composition		275

Pattern	Stamping	Years Made	Handle	Variation / Blade	Mint Price
3308	Tested	Prior 1940	Yellow Composition		$325
5308	Tested	Prior 1940	Stag		350
6308	Tested	Prior 1940	Green Bone		275
6308	XX	1940s	Rough Black		175
	XX	1940–1955	Green Bone		210
	XX	1940–1955	Red Bone		175
	XX	1950–1965	Bone		50
	USA	1965–1970	Bone		35
	10 Dots	1970–1971	Bone		35
	Dots	1970s	Bone		30
	Dots	1970s	Delrin		25
	Lightning S 10 Dots	1980	Bone		24
6308	Lightning S Dots	1980	Bone		22

3¼″ Swell Center

| 8308 | Tested | Prior 1940 | Pearl | | 550 |

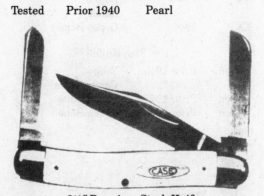

3½″ Premium Stock Knife

2318	Lightning S Dots	1984	Black Composition		22
3318SHSP	Tested	Prior 1940	Yellow Composition		150
3318 SHPEN	Tested	Prior 1940	Yellow Composition		150
3318 SHPEN	XX	1940–1965	Yellow Composition		50

Pattern	Stamping	Years Made	Handle	Variation / Blade	Mint Price
	USA	1965–1970			$35
	10 Dots	1970–1971			35
3318	Lightning S 10 Dots				18
3318	Lightning S Dots	1980s			18
	Dots	1970s			15
4318PP	XX	1950–1957			50
4318SHSP	XX	1957–1965	White Composition		50
	XX	1957–1965		Calif. Clip blade	50
	USA	1965–1970			40
	10 Dots	1970–1971			40
	Dots	1970s			32
5318SHSP	Tested	Prior 1940	Stag		200
6318SHP	Tested	Prior 1940	Green Bone		200

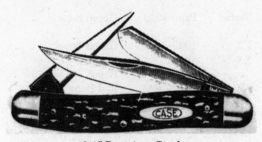

3½″ Premium Stock

6318SPP	Tested	Prior 1940	Green Bone		200
	XX	1940–1955	Green Bone		145
	XX	1940s	Rough Black		100
	XX	1950–1955	Red Bone		65
	XX	1962–1965	Bone		40
	USA	1965–1970	Bone		30
	10 Dots	1970–1971	Bone		30
	Dots	1970s	Bone		25
	Lightning S 10 Dots	1908	Bone		22
	Lightning S Dots	1980s	Bone		22

Pattern	Stamping	Years Made	Handle	Variation / Blade	Mint Price
6318SHSP	Tested	Prior 1940	Green Bone		$175
	XX	1940–1955	Green Bone	Long Pull	175
	XX	1940–1955	Green Bone		125
	XX	1940s	Rough Black		125
	XX	1950–1965	Red Bone		70
	XX	1950–1965	Bone		40
	USA	1965–1970	Bone		32
	10 Dots	1970–1971	Bone		32
	Dots	1970s	Bone		20
	Dots	1970s	Delrin		18
	Lightning S 10 Dots	1980	Bone		18
	Lightning S Dots	1980s	Bone		16
6318 SPPEN	Tested	Prior 1940	Green Bone		175
6318 SHPEN	Tested	Prior 1940	Green Bone		175
	XX	1940–1955	Green Bone		165
	XX	1940s	Rough Black		75
	XX	1950–1965	Red Bone		65
	XX	1950–1965	Bone		45
	USA 10 Dots	1965–1970	Bone		30
	10 Dots	1970–1971	Bone		30
	Dots	1970s	Bone		22
	Dots	1970s	Delrin		20
	Lightning S 10 Dots	1980	Bone		18
	Lightning S Dots	1980s	Bone		18
6318 SHSPSSP	USA	1965–1966	Bone	Flat Ground etched "Tested"	75
	USA	1965–1970	Bone	Concave Ground, polished	50
	10 Dots	1970–1971	Bone		50

Pattern	Stamping	Years Made	Handle	Variation / Blade	Mint Price
	10 Dots	1970–1971	Bone	Entire blade polished	$55
	Dots	1970s	Bone		30
	Lightning S 10 Dots	1980	Bone		25
	Lightning S Dots	1980s	Bone		22
5318SSP	1 Dot	1979	Genuine Stag		45
	Dots	1979	Delrin		15
8318		Prior 1940	Pearl		350
9318 SHPEN		Prior 1940	Imitation Pearl		200

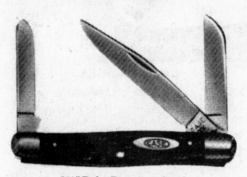

2¾″ Baby Premium Stock

Pattern	Stamping	Years Made	Handle	Variation / Blade	Mint Price
6327SHSP	XX	1957–1965	Bone		32
	USA	1965–1 970	Bone		28
	10 Dots	1970–1971	Bone		28
	10 Dots	1970–1971	Delrin		20
	Dots	1970s	Delrin		15
9327SHSP	XX	1957–1965	Imitation Pearl		45
	USA	1965–1970	Imitation Pearl		30
	10 Dots	1970–1971	Imitation Pearl		30
	Dots	1971–1974	Imitation Pearl		18
63027	3 Dots	1978	Delrin		15

Pattern	Stamping	Years Made	Handle	Variation / Blade	Mint Price
	Lightning S 10 Dots	1980	Delrin		$15

3⅝″ Canoe

Pattern	Stamping	Years Made	Handle	Variation / Blade	Mint Price
53131	Tested	Prior 1940	Stag		1200

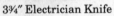

3¾″ Electrician Knife

Pattern	Stamping	Years Made	Handle	Variation / Blade	Mint Price
13031LR	XX	1964–1965	Walnut		50
	USA	1965–1970			45
	10 Dots				45
	Dots	1970–1974			25
	8 Dots	1970–1974			22

3⅝″ Gunstock Stockman

Pattern	Stamping	Years Made	Handle	Variation / Blade	Mint Price
5332	Tested	Prior 1940	Stag		185
	XX	1960–1965	Stag		100

Pattern	Stamping	Years Made	Handle	Variation/ Blade	Mint Price
	USA	1965–1970	Stag		$65
	10 Dots	1970–1971	Stag		65
6332	Tested	Prior 1940	Green Bone		185
	XX	1940–1955	Green Bone		155
	XX	1940s	Rough Black		120
	XX	1950–1955	Red Bone		75
6332	XX	1950–1965	Bone		50
	USA	1965–1970	Bone		35
	10 Dots	1970–1971	Bone	ABC Club Knife	35
	Dots	1970s	Bone		25
	Dots	1970s	Delrin		20
63032	Lightning S 10 Dots	1980	Bone		18
63032	Lightning S Dots	1980s	Bone		15
	USA	1965–1970	Black Composition		20

2⅝″ Baby Premium Stock

6333	Tested	Prior 1940	Green Bone		150
	XX	1940–1955	Green Bone		125
	XX	1940s	Rough Black		85
	XX	1940s	Rough Black	Long Pull	100
	XX	1950–1965	Bone		45
	USA	1965–1970	Bone		35

Pattern	Stamping	Years Made	Handle	Variation / Blade	Mint Price
	10 Dots	1970–1971	Bone		$35
	10 Dots	1970–1971	Delrin		30
	Dots	1970s	Delrin		15
9333	Tested	Prior 1950	Imitation Pearl		115
	XX	1950–1965	Imitation Pearl	Long Pull	75
	XX	1950–1965	Imitation Pearl		30
	USA	1965–1970	Imitation Pearl		22
	10 Dots	1970–1971	Imitation Pearl		25
	Dots	1970–1974	Imitation Pearl		15
63033	1 Dot	1979	Delrin		15
93033	1 Dot	1979	Imitation Pearl		15
63033	Lightning S 10 Dots	1980	Delrin		15
63033	Lightning S Dots	1980s	Delrin		12

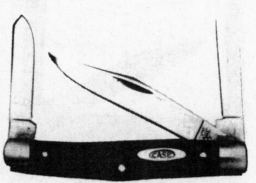

3¼″ Premium Stock

Pattern	Stamping	Years Made	Handle	Variation / Blade	Mint Price
3344SPP	Tested	Prior 1940	Imitation Onyx		150
3344SHP	Tested	Prior 1940	Yellow Composition		125

Pattern	Stamping	Years Made	Handle	Variation / Blade	Mint Price
3344SPP	Tested	Prior 1940	Yellow Composition		$125
3344SHSP	Tested	Prior 1940	Green Bone		125
3344 SHPEN	Tested	Prior 1940	Rough Black		125
5344SHSP	Tested	Prior 1940	Stag		220
5344 SHPEN	Tested	Prior 1940	Stag		220
6344SHP	Tested	Prior 1940	Green Bone		150
6344SSP	Tested	Prior 1940	Green Bone		150
6344 SPPEN	Tested	Prior 1940	Green Bone		150
6344SHSP	Tested	Prior 1940	Green Bone		150
	XX	1940–1955	Green Bone		125
	XX	1950–1965	Red Bone		60
	XX	1960–1965	Bone		40
	USA	1965–1970	Bone		30
	10 Dots	1970–1971	Bone		30
	10 Dots	1970–1971	Delrin		25
	9 Dots	1971–1972	Bone	Limited # in bone	25
	Dots	1970s	Delrin		18
	Lightning	1980	Delrin		
	S 10 Dots				15
6344 SHPEN	Tested	Prior 1940	Green Bone		150
	XX	1940–1955	Green Bone	Long Pull	125
	XX	1950–1965	Red Bone	Long Pull	65
	XX	1950–1965	Bone	Long Pull	40
	USA	1965–1970	Bone		30
	10 Dots	1970–1971	Bone	Long Pull	30
	10 Dots	1970–1971	Delrin		25
	Dots	1970s	Delrin		15
9344 SHPEN	Tested	Prior 1940	Imitation Pearl		135
9344SHSP	Tested	Prior 1940	Imitation Pearl		135
6344 SHPEN SS	Lightning S	1950–1965	Delrin		15

Pattern	Stamping	Years Made	Handle	Variation / Blade	Mint Price

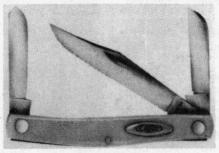

3¼″ Birdseye

Pattern	Stamping	Years Made	Handle	Variation / Blade	Mint Price
33044 SHSP	XX	1964–1965	Yellow Composition		$95
	USA	1965–1970	Yellow Composition		50
	10 Dots	1970–1971	Imitation Onyx		50
	Dots	1970s	Yellow Composition		30

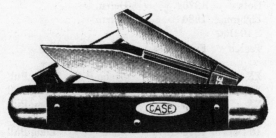

3⅝″ Equal End Cattle Knife

Pattern	Stamping	Years Made	Handle	Variation / Blade	Mint Price
2345½ SPPEN	Tested	Prior 1940	Black Composition		150
2345½P	Tested	Prior 1940	Black Composition		225
2345½P	Tested	1940s	Black Composition	Long Pull	150
2345½SH	XX	1950–1965	Black Composition		75
2345½SH	USA	1965–1967	Black Composition		140

Pattern	Stamping	Years Made	Handle	Variation / Blade	Mint Price
6345½SH	Tested	Prior 1940	Green Bone		$225
	XX	1940–1955	Green Bone		150
	XX	1950–1965	Red Bone		100
	XX	1950–1965	Bone		65

3⅞" Premium Stock

Pattern	Stamping	Years Made	Handle	Variation / Blade	Mint Price
3347SHP	Tested	Prior 1940	Yellow Composition	"A" Blade	150
3357SHSP	Tested	Prior 1940	Yellow Composition		150
3347 SPPEN	Tested	Prior 1940	Yellow Composition	"A" Blade	150
3347SHSP	XX	1940–1953	Yellow Composition	Long Pull	80
	XX	1950–1965	Yellow Composition		40
	USA	1965–1970	Yellow Composition		32
	10 Dots	1970–1971	Yellow Composition		32
	Dots	1970s			20
	Lightning	1980		"A" Blade	
	S 10 Dots				18
5347 SHPEN	Tested	Prior 1940	Stag		275
5347SHSP	Tested	Prior 1940	Stag		275
	XX	1950–1965	Stag	Long Pull	200
	XX	1950–1965	Stag		125
	USA	1965–1970	Stag		75
	10 Dots	1970–1971	Stag		75

Pattern	Stamping	Years Made	Handle	Variation / Blade	Mint Price
5347SSP	4 Dots	1977	Stag		$55
5347SS	3 Dots	1978	Stag	1978 Sets	42
5347SSP	2 Dots	1979	Stag		42
5347SHSP SS	XX	1950–1965	Stag		150
	USA	1965–1970	Stag		65
	10 Dots	1970–1971	Stag		190
5347SHSP SSP	9 Dots	1873	Stag	From collector set	50
6347J	Tested	Prior 1940	Green Bone		500
6347PJ	Tested	Prior 1940	Green Bone		500
6347SHP	Tested	Prior 1940	Green Bone		300
	XX	1940–1955	Green Bone	Long Pull	250
	XX	1940–1955	Green Bone		175
	XX	1940s	Rough Black	Long Pull	135
	XX	1950–1965	Bone		50
	USA	1965–1966	Bone		35
6347PP	Tested	Prior 1940	Green Bone		295
6347PP	XX	1940–1955	Green Bone	Long Pull	250
	XX	1940–1955	Green Bone		175
	XX	1950–1965	Red Bone		100
	XX	1950–1965	Bone		50
	USA	1965–1970	Bone		40
	10 Dots	1970–1971	Bone		40
	Dots	1970–1975	Bone		32
6347 SPPEN	Tested	Prior 1940	Green Bone		275
6347 SHPEN	Tested	Prior 1940	Green Bone		275
	XX	1955–1965	Bone		50
	XX	1940–1955	Green Bone		175
	XX	1940s	Rough Black		85
	XX	1950–1965	Red Bone		75
	XX	1950–1965	Bone		50
	USA	1965–1970	Bone		40
	10 Dots	1970–1971	Bone		40
	Dots	1970–1976	Bone		25
6347SHSP	Tested	Prior 1940	Green Bone		150
	XX	Prior 1940	Green Bone	Long Pull	300

Pattern	Stamping	Years Made	Handle	Variation / Blade	Mint Price
	XX	1957–1965	Green Bone		$175
	XX	1940s	Rough Black	Long Pull	135
	XX	1940s	Rough Black		125
	XX	1950–1965	Red Bone		75
	XX	1950–1965	Bone		50
	USA	1965–1970	Bone		35
	Lightning S 10 Dots	1980	Bone		20
6347	Lightning S Dots	1980s	Bone		18
6347SHSP SSP	10 Dots	1970–1971	Bone		45
	Dots	1970s	Bone		25
	Dots	1970s	Delrin		22
6347SHSP SS	XX	1950–1955	Green Bone		200
6347SHSP SSP	XX	1950–1965	Bone		75
	XX	1955–1965	Red Bone		85
6347SHSP SSP	USA	1965–1970	Bone		40
	Lightning S 10 Dots	1980	Bone		20
	Lighting S Dots	1980s	Bone		20
	USA	1965	Green Bone	"Tested XX Stainless"	75
	USA	1965–1970	Bone	Polished Blade	45
	10 Dots	1940–1955	Green Bone		40
53047	XX	1955–1965	Stag		140
	USA	1965–1970	Stag		65
	10 Dots	1970	Stag		75
63047	XX	1955–1965	Bone		75
	USA	1965–1970	Bone		50
	10 Dots	1970–1971	Bone		45
	Dots	1970s	Bone		30
	Dots	1970s	Delrin		22
SR63047	1 Dot	1980s	Smooth Rose Bone		40

Pattern	Stamping	Years Made	Handle	Variation / Blade	Mint Price
SR63047	1 Dot	Prior 1940	Smooth Green Bone		$40
93047	XX	1950–1956	Imitation Pearl		225

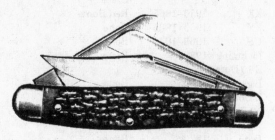

4″ Premium Stock

Pattern	Stamping	Years Made	Handle	Variation / Blade	Mint Price
630047	Tested	Prior 1940	Green Bone		225
630047P	Tested	Prior 1940	Green Bone		225
630047 SHPEN	Tested	Prior 1940	Green Bone		225

3½″ Congress

Pattern	Stamping	Years Made	Handle	Variation / Blade	Mint Price
63052	Tested	Prior 1940	Green Bone		700
33055P	Tested	Prior 1940	Yellow Composition		250
23055	XX	1942	Black Composition	Long Pull	325
73055	Tested	Prior 1940	Imitation Tortoise	Whittler	325
5355	Tested	Prior 1940	Stag	Wharncliffe Whittler	375

3⁷⁄₁₆″ Senator Pen

Pattern	Stamping	Years Made	Handle	Variation / Blade	Mint Price
8360SCI	Tested	Prior 1940	Pearl		190

A group of old and exceptionally fine Case green bone handled knives from the Case Factory Collection. *(Courtesy of Smoky Mountain Knifeworks; photo by Cynthia Pipes)*

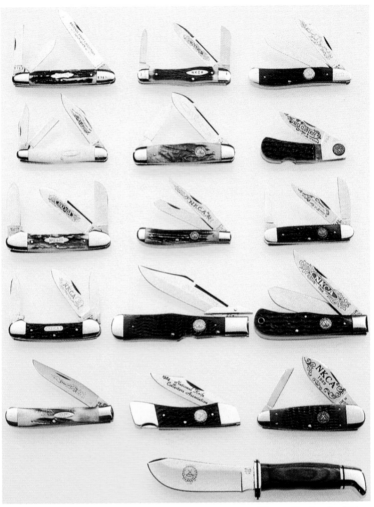

N.K.C.A. club knives from 1975 to the present. These limited edition knives are made under contract by various manufacturers and offered each year to members of the National Knife Collectors Association. *(Courtesy of N.K.C.A.; photo by Weyer)*

Knives by various manufacturers made into unique collectibles. These were made as one-of-a-kind knives by rehandling in mastodon ivory, decorated with original color scrimshaw. Blade backs and backsprings are hand filed with individual and distinctive patterns. *Courtesy of Knife World Publications; photo by Weyer)*

Classic cutlery collectibles. Featured are a variety of knives and razors made from fifty to more than one hundred years ago. *(Courtesy of Smoky Mountain Knifeworks; photo by Cynthia Pipes)*

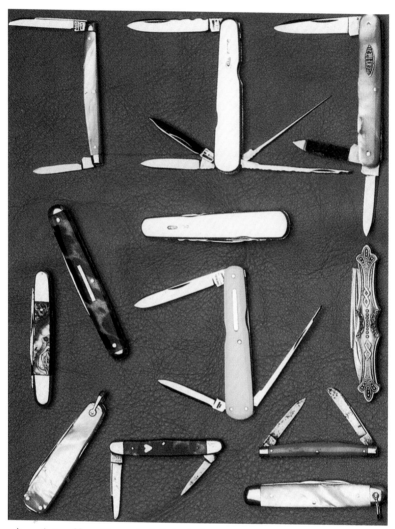

A variety of handle materials including ivory, pearl, abalone, coin silver, genuine tortoise shell and waterfall celluloid. These antique knives were made by manufacturers such as Schatt & Morgan, Robeson, Geo. Wostenholm, Remington, and W. Mills & Son. *(Courtesy of Smoky Mountain Knifeworks; photo by Cynthia Pipes)*

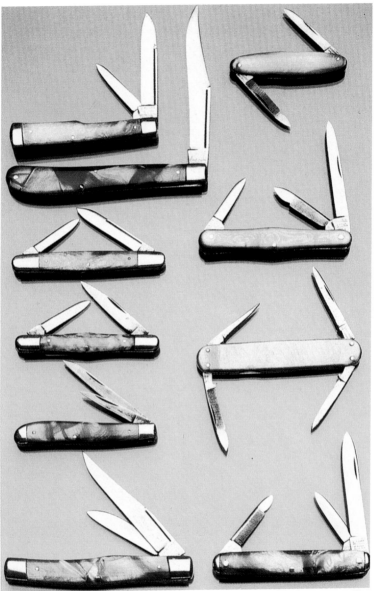

A group of very rare mottled green celluloid handled knives, manufactured by Case in the early 1900s. *(Courtesy of Smoky Mountain Knifeworks; photo by Cynthia Pipes)*

Pattern	Stamping	Years Made	Handle	Variation/ Blade	Mint Price

3⅛″ Senator Pen

Pattern	Stamping	Years Made	Handle	Variation/ Blade	Mint Price
5364T	Tested	Prior 1940	Stag		$225
8364SCIS	Tested	Prior 1940	Pearl		200
8364T	Tested	Prior 1940	Pearl		200
8364TSS	XX	1950–1960	Pearl		125
8364SCIS SS	XX	1950–1965	Pearl		125
	USA	1965–1970	Pearl		125
	10 Dots	1970–1971	Pearl		100
	Dots				60

3⅛″ Jr. Premium Stock

Pattern	Stamping	Years Made	Handle	Variation/ Blade	Mint Price
6366	Tested	Prior 1940	Green Bone		250
6366PEN	Tested	Prior 1940	Green Bone		250

3⅛″ Swell Center

Pattern	Stamping	Years Made	Handle	Variation/ Blade	Mint Price
6370	Tested	Prior 1940	Green Bone		425
8370F	Tested	Prior 1940	Mother-of-Pearl		475

Pattern	Stamping	Years Made	Handle	Variation / Blade	Mint Price

4⁵⁄₁₆″ Gunstock Stockman

Pattern	Stamping	Years Made	Handle	Variation / Blade	Mint Price
5375	Tested	Prior 1940	Stag		$400
	XX	1940–1954	Stag	Long Pull	250
	XX	1950–1965	Stag		125
	XX	1960–1965	Stag (second cut)		600
5375	USA	1965–1970	Stag (second cut)		600
	USA	1965–1970	Stag		75
	10 Dots	1970s	Stag		75
6375	Tested	Prior 1940	Green Bone		450
	XX	1940–1955	Green Bone	Long Pull	300
	XX	1940s	Rough Black	Long Pull	150
	XX	1940–1955	Red Bone	Long Pull	200
	XX	1950–1965	Red Bone		150
	XX	1950–1955	Bone	Long Pull	150
	XX	1950–1965	Bone		75
	USA	1965–1970	Bone		50
	10 Dots	1970–1971	Bone		50
	Dots	1970s	Bone		30
	Dots	1970s	Delrin		20
	Lightning S 10 Dots	1980	Bone		22
	Lightning S Dots	1980s	Bone		22

4″ Sleeveboard Whittler

Pattern	Stamping	Years Made	Handle	Variation / Blade	Mint Price
2376	Tested	Prior 1940	Black Composition		225

Pattern	Stamping	Years Made	Handle	Variation / Blade	Mint Price

3⅝″ Sleeveboard Whittler

Pattern	Stamping	Years Made	Handle	Variation / Blade	Mint Price
2376½	Tested	Prior 1940	Black Composition		$290
5376½	Tested	Prior 1940	Stag		450
6376½	Tested	Prior 1940	Green Bone		450

3¼″ Sleeveboard Pen

Pattern	Stamping	Years Made	Handle	Variation / Blade	Mint Price
63079½F	Tested	Prior 1940	Green Bone		375

3⅞″ Whittler

Pattern	Stamping	Years Made	Handle	Variation / Blade	Mint Price
6380	Tested	Prior 1940	Green Bone		650
	XX	1940–1955	Green Bone		400
	XX	1940–1955	Red Bone		225

Pattern	Stamping	Years Made	Handle	Variation / Blade	Mint Price
	XX	1955–1965	Bone		$100
	USA	1965–1970	Bone		65
	10 Dots	1970–1971	Bone		65
	Dots	1970s	Bone		40
	Dots	1970s	Delrin		35

3″ Lobster Pen

| 83081 | Tested | Prior 1940 | Pearl | | 175 |

3⁹⁄16″ Oval Lobster

| 83083 | Tested | Prior 1940 | Pearl | | 225 |

3½″ Balloon Whittler

2383	Tested	Prior 1940	Black Composition		250
2383SAB	XX	1940s	Black Composition		250
2383	XX	1950–1965	Black Composition		100
2383	USA	1965–1966	Black Composition		100
5383	Tested	Prior 1950	Stag		400
	XX	1950–1965	Stag		150

Pattern	Stamping	Years Made	Handle	Variation / Blade	Mint Price
	USA	1965–1970	Stag		$100
	10 Dots	1970–1971	Stag		100
6383SAB	Tested	Prior 1940	Green Bone		500
6383SAB	XX	1940–1942	Bone		300
6383SAB	XX	1940s	Rough Black		250
6383	Tested	Prior 1940	Green Bone		475
6383	XX	1940s	Rough Black		185
6383	XX	1940–1955	Red Bone		100
6383	XX	1955–1965	Bone		95
6383	USA	1965–1970	Bone		55
6383	10 Dots	1970–1971	Bone		55
6383	Dots	1970s	Bone		30
6383	Dots	1970s	Delrin		20
6383	Lightning S 10 Dots	1980	Bone		24
9383SAB	Tested	Prior 1940	Imitation Pearl		325
9383SAB	Tested	1940–1942	Imitation Pearl		275
	XX	1940–1942	Imitation Pearl		220

3¼″ Premium Stock

23087 SHPEN	Tested	Prior 1940	Black Composition		125
	XX	1950–1965			30
	USA	1965–1970			25
	10 Dots	1970–1971			25
	Dots	1970s			18

Pattern	Stamping	Years Made	Handle	Variation / Blade	Mint Price
23087	Lightning S 10 Dots	1980			$15
23087	Lightning S Dots	1980s	Black Composition		15
43087SH SP	Tested	Prior 1950	White Composition		135
63087 SPPEN	Tested	Prior 1950	White Composition		150
53087 SHPEN	XX	1940–1965	Stag		75
	USA	1965–1970	Stag		65
	10 Dots	1970–1971	Stag		65
	9 Dots	1973	Stag	In 1st collector set only	45
63087 SHPEN	XX	1940–1955	Green Bone		125
	XX	1940s	Rough Black		95
	XX	1950–1965	Red Bone		60
	XX	1950–1965	Bone		40
	USA	1965–1970	Bone		30
	10 Dots	1970–1971	Bone		30
	10 Dots	1970–1971	Delrin		25
	Dots	1970s	Delrin		20
63087	Lightning S 10 Dots	1980	Delrin		20
63087	Lightning S Dots	1980s	Delrin		15

3⅛" Lobster Pen

| 83088SS | Tested | Prior 1950 | Pearl | | 215 |
| 83088SS | XX | 1950–1964 | Pearl | | 225 |

Pattern	Stamping	Years Made	Handle	Variation/ Blade	Mint Price
3¹⁄₁₆″ Lobster Pen					
83089	Tested	Prior 1950	Pearl		$200
83089 SCFSS	XX	1950–1965	Pearl		200
83089 SCFSS	USA	1965–1966	Pearl		225

2¼″ Lobster Pen					
83090 SCRSS	Tested	Prior 1940	Pearl		215
83090 SCRSS	XX	1940–1965	Pearl		250

4½″ Whittler					
3391	Tested	Prior 1940	Yellow Composition		1700
5391	Tested	Prior 1940	Stag		2150
5391	Tested	Prior 1940	Stag (second cut)		2150
	XX	1940–1942	Red Stag		1950
6391	Tested	Prior 1940	Green Bone		2400
2¼″ Lobster Pen					
83091	Tested	Prior 1940	Pearl		200

Pattern	Stamping	Years Made	Handle	Variation / Blade	Mint Price

4″ Birdseye

33092	Tested	Prior 1950	Yellow Composition		$175
	XX	1950–1965	Yellow Composition	Without Shield	75
	XX	1950–1965	Yellow Composition	With Shield	75
	USA	1965–1970	Yellow Composition		50
	10 Dots	1970–1971	Yellow Composition		45
	Dots	1970s	Yellow Composition		35

4″ Premium Stock

| 630092 | Tested | Prior 1940 | Green Bone | | 315 |
| 630092P | Tested | Prior 1940 | Green Bone | | 315 |

Pattern	Stamping	Years Made	Handle	Variation / Blade	Mint Price

4″ Premium Stock

Pattern	Stamping	Years Made	Handle	Variation / Blade	Mint Price
5392	Tested	Prior 1950	Stag		$315
	XX	1950–1965	Stag		125
	USA	1965–1970	Stag		75
	10 Dots	1970	Stag		75
6392P	Tested	Prior 1950	Green Bone	Punch Blade	375
6392	Tested	Prior 1950	Green Bone		400
6392	XX	1940s	Rough Black		200
6392	XX	1940–1950s	Green Bone		225
6392	XX	1940–1950s	Red Bone		110
6392	XX	1950–1965	Bone		65
6392	USA	1965–1970	Bone		40
6392	10 Dots	1970–1971	Bone		40
6392	Dots	1970s	Bone		25
	Lightning S 10 Dots	1980	Bone		20
	Lightning S Dots	1980s	Bone		20

3¹⁵⁄₁₆″ Premium Stock

Pattern	Stamping	Years Made	Handle	Variation / Blade	Mint Price
6393 PEN	Tested	Prior 1940	Green Bone		325

Pattern	Stamping	Years Made	Handle	Variation / Blade	Mint Price
6393	Tested	Prior 1940	Green Bone		$325
5393	Tested	Prior 1940	Stag		325
9393	Tested	Prior 1940	Imitation Pearl		325

4¼″ Cattle Knife

Pattern	Stamping	Years Made	Handle	Variation / Blade	Mint Price
6394½	Tested	Prior 1940	Green Bone		1000
5394½	Tested	Prior 1940	Stag		950
6394½	XX	1940s	Green Bone	Long Pull	750
6394½	XX	1940s	Red Bone		625

4¼″ Gunboat

Pattern	Stamping	Years Made	Handle	Variation / Blade	Mint Price
5394	Tested	Prior 1940	Stag		2000

4¹³⁄₁₆″ Navy Knife

Pattern	Stamping	Years Made	Handle	Variation / Blade	Mint Price
Case	XX	1942–1945	Metal		125
Case	XX	1942–1945	Metal	British Ordmarks	125

Pattern	Stamping	Years Made	Handle	Variation/Blade	Mint Price
		3⅞″ Fly Fisherman			
Fly Fisherman	Tested	Prior 1950	Stainless Steel		$200
Fly Fisherman	XX	1950–1955	Stainless Steel	Blades not stainless	150
Fly Fisherman	XX	1950–1955			150
Fly Fisherman	Transition	1964–1965			140
Fly Fisherman	USA	1965–1970			140
Fly Fisherman	Transition	1969–1970	USA to 10 Dots		125
Fly Fisherman	10 Dots	1970–1971			175
	Dots	1970s			100

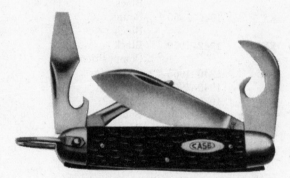

3⅝″ Scout Knife

Pattern	Stamping	Years Made	Handle	Variation/Blade	Mint Price
640045R	Tested	Prior 1940	Black Composition		75
	XX	1950–1965	Black Composition		35
	XX	1950–1965	Brown Composition		35
	USA	1965–1970	Brown Composition		25
	10 Dots	1970–1971	Brown Composition		25
	Dots	1970s	Brown Composition		18

Pattern	Stamping	Years Made	Handle	Variation / Blade	Mint Price

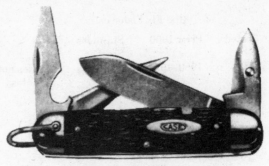

3¾" Utility Knife

Pattern	Stamping	Years Made	Handle	Variation / Blade	Mint Price
6445R	Tested	Prior 1940	Green Bone		$200
6445R	Tested	Prior 1940	Black Composition		150
6445R	Tested	Prior 1940	Rough Black		150
6445R	XX	1940–1950	Rough Black		100
	XX	1942–1950	Black Composition		50
	XX	1940–1955	Red Bone		100
	XX	1940–1965	Bone		55
	US	1965–1970	Bone		45
	10 Dots	1970–1971	Bone		45
	Dots	1970s	Bone		20
	Dots	1970s	Delrin		20

4" Serpentine Stock

Pattern	Stamping	Years Made	Handle	Variation / Blade	Mint Price
64047P	Tested	Prior 1940	Green Bone		285

Pattern	Stamping	Years Made	Handle	Variation / Blade	Mint Price
94047P	Tested	Prior 1940	Imitation Pearl		$285
64047P	XX	1940–1955	Green Bone		250
	XX	1942–1955	Rough Black		225
	XX	1950–1965	Bone		75
	USA	1965–1970	Bone		45
	10 Dots	1970–1971	Bone		45
	Dots	1970s	Bone		30
	Dots	1970s	Delrin		20
	Dots	1979	Bone		30

4" Hobo

3452	Tested	Prior 1940	Yellow Composition		450
6452	Tested	Prior 1940	Green Bone		450

3½" Congress

54052	Tested	Prior 1950	Stag		475
	XX	1950–1965	Stag		140
	Transition	1964–1965	Stag	XX to USA	140
	USA	1965–1970	Stag		85
	Transition	1969–1970	Stag	USA to 10 Dots	100
	10 Dots	1970–1971	Stag		75
64052	Tested	Prior 1940	Green Bone		425
	XX	1940–1955	Green Bone		250
	XX	1940–1955	Red Bone		125
	XX	1955–1965	Bone		75
64052	Transition	1964–1965	Bone	XX to USA	100
	USA	1965–1970	Bone		50

Pattern	Stamping	Years Made	Handle	Variation / Blade	Mint Price
	Transition	1969–1970	Bone	USA to 10 Dots	$65
	10 Dots	1970–1971	Bone		50
	Dots	1970s	Bone		30
	Dots	1970s	Delrin		25
	Lightning	1980	Bone		
	S 10 Dots				25

3⁷⁄₁₆″ Cattle Knife

64055P	Tested	1940–1942	Green Bone		550

3⅜″ Senator Pen

5460	Tested	Prior 1940	Stag		375

3⁵⁄₁₆″ Bartender's Knife

84062K	Tested		Pearl		475
94062K	Tested		Imitation Pearl	Cracked Ice	400

Pattern	Stamping	Years Made	Handle	Variation / Blade	Mint Price
		5¼″ Folding Hunter			
6465 CLASP	Tested	Prior 1940	Green Bone		$2200
9465 CLASP	Tested	Prior 1940	Cracked Ice		2000

		3⅛″ Swell Center			
6470	Tested	Prior 1940	Green Bone		450

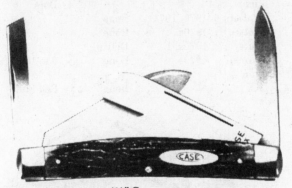

		4⅛″ Congress			
5488	Tested	Prior 1940	Stag		900
5488	XX	1940–1954	Stag	Long Pull	650
5488	XX	1950–1965	Stag		200
5488	XX	1960–1965	Stag (second cut)		525
5488	Transition	1964–1965	Stag	XX to USA	200
5488	Transition	1964–1965	Stag (second cut)	XX to USA	525

Pattern	Stamping	Years Made	Handle	Variation / Blade	Mint Price
5488	USA	1965–1970	Stag		$135
	USA	1965–1970	Stag (second cut)		500
	10 Dots	1970	Stag		155
6488	Tested XX	Prior 1940	Green Bone		900
6488	XX	1940–1955	Green Bone	Long Pull	750
	XX	1940–1955	Rough Black	Long Pull	350
	XX	1940–1955	Red Bone	Long Pull	525
	XX	1940–1955	Red Bone		275
	XX	1940–1955	Bone	Long Pull	450
	Transition	1964–1965	Bone	XX to USA	150
	USA	1965–1970	Bone		75
	USA	1965–1970	Stag (second cut)	Stamped either "5" or "6"	525
	Transition	1969–1970	Bone	USA to 10 Dots	100
	10 Dots	1970–1971	Bone		75
	Dots	1970s	Bone		50
	Dots	1970s	Delrin		50
	Transition	1970s	Bone	8 to 10 Dots	50
6488	XX		Bone	Reg Pull	140

3⅜″ Baby Scout Knife

| 640090 | Tested | Prior 1940 | Green Bone | | 175 |

4″ Premium Stock

| 6592 | Tested | Prior 1940 | Green Bone | | 1950 |

OLDER CASE KNIVES

Older Case knives, those marked with stampings used prior to or near 1920, are included in the following listing. In this instance, the name "Case" does not necessarily mean a W. R. Case & Sons stamped knife. Knives by Case Brothers, bearing marks of the several locations, are included because the patterns were usually very similar. The values are for knives stamped "W. R. Case & Sons" and those with different stampings are normally valued at an additional premium of 20 to 40 percent.

Pattern	Mint Price	Pattern	Mint Price
5200	$575	6106 25C knife	$225
6200	600	5206½	185
9200	525	6206	165
2201	95	6206½	165
3201	90	62006½	165
3201R	95	7206	200
6201	120	8206	230
62001	115	3207	250
8201	145	5207	325
82001	145	6207	310
9201	90	8407	600
9201R	95	5208	325
P202	150	6208	150
R202	175	3308	50
1202 D&B	400	5308	290
5202RAZ	355	6308	265
5202½	225	8308	375
6202	225	6209	175
62021	225	62009	190
62025	225	62009RAZ	250
6202½	190	62009SH	225
B3102	125	62009SP	185
63102	175	62009½	175
83102	200	B-3109-Christmas	500
6103 B&G	140	63109	380
6203	350	83109	475
2104	100	3210½	175
6104 BUD	235	5210½	210
6204½	220	6210	200
5205	350	62105	180
5205RAZ	365	62101	165
5205½	350	6210½	190
6205	325	B1011	175
6205RAZ	340	R111½	450
6205½	300	11011	115
6106	150	3111½	450

Pattern	Mint Price	Pattern	Mint Price
6111½	$520	9220	$300
6111½	600	B221	275
61011	195	OB221	175
6211	520	6221	200
6211½	500	06221	185
1212L	125	06221½	185
62012	135	08221	250
61013	200	6321	275
6213	375	G222	160
5214½	225	6222	160
6214	250	8222	225
6214½	200	P223	165
P125	115	6223	175
6116	140	9223	175
6116½	175	3124	110
61016½	110	3124½	110
22016	135	6124	110
22016½	130	6124½	110
6216	150	B224	175
62161	120	3224	120
6216S	120	3224½	120
6216EO	150	5224	190
62016	125	52024	190
62016½	125	5224½	190
62016S	125	52024½	190
6216½	135	6224	115
6216½L	125	62024	120
62116	95	62024RAZ	200
2217	225	62024SH	190
6217	220	62024½	130
3318SHSP	170	8224	275
3318SHPEN	170	32025½	200
5318SHSP	275	5225½	275
6318SHSP	200	6225	250
6318SHP	200	6225½	225
6318SHPEN	200	62025½	210
8318SHSP	300	8225	325
9318SPPEN	225	B226	220
6219	275	6226	175
62019	285	62026	125
Y220	300	6226½	170
3220	250	82026	160
5220	325	62027	125
6220	300	62027½	125
62020	250	82027	185
62020S	200	92027	110
62020½	200	92027½	190
8220	400	P228EO	200

Pattern	Mint Price	Pattern	Mint Price
2228	$180	3235½	$125
2228EO	250	5235½	190
2228P	200	6235	125
6228	185	6235EO	175
6228EO	240	62035	135
6228P	175	6235½	125
6202B	225	62035½	175
82028	290	2237	210
6229½	140	2237½	210
9229½	140	6237	275
P0230	160	6237½	250
02230	165	5238	225
02230½	165	5438	375
05230½	235	8348	475
06230	230	1139	185
06230½	225	B239	300
09230	210	G2039	275
09230½	210	6239	200
6230SH	200	B339	300
1131SH	90	G3039	300
2231	140	6339	375
22031	140	63039	275
2231½	200	6539	2200
2231½SAB	250	11040	120
22031½	140	3240P	350
52031	225	6240	500
52031½	275	6240SP	600
52131	525	6241	150
6231	160	G242	135
62031	160	52042	140
6231½	175	6242	135
62031½	175	62042	120
53131	1200	82042	175
53131 PUNCH	1250	92042	95
G232	225	63042	200
3232	150	83042	300
6232	155	93042	300
5332	225	6143	200
6332	210	5343	400
3233	175	B224	190
6233	225	3244	120
62033	145	5244	150
8233	275	05244	155
9233	225	6244	140
6333	140	06244	120
9333	110	62044	120
5234	325	62044 FILE	125
G2035	225	8244	185

Pattern	Mint Price	Pattern	Mint Price
82044	$185	3347SHSP	$200
82044 FILE	185	3347SPPEN	185
08244	175	43037	220
9244	175	5347SHPEN	240
B344SHSP	200	53047	240
3344SHSP	135	6347SHPEN	215
5344SHSP	250	6347SHP	215
6344SHSP	160	634PPEN	225
6344SHPEN	160	6347PH	450
8344	250	6347SHSP	225
9344SHPEN	125	63047	225
02445	150	630047	225
02245½·	150	630047P	225
04245 B&G	235	8347SHSP	350
05245	250	83047	350
05245½	250	9347SHSP	300
06245	200	9347PJ	400
06245½	200	93047	225
2345½	190	5447SHSP	370
5345	350	5447SPP	370
5345P	350	64047P	325
5345½	300	94047P	365
6345	270	B1048	250
6345P	325	G1048	250
6345½	270	R1048	215
6345½P	275	61048	125
62345½SH	275	B2048	275
B445R	195	B2048SP	300
6445R	225	G2048	225
640045R	110	G2048S	225
G2046	175	R2048	270
3246	165	R2048S	250
6246	220	62048	175
62046	175	62048SP	200
2346	180	R1049L	450
B346P	210	61049	290
G3046	200	61049L	375
6346	250	B249	250
63046	200	R2049	300
04247SP	175	6249	275
5247J	725	62049	250
05247SP	200	B10050	800
6247J	500	CB1050SAB	800
06247	175	C31050SAB	600
06247PEN	125	310050	600
06247SP	125	C51050SAB	1200
B3047	300	610050	650
P347SHSP	250	61050	700

Pattern	Mint Price	Pattern	Mint Price
C61050	$700	83056	$275
C61050SAB	625	4257	100
C61050L	2200	42057	100
C91050SAB	625	8257	225
6250	850	92057	100
8250	1250	32058	100
B1051	325	6258	200
G1051	325	8258	225
R1051	300	92058	100
R1051L	425	8358	250
6151	650	P259	200
6151L	750	62059	110
61051	300	62059SP	115
61051L	380	8259	200
81051	400	5260	250
9151	725	8260	250
6251	600	8360SCI	215
P2052	165	5460	325
3252	300	8460	400
32052	200	5161L	1000
52052	210	6161L	1000
6252	300	82062K	200
62052	150	83062K	275
63052	600	84062K	360
3452	350	94062	275
54052	450	B2063	225
6452	375	P263	150
64052	525	05263	150
GA253	150	62063	115
5253	150	06263	115
6253	140	61063½	115
62053	120	82063	150
8253	190	08263	175
82053	165	82063½	175
82053SR	115	92063½	115
9253	100	B3063	200
6353	250	63063	225
6353P	190	83063	200
53053	185	6264	125
22055	165	6264 FILE	125
32055	175	62064	125
62055	190	8264T	225
82055	275	8264T FILE	225
92055	190	9264T FILE	185
64055P	525	3165SAB	450
62056	195	5165SAB	600
82056	220	6165SAB	550
63056	250	8165	1500

Pattern	Mint Price	Pattern	Mint Price
9165SAB	$400	06275½	$350
G265	425	G375	375
3265SAB	400	5375	400
5265SAB	475	6375	350
6265 SAB	450	6276½	200
8265	1600	06276	240
9265SAB	450	06276½	240
6366	225	2376½	425
6366PEN	225	6376	475
8366PEN	300	6376½	475
62067	115	4277	160
06267	125	8277	210
82067	185	6278T	200
08267	185	GM279	115
B3067	250	M279R	125
6367	200	3279	115
63067	175	3279R	115
8367	200	5279	150
83067	225	6279	125
9367	200	62079	165
6268	175	62079½	165
8268	225	8279	175
G2069	155	8279 SHAD	175
6269	110	82079	200
8269	175	820279½	200
9269	110	92079½	140
6369	225	B3079	425
8369	375	63079	350
6370 FILE	350	63079½ FILE	350
8370 FILE	425	73079	350
6470 FILE	350	83079	350
5171L	1400	P280	250
8271	275	6280	285
8371	475	G281	175
6172	1350	6281	165
5372	300	9281	150
22074½P	225	83081	200
62074½	250	64081	300
B3074	350	84061	350
B3074½	350	6282	375
B3074½P	350	P383	425
5374	375	2383	350
63074	400	5383	500
63074½	325	6383	425
63074½P	325	6383SAB	525
83074	375	63083	220
5275SP	475	8383	600
6275SP	375	83083	220

Pattern	Mint Price	Pattern	Mint Price
9383	$350	6393	$275
3185	250	6393S	275
6185	275	6393PEN	250
B285	425	9393	325
G285	425	93093	225
R185	325	05294	350
3285	325	6294	500
6285	340	6294 J	900
G2086	400	5394	1500
52086	450	6394	1300
82086	450	B1095	325
5287	475	G1095	275
5387	775	HA1095	350
6288	400	R1095	350
6388	525	31095	240
83088	200	61095	250
5488	850	B2095 F	200
6488	850	32095 F	175
83089	200	B296	275
M2090R	110	6296	300
83090SCI	250	B396	300
B490R	325	6396	350
6490R	250	B1097	475
640090R	140	G1097	500
GM3091	160	GS1097	500
GM3091R	160	R1097	400
5391	2200	P297	350
83091	220	R297	350
3292	220	3297	325
5292	225	8297	425
6292	220	61098	275
33092	220	32098 F	175
5392	375	62098 F	200
6392	225	6199	175
6392P	250	GM2099 R	140
630092	225	3299	225
630921P	300	3299½	200
B1093	300	5299½	300
G1093	300	6299	300
R1093	300	6299½	300
61093	275	82099R	225
32093F	140	31100	500
6293	150	61100	650
62093F	150	62100	700
B393	325	82101 R	175
H393	300	92101 R	125
4393	275	M3102 R	115
5393	275	83102 R	150

Pattern	Mint Price	Pattern	Mint Price
63109 K	$375	MUSKRAT	$550
31113	350	FLY FISHER-	225
61113	375	MAN	
32113	375	1502 SCOUT	125
62113	400	1503 JUNIOR	100
MAIZE #1	175	SCOUT	
MAIZE #2	175		

Case—the Second Century

In 1989, ownership of the W. R. Case & Sons Cutlery Co. changed for only the second time in its long history when the company was sold by American Brands to James F. Parker. Within a very short time, significant changes were already in the making.

Knife patterns, stampings, and handle materials used many years ago but discontinued over the past several decades were reintroduced. Among the handle materials used on "the new Case" knives is Rogers bone, Christmas Tree celluloid, Goldstone celluloid, red bone, green bone, curly maple, and India stag. The reintroduction of old-time patterns and stampings was accomplished through a series started in 1989 known as Commemorative Case Classics. This series was announced as "basically

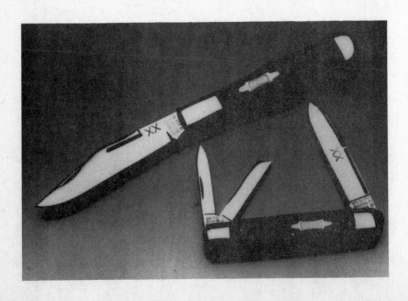

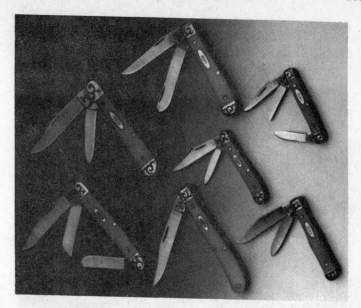

handmade just as they were in the late 1800s," and many of the original dies were used. The commemorative knives are very close in appearance to the originals, but their stamping includes the year of manufacture.

The first patterns revived in the Classic series included #91, #50, #75, and #72. Earliest knives with revived stampings were patterns 3611 (ROG6391, Case Brothers), 3612 (G6391, W. R. Case & Sons), 3619 (CT1072, Case Tested XX), 1626 (ROG-61050SAB, Case Brothers), 3620 (51050SAB, W. R. Case), 3622 (G62075, W. R. Case & Sons), and 3621 (ROG62075, Case Brothers). The handle materials, shields, blade pulls, and blade marks were matched to the original period of the knife's production by the old companies. These knives were limited in production to three thousand of each, and five hundred of each were reserved for the Centennial Mint Set. Retail prices of the Classics ranged from $120 to $150, and it is too soon to determine their collector values.

The Centennial Mint Set contained a total of one hundred knives with a wide variety of patterns and handle materials. Most of their blades were etched "Case XX Tested Centennial 1889–1989." Retail price of the complete matching serial number sets was $5,000.

Beginning in 1990, the new tang stamping for regular production knives was changed to "Case XX Bradford, PA 19 USA 90," and subsequent years' production will reflect in the tang marking the year of manufacture.

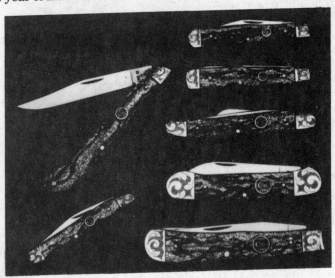

CATTARAUGUS CUTLERY COMPANY

Cattaraugus founder John Brown Francis Champlin first became associated with cutlery at the age of twenty-five, when he became a cutlery salesman for importers Friedman and Lauterjung. After working for about sixteen years, Champlin left his employer in 1882 to join with his son Tint in starting their own business. The cutlery jobbing firm was named J. B. F. Champlin & Son.

In 1886, four of the elder Champlin's brothers-in-law joined in the J. B. F. Champlin & Son business. The relatives were W. R., Jean, John, and Andrew, sons of Job Russell Case and brothers of Champlin's wife, Theresa. When the Case brothers entered the business, its name was changed to Cattaraugus Cutlery Company. Although the Case brothers soon dropped out of the new business, it was the beginning of the longtime association of the Case family with cutlery.

In 1890, the Champlins purchased the knife-making equipment owned by Beaver Falls Cutlery Company of Beaver Falls, Pennsylvania. With the purchase of this equipment and the building of their factory in Little Valley, New York, Cattaraugus had changed from a jobbing operation to a cutlery manufacturer.

Under the leadership of the Champlin family, Cattaraugus remained in business until 1963. During this time the company name was a respected one within the industry as well as with consumers. Cattaraugus made knives for the armed forces and the Byrd Polar expedition and sponsored whittling competitions in promotional efforts, offering up to $50,000 in prizes.

In 1984, A. G. Russell revived the Cattaraugus brand name for special-issue knives sold by the Knife Collectors Club. These should not be confused with knives made by the original company.

Cattaraugus knife production seemed to favor bone-handled, large-pattern knives, but they also produced some knives with plastic handles. The company's knives were stamped "Whittle Craft," "3," a "C" inside a circle, and "Cattaraugus Cutlery Company, Little Valley, New York."

Most Cattaraugus knives were stamped with pattern numbers. The first digit indicates the number of blades (up to 5-blade knives were made by Cattaraugus), and the second digit indicates the type of bolsters as follows:

0—no bolsters	3—tip bolsters
1—one bolster	4—unknown
2—two bolsters	5—slant bolsters

The third and fourth digits are the factory handle-frame pattern numbers. Unlike those of Case and some other manufacturers, the Cattaraugus numbers were not consistent to the point that they are a reliable reference. The 20224 pattern will be a different knife from the 22223 pattern, although both knives are 22 patterns. And the company made so many patterns—more than one hundred—that few collectors, if any, have memorized them. We recommend that you learn the pattern number from the knife itself and, for pricing reference, find it on the following list, which is published in numerical order.

The last digit of the number indicates the knife's handle material, as follows:

0—White Fiberloid	6—Ebony
2—Pearl (French)	7—Cocobolo, Fancy Fiberloid,
3—Mother-of-Pearl	Burnt Bone
4—Fiberloid	8—White Bone
5—Genuine Stag	9—Stag Bone

Pattern No.	Mint Price
P-1	$175

1-W—(4½″) **Strong cutting blade and a combination cap lifter/screw-driver in the handle of the wrench; brass lined; nickel silver bolsters; glaze finish; bone stag handles**   *$300*

Pattern No.	Mint Price
3-W	$300
10101	45
10484	70
10851	55
1159 (BW)	95
11067-S	80
11079	155
11227	65
11247	55
11404	45
11486	110
11704 (L)	105

11709—(4″) Small Hunter; **long clip blade; brass-lined; nickel silver bolsters; glaze finish; stag handles; shielded spring lock holds the blade in position when open**   *$85*

Pattern No.	Mint Price
11709 (L)	$115
11804	35
11827	95
11839	120
11844	100
11996-S	70

12099—(4½″) The Deer Slayer; long clip blade with spring lock; brass-lined; nickel silver bolsters; shield; glaze finish; stag handles   *$175*

Pattern No.	Mint Price
12099 (L)	$300
12114	150
12134 (Y)	55
12144	65

12819—(5⅜″) King of the Woods; blade has a clip point and 3¾″ cutting surface; brass-lined; long nickel silver bolsters on one end and round nickel silver bolsters on other; hole drilled for ring or thong; glaze finish; stag handles   *$550*

Pattern No.	Mint Price
12839	$800
12829	500
12829 (L)	700
200-OP	55
200-PP	55
2000	45
2013	70
2022	35
2022-OP	60
2022-PP	75
20223	115
20224	55

20228—(3⁵/₁₆″) Emblem Knife; two blades; brass-lined; crocus finish; pearl-luster celluloid handle; special emblem in handles   *$175*

Pattern No.	Mint Price
20232	$50
20233	60
20234	45
203-G	40
203-Orl	55
203-O	35
203-OP	35
20371	50
2059-Orl	85
2059-OP	85

2059PP—(3¼″) One large and one pen blade; brass milled liners; full- crocus finish; peacock pearl handles   *$85*

Pattern No.	Mint Price
20594	$60
206-Shrine	55
206-32nd	55
206-O	35
206K of P	60
206-IOOF	35
2066-Ori	35
2066-G	35
2066-OP	35
2066-O	35
2066-PP	35
20664	35

20673 —(3") Two blades; brass-lined; full polish; mother-of-pearl handles $50

Pattern No.	Mint Price
20677	$45
20701	40
20853	55
B2109	100
21046	80
21049	90
21087	55
21089	55
21169	60
21169-G	65
21229	75
21246	45
21249	65
21259	90
21266	80
21269	110
21269-C	110
21269-CC	110
2139 (BW)	140
21356	85
21359	95
21411	130

21419—(3¾") *Come-apart camp knife;* knife and fork may be used separately; brass-lined; nickel silver bolster; full polish; shield; stag handles $125

Pattern No.	Mint Price
21476	$50
21479	65
21484	40
21486	55
21489	70
2149	130
2159 (BW)	120

21709—(4") Long spear point and pen blades in the same end; brass-lined; nickel silver bolsters and shield; glaze finish; stag handles   *$60*

Pattern No.	Mint Price
21816	$65
21819	110
21826	65
21829	105
21839	95
21899-C	55
21899-S	55
22029	70
22039	95
22053	60
22069	90
22079	75
22084	80
22099	180
22099-F	180
22104	70
22109	180

22109-F—(4½") One long clip blade and one long pen blade in the same end; brass-lined; nickel silver bolsters and shield; glaze finish; stag handle   *$180*

Pattern No.	Mint Price
22109-F	$180
22119	65
22139	70
22149	150
22153	75
22159	65
22162	65
22163	95
22169	100
22182	60
22182 (SS)	60
22186	65
22187	60
22104	70
2219	150
221039	95
221049	175

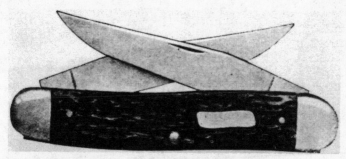

22199—(3½") Two sabatur blades; brass-lined; nickel silver bolsters and shield; full polish; stag handles *$150*

Pattern No.	Mint Price
22209	$45
22213	95
22219	65
22223	75
22226	70
22229	70
22233	70
22239	70
2224B	65
22246	65
22248	90

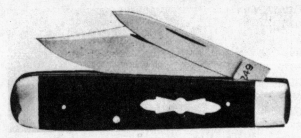

22249—(3⅝″) Large clip and pen blades; brass-lined; nickel silver bolsters and shield; full polish; stag handles   *$80*

Pattern No.	Mint Price
22256	$65
22258	95
22259	80
22269	85
2227	65
22276	65
22278	80
22279	70
22286	65
22289	85
22292	50
22299	70
22329 (SS)	45
22336	180

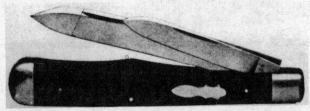

2239—(4½″) Long spear point and long pen blades; brass-lined; nickel silver bolsters and shield; glaze finish; stag handles   *$225*

Pattern No.	Mint Price
22339	$290
22349	90
22356	90
22359	110
22366	155
22369	185

Pattern No.	Mint Price
22376	$85
22378	125
22379	100
22389	70
22389 (SS)	70
22396	95
22399	90
22406	60
22419	110

22429—(3⅝″) Gunstock pattern; large spear point and pen blades; brass-lined; flat nickel silver bolsters and shield; glaze finish; stag handles

$230

Pattern No.	Mint Price
22439	$105
22449	90
22459	65
22463	65
22469	40
22474	55
22476	55
22479	85
22486	65
22489	75
2249	70
2259	150
22509	80

22519—(3½″) Clip and pen blades; milled silver lining; nickel silver bolsters; full polish; shield; stag handles   *$75*

Pattern No.	Mint Price
22526	$60
22529	80
22536	75
22539	90
22549	65

22554—(3⅜") Large spear and pen blade; brass-lined; nickel silver bolsters; full polish; transparent Fiberloid handles　　　　*$55*

Pattern No.	Mint Price
22557	$55
22559	65
22556	60
22569	80
22576	70
22579	75
2586	75

22586 —(3⅜") Two blades; brass-lined; nickel silver bolsters; glaze finish; shield; ebony handles　　　　*$75*

Pattern No.	Mint Price
22589	$110
22594 (SS)	40
22599 (SS)	45
22599	40
22609	45
22612	40
22614	45
22622	55
22624-Y	60
22628 (SS)	55
22629 (SS)	70

22629—(3") Spear and pen blades; brass-lined; nickel silver bolsters; shield; stag handles   *$70*

Pattern No.	Mint Price
22633 (SS)	$55
22639	50
22642	55
22643 (SS)	90
22649	65
22652	40
22653	65
22654	45
22659 (SS)	40
22659	40
22663	55
22664	40
22673	50

2269—(4") Large spear point and long pen blades; brass-lined; nickel silver bolsters and shield; glaze finish; stag handles   *$150*

Pattern No.	Mint Price
22682 (SS)	$50
22683	100
22684	65
22686	70
22689	85
22689 (SS)	85

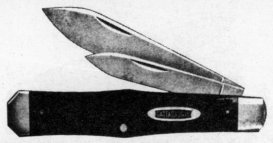

22729—*(3⅝″)* Large spear and pen blades; milled silver lining; nickel silver bolsters and shield; full polish; stag handles   *$125*

Pattern No.	Mint Price
22739	$100
22749	80
22753	100
22754	70
22759	70
22762	70
22763	155
22766	70
22769	95
22772	65
22773	100
22779	75
22783	45
2279	70
2279-P	70
22793	90
22793 (SS)	90

22794—*(3″)* Two blades; brass-lined; nickel silver bolsters; full polish; Fiberloid handles   *$55*

Pattern No.	Mint Price
22796	$55
22799	65

Pattern No.	Mint Price
22799-N	$60
22813	40
22814	40
22819	40
22822	40
22823	45
22833	45
2284	80
22849	60

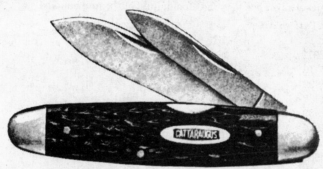

22859—(3¼") Spear and pen blades; brass-lined; nickel silver bolsters and shield; full polish; stag handles   *$80*

Pattern No.	Mint Price
22869	$60
22874	65
22877	60
B2879	70
22879	70
22879 (SS)	70
22882	65
22883	65
22884	55
22886	55
22889	70
22893	75
22894	70
22896	60
22899	75
22899-Jr.	70
B2909	55

22909 (SS)—(3⅛″) Stainless steel spear and pen blades; milled silver lining; nickel silver bolsters and shield; full polish; stag handles   *$65*

Pattern No.	Mint Price
22911	$120
B2919	70
22919	180
22929	360
22936	90
22939	90
22949	180
22952	65
22959	85
22963	70
22964	55
22967	60
22969	60
22979	75
2319	55
23009	115
23224	50
23229	50
23232	45
23232 C-SS	45

23234—(2⅞″) Clip and pen blade; brass-lined; nickel silver tips; full polish; Fiberloid handle   *$45*

Pattern No.	Mint Price
2342	$45
2343	65
2344	40
2349	50
2379	75
2389	65
23642 (SS)	60
23649	60
23662	55
23663	60
23669	40
23669- N	65
23672	50

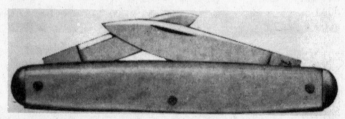

23673—(3") Two blades; brass-lined; nickel silver tips; crocus finish; mother-of-pearl handles   *$75*

Pattern No.	Mint Price
23679	$55
23689	65
24337	72
24376	75
24379	90
24396	90
24399	95
24409	65
24889	85
C2589	160
D2589	160
B2672	55
B2874-Y	85
B2879	95
B 2909 (SS)	75
B2919 (SS)	55
2929	200

300-Ori—(3") One large blade; 2 pen blades and 1 flexible file blade; brass-lined; milled; full-crocus finish; Oriental pearl handles   *$50*

Pattern No.	Mint Price
300-G	$55
300-OP	75
3003	75
3009	75
301	40
301-IOOF	35
301-BPOE	35
301-F & AM	35
301-Shrine	35
301-Ori	50
303-G	40

303-D-Ori—(2⅝") Two blades with flexible file in back; full-crocus finish; Oriental pearl handle   *$50*

Pattern No.	Mint Price
304-Ori	$75
304-G	75
305-F & AM	55
305-FOE	55
305-KT	55

Pattern No.	Mint Price
305-Shrine	$55
305-K of P	60
305-IOCF	45
305-32nd	50
305-BPOE	50
3013	50
30673	75
309-Ori	50
309-OP	55
32009	120
32019	110
32019-S	110

32019-G—(3⅜") Large spear, pen, and punch blades; brass-lined; nickel silver bolsters and shield; full polish; stag handles   *$110*

Pattern No.	Mint Price
32029	$110
32039	110
32053 (WH)	95
32059 (WH)	110
32099 (WH)	110
32125	80
32126 (WH)	95
32139—	170
32141	80
32144	115
32145	160
32149	120
32149-G	120
32149-SH & G	120
32149-P & SH	120
32164 (WH)	110

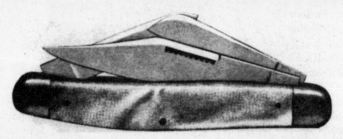

32173—(3⅞″) Fine stock pattern; large clip, sheepfoot, and spey blades; brass-lined; nickel silver bolsters; crocus finish; mother-of-pearl handles $255

Pattern No.	Mint Price
32174	$150
32175	145
32179	115
32183	200
32184	155

32189—(3⁷⁄₁₆″) Large clip, spey, and pen blades; crocus-polished; brass-lined; nickel silver bolsters and shield; stag handle $125

Pattern No.	Mint Price
32189-S	$155
32189-G	150
32189-S & G	150
32203	245
32204	140
32204-G	140
32204-C & G	140
32205	195
32206-G	120
32206-C & G	120
32206	110
32209	155

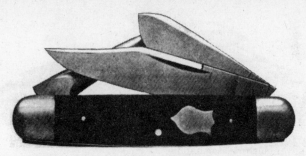

32209-G— (3⅝") Large spear, spey, and punch blades; crocus-polished; brass-lined; nickel silver bolsters and shield; bone stag handle   *$125*

Pattern No.	Mint Price
32209-G & P	$125
32209-C & G	125
32233 (WH)	170
32243	170
32244	95
32245	110
32249	105
3229	105
3233	110

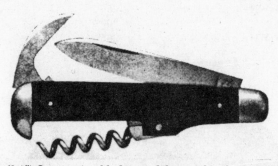

3239-H—(3¼") One cutting blade, cap lifter, and corkscrew; crocus-polished; brass-lined; nickel silver tip bolsters; bone stag handle   *$70*

Pattern No.	Mint Price
3299	$75
32389	125
32403 (WH)	145
32404 (WH)	130
32406 (WH)	110
32409 (WH)	155
32443	120

32449—(3") Whittler; three blades; full crocus-polished; brass-lined; nickel silver bolsters; stag handle   *$125*

Pattern No.	Mint Price
32566 (WH)	$165
32569 (WH)	210
32575 (WH)	210
32576 (WH)	165
32579 (WH)	170
32586 (WH)	130
32589 (WH)	170
32599 (WH)	165
32643 (WH)	170
32644 (WH)	150
32646 (WH)	155
32649 (WH)	250
32653	300
32656 (WH)	265

32659—(3½") Large swedge clip, small clip, and scribing blades; full-polished; brass-lined; nickel silver bolsters and shield   *$265*

Pattern No.	Mint Price
32683 (WH)	$265
32689 (WH)	225
32734 (WH)	230
32739 (WH)	250

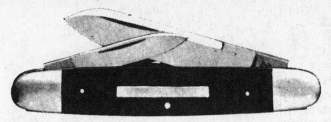

32779 (WH)—(3¾") Three blades; brass-lined; nickel silver bolster and shield; crocus finish, stag handle **$240**

Pattern No.	Mint Price
32793 (WH)	$250
32794 (WH)	190
32799 (WH)	210
32866 (WH)	190
32869	265
32876 (WH)	165
32879 (WH)	265
3289 (WH)	190
32889 (WH)	275
32916 (WH)	400

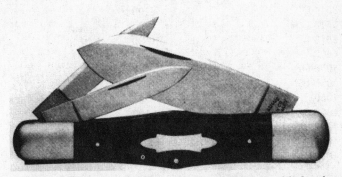

32919 (WH)—(4⅜") Large heavy spear point and 2 pen blades; brass-lined; nickel silver bolsters and shield; crocus finish, stag handle **$490**

Pattern No.	Mint Price
3293	$120
32956 (WH)	190
32959 (WH)	225
32973 (WH)	160
32976 (WH)	135
32979 (WH)	150

Pattern No.	Mint Price
3299	$90
33073	110
33079	100
3343	135
3349	120
33673 (WH)	230
33674 (WH)	205
33679 (WH)	215
33683 (WH)	260
33689 (WH)	215

35141—(3⅞″) Large clip, spey, and scribing blades; brass-lined; nickel silver bolster and shield; full polish, white Fiberloid handle   *$100*

Pattern No.	Mint Price
35144	$100
35151	90
3913	90
4403	135
4059-Ori	180
4059-OP	180
40503	190
4053	190
40593	180
4059-OP	175
40593	180

40673—(3 ″) One large blade, 2 pen blades, and flexible file blade; brass-lined; crocus finish, mother-of-pearl handle   *$240*

Pattern No.	Mint Price
40863	$265
42049	165
42053	210
42059	155
42069	260
42070	185
42099	255

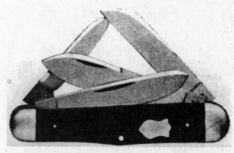

42109—(3⅝") Large spear point, large sheepfoot, large spey, and pen blades; iron-lined; nickel silver bolsters and shield; crocus finish and stag handle   *$230*

Pattern No.	Mint Price
42172	$140
42179	160
42009-B	115
42363	180
42369	175
42369	165
42459	130
42469	100
42509	175
42519	175

42559—(3⅜") Spear blade, 2 pen blades, and nail file; brass-lined; nickel silver bolsters and shield; full polish; stag handle   *$180*

Pattern No.	Mint Price
42689	$190
42793	195
42795	165
4303	230
4309	190
43559	170
43593	190
43673	180
43679	165
43683	195
43689	160
4503 (WE)	145
4509 (WE)	135
5003	155
5009	120

CHALLENGE CUTLERY

Challenge knives were made in Sheffield by the B. J. Eyre Company as early as 1867. When the Frederick Wiebusch Company purchased the Eyre company in 1877, the trade name was a part of that purchase. After the 1893 death of Wiebusch, his company became the Wiebusch and Hilger Company of New York.

The first U.S. factory to produce Challenge knives was opened in 1891 in Bridgeport, Connecticut. The factory was owned by the Hatch Cutlery Company and later by the Griffon Cutlery Works. Both companies made knives under contract for the Wiebusch companies. In 1905, Challenge purchased the factory and continued to make knives until 1928.

About 1920, under license from the inventor George Schrade, the company introduced their Flylock knife in two sizes. The smaller size was a two-blade pen knife handled with pearl, shell rosewood, smoked pearl, nickel silver with a beaded edge, or sterling silver. The larger pattern was the same pattern as the Schrade HUNTERS PRIDE.

Knives marked with the name and "company" were manufactured in Sheffield and imported by the Wiebusch company. Those made in the United States were marked with the brand name and "corporation." The various stampings used were

1867–1914—Challenge Cutlery Co. New York
Challenge Cutlery Co. Sheffield

1905–1928—Challenge Cut'l Co. Bridgeport
    Challenge Cut. Corp.
    Challenge Cut. Corp. B'port Conn.
    Challenge CC Bridgeport CT

CLAUSS CUTLERY COMPANY

Located in Fremont, Ohio, Clauss is a shears and scissors manufacturer that has been in business since 1887. For a short time during the mid-1920s, Clauss sold pocketknives made under contract by companies such as Schatt & Morgan Cutlery Company and W. R. Case & Sons, and it is possible that Clauss actually made some of their own knives. Clauss Cutlery Company knives were marketed in an assortment of patterns, using both bone and celluloid for handles.

COLONEL COON KNIVES

Adrian Harris formed Tennessee Knife Works in 1978 and operated the company in Columbia, Tennessee, until 1988. The shop hand-assembled and finished knives made from parts stamped out by major knife manufacturers. The patterns made were pri-

marily barlow, muskrat, stockman, and congress. Although a few knives were handled in pearl, most Colonel Coon knives were handled in bone or genuine stag. The knives were well made and their quality was recognized in the southeastern area where they were primarily marketed. They have become desirable collectibles in those areas, and their values are substantially higher than their original sales price.

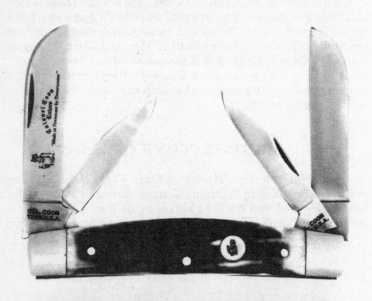

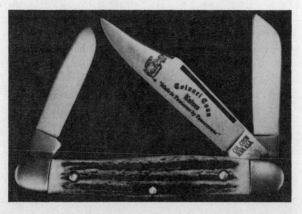

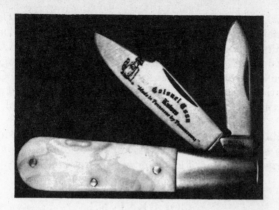

COLONIAL KNIFE COMPANY

Colonial knives and the several trade names used on them have been a mainstay in the American cutlery industry since the company's beginning in 1926. Names such as Forest Master, Topper, Ranger, Old Cutler, and Snappy are but a few that may be recalled from the collectors' memories.

The family that founded and still owns Colonial was experienced in cutlery manufacture prior to establishment of their Providence, Rhode Island, company. Frederick Paolantonio, the founder of Colonial, was first trained in the cutler's art in his home town of Frosolone, Italy. He arrived in the United States in 1903, worked briefly in a Rhode Island cutlery shop, and then went to work for Empire Knife Company, where he remained for five years.

He next went to work for Miller Brothers Cutlery Company and became production foreman there in 1914. While there he met Edward Oefinger, and together they started their own company, named Meriden, to make skeleton knives for Miller Brothers. (These knives were not stamped MERIDEN and should not be confused with the older Meriden Cutlery Company knives.) In 1920, they started P. & S. Cutlery Company in Meriden, Connecticut, but sold it the following year to Imperial, a company also started by former Empire employees. Paolantonio's brothers, Dominick and Anthony, immigrated in 1910 and worked for Empire until 1917. At that time, they started the Providence Cutlery Company, making skeleton knives.

In 1920, Anthony formed the A. Paolantonio Cutlery Company in Providence, making gold- and pearl-handled knives. Dominick sold his Providence Cutlery Company in 1925 and joined Anthony in his business. By 1926, the three brothers had joined together to form and organize the Colonial Knife Company. The Colonial organization took over the A. Paolantonio business and soon expanded the factory to manufacture a standard line of pocketknives.

Colonial Knife Company, under the leadership of the founding brothers' sons and grandsons, still operates today and manufactures large quantities of lower-priced pocketknives.

COLT KNIVES

Like other major gun manufacturers, Colt made knives, and most of them have become collectibles—a few were originally intended for the collector market. Unlike their firearms competitors, Remington and Winchester, Colt's entry into the knife market came in recent years, and their tenure lasted only four years—from 1969 until 1973.

About fifteen different models, primarily fixed-blade knives, were made. The most unique of Colt's knives and the one that is in greatest demand by collectors was designed by Barry Wood of Venice, California. Wood had been using the patented design since 1967 on his own handmade knives and was approached by Colt about making the knives for them in 1968. Production on the first knives was completed in October 1969, with Wood having the blades made by Russell Harrington Company and several other components made by different manufacturers. He then assembled and finished the knives in his own California shop.

During the next four years, 15,300 of the Colt folders were made in several variations. The first five hundred knives, stamped with the Colt rearing horse trademark, have a handle shaped like a rectangle with rounded edges. These knives have canvas Micarta handles and are probably the rarest of the Colt knife variations.

The second model is similar to the first, with the same shape and handle, but is stamped with the "Rampant Colt" trademark and COLT, HARTFORD, CONN. in large letters. With the knife's blade at a half-open position, it is possible to see these markings and the Colt Serpentine trademark as well. Two thousand of these knives were made.

The most common Colt Woods Folder is the third model, which features a change in shape and handle material on most of them. Their shape is slightly curved, and although a few knives used the canvas Micarta handles, the majority had a burgundy Micarta handle. This model did not have the Colt lettering stamp on the liner.

These knives were originally sold at prices in the $30 range. Those of the third variation are now valued in the $200 to $250 range, with premiums paid for knives with original sheaths and boxes. The first and second variation models are valued more highly and may range up to $400, especially with the original sheath and box.

There were two other variations made, but they will rarely, if ever, be found in the collector market. Twelve knives were made with black Micarta handles and used as salesman samples. Two knives with stag handles were made especially for Colt executives. If found, these knives would be quite expensive, and a prospective buyer should expect to receive letters of verification to accompany the rare knife.

Although Wood terminated his agreement with Colt in 1978, he continued to make a similar knife, using 154CM steel and a variety of handle materials. Prices for these handmade knives stamped with the maker's name range from $200 upward.

The Colt sheath knives were packaged in a wood-grain paper box embossed with the Rampant Colt emblem, with the knife contained in a red velvet drawstring pouch. Sheath knives stamped SHEFFIELD were made by J. and F. Hopkins & Sons of Sheffield, England. They were imported through Indian Ridge Traders in quantities of approximately 2,500 each. There were four variations of the Sheffield-made knives, each with sweeping clip blades. The three larger patterns include a sheath with a snap that closes over the bottom of the guard. The smallest skinner came with a pouch sheath.

There were about twenty thousand sheath knives made in this country by the Olsen Knife Company of Howard City, Michigan. They were stamped with the Cold Serpentine trademark and the words "Hartford Conn." Most of these knives were equipped with black leather sheaths, and the Sheffield knives came with brown sheaths. Both included the red velvet pouches.

Retail prices of the fixed-blade knives ranged from $29 to $49 in 1973. Current collector values are about $100, with large patterns valued slightly higher and smaller knives valued at slightly less.

CRANDALL CUTLERY COMPANY

This company was founded in 1902 by Herbert Crandall and was located in Bradford, Pennsylvania. Cutlery historians may recall that Crandall was married to Theresa Case, the daughter of W. R. Case. Most of the company's knives were bone-handled and were stamped CRANDALL, BRADFORD, PA. In 1912, Crandall merged his company with W. R. Case & Sons Cutlery Company. Knives made during the company's ten-year existence are rarely found and, when found, are desirable collectibles.

CRIPPLE CREEK CUTLERY

In 1981 Cripple Creek Cutlery was formed in Lockport, Illinois, by Bob Cargill. His goal was the revival of old-time patterns and production of them in limited numbers. Cargill had been involved in collecting antique factory-made knives for a number of years and had served several years as a factory-authorized repairman for W. R. Case & Sons Cutlery. More recently, he had been a custom knife maker for a half dozen years, and many of his custom knives were patterned after the antique favorites. Cripple Creek was the fruition of a dream to apply modern-day handcrafting methods to age-old favorite knives.

The first patterns to be produced were narrowed down to ten favorites, designated LI 1 through LI 10 and referred to as the "ten little Indians" because of Cargill's devotion to American Indian lore. Distribution of the new brand was to be through a limited number of distributor/dealers, and seven display sets containing one each of these ten knives were made. Those sets were valued at about $350 when produced in 1981 but will command prices of about $3,000 in today's collector market.

Identification of a Cripple Creek is made primarily by noting the shield and stamping. Except for knives made in 1981, all knives have the year of manufacture stamped on the master blade's reverse tang. The shield found on most Cripple Creek knives is an oval embossed with a three-legged buffalo, modeled after the one on the 1937 "D" nickel. The very earliest knives produced, however, used an oval shield with C.C.C. or CRIPPLE CREEK stamped on it. These knives, which retailed in the $30 to $45 range, are now valued at about ten times that amount.

Production of the standard Cripple Creek patterns was approximately 500 knives in 1981 and approximately 250 in 1982.

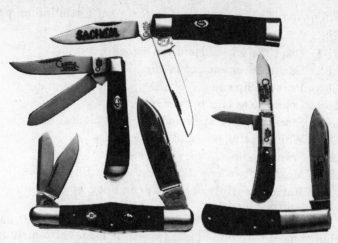

Gunstock, Trapper, Balloon Whittler, and two sizes of Barlow patterns made by Cripple Creek in 1983.   *(Photo by Weyer)*

Shortly after introduction of the brand, Cripple Creek contracted to make a special knife for Knife World Publications. The 1st Edition Knife World knife was limited to two thousand pieces, but their production required most of Cargill's time during the latter portion of 1981 and much of 1982. Therein lies the reason for the very low production of regular Cripple Creek LI series knives during this period.

Most Cripple Creek knives have bone and genuine stag handles; another favorite handle material used, although less frequently, is mother-of-pearl. Although other patterns have been added to the line or substituted for the original ten, most follow the patterns of knives made during the earlier part of this century.

In 1986, Cripple Creek was relocated to Tennessee, and in 1987 the name "Old Fort, TN" was added to knife stampings.

A variety of handle materials has been used for Cripple Creek, but the majority have been handled in bone. During the first three years, a light brown bone, referred to as "Honey Bone," was used. It became a favorite for collectors of the brand. Other colors used have been brown bone, strawberry bone, green bone, and white bone. Except for 1986, when Christmas celluloid and Red-White-Blue Micarta were used on two special knives, natural handle materials have been used. Stag has been second in use to bone, followed by mother-of-pearl.

Following is a description of the original Little Indian patterns.

LI-1   Dog Leg Jack; clip and pen blades

LI-2   Canoe; spear and pen blades

LI-3   Peanut; clip and pen blades

LI-4   Coke Bottle; clip and pen blades

LI-5   Stockman; clip, spey, and sheepfoot blades

LI-6   Whittler; clip, pen, and coping blades

LI-7   Trapper; clip and spey blades

LI-8   Muskrat; two long clip or "California Clip" blades

LI-9   Barlow; variety of clip, spear, spey, or razor master blades and pen blade

LI-10   Buffalo Skinner (Large Dog Leg Folding Hunter); one-blade model with clip blade; two-blade model also included skinner blade.

As with all knives, values of Cripple Creeks vary depending on pattern, year made, and handle material used. With this brand of knives, however, it is possible to offer some general value guidelines for mint condition knives that apply to all or most patterns.

Any knife bearing the "C.C.C." or "Cripple Creek" shields will have a minimum collector value of $350, and some will range up to $600.

Early Cripple Creeks made in 1981 and 1982. Note the "Cripple Creek" shields and blade etchings . *(Photo by Weyer)*

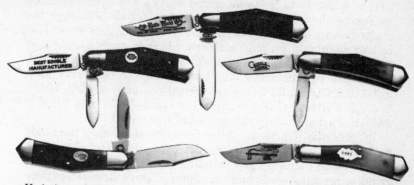

Variations of the LI-1 pattern made during the 1981–1983 period.   *(Photo by Weyer)*

Any knife made in 1981, regardless of shield type, will have a minimum collector value of $200, ranging upward to $350. With the limited production of regular patterns in 1982, any standard Cripple Creek pattern knife dated that year will be valued as highly as one produced in 1981.

Any knife bearing an Oak Leaf shield is an especially desirable collectible, varying in value from $150 for the LI-1 pattern one-blade "White Hawk," made in 1983, to $350 for the LI-4 made in 1981.

In 1984, Cripple Creek produced the five-blade sowbelly stockman in three handle materials. Those handled in Stag have a collector value of $225, while the Honey Bone and Strawberry Bone models are valued at $175 to $200.

Finally, any mint condition Cripple Creek knife bearing a date stamp up to 1986 will have a minimum collector value of $100.

EAGLE POCKETKNIFE COMPANY

This firm was founded in 1916 by the Hemming brothers, Otto, Frank, and Carl, and operated in New Haven, Connecticut. Their primary product was the all-metal knife with wrap-around handles. The brothers invented machinery that made it possible to manufacture knives of this type on an assembly line basis.

Markings used on this company's knives included EAGLE KNIFE CO. PAT PEND. MADE IN U.S.A. and EAGLE KNIFE

CO. In addition to these all-metal knives, the company made knives handled with black fiber-based materials. Although the majority were of lesser quality, some of Eagle's knives were of excellent quality, in keeping with other brands made during that time. Knives made by this company should not be confused with those made by other companies but bearing similar marks, such as EAGLE CUTLERY CO. (Eagle Pencil Company, c. 1883–1945), EAGLE, PHILA. (G. F. Creutzberg, c. 1875–1943), and EAGLE JAPAN (Parker Cutlery Company, 1974–present).

In 1919, the Winchester Arms Company purchased the Eagle firm, primarily for the Hemming-designed and patented machinery for blade blanking and grinding. The Hemming automatic grinding machine would allow mechanization of their own cutlery manufacture. The machine became widely used among cutlery manufacturers, and many that were manufactured during this era are still in use today.

ELECTRIC CUTLERY COMPANY

This was a trademark of Friedman and Lauterjung, a cutlery-importing firm that was in business from 1866 until 1909. Knives stamped with Electric's brand were of excellent quality, with bone, celluloid, and rosewood handles. Made under contract in Walden, New York, by both New York Knife Company and Walden Knife Company, the knives were stamped ELECTRIC CUTLERY COMPANY, WALDEN, NEW YORK, and ELECTRIC CUTLERY COMPANY, NEWARK, NEW JERSEY.

EYE BRAND—CARL SCHLIEPER

The best-known trademark for knives manufactured by Carl Schlieper is popularly called "Eye Brand" or sometimes "German Eye." These names aptly describe the tang marking of this Solingen, Germany, company's logo: an eye plus the word GERMANY or the words C. SCHLIEPER or CARL SCHLIEPER plus the eye.

This company was established by Carl Schlieper in 1898 as a branch of the Schlieper Tool and Cutlery Company. It is now managed by a sixth-generation member of the family, Hanspeter Schlieper. Knives exported by the company to the United States include pocketknives, hunting knives, kitchen cutlery, and scissors. The company's pocketknives have been handled in stag, bone, composition, and genuine pearl.

Other, lesser-known trademarks for pocketknives made by Schlieper include JIM BOWIE/GERMANY and EL GALLO/ GERMANY, but the "Eye Brand" line is best recognized for excellent quality and will be the brand most often found by collectors.

FIGHT'N ROOSTER

The first Fight'n Rooster brand pocketknives were produced in 1976 in Solingen, Germany. Their production, as well as their acceptance within the collector market, has been the realization of the goals set by a dealer and collector of old pocketknives. Frank Buster had been a trader and collector of knives for a number of years when he recognized that finding old knives at reasonable prices was becoming more and more difficult. His answer to the problem was to have limited numbers of traditional-pattern knives produced for collectors, but finding U.S. manufacturers who were willing or able to produce these knives in relatively small numbers was nearly impossible. Finally, Buster located a small factory in Germany that would cooperate in making a few patterns.

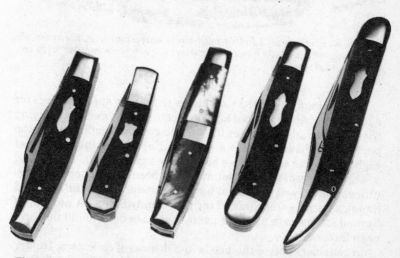

The handles on these knives are typical of those used by Fight'n Rooster. Left to right: Christmas Tree celluloid, Metal Flake celluloid, pearl, bone stag, and genuine stag.   *(Photo by Weyer)*

The Frank Buster Cutlery Company was formed in Lebanon, Tennessee, and the first knives produced bore a logo that has become recognized and respected by collectors from most parts of the county. The knives are stamped with two fighting roosters and SOLINGEN or GERMANY. Other stampings used, often in combination with the logo, are FRANK BUSTER CUTLERY CO./ GERMANY or FRANK BUSTER CELEBRATED CUTLERY/ GERMANY.

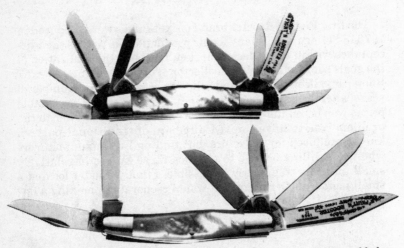

Fight'n Rooster's pearl-handled multiblade knives, such as the ten-blade Congress and six-blade Stockman patterns, have been popular with collectors. *(Photo by Weyer)*

The company has been very active in making special knives for a large number of regional knife-collecting clubs and in supplying the regular Fight'n Rooster line to collectors through dealers who participate in knife shows and mail order businesses. Most Fight'n Rooster knives have been made in traditional styles, and a large variety of handle materials has been used. Especially significant have been those that have reintroduced colorful celluloid handles such as Christmas Tree and Candy Stripe. A number of limited issues have used old parts that have been found in European factories.

In consideration of the needs and desires of collectors, Buster has kept the quantity of his knives low and the quality high. Recognizing that statistics are important to collectors, the company

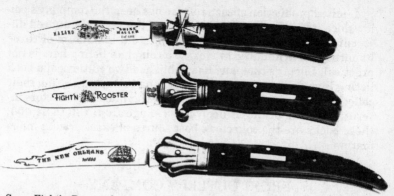

Some Fight'n Rooster knives are made with genuine old parts, such as these fancy bolsters found in the old German factory.   *(Photo by Weyer)*

has maintained records of the numbers of each knife produced and the year of production. Noteworthy among the company's other activities within the collector market have been encouragement and support of participation by women and youngsters in a hobby that has too often been considered one for men only. Visitors to knife shows, especially those held in the southeast, will find several elaborate and informative displays of Fight'n Rooster knives.

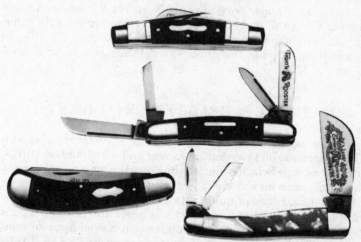

Traditional patterns with modern expression are typical of many Fight'n Rooster releases.   *(Photo by Weyer)*

Limited production of each release has been the company's policy since its beginning. The majority of the several hundred different knives made have been limited to a maximum of three hundred to five hundred knives, so a complete listing here is not practical. Buster's company has published two editions of a book listing Fight'n Rooster knives, describing them and stating their collector values. A third edition is being complied for collectors interested in the brand. Since values range from $30 to $4,000, these books are the collector's best source of exact pricing information.

FROST CUTLERY COMPANY

This Chattanooga, Tennessee–based company was formed in 1978 by James A. Frost, a former partner of the Parker-Frost Cutlery Company. The company is a major importer of knives made in Japan but bearing the Frost name and "Falcon" trademark. In addition, the company serves as a distributor of several other knife brands made in the United States as well as in other countries. Several limited-edition or commemorative issues, primarily knives made by Case and creatively packaged by Frost, have been marketed. Some of these, along with limited editions bearing the Parker-Frost stamping are listed in the commemorative section of this book.

Although a major portion of Frost knives are made and sold for regular knife use, many of these are decorated with color-engraved (panagraphed) handles and blade etching. Wildlife and sports teams are but two of the several themes used for decorations.

GEORGE SCHRADE KNIFE COMPANY

George Schrade is best recognized as a knife inventor, especially for patents on push-button knives and wire-handled knives. In 1893, George Schrade formed the Press Button Knife Company to manufacture his switchblade knife patented two years earlier. Because of the lack of qualified cutlers, production at his New York City shop was at low volume. Schrade entered into a joint venture with Walden Knife Company and moved his own company to Walden, New York. Knives stamped PRESS BUTTON KNIFE CO. WALDEN N.Y. were made in large quantities and in at least a dozen patterns from 1893 until the 1920s but not always with George Schrade's personal involvement. In 1903, he sold his interest in the company and his patent rights to Walden Knife Company and joined with his brothers in forming Schrade Cutlery Company. The purpose of the new company was to manufacture improved versions of his switchblade designs.

George Schrade left the brothers' company about 1910 to pursue his interest in another patent, the automatic shielding machine. In 1916, Schrade's new patent switchblade design was introduced under the name FLYLOCK and was made by Challenge Cutlery Company, which later purchased the trademark from Schrade. Near the mid-1920s George Schrade Knife Company was formed in Bridgeport, Connecticut, and the knife was made with the trademark PRESTO. In the early 1940s, Schrade patented his wire-handled jackknives and produced them in large quantities.

Although George Schrade died in 1945, his company remained in business until 1958. Knife stampings used by the company include GEO. SCHRADE B'PORT CONN. and GEORGE SCHRADE KNIFE CO. B'PORT CONN. Some stampings used during the company's later years included patent dates for wire jackknives.

GERBER LEGENDARY BLADES

The formation of this company began in 1939, when an advertising executive, Joseph R. Gerber, arranged for the production of a couple of dozen knives for use as Christmas gifts to his clients. The local craftsman who made the knives was David Z. Murphy, a knife maker who would soon be supplying a large number of Murphy Combat knives for use by servicemen fighting in World War II. When an executive of Abercrombie & Fitch offered to buy as many knives as could be produced, a business was started.

The earliest knives featured a cast-aluminum handle, and the design gained early recognition, especially as household cutlery. When Gerber branched out into sportsmen's knives in 1950, a variation of the cast handle was followed through in their Magnum series. Like the earlier knives, these would earn recognition as well as respect for their high quality.

Gerber added folding knives to its line and became an innovator of new knife designs, some of which were produced in Japan as a supplement to those produced in the company's own Portland, Oregon, factory. In addition to their own designs, knives designed by Paul Poehlmann, Bob Loveless, and "Blackie" Collins were produced bearing the stamping GERBER/PORTLAND, or 97223/ USA. A large number of the company's products were stamped with its trademark, the "Excalibur" sword embedded in a large rock.

Ownership of Gerber Legendary Blades remained with the Gerber family until 1987, when the company was sold to Fiskars.

HUMASON & BECKLEY

The Humason & Beckley Manufacturing Company was founded in 1853 by William L. Humason and F. W. Beckley. Along with several hardware items, the New Britain, Connecticut, company manufactured pocketknives of exceptionally good quality.

Handle materials used for their knives included buffalo horn, ebony, stag, bone, pearl, and sterling silver. Trademark stamping was H&B MFG. CO./NEW BRITAIN/CONN, and the initials H. & B. were often stamped on the center of the knife's main blade as well.

H & B knives are rarely found in the collector market because the numbers made were never high, compared to knives of larger manufacturers such as this company's own successor. The company was purchased in 1912 by another New Britain cutlery firm, Landers, Frary & Clark. Although L. F. & C. was probably the world's top cutlery producer at the time, their line did not include pocketknives. The Humason & Beckley factory became their pocketknife division and continued to manufacture H & B knives until 1916.

J. A. HENCKELS

One of the best-known trademarks in imported knives is that of the J. A. Henckels company of Solingen, Germany, established in 1731. Henckels "Twinworks" knives are stamped with the name J. A. HENCKELS and the logo of two men in silhouette joined at the arm and leg. Collectors normally refer to these high-quality pocketknives as "Twin Henckles."

Expansion of the brand began in its home country in the early 1800s, when Johann Abraham Henckels established his second cutlery showroom in Berlin, a three-week journey from Solingen. The first American showroom was opened in New York City in 1883, when the brand became associated with the importing firm of Graef & Schmidt.

The Henckels factory continues to operate today and is an extremely large cutlery manufacturing complex. The company produces a wide line of products—over two thousand different patterns of cutlery, including pocketknives, kitchen cutlery, and scissors.

HOLLEY MANUFACTURING COMPANY

Alexander H. Holley first entered the knife manufacturing business in 1844, after hearing of the efforts of a small group of English workmen to introduce "spring cutlery" (folding pocketknives) to this country. Holley bought out their failing business, hired the former owners, and built a new building to house the manufacturing of pocketknives in Salisbury, Connecticut. He soon took in Nathan W. Merwin, and a little later the two were joined by George P. Burrell. The partners made knives and conducted business under the name Holley & Company. The knife stamping used at that time was HOLLEY & CO. SALISBURY (1844–1846). The town's name was changed in 1846 to Lakeville, and the stamping was changed to HOLLEY & CO. LAKEVILLE (1846–1854). A new stamping was introduced in 1854, when the partners incorporated their business under the name of Holley Manufacturing Company. From that year until the 1930s, their knives were marked HOLLEY LAKEVILLE CONN.

Holley made high-quality knives and for a number of years enjoyed good business. About the turn of the century, Holley's market share began to dwindle as newer and more modernized manufacturers began to compete. The company delayed too long in updating manufacturing methods and had lost much of its national sales volume by 1904. The firm continued to make knives in a much smaller volume until 1930, when it ceased production.

The company handled its knives in horn, bone, ivory, metal, and wood, always using brass liners. Because of the very low production during the company's latter years, Holley knives are difficult to find and are quite desirable in the collector market.

HONK FALLS KNIFE COMPANY

This firm was formed in Napanoch, New York, about 1921 by four former employees of the Napanoch Knife Company. When Winchester purchased the Napanoch business and moved production to Connecticut, one of the employees who moved also was

John J. Cushner. By 1920, Cushner had returned home to Napanoch and joined with Melvin Quick, Melvin Schoonmaker, and George Brackley in buying the old knife company's factory from Winchester. They formed the Honk Falls Knife Company and employed their beginning work force of ten men to produce their own brand of pocketknives.

Knives stamped HONK FALLS, NAPANOCH, NEW YORK, U.S.A. were produced until the factory burned in 1929. These knives were of high quality and, when found, are valuable collectibles.

HOWARD CUTLERY COMPANY

A sewing machine parts distributor, the C. B. Barker Co. of New York City, introduced the name "Howard" as a knife brand during the early 1880s. The brand was made until 1905. Barker contracted with Canastota Knife Company for knives to be made under the Howard name. In addition, since the Barker firm was an importer, some of their knives were made in Germany. Stampings used included HOWARD CUTLERY CO./GERMANY and HOWARD (with the logo of an owl on a limb and "Howard Cutlery Co" stamped on the reverse tang). While either is a desirable brand, those knives made by Canastota are of higher value than those made in Germany.

HIBBARD, SPENCER AND BARTLETT

Founded in 1855, this company was a large wholesaler of hardware until 1960. The Chicago-based company's best-known and most collectible pocketknife brand was OVB (Our Very Best). Other knives were marked TRUE VALUE, HIBBARD, and HIBSPEBAR. Hibbard, Spencer and Bartlett was not a cutlery manufacturer; knives were made for them under contract by manufacturers such as Camillus, Ulster, and Schrade.

HENRY SEARS & SON

The firm of Henry Sears & Co. was started about 1865 as a Chicago-based manufacturer. It became Henry Sears & Son in 1883, with ownership by Henry Sears, E. B. Sears, and E. W. Beattie. Cutlery stamped H. SEARS MFG. CO. was marketed between 1865 and 1883. From 1883 until 1897 the stamping was HENRY SEARS & SON CHICAGO. During this latter period (about 1887), the business was sold to the Farwell-Ozmun-Kirk & Co. Hardware firm of St. Paul, Minnesota, but the stamping continued until 1897. From 1897 until 1959, the stamping HENRY SEARS & SON 1865 was used by the hardware distributor. Although the date 1865 was included in the stamping or as a blade etching, the knives do not date to that year of manufacture. The knives sold by Farwell-Ozmun-Kirk using that date marking were made under contract by several prominent cutlery manufacturers.

GEORGE IBBERSON & COMPANY

This company was founded in Sheffield, England, in 1700, and the first knife marking used was an *S* over a *T*. The trademark that is most often associated with Ibberson knives is the Violin logo, first used in 1880. During its long history, the company has used thirty-three trademarks.

Although Ibberson's includes table cutlery, letter openers, and scissors, none of its products compare in terms of quality of workmanship and personal appeal with its pocketknives. Besides a regular line of pocketknives, Ibberson has produced several patterns of "chaised knives" (backsprings and liners filed with artistic designs); they usually have mother-of-pearl handles.

IMPERIAL KNIFE COMPANY

In 1916, the brothers Michael and Felix Mirando arrived in Providence, Rhode Island, from Winsted, Connecticut, where they had worked for the Empire Knife Company. The Mirando family had made knives in Italy for several generations, and the move from Empire was with the intent of starting their own cutlery business. Their first knives were made during 1917 in a small rented blacksmith shop, and the Imperial Knife Company was formed. The company at first made only knife skeletons that were used by the area's jewelry trade in making watch chain knives, and within less than a year of the company's founding, Imperial was producing more than a thousand pieces per week.

Business grew, and in 1919 the Mirandos were joined in business by Domenic Fazzano, a boyhood friend from Italy's Frosilone cutlery center. By the early 1920s, wristwatches began replacing pocketwatches, and necessity became the mother of invention for Imperial. Their innovation of the shadow knife (skeletons with mounted plastic scales) was responsible for their continuing success. In fact, continued practical application of innovative ideas not only helped Imperial to weather the storm of the Great Depression but also helped make the company into the giant it is today. During a time when knives had handles in bone, stag, cocobolo, and horn, Imperial pioneered knives with colorful plastic handles. When the buying public was exceptionally cost-conscious, Imperial's sales of bumped tip bolstered knives and those of shell-wrapped handle construction offered reasonable alternatives.

By 1940, Imperial was the world's largest cutlery manufacturer, producing as many as one hundred thousand knives per day. During World War II, production of knives for civilian use was restricted, and Imperial converted to full wartime production. The company produced more than half of the trench knives used by the various branches of the armed forces. After playing the key role in designing the M-4 bayonet, Imperial produced the largest quantity of all bayonets purchased by the government. With wartime production priorities, Imperial began to work cooperatively with the Ulster Knife Company, owned by Albert and Henry Baer.

In 1947, the three established company names of Imperial, Schrade, and Ulster came together under the leadership of the Mirandos, the Fazannos, and the Baers in a company named the Imperial Knife Associated Companies. The Baer brothers bought out their partners in 1984, and the company name was changed to Imperial Schrade Corporation.

Some of the stampings used by Imperial included IMPERIAL KNIFE CO., IMPERIAL/PROV. R. I., HAMMER BRAND, I. K. CO., JACK-MASTER, KAMP KING, and FRONTIER, as well as several contract brands. Although older knife handles were of traditional materials such as bone and celluloid, those using plastic, metal, and Delrin are more commonly found.

KA-BAR CUTLERY COMPANY, INC.

Originally named Union Razor Company, this cutlery firm was started about 1898 by Wallace R. Brown, a grandson of Job R. Case. Founded in Tidioute, Pennsylvania, the company specialized in straight razors but also made pocketknives as well as other lines of cutlery. After operating for fourteen years in

Tidiuote, the company relocated to the nearby town of Olean, New York.

Olean offered Union Razor Company several enticements to bring its industry to the small town. During the next two years the company moved, and by 1921 it was in full operation at the Olean facility. The knives made at this time were stamped "Union Cutlery Company, Olean New York" (the Razor Company trademark had been dropped on January 15, 1909).

Union was soon making an extensive line of pocketknives bearing such stampings as "Olcut," "Keenwell," and another trademark that was popular on their large folding hunter patterns, "KA-BAR."

According to legend, this latter trademark came from a testimonial letter. It was written by an old trapper whose life had allegedly been saved in a bear fight by a well-made Union Cutlery Company knife. Because of his lack of education, he wrote of how he had been able to "kil a bar." This was shortened and appeared as KA-BAR.

A trademark was born, and the Ka-bar name soon became more popular than the Union Cutlery name stamping. In 1951 the corporate name was changed to KA-BAR Cutlery Company, Inc., and the tang stamping was changed from KA-BAR to Kabar.

In the early 1950s, Ka-bar attempted to move the production of their pocketknives to Dawsonville, Georgia, hoping to take advantage of the inexpensive labor supply in the North Georgia mountains. Ka-bar management, however, failed to reckon with the area residents taking off work completely for much of the planting and harvest seasons. Then too, although laborers were plentiful, there was a general lack of skilled workers in the area. Within a year the company was moving back to Olean.

After Danforth Brown's death, the company changed ownership several times and, for a brief while in the 1960s, completely stopped knife production. Then, in 1966, Cole National Corporation purchased the company and again started national distribution, with emphasis on marketing through several large discount stores.

By 1977, Ka-bar had ceased all knife production by their own employees, but the old factory is still used for storage and shipping purposes. The company has recently moved more toward importation of knives made in Japan and other cutlery production—oriented countries.

Unfortunately for collectors, the company failed to stamp pattern numbers on the majority of its knives. Once one becomes familiar with those that are stamped, the pattern numbers on Ka-bar knives can tell quite a bit about them. The first number represents the handle material designated as follows:

1—Ebony

2—Natural Stag

3—Redwood

4—White Imitation Ivory

5—Black Celluloid

6—Bone Stag

7—Mother-of-Pearl

8—Unknown

9—Silver Pyraline

O—Pyraline Candy Stripe
and Fancy Celluloid

P—Imitation Pearl

H—Horn

T—Fancy Pearl (early)
Cream Celluloid (late)

R—Rainbow Celluloid

C—Unknown

The second digit in the pattern number signifies the number of blades. The company made knives with up to seven blades. Four-blade knives by Ka-bar are not very commonplace, but the seven-blade knife is a very rare find.

The remaining digits designate the factory pattern number. Knives listed in this guide are arranged by that pattern number.

Although a few early knives were made with iron liners, most Ka-bars will be found with brass liners and nickel silver bolsters. Knives with every blade stamped will bring a 10 to 15 percent premium over those with just the master blade stamped. Of extra rarity and extra value is a "Ka-bar USA"–stamped knife with bone handles. Rarer still is the "Ka-bar"-stamped, bone-handle knife because by the time that stamping was used, almost all of the company's knives were made with plastic handles. Several KA-BAR folding hunters featured a shield shaped like the silhouette of a dog's head. Popularly known as "dog's head Ka-Bars," these knives are quite desirable and are valued considerably higher than most other knives produced by the company.

Value estimates listed in this section are not for an extra-rare Union Razor stamping. Knives with this stamping should be worth 1½–2 times the value of the same pattern in a "Union Knife Co." or "Ka-Bar" stamping. Also of greater value are the knives stamped "KA-BAR Olean, New York." A knife with this stamping should be valued about 50 percent higher than one of like pattern but with the "Kabar, USA" stamping.

Ka-Bar Stampings

Ka-Bar has used numerous tang stampings during the several stages of its long tenure. Some that the collector may encounter are listed below.

UNION RAZOR CO. Tidioute, PA
UNION CUTLERY CO. Tidioute, PA
UNION CUT. CO. Tidioute
Union (inside an American shield)
Union Cut. Co. Olean, N. Y.
Union Cut. Co.
Unionco
KA-BAR
KA-BAR Olean, N. Y.
Ka-Bar Olean, N. Y.
Ka-Bar Stainless
Kabar Stainless
Olcut
Kabar (pattern no.) USA
KA-BAR-LO

Ka-Bar Knives with Dog's-Head Shields

Pattern	Length	Stamping	Handle	Mint Price
22 Bullet	4½″	KA-BAR/ UNION CUT.	Genuine Stag	$600
62 Bullet	4½″	KA-BAR/ UNION CUT.	Bone Stag	500
6191LG	5¼″	KA-BAR/ UNION CUT.	Bone Stag	500
P191 LG	5¼″	KA-BAR/ UNION CUT.	Imitation Pearl	475
6291 KF	5¼″	UNION in a shield	Bone Stag	450
6291 KF	5¼″	UNION CUT. CO.	Bone Stag	400
2291 KF	5¼″	UNION CUT. CO.	Genuine Stag	425
6291 KF	5¼″	KA-BAR/ UNION CUT.	Bone Stag	375

Pattern	Length	Stamping	Handle	Mint Price
6391 K-F-S	5¼″	KA-BAR/ UNION CUT.	Bone Stag	$650
61106 LG	5⅜″	UNION	Bone Stag	800
61106 LG	5⅜″	UNION CUT. CO. (circle)	Bone Stag	550
61106 LG	5⅜″	UNION CUT. CO. (straight)	Bone Stag	550
61106 LG	5⅜″	KA-BAR/ UNION CUT.	Bone Stag	525
61106	5⅜″	UNION in a shield	Bone Stag	650
61106	5⅜″	UNION CUT. CO. (circle)	Bone Stag	500
61106	5⅜″	UNION CUT. CO. (straight)	Bone Stag	500
21106	5⅜″	KA-BAR/ UNION CUT.	Genuine Stag	625
61106	5⅜″	KA-BAR/ UNION CUT.	Bone Stag	475
P1106	5⅜″	KA-BAR/ UNION CUT.	Pearl Celluloid	350
21107	5¼″	UNION CUT. CO. (straight)	Genuine Stag	425
21107	5¼″	KA-BAR/ UNION CUT.	Genuine Stag	350
21107	5¼″	Current Model Dated	Genuine Stag	80
22107	5¼″	UNION CUT. CO. (straight)	Genuine Stag	400
22107	5¼″	KA-BAR/ UNION CUT.	Genuine Stag	375
22107	5¼″	Ka-Bar Olean, N.Y.	Genuine Stag	325
22107	5¼″	kabar (number)	Genuine Stag	80
61107 LG	5¼″	KA-BAR/ UNION CUT.	Bone Stag	600
22107 LG	5¼″	KA-BAR/ UNION CUT.	Genuine Stag	675
T1107 LG	5¼″	KA-BAR/ UNION CUT.	Cream Celluloid	475
61107	5¼″	UNION in a shield	Bone Stag	625
61107	5¼″	UNION CUT. CO. (straight)	Bone Stag	425
61107	5¼″	KA-BAR/ UNION CUT.	Bone Stag	350
62107	5¼″	UNION CUT. CO. (straight)	Bone Stag	400

Pattern	Length	Stamping	Handle	Mint Price
62107	5¼″	KA-BAR/ UNION CUT	Bone Stag	$350
62107	5¼″	Ka-Bar Olean, N.Y.	Bone Stag	300
61110	4⅝″	UNION in a shield	Bone Stag	475
02118	4″	Bicentennial Model	R/W/B Celluloid	75
61126 L	4⅝″	UNION CUT. CO. (circle)	Bone Stag	850
22156	5¼″	UNION in a shield	Genuine Stag	700
22156	5¼″	UNION CUT. CO. (straight)	Genuine Stag	525
62156	5¼″	UNION in a shield	Bone Stag	575
62156	5¼″	UNION CUT. CO. (straight)	Bone Stag	450

One-Blade Knives

Pattern	Length	Stamping	Handle	Mint Price
Cigar Cutter	2″	UNION CUT CO.	Cream Celluloid	$45
T-19	5″	KA-BAR Stainless	Cream Celluloid	30
6111	3⅞″	UNION CUT CO.	Bone Stag	100
0111	3⅞″	UNION CUT CO.	Pyraline	75

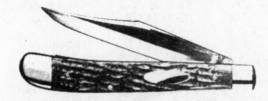

6112	4″	UNION CUT CO.	Bone Stag	70
0112	4″	UNION CUT CO.	Pyraline	60
6112	4″	KA-BAR	Bone Stag	60
0112	4″	KA-BAR	Pyraline	55
6112	4″	kabar	Rough Black	35

Pattern	Length	Stamping	Handle	Mint Price
T112	4″	kabar	Cream Celluloid	$30
T118	3″	KA-BAR	Cream Celluloid	30
3163	3½″	UNION CUT CO.	Redwood	35
6163	3½″	UNION CUT CO.	Bone Stag	55
6165	4½″	UNION CUT CO.	Bone Stag	90
0165	4½″	UNION CUT.	Fancy Celluloid	80
6165 LG	4⅜″	UNION CUT CO.	Bone Stag	175
6165 LG	4⅜″	KA-BAR	Bone Stag	140
2165 LG	4⅜″	kabar	Genuine Stag	85
6165 LG	4⅜″	kabar	Rough Black	50
6165 LG	4⅜″	kabar (number) USA	Delrin	10
3170	4″	UNION CUT CO.	Redwood	90
3174	3¾″	UNION CUT CO.	Redwood	30
6174	3¾″	UNION CUT CO.	Bone Stag	45
3174	3¾″	KA-BAR	Redwood	25
6174	3¾″	KA-BAR	Bone Stag	40
6175RG	4½″	UNION CUT CO.	Bone Stag	50
2179-L Grizzly	5½″	KA-BAR	Genuine Stag	1500
T179	5½″	KA-BAR	Cream Celluloid	400
9179	5½″	KA-BAR	Silver Pyraline	600
6191 L	5½″	UNION CUT CO	Bone Stag	600
6191 L	5½″	UNION CUT CO	Genuine Stag	750

Pattern	Length	Stamping	Handle	Mint Price
61103	3⅜″	UNION CUT CO	Bone Stag	70
01103	3⅜″	UNION CUT. CO.	Fancy Celluloid	55

Pattern	Length	Stamping	Handle	Mint Price
71103	3⅜″	UNION CUT CO	Pearl	$85
61103	3⅜″	KA-BAR	Bone Stag	70
01103	3⅜″	KA-BAR	Fancy Celluloid	50
21105	4½″	UNION CUT CO	Genuine Stag	500
21105	4½″	KA-BAR	Genuine Stag	400
61105	4½″	KA-BAR	Bone Stag	400
T1105	4½″	KA-BAR	Cream Celluloid	350
61106	5⅜″	UNION CUT CO	Bone Stag	300
66106	5⅜″	KA-BAR	Bone Stag	250
T1106	5⅜″	Ka-Bar	Cream Celluloid	275
61106 L	5⅜″	UNION CUT CO	Bone Stag	450
21107 L. Grizzly	5¼″	KA-BAR	Genuine Stag	1500
61107	5¼″	UNION CUT CO	Bone Stag	300
61107	5¼″	KA-BAR	Bone Stag	250
61107	5¼″	KA-BAR	Rough Black	125
P-2207	5¼″	KA-BAR	Imitation Pearl	150
61107	5¼″	kabar	Rough Black	75
31108	5¼″	kabar	Redwood	30
31108	5¼″	kabar (number) USA	Redwood	15
61110	4½″	UNION CUT CO	Bone Stag	95
61118	4¼″	UNION CUT CO	Bone Stag	200
01118	4¼″	UNION CUT CO	Fancy Celluloid	140
61125 L	4½″	UNION CUT CO	Bone Stag	275
61126 L	4½″	UNION CUT CO	Bone Stag	600

Pattern	Length	Stamping	Handle	Mint Price
61129	5″	UNION CUT CO	Bone Stag	125

Pattern	Length	Stamping	Handle	*Mint* Price
G1129	5″	UNION CUT CO	Pyraline	$90
61129	5″	KA-BAR	Bone Stag	90
K1129	5″	KA-BAR	Fancy Celluloid	90
T1129	5″	KA-BAR	Cream Celluloid	75
31130	4″	kabar	Redwood	15
31130	4″	kabar (number) USA	Redwood	10
31131	4⅝″	UNION CUT CO	Redwood	50
31131	4⅝″	KA-BAR	Redwood	40

Pattern	Length	Stamping	Handle	Price
61132	5½″	UNION CUT CO	Bone Stag	250
11132	5½″	UNION CUT CO	Ebony	150
91132	5½″	UNION CUT CO	Silver Pyraline	200
61132	5½″	KA-BAR	Bone Stag	200
P-1147	4½″	KA-BAR	Imitation Pearl	50
T-1147	4½″	KA-BAR	Cream Celluloid	50

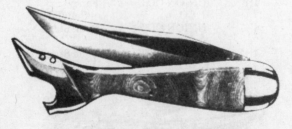

Pattern	Length	Stamping	Handle	Price
P-1154	4¾″	UNION CUT CO	Fancy Celluloid	175
P-1154	4¾″	KA-BAR	Fancy Celluloid	140

Pattern	Length	Stamping	Handle	Mint Price
71155	1½"	UNION CUT CO	Genuine Pearl	
				$75
X 1157	5¾"	UNION CUT CO	Metal	
				125
X 1157	5¾"	KA-BAR	Metal	100
R-1160	4¼"	U NION CUT CO	Fancy Celluloid	
				50
61161	4½"	UNION CUT CO	Bone Stag	
				200
61161-BAIL	4½"	KA-BAR	Bone Stag	
				175
T-1161	4½"	KA-BAR	Cream Celluloid	
				225

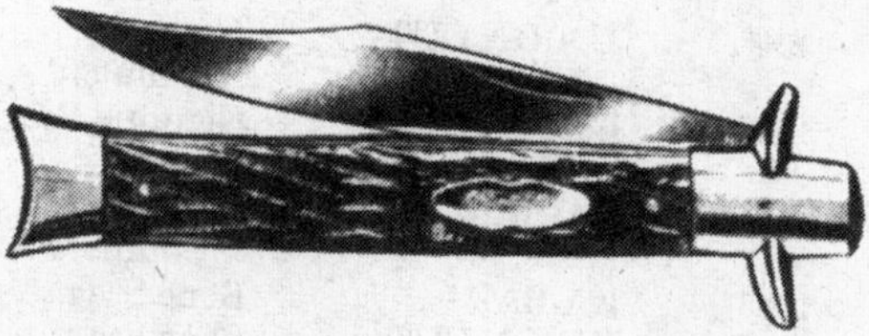

Pattern	Length	Stamping	Handle	Mint Price
61169	4½"	KA-BAR	Bone Stag	150
T-1175	4½"	KA-BAR	Cream Celluloid	
				45
21187	5¼"	KA-BAR	Genuine Stag	350
61187	5¼"	KA-BAR	Bone Stag	290
31187	5¼"	KA-BAR	Redwood	175
61187	5¼"	UNION CUT CO	Smooth Bone	
				125
61187	5¼"	KA-BAR	Smooth Bone	100
51187	5¼"	kabar	Black Composition	
				40
51187	5¼"	kabar (number) USA	Black Celluloid	
				10
51198	4"	kabar	Black Celluloid	
				20
51198	4"	kabar (number) USA	Black Celluloid	
				10

Two-Blade Knives

Pattern	Length	Stamping	Handle	Mint Price
42027 S	3½"	UNION CUT CO	Imitation Ivory	
				$80
42027 S	3½"	UNION CUT CO	Imitation Ivory	
				70

Pattern	Length	Stamping	Handle	Mint Price
5-29	5″	KA-BAR	Black Celluloid	$35
T-29	5″	KA-BAR	Cream Celluloid	25
R-29	5″	KA-BAR	Red Celluloid	25
T-29	5″	kabar	Cream Celluloid	12
R-29	5″	kabar	Red Celluloid	12
T-29	5″	kabar (number) USA	Cream Celluloid	8
6200	2½″	UNION CUT CO	Bone Stag	45
T 200	2½″	UNION CUT CO	Cream Celluloid	25
T 200 RG	2½″	UNION CUT CO	Cream Celluloid	25
T 200 RG	2½″	UNION CUT CO	Genuine Pearl	50
T 200 RG	2½″	KA-BAR	Rainbow Celluloid	30
6200	2½″	KA-BAR	Bone Stag	50
6201 T	2⅞″	UNION CUT CO	Bone Stag	45
7201 T	2⅞″	UNION CUT CO	Genuine Pearl	70
6201	2⅞″	KA-BAR	Bone Stag	40
6202	3″	UNION CUT CO	Bone Stag	45
7202	3″	UNION CUT CO	Genuine Pearl	45
6202	3″	KA-BAR	Bone Stag	40
7202	3″	KA-BAR	Genuine Pearl	70
6203½	3″	UNION CUT CO	Bone Stag	40
0203½	3″	UNION CUT CO	Fancy Pyraline	45
7203½	3″	UNION CUT CO	Genuine Pearl	70
6204	3″	UNION CUT CO	Bone Stag	50
7204	3″	UNION CUT CO	Genuine Pearl	70
6204	3″	KA-BAR	Bone Stag	45
6204	3″	KA-BAR	Rough Black	25
6205	3⅛″	UNION CUT CO	Bone Stag	50

Pattern	Length	Stamping	Handle	Mint Price
6205	3⅛″	KA-BAR	Bone Stag	$40
1206	3¼″	UNION CUT CO	Ebony	30
2206	3¼″	UNION CUT CO	Genuine Stag	45
6206	3¼″	UNION CUT CO	Bone Stag	40
7206	3¼″	UNION CUT CO	Genuine Pearl	65
9206	3¼″	UNION CUT	Silver Pyraline	35
2206	3¼″	KA-BAR	Genuine Stag	40
6206	3¼″	KA-BAR	Bone Stag	40
P206	3¼″	KA-BAR	Imitation Pearl	35
2206	3¼″	kabar	Genuine Pearl	30
6206	3¼″	kabar	Bone Stag	25
P206	3¼″	kabar	Pearl Celluloid	20
7206	3¼″	kabar	Genuine Pearl	40
6206	3¼″	kabar (number) USA	Delrin	5
6209½	3¼″	UNION CUT CO	Bone Stag	125
6210	3½″	UNION CUT CO	Bone Stag	120
6210	3½″	KA-BAR	Bone Stag	95

Pattern	Length	Stamping	Handle	Mint Price
6212 J	4⅛″	UNION CUT CO	Bone Stag	75
0212 J	4⅛″	UNION CUT CO	Pyraline	55
6212 J	4⅛″	KA-BAR	Bone Stag	65
6212 J	4⅛″	kabar	Bone Stag	50
5212 J	4⅛″	kabar	Black Celluloid	25
6213 J	3⅞″	UNION CUT CO	Bone Stag	135
2213 J	3⅞″	KA-BAR	Genuine Stag	145
6213 J	3⅞″	KA-BAR	Bone Stag	120

Pattern	Length	Stamping	Handle	Mint Price
1215	3⅝″	UNION CUT CO	Ebony	$80
6215	3⅝″	UNION CUT CO	Bone Stag	140
6215 PU	3⅝″	UNION CUT CO	Bone Stag	130
6215	3⅝″	KA-BAR	Bone Stag	110
6215½	3⅝″	KA-BAR	Bone Stag	110
6215	3⅝″	kabar	Bone Stag	80
6215	3⅝″	kabar	Rough Black	40
6215	3⅝″	kabar (number) USA	Delrin	10
1218	3¼″	UNION CUT CO	Ebony	50
2218	3¼″	UNION CUT CO	Genuine Stag	90
6218	3¼″	UNION CUT CO	Bone Stag	75
7218	3¼″	UNION CUT CO	Pearl	120
1218	3¼″	KA-BAR	Ebony	40
6218	3¼″	KA-BAR	Bone Stag	75
6219½	3¼″	UNION CUT CO	Bone Stag	65
6220 J	3½″	UNION CUT CO	Bone Stag	95
2220 J	3½″	KA-BAR	Genuine Stag	100
6220 J	3½″	KA-BAR	Bone Stag	85
7220 J	3½″	KA-BAR	Genuine Pearl	135
6221	3¼″	UNION CUT CO	Bone Stag	65
6221	3¼″	KA-BAR	Bone Stag	50
6221	3¼″	kabar	Rough Black	25
T221	3¼″	kabar	Cream Composition	120
1222T	3⅜″	UNION CUT CO	Ebony	40
6222 T	3⅜″	UNION CUT CO	Bone Stag	65
7222 T	3⅜″	UNION CUT CO	Genuine Pearl	90
9222 T	3⅜″	UNION CUT CO	Silver Pyraline	60
5223	3¼″	KA-BAR	Black Composition	60
6223	3¼″	KA-BAR	Smooth Bone	90
6223½	3¼″	KA-BAR	Smooth Bone	90

Pattern	Length	Stamping	Handle	Mint Price
5223 SH	3¼″	kabar	Black Composition	$40
5223	3¼″	kabar	Black Composition	30
5223½	3¼″	kabar	Black Composition	30
6223	3¼″	kabar (number) USA	Delrin	10
6223½	3¼″	kabar (number)	Delrin	10
6224	2¾″	UNION CUT. CO.	Bone Stag	55
6224	2¾″	KA-BAR	Bone Stag	45
P225	3¾″	UNION CUT CO	Imitation Pearl	70
6225½	3¾″	KA-BAR	Bone Stag	125
6225	3¾″	KA-BAR	Bone Stag	125
5226 Emb	3″	UNION CUT CO	Black Pyraline	35
7226 Emb	3″	UNION CUT CO	Genuine Pearl	65
6226	3″	KA-BAR	Bone Stag	50
7226	3″	KA-BAR	Genuine Pearl	60
1228 EO	3⅝″	UNION CUT CO	Ebony	90
2228 EO	3⅝″	UNION CUT CO	Genuine Stag	150
6228 EO	3⅝″	UNION CUT CO	Bone Stag	130
9228 EO	3⅝″	UNION CUT CO	Silver Pyraline	115
6229	3¼″	UNION CUT CO	Bone Stag	55
6229½	3¼″	UNION CUT CO	Bone Stag	55
6229	3¼″	KA-BAR	Bone Stag	50
6229½	3¼″	kabar	Rough Black	25
6229½	3¼″	kabar (number) USA	Delrin	8
6230	3¼″	UNION CUT CO	Bone Stag	60
7230	3¼″	UNION CUT CO	Genuine Pearl	100
1232	3⅜″	UNION CUT CO	Ebony	50
6232	3⅜″	UNION CUT CO	Bone Stag	80
9232	3⅜″	UNION CUT CO	Silver Pyraline	70

Pattern	Length	Stamping	Handle	Mint Price
1232	3⅜"	KA-BAR	Ebony	$35
6232	3⅜"	KA-BAR		75
6232	3⅜"	kabar	Rough Black	30
6232½	3⅜"	kabar (number) USA	Delrin	8
1233	3⅝"	UNION CUT CO	Ebony	90
2233	3⅝"	UNION CUT CO	Genuine Stag	130
6233	3⅝"	UNION CUT CO	Bone Stag	120
9233	3⅝"	UNION CUT CO	Silvery Pyraline	105
2233	3⅝"	KA-BAR	Genuine Stag	115
6233	3⅝"	KA-BAR	Bone Stag	100
6236 LL	3⅜"	KA-BAR	Bone Stag	60
6236 LL	3⅜"	kabar	Rough Black	25
Gunstock 6237	3⅛"	UNION CUT CO	Bone Stag	135
Gunstock P237	3⅛"	UNION CUT CO	Imitation Pearl	110
Gunstock 6237	3⅛"	KA-BAR	Bone Stag	115
Gunstock 2237	3⅛"	KA-BAR	Genuine Pearl	135
Gunstock 7237	3⅛"	KA-BAR	Genuine Pearl	160
Gunstock P237	3⅛"	KA-BAR	Imitation Pearl	100
6239	3"	UNION CUT CO	Bone Stag	45
9239	3"	UNION CUT CO	Fancy Celluloid	40
6240 J	3¼"	UNION CUT CO	Bone Stag	120
6240 J	3¼"	KA-BAR	Bone Stag	95
6241	2¾"	UNION CUT CO	Bone Stag	40
7241	2¾"	UNION CUT CO	Genuine Pearl	50
P241	2¾"	KA-BAR	Pearl Celluloid	20
6241	2¾"	KA-BAR	Bone Stag	30
7241 G	2¾"	KA-BAR	Genuine Pearl	35
P241	2¾"	kabar	Pearl Celluloid	15
2241	2¾"	kabar	Genuine Stag	30
6242	3½"	UNION CUT CO	Bone Stag	55

Pattern	Length	Stamping	Handle	Mint Price
6242	3⅛″	KA-BAR	Bone Stag	$65
T242	3⅛″	KA-BAR	Cream Celluloid	50
6242	3⅛″	kabar	Bone Stag	50
6244	3⅝″	UNION CUT CO	Bone Stag	150
7244	3⅝″	UNION CUT CO	Genuine Pearl	175
1246	3½″	UNION CUT CO	Ebony	80
2246	3½″	UNION CUT CO	Genuine Stag	150
6246	3½″	UNION CUT CO	Bone Stag	140
P246	3½″	UNION CUT CO	Imitation Pearl	110
2246	3½″	KA-BAR	Genuine Pearl	135
6246	3½″	KA-BAR	Bone Stag	120
6247	3¼″	UNION CUT CO	Bone Stag	65
6249	3⅝″	UNION CUT CO	Bone Stag	120
6250	4½″	UNION CUT CO	Bone Stag	350
R250	4½″	UNION CUT CO	Rainbow Celluloid	275
6250	4½″	KA-BAR	Bone Stag	275
6251	4″	KA-BAR	Bone Stag	135
6251½	4″	KA-BAR	Bone Stag	135
1252	3¾″	UNION CUT CO	Ebony	65
2252½	3¾″	UNION CUT CO	Genuine Stag	130
6252	3¾″	UNION CUT CO	Bone Stag	110
6252 Saber	3¾″	UNION CUT CO	Bone Stag	125
2253	3⅛″	UNION CUT CO	Genuine Stag	60
7253	3⅛″	UNION CUT CO	Genuine Stag	75
2253	3⅛″	KA-BAR	Genuine Stag	65
3253	3⅛″	KA-BAR	Redwood	35
6253	3⅛ ″	KA-BAR	Bone Stag	55
7253	3⅛″	KA-BAR	Genuine Pearl	75
T253	3⅛″	KA-BAR	Cream Celluloid	40

Pattern	Length	Stamping	Handle	Mint Price
6253	3⅛″	kabar	Rough Black	$25
T253	3⅛″	kabar	Celluloid	20
2255	3⅛″	UNION CUT CO	Genuine Stag	85
6255	3⅛″	UNION CUT CO	Bone Stag	80
7255	3⅛″	UNION CUT CO	Genuine Pearl	120
9255	3⅛″	UNION CUT CO	Fancy Celluloid	60
6255	3⅛″	KA-BAR	Bone Stag	70
7255	3⅛″	KA-BAR	Genuine Pearl	100
6255	3⅛″	kabar	Rough Black	30
T255	3⅛″	kabar	Cream Celluloid	25
6256 J	3¼″	UNION CUT CO	Bone Stag	75
7256 J	3¼″	UNION CUT CO	Genuine Pearl	110
R256 J	3¼″	UNION CUT CO	Imitation Pearl	60
6256 J	3¼″	KA-BAR	Bone Stag	65
2256 J	3¼″	KA-BAR	Genuine Stag	75
7256 J	3¼″	KA-BAR	Genuine Pearl	100
P256 J	3¼″	KA-BAR	Imitation Pearl	50
6256 J	3¼″	kabar	Bone Stag	45
2256 J	3¼″	kabar	Genuine Stag	50
T256 J	3¼″	kabar	Cream Celluloid	25
6256	3¼″	kabar (number) USA	Delrin	9
6257 mu	3⅝″	KA-BAR	Bone Stag	120
6257 mu	3⅝″	kabar	Imitation Bone	60
2257 mu	3⅝″	kabar	Genuine Stag	85
2260 K&F	3⅞″	UNION CUT CO	Genuine Stag	145
6260 K&F	3⅞″	UNION CUT CO	Bone Stag	130
6260 K&F	3⅞″	KA-BAR	Bone Stag	100
T260 K&F	3⅞″	KA-BAR	Cream Celluloid	80
6261	4″	UNION CUT CO	Bone Stag	150
6261	4″	KA-BAR	Bone Stag	120
6261	4″	KA-BAR	Rough Black	60
6261	4″	kabar	Rough Black	40

Pattern	Length	Stamping	Handle	Mint Price
6263	3⅜"	UNION CUT CO	Bone Stag	$60
6263 PU	3⅜"	UNION CUT CO	Bone Stag	60
6263	3⅜"	KA-BAR	Bone Stag	50
6263	3⅜"	kabar	Rough Black	20
6263	3⅜"	kabar (number) USA	Delrin	7
6265	4½"	UNION CUT CO	Bone Stag	200
0265	4½"	UNION CUT CO	Fancy Celluloid	160
6265	4½"	KA-BAR	Bone Stag	170
2266 J	4⅜"	UNION CUT CO	Genuine Stag	275
6266 J	4⅜"	UNION CUT CO	Bone Stag	250
2266 J	4⅜"	KA-BAR	Genuine Stag	240
6266 J	4⅜"	KA-BAR	Bone Stag	210
6267	4"	UNION CUT CO	Bone Stag	250
6267	4"	KA-BAR	Bone Stag	210
P269 J	4"	UNION CUT CO	Imitation Pearl	80
2269 J	4"	UNION CUT CO	Genuine Stag	140
6269 J	4"	UNION CUT CO	Bone Stag	120
P269 J	4"	KA-BAR	Imitation Pearl	60
2269 J	4"	KA-BAR	Genuine Stag	110
6269 J	4"	KA-BAR	Bone Stag	95
5269 J	4"	KA-BAR	Black Celluloid	35
6270	4½"	UNION CUT CO	Bone Stag	150
2270½	4½"	KA-BAR	Genuine Stag	130
6270½	4½"	KA-BAR	Bone Stag	110
2270½	4½"	kabar	Second Cut Stag	85
2270½	4½"	kabar	Genuine Stag	70
6270½	4½"	kabar	Delrin	30
6271 J	4¼"	UNION CUT CO	Bone Stag	110
2271 J	4¼"	UNION CUT CO	Genuine Stag	135
6271	4¼"	UNION CUT CO	Bone Stag	130

Pattern	Length	Stamping	Handle	Mint Price
6271 J	4¼″	KA-BAR	Bone Stag	$95
2271 J	4¼″	KA-BAR	Genuine Stag	115
3273	3⅝″	UNION CUT CO	Redwood	30
3273	3⅝″	KA-BAR	Redwood	35
TL-29	3⅝″	Ka-Bar	Redwood	35
5273	3⅝″	kabar (number) USA	Black Celluloid	8
T275	4¼″	KA-BAR	Cream Celluloid	20
T275	4¼″	kabar	Cream Celluloid	15
7285	2⅝″	UNION CUT CO	Genuine Pearl	75
7285 Emblem	2⅝″	UNION CUT CO	Genuine Pearl	95
7286 RG	2½″	UNION CUT CO	Genuine Pearl	75
6288	4¼″	UNION CUT CO	Bone Stag	175
6288	4¼″	KA-BAR	Bone Stag	150
7289 R	2¼″	KA-BAR	Genuine Pearl	120
6290	3⅛″	UNION CUT CO	Bone Stag	70

2291 K&F	5¼″	UNION CUT CO	Genuine Stag	350
6291 K&F	5¼″	UNION CUT CO	Bone Stag	300
7291 K&F	5¼″	UNION CUT CO	Genuine Pearl	450
0291 K&F	5¼″	UNION CUT CO	Fancy Celluloid	250
6291 K&F	5¼″	KA-BAR	Bone Stag	225

Pattern	Length	Stamping	Handle	Mint Price
6295 EX	3½″	UNION CUT CO.	Bone Stag	$90
9295 EX	3½″	UNION CUT CO.	Genuine Pearl	130
6295 EX	3½″	UNION CUT CO.	Genuine Stag	120
9295 EX	3½″	KA-BAR	Bone Stag	90
6299	2⅞″	UNION CUT CO.	Bone Stag	80
7299	2⅞″	UNION CUT CO.	Genuine Pearl	110
22110	3⁹⁄₁₆″	UNION CUT CO.	Genuine Stag	110
62110	3⁹⁄₁₆″	UNION CUT CO.	Bone Stag	90
62110	3⁹⁄₁₆″	KA-BAR	Bone Stag	80
22106 Cleaver	5¼″	KA-BAR	Genuine Stag	475
62107	5¼″	UNION CUT CO.	Bone Stag	275
62107	5¼″	KA-BAR	Bone Stag	225
62107	5¼″	KA-BAR	Rough Black	125
P2107	5¼″	KA-BAR	Imitation Pearl	125
22107	5¼″	kabar	Genuine Stag	80
62107	5¼″	kabar	Rough Black	45
62107	5¼″	kabar	Aster Felts Model	100
22107	5¼″	kabar (number) USA	Imitation Stag	15
P2109	3⅛″	UNION CUT CO.	Imitation Pearl	45
52109	3⅛″	UNION CUT CO.	Black Celluloid	45
72109	3⅛″	UNION CUT CO.	Genuine Pearl	95
52109	3⅛″	KA-BAR	Black Celluloid	35
02109	3⅛″	KA-BAR	Fancy Celluloid	75
72110	2″	UNION CUT CO.	Abalone Pearl	175
72111	2″	UNION CUT CO.	Abalone Pearl	175
62118	4¼″	UNION CUT CO.	Bone Stag	250

Pattern	Length	Stamping	Handle	Mint Price
22118	4¼″	KA-BAR	Genuine Stag	$225
62118	4¼″	KA-BAR	Bone Stag	200
P2118	4¼″	KA-BAR	Imitation Pearl	200
R2118	4¼″	KA-BAR	Rainbow Celluloid	200
22118	4¼″	kabar	Genuine Stag	80
62118	4¼″	kabar	Bone Stag	120
62118	4¼″	kabar	Rough Black	60
T2118	4¼″	kabar	Cream Composition	45
62118	4¼″	kabar (number) USA	Delrin	12
T2118	4¼″	kabar (number) USA	Cream Composition	15
72124 RG	2¼″	UNION CUT CO.	Genuine Pearl	60
P2127	3¼″	UNION CUT CO.	Imitation Pearl	60
R2127	3¼″	UNION CUT CO.	Rainbow Celluloid	70
52125	3¼″	KA-BAR	Black Celluloid	55
P2127	3¼″	KA-BAR	Imitation Pearl	55
62128 F	3¼″	UNION CUT CO.	Bone Stag	75
62128 Scout	3¼″	KA-BAR	Bone Stag	100
62128 Scout	3¼″	KA-BAR	Bone Stag	75
62132	5¼″	UNION CUT CO.	Bone Stag	225
62132	5¼″	KA-BAR	Bone Stag	180
T2132	5¼″	KA-BAR	Cream Celluloid	150
62133	2¾″	UNION CUT CO.	Bone Stag	50
72133	2¾″	UNION CUT CO.	Genuine Pearl	70
R2133	2¾″	UNION CUT CO.	Rainbow Celluloid	40
62133	2¾″	KA-BAR	Bone Stag	45
72133	2¾″	KA-BAR	Genuine Pearl	65
62133	2¾″	kabar	Bone Stag	30
T2133	2¾″	kabar	Cream Composition	20
P2133	2¾″	kabar	Pearl Celluloid	20

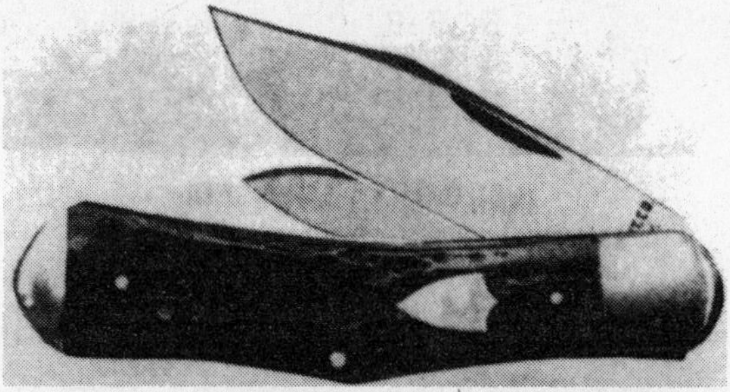

Pattern	Length	Stamping	Handle	Mint Price
62134	3⅜″	UNION CUT CO.	Bone Stag	$175
62134	3⅜″	KA-BAR	Bone Stag	160
62135	3⅞″	UNION CUT CO.	Bone Stag	60
B2135	3⅞″	UNION CUT CO.	Goldstone Celluloid	50
72135	3⅞″	KA-BAR	Genuine Pearl	90
62140	3⅛″	UNION CUT CO.	Bone Stag	80
72140	3⅛″	UNION CUT CO.	Genuine Pearl	110
H2140	3⅛″	UNION CUT CO.	Horn	65
62140	3⅛″	KA-BAR	Bone Stag	65
62141	3″	UNION CUT CO.	Bone Stag	80
72141	3″	UNION CUT CO.	Genuine Pearl	110
62141	3″	KA-BAR	Bone Stag	75
T2141	3″	KA-BAR	Cream Celluloid	45
62141	3″	kabar	Rough Black	30
T2141	3″	kabar	Cream Celluloid	30
62141	3″	kabar (number) USA	Delrin	8
62142	3″	UNION CUT CO.	Bone Stag	70
72142	3″	UNION CUT CO.	Genuine Pearl	95
62142	3″	KA-BAR	Bone Stag	60
72142	3″	KA-BAR	Genuine Pearl	85
62143	3″	UNION CUT CO.	Bone Stag	75
72143	3″	UNION CUT CO.	Genuine Pearl	120

Pattern	Length	Stamping	Handle	Mint Price
62143	3″	KA-BAR	Bone Stag	$70
72143	3″	KA-BAR	Pearl	110
92143	3″	KA-BAR	Silver Pyraline	80
22144	2⅞″	UNION CUT CO.	Genuine Stag	150
62144	2⅞″	UNION CUT CO.	Bone Stag	150
72144	2⅞″	UNION CUT CO.	Genuine Pearl	200
22144	2⅞″	KA-BAR	Genuine Stag	150
62144	2⅞″	KA-BAR	Bone Stag	150
72144	2⅞″	KA-BAR	Genuine Pearl	200
62145	2⅝″	UNION CUT CO.	Bone Stag	50
72145	2⅝″	UNION CUT CO.	Genuine Pearl	90
62145	2⅝″	KA-BAR	Bone Stag	45
72145	2⅝″	KA-BAR	Genuine Pearl	80
92145	2⅝″	KA-BAR	Fancy Celluloid	75
22146	3¼″	UNION CUT CO.	Genuine Stag	65
62146	3¼″	UNION CUT CO.	Bone Stag	55
72146	3¼″	UNION CUT CO.	Genuine Pearl	90
P2146 EX	3¼″	UNION CUT CO.	Fancy Celluloid	60
H2147	2⅞″	UNION CUT CO.	Horn Celluloid	35
62147	2⅞″	UNION CUT CO.	Bone Stag	50
72147	2⅞″	UNION CUT CO.	Genuine Pearl	75
62147	4¾″	KA-BAR	Bone Stag	75
M2147	4¾″	KA-BAR	Metal Handle	50
P2147	4¾″	kabar	Pearl Celluloid	30
T2147	4¾″	kabar	Cream Celluloid	30
62148	3¼″	UNION CUT CO.	Bone Stag	85
72148	3¼″	UNION CUT CO.	Genuine Pearl	120
62148	3¼″	KA-BAR	Bone Stag	70
72148	3¼″	KA-BAR	Genuine Pearl	100
62149	3″	UNION CUT CO.	Bone Stag	70

Pattern	Length	Stamping	Handle	Mint Price
72149	3″	UNION CUT CO.	Genuine Pearl	$90
P2149	3″	KA-BAR	Imitation Pearl	45
22150	3¾″	UNION CUT CO.	Genuine Stag	140
22150 R	3¾″	UNION CUT CO.	Genuine Stag	160
22150½	3¾″	UNION CUT CO.	Genuine Stag	120
22150	3¾″	KA-BAR	Genuine Stag	115
220151	3¼″	UNION CUT CO.	Genuine Stag	175
620151	3¼″	UNION CUT CO.	Bone Stag	150

Pattern	Length	Stamping	Handle	Mint Price
22151	3¼″	UNION CUT CO.	Stag	200
62151	3¼″	UNION CUT CO.	Bone Stag	175
02151	3¼″	UNION CUT CO.	Fancy Celluloid	150
22151	3¼″	KA-BAR	Stag	175
62151	3¼″	KA-BAR	Bone Stag	150
72151	3¼″	KA-BAR	Genuine Pearl	200
62152	3½″	UNION CUT CO.	Bone Stag	150
62152	3½″	KA-BAR	Bone Stag	135

Pattern	Length	Stamping	Handle	Mint Price

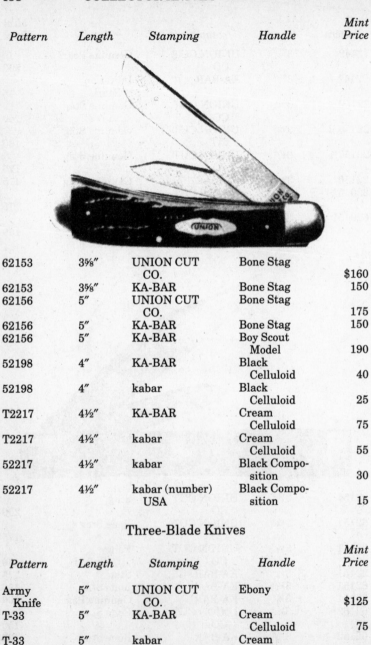

Pattern	Length	Stamping	Handle	Mint Price
62153	3⅝″	UNION CUT CO.	Bone Stag	$160
62153	3⅝″	KA-BAR	Bone Stag	150
62156	5″	UNION CUT CO.	Bone Stag	175
62156	5″	KA-BAR	Bone Stag	150
62156	5″	KA-BAR	Boy Scout Model	190
52198	4″	KA-BAR	Black Celluloid	40
52198	4″	kabar	Black Celluloid	25
T2217	4½″	KA-BAR	Cream Celluloid	75
T2217	4½″	kabar	Cream Celluloid	55
52217	4½″	kabar	Black Composition	30
52217	4½″	kabar (number) USA	Black Composition	15

Three-Blade Knives

Pattern	Length	Stamping	Handle	Mint Price
Army Knife	5″	UNION CUT CO.	Ebony	$125
T-33	5″	KA-BAR	Cream Celluloid	75
T-33	5″	kabar	Cream Celluloid	60

Pattern	Length	Stamping	Handle	Mint Price
6306	3¼"	UNION CUT CO.	Bone Stag	$200
6306	3¼"	KA-BAR	Bone Stag	180
2307	3"	UNION CUT CO.	Genuine Stag	70
7307	3"	UNION CUT CO.	Genuine Pearl	120
7307	3"	UNION CUT CO.	Abalone Pearl	175
1309½	3⅞"	UNION CUT CO.	Ebony	200
6309	3⅞"	UNION CUT CO.	Bone Stag	300

6313	3⅞"	UNION CUT CO.	Bone Stag	160
9313 F	3⅞"	UNION CUT CO.	Silvery Pryaline	145

6314	3⅝"	UNION CUT CO.	Bone Stag	225
6314	3⅝"	KA-BAR	Bone Stag	190

Pattern	Length	Stamping	Handle	Mint Price
2314 EX PU	3⅝″	UNION CUT CO.	Genuine Stag	$700
6314 EX	3⅝″	UNION CUT CO.	Bone Stag	600
6314 PU	3⅝″	UNION CUT CO.		225
6314 PU	3⅝″	KA-BAR	Bone Stag	200
2320½	3½	UNION CUT CO.	Genuine Stag	300
6320½	3½″	UNION CUT CO.	Bone Stag	275
7320½	3½″	UNION CUT CO.	Genuine Pearl	400
2320½	3½″	KA-BAR	Genuine Stag	250
6320½	3½″	KA-BAR	Bone Stag	225
7320½	3½″	KA-BAR	Genuine Pearl	350
6322 T	3⅜″	UNION CUT CO.	Bone Stag	275
6324 RG	3½″	KA-BAR	Bone Stag	80
6326	3″	KA-BAR	Bone Stag	180
P326	3″	kabar	Imitation Pearl	125

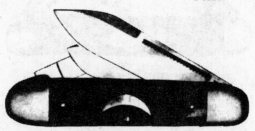

Pattern	Length	Stamping	Handle	Mint Price
6331 EX PU	3¼″	UNION CUT CO.	Bone Stag	600
7331 EX PU	3¼″	UNION CUT CO.	Genuine Pearl	900
6331 EX PU	3¼″	KA-BAR	Bone Stag	600
6340½	3¼″	UNION CUT CO.	Bone Stag	250
7340½	3¼″	KA-BAR	Genuine Pearl	300
2345	3⅜″	UNION CUT CO.	Genuine Stag	110
7345	3⅜″	UNION CUT CO.	Genuine Pearl	140
6349	3⅝″	UNION CUT CO.	Bone Stag	375
6349½	3⅝″	KA-BAR	Bone Stag	325

Pattern	Length	Stamping	Handle	Mint Price
T3256 CC	3⅜″	KA-BAR	Cream Celluloid	$90
T3256 CC	3⅜″	kabar	Cream Celluloid	50
6356	3¼″	UNION CUT CO.	Bone Stag	135
7356	3¼″	UNION CUT CO.	Genuine Pearl	175
6356	3¼″	KA-BAR	Bone Stag	120
2356	3¼″	kabar	Genuine Stag	60
6356	3¼″	kabar	Bone Stag	50
P356	3¼″	kabar	Imitation Pearl	35
6356	3¼″	kabar (number) USA	Delrin	10
T3257 CC	3⅝″	KA-BAR	Cream Celluloid	120
T3257 CC	3⅝″	kabar	Cream Celluloid	60
2357	3⅝″	UNION CUT CO.	Genuine Stag	160
6357	3⅝″	UNION CUT CO.	Bone Stag	150
9357	3⅝″	UNION CUT CO.	Fancy Celluloid	125
2357	3⅝″	KA-BAR	Genuine Stag	135
6357	3⅝″	KA-BAR	Bone Stag	120
9357	3⅝″	KA-BAR	Fancy Celluloid	110
2357	3⅝″	kabar	Genuine Stag	60
6357	3⅝″	kabar	Rough Black	40
P357	3⅝″	kabar	Imitation Pearl	40
6357	3⅝″	kabar (number) USA	Delrin	8

6360	3⅞″	UNION CUT CO.	Bone Stag	140

Pattern	Length	Stamping	Handle	Mint Price
9360	3⅞″	UNION CUT CO.	Rainbow Stag	$120
6360	3⅞″	KA-BAR	Bone Stag	120

Pattern	Length	Stamping	Handle	Mint Price
2366 EX	4½″	UNION CUT CO.	Genuine Stag	750
6366 EX	4½″	UNION CUT CO.	Bone Stag	500
2366 EX	4½″	KA-BAR	Genuine Stag	650
6366 EX	4½″	KA-BAR	Bone Stag	600

Pattern	Length	Stamping	Handle	Mint Price
2367	4″	UNION CUT CO.	Genuine Stag	700
6367	4″	UNION CUT CO.	Bone Stag	600
2369	3⅞″	UNION CUT CO.	Genuine Stag	175
6369	3⅞″	UNION CUT CO.	Bone Stag	160
6369 PU	3⅞″	UNION CUT CO.	Bone Stag	165

Pattern	Length	Stamping	Handle	Mint Price
P367 PU	3⅞″	UNION CUT CO.	Imitation Pearl	$130
2369	3⅞″	KA-BAR	Genuine Stag	150
2369	3⅞″	KA-BAR	Second Cut Stag	175
6369	3⅞″	KA-BAR	Bone Stag	135
P369	3⅞″	KA-BAR	Imitation Pearl	100
2369	3⅞″	kabar	Genuine Stag	75
6369	3⅞″	kabar	Bone Stag	70
6369	3⅞″	kabar	Rough Black	45
P369	3⅞″	kabar	Imitation Pearl	40
P369	3⅞″	kabar (number) USA	Delrin	10

Pattern	Length	Stamping	Handle	Mint Price
2371	4¼″	UNION CUT CO.	Genuine Stag	250
6371	4¼″	UNION CUT CO.	Bone Stag	225
2371	4¼″	KA-BAR	Genuine Stag	225
6371	4¼″	KA-BAR	Bone Stag	200
9371	4¼″	KA-BAR	Fancy Celluloid	180
T371	4¼″	kabar	Cream Celluloid	45
2381	2¾″	UNION CUT CO.	Genuine Stag	95
7381	2¾″	UNION CUT CO.	Genuine Pearl	125
7381	2¾″	KA-BAR	Genuine Pearl	110
P381	2¾″	KA-BAR	Imitation Pearl	60
6390	2⅝″	KA-BAR	Bone Stag	70
P390	2⅝″	KA-BAR	Cream Celluloid	45

Pattern	Length	Stamping	Handle	Mint Price
6390	2⅝″	kabar	Rough Black	$30
P390	2⅝″	kabar	Cream Celluloid	30
6390	2⅝″	kabar (number) USA	Delrin	6
6397	3⅝″	UNION CUT CO.	Bone Stag	400
6397	3⅝″	KA-BAR	Bone Stag	300
23101	2⅝″	UNION CUT CO.	Genuine Stag	55
73101	2⅝″	UNION CUT CO.	Genuine Pearl	100
73101	2⅝″	KA-BAR	Genuine Pearl	90
73101	3″	UNION CUT CO.	Abalone Pearl	190
63104	4¼″	UNION CUT CO.	Bone Stag	800
73104	4¼″	UNION CUT CO.	Genuine Pearl	1200
P3104	4¼″	UNION CUT CO.	Imitation Pearl	650
63111	4¼″	UNION CUT CO.	Bone Stag	190
P3111	4¼″	UNION CUT CO.	Imitation Pearl	150
P3111 PU	4¼″	UNION CUT CO.	Imitation Pearl	150
63111	4¼″	KA-BAR	Bone Stag	160
P3111	4¼″	KA-BAR	Imitation Pearl	120
P3111 PU	4¼″	KA-BAR	Imitation Pearl	120
23116	4″	UNION CUT CO.	Genuine Stag	175
63116	4″	UNION CUT CO.	Bone Stag	160
P3116	4″	UNION CUT CO.	Imitation Pearl	110
23116	4″	KA-BAR	Genuine Stag	150
63116	4″	KA-BAR	Bone Stag	130
P3116	4″	KA-BAR	Imitation Pearl	90
23116	4″	kabar	Genuine Stag	65
63116	4″	kabar	Rough Black	45
63116	4″	kabar (number) USA	Delrin	10
63118	4¼″	UNION CUT CO.	Bone Stag	300

Pattern	Length	Stamping	Handle	Mint Price
63152	3½″	UNION CUT CO.	Bone Stag	$200
W3152	3½″	UNION CUT CO.	Golden Celluloid	180
63152	3½″	KA-BAR	Bone Stag	175
62163	3¼″	KA-BAR	Bone Stag	120
62195 TJ	4″	KA-BAR	Bone Stag	90
62195 TJ	4″	KA-BAR	Rough Black	45
T2195 TJ	4″	KA-BAR	Cream Celluloid	40
62195 TJ	4″	kabar	Rough Black	35
T2195 TJ	4″	kabar	Cream Celluloid	30
62195 TJ	4″	kabar (number) USA	Delrin	12

Multiblade Knives

Pattern	Length	Stamping	Handle	Mint Price
6401 T	2⅞″	UNION CUT CO.	Bone Stag	$200
7401 T	2⅞″	UNION CUT CO.	Genuine Pearl	275
R466	4″	KA-BAR	Fiberoid	125
T4107	5¼″	KA-BAR	Cream Celluloid	1000
64107	5¼″	KA-BAR	Green Bone	1500
24107	5¼″	KA-BAR	Genuine Stag	2000

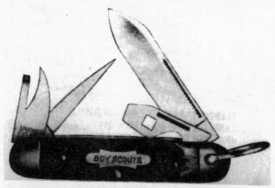

| 6415 RG | 3⅝″ | UNION CUT CO. | Bone Stag | 100 |

Pattern	Length	Stamping	Handle	Mint Price
6415 RG	3⅝″	KA-BAR	Bone Stag	$80
P415 RG	3⅝″	KA-BAR	Imitation Pearl	90
6415 RG	3⅝″	kabar	Rough Black	20
6415 RG	3⅝″	kabar (number) USA	Rough Black	8
6421	3¼″	UNION CUT CO.	Bone Stag	250
6421	3¼″	KA-BAR	Bone Stag	225
6426	3″	UNION CUT CO.	Bone Stag	140
7426	3″	UNION CUT CO.	Genuine Pearl	180
7426	3″	KA-BAR	Genuine Pearl	160
7455	3⅛″	UNION CUT CO.	Genuine Pearl	225
7455	3⅛″	KA-BAR	Genuine Pearl	225
6460	3⅞″	UNION CUT CO.	Bone Stag	150
6460	3⅞″	KA-BAR	Bone Stag	135
2461 PU	4″	UNION CUT CO.	Genuine Stag	250
6461 PU	4″	UNION CUT CO.	Bone Stag	240
6461 PU	4″	KA-BAR	Bone Stag	225
2461	4″	kabar	Genuine Stag	100
6461	4″	kabar	Rough Black	75
2462	4⅛″	UNION CUT CO.	Genuine Stag	200
6766	4⅛″	KA-BAR	Bone Stag	2500
T766	4⅛″	kabar	Cream Celluloid	2000
6469 PU	4″	UNION CUT CO.	Bone Stag	250
5480	3⅛″	UNION CUT CO.	Black Celluloid	125
P480	3⅛″	UNION CUT CO.	Imitation Pearl	125
P480	3⅛″	KA-BAR	Imitation Pearl	110
7487	3″	UNION CUT CO.	Genuine Pearl	150
T487	3″	UNION CUT CO.	Abalone Pearl	175

Pattern	Length	Stamping	Handle	Mint Price
2488	4¼″	UNION CUT CO.	Genuine Stag	$325
6488	4¼″	UNION CUT CO.	Bone Stag	300
2488	4¼″	KA-BAR	Genuine Stag	250
6488	4¼″	KA-BAR	Bone Stag	250
7489	3″	UNION CUT CO.	Genuine Pearl	200
7489	3″	KA-BAR	Genuine Pearl	175
24100	3½″	UNION CUT CO.	Genuine Stag	225
64100	3½″	UNION CUT CO.	Bone Stag	225
66158	3¼″	KA-BAR	Bone Stag	150
24163	3¼″	UNION CUT CO.	Genuine Stag	175
64163	3¼″	UNION CUT CO.	Bone Stag	175
74163	3¼″	UNION CUT CO.	Genuine Pearl	250
64168	4″	KA-BAR	Bone Stag	85
54202	4″	KA-BAR	Black Celluloid	90
T4202	4″	KA-BAR	Cream Celluloid	120
M4202	4″	KA-BAR	Metal Handles	110
54202	4″	kabar	Black Celluloid	80
T4202	4″	kabar	Cream Celluloid	80

KEEN KUTTER

The Keen Kutter brand was used for pocketknives as well as numerous tools and hardware items marketed during the late nineteenth and early twentieth centuries. It was a brand stamping used by the E. C. Simmons Hardware Company of St. Louis, Missouri, beginning about 1870. Simmons Hardware owned controlling interest in Walden Knife Company, and testimony to the quality of their products is evidenced by an award, presented at the 1905 Lewis & Clark Exposition, held in Portland, Oregon, for the "Superior excellence of quality and finish of their Walden and Keen Kutter pocketknives."

The 1923 merger of Simmons Hardware and Winchester resulted in the movement of Walden Knife Company equipment to New Haven, Connecticut. Walden had made Keen Kutter knives; for the next ten years, they would be made by Winchester.

In 1940, the merged companies were again split when Shapleigh Hardware purchased the assets (including controlling interest in Walden Knife Company) of Simmons Hardware. The brand and knife patterns were continued by Shapleigh.

K7WCCEE—(3⅛") Green celluloid handle; spear and pen blades; nickel silver bolster, liner, cap, and shield   *$60*

K7WCS—As above, stag handle   *$65*

K7WPC—As above, pearl handle   *$130*

K013—(2¼") Pearl handle; pen blade and nail file; nickel silver bolsters and liners   *$50*

K013/S—As above, stag handle and shackle   *$50*

K38¾—(3¾") Stag handle; clip, spey, and pen blades; nickel silver bolsters and shield; brass liners   *$185*

K50—(3⅜") Cocobolo handle; spear and pen blades; glazed-finish blades; nickel silver shield; polished steel bolster and cap; brass liners   *$45*

K50K—(3½") Red and black celluloid handle; spear and pen blades; glazed finish; steel caps and bolsters; crest shield; brass liners   *$67*

K50¾K—As above, clip and pen blades   *$67*

K51¾—(3⅜") Ebony handle; spear and pen blades; glazed finish; nickel silver shield; polished steel bolster and cap; brass liners   *$50*

K53—(3⅜") Stag handle; spear and pen blades; glazed finish; nickel silver shield; polished steel bolster and cap; brass liners   *$50*

K080—(3⅛") Pearl celluloid handle; spear and pen blades; nickel silver tip bolsters and liners   *$60*

K083T—(3⅛") Pearl handle; spear and pen blades; nickel silver tip bolsters and liners   *$105*

K094T—(3¼") Pearl handle; spear and pen blades; nickel silver bolsters; shield and liners   *$85*

K099T—(3⅜") Pearl handle; spear and pen blades; nickel silver tip bolsters and liners   *$125*

K0147¾—(4") Muskrat; two long, narrow blades etched "Muskrat"; nickel silver bolsters and liners   *$185*

K0151—(3") Stag handle; spear blade and long nail file; nickel silver tip bolsters and liners   *$65*

K0153—(3") Pearl handle; spear blade and long nail file; nickel silver tip bolsters and liners; fully milled   *$80*

K153—(3") Stag handle; spear blade and long nail file; nickel silver tip bolsters and liners; fully milled   *$75*

K0195¾K—(3⅜") Pearl blue celluloid handle; clip and spey blades; nickel silver bolsters, shield, and liners   *$42*

*K0195¾P—*As above, red and black celluloid handle   *$42*

K0196—(3⅜") Ebony handle; spear and pen blades; nickel silver bolsters, shield, and liners   *$55*

K0197¾K—(3⅜") Red and black celluloid handle; clip and pen blades; nickel silver bolsters, liners, and crest shield   *$65*

K0198—(3⅜") Stag handle; spear and pen blades; nickel silver bolsters, shield, and liners   *$60*

*K0198¾—*As above, clip and spey blades   *$60*

K0207R—(3") Stag handle; spear and pen blades; nickel silver bolsters and liners   *$55*

K0109R—(3") Pearl handle; spear and pen blades; nickel silver bolsters and liners   *$90*

K0214—(3") Stag handle; spear and pen blades; nickel silver bolsters and shield; brass liners   *$55*

*K0214K—*As above, red and black celluloid handle   *$50*

*K0214TC—*As above, pearl celluloid handle and nickel silver tip bolsters   *$65*

K0247—(3⅞″) Stag handle; spear and clip blades; nickel silver bolsters and shield; brass liners $115

K0256—(3¼″) Stag handle; spear and pen blades; nickel silver tip bolsters, liners, and crest shield $55

K0258—(3¼″) Pearl handle; spear and pen blades; nickel silver tip bolsters, shield, and liners $95

K264—(3¼″) Stag handle; spear and pen blades; nickel silver bolster, cap, shield, and liners $40

*K264¾—*As above, clip and pen blades $75

K0281T—(3⅜″) Stag handle; spear and pen blades; nickel silver tip bolsters, shield, and liners $60

K309R—(3″) Pearl handle; spear and pen blades, curly nail file; fully polished $85

K0333—(3¼″) Stag handle; sheepfoot and pen blades; nickel silver bolsters, shield, and liners $85

K341—(3¼″) Stag handle; spear and pen blades, curly nail file; nickel silver tip bolsters, shield, and liners $85

K343—(3¼″) Pearl handle; nickel silver tip bolsters, liners, and shield; spear and pen blades, nail file; milled liners $75

K0348—(3½″) Stag handle; clip and pen blades; nickel silver bolsters, shield, and liners $110

K356—(3⅛″) Stag handle; spear, two pen blades, and nail file; nickel silver tip bolsters and shield; milled liners $100

K357—(3⅛″) Pearl handle; spear and two pen blades, pick nail file; nickel silver tip bolsters, shield, and liners; fully milled   *$140*

K0388/S—(2⅞″) Pearl handle; spear and pen blades; nickel silver tip bolsters, shield, shackle, and liners   *$100*

K443—(3¼″) Pearl handle; spear and two pen blades, curly nail file; fully polished; nickel silver tip bolsters, shield, and liners   *$130*

K0486—(2⅞″) Stag handle; spear and pen blades; fully polished; nickel silver tip bolsters and liners   *$30*

K0488—(2⅞″) Pearl handle; spear and pen blades; nickel silver tip bolsters and liners   *$55*

K0498—(3″) Stag handle; sheepfoot and pen blades; nickel silver rat-tail bolsters, shield, and liners   *$55*

K0499—(3″) Pearl handle; sheepfoot and pen blades; nickel silver rat-tail bolsters and liners   *$95*

K0529—(2¾″) Pearl handle; spear and pen blades; long nickel silver bolsters; nickel silver liners   *$55*

K0612R—(3″) Pearl handle; spear and pen blades; long nickel silver bolsters; nickel silver liners   *$65*

K0643—(2¾″) Pearl handle; spear and pen blades, pick nail file; nickel silver shield, shackle, and liners; fully milled   *$90*

K0698—(3½″) Stag handle; spear and pen blades; nickel silver bolsters and shield; brass liners   *$125*

K711—(2¾″) Curved pearl handle; spear and pen blades; nickel silver bolster, cap, and liners   *$95*

K711G—As above, gold celluloid handle   *$35*

K711/SC—As above, silver celluloid handle   *$45*

K713—(2¾″) Stag handle; spear and pen blades; nickel silver bolsters, liners, and cap   *$45*

K713¾—(2⅞″) Stag handle; clip and pen blades; nickle silver bolsters, liners, and cap   *$45*

K713¾A—(3⅝″) Abalone celluloid handle; clip, spey, and punch blades; nickel silver bolsters, shield, and liners   *$110*

K735¾A—(3⅝″) Abalone celluloid handle; clip, spey, and punch blades; nickel silver bolsters, shield, and liners   *$110*

K735¾—As above, red celluloid handle   *$110*

K737¾—As above, red and white celluloid handle   *$150*

K738¾—(3¾″) Stag handle; clip, spey, and punch blades; nickel silver bolsters, shield, and liners   *$180*

K0797—(2⅞″) Stag handle; spear and pen blades; nickel silver bolsters and liners   *$45*

K0798—(2⅞″) Pearl handle; spear and pen blades; nickel silver bolsters and liners   *$55*

K0799—(2⅞″) Pearl celluloid handle; spear and pen blades; nickel silver bolsters and liners   *$50*

K0814—(3″) Nickel silver handle; spear and pen blades; fully polished *$45*

K0815/S—(3″) Nickel silver handle; spear and pen blades; nickel silver shackle   *$45*

K0878—(3¾″) Stag handle; sheepfoot and pen blades; nickel silver rat-tail bolsters and shield; brass liners   *$55*

K0883—(3⅛″) Pearl handle; spear blade and curly nail file; nickel silver bolsters, shield, and liners   *$100*

K1704¼—(3¾") Cocobolo handle; spey blade; nickel silver bolster and liners   *$45*

K1734½—(3½") Stag handle, spey blade; nickel silver bolster, cap, shield, and liners   *$80*

K0188A—(3⅛") Abalone celluloid handle; spear and pen blades; nickel silver bolsters, shield, and liners   *$40*

K01880R—As above, iridescent celluloid handle   *$35*

K01881—(3½") Stag handle; spear and pen blades; nickel silver bolsters, shield, and liners   *$110*

K01884—(3⅛") Stag handle; spear and pen blades; nickel silver bolsters, shield, and liners   *$100*

K02070M—(3") Stag handle; spear and pen blades; nickel silver bolsters and liners   *$55*

K02071—(3⅜") Stag handle; spear and pen blades; nickel silver bolsters, shield, and liners   *$55*

K02074—(3⅜") Stag handle; spear and pen blades; nickel silver bolsters, shield, and liners   *$65*

K02074L—(3⅜") Varicolored celluloid handle; spear and pen blades; nickel silver bolsters, shield, and liners   *$50*

K02120—(3⅜") Office knife; white celluloid handle with etching; spear and eraser blades; nickel silver liners $55

K02220—(3⅜") White celluloid handle with etching; spear and eraser blades; nickel silver liners $50

K02235N—(3") Silverlour-finish celluloid handle; spear and pen blades; nickel silver tip bolsters, shield, and liners $80

K02237—(3") Stag handle; spear and pen blades; nickel silver tip bolsters, shield, and liners $65

K02238—(3½") Pearl celluloid handle; spear and pen blades; nickel silver tip bolsters, and liners $80

K02239—(3") Pearl handle; spear and pen blades; nickel silver shield, tip bolsters, and liners $100

K02423—(3¾") Stag handle; spear and pen blades; glazed blades; nickel silver bolster and shield; brass liners $60

K02436¾—(3⅜") Black celluloid handle; clip and pen blades; nickel silver bolsters, shield, and liners $60

K02437¾—(3⅜") Stag handle; clip and pen blades; nickel silver bolsters, shield, and liners $50

K02463—(3") Pearl handle; spear blade and nail file; nickel silver bolsters, shield, and liners $85

K02527—(2⅝") Stag handle; spear and pen blades; nickel silver bolsters and liners $45

K02529—(2¾") Pearl handle; spear and pen blades; long nickel silver bolsters; nickel silver liners $55

K02529/S—As above except with shackle $55

K2720—(3") Cocobolo handle; spear and pen blades; nickel silver bolster, cap, and shield; brass liners $45

K2723—(3") Stag handle; spear and pen blades; nickel silver bolster, cap, and shield; brass liners $45

K02736—(3") Smooth fiber handle; spear and pen blades; nickel silver turned edge and liners $45

K02878—(3⅝") Stag handle; clip and spear blades; nickel silver bolsters and shield; brass liners $70

K2878¾—(3⅝") Stag handle; clip and spear blades; nickel silver bolsters and shield; brass liners $75

K3036T—(3") Stag handle; spear, pen blades, and pick nail file; nickel silver tip bolsters, shield, and liners $90

K3037T—(3") Pearl handle; spear, pen blades, and pick nail file; nickel silver shield, tip bolsters, and liners; milled $80

K3070J—(3⅜") Green and black celluloid handle; spear and two pen blades; fully polished; nickel silver bolsters, shield, and liners $125

K3070FK—As above except with spear, pen, and nail file; red and black celluloid handle $125

K3070FL—Red and green celluloid handle $110

K3071F—(3⅜″) Stag handle; spear, pen blades, and regular nail file; nickel silver bolsters, shield, and liners   *$120*

K3071¼— As above except with clip, spey, and pen blades   *$125*

K3071½— As above except with clip, sheepfoot, and pen blades   *$125*

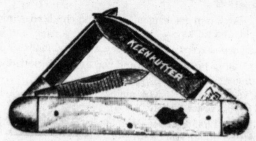

K3073—(3¼″) Pearl handle; spear, pen blades, and curly nail file; nickel silver bolsters, shield, and liners   *$160*

K3215¾G—(3⅜″) Gold celluloid handle; clip, sheepfoot, and pen blades; nickel silver bolsters and shield; brass liners   *$120*

K3218¾—(3⅜″) Stag handle; clip, sheepfoot, and pen blade; nickel silver bolsters and shield; brass liners   *$120*

K3278—(3⅝″) Stag handle; spear, clip, and spey blades; nickel silver bolsters, shield, and liners   *$125*

K3305RJ—(3″) Green and black brilliant-finish celluloid handle; spear, pen blades, and curly nail file; nickel silver bolsters, shield, and liners   *$90*

K3307R—(3″) Stag handle; spear, pen blades, and curly nail file; nickel silver bolsters, shield, and liners   *$120*

K3310—(3⅝″) Black celluloid handle; clip and pen blades; nickel silver bolsters, shield, and liners   *$120*

K03311—(3⅝″) Stag handle; clip and pen blades; nickel silver bolsters, shield, and liners   *$80*

K3311¼—(3⅝″) Stag handle; clip, small spey, and pen blades; nickel silver bolsters, shield, and liners   *$135*

K3316—(3⅝″) Stag handle; saber clip, small clip, and pen blades; nickel silver bolsters, shield, and liners   *$160*

K3317—(3⅝″) Golden celluloid handle; saber clip, clip, and pen blades; fully polished; nickel silver bolsters and liners   *$125*

K0334—(3¼″) Stag handle; spear, pen blades, and file, polished; brass liners   *$60*

K03342J—(3¼″) Green and black brilliant-finish celluloid handle; spear and pen blades; brass liners   *$45*

K03342K— As above, red and black celluloid handle   *$45*

K03344/S—(3¼″) Nickel silver engine-turned handle; spear and pen blades; skeleton trim with shackle   *$45*

K3430—(4") Genuine buffalo horn handle; clip, sheepfoot, and spey blades highly finished; nickel silver bolsters, shield, and liners; fully milled *$125*

K03433—(4") Stag handle; clip and spey blades; nickel silver bolsters, shield, and liners *$100*

K3433—(4") Stag handle; sheepfoot, spey, and clip blades; nickel silver bolsters, shield, and liners *$125*

K3433¼— As above except with clip, spey, and pen blades *$120*

K03471—(3⅜") Stag handle; spear and pen blades; nickel silver tip bolsters; brass liners *$55*

K3472—(3⅜") Stag handle; spear, pen blades, and file; nickel silver tip bolsters and shield; brass liners *$90*

K3483—(3⅛") Pearl handle; spear, pen blades, and curly nail file; nickel silver tip bolsters, shield, and liners *$120*

K3527—(3¼") Stag handle; sheepfoot, pen blades, and nail file; nickel silver rat-tail bolsters, shield, and liners *$130*

K3553—(3⅜") Stag handle; spear, clip, and spey blades; nickel silver bolsters, shield, and liners *$110*

K3599T—(3⅜") Pearl handle; spear and two pen blades; nickel silver tip bolsters and liners *$150*

K3619—(3⅜") Pearl handle; spear, clip, and spey blades; nickel silver bolsters, shield, and liners *$175*

K3681T—(3⅜") Stag handle; spear and two pen blades; nickel silver tip bolsters, shield, and liners *$125*

K3698¾—(3½") Stag handle; clip and two pen blades; nickel silver bolsters and shield; brass liners $160

K3706¼D—(3¼") Red celluloid handle; clip, spey, and pen blades; nickel silver bolsters, shield, and liners $115

K03706—(3¼") Stag handle; clip and pen blades; nickel silver bolsters, shield, and liners $50

K3705½—(3½") Stag handle; clip, sheepfoot, and pen blades; nickel silver bolsters and liners; crest shield $90

K03706¼—(3¼") Stag handle; clip and spey blades; nickel silver bolsters, shield, and liners $50

K03707—(3¼") Ebony handle; clip and pen blades; nickel silver bolsters and liners; crest shield $40

K3708¼—(3¼") Pearl handle; clip, spey, and pen blades; nickel silver bolsters, shield, and liners $150

K3732—(3½") Gold color celluloid handle; clip, spear, and spey blades; nickel silver bolsters, shield, and liners $90

K3733—(3½") Stag handle; clip, spear, and spey blades; nickel silver bolsters, shield, and liners $100

K3825—(4") Black celluloid handle; clip, sheepfoot, and spey blades; nickel silver bolsters, shield, and liners $115

K3825H— As above, pearl celluloid handle $90

K3826—(4") Red and white celluloid handle; clip, sheepfoot, and spey blades; nickel silver bolsters, shield, and liners $155

K3828—(4") Stag handle; clip, sheepfoot, and spey blades; nickel silver bolsters, shield, and liners $130

K3878¾—(3⅝") Stag handle; clip, sheepfoot, and pen blades; nickel silver bolsters, shield, and liners $140

K3908/S—(2⅞") Pearl handle; spear, pen blades, and curly nail file; nickel silver tip bolsters, shield, shackle, and liners $120

K4208—(3¼") Pearl handle; spear, two pen blades, and file; nickel silver bolsters and liners; crest shield $125

K4428—(4") Stag handle; clip, sheepfoot, spey, and pen blades; nickel silver bolsters, shield, and liners   *$185*

K04527—(3¼") Stag handle; sheepfoot and pen blades; nickel silver rattail bolsters, shield, and liners   *$120*

K4527—(3¾") Stag handle; sheepfoot, two pen blades, and nail file; nickel silver rat-tail bolsters, liners, and shield   *$120*

K04529—(3¼") Pearl handle; sheepfoot and pen blades; nickel silver rattail bolsters, shield, and liners   *$120*

K4843—(2¾") Pearl handle; spear, pen blades, nail scissor, and pick nail file; nickel silver shield and liners; fully milled   *$120*

K5328—(3") Stag handle; spear and pen blades; nickel silver bolster, cap, and shield; brass liners   *$150*

K4738/S—(3⅛") Skeleton pearl handle; spear, pen blades, and flexible nail file; nickel silver shackle   *$70*

K06256F—(3¼") Stag handle; spear blade and curly nail file; nickel silver tip bolsters, shield, shackle, and liners   *$65*

K6353—(3½") Stag handle; spear blade, punch, can opener, combination screwdriver and bottle opener; nickel silver bolsters, shield, and shackle; brass liners, with steel center liners   *$80*

K6559—(3⅝") Stag handle; spear blade, punch, can opener, combination screwdriver and bottle opener; nickel silver bolsters, shield, shackle; brass liners, with steel center liners   *$80*

K07243—(*3¾″*) Stag handle; clip and spey blades; nickel silver bolsters, shield, and liners   *$90*

K78433—(*3¾″*) Stag handle; spear, clip, and spey blades; nickel silver bolsters, shield, and liners; fully polished   *$120*

K7530J—(*3¼″*) Green and black brilliant-finish celluloid handle; clip, spey, and pen blades; nickel silver bolsters, shield, and liners   *$105*

K7733—(*3⅛″*) Stag handle; spear and pen blades; nickel silver bolster, cap, and shield; brass liners   *$80*

K7733¾—As above except with clip and pen blades   *$80*

K8464¼—(*3⅝″*) Ivory handle with etching, "Keen Kutter Kattle Knife," on side and steer's head on other; spear, sheepfoot, and spey blades; nickel silver bolsters and liners   *$175*

K23628¾—(*3″*) Stag handle; clip and pen blades; nickel silver bolsters, shield, and liners   *$45*

K27122—(*2⅝″*) Pearl celluloid handle; spear and pen blades; nickel silver tip bolsters and liners   *$40*

K27233¾—(*2¾″*) Stag handle; saber clip and pen blades; nickel silver bolster, cap, and shield; brass liners   *$50*

K32436¾—(*3⅜″*) Black celluloid handle; clip, pen blades, and nail file; nickel silver bolsters, shield, and liners   *$85*

K32437—(*3⅜″*) Stag handle; spear, pen blades, and nail file; nickel silver bolsters, shield, and liners   *$100*

K33251—(*3¼″*) Stag handle; spear blade, bottle decapper, and corkscrew; nickel silver bolsters, shield, and liners   *$60*

K33253—(*3¼″*) Pearl handle; spear blade, bottle decapper, and corkscrew; nickel silver bolsters and liners   *$140*

K33433—(*4″*) Stag handle; clip, sheepfoot, and pen blades; nickel silver bolsters, shield, and liners   *$135*

K33720R—(*3¼″*) Iridescent celluloid handle; spear, sheepfoot, and spey blades; nickel-silver bolsters, shield, and liners   *$90*

K33721—As above, stag handle   *$100*

K33732K—(*3½″*) Red and black brilliant-finish celluloid handle; clip, spear, and pen blades; nickel silver bolsters, shield, and liners   *$90*

K37334—(3½") Stag handle; clip, spear, and spey blades; nickel silver bolsters, shield, and liners   *$125*

K72286—(3½") Ebony handle; two glazed-finish blades; spear blade and punch; steel bolster; nickel silver shield; brass liners   *$25*

K72288¾—(3½") Stag handle; clip blade and punch, glazed finish; steel bolster; nickel silver shield; brass liners   *$35*

K72423—(3¼") Fiber handle; spear blade and punch; nickel silver bolsters and shield; brass liners   *$65*

K72783—(3½") Stag handle; spear blade and punch; nickel silver caps and bolsters; brass liners; crest shield   *$65*

*K72783¾—*As above except with clip and pen blades   *$65*

K73310¼R—(3⅝") Iridescent celluloid handle; clip, spey blades, and punch; nickel silver bolsters, shield, and liners   *$150*

K73311½—(3⅝") Stag handle; clip, spey blades, and punch; nickel silver bolsters, shield, and liners   *$65*

K73433¼—(4") Stag handle; clip, spey blades, and punch; nickel silver bolsters, shield, and liners   *$140*

K73477¾—(3⅝") White celluloid handle with etching, "Keen Cutter Kattle Knife," and steer's-head shield; clip, spey blades, and punch; nickel silver bolsters; nickel liners   *$160*

K73553¾—(3⅛") Stag handle; clip, spey blades, and punch; nickel silver bolsters and liners; crest shield $90

K73625A—(3") Gold celluloid handle; leather spear, spey, and punch; nickel silver bolsters, shield, and liners $90

K73628—(3") Stag handle; spear, spey blades, and punch; nickel silver bolsters, shield, and liners $90

K73706—(3¼") Stag handle; clip, pen blades, and punch; nickel silver bolsters, shield, and liners $110

K73733—(3½") Stag handle; clip, spey blades, and punch; nickel silver bolsters, shield, and liners $130

K73828—(4") Stag handle; clip, spey blades, and punch; nickel silver bolsters, shield, and liners $150

K73845¼L—(3⅛") Varicolored brilliant-finish celluloid handle; spear, spey blades, and punch; nickel silver bolsters, shield, and liners $130

K73845¼D—As above, red celluloid handle $130

K73848—(3½") Stag handle; spear, pen blades, and punch; nickel silver bolsters, shield, and liners $90

K73848¼—As above except with spear, spey blades, and punch $135

K73875¾P—(3⅝") Pearl blue celluloid handle; clip, spey blades, and punch; nickel silver bolsters, shield, and liners $125

K73878¼—(3⅛") Stag handle; spear, spey blades, and punch; nickel silver bolsters and liners; crest shield $125

K73878¾—As above except with clip, spey blades, and punch $125

K74825E—(4") Pearl celluloid handle; clip, sheepfoot, spey blades, and punch; nickel silver bolsters, shield, and liners $125

K74828—(4") Stag handle; clip, sheepfoot, spey blades, and punch; nickel silver bolsters, shield, and liners $150

KINFOLKS, INC.

The brand name KINFOLKS was derived from the fact that the company's founders were cousins. The company was formed in Little Valley, New York, in 1927 by J. Russell Case, Dean J. Case, and Tint Champlin. Champlin served as the company's first president and was succeeded in that office by Dean J. Case in 1929.

The firm produced sheath knives, household knives, razors, hatchets, and pocketknives. The majority of their knife production was in sheath knives, and a large number was made for World War II military use. In addition to knives stamped KINFOLKS USA, the factory also produced knives marked JEAN CASE or J. CASE until it ceased operation in 1948.

When Emerson Case went to work for Robeson in the 1950s, he had somehow obtained rights to the Kinfolks trademark. Robeson made a line of approximately ten knives bearing that brand and with the "Kinfolks" brand and marketed them through the Robeson dealers. These knives usually had green bone handles, and when Robeson changed to the traditional strawberry bone, the Kinfolks stamping was dropped.

ROBERT KLAAS COMPANY—KISSING CRANE

This company's story began when a scissors maker named Peter Daniel Pauls married Johanne Amalie Storsberg, whose father was a maker of pen knives. Shortly thereafter, in 1834, Pauls began his own production of pen knives. In 1850, when the first shipment of Pauls's knives to the United States was made, the high quality of his three- and four-blade knives was recognized and appreciated. Pauls's daughter married a young scissors maker named Frederich Robert Klass, and after Pauls's death, the old company was merged with the Robert Klaas Company in 1869. The Klass business grew in reputation and sales under Robert Klass's leadership, and in 1895 he registered the "Kissing Crane" logo as its trademark.

Ownership and management of the Klass firm has been passed through several generations succeeding Robert Klass. Although the owners' names changed through marriage of Klass's daughters, the company still carries the Robert Klass name and the trademark he designed. Hugo Schiesen, great-grandson of Robert Klass, began work with the company in 1930. Presently, leadership of the company rests with the brothers Hans-Gerd and

Ernst-Jorgen Schiesen, sixth-generation descendants of the company's founder.

Kissing Crane knives were distributed exclusively by Star Sales of Knoxville, Tennessee, for a number of years. U.S. distribution rights were purchased in 1987 by a group of leading knife distributors.

In 1972, Klaas began to use a dating system on its knives. The first two numbers indicate the pattern number, the third number indicates the number of blades, and the fourth number indicates handle material, as follows:

1—Imitation ivory   6—Yellow composition
2—Black composition   7—Mother-of-Pearl
3—Imitation bone   8—Wood
4—Imitation pearl   9—Genuine bone
5—Genuine deer stag   0—Red composition

Following those numbers are Roman numeral keys beginning with "XI," signifying the year of manufacture as 1972, and incrementing one numeral for each year thereafter. For example, the number 2929XII would indicate a small canoe pattern with two blades, handled in bone and made in 1973.

LACKAWANNA CUTLERY COMPANY

This firm was originally started in Nicholson, Pennsylvania, in 1911 as the Eureka Cutlery Company. Its owner was unable to build a successful business, and the factory was sold to some local businessmen, who reopened it as the Lackawanna Cutlery Company. The company manufactured knives at that factory from about 1917 until the factory burned in 1923. From 1923 until 1930, the company owners purchased parts from other manufacturers and assembled them under their company's name. Knives from the latter era were primarily celluloid and picture-handle knives. Stampings used included LACKAWANNA (curved) and L. C. CO. NICHOLSON PA.

LANDERS, FRARY AND CLARK

This firm was first organized in 1865, with its major production focused on tableware and kitchen knives. James Frary, the company's president, patented a hollow handle for table cutlery in 1869. In 1871, his patent for making knife bolsters from sheet metal, as well as other innovations for pocketknife making, led Frary to resign and to open his own company, Frary Cutlery Company, in Bridgeport, Connecticut. His company lasted only from 1876 to 1884.

In the meantime, Landers, Frary & Clark had grown into a major cutlery producer, and the company name was shortened to L. F. & C. in 1898. Using the tradename UNIVERSAL (purchased from the Universal Knife Company), L. F. & C. entered pocketknife manufacture in 1912. That same year, the company purchased the Humason & Beckley Manufacturing Company and used that company's knife patterns along with new ones of their own. Another major acquisition was made in 1918, when the company purchased the Meriden Cutlery Company. In 1950, L. F. & C. of New Britain, Connecticut, discontinued its cutlery division.

MAHER AND GROSH

Established by two dentists in 1877, the Maher and Grosh firm is probably the oldest mail-order knife business in the United States. Located in Toledo, Ohio, during its earlier years, the company manufactured none of the numerous knives stamped with its name. Knives were made under contract by companies such as Schatt and Morgan, Schrade, Queen, and Miller Brothers and were stamped MAHER & GROSH TOLEDO OHIO (or the city name followed by "O.").

The company actively pursued the agricultural trade with horticultural knives as well as the quality line of pocketknives. A late 1880s catalog listed more than 125 knives. Some Maher & Grosh knives bore pattern numbers, while others were given colorful names such as "The Indian Trapper," "Old Dixie Knife," or "Kattle King" etched on the master blades.

The firm was moved to Clyde, Ohio, in 1963 and continues in business, offering knives of other brand stampings as well as other supplies.

AL MAR KNIVES

Al Mar, the founder of this company, was employed as a knife designer by Gerber Legendary Blades and is credited with many

of the successful Gerber designs of the 1970s. In 1979, he determined to have knives of his design produced with his own trademark, and the company—Al Mar Knives—was formed.

Not unlike most of the knives that are collected today, Mar knives were made for using, not necessarily for collecting. Before long, Mar products earned an excellent reputation for quality of design, materials, and workmanship. Each knife was designed by Mar and manufactured to his rigid specifications by Sakai Cutlery, a respected knife maker of Japan's Seki City cutlery center. Several of the earlier Mar series were manufactured in relatively low quantities and are becoming of increasing interest to collectors. More recent additions to the AMK line, such as the earlier S.E.R.E. knives, are of significance as trendsetting examples of modern cutlery.

For dating information, the first five thousand of each utility series knife was marked with the Al Mar name and logo, and the blade tangs were stamped USA SEKI, JAPAN; the stamping was later changed to SEKI JAPAN. A fixed-blade model, the Fang I, was at first produced (3,000 knives) with tapered tangs, but subsequent knives were made with nontapered tangs.

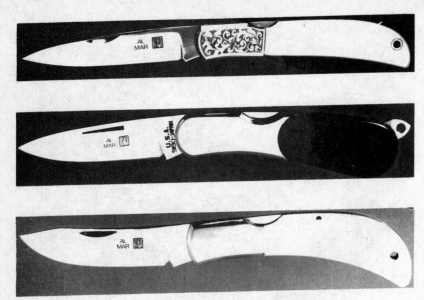

MARBLE'S ARMS
AND MANUFACTURING COMPANY

Born in 1854, Webster L. Marble grew up learning the skills of hunter, fisherman, and trapper. During his early adult life, Marble worked as a timber surveyor and cruiser. These experiences might not have been important except for the effect they would have on the knives we used and trusted years ago—knives that have become highly regarded collectibles today. Webster Marble recognized needs and used his talents to fill them. His earliest contributions were the waterproof matchbox and safety pocket ax. Marble made these items part-time until 1898, when he built a 64-square-foot building for his growing business.

Operating as W. L. Mable, Gladstone, Michigan, he started full-time manufacturing and national advertising in 1899. That year, he was joined in the business by a partner, Frank H. Van Cleeve. The company name was then changed to The Marble Safety Ax Company, and a move was made into a 9,000-square-foot building.

Marble's first knife was introduced in 1901 and was named "The Ideal"; in 1902, it became the Dall DeWeese Model. The

Marble's Safety Hunting Knife, introduced in 1902, was deserving of the success it achieved. The knife combined features of the safety ax with a quality hunting or sporting blade. That knife is one of today's choice collectibles. About this time, the company introduced a line of pocketknives, probably made by the Case Brothers, Union Cutlery, and German manufacturers as well.

In 1911, the company name changed again, this time to The Marble's Arms and Manufacturing Company, and another move was made into even larger quarters. Marble's knives were so respected that they were used by Teddy Roosevelt, the Perry Arctic expedition, and Smithsonian Instituion expeditions.

Many of Marble's patents expired during the 1920s, and other manufacturers began to capitalize on his designs. Although their quality was usually lower, so were their prices, and the competition began to take its toll on Marble's company. Business was still quite good when Webster Marble died in 1930, but by the end of World War II, Marble's sales volume and profits were declining. The ax and folding-knife lines were dropped, and sheath knife patterns were cut back to four models. In 1977 the company ceased knife manufacturing.

MERIDEN CUTLERY COMPANY

The origin of this Meriden, Connecticut, company can be traced to a table cutlery manufacturing company started in 1832 by David Ropes. When Ropes was joined by new business partners, the company became Platt, Ropes, Webb and Company. In 1855, the company was incorporated as the Meriden Cutlery Company. Although primary manufacture was in table cutlery, some smaller knife patterns, such as lobster pen knives and watch fob knives, with the company's stamping can be found. Meriden Cutlery became a part of Landers, Frary & Clark in 1918.

MILLER BROTHERS CUTLERY COMPANY

The Miller brothers, William H. and George W., were toolmaker and gunsmith apprentices at a young age, and their first work experiences were in the gun manufacturing industry. Desiring their own business, they began to make cutlery products in Yalesville, Connecticut, about 1863. They soon relocated their shop to nearby Wallingford and later moved to Meriden, Connect-icut, where they purchased the Pratt, Read & Co. facilities.

The larger factory enabled the Miller Brothers company to ex-pand their knife line and to make knives under contract for a number of other firms as well as for the government. Their knives were of very high quality, and a good number of their patterns fea-tured handles attached with small brass screws rather than pins—a feature unique to Miller Brothers manufacture. The brothers and their employees were indeed innovative, and their contributions to the knife industry include methods and machin-ery to stamp knife parts and methods to manufacture bolsters.

In spite of the high quality of their knives and their innovative methods, the business failed in 1878. It was reorganized, with William Rockwell serving as general manager, and continued to use the Miller Brothers company name. The firm sold its cutlery division in 1917 to Meriden Knife Company, favoring the busi-ness of steel pen manufacture. In 1926, they ceased knife manu-facturing entirely, and the name was changed to Miller Brothers Pen Company.

Stampings used during the years of cutlery manufacture include MILLER BROS. CELEBRATED CUTLERY, MILLER BROS., MIL-LER BROS. CUT. CO. MERIDEN, and MILLER BROS. U.S.A.

NAPANOCH KNIFE COMPANY

A knife manufacturing company was formed in 1900 when the brothers Irving and William Carmen joined with William Hoorn-beek in leasing the DuVall Rake Manufactory in Napanoch, New York. Using water as a power source and employing between fif-teen and twenty-five craftsmen, the factory produced knifes of ex-ceptionally good quality. The company was renamed Napanoch Knife Company in 1905 and was incorporated in 1909.

In addition to knives branded Napanoch, the company made knives on contract for other companies such as Wilbert Cutlery Co., Ulery, Keene Cutlery Co., and Hibbard, Spencer & Bartlett.

The corporation was sold to Winchester Repeating Arms Com-pany in 1919, about the same time that Winchester acquired the Eagle knife manufacturing facilities. Some of the skilled crafts-men were transferred by Winchester to the Eagle factory, and the brand Napanoch was continued for two or three years on knives produced in that factory.

The factory in Napanoch was purchased from Winchester in 1921 by four former employees, and it again manufactured knives, this time stamped Honk Falls Knife Company, from 1921 until it burned in 1929.

In 1931 the Napanoch trademark was revived when John Cushner converted an old barn into a knife shop near his Napanoch, New York, home. These knives, stamped "Napanoch Knife Co., Napanoch, New York U.S.A." were made until his death in 1938.

NEW YORK KNIFE COMPANY

This manufacturer of some of the finest-quality pocketknives ever made in America was founded in 1852. The New York Knife Company was started by a group of English cutlers who had previously worked for the Waterville Company in Waterbury, Connecticut. They began making knives in the town of Matteawan and operated there until 1856, using the stamping "New York Knife Co. Matteawan."

The town of Walden, New York, was just across the Hudson River, and Walden's town fathers offered factory facilities as inducement for the company to move there. The company's management accepted the offer, and when the move was made, the entire populace of Walden reportedly turned out with their wagons and horses to assist. The company's president at the time of this move was Thomas W. Bradley, and under his management the New York Knife Company had become the nation's largest knife manufacturer by the time of his death in 1879.

In 1878, the company adopted as a trademark the picture of a muscular arm with sleeve rolled up, the hand holding a hammer. Four years later, the words "Hammer Brand" were added to the pictorial logo. From that time, most of the company's pocketknives had the trademark etched on the blades, and some knives will be found with tangs stamped with both the company name and the trademark. In addition to the high-quality knives marketed with the "New York Knife Co. Walden, N.Y." stamping and the Hammer Brand trademark, the company made a less expensive and lower-quality knife under the name of Walkill River Works, beginning about 1928. In 1931, New York Knife Company went out of business.

Collectors should be aware that the Hammer Brand trademark was purchased in 1936 by Imperial Knife Company for use on its shell-handled knives. These knives will normally have patent numbers on a second blade, crimped bolsters, and no New York Knife Co. stamping. Although the New York Knife Company's Hammer Brand knives are choice collectibles, the inexpensive knives are not as desirable to collectors.

NORTHFIELD KNIFE COMPANY

This company was formed when Samuel Mason, who had learned the cutlery trade working in the Sheffield factory of Joseph Mappin & Son, joined with several businessmen and lured a group of former Sheffield cutlers from their jobs in Waterville to Northfield, Connecticut, for the purpose of establishing a knife manufactory. The Northfield Knife Company was established in 1858 and made the first cast-iron-handled knives, patented by Mason in 1862.

Although the business prospered, Mason left the company in 1865 when ownership control passed to Franklin H. and John H. Catlin. Mason joined Edward Binns in making knives at Rochester, Pennsylvania, in a company that would later become Beaver Falls Cutlery Company.

Northfield's success led the Catlin brothers to expand through the purchase of several of the area's smaller knife companies. American Knife Company of Plymouth Hollow (Thomaston), Connecticut, was purchased in 1865, and the Excelsior Knife Company of Torrington, Connecticut, was purchased in 1884.

In 1872, Charles N. Platts (see Cattaraugus) became plant superintendent and continued in that capacity until 1896. Platts's sons worked at the Northfield company and gained there the early cutlery experiences that would influence much of America's cutlery industry. Platts and other Sheffield-trained cutlers provided the leadership and expertise for the company to produce an excellent grade of knives. The trademark UN-X-LD, meaning unexcelled, was adopted in 1876. The company's exhibit at the 1901 Pan American Exposition displayed over a thousand different knife styles.

The Northfield Knife Company was sold to Clark Brothers Cutlery of St. Louis, Missouri, in 1919. The new owner dropped the Northfield name and stamped the knives made in the Northfield factory with their own logo. The company was declared bankrupt in 1929.

PAL CUTLERY COMPANY

Pal was first a trademark of Utica Knife and Razor Company of Utica, New York, for knives made in Germany. Stampings used from 1924 to 1939 were PAL and PAL BRAND; both included "Germany." The Pal Blade Company of Chicago was started in 1934 by Otto E. Kraus. The two firms joined together in 1935 as Pal Blade Company and opened manufacturing facilities in Plattsburg, New York. The company's knife stampings from 1934 to 1953 were PAL BLADE CO. MADE IN USA and PAL CUTLERY CO. MADE IN USA.

Around 1940, Pal purchased the cutlery division of Remington Arms Co., and their purchase included Remington's stock of knives and knife parts as well as the factory in Holyoke, Massachusetts. Some knives made by Pal at this time may have blades stamped with both Pal and Remington markings. One may find a "Pal" knife with at least one Remington blade or a "Remington" knife with one or more Pal blades. These transition knives represented expediency and production economy and should not be considered counterfeits.

Prior to the Remington purchase, Pal's knife production had been primarily pocketknives. Afterward, the company was a prolific manufacturer of fixed-blade, or hunting knives, made in styles identical to the Remingtons of earlier years. The company produced these knives under several government contracts during World War II. In 1953, Pal ceased production of knives.

PARKER CUTLERY COMPANY

Several company and brand names have been initiated by and associated with James F. Parker, the founder of this company. During the 1960s, when his primary employment was as a sales representative for a major paint manufacturer, Parker conducted a sideline business of buying and selling knives. In addition to his activity within the gun and knife show circuit, Parker was one of the first to effectively utilize direct mail for selling and buying antique or collectible knives. In 1970, Parker Distributing Company was formed, with headquarters in Chattanooga, Tennessee.

Parker began to import knives from Japan, using the company name as well as EAGLE BRAND or the logo of an eagle with widespread wings for tang stampings. In 1976, the Parker-Frost Cutlery Company was formed as a partnership with James F. Frost, and the PARKER-FROST CUTLERY CO. (Eagle Logo) brand stamp was used. In addition to knives made in Japan, the company marketed several commemorative issues and individual knives made by manufacturers such as Schrade and Rodgers-Wostenholm. The partnership was dissolved in 1978, but some knives that had already been ordered prior to that time were marketed for a short while afterward. Parker Cutlery Company concentrated its efforts on promotion of the EAGLE BRAND knives, stamped with the Parker company name and logo.

In addition to the above-named companies and stampings, Parker has been responsible for the formation of several other companies and brand stampings. In 1978, PARKER BROTHERS (Eagle Logo) CHATTANOOGA, TN knives were introduced, and about three dozen different models were sold for a short while under the partnership of the brothers James and Mack Parker. PARKER & SON (Eagle Logo) CHATTANOOGA, TN was used on a limited number of knives handled in stag and second-cut stag from 1982 until about 1985.

In 1982, Parker invested in the Japanese cutlery manufacturer, Imai. The Imai factory was enlarged, and new quality control measures were instituted, giving birth to the PARKER-IMAI stamping that replaced the Parker Brothers' stamping on most patterns. This stamping was discontinued in 1984, when most of the stag-handled knives were no longer manufactured.

In 1984, Parker Cutlery purchased Rodgers Wostenholm USA LTD., including its inventory and the right to use the IX*L trademark for a period of twelve years. Subsequently, high-quality bench-made pocket folders with the I*XL trademark were produced. Knives of this special series had mother-of-pearl, black pearl, abalone, buffalo horn, and stag handles. Except for twelve hundred butterfly knives, these patterns were limited to three hundred knives each.

In 1984, Parker Cutlery contracted with Fain Edwards Ironworks to produce Damascus steel for thirty thousand folding knives with stag handles. Edwards, a bladesmith and knife maker, had begun producing Damascus steel in sufficient quantities to make Damascus knives commercially. Edwards and Parker formed a corporation, the Parker-Edwards Cutlery Co. Inc., in 1985. Located in Jacksonville, Alabama, the company was formed to manufacture Damascus folders and hunting knives, as well as pocketknives and sporting knives, from 440C steel. In 1986, Parker became the sole owner of the company through the purchase of Edwards's stock. Because a supply of knife blades had already been produced, the PARKER-EDWARDS stamp was used on some knives made during the next two years. These knives, along with those from earlier years stamped PARKER-FROST, are becoming of greater interest to collectors.

With total ownership of the Jacksonville factory, manufacture of a number of Parker Cutlery Company knives was moved to that location, and the stamping, PARKER U.S.A., was used.

During recent years, James F. Parker and the companies he has started or acquired have had a significant impact on the cutlery industry. In 1987, Parker purchased Cutlery World, the nation's largest retail cutlery chain. With stores located in major shopping malls in most parts of the country, Cutlery World offers a wide line of both using and collectible knives. Parker's experience in mail-order merchandising has been instrumental in this company's new use of knife catalogs to supplement sales to local customers and prospects.

Perhaps the most significant of Parker's acquisitions was accomplished in January 1989 with the purchase of W. R. Case & Sons Cutlery Company.

Near the end of 1990, the James F. Parker Companies were involved in reorganization through Chapter 11 Bankruptcy.

Parker-Frost 3¾" Canoe; stamped Rodgers-Wostenholm on back of tang; manufactured in several handle materials as follows:

Christmas Tree celluloid, 12,000 produced	*$40*
Tiger Eye celluloid, 1,000 produced	*$55*
Red and brown bone, 1,000 produced	*$50*
Genuine stag, 6,000 produced	*$45*

Parker-Frost Coffin Knife—3¾" Coffin pattern with pearl handles; 1,200 produced   *$80*

Colony Bicentennial—Set of 13 metal-handled knives and one stag clasp knife   *$550*

Deerslayer—5½" clasp knife; back blade marked "made especially for Parker-Frost"; 1,000 produced   *$55*

Eagle display knife—12" closed-length display knife made in limited quantity of 25   *$700*

Longhorn—one-blade 3¾" lockback with smooth bone handles   *$40*
    As above except with pearl handles   *$70*

Indian Series #1—4 Trapper-pattern knives; 2 handled in bone and 2 in tortoise celluloid; blade etching of Indian tribes   *$125 set*

Indian Series #2—same as above except different blade etching   *$115*

North American Whittler—set of 4 stag-handled Whittler-pattern knives   *$250*

American Series—various patterns made in 1978 for Parker-Frost by Schrade as follows:

> *Tennessee Stockman*—4″ 3-blade Stockman pattern handled in stag   *$60*
>
> *Kentucky Stockman*—same as above except different blade etching   *$60*
>
> *Stockman*—4″ 3-blade Stockman with bone handles   *$30*
>
> *Stockman*—same as above except with black sawcut bone handles *$22*
>
> *Muskrat*—4″ 2-blade Muskrat pattern with bone handles   *$27*
>
> *Muskrat*—same as above except with black sawcut bone handles *$22*
>
> *Trapper*—3⅞″ Trapper pattern with bone handles   *$30*
>
> *Trapper*—same as above except with black sawcut bone handles *$22*
>
> *Lockback*—3⅞″ 1-blade lockback with bone handles   *$25*
>
> *Lockback*—same as above except with stainless steel handles   *$22*
>
> *Peanut*—3⅛″ Peanut pattern with black sawcut bone handles   *$18*
>
> *Folding Hunter*—5½″ 2-blade folding Hunter pattern with scrimshaw composition handles   *$40*

Copperhead Set—3¾″ 2-blade Copperhead pattern knives; 1,200 matching serial-numbered sets made; stag handles   *$150*

Parker Cutlery Co. American Lockback Whittler—4″ Whittler pattern with front lock release; Eagle shield; 6,000 each made with smooth-bone and pick-bone handles   *$50*

Bullet—3½″ knife made by Parker Eagle Brand with 4 different handle materials; Christmas Tree celluloid, pickbone, and smooth bone   *$24*

> *Mother-of-pearl handles;* blade etched "Christmas 1982"   *$120*

Celebrated Dirk Knife—4″ 3-blade Whittler with front lock release made by Parker Eagle Brand; master blade etched; handled in pearl   *$100*

Country Doctor Set—3½″ Doctor's pattern handled in 5 different handle materials: abalone, stag, pearl, pick bone, and smooth bone   *$125*

Desperado—made by Parker Eagle Brand; large pearl-handled folder decorated with scrimshawed handles and engraved bolsters; 24 produced   *$250*

Hercules—3″ Coffin-pattern folder handled in abalone, black pearl, and mother-of-pearl; 200 of each produced by Parker Cutlery   *$75*

Little Pillbuster—3⅔″ Doctor's pattern by Parker Cutlery; 3 handle materials: pearl, pick bone, and smooth bone; 7 serial-numbered sets were produced   *$120*

> *Individual knives,* not numbered   *$25*

Old Remington—3¾″ Wharncliffe pattern whittler with locking master blade; master blade etched; 3,000 each produced in smooth bone and pick bone; Eagle Brand   *$45*

Saturday Night Special—5″ Texas Toothpick or Powderhorn pattern handled with 9 different materials; 1,000 sets produced   *$190 set*

Sowbelly I—4¼″ serpentine pattern made by Eagle Brand; handled in smooth bone and pick bone   *$25*

Sowbelly III—4¼″ serpentine 3-blade Stockman pattern handled in smooth bone and pick bone   *$30*

Sowbelly V—4¼″ serpentine 5-blade Stockman pattern handled in smooth bone, second-cut stag, and pick bone   *$50*

*Second-Cut Stag Set—*300 serial-numbered sets produced by Parker & Sons; 19 knives assembled in framed display case   *$600*

PLATTS

Platts Brothers Cutlery Company

The Platts brothers, Charlie, Ray, Joe, and Frank, had been employees and shareholders in the cutlery company started by their father in 1897, and after their father's death in 1900, had continued ownership along with their brother, H. N. Platts. When H. N. purchased his brothers' shares in the old company in 1905 and merged it with W. R. Case & Son Cutlery, the other brothers began plans for their own cutlery company.

The stamping PLATTS BROS. UNION N.Y. likely dates to 1905–1907 and indicates that the brothers began as a jobbing firm. Their own factory in Andover, New York, was started in 1907 but lasted only a few years. The stamping PLATTS BROS. ANDOVER N.Y. was used from about 1907 to 1909.

After the demise of their company, each of the brothers worked with a variety of cutlery companies, including Thomaston, Eureka, W. R. Case & Sons, and Remington.

C. Platts & Sons Cutlery Company

Charles Platts began his apprenticeship as a cutler in Sheffield, England, in 1854 when he was fourteen years old. Before emigrating to the United States in 1864, he worked at both Joseph Rodgers and George Wostenholm cutlery factories. Shortly after his arrival, he began work for the American Cutlery Company in Reynolds Bridge, Connecticut.

Platts became plant superintendent for Northfield Knife Company in 1872 and remained in that capacity until 1893, when he was hired as superintendent of Cattaraugus Cutlery Company. Charles Platts's son, Harlow Nixon (H. N.), was already employed by Cattaraugus, and the other four sons joined their father in the move to that company.

With five trained cutlers as sons, Platts conceived the idea of a family-owned business, and in 1896 they started the C. Platts & Sons Cutlery Company. Their first factory was in the Gowanda, New York, building that had been vacated when Schatt and Morgan moved to Titusville, Pennsylvania. Knife stamping during this 1896–1897 period was C. PLATTS & SONS GOWANDA N.Y.

The company's business was very good, and the manufacturing was moved to Eldred, Pennsylvania. In addition to knives stamped C. PLATTS & SONS ELDRED PA., the firm made knives on contract for other companies, such as Case Brothers and W. R. Case & Son.

When Charles Platts died in 1900, his sons renamed the company C. Platts's Sons Cutlery Company and operated it until 1905.

PUMA

Puma-Werk Lauterjung & Sohn of Solingen, Germany, is a cutlery manufacturer with a tenure of more than two hundred years. In 1769, Johann Wilhelm Lauterjung received his first trademark from the Solingen Master Cutlers Guild. Along with his son, Johann Wilhelm II, he established a knife works on the bank of the Wupper River near Solingen. The shop produced knives, razors, tableware, and shears along with swords and daggers for military use. Ownership of the business passed through several generations of the founder's descendants. In the mid-1800s, Nathanael Lauterjung, the founder's great-grandson, relocated the cutlery shop to Solingen, where it continued to prosper. In the early part of the 1900s, the succeeding generation, Eugen and Franz Lauterjung, led the company in its boldest move—building a complete production factory and major expansion into the export market.

The Lauterjung business, which had become known as the Puma Works, began to change after World War II. Renate Lauterjung von Frankenberg's husband, Baron Oswald von Frankenberg, became the first company chief executive not born into the Lauterjung family. His decision to concentrate on sporting knives brought a number of new products into production. Most noteworthy, at least in terms of the company's recognition in the United States, was the introduction of a knife of his design known as the Puma White Hunter. His experience as a hunter of all types of game, as well as his association with Germany's Forest Rangers, allowed for testing and evaluation of each product. The White Hunter was first imported into the United States by Kurt Gutmann, founder of Gutmann Cutlery, and it led the way for Puma's knives to become known for their quality and performance in the field. Many other types of knives for the sportsman were developed and received the most severe and rugged testing.

The Puma name and logo have been associated not only with fixed-blade hunting knives but quality pocketknives as well. The Puma line today consists of more than seventy-five regular models. In addition to older knives such as early White Hunters and Scale Knives (for fishermen), the company has produced several fine commemorative or limited-edition series that attract serious collectors.

Dating the manufacture of Puma knives is no easy task, especially those not intended for the export market. Puma did develop a control number coding system in 1964 that indicated not only the year but also the quarter during which a knife was manufactured. Had the system not changed four times since, explanation might have been possible. The collector interested in Puma knives should not be discouraged, however, because information can be found. The company produced a chart in 1985 that explained the coding system and listed the years that Puma knife models were exported to this country. The older knives in good condition have appreciated in value, as have most of the special issues. If found, one of the 1985 charts will be extremely helpful, and it may well be a collectible in itself.

QUEEN CUTLERY COMPANY

This well-known company was started shortly after World War I as a "moonlighting operation" of several foremen of the Schatt & Morgan factory. The story is that each foreman would make and steal a few extra knife parts before ending his day's work. They would then use the parts to assemble their own knives and sell them under the brand QUEEN CITY CUTLERY COMPANY. The operation of these foremen officially became Queen City Cutlery about 1920 or 1921.

Schatt & Morgan's sales were depressed, and management recognized that part of their problem was that the competing sales of Queen City's knives were made at their own expense. The disloyal foremen were fired, but the loss of experienced supervisors added other problems. Schatt & Morgan went out of business around 1931, and the six Queen City founders pooled their savings to buy the old factory. They moved into it in 1932, and Queen knives are still made in that same factory today.

As members of the original founding group died, those remaining bought out their interests. Eventually, only two of the original families were in the business, the Mathewses and the Ericsons. Soon after, Will Mathews and Ericson decided to make knife blades of 440C steel. Their knives were stamped QUEEN CITY until 1945, when the mark was changed to the letter *Q* or *Q* with a crown on top. Some of these knives were also stamped STAINLESS on the tang, but many consumers would not buy them because they considered stainless steel an inferior product for pocketknife blades. Consequently, the company discontinued use of the STAINLESS stamping and adopted QUEEN STEEL instead—the steel did not change.

During the early 1960s, the company discontinued stamping of blade tangs in favor of etching QUEEN STEEL on the master blade. In 1971, using old dies, the company again began stamping their knives on the tang, and a new stamping was used: a crown and the word QUEEN (with the long pointed tail of the *Q* extending the length of the word). In 1976 and 1977, the stamping became a large *Q* with a crown on top, the long tail, and the numbers 76 or 77 over the tail. Queen Cutlery was sold to Servotronics, Inc., in 1969 and continues to make knives.

REMINGTON

The company that began manufacturing knives branded Remington in 1920 had started about a century before, when Eliphalet Remington forged his first gun barrel. Shortly thereafter, Union Metallic Cartridge Company was founded by Marcellus Hartley. Upon the death of Remington, the two businesses would come together through Hartley's purchase of the firearms company. Years later, Marcellus Hartley Dodge became chief executive of the two companies and consolidated them under the name of the Remington Union Metallic Cartridge Company. The cartridge company was the smaller of the two entities, and the Remington trademark had far greater recognition, so the UMCC portion of the name was dropped. But it was not forgotten. Knife collectors today will find the initials UMC stamped along with the name "Remington" on knives, and sportsmen will find a "U" stamped on rimfire cartridges made by the company.

Remington prospered during the early part of this century but, at the end of World War I, found itself with extensive manufacturing facilities and without government contracts to keep the plant busy. The relatively new Bridgeport, Connecticut, factory was nearly idle, and management knew that cutlery manufacture was not an entirely new endeavor since Remington had made a large number of bayonets, beginning about 1915. A decision was made to enter the cutlery field, and Remington's first pocketknives (R-103) were made in February 1920.

The manufacture of pocketknives quickly got underway, and by 1921 more than two thousand dealers sold Remington knives in most parts of the country. Further expansion came during the 1920s, and by 1931 Remington was producing almost 3 million knives per year in as many as one thousand patterns.

Near the end of 1922, the company announced the first "Bullets"—large trappers or folding hunters—and a dozen different knives of this high-quality line had been produced by the end of the decade. Further success came in 1923 with Remington's production of the Official Boy Scout Knife, the R-3333 pattern with an official scout shield. By 1925, the number of patterns produced approached one thousand, and fixed-blade, or sheath, knives were added to the line. Quality remained high, as did production; ten thousand knives per day were made by the Bridgeport factory at the beginning of the century's third decade. But the Great Depression took its toll, and the failure of a large number of Remington's distributors and dealers brought financial difficulty to the manufacturer.

In 1933, controlling interest in the company was sold to E. I. DuPont Company. The number of knife patterns was reduced to about a third of their earlier number by 1936; with this reduction in knife selections came a reduction in quality, and many of those patterns were made under contract. The 1940 announcement of Remington's revival of military small arms production was in keeping with the rumored $2 million loss in its cutlery division. The company's cutlery equipment, parts, and supplies were sold to the Pal Blade Company.

Remington made several million knives during its twenty-year production period, and those numbers could make one wonder why the brand is considered rare and is so popular with collectors. But the knives were highly advertised, widely distributed, easily sold, and faithfully used in all parts of the country. Finding a Remington knife today may not be really difficult, but one found in mint condition is a prized possession, especially one of the rarer patterns. There has probably been no other knife type, manufactured in reasonably large quantities, that can approach the "Remington Bullet" in collector demand.

Shields

Remington used a variety of handle shields, but the most recognized and most desirable are the replicated cartridge ("Bullet") or the acorn shield. Knives bearing the bullet shield are normally the larger folding-hunter patterns and are recognized, respected, and highly valued by collectors. The acorn shield was used by Remington on knives with a leather punch blade. A good rule of thumb in evaluating these knives is that a Remington knife with an acorn shield and without a punch blade should be subject to suspicion.

Pattern Numbers

Collectors are fortunate in that Remington stamped pattern numbers on most knives produced, and several of the company's catalogs have been reprinted for reference use. The letter *R* before the pattern number indicates a pocketknife, and the last digit indicates its handle material, as follows:

1—Redwood	6—Genuine Stag
2—Black	7—Ivory or White Bone
3—Bone	8—Cocobolo
4—Pearl	9—Metal
5—Pyremite	0—Buffalo Horn

"Ch" after the numbers means a chain attached. Pattern numbers R1 through R2999 are jackknives; R-3000 through R-5999 are cattle, premium stock, farmers, mechanics, and scout knives; and R6000 through R9000 are pen knives.

Stamping

Most Remington knife stampings are either the so-called Circle Remington stamping or the Straight Line stamping. As a general rule, the company's higher-quality pocketknives have the circle stamping, and the straight-line stamp will be found on those of lesser quality.

A variety of stampings were used by Remington, but, primarily, they were REMINGTON in straight-line script stamped horizontally on the tang or REMINGTON inside a circle in several variations as shown below.

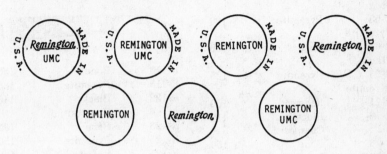

Pattern No.	Handle	Mint Price	Pattern No.	Handle	Mint Price
R-1	Redwood	$70	R-23ch	Bone	$115
R-2	Black Composition	70	R-25	White Pyremite	90
R-3	Bone	85	R-31	Redwood	90
R-01	Redwood	65	R-32	Black Composition	90
R-02	Black Composition	65	R-33	Bone	110
R-03	Bone	80	R-35	Pyremite	105
R-A1	Redwood	65	R-B040 (B)	Brown Bone	95
R-C5	Pyremite	70			
R-C6	Stag	70	R-041 (B)	Brown Bone	95
R-C7	Ivory	70			
R-C8	Cocobolo	70	R-B43 (B)	Brown Bone	130
R-C9	Metal	70			
R-15	Pyremite Leg Pattern	200	R-B44 (B)	Brown Bone	130
R-015	Pyremite	95	R-B45 (B)	Brown Bone	140
R-17	White Composition	95	R-B44W (B)	White Bone	120
R-21	Redwood	90			
R-21ch	Redwood	110	R-B46 (B)	Brown Bone	135
R-22	Black Composition	95	R-B47 (B)	Brown Bone	150
R-23	Bone	110			

Pattern No.	Handle	Mint Price
R-51	Redwood	$90
R-52	Black	165
Black	Composition	
R-53	Stag	190
Stag		
R-55	Pyremite	180
Pyremite		
R-63	Stag	180
Stag		
R-65	Pyremite	125
Pyremite		
R-71	Redwood	100
R-72	Black	110
	Composition	
R-73	Bone	150
R-75	Pyremite	125
R-81	Redwood	100
R-82	Black	110
	Composition	
R-83	Bone	155
R-85	Pyremite	125
R-CO90	Black Bone	80
R-CO91	Black Bone	80

Pattern No.	Handle	Mint Price
R-91	Redwood	135
R-92	Black	145
Black	Composition	
R-93	Stag	180
Stag		
R-95	Pyremite	140
Pyremite		
R-103	Bone	155
R-103ch		165

Pattern No.	Handle	Mint Price
R-105		135
R-105A	Onyx	135
R-105B	Pyremite	135

Pattern No.	Handle	Mint Price
R-108ch	Cocobolo	$130
R111	Redwood	120
R-112	Black	120
	Composition	

Pattern No.	Handle	Mint Price
R-113	Bone	150
R-115	Pyremite	135
R-122	Black	140
	Composition	
R-123	Bone	165
R-125	Pyremite	150
R-131	Redwood	140
R-132	Black	140
	Composition	

Pattern No.	Handle	Mint Price
R-133	Stag	170
R-135	Pyremite	160
R-141	Redwood	130
R-142	Black	130
	Composition	
R-143	Bone	175
R-145	Pyremite	150
R-151	Redwood	135
R-152	Black	135
	Composition	
R-153	Bone	175
R-155	Pyremite	150
R-155B		150
R-155M		150
R-155Z		150
R-161	Redwood	135
R-162	Black	135
	Composition	
R-163	Bone	175
R-165	Pyremite	150

Pattern No.	Handle	Mint Price	Pattern No.	Handle	Mint Price
R-171 (T)	Redwood	$150			
R-172 (T)	Black Composition	150			
R-173 (T)	Brown Bone	175			
R-175 (T)	Pyremite	165	R-213 (E.O.)	Bone	$210
			R-219 (E.O.)	Brass	175
			R-222 (T)	Black Composition	150
			R-223 (T)	Bone	200
R-181 (T)	Redwood	165	R-225 (T)	Pyremite	165
R-182 (T)	Black Composition	165	R-228 (T)	Cocobolo	150
R-183 (T)	Bone	200	R-232 (T)	Black Composition	150
R-185 (T)	Pyremite	170	R-233 (T)	Bone	210
R-191 (T)	Redwood	160	R-235 (T)	Pyremite	195
R-192 (T)	Black Composition	160	R-238 (T)	Cocobolo	145
R-193 (T)	Bone	200	R-242 (E.O.)	Black Composition	195
R-195 (T)	Pyremite	180	R-243 (E.O.)	Bone	225
R-201 (E.O.)	Redwood	175	R-245 (E.O.)	Pyremite	200
R-202	Black Composition	175	R-248 (E.O.)	Cocobolo	165
R-203 (E.O.)	Brown Bone	215	R-252 (T)	Black Composition	160
R-205 (E.O.)	Pyremite	200	R-253 (T)	Bone	210
R-211 (E.O.)	Redwood	175	R-255 (T)	Pyremite	190
R-212 (E.O.)	Black Composition	175	R-258 (T)	Cocobolo	170

Pattern No.	Handle	Mint Price	Pattern No.	Handle	Mint Price
R-262	Black Composition	$150	R-372	Black Composition	$190
R-263	Bone	210	R-373	Bone	225
R-265	Pyremite	195	R-375	Pyremite	190
R-272	Black Composition	180	R-378	Cocobolo	180
			R-383	Bone	225
R-273	Brown Bone	225	R-391 (T)	Redwood	180
R-275	Pyremite	195	R-392 (T)	Black Composition	180
R-282	Black Composition	185	R-393 (T)	Bone	225
R-283	Bone	230			
R-293 (S.T.)		325	R-395 (T)	Pyremite	180
R-293 (S.T.2)		750	R-402	Black Composition	160
R-293 (L.B.)	Brown Bone	1750	R-403	Bone	220
			R-405	Pyremite	190
R-303	Bone	180	R-410	Buffalo Horn	165
R-305	Pyremite	170	R-412 (E.O.)	Black Composition	165
R-313	Brown Bone	235	R-413 (E.O.)	Bone	200
R-315	Pyremite	185			
R-322	Black Composition	175	R-415 (E.O.)	Pyremite	175
R-323	Bone	225			
R-325	Pyremite	200			
R-328	Cocobolo	185			
R-333	Bone	190			
R-341	Redwood	185	R-423	Bone	190
R-342	Black Composition	185	R-432 (D.K.)	Black Composition	275
R-343	Bone	235	R-433 (D.K.)		375
R-352	Black Composition	160	R-435 (D.K.)	Pyremite	300
R-353	Bone	225			
R-355	Pyremite	195	R-443 (D.K.)	Bone	275
R-358	Cocobolo	185			
R-363	Bone	235	R-444 (D.K.)	Pearl	425
R-365	Pyremite	185			

Pattern No.	Handle	Mint Price	Pattern No.	Handle	Mint Price
R-453 (D.K.)	Bone	$400	R-595	Pyremite	$175
			R-603	Bone	175
R-455 (D.K.)	Pyremite	300	R-604		160
			R-605	Pyremite	160
R-463	Bone	200	R-609	Metal	200
R-465	Pyremite	175			
R-473	Bone	200			
R-475	Pyremite	175			
R-482	Black Composition	175	R-613	Bone	225
			R-615	Pyremite	160
R-483	Bone	200	R-622	Black Composition	175
R-485	Pyremite	175			
R-488	Cocobolo	175	R-623	Bone	200
R-493	Bone	200			
R-495	Pyremite	175			
R-503	Bone	200	R-625	Pyremite	200
R-505	Pyremite	175	R-633	Bone	200
R-512	Black Composition	175			
R-513	Bone	200			
R-515	Pyremite	175	R-635	Pyremite	160
R-523	Bone	225	R-643 (F)	Bone	275
R-525	Pyremite	180			
R-551	Redwood	130	R-645 (F)	Pyremite	250
R-552	Black Composition	130	R-645 (F2)	Candy Stripe	450
R-553	Brown Bone	175	R-653 (F)	Black Composition	260
R-555	Candy Stripe	165	R-655 (F)		220
R-563	Brown Bone	175			
R-572	Black Composition	165	R-655 (S)	Pyremite	500
R-573		190	R-662		275
R-575	Pyremite	170	R-663	Bone	375
R-583	Bone	200	R-668	Cocobolo	325
R-585	Pyremite	175	R-672 (D)	Black Composition	165
R-590	Buffalo Horn	275	R-673 (D)	Bone	200
R-593	Bone	200			

Pattern No.	Handle	Mint Price	Pattern No.	Handle	Mint Price
R-674 (D)	Pearl	$325	R-745	Pyremite	$165
R-675 (D)	Pyremite	190	R-753	Bone	190
R-677	Ivory	200	R-755	Pyremite	150
R-679 (D)	Metal	170	R-756	Stag	180
R-682 (G)	Black Composition	275	R-763	Bone	180
R-683 (G)	Brown Bone	375	R-772 (T)	Black Composition	185
R-684 (G)	Pearl	475	R-773 (T)	Bone	210
R-685 (G)	Pyremite	375	R-775 (T)	Pyremite	185
R-693 (HA)	Bone	175	R-783 (T)	Bone	220
R-698 (HA)	Cocobolo	150	R-793	Bone	250
R-703 (HA)	Bone	125	R-803	Bone	125
R-706 (HA)	Stag	90	R-805	Pyremite	125
R-708 (HA)	Cocobolo	100	R-C803	Bone	65
R-713 (HA)	Bone	195	R-813	Bone	250
R-718 (HA)	Cocobolo	170	R-823	Bone	210
R-723 (HA)	Bone	225	R-825	Pyremite	180
R-728 (HA)	Cocobolo	180	R-833	Bone	190
R-732	Black Composition	150	R-835	Pyremite	160
R-733	Bone	185	R-843	Bone	190
R-735	Pyremite	160	R-845	Pyremite	160
R-738	Cocobolo	150	R-853	Bone	200
			R-855	Pyremite	180
			R-863	Bone	225
			R-865	Pyremite	190
			R-873	Bone	125
			R-874	Pearl	160
			R-875	Pyremite	125
			R-881	Redwood	125
			R-882	Black Composition	135
			R-883	Bone	175
R-743	Bone	190	R-892 (E.O.)	Black Composition	165
			R-893 (E.O.)	Bone	220

Pattern No.	Handle	Mint Price	Pattern No.	Handle	Mint Price
R-895 (E.O.)	Pyremite	$200	R-985 (D)	Pyremite	$120
R-901	Redwood	150	R-992	Black Composition	125
R-913	Bone	240	R-993	Bone	150
R-921	Redwood	130	R-995	Blue/wh Composition	125
			R-1002	Black Composition	125
			R-1003	Bone	150
			R-1005	Pyremite	125
R-932 (T.T.)	Black Composition	250	R-1012	Black Composition	165
R-933 (T.T.)		300	R-1013	Bone	175
R-935 (T.T.)	Pyremite	325	R-1022	Black Composition	300
R-942 (T.T.)	Black Composition	275	R-1023	Bone	325
R-943 (T.T.)	Bone	325	R-1032	Black Composition	120
R-945 (T.T.)	Pyremite	275	R-1033	Bone	140
R-C953 (T.T.)	Bone	250	R-1035	Pyremite	120
R-953 (T.T.)	Bone	700	R-1042	Black Composition	150
R-955 (T.T.)	Pyremite	250	R-1043	Bone	175
R-962 (E.O.)	Black Composition	175	R-1045	Pyremite	150
R-963 (E.O.)	Imitation Bone	300	R-1051	Redwood	110
R-965 (E.O.)	Pyremite	165	R-1053	Bone	100
R-971 (C.S.)	Redwood	250	R-1055	Pyremite	100
R-982 (D)	Black Composition	110	R-1061	Redwood	110
R-983 (D)	Bone	150	R-1062	Black Composition	125
			R-1063	Bone	150
			R-1065W	White Pyremite	110
			R-1071	Cocobolo	125
			R-1072	Black Composition	125
			R-1073	Bone	150
			R-1075	Pyremite	125
			R-1082	Black Composition	75

Pattern No.	Handle	Mint Price	Pattern No.	Handle	Mint Price
R-1083	Bone	$95	R-1240 (D.B.)	Brown Bone	$300
R-1085	Pyremite	70	R-1241 (D.B.)	Redwood	310
R-1092	Black Composition	65	R-1242 (D.B.)	Black Composition	400
R-1093	Bone	100	R-1243 (D.B.)	Bone	425
R-1102	Black Composition	120			
R-1103	Brown Bone	150			
R-1112	Black Composition	120			
R-1113	Bone	160	R-1253 (BL)	Brown Bone	1350
R-1123 (BL)	Bone	1000			
R-1128 (BL)	Cocobolo	1500			
R-1133	Bone	180	R-1263 (BL)	Brown Bone	1400
R-1143	Bone	180			
R-1153	Bone	350			
R-1163	Bone	350			
R-1173 (BL)	Brown Bone	1800			
R-1182	Black Composition	140	R-1273 (BL)	Brown Bone	1750
R-1183	Bone	175	R-1283	Bone	140
R-1192	Black Composition	120	R-1284	Pearl	210
R-1193	Bone	140	R-1285	Tortoise Shell	110
R-1202	Black Composition	145	R-1293	Bone	225
R-1203	Bone	175	R-1295 (TP)	Pyremite	250
R-1212	Black Composition	265	R-1303 (BL)	Brown Bone	1350
R-1213	Bone	325	R-1306 (BL)	Stag	1150
R-1222	Black Composition	285	R-1315	Pyremite	165
R-1223	Bone	325	R-1323 (D)	Bone	175
R-1225W (E.E.)	White Composition	285	R-1324 (D)	Pearl	250
R-1232	Black Composition	160	R-1325 (D)	Pyremite	150
R-1233	Bone	200			

Pattern No.	Handle	Mint Price	Pattern No.	Handle	Mint Price
R-1333	Bone	$150	R-1592	Black Composition	$110
R-1343	Bone	310			
R-1353	Bone	235	R-1593	Bone	125
R-1363	Bone	235	R-1595	Pyremite	110
R-1373	Bone	325	R-1608 (B.K.)	Cocobolo	90
R-1379	Metal	140			
R-1383	Brown Bone	350	R-1613 (BL)	Bone	1400
R-1383 (FSL)		230	R-1613	Bone	700
			R-1615 (R.B.)	Pyremite	300
R-1389	Metal	150			
R-1399	Metal	120	R-1622	Black Composition	110
R-1409	Metal	120			
R-1413	Bone	145	R-1623	Bone	125
R-1423	Bone	145	R-1623ch	Imitation Bone	135
R-1437	Ivory	150			
R-1447 (BU)	Ivory	150	R-1630 (D.B.)	Bone	425
R-1457 (BU)	Ivory	165	R-1643	Bone	135
			R-1644	Pearl	225
R-1465 (BU)	Pyremite	175	R-1645	Pyremite	125
R-1477 (BU)	Ivory	140	R-1653 (P)	Bone	140
			R-1655 (P)	Pyremite	110
R-1483	Bone	150			
R-1485	Pyremite	125	R-1668	Cocobolo	165
R-1493	Bone	150	R-1671 (E.O.)	Redwood	80
R-1495	Pyremite	130			
R-1535 (FL)	Imitation Ivory	100	R-1673 (E.O.)	Bone	110
R-1545	Imitation Ivory	100	R-1685	Pyremite	115
			R-1687	Ivory	115
R-1555 W	Pyremite	145	R-1688 (BK)	Cocobolo	115
R-1568	Cocobolo	130	R-1697 (BK)		115
R-1572	Black Composition	100			
			R-1707 (BK)	Ivory	115
R-1573	Bone	120			
R-1573ch	Imitation Bone	135	R-1715 (BK)	Pyremite	85
R-1582	Slick Black	100	R-1717 (BK)	Ivory	110

Pattern No.	Handle	Mint Price	Pattern No.	Handle	Mint Price
R-1723	Bone	$165	R-2065	Pyremite	$60
R-1751	Redwood	100	R-2073	Bone	65
R-1752	Black Composition	100	R-2075	Pyremite	60
			R-2083	Bone	65
R-1753	Bone	125	R-2085	Pyremite	60
R-1755	Pyremite	100	R-2093	Bone	80
R-1763	Bone	140	R-2095	Black/Wh Composition	65
R-1772 (E.O.)	Black Composition	135			
			R-2103	Bone	80
R-1782	Black Composition	135	R-2105MW	Pyremite	65
			R-2111(elec)	Redwood	125
R-1783	Bone	145	R-2203	Bone	115
R-1785	Pyremite	115	R-2205D	Pyremite	70
R-1803	Bone	120	R-2213	Bone	75
R-1823	Brown Bone	135	R-2215M	Red/Black Pyremite	75
R-1825	Imitation Tortoise	140	R-2223	Bone	65
R-1833	Bone	155	R-2303 (S)	Bone	375
R-1853	Bone	125	R-2403 (S)	Bone	500
R-1855 M	Pyremite	100			
R-1863	Bone	130	R-2503	Bone	65
R-1873	Bone	125	R-2505B	Pyremite	65
R-1882B	Black Composition	125	R-2505M	Pyremite	65
			R-2505R	Pyremite	65
R-1903	Bone	100	R-2603	Bone	75
R-1905	Pyremite	90	R-2605B	Red Composition	80
R-1913	Bone	140			
R-1915	Candy Stripe	140	R-3003	Bone	310
			R-3005	Pyremite	275
R-1962	Black Composition	120	R-3013	Bone	310
			R-3015	Pyremite	275
R-1973 (E)	Bone	200	R-3033	Bone	350
			R-3035	Pyremite	275
R-1995 (BG)	Pyremite	125			

Pattern No.	Handle	Mint Price
R-2043	Bone	65
R-2045	Pyremite	65
R-2053	Bone	65
R-2055	Pyremite	65
R-2063	Bone	65

R-3050 Buf (ST)	Buffalo Horn	275
R-3053 (ST)	Bone	310

Pattern No.	Handle	Mint Price	Pattern No.	Handle	Mint Price
R-3054 (ST)	Pearl	$425			
R-3055 (ST)	Pyremite	275			
R-3056 (ST)	Stag	375	R3133	Bone	$330
R-3059 (ST)	Metal	275	R-3143 (BL.S.)	Bone	1150
R-3062 (ST)	Black Composition	275	R-3153 (C)	Brown Bone	275
R-3063 (ST)	Bone	310	R-3155 (C)	Pyremite	225
R-3064 (ST)	Pearl	450	R-3155B (C)	Pyremite	225
R-3065A (ST)		275	R-P (C)		175
R-3065W (ST)	Pyremite	275	R-3163 (C)	Bone	310
R-3065L (ST)	Yellow Composition	250	R-3154T (C)		250
R-3707	Buffalo Horn	275	R-3173 (C)	Bone	300
R-3073	Bone	250	R-3183 (C)	Bone	300
R-3075	Pyremite	250			
R-3083LP	Bone	425	R-3185 (C)	Pyremite	275
R-3085 (ST)	Pyremite	350	R-3193	Bone	300
R-3093 (ST)	Bone	275	R-3202	Black Composition	275
R-3095 (ST)	Pyremite	210	R-3203	Bone	300
R-3103 (ST)	Bone	310	R-3212	Black Composition	275
			R-3213	Bone	325
			R-3215	Pyremite	275
			R-3222	Black Composition	210
R-3105 (ST)	Pyremite	250	R-3223	Bone	275
R-3113	Bone	200	R-3225	Pyremite	250
R-3115G	Pyremite	165	R-3232	Black Composition	225
R-3115W	Pyremite	165	R-3233	Bone	300
R-3123 (M)	Bone	270	R-3235	Pyremite	270
			R-3242	Black Composition	290

Pattern No.	Handle	Mint Price
R-3243 (W)	Pyremite	$300
R-3245		285
R-3253 (C)	Bone	325
R-3255 (C)	Pyremite	275
R-3263 (C)	Bone	325
R-3265 (C)	Pyremite	275
R-3273 (C)	Brown Bone	300
R-3274 (C)	Pearl	425
R-3275 (C)	Pyremite	290
R-3283	Bone	300

Pattern No.	Handle	Mint Price
R-3285	Pyremite	270
R-3293	Bone	300
R-3295	Pyremite	270
R-3302	Black Composition	400
R-3303	Bone	400
R-3305D	Pyremite	325

Pattern No.	Handle	Mint Price
R-3312	Black Composition	325
R-3313	Bone	425
R-3315B	Pyremite	375
R-3322 (SC)	Black Composition	220
RS-3333 (OSC)	Brown Bone	245

Pattern No.	Handle	Mint Price
R-3333 (SC)	Brown Bone	$265

Pattern No.	Handle	Mint Price
R-3335	Red/White/ Blue	300
R-3352	Black Composition	185
R-3353	Bone	250
R-3363	Brown Bone	225
R-3372	Black Composition	190
R-3373	Bone	225
R-3375	Pyremite	200
R-3382	Black Composition	225
R-3383	Bone	240
R-3385S	Pyremite	225
R-3393	Bone	230
R-3395 T	Pyremite	200
R-3403	Bone	275
R-3405J	Pyremite	235
R-3413	Brown Bone	220
R-3414	Pearl	325
R-3415	Pyremite	225
R-3415 H	Pyremite	225
R-3423 (W)	Bone	250
R-3424 (W)	Pearl	390
R-3425P (W)	Pyremite	230
R-3432	Black Composition	190
R-3433	Bone	225
R-3435	Pyremite	190

Pattern No.	Handle	Mint Price	Pattern No.	Handle	Mint Price
R-3442	Black Composition	$190	R-3524 (W)	Pearl	$380
R-3443	Bone	200	R-3525 (W)	Pyremite	220
R-3445B	Pyremite	185			
R-3453 (W)	Bone	225	R-3533	Bone	200
			R-3535	Pyremite	160
R-3455 (W)	Pyremite	190	R-3545	Pyremite	155
			R-3553 (ST)	Brown Bone	250
R-3463 (W)	Bone	300			
			R-3554 (ST)	Pearl	385
R-3465B (W)	Pyremite	260			
			R-3555G (ST)	Pyremite	235
R-3475K (W)	Pyremite	250			
			R-3555 IW (ST)	Red Composition	235
R-3475J (W)	Pyremite	230			
			R-3563 (ST)	Bone	265
R-3480	Buffalo Horn	200			
			R-3565D (ST)	Pyremite	225
R-3483	Bone	255			
R-3484	Pearl	325	R-3573 (W)	Bone	265
R-3485J	Gold Pyremite	225			
			R-3575	Pyremite	230
R-3489	Metal	160	R-3580Buf	Buffalo Horn	140
R-3494	Pearl	325			
R-3495M	Pyremite	170	R-3583	Bone	170
R-3499	Metal	265	R-3585	Pyremite	140
R-3500Buf	Buffalo Horn	235	R-3593	Bone	340
			R-3595	Pyremite	300
R-3503	Bone	245	R-3596	Stag	395
R-3504	Pearl	340	R-3600	Buffalo Horn	200
R-3505	Pyremite	245			
R-3513 (W)	Brown Bone	250	R-3603	Bone	230
			R-3604	Pearl	350
R-3514 (W)	Pearl	350	R-3605	Pyremite	210
			R-3613	Bone	240
R-3515 (W)	Pyremite	220	R-3615	Pyremite	210
			R-3620Buf	Buffalo Horn	155
R-3520Buf (W)	Buffalo Horn	225			
			R-3623	Bone	185
R-3523 (W)	Bone	275	R-3625	Pyremite	160
			R-3633	Bone	170

Pattern No.	Handle	Mint Price
R-3635	Pyremite	$150
R-3643 (ST)	Bone	350
R-3644 (ST)	Pearl	450
R-3645 (ST)	Pyremite	325
R-3653	Bone	280
R-3655	Pyremite	250

Pattern No.	Handle	Mint Price
R-3665	Pyremite	345
R-3675	Pyremite	350
R-3683 (C)	Bone	250
R-3685 (C)	Pyremite	200
R-3693 (W)	Brown Bone	570
R-3695G	Pyremite	485
R-3700Buf	Buffalo Horn	250
R-3703	Bone	265
R-3704	Pearl	425
R-3705	Pyremite	245
R-3710Buf	Buffalo Horn	250
R-3713	Bone	295

Pattern No.	Handle	Mint Price
R-3714	Pearl	435
R-3715F	Pyremite	275
R-3722 (W)	Black Composition	350
R-3723 (W)	Bone	550
R-3725 (W)	Pyremite	395

Pattern No.	Handle	Mint Price
R-3732 (W)	Black Composition	$355
R-3733 (W)	Bone	425
R-3735 (W)	Pyremite	365
R-3843 (SC)	Brown Bone	370
R-3853 (PR)	Bone	240
R-3855	Imitation Ivory	230
R-3858	Cocobolo	225
R-3863 (SC)	Brown Bone	215
R-3870Buf (ST)	Buffalo Horn	245
R-3873 (ST)	Bone	265
R-3874 (ST)	Pearl	390
R-3875A (ST)	Pyremite	245
R-3883	Bone	300
R-3885	Pyremite	255
R-3893	Bone	170
R-3895	Pyremite	155
R-3903 (M)	Bone	245
R-3926	Stag	450
R-3932 (W)	Black Composition	400
R-3933 (W)	Stag	475
R-3935 (W)	Pyremite	400
R-3952	Black Composition	190
R-3953	Bone	245

Pattern No.	Handle	Mint Price	Pattern No.	Handle	Mint Price
R-3955	Pyremite	$210	R-4055 (ST)	Pyremite	$200
R-3962	Black Composition	215			
R-3963	Bone	240			
R-3965	Pyremite	200			
R-3973 (ST)	Bone	245			

Pattern No.	Handle	Mint Price	Pattern No.	Handle	Mint Price
			R-4063 (ST)	Bone	265
R-3975 (ST)	Pyremite	200	R-4065 (ST)	Pyremite	225
R-3983 (W)	Bone	225	R-4073 (ST)	Brown Bone	255
R-3985 (W)	Pyremite	185	R-4075 (ST)	Pyremite	210
R-3993 (ST)	Bone	260	R-4083 (ST)	Bone	265
R-3995 (ST)	Pyremite	225	R-4085 (ST)	Pyremite	225
R-4003	Bone	175	R-4093 (ST)	Bone	235
R-4005	Pyremite	135	R-4095 (ST)	Pyremite	200
R-4013 (M)	Bone	225	R-4103	Bone	170
R-4015 (M)	Pyremite	185	R-4105	Pyremite	140
R-4023 (ST)	Bone	265	R-4113 (ST)	Bone	250
R-4025 (ST)	Pyremite	220	R-4114 (ST)	Pearl	385
R-4033 (ST)	Bone	275	R-4123 (ST)	Bone	325
R-4035 (ST)	Pyremite	215	R-4124 (ST)	Pearl	375
R-4043 (ST)	Bone	245	R-4133 (ST)	Bone	225
R-4045 (ST)	Pyremite	210	R-4134 (ST)	Pearl	340
R-4053 (ST)	Bone	225	R-4135 (ST)	Pyremite	210
			R-4143	Bone	155
			R-4144	Pearl	255
			R-4145	Pyremite	140

Pattern No.	Handle	Mint Price	Pattern No.	Handle	Mint Price
R-4163	Bone	$225	R-4313	Bone	$240
R-4173 (W)	Bone	225	R-4323 (ST)		250
R-4175 (W)	Pyremite	200	R-4334 (BR)	Pearl	265
R-4200 (ST)	Buffalo Horn	230	R-4336 (BR)	Stag	225
R-4203 (ST)	Bone	265	R-4343	Bone	300
			R-4345	Pyremite	300
			R-4353 (R.G.)		1000
R-4213 (ST)	Bone	270	R-4353 (BL)	Brown Bone	1500
R-4223	Bone	275	R-4363 (ST)	Bone	325
R-4225	Pyremite	245	R-4365	Pyremite	300
R-4233 (SC)	Bone	215	R-4373 (O.G.S.)	Bone	225
RS-4233 (O-SC2)	Brown Bone	245	R-4375	Pyremite	200
R-4234 (SC)	Pearl	325	R-4383	Bone	225
R-4235	Pyremite	240	R-4384	Pearl	315
R-4243 (BL)	Brown Bone	1100	R-4394	Pearl	375
R-4253	Bone	255	R-4403	Bone	230
R-4263 (H)	Bone	335	R-4405	Christmas Tree	245
R-4273 (H)	Bone	425	R-4413	Bone	220
R-4274 (H)	Pearl	575	R-4423	Bone	220
			R-4425	Pyremite	200
R-4283 (H2)	Brown Bone	1850	R-4433 (W)	Bone	300
R-4293 (ST)	Bone	240	R-4443	Bone	200
			R-4466 (BL)	Bone	1850
R-4303 (ST)	Bone	240	R-4473	Bone	170
			R-4483 (C)	Bone	300
			R-4493	Bone	220

Pattern No.	Handle	Mint Price	Pattern No.	Handle	Mint Price
R-4495		$135	R-4713	Bone	$170
R-4505	Pyremite	235	R-4723 (O.G.S.)	Bone	80
			R-4733 (D.G.)	Bone	225
R-4506	Stag	270	R-4783 (SC)	Bone	175
R-4513	Brown Bone	320			
R-4523 (OSS)	Bone	225	R-4813	Bone	140
			R-4815	Pyremite	115
R-4533 (SS)	Bone	215	R-4823	Bone	100
			R-4825	Pyremite	85
R-4548 (E)	Cocobolo	210	R-4833	Bone	90
			R-4835	Pyremite	85
R-4555	Pyremite	225	R-4843	Imitation Bone	85
R-4563	Bone	350	R-4845	Black Composition	85
R-4573	Bone	270			
R-4583	Bone	175	R-4853	Bone	95
R-4593 (MSB)	Brown Bone	215	R-4855	Pyremite	85
			R-4863	Bone	90
R-4593 (MRB)	Brown Bone	245	R-4865	Pyremite	80
R-4603	Brown Bone	200			
R-4605	Pyremite	170			
R-4613	Bone	155	R-6013	Bone	225
R-4623 (W)	Brown Bone	175	R-6014	Pearl	270
			R-6015	Pyremite	185
R-4625 (W)	Pyremite	160	R-6023 (W)	Bone	250
R-4633	Bone	125	R-6024 (W)	Pearl	325
R-4635G	Pyremite	115			
R-4643	Bone	150	R-6025	Bone	170
R-4679	Metal	125			
R-4683	Bone	175			
R-4685	Pyremite	145			
R-4695	Pyremite	180	R-6032 (CO)	Black Composition	250
R-4702	Black Composition	175			
R-4703 (M)	Brown Bone	200	R-6033 (CO)	Bone	275

Pattern No.	Handle	Mint Price	Pattern No.	Handle	Mint Price
R-6034 (CO)	Pearl	$450	R-6195	Brown Composition	$110
R-6043 (CO)	Bone	450	R-6203	Bone	110
R-6053 (CO)	Bone	420	R-6204	Pearl	175
R-6063 (CO)	Brown Bone	245	R-6205	Pyremite	80
			R-6213 (W)	Bone	135

			R-6214	Pearl	215
			R-6215	Pyremite	100
R-6073 (CO)	Brown Bone	275	R-6223 (W)	Bone	150
R-6083 (CO)	Bone	275	R-6224 (W)	Pearl	220
R-6093 (CO2)	Bone	155	R-6225 (W)	Green Pyremite	125

R-6103	Bone	145	R-6233	Bone	165
R-6104	Pearl	200	R-6234	Pearl	210
R-6105	Pyremite	125	R-6235	Pyremite	125
R-6113 (CO)	Bone	275	R-6243 (L)	Bone	95
R-6123 (CO)	Brown Bone	200	R-6244 (L)	Pearl	120
R-6133 (W)	Brown Bone	285	R-6245 (L)	Pyremite	75
R-6143	Bone	150	R-6249	Metal	70
R-6145	Pyremite	120	R-6255 (L)	Pyremite	75
R-6153	Bone	150	R-6259 (L)	Metal	70
R-6155	Pyremite	120	R-6265 (W)	Pyremite	150
R-6163 (CO2)	Bone	145	R-6275 (W)	Pyremite	350
R-6175W (O.K.)	Pyremite	140	R-6285 (W)	Pyremite	350
R-6182	Black Composition	75	R-6295 (W)	Pyremite	350
R-6183	Bone	100	R-6303	Bone	150
R-6184	Pearl	155	R-6313 (W)	Bone	225
R-6185	Pyremite	90			
R-6192	Black Composition	110			
R-6193	Bone	145			
R-6194	Pearl	185			

Pattern No.	Handle	Mint Price	Pattern No.	Handle	Mint Price
R-6323 (W)	Bone	$250	R-6405 (W)	Pyremite	$175
R-6325 (W)	Pyremite	215	R-6423	Bone	80
R-6330 (W)	Buffalo Horn	175	R-6424	Pearl	140
			R-6429	Metal	70
R-6333 (W)	Bone	185	R-6433	Bone	110
			R-6434	Pearl	145
R-6334 (W)	Pearl	240	R-6439	Metal	75
R-6335 (W)	Pyremite	160	R-6443	Bone	85
			R-6444	Pearl	135
R-6340Buf (W)	Buffalo Horn	225	R-6445	Pyremite	80
			R-6448	Cocobolo	55
R-6343 (W)	Bone	275	R-6454 (L.W.)	Pearl	235
R-6344 (W)	Pearl	375	R-6456 (L.W.)	Stag	220
R-6345T (W)	Pyremite	200	R-6463	Bone	75
			R-6464	Pearl	110
R-6350 (W)	Buffalo Horn	235			

Pattern No.	Handle	Mint Price	Pattern No.	Handle	Mint Price
R-6353 (W)	Bone	250	R-6465	Onyx	95
R-6355G (W)	Pyremite	230	R-6473	Bone	100
			R-6474	Pearl	140
R-6363	Bone	145	R-6483	Bone	110
R-6365A (W)	Pyremite	110	R-6484	Pearl	155
			R-6494	Pearl	120
R-6390 (W)	Buffalo Horn	140	R-6495	Pyremite	65
			R-6499	Metal	60
R-6393 (W)	Brown Bone	340	R-6504	Pearl	125
			R-6505	Pyremite	75
R-6394 (W)	Pearl	425	R-6513	Bone	80
			R-6514	Pearl	125
R-6394G (W)	Pearl	495	R-6519	Metal	100
R-6400 (W)	Buffalo Horn	130	R-6520 (W)	Buffalo Horn	150
R-6403 (W)	Bone	150	R-6523 (W)	Bone	155
R-6404 (W)	Pearl	295	R-6524 (W)	Pearl	240
			R-6533 (W)	Brown Bone	175

Pattern No.	Handle	Mint Price	Pattern No.	Handle	Mint Price
R-6534 (W)	Pearl	$225	R-6633	Bone	$110
			R-6634	Pearl	145
R-6535 (W)	Pyremite	135	R-6635	Pyremite	100
R-6542 (W)		145	R-6643	Bone	120
			R-6644	Pearl	185
R-6543 (W)	Bone	200	R-6645	Cracked Ice	110
R-6545 (W)	Pyremite	145	R-6653 (W)	Bone	145
R-6554 (L)	Pearl	110	R-6654 (W)	Pearl	195
R-6559 (L)	Metal	90	R-6655 (W)	Pyremite	110
R-6563	Brown Bone	125	R-6662 (CO2)		100
R-6565	Pyremite	100	R-6664	Pearl	185
R-6573	Bone	110	R-6673 (CO)	Bone	190
R-6575	Pyremite	85	R-6674 (CO)	Pearl	255
R-6583	Bone	145			
R-6585	Pyremite	125	R-6683 (CO)	Bone	175
R-6593 (W)	Bone	150	R-6693 (CO)	Bone	190
R-6595 (W)	Pyremite	115	R-6694 (CO)	Pearl	235
R-6603 (W)	Bone	140	R-6695 (CO)	Pyremite	140
R-6604 (W)	Pearl	230	R-6703	Bone	150
R-6605 (W)	Pyremite	125	R-6704	Pearl	195
			R-6705Q	Pyremite	125
R-6613 (W)	Bone	165	R-6713	Bone	150
R-6615 (W)	Pyremite	135	R-6714	Pearl	195
			R-6723 (W)	Bone	195
R-6623	Bone	110			
R-6624	Pearl	175	R-6724 (W)	Pearl	295
R-6625	Cracked Ice	95	R-6725F (W)	Pyremite	165

Pattern No.	Handle	Mint Price
R-6733 (E.E.)	Bone	$150
R-6735 (E.E.)	Pyremite	110
R-6744	Pearl	130
R-6745F	Pyremite	90
R-6754 (W)	Pearl	215
R-6755A (W)	Pyremite	140
R-6763 (W)	Bone	175
R-6764 (W)	Pearl	280
R-6765A (W)	Pyremite	155
R-6773 (W)	Bone	250
R-6775 (W)	Pyremite	190
R-6781	Redwood	100
R-6785 (O.K.)	Imitation Ivory	125
R-6793	Bone	125
R-6795	Pyremite	100
R-6803 (W)	Bone	170
R-6805 (W)	Pyremite	150
R-6816 (L.W.)	Stag	1050
R-6823 (W)	Stag	750

Pattern No.	Handle	Mint Price
R-6825 (W)	Pyremite	$550
R-6834 (W)	Pearl	500
R-6835 (W)	Pyremite	400
R-6836 (W)	Stag	425
R-6843	Bone	75
R-6844	Pearl	100
R-6845	Pyremite	60
R-6854	Pearl	95
R-6859	Metal	60
R-6863	Bone	60
R-6864	Pearl	80
R-6865	Pyremite	55
R-6872	Black Composition	55
R-6873	Bone	75
R-6874	Pearl	110
R-6875	Pyremite	70
R-6883	Bone	175
R-6885	Pyremite	145
R-6893 (W)	Bone	200
R-6894 (W)	Pearl	285
R-6895 (W)	Pyremite	165
R-6903	Bone	55
R-6904	Pearl	80
R-6905	Onyx	50
R-6914	Pearl	65
R-6919	Metal	50
R-6923	Bone	130
R-6924	Pearl	195
R-6925	Imitation Ivory	105
R-6933 (CO)	Bone	185

Pattern No.	Handle	Mint Price	Pattern No.	Handle	Mint Price
R-6934 (CO)	Pearl	$250	RG-7049/21	Metal	$80
			RG-7049/22	Metal	80
R-6949	Metal	65	RG-7049/23	Metal	80
R-6954 (W)	Pearl	350	RG-7049/24	Metal	80
			R-7054	Pearl	95
R-6956 (W)	Stag	325	RG-7059/17	Metal	80
			RG-7059/18	Metal	80
R-6964 (W)	Pearl	350	RG-7059/19	Metal	80
			RG-7059/20	Metal	80
R-6966 (W)	Stag	225	RG-7059/39	Metal	80
			RG-7059/40	Metal	80
R-6973	Bone	200	R-7064	Pearl	85
R-6974	Pearl	400	R-7069/25	Metal	80
			R-7069/26	Metal	80
			R-7069/27	Metal	80
			R-7069/28	Metal	80
R-6984 (W.B.)	Pearl	650	R-7074	Pearl	95
			RG-7079/10	Metal	80
R-6993	Bone	175	RG-7079/11	Metal	80
R-6994	Pearl	265	RG-7079/12	Metal	80
R-6995	Pyremite	160	RG-7079/35	Metal	80
R-7003 (W)	Bone	250	RG-7079/36	Metal	80
			RG-7079/37	Metal	80
R-7004 (W)	Pearl	325	R-7084	Pearl	110
			RG-7089/13	Metal	80
R-7005 (W)	Pyremite	210	RG-7089/14	Metal	80
			RG-7089/15	Metal	80
R-7023 (W)	Bone	140	RG-7089/16	Metal	80
			RG-7089/32	Metal	80
R-7024 (W)	Pearl	220	RG-7089/33	Metal	80
			RG-7089/34	Metal	80
R-7026 (W)	Stag	165	R-7090	Buffalo Horn	100
R-7034 (W)	Pearl	80	R-7091	Redwood	95
R-7045	Pyremite	65	R-7094 (L)	Pearl	145
R-7039/5	Metal	80	RG-7099/1	Metal	100
R-7039/6	Metal	80	RG-7099/2	Metal	100
R-7039/7	Metal	80	RG-7099/3	Metal	100
R-7039/8	Metal	80	RG-7099/4	Metal	100
R-7044	Pearl	95	RG-7099/29	Metal	100

Pattern No.	Handle	Mint Price	Pattern No.	Handle	Mint Price
RG-7099/30	Metal	$100	R-7244 (W)	Pearl	$300
RG-7099/31	Metal	100			
RT-7099	Metal	95			
R-7103	Bone	80			
			R-7246 (W)	Stag	250
R-7104	Pearl	120	R-7254	Pearl	90
R-7114	Pearl	120	R-7264	Pearl	80
R-7116	Stag	95	R-7274	Pearl	80
R-7120	Buffalo Horn	100	R-7284 (L)	Pearl	85
R-7124	Pearl	225			
R-7126	Stag	195	R-7284		100
R-7134	Pearl	175	R-7284-6 (L)		100
R-7144	Pearl	275			
R-7146	Stag	215	R-7293 (W)	Bone	275
			R-7309	Metal	80
			R-7319	Metal	80
R-7153	Bone	170	R-7324 (L)	Pearl	100
R-7163	Bone	150			
R-7176	Stag	185	R-7329 (L)	Metal	55
R-7183 (W)	Bone	265			
			R-7335	Pyremite	65
R-7196 (W)	Stag	250	R-7339	Metal	65
			R-7343	Bone	115
R-7203 (W)	Bone	275	R-7344	Pearl	145
			R-7353	Bone	100
R-7216	Stag	285	R-7363	Bone	100
R-7223	Bone	110	R-7364 (L)	Pearl	155
R-7224	Pearl	160			
R-7225	Pyremite	100	R-7366	Stag	140
R-7233	Bone	80	R-7374	Pearl	100
R-7234	Pearl	110	R-7375	Pyremite	90
			R-7384	Pearl	100
			R-7394 (L)	Pearl	110
R-7236	Stag	85	R-7396	Stag	100
R-7243 (W)	Bone	175	R-7403	Bone	85
			R-7404	Pearl	120
			R-7414	Pearl	125

Pattern No.	Handle	Mint Price	Pattern No.	Handle	Mint Price
R-7423	Bone	$85	R-7594	Pearl	$180
R-7425	Onyx	80	R-7596	Stag	140
R-7433 (W)	Bone	160	R-7603	Bone	145
			R-7604	Pearl	195
R-7443	Bone	110	R-7606	Stag	175
R-7453	Bone	110	R-7613	Bone	80
R-7463	Bone	110	R-7614	Pearl	110
R-7465	Pyremite	95	R-7623	Bone	80
R-7473	Bone	115	R-7624	Pearl	115
R-7475	Pyremite	95	R-7633 (W)	Bone	165
R-7483 (W)	Bone	215	R-7643	Bone	90
R-7485 (W)	Pyremite	200	R-7645	Pyremite	80
			R-7653 (W)	Bone	185
R-7493 (W)	Bone	310	R-7654 (W)	Pearl	225
R-7495 (W)	Pyremite	275	R-7663 (W)	Bone	180
R-7500Buf (W)	Buffalo Horn	210	R-7664 (W)	Bone	250
R-7503 (W)	Bone	245	R-7674	Pearl	85
R-7513 (W)	Bone	245	R-7683	Bone	65
			R-7684	Pearl	100
R-7526	Stag	150	R-7696 (W)	Stag	250
R-7536	Stag	150	R-7706	Stag	155
R-7543	Bone	115	R-7713	Bone	65
R-7544	Pearl	155	R-7725 (BU.K)	Pyremite	75
R-7546	Stag	145			
R-7554	Pearl	125	R-7734	Pearl	85
R-7564	Pearl	125	R-7744	Pearl	85
R-7566	Stag	110	R-7756	Stag	825
R-7573	Bone	75	R-7766	Stag	875
R-7574	Pearl	125	R-7772	Black Composition	55
R-7576	Stag	110	R-7773	Bone	70
R-7584 (W)	Pearl	225	R-7775	Pyremite	65
R-7586 (W)	Stag	165	R-7783 (W)	Bone	100
R-7593	Bone	120			

Pattern No.	Handle	Mint Price	Pattern No.	Handle	Mint Price
R-7785	Pyremite	$120	R-7995 (BR)	Pyremite	$85
R-7793	Bone	75			
R-7795	Pyremite	80	R-8003	Bone	70
R-7803	Bone	130	R-8004	Pearl	95
R-7805	Pyremite	155	R-8013	Bone	60
R-7813	Bone	75	R-8023 (W)	Bone	175
R-7814	Pearl	115			
R-7823	Bone	110	R-8039 (BR)		75
R-7825	Pyremite	100			
R-7833	Bone	350	R-8044 (L)	Pearl	175
R-7853	Bone	85			
RC-7853	Bone	85	R-8055 (S)	Pyremite	100
R-7854	Pearl	135			
R-7857	Ivory	85	R-8059 (BR)	Metal	65
R-7863	Bone	75			
R-7873	Bone	75	R-8063 (S)	Bone	250
R-7895	Pyremite	60			
R-7925	Pyremite	55	R-8065	Pyremite	210
R-7985	Pyremite	95	R-8069 (S)	Metal	175
R-7993 (BR)	Bone	75			
			R-9003SS	Bone	175

Remington Bullet Reproductions

In 1982, Remington Arms began a series of knives to be issued annually as reproductions of the famous Remington Bullets. The knives are made for Remington by other manufacturers, such as Camillus, but are distributed through Remington's dealer network.

The success and value increases of most of these reproductions has been quite good. The earlier releases are in growing demand, and so are the companion posters, issued concurrently with the knives and reproducing posters of some fifty years ago. Although this is not a price guide of reproduction posters, knife collectors should be aware of their value appreciation along with that of the reproduction knives. For instance, one thousand posters were produced in 1982 for use by Remington's sales force and dealer network. Just as the 1982 knife has skyrocketed in price, so has the poster. Originally selling for $10, some have recently sold for about $300.

The first knife retailed at $39.95 and now commands prices near $550 when accompanied by the original box and papers.

Remington Bullet reproduction knives are etched "Remington/Trade Mark" on their master blades, and tang brand stampings are the circle Remington marking used years ago. Except for the first knife, issued in 1982, the reproduction series knives are also stamped with the year of their release. Bullet shields are used on the handles.

1982—R1123 pattern with Delrin handles   *$550*

1983—R1173 pattern Baby Bullet; Remington blade etch, Delrin handles, stamped 1983 on reverse blade tang   *$250*

1984—R1173L pattern lockback Baby Bullet; Delrin handles, single blade   *$125*

1984—R1303 pattern large lockback; Delrin handles; single blade   *$150*

1985—R1988 pattern Woodsman Muskrat 2-blade knife; Delrin handles; stainless steel long clip and spey blades   *$150*

1986—R1263 pattern 2-blade hunter; Delrin handles   *$200*

1987—R1613 pattern Fisherman's Bullet; Delrin handles   *$100*

1988—R4466 pattern Muskrat with Delrin handles $85

1989—R1128 pattern large 2-blade trapper with cocobolo handles $60

1990—R1306 pattern, "The Tracker" lockback with Staglon
(imitation stag) handles $45

ROBESON CUTLERY COMPANY

Millard F. Robeson founded the company that bore his name in 1879 as a cutlery jobbing firm, operating from his home in Elmira, New York. Selling knives was at first a sideline, but business grew. Robeson's first storage area was his dresser drawers, but as additional space was needed, they overflowed into the closet and underneath the bed. Upon returning from a business trip and finding his cutlery inventory moved to the porch, he agreed with Mrs. Robeson that larger facilities were needed. They first came in the form of a new room added to the house, next a new building adjacent to the home, and finally a move to the town of Camillus, New York.

After leasing the cutlery works in Camillus, Robeson employed about three dozen workers to make knives. Their tenure at this factory lasted about four years, until 1898. Robeson had purchased an interest in Rochester Stamping Works, which became Robeson Rochester Corporation. A move of the Robeson Cutlery Company's headquarters and manufacturing was made to Rochester and, about two years later, an additional location in Perry, New York.

In 1901, the trade name SHUREDGE was adopted for Robeson's quality line of cutlery. After Millard Robeson's death in 1903, his company remained although business declined. In 1940, the then bankrupt company was purchased by Saul Frankel, a Rochester businessman. Frankel was not like Robeson, who had the knowledge and expertise for manufacturing high-quality knives. But he was an excellent businessman and recognized his shortcomings. In order to build a successful company, Frankel sought out and hired Emerson Case to serve as Robeson's vice-president and general manager. Case reorganized the company and became its president in 1948. Robeson continued to make knives until 1965, when Case retired.

The company had been purchased by Federal Cutlery Inc. in 1964 and, from 1965 until 1977, sold knives marked with the Robeson stamping but manufactured by other companies. For about six years Robeson knives were made by Camillus Cutlery

Co. but were shipped from the Perry headquarters. In 1971, the Ontario Knife Company bought Robeson and made Robeson-brand knives until 1977, when the trademark was dropped.

Robeson knives were stamped ROBESON CUTLERY CO. from 1894 until 1922. During the years from 1922 to 1977, the well-known stampings of "ROBESON SHUREDGE ROCHESTER" and ROBESON SHUREDGE USA was used. A few Robeson knives will be found with a German stamping, indicating their country of manufacture.

A trademark popular with collectors is the line of Robeson knives named POCKETEZE and identified by the shield name. Registered in 1914, the trademark meant that the blade backs were recessed below the knife handles, reducing their wear on pants pockets. MASTERCRAFT was another Robeson trademark, and these knives were also identified by shield marking. Etched on the blades of some Robeson knives are the words "Frozen Heat," indicating a tempering process developed in 1950 by Emerson Case.

Older Robeson knives are handled in green bone, brown bone, and a unique red bone referred to as strawberry bone. Of the bone handles used, strawberry bone was used later in the company's manufacturing years. It was dropped from the line in the 1950s in favor of plastic or composition handles of a similar color. The last Robeson knives made had darker Delrin handles.

Although Robeson Bone was and is quite popular, in its best days Robeson also made handles of mother-of-pearl, genuine stag, and the various composition materials. The shortage of bone during World War II forced the company to use rough black composition materials for handles.

The Robeson line used a six-digit pattern number. The first number signifies handle material, as follows:

1—Black Composition	6—Bone
2—Rosewood	7—Pearl
3—Black Pyralin	8—Swirl Composition
4—White Composition	9—Gun Metal
5—Metal or sometimes Stag	

The second number signifies the number of blades, and the third number indicates the liner and bolster materials, as follows:

1—Steel liners and bolsters

2—Brass liners, nickel silver bolsters

3—Nickel silver liners and bolsters
6—Brass liners, nickel silver bolsters
9—Stainless steel or chrome-plated

The remaining numbers are the factory pattern numbers.

4525—Stainless steel scissor knife; 2 blades, engine-turned; German import   *$20*

4821—Senator pen knife, German import   *$35*
4822—Jacknife   *$35*
4833—Premium stock knife, German import   *$70*
4864—Swiss-type army knife, red celluloid handles, German import *$60*
026319—Father and Son set, contains No. 622026 and 622319, gift-boxed   *$375*

033750—(4") Metal handle, nickel silver liners and bolsters, premium stock knife   *$85*
126056—(3¾") Black Pyralin handle, mirror-finished blades, nickel silver bolsters, brass liners   *$50*
126240—(3⅝") Black Pyralin handle, mirror-finished blades, nickel silver bolsters, brass liners   *$50*
126636—(3⅜") Black Pyralin handle, mirror-finished blades, nickel silver bolsters, brass liners   *$50*
128105—(3") Lifelong ebonized handle, black Pyralin handle, nickel silver bolsters, nickel silver liners   *$30*

132433—(3⅝″) Black Pyralin handle, mirror-finished blades, nickel silver bolsters, brass liners   *$60*

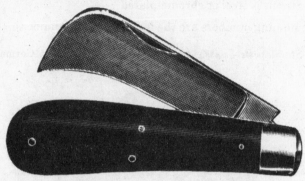

211007—(4″) Rosewood handle, mirror-finished blades, nickel silver bolsters, steel liners $30

211008—(4″) Rosewood handle, mirror-finished blades, nickel silver bolsters, steel liners $40

211035—(3⅜″) Rosewood handle, steel bolsters, blades fine-glazed, steel liners $30

222030—(3½″) Walnut handle, brass liners $30

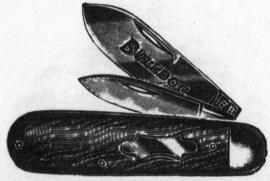

222050—(3⅞″) Rosewood handle, mirror-finished blades, nickel silver bolsters, brass liners $160

322013 —Black Pyralin handle, mirror-finished blades, nickel silver bolsters, brass liners $60

322027—(3¾″) Black Pyralin handle, mirror-finished blades, nickel silver bolsters, brass liners $60

322286—(3⅜″) Black Pyralin handle, mirror-finished blades, nickel silver bolsters, brass liners $40

323404—(2¾″) Black Pyralin handle, mirror-finished blades, nickel silver bolsters, all joints sunk flush with handle   *$35*

323480—(3⅜″) Black Pyralin handle, mirror-finished blades, nickel silver bolsters   *$35*

323617—(2⅞″) Black Pyralin handle, mirror-finished blades, nickel silver bolsters, milled nickel silver liners, frictionless bronze bearings built into spring   *$45*

323646—(3″) Black Pyralin handle, mirror-finished blades, nickel silver bolsters   *$35*

323657—(3⅜″) Black Pyralin handle, mirror-finished blades, nickel silver bolsters, milled nickel silver liners, frictionless bronze bearings built into spring   *$50*

323669—(3½″) Black Pyralin handle, mirror-finished blades, nickel silver bolsters, milled nickel silver liners, frictionless bronze bearings built into spring   *$70*

323675—(3″) Black Pyralin handle, mirror-finished blades, nickel silver bolsters, all joints sunk flush with handle   *$45*

323676—(3″) Black Pyralin handle, mirror-finished blades, nickel silver bolsters, milled nickel silver liners, frictionless bronze bearings built into spring   *$50*

323817—(2⅞″) Black Pyralin handle, mirror-finished blades, nickel silver bolsters, all joints sunk flush with handle   *$45*

323826—(3⅝″) Black Pyralin handle, mirror-finished blades, nickel silver bolsters   *$35*

323865—(3⅜") Black Pyralin handle, mirror-finished blades, nickel silver bolsters, brass liners   **$35**

326011—(3") Black Pyralin handle, mirror-finished blades, nickel silver bolsters, brass liners   **$30**

326015—(3") Black Pyralin handle, mirror-finished blades, nickel silver bolsters, brass liners   **$40**

326242—(3⅜") Black Pyralin handle, mirror-finished blades, nickel silver bolsters, brass liners   **$50**

333633—(3⅝") Black Pyralin handle, mirror-finished blades, nickel silver bolsters, milled nickel silver liners, frictionless bronze bearings built into spring   **$75**

421179—(3⅜") White Pyralin handle, steel bolster, blades fine glazed, steel liners   **$85**

421200—(3⅜") White Pyralin handle, steel bolsters, blades fine glazed, steel liners   **$90**

422064—(2¾") White Pyralin handle, mirror-finished blades, nickel silver bolsters, brass liners   **$30**

422174—(3¾") White Pyralin handle, mirror-finished blades, nickel silver bolsters, brass liners   **$40**

422274—(3¼") White Pyralin handle, mirror-finished blades, nickel silver bolsters, brass liners   **$40**

423405—(3¼") White Pyralin handle, mirror-finished blades, nickel silver trim, all joints sunk flush with handle   **$35**

423430—(3⅜") White Pyralin handle, mirror-finished blades, nickel silver trim, all joints sunk flush with handle   **$40**

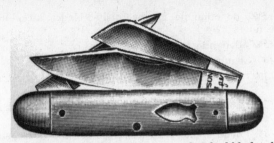

432868—(3⅜″) White Pyralin handle, mirror-finished blades, brass liners   *$45*

433594—(3⅞″) White celluloid handle, mirror-finished blades, nickel silver bolsters, nickel silver liners   *$55*

433595—(3⅞″) White Pyralin handle, mirror-finished blades, nickel silver bolsters, nickel silver liners   *$55*

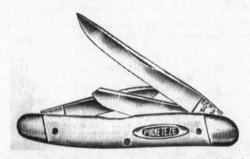

433727—(3⅝″) White Pyralin handle, mirror-finished blades, nickel silver liners   *$45*

511168—(3⅜″) Bone handle, steel bolsters, blade fine-glazed, steel liners   *$85*

511178—(3⅜″) Bone stag handle, brass liners   *$60*

511179—(3⅜″) Bone handle, steel bolsters, blades fine glazed, steel liners   *$100*

511224—(3¾") Bone handle, mirror-finished blades, nickel silver bolsters, steel liners $120

512224—(3¾") Bone stag handle, brass liners $145

512872—(4") Genuine stag handle, brass liners $145

521168—(3⅜") Bone handle, steel bolsters, blades fine glazed, steel liners $110

521178—(3⅜") Bone handle, steel bolsters, blades fine-glazed, steel liners $110

521179—(3⅜") Bone handle, steel bolsters, blade fine-glazed, steel liners $110

521199—(3⅜") Bone handle, steel bolsters, blade fine-glazed, steel liners $125

522482—(4½") Genuine stag handle, brass liners $260

523858—(2⅞") Genuine stag handle, nickel silver liners $50

529003—(2¾") Chromium-plated metal handle, blades, springs, liners completely protected with durable lustrous chrome plating $25

529007—(2¾") Chromium-plated metal handle, blades, springs, liners completely protected with durable lustrous chrome plating $25

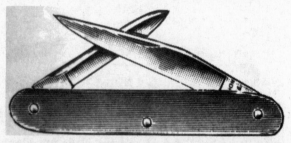

529404—(2¾") Chromium-plated metal handle, blades, springs, liners completely protected with durable lustrous chrome plating $25

529735—(2½") Chromium-plated metal handle, blades, springs, liners completely protected with durable lustrous chrome plating $25

529740—(2¾") Chromium-plated metal handle, blades, springs, liners completely protected with durable lustrous chrome plating $25

533167—(3") Genuine stag handle, nickel silver liners $120

533278—(3⅜") Solid nickel silver handle, mirror-finished blade, nickel silver liners $30

533729—(3⅜") Solid nickel silver handle, mirror-finished blade $50

533750—(4") Solid nickel silver handle, mirror-finished blade, nickel silver bolsters $70

539445—(2¾") Chromium-plated metal handle, blades, springs, liners completely protected with durable lustrous chrome plating $25

612060—(4⅛") Bone stag handle, brass liners $85

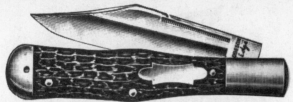

612118—(5½") Bone stag handle, mirror-finished blade, nickel silver bolsters, brass liners   *$470*

612407—(5") Bone stag handle, brass liners   *$265*

612610—(5") Bone stag handle, lock blade hunting knife, mirror-finished blade, nickel silver bolsters, brass liners   *$220*

616407—(5") Bone stag handle, mirror-finished blade, nickel silver bolsters, brass liners   *$130*

621105—(3") Bone stag handle, mirror-finished blade, nickel silver bolsters, steel liners   *$45*

621177—(3") Bone stag handle, mirror-finished blade, nickel silver bolsters, steel liners   *$55*

622001—(3¼") Bone stag handle, mirror-finished blade, nickel silver bolsters, brass liners   *$70*

622003—(2¾") Bone stag handle, mirror-finished blade, nickel silver bolsters, brass liners   *$55*

622013—(3⅝") Bone stag handle, mirror-finished blade, nickel silver bolsters, brass liners   *$85*

622020—(3⅝") Bone stag handle, mirror-finished blade, nickel silver bolsters, brass liners   *$90*

622022—(3⅝") Bone stag handle, mirror-finished blade, nickel silver bolsters, brass liners   *$75*

622026—(3") Bone stag handle, mirror-finished blade, nickel silver bolsters, brass liners   *$50*

622027—(3¾") Bone stag handle, mirror-finished blade, nickel silver bolsters, brass liners   *$125*

622037—(4") Bone stag handle, mirror-finished blade, nickel silver bolsters, brass liners   *$135*

622048—(1⅞″) Bone stag handle, mirror-finished blade, nickel silver bolsters, brass liners   *$45*

622056—(3¾″) Bone stag handle, brass liners   *$80*

622061—(4⅛″) Bone stag handle, brass liners   *$105*

622062—(4⅛″) Bone stag handle, mirror-finished blade, nickel silver bolsters, brass liners   *$270*

622064—(2¾″) Bone stag handle, mirror-finished blade, nickel silver bolsters, brass liners   *$45*

622083—(2¾″) Bone stag handle, mirror-finished blade, nickel silver bolsters, brass liners   *$45*

622088—(3¾″) Bone stag handle, mirror-finished blade, nickel silver bolsters, brass liners   *$100*

622102—(3¾″) Bone stag handle, mirror-finished blade, nickel silver bolsters, brass liners   *$60*

622105—(3″) Bone stag handle, mirror-finished blade, nickel silver bolsters, steel liners   *$50*

622119—(4½″) Bone stag handle, mirror-finished blade, nickel silver bolsters, brass liners   *$130*

622138—(3¾″) Bone stag handle, mirror-finished blade, nickel silver bolsters, brass liners   *$165*

622151—(4½″) Bone stag handle, mirror-finished blade, nickel silver bolsters, brass liners   *$110*

622167—(3″) Bone stag handle, mirror-finished blade, nickel silver bolsters, brass liners   *$55*

622177—(3") Bone stag handle, mirror-finished blade, nickel silver bolsters, steel liners   *$55*

622183—(2¾") Bone stag handle, mirror-finished blade, nickel silver bolsters, brass liners   *$45*

622187—(4") Bone stag handle, mirror-finished blade, nickel silver bolsters, brass liners   *$165*

622193—(3¾") Bone stag handle, mirror-finished blade, nickel silver bolsters, brass liners   *$100*

622195—(3") Bone stag handle, mirror-finished blade, nickel silver bolsters, brass liners   *$165*

622225—(3⅝") Bone stag handle, mirror-finished blade, nickel silver bolsters, nickel silver liners   *$130*

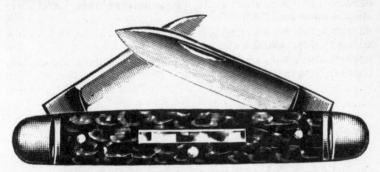

622253—(3⅝") Bone stag handle, mirror-finished blade, nickel silver bolsters, brass liners   *$50*

622295—(3⅜") Bone stag handle, mirror-finished blade, nickel silver bolsters, brass liners   *$45*

622229—(2⅝") Bone stag handle, mirror-finished blade, nickel silver bolsters, brass liners   *$30*

622319—(3") Bone stag handle, mirror-finished blade, nickel silver bolsters, brass liners   *$45*

622331—(2⅝") Bone stag handle, brass liners   *$85*

622382—(4⅛") Bone stag handle, brass liners   *$160*

622393—(2¾") Bone stag handle, mirror-finished blade, nickel silver bolsters, nickel silver liners   *$40*

622457—(4⅛") Bone stag handle, mirror-finished blade, nickel silver bolsters, brass liners   *$40*

622597—(3⅞") Bone stag handle, brass liners   *$65*

622636—(3½") Bone stag handle, mirror-finished blade, nickel silver bolsters, brass liners   *$55*

622841—(3⅜") Bone stag handle, mirror-finished blade, nickel silver bolsters, brass liners   *$75*

623177—(3") Bone stag handle, nickel silver liners   *$60*

623191—(3¼") Bone stag handle, mirror-finished blade, nickel silver bolsters, brass liners   *$55*

623405—(3¼") Bone stag handle, mirror-finished blade, nickel silver trim, all joints sunk flush with handle   *$60*

623422—(3⅝") Bone stag handle, mirror-finished blade, nickel silver trim, all joints sunk flush with handle   *$85*

623480—(3⅜") Bone stag handle, mirror-finished blade, nickel silver trim, all joints sunk flush with handle   *$85*

623500—(3⅜") Bone stag handle, mirror-finished blade, nickel silver trim, all joints sunk flush with handle   *$130*

623501—(3") Bone stag handle, mirror-finished blade, nickel silver trim, all joints sunk flush with handle   *$60*

623505—(3¼") Bone stag handle, mirror-finished blade, nickel silver trim, all joints sunk flush with handle   *$60*

623595—(3⅞") Bone stag handle, mirror-finished blade, nickel silver trim, all joints sunk flush with handle   *$95*

623603—(2¾″) Bone stag handle, mirror-finished blade, nickel silver bolsters, milled nickel silver liners, frictionless bronze bearings built into spring   *$50*

623662—(3¼″) Bone stag handle, mirror-finished blade, nickel silver bolsters, milled nickel silver liners, frictionless bronze bearings built into spring   *$50*

623667—(3⅞″) Bone stag handle, mirror-finished blade, nickel silver trim, all joints sunk flush with handle   *$55*

623671—(3″) Bone stag handle, mirror-finished blade, nickel silver trim, all joints sunk flush with handle   *$45*

623681—(3″) Bone stag handle, mirror-finished blade, nickel silver bolsters, milled nickel silver liners, frictionless bronze bearings built into spring   *$50*

623698—(3⅝″) Bone stag handle, mirror-finished blade, nickel silver trim, all joints sunk flush with handle   *$50*

623777—(3⅝″) Bone stag handle, mirror-finished blade, nickel silver trim, all joints sunk flush with handle   *$45*

623851—(2¹¹⁄₁₆″) Bone stag handle, nickel silver liners   *$65*

623858—(2⅞″) Bone stag handle, mirror-finished blade, nickel trim, all joints sunk flush with handle   *$70*

623875—(3⅝″) Bone stag handle, woodcraft knife, mirror-finished blade, nickel silver trim, all joints sunk flush with handle   *$85*

626041—(3⅜″) Bone stag handle, mirror-finished blade, nickel silver bolsters, brass liners   *$60*

626052—(3¾″) Bone stag handle, mirror-finished blade, nickel silver bolsters, brass liners   *$70*

626054—(3¾″) Bone stag handle, mirror-finished blade, nickel silver bolsters, brass liners   *$60*

626056—(3¾″) Bone stag handle, mirror-finished blade, nickel silver bolsters, brass liners   *$65*

626094—(3⅜″) Bone stag handle, mirror-finished blade, nickel silver bolsters, brass liners   *$45*

626104—(3⅜″) Bone stag handle, mirror-finished blade, nickel silver bolsters, brass liners   *$55*

626204—(3⅜″) Bone stag handle, mirror-finished blade, nickel silver bolsters, brass liners   *$50*

626240—(3⅜″) Bone stag handle, mirror-finished blade, nickel silver bolsters, brass liners   *$60*

626241—(3⅜″) Bone stag handle, mirror-finished blade, nickel silver bolsters, brass liners   *$75*

626242—(3⅜″) Bone stag handle, mirror-finished blade, nickel silver bolsters, brass liners   *$75*

626331—(2⅝″) Bone stag handle, mirror-finished blade, nickel silver bolsters, brass liners   *$45*

626636—(3⅜″) Bone stag handle, mirror-finished blade, nickel silver bolsters, brass liners   *$55*

626637—(3⅜″) Bone stag handle, mirror-finished blade, nickel silver bolsters, brass liners   *$60*

626765—(3⅜″) Bone stag handle, mirror-finished blade, nickel silver bolsters, brass liners   *$45*

626766—(3⅜″) Bone stag handle, mirror-finished blade, nickel silver bolsters, brass liners   *$85*

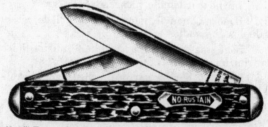

629005—(3¼″) Bone stag handle, mirror-finished blade, nickel silver bolsters, stainless, nickel silver liners   *$65*

629675—(3") Bone stag handle, mirror-finished blade, nickel silver bolsters, nickel silver liners   *$80*

632102—(3⅝") Bone stag handle, mirror-finished blade, nickel silver bolsters, brass liners   *$120*

632167—(3") Bone stag handle, mirror-finished blade, nickel silver bolsters, brass liners   *$45*

632225—(3⅝") Bone stag handle, mirror-finished blade, nickel silver bolsters, brass liners   *$85*

632295—(3⅝") Bone stag handle, mirror-finished blade, brass liners   *$100*

632319—(3") Bone stag handle, mirror-finished blade, nickel silver bolsters, brass liners   *$50*

632596—(3⅞") Bone stag handle, mirror-polished blade, nickel silver bolsters, brass liners   *$85*

632750—(4") Bone stag handle, mirror-finished blade, nickel silver bolsters, brass liners   *$150*

632751—(4") Bone stag handle, mirror-finished blade, nickel silver bolsters, brass liners   *$150*

632768—(2½") Bone stag handle, mirror-finished blade, nickel silver bolsters, brass liners   *$45*

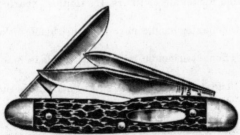

632831—(3⅜") Bone stag handle, brass liners   *$70*

632838—(3⅜") Horn Pyralin handle, mirror-finished blade, nickel silver bolsters, brass liners   *$45*

632868—(3⅜") Bone stag handle, mirror-finished blade, brass liners   **$70**

632882—(3⅝") Bone stag handle, mirror-finished blade, nickel silver bolsters, brass liners   **$85**

633295—(3⅜") Bone stag handle, nickel silver liners   **$95**

633295TC—(3⅜") Bone stag handle, nickel silver liners, large blade with flame edge   **$100**

633593—(3⅞") Bone stag handle, mirror-finished blade, nickel silver bolsters, nickel silver liners   **$90**

633594—(3⅞") Bone stag handle, mirror-finished blade, nickel silver bolsters, nickel silver liners   **$75**

633595—(3⅞") Red Pyralin handle, mirror-finished blade, nickel silver bolsters, nickel silver liners   **$70**

633596—(3⅞") Bone stag handle, nickel silver liners   **$120**

633662—(3¼") Bone stag handle, mirror-finished blade, milled nickel silver liners   **$85**

633670—(3⅜") Bone stag handle, mirror-finished blade, nickel silver bolsters, milled nickel silver liners, frictionless bronze bearings built into spring   **$165**

633681—(3") Bone stag handle, mirror-finished blade, nickel silver bolsters, milled nickel silver liners, frictionless bearing built into spring   **$85**

633727—(3⅝") Bone stag handle, mirror-finished blade, nickel silver liners   **$85**

633728—(3⅜") Bone stag handle, mirror-finished blade, nickel silver liners   **$85**

633750—(4") Bone stag handle, nickel silver liners and bolsters   **$80**

633830—(3⅜") Bone stag handle, mirror-finished blade, nickel silver liners   **$80**

633850—(2⅝") Bone stag handle, nickel silver liners   **$55**

633865—(3⅜") Bone stag handle, mirror-finished blade, nickel silver liners   **$95**

633866—(3⅜") Bone stag handle, mirror-finished blade, nickel silver bolsters, nickel silver liners   **$95**

633875—(3⅝″) Bone stag handle, Woodcraft PocketEze, nickel silver bolsters, nickel silver liners, milled   *$165*

633880—(3⅝″) Bone stag handle, mirror-finished blade, nickel silver bolsters, nickel silver liners   *$100*

633881—(3⅝″) Bone stag handle, mirror-finished blade, nickel silver bolsters, nickel silver liners   *$115*

633884—(3⅝″) Bone stag handle, mirror-finished blade, nickel silver bolsters, nickel silver liners   *$115*

633885—(3⅝″) Bone stag handle, mirror-finished blade, nickel silver bolsters, nickel silver liners   *$115*

633886—(3⅝″) Bone stag handle, mirror-finished blade, nickel silver bolsters, nickel silver liners   *$115*

642088—(4⅛″) Bone stag handle, brass liners   *$170*

642208—(4⅛″) Bone stag handle, mirror-finished blade, nickel silver bolsters, brass liners   *$175*

642214—(3⅝″) Bone stag handle, mirror-finished blade, nickel silver bolsters, brass liners   *$145*

643453—(3½″) Bone stag handle, mirror-finished blade, nickel silver bolsters, nickel silver liners   *$105*

643645—(3⅝″) Bone stag handle, mirror-finished blade, nickel silver bolsters, nickel silver liners   *$105*

643777—(3⅜") Bone stag handle, mirror-finished blade, nickel silver bolsters, nickel silver liners $105

722007—(2¾") Genuine pearl handle, brass liners, nickel silver tip bolsters, bail $60

722110—(2¾") Genuine pearl handle, brass liners, nickel silver bolsters $55

722120—(2½") Genuine pearl handle, brass liners, blade and file $60

722159—(2⅜") Genuine pearl handle, brass liners, marked "R. C. Co.," nickel silver bolsters $55

722236—(2⅜") Genuine pearl handle, brass liners, long nickel silver bolsters $50

722237—(2⅜") Genuine pearl handle, blade and button hook, brass liners $60

722273—(3") Genuine pearl handle, milled brass liners, blade and nail file, tip nickel bolsters $55

722319—(3") Genuine pearl handle, brass liners, bail $65

722320—(3") Genuine pearl handle, brass liners, long bolster $65

722380—(2½") Genuine pearl handle, brass liners, nickel silver bolsters, marked "R.C." $55

722381—(3") Genuine pearl handle, milled brass liners, blade and file, marked "R.C. Co." $70

723167—(3") Genuine pearl handle, nickel silver liners $65

723317—(3") Genuine pearl handle, nickel silver liners, blade and file, bail $70

723442—(2¾") Genuine pearl handle, milled nickel silver liners, no bolsters $65

723681—(3") Pearl handle, mirror-finished blade, nickel silver bolsters, milled nickel silver liners $60

727304—(3⅛″) Genuine pearl handle, no liners, one-piece wrap-around handle   *$95*

732118—(3″) Genuine pearl handle, milled brass liners, tip nickel silver bolsters, 2 blades and scissors   *$70*

732167—(3″) Genuine pearl handle, Whittler pattern, brass liners, 2 blades and file   *$65*

732200—(2¼″) Genuine pearl handle, milled brass liners, 2 blades and file   *$55*

733505—(3¼″) Genuine pearl handle, nickel silver liners and bolster, Whittler pattern   *$65*

742198—(3¼″) Genuine pearl handle, milled brass liners, shield   *$90*

812118—(5¼″) Maize Pyralin handle, mirror-finished blade, nickel silver bolsters, brass liners   *$190*

812872—(4½″) Maize composition handle, brass liners   *$130*

816407—(5″) Red and white Pyralin handle, mirror-finished blade, nickel silver bolsters, brass liners   *$100*

822023—(3¼″) Horn Pyralin handle, mirror-finished blade, nickel silver bolsters, brass liners   *$45*

822048—(2⅞″) Gold Pyralin handle, mirror-finished blade, nickel silver bolsters, brass liners   *$45*

822061—(4⅛") Maize composition handle, brass liners   *$65*

822064—(2¾") Black Pyralin handle, mirror-finished blade, nickel silver
bolsters, brass liners   *$30*

822094—(3⅜") Maize Pyralin handle, mirror-finished blade, nickel silver
bolsters, brass liners   *$40*

822183—(2¾") Gold Pyralin handle, mirror-finished blade, nickel silver
bolsters, brass liners   *$40*

822253—(3⅝") Maize Pyralin handle, mirror-finished blade, nickel silver
bolsters, brass liners   *$35*

822295—(3⅝") Horn Pyralin handle, mirror-finished blade, nickel silver
bolsters, brass liners   *$35*

822319—(3") Russed Pyralin handle, mirror-finished blade, nickel silver
bolsters, brass liners   *$35*

822355—(3⅜") Imitation pearl handle, brass liners   *$30*

822393—(2¹³/₁₆") Maize composition handle, brass liners   *$50*

822482—(4½") Maize composition handle, brass liners   *$185*

822497—(5") Maize Pyralin handle, fishing knife, mirror-finished blade,
nickel silver bolsters, brass liners   *$110*

822728—(3⅜") Maize Pyralin handle, mirror-finished blade, nickel silver
trim   *$60*

822850—(2¾") Gold Pyralin handle, mirror-finished blade, nickel silver
bolsters, brass liners   *$35*

823505—(3¼") Gray mottled Pyralin handle, mirror-finished blade,
nickel silver trim, all joints sunk flush with handle   *$50*

823724—(3½") Black Pyralin handle, mirror-finished blade, nickel silver
trim, all joints sunk flush with handle   *$60*

823851—(3¹¹/₁₆") Maize composition handle, nickel silver liners   *$30*

823881—(3⅝") Maize Pyralin handle, mirror-finished blade, nickel silver trim, all joints sunk flush with handle   *$65*

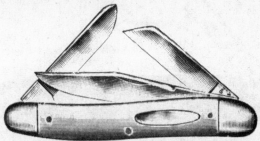

832597—(3⅞") Maize celluloid handle, mirror-finished blade, nickel silver bolsters, brass liners   *$80*

832726—(3⅜") Maize Pyralin handle, mirror blade, brass liners   *$50*

832838—(3⅜") Horn Pyralin handle, mirror-finished blade, nickel silver bolsters   *$80*

832883—(3⅝") Horn Pyralin handle, mirror-finished blade, nickel silver bolsters, brass liners   *$80*

833295—(3⅜") Maize composition handle, nickel silver liners   *$45*

833595—(3⅞") Red Pyralin handle, mirror-finished blade, nickel silver bolsters, nickel silver liners   *$55*

833850—(2⅝") Imitation pearl handle, nickel silver liners   *$40*

833865—(3⅜") Maize Pyralin handle, mirror-finished blade, nickel silver liners   *$95*

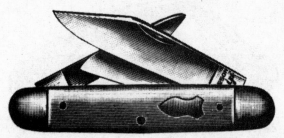

833867—(3⅜") Maize Pyralin handle, mirror-finished blade, nickel silver bolsters, nickel silver liners   *$55*

833880—(3⅝") Maize Pyralin handle, mirror-finished blade, nickel silver bolsters, nickel silver liners   *$85*

833881—(3⅝") Maize Pyralin handle, mirror-finished blade, nickel silver liners   *$85*

833887—(3⅝") Red Pyralin handle, mirror-finished blade, nickel silver bolsters, nickel silver liners   *$85*

922253—(3⅜″) Brown "Shur Wood" handle, brass liners   *$45*

922295—(3⅜″) Brown "Shur Wood" handle, brass liners   *$45*

922295TC—(3⅜″) Brown "Shur Wood" handle, brass liners, large blade
with flame edge   *$45*

922296TC—(3⅜″) Brown "Shur Wood" handle, brass liners, large blade
with flame edge   *$45*

922497—(5″) Brown "Shur Wood" handle, brass liners   *$55*

929004—(2¾″) Fine gunmetal handle, blade completely protected with
durable lustrous chrome plate   *$25*

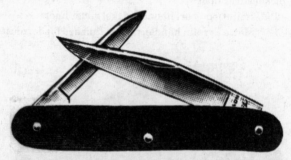

929404—(2¾″) Fine gunmetal handle, blade completely protected with
durable lustrous chrome plate   *$30*

929007—(2¾″) Fine gunmetal handle, blade completely protected with
durable lustrous chrome plate   *$35*

929735—(2½″) Fine gunmetal handle, blade completely protected with
durable lustrous chrome plate   *$35*

929740—(2¾″) Fine gunmetal handle, blade completely protected with
durable lustrous chrome plate   *$30*

939445—(2¾″) Fine gunmetal handle, blade completely protected with
durable lustrous chrome plate   *$35*

J. RUSSELL & COMPANY

Although John Russell entered the cutlery manufacturing business in 1834, it was forty-one years later that the company began to make pocketknives. His first factory was located in Greenfield, Massachusetts, where it sat on the banks of the Green River. Russell's first products were cast-steel socket chisels and ax heads, followed shortly thereafter by the addition of butcher knives and an assortment of kitchen knives.

Although the company's products were well accepted for their high quality, its own fortunes were not so good. The first facility was destroyed by fire, and its replacement, Russell's second shop, was severely damaged by a flood some two years after the company's founding.

In 1836, Russell was joined in business by his brother Francis and an investor named Henry Clapp. The new factory they built was christened the "Green River Works," a trade name that would soon be carried on knives across America. The Russells developed several labor-saving devices and introduced a steam engine to power much of their equipment. Their innovative ideas also included setting wages at a rate that would lure skilled cutlery workers from the Sheffield, England, factories. The net result was a reputation for quality and a profitable business.

In the late 1830s, Russell began to make what was called "An American Hunting Knife" and stamped it with the company name and trademark. The knives were such a success that, during the next couple of decades, well over a half-million knives marked J. Russell & Co., Green River Works, were sold to the western trade. The fame of these butcher and skinning-style knives was such that Sheffield capitalized on it by flooding the American market with their own "Green River" knives.

In 1868, a fire destroyed much of the Greenfield factory, and a new one was built in Turner Falls, Massachusetts. The John Russell Manufacturing Company's new cutlery factory was the largest in the world and featured many conveniences not found in the company's previous facilities. Nearly five hundred employees worked there, but it was reported that the factory was large enough to employ over a thousand workmen. Although business was good, with sales volume near $750,000, the new factory had drained the company's financial resources. The company went bankrupt in 1873, and reorganization took place soon thereafter, with no members of the John Russell family remaining as investors.

Manufacture of pocketknives began in 1875, and by 1877 Russell had made more than four hundred different patterns and had sold over a half-million pieces. Similar to the fame earned by Russell's Green River knives, another knife pattern's name would become synonymous with that of its manufacturer. The first "Barlow" had been invented about 1667 by a Sheffield cutler, Obadiah Barlow, but it was Russell who would make it America's favorite for several decades. It became famous by selling for 15 cents and 25 cents for the one-blade and two-blade models, respectively. When the post–World War I steel price increases dictated a price increase on Russell's Barlows, consumers were unhappy, and the company discontinued its manufacture in the early 1930s.

In 1933, the John Russell Manufacturing Company merged with the Harrington Cutlery Company to become the Russell-Harrington Company, and it was moved to Southbridge, Massachusetts. When a popular Louisville *Courier Journal* columnist, Allen Trout, founded the Barlow Bobcats Club in the early 1950s (a requirement was to own an original Russell Barlow), the company participated for a while in the knife's renewed popularity by restoring Russell Barlows for $1. Knife production today is primarily in kitchen cutlery, and pocketknives have not been made since about 1930. The twelve thousand Russell Barlow Commemorative knives introduced by the company in 1974 were manufactured by another company, probably Schrade.

SCHATT & MORGAN

This company, which at one time was one of the largest cutlery manufacturers in this country, originated when J. W. Schatt and C. B. Morgan formed the New York Cutlery Company about 1890. Both men had considerable previous experience within the cutlery industry. Schatt had worked with the J. R. Torrey Razor Company, and Morgan had sold knives manufactured by the Canastota Knife Company and his brother's Bayonne Knife Company.

At first, their business was a cutlery-importing firm, but the partners soon opened their own factory in Gowanda, New York, and named it Schatt & Morgan Cutlery Company. Knives sold during the 1890–1895 period were stamped S & M NEW YORK and S & M GOWANDA N. Y., crossed with an elongated *X*. When this facility was sold in 1895 to the Platts family, the partners' business was moved to nearby Titusville, Pennsylvania, and incorporated there.

Although the business headquarters had moved, Schatt continued to reside in Gowanda and work out of his hometown. In 1911, Morgan purchased Schatt's interest in the company but continued the dual name.

The demise of this producer of fine knives began about 1922 and was heralded with the announcement by *American Cutler* that "the Queen City Cutlery Company of Titusville, Pa., manufacturers of pocketknives, has been incorporated with a capital stock of $25,000." Another announcement that year reported that Schatt & Morgan's staff was sixty men, about one-third of its usual work force. The new company had been started, at the expense of Schatt & Morgan, by six of the factory foremen, who produced extra parts after the shift and then assembled them into knives marked with the QUEEN CITY brand. The company fired these employees but found it difficult to continue to operate efficiently with inadequate supervisory personnel and with the former employees now devoting full time to making the competitive brand. Schatt & Morgan Cutlery Company was forced to close its doors in 1930. The irony of this saga was Queen City Cutlery's 1932 purchase of the building, machinery, and stock of parts owned by the old company and subsequent move into the S & M factory.

Schatt & Morgan produced a large variety of knives in considerable quantities—nearly six hundred different patterns were offered in 1911, and a few million knives were sold. Still, when compared to several other brands, Schatt & Morgan knives are not easy to find. When found, they are not easy to identify because few were stamped with standardized pattern numbers offering information about number of blades, handle material, or bolster type. The suffixes can offer some information as follows:

½—Sheepfoot blade	S—Equal end jack with pen blade
¼—Clip blade	
EO—Easy open pattern	B—Black celluloid handles
JS—Swell center balloon pattern	W—White celluloid handles
CH—Chain	S—Shell celluloid handles

A large variety of bolster and liner materials was used, including brass, nickel, silver, steel, and Norway iron. Shield variety was also plentiful, with most common styles of the period being used.

In general, the company used the last number to indicate handle material. Although not always consistent, the numbers listed below will be helpful in many instances.

0—Cocobolo
1—Genuine mother-of-pearl
2—Ebony
3—Ebony or stag
4—Cocobolo
5—Rosewood, sometimes bone
6—Bone, called "imitation stag"
7—Stag
8—Transparent celluloid, sometimes ebony
9—Stag

Knives marked SCHATT & MORGAN KNIVES GOWANDA N.Y. and S & M NEW YORK are the rarest; most will be found bearing an S & M TITUSVILLE PA. or SCHATT & MORGAN, TITUSVILLE, PA. stamp. In addition to its own high-quality knife line, the company also produced knives under contract for other marketing firms.

152½—(3⅜") Ebony handle; nickel silver bolsters; brass liners   *$100*

156—(3⅝") Imitation stag handle; brass liners   *$100*

336¼—(3¾") Imitation stag handle; nickel silver bolsters; brass liners   *$60*

370—(4") Cocobolo handle; nickel silver bolsters; brass liners   *$65*

370¼—(4") Cocobolo handle; nickel silver bolsters; brass liners   *$65*

386—(3⅝") Imitation stag handle; nickel silver bolsters; brass liners   *$80*

396—(4") Imitation stag handle; brass liners   *$170*

1016—(3⅝") Imitation stag handle; brass liners   *$60*

1092EO—(3¾") Ebony handle; nickel silver bolsters; brass liners   *$65*

1096—(3¾") Imitation stag handle; nickel silver bolsters; brass liners   *$65*

1099—(3⅝") Imitation stag handle; brass liners   *$65*

1126½—(3¾") Imitation stag handle; nickel silver bolsters; brass liners   *$75*

1136¼—(3½") Imitation stag handle; brass liners   *$70*

1152—(3⅝") Ebony handle; nickel silver bolsters; brass liners   *$60*

1166—(3⅝") Imitation stag handle; nickel silver bolsters; brass liners   *$225*

1170—(4") Cocobolo handle; nickel silver bolsters; brass liners   *$75*

1206—(4") Imitation stag handle; nickel silver bolsters; brass liners   *$70*

1396—(4") Imitation stag handle; brass liners   *$60*

2036—(3¾") Imitation stag handle; brass liners $65

2066—(3½") Imitation stag handle; nickel silver bolsters; brass liners; extra heavy blades $50

2072½—(4") Ebony handle; nickel silver bolsters; brass liners $60

2076¼—(4") Imitation stag handle; brass liners $65

2076½—(4") Imitation stag handle; nickel silver bolsters; brass liners $65

2156—(3⅝") Imitation stag handle; brass liners $70

2195—(3⅝") Ebony handle; nickel silver bolsters; brass liners $60

2356—(4") Imitation stag handle; nickel silver bolsters; brass liners $75

2357—(4") Imitation stag handle; nickel silver bolsters, brass liners $75

2700—(4") Cocobolo handle; nickel silver bolsters; brass liners $75

2700¼—(4") Cocobolo handle; nickel silver bolsters; brass liners $75

3096S—(3⅝") Imitation stag handle; nickel silver bolsters; brass liners $95

3306—(4") Imitation stag handle; nickel silver bolsters; brass liners *$120*

3593—(2½") Genuine stag handle; nickel silver bolsters $65

3706—(3⅞") Imitation stag handle; nickel silver bolsters; brass liners $95

3766¼—(4") Imitation stag handle; nickel silver bolsters; brass liners   *$100*

4126½—(3¾") Imitation stag handle; Norway iron bolsters; brass liners $95

4146½—(4") Imitation stag handle; Norway iron bolsters; brass liners $80

4197—(4½") Imitation stag handle; Norway iron bolsters; brass liners $80

4593—(2½") Genuine stag handle; nickel silver liners $65

4743—(3".) Genuine stag handle; nickel silver liners $65

5016—(3⅝") Imitation stag handle; Norway iron bolsters; steel liners $55

5226—(3⅝") Imitation stag handle; Norway iron bolsters; steel liners $70

5286—(3½") Imitation stag handle; Norway iron bolsters; steel liners $45

24143—(3⅝") Genuine stag handle; nickel silver bolsters; brass liners $50

34173—(3⅝") Genuine stag handle; Norway iron bolsters; brass liners $85

34263—(3⅜") Genuine stag handle; brass liners $95

37153—(3⅛") Genuine stag handle; nickel silver liners $50

37193—(3⅝") Genuine stag handle; nickel silver liners $200

37203—(3⅜") Genuine stag handle; nickel silver liners $70

37283—(3") Genuine stag handle; nickel silver liners   *$55*

44133—(4") Genuine stag handle; Norway iron bolsters; brass liners   *$80*

46163—(3⅞") Genuine stag handle; nickel silver liners   *$60*

47283—(3") Genuine stag handle; nickel silver liners   *$60*

SCHRADE CUTLERY

Schrade Cutlery Company was incorporated in 1904 by the Schrade brothers, Louis, William, and George. As former employees of Walden Knife Company, the brothers were well indoctrinated in the cutlery business and began their own in a building about 2,000 square feet in size. At first the primary goal was to produce and market the Push Button Knife that had been invented by George a dozen years earlier. Their business grew, and in 1915 Schrade purchased the Walden Cutlery Handle Company. This company had been formed by the Schrade brothers' company in cooperation with two other New York cutlery firms, New York Knife Company and Walden Knife Company.

About this time, George Schrade left the company and formed his own, the George Schrade Cutlery Company, in Bridgeport, Connecticut, in an effort to manufacture the switchblade knife he had invented. Upon his departure, Louis Schrade filled the office of president, left vacant by George. The new leader took immediate steps to revolutionize his factory into mass production. A second factory in Middletown, New York, was established in 1918 and was managed by Joseph Schrade, another brother. This branch was closed in 1932 as a result of the economic depression.

But the parent company continued to survive and to produce quality knives. In addition to their own extensive line, Schrade Cutlery Company made knives under contract for several major hardware distributing firms. Their capacity for producing large quantities of quality knives would stand them in good stead with the business that came during World War II through government contracts.

Schrade Cutlery Company remained under the ownership and leadership of the Schrade family until 1947. At that time, the brothers Henry and Albert Baer of Ulster Knife Company bought Schrade. The company name and knife stamping was then changed to Schrade-Walden. Ten years later, production of the company's knives was moved to Ellenville, New York. Although the Walden factory was closed, most of the employees remained with the company, many of them transported daily by bus from Walden to Ellenville.

Schrade's earliest knife stamping is the rarest to be found. Used at the time of the company's founding, it is SCHRADE CUT CO. WALDEN, N.Y. GERMANY, and it dates to about 1904. The next marking was SCHRADE CUT CO. in a half circle over WALDEN, NY in a straight line. Although no records can be found showing how long this marking was used, it is believed to have continued until the World War I era. The straight-line "Schrade Cut Co." marking was adopted after World War I and was used until World War II or shortly afterward, when the company was sold. The USA stamping was not used until the early or mid-1950s, when it was changed to SCHRADE WALDEN NY USA. This tang stamp was used until the change, in 1973, to SCHRADE NY USA. Beginning in the early 1970s, knives made by the company on contract and for special limited editions sold by Schrade were often stamped SW. CUT USA. on the blade's rear tang.

Through the years, Schrade has used practically every popular handle material on its knives. The favorite for collectors, however, has been bone. Knives made during the 1920 to 1955 era are especially favored and are commonly referred to as peach tree seed bone or peach seed bone because of the material's resemblance to a dried and cut peach seed. This bone, dyed a medium tan to brown, was made for Schrade by the old Rogers Bone Company until its factory burned in 1956. The company made very few genuine bone-handled knives after that. Even though peach seed bone has a distinctive appeal all its own, knives made by Schrade with red bone and smooth tan bone handles are considered by collectors to be much rarer. From 1960 until 1978, Schrade did not produce any bone-handle knives but used Delrin or manmade materials instead. In 1978, several different bone-handled knives were produced on contract for Parker-Frost Cutlery Company. Approximately six thousand knives each were produced in green, red, and brown bone; these knives were stamped "Schrade" on the rear tang. In 1983, Schrade's own knives, with genuine bone handles were reintroduced in the company's "Heritage" series.

During its nearly ninety-year existence, Schrade has manufactured knives for a large number of other companies, including Shapleigh Hardware, Hibbard, Spencer and Bartlett, L. L. Bean, and Buck, as well as the Parker-Frost company.

Schrade has also been a major producer of commemorative knives and has played an important role in building the popularity of commemoratives during the "early days" of the 1970s. They were produced in quantities of many thousands, but special issues such as Minuteman, Paul Revere, Liberty Bell, Jim Bowie, Will Rogers, Service Series, Buffalo Bill, and Custer's Last Fight found homes with many would-be knife collectors. Although the company's aim was profitable sales and collectors were a means to that end, its activities proved a benefit to the collector movement as the general public was made aware of limited-edition knives as collectibles. Because of the numbers produced (18,000 to 24,000), most of those knives sold nearly twenty years ago are valued in the collector market at prices only slightly higher than their retail price at issue.

This book's first listing of Schrade knives consists of those produced from 1904 to 1947, stamped "SCHRADE CUTLERY CO., WALDEN N.Y." The next listing includes some of the knives produced during the era of the "Schrade-Walden" stamping, 1948 to 1973. Knives produced during the first ten years of this period are becoming as popular with collectors as the older "Schrade Cuts," and their values are usually nearly the same. When Schrade's knife production moved in 1957 from the Walden factory to the Ulster factory in Ellenville, construction changes included a switch from bone to Delrin and to different blade finishes. Knives produced during this latter portion of the Schrade-Walden era are not included except for those listed in the commemorative section. Their values are generally less than half that of knives from the early Schrade-Walden era.

Key to Schrade Cutlery Company (1904–1946) Numbering System

The number of blades is denoted by the first number as follows:

1 represents a 1-blade knife.

2 represents a 2-blade knife with both blades in one end.

3 represents a 3-blade knife with all blades in one end.

7 represents a 2-blade knife with a blade in each end.

8 represents a 3-blade knife with 2 blades in one end and 1 blade in the other end.

9 represents a 4-blade knife with 2 blades in each end.

The second and third digit of the knife number indicate the handle die pattern of the knife. An example would be the 2013, with the 01 indicating the Easy Open pattern.

The fourth digit indicates the kind of handle material used, as follows:

1—Cocobolo	6—Mother-of-Pearl
2—Ebony	7—Stained or dyed bone
3—Bone Stag	8—Buffalo horn
4—Celluloid	9—Miscellaneous
5—White Bone	

The type or color of celluloid handles is indicated by a letter or letters after the fourth digit (always "4"), as follows:

AC—	Assorted colors	J—	Red, white, amber-striped
AP—	Abalone Pearl		
B—	Black	K—	Brown-lined cream
BLUE—	Blue	M—	Marine Pearl
BP—	Black Pearl	MB—	Mottled Blue
BRNZ—	Bronze	MR—	Mottled Red
C—	Cocobolo	O—	Onyx
GL—	Goldaleur	P—	Smoked Pearl
GP—	Golden Pearl	PP—	Persian Pearl
G—	Green Pearl	S—	Tortoise Shell
H—	Black and White stripe	US—	Red, white, blue striped
HORN—	Horn	W—	(White) Ivory
		X—	Mottled Green

Miscellaneous handles are indicated by a letter or letters after the figure 9, as follows:

BR—	Solid Brass	GS—	Genuine Stag
GM—	Gun Metal	GSIL—	Nickel Silver
GOLD—	12 Karat Gold Plate	SS—	Sterling Silver

A fraction at the end of a number indicates the kind of blade substituted for a spear blade, as follows:

¼—Spey		¾—Clip	
½—Sheepfoot		⅞—Razor point	

Other designations included:

T after the pattern number indicates tip bolsters.

S before the pattern number indicates a special combination or finish.

SS before the pattern number indicates stainless steel blades and backsprings.

B before the pattern number indicates a knife with brass liners that was usually made with steel liners.

F before the pattern number indicates a knife with nail file blade that was usually made with cutting blades.

LB after the pattern number indicates the substitution of a punch blade.

Schrade Cutlery Company, Walden, N.Y.

Note. Unless noted otherwise, blades are either crocus-polished on one side of master blade or fully crocus-polished; knives are cleaned inside; N/S denotes nickel silver.

SSC114¾S—(5″) Lockback Easy Opener Fisherman's Knife with stainless steel blade and spring; special clip blade with fish scaler back; brass-lined; N/S bolsters, cleaned inside; glaze-finished blade; bone stag handle   *$300*

123EW—(4⁵/₁₆″) Pruning Knife; pruner blade; brass-lined; black inside; glaze-finished blade; walnut handle   *$85*

M1001—(4″) Maize Knife; spey-type blade; steel-lined; black inside; glaze-finished blade; cocobolo handle   *$60*

1003—(4″) Pruning Knife; pruning blade; steel-lined; steel bolsters; black inside; glaze-finished blade; bone stag handle   *$80*

1001—cocobolo handle   *$65*

1083—(5″) Sportsman's Knife; saber clip blade; brass-lined; N/S bolsters and caps; bone stag handle   *$150*

1084J—red-white-amber striped Pyralin handle   *$160*

1083¾—long clip blade; bone stag handle   *$150*

1091—(3⅝") Jackknife; spear blade; steel-lined; steel bolsters; black inside; glaze-finished blade; cocobolo handle   *$60*

1104¾Stg—(5¼") Hunting Knife; flat clip blade; brass-lined; N/S bolsters and caps; celluloid stag handle   *$125*

1104⅜M—as above except with full saber clip blade; marine pearl Pyralin handle   *$145*

1104⅜PO—plain onyx celluloid handle   *$145*

11034⅝W—(3⅝") Florist's Pruning Knife; one pruning blade; brass-lined; black inside; glaze-finished blade; ivory celluloid handle (stamped)   *$45*

11034½W—as above except with grafting blade substituted for pruning blade   *$45*

1131—(3½") Jackknife; spear blade; steel-lined; steel bolsters; black inside; glaze-finished blade; cocobolo handle   *$65*

1133—bone stag handle   *$70*

1131¾—as above except with clip blade; cocobolo handle   *$65*

1147¾—(5") Barlow; clip blade; steel-lined; steel bolsters; black inside; glaze-finished blade; stained bone handle   *$175*

115S—(3⅜") Barlow; spear blade; steel-lined; steel bolsters; black inside; glaze-finished blade; bone stag handle   *$80*

1157—(3⅜") Barlow; spear blade; steel-lined; steel bolsters; black inside; glaze-finished blade; stained bone handle   *$75*

1157¼—spey blade   *$85*

1157½—one sheepfoot blade   *$85*

1157¾—one clip blade   *$80*

1153—(3⅜") Jackknife; spear blade; steel-lined; steel bolsters; black inside; glaze-finished blade; bone stag handle   *$65*

L1153—as above except has long bolsters   *$70*

1151—cocobolo handle   *$50*

1152—ebony handle   *$50*

1153¾—one clip blade; bone stag handle   *$65*

1251—(3¼") Jackknife; spear blade; steel-lined; steel bolsters; black inside; glaze-finished blades; cocobolo handle   *$55*

1251 Chain—as above except has chain   *$65*

1253 Chain—bone stag handle   *$70*

1253—bone stag handle as above but no chain   *$65*

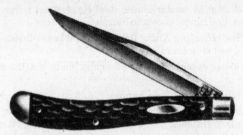

1293⅜—(4⅛") Slim Serpentine Jackknife; half saber clip blade; brass-lined; N/S bolsters, caps, and shield; bone stag handle $100

1294⅜J—red-white-amber striped Pyralin handle $90

1294⅜K—brown-lined cream Pyralin handle $85

1309GSIL—(3⅛") Senator Slim Pattern Knife; spear blade; black crocus polished one side; thin oval nickel silver handles $35

1354¼W—(4") Budding Knife; flat-sided budding blade with bark loosener on back; thick brass lining; glaze-finished blade; white celluloid handle $65

1354¼B—black celluloid handle $65

1354½B—Grafting Knife; flat-sided grafting blade; black celluloid handle $55

1354½W—white celluloid handle $55

S1354¼B—black celluloid handle $55

1361—(4⁷⁄₁₆") Pruning Knife; one pruning blade; steel-lined; steel bolsters; black inside; glaze-finished blade; cocobolo handle $45

1361 Sha—(4⁷⁄₁₆") Lineman's Skinning Knife; with shackle; skinning blade; steel-lined; steel bolsters; black inside; glaze-finished blade; cocobolo handle $55

SN1364Stg Shac—Sailor's Knife; as above except with square-point blade; Fibestos handle $75

N1361—Rope or Hawser Knife; as above except no shackle; cocobolo handle $50

1391—(3⁹⁄₁₆") Pruning Knife; one medium pruning blade; brass-lined; rattail N/S bolsters; glaze-finished blade; cocobolo handle $45

1392½—(3⁹⁄₁₆″) New England Whaler; large sheepfoot blade; brass-lined; rat-tail N/S bolsters; glaze-finished blades; ebony handle $60

L1404W—(8⅞″ overall) Combination letter opener and safety push-button knife, handle is 3⅜″ long; 1 cutting blade; brass-lined; white celluloid handle; letter opener is 5½″ long; steel, nickel-plated $175

LR1429GSIL—as above except ring opening pen knife, 3⅛″ long, with N/S handle substituted for safety push-button knife $120

L1784M—as above except Senator-pattern pen knife, 3⁵⁄₁₆″ long with marine pearl Pyralin handle substituted for safety push-button knife $120

SS1564W—(3⅜″) Equal-end Jackknife with stainless steel blade and spring; spear blade; brass-lined; N/S bolsters and shield; ivory celluloid handle $40

1694B—(4⅝″ overall) Budding Knife with stationary genuine ivory budder; handle—3⅛″ long; one budding blade; brass-lined; N/S bolsters; glaze-finished blade; black celluloid handle $65

1693—bone stag handle $85

C1824W—(3⅛″) Corn Knife, Sleeveboard pattern; 1 surgical blade; brass-lined; ivory celluloid handle (stamped) $45

L1824M—(6″ overall) Combination letter opener and Sleeveboard-pattern penknife; handle—3⅛″ long; 1 office blade; brass-lined; N/S bolsters at one end; Marine Pearl Pyralin handle; letter opener is 2⅞″ long, steel-polished $75

1863¾—(4½″) Jackknife; 1 clip blade; brass-lined; steel bolsters and caps; N/S shield; glaze-finished blade; bone stag handle $140

1864¾J—as above except with N/S bolsters and caps; red-white-amber striped Pyralin handle $120

S1944⅝W—(3⅞″) Florist's Pruning Knife with shackle; one small pruning blade; brass-lined; N/S shackle; glaze-finished blade; ivory celluloid handle (stamped) $50

S1944½W—as above except with grafting blade substituted for pruning blade $50

S1944W—(3⅞″) Florist's Knife; 1 budding blade; brass-lined; glaze-finished blade; ivory celluloid handle (stamped) $50

C1944W—(3⅞″) Stockman's Knife; surgical spey blade; N/S-lined; ivory celluloid handle (stamped) $50

1974½W—(4¼″) Florist's Knife; sheepfoot blade; brass-lined; glaze-finished blade; white celluloid handle $45

2013—(3⅝″) Easy Opener Jack; spear and pen blades; brass-lined; N/S bolsters, caps, and shield; bone stag handle $120

2011—cocobolo handle $85

2012—ebony handle $75

2014—assorted celluloid handles $110

2019BR—solid brass handle $100

2014X—mottled green celluloid handle $95

SS2013—with stainless steel blades and springs; bone stag handle $165

2022—(3⅝″) Easy Opener Jack; spear and pen blades; brass-lined; N/S bolsters and shield; ebony handle $90

2021—cocobolo handle $85

2023—bone stag handle $130

2023 Chain—bone stag handle as above except with chain $135

2033EO—(3⅜″) Easy Opener Jack; spear and pen blades; brass-lined; N/S bolsters, caps, and shield; bone stag handle $115

2034KEO—brown-lined cream Pyralin handle $105

2033¾—(3 ⅜″) Jackknife; clip and pen blades; brass-lined; N/S bolsters, caps and shield; bone stag handle $100

2042SD—(3¾″) Electrician's Knife (lockback); large spear blade and a lockback screwdriver–wire scraper blade; brass-lined; N/S bolsters and shield; ebony handle $75

2042SD Shackle—as above except with N/S shackle $95

2043SD Shackle—bone stag handle $120

C2041SD—as above except with center lock screwdriver blade; cocobolo handle $75

C2041SD Shac—as above except with shackle $75

2043—(3¾″) Jackknife; spear and pen blades; brass-lined; N/S bolsters and shield; bone stag handle $85

2042—ebony handle $70

2043¾—bone stag handle as above except with pen and clip blades $85

C2043¾—(3¾″) Jackknife; spear and screwdriver blades; brass-lined; N/S bolsters, caps, and shield; bone stag handle $115

2054K—(3¹⁄₁₆″) Serpentine Jackknife; spear and pen blades; brass-lined; N/S bolsters, caps, and shield; brown-lined cream Pyralin handle $80

2053—bone stag handle $85

2054M—Marine Pearl Pyralin handle $80

S2053—as above except with fancy bolsters; bone stag handle $90

2053½—*(3⅝″) Electrician's Knife;* screwdriver–wire scraper and sheep-foot blades; brass-lined; N/S bolsters, caps, and shield; bone stag handle $135

2063—*(3⅝″) Jackknife;* spear and pen blades; brass-lined; N/S bolsters, caps, and shield; bone stag handle $110

2061—cocobolo handle $100

2062—ebony handle $100

2064—assorted celluloid handles $100

2063½—sheepfoot and pen blades; bone stag handle $120

2061¾—cocobolo handles $100

2062¾—clip and pen blades; ebony handle $90

2063¾—bone stag handles $115

2069BR—*(3⅝″) Jackknife;* spear and pen blades; brass-lined, cleaned in-side; solid brass handle $100

2069¾BR—clip and pen blades $100

2072—*(3⅝″) Jackknife;* spear and pen blades; brass-lined; N/S bolsters and shield; ebony handle $90

2071—cocobolo handle $85

2073—bone stag handle $110

2073¾—clip and pen blades; bone stag handle $110

2071¾—cocobolo handle $90

2072¾—ebony handle $90

2083B—*(3″) Small Equal-end Jackknife;* spear and pen blades; N/S lin-ings and bolsters; bone stag handle $75

2084—assorted celluloid handles $65

SSD2084PO—*(5″) Fisherman's Knife* with stainless steel blades and springs; disgorger–scaler–cap-lifter blade and long clip cutting blade; brass-lined; N/S bolsters and caps; hole in cap for straightening fish hooks; plain onyx celluloid handle $100

P2088—*(3″) Smoker's Knife;* Senator pattern; sunk joint, spear blade and punch for piercing cigars or clearing pipe; N/S tamper on end; thick oval N/S blade $80

2093—*(3⅝″) Jackknife;* spear and pen blades; steel-lined; steel bolsters; N/S shield; glaze-finished blades; bone stag handle $110

2091—cocobolo handle ... $100

2092—ebony handle ... $100

2102⅜—(5¼") *Hunter's and Trapper's Knife;* full saber clip and skinning blades; brass-lined; N/S bolsters and caps; bone stag handle ... $210

2104⅜M—Marine Pearl Pyralin handle ... $195

2104⅜PO—plain onyx celluloid handle ... $300

2109⅜GS—genuine stag handle ... $275

2122—(3½") *Jackknife;* spear and pen blades; steel-lined; steel bolsters; N/S shield; glazed-finished blades; ebony handle ... $70

2121—cocobolo handle ... $70

2123—bone stag handle ... $90

2121¾—as above except with pen and clip blades; cocobolo handle ... $70

2123¾—bone stag handle ... $95

2133—(3½") *Jackknife;* spear and pen blades; steel-lined; steel bolsters; black inside; glaze finished blades; bone stag handle ... $80

2131—cocobolo handle ... $70

2132—ebony handle ... $70

2133 *Chain*—with chain; bone stag handle ... $85

2134¾GP—(3¼") *Norfolk-pattern Jackknife;* clip and pen blades; brass-lined; N/S bolsters and shield; Golden Pearl Pyralin handle ... $105

2133¾—bone stag handle ... $130

2134¾M—Marine Pearl Pyralin handle ... $105

215S—(3⅜") *Barlow;* spear and pen blades; steel-lined; steel bolsters; black inside; glaze-finished blades; bone stag handle ... $100

215¾S—pen and clip blades ... $95

215¾M—pen and clip blades; Marine Pearl Pyralin ... $85

2157—(3⅜") *Barlow;* spear and pen blades; steel-lined; steel bolsters; black inside; glaze-finished blades; stained bone handle ... $100

2155—white bone handle ... $115

2157¼—pen and spey blades; stained bone handle ... $105

2157½—pen and sheepfoot blades; stained bone handle ... $110

2157¾—pen and clip blades; stained bone handle ... $100

2157⅞—pen and razor point blades; stained bone handle ... $110

L2153—(3⅜") Jackknife; spear and pen blades; steel-lined; long steel bolsters; black inside; glaze-finished blades; bone stag handle $85

L2153¾—pen and clip blades $80

2151—(3⅜") Jackknife; spear and pen blades; steel-lined; steel bolsters; black inside; glaze-finished blades; cocobolo handle $65

2152—ebony handle $65

2153—bone stag handle $75

2153 Chain—with chain; bone stag handle $100

2151 Chain—cocobolo handle $85

2152½—sheepfoot and pen blades; ebony handle $70

2153½—bone stag handle $90

2153¾—clip and pen blades; bone stag handle $80

2151¾—cocobolo handle $60

2152¾—ebony handle $60

B2151—(3⅜") Jackknife; spear and pen blades; brass-lined; steel bolsters; black inside; glaze-finished blades; cocobolo handle $60

B2152—ebony handle $60

B2153—bone stag handle $70

B2152½—sheepfoot and pen blades; ebony handle $70

B2153½—bone stag handle $85

B2153¾—clip and pen blades; bone stag handle $75

B2151¾—cocobolo handle $65

B2152¾—ebony handle $65

C2153SD—(3⅜") Screwdriver Jackknife; cutting blade and combination screwdriver—cap lifter; brass-lined; steel bolsters and caps; N/S shield; black inside; glaze-finished blades; bone stag handle $110

2151SD—as above except without caps and shield; steel linings; cocobolo handle $80

2154¾M—(3⅜") Barlow; clip and pen blades, steel-lined; steel bolsters; black inside; Marine Pearl Pyralin handle $105

C2154¾KLB—(3⅜") Jackknife; leather punch and clip blade; brass-lined; steel bolsters and caps; N/S shield; black inside; brown-lined cream Pyralin handle $90

C2154¾APLB—Abalone Pearl Pyralin handle $90

C2154¾—assorted celluloid handles $90

C2152¾LB—as above except with glaze-finished blades; ebony handle $90

C2151LB—as above except with spear blade substituted for clip blade; glaze-finished blades; cocobolo handle $90

C2154—as above except with large blade, crocus-polished one side; assorted celluloid handles $90

S2151—(3⅜") Jackknife; spear and pen blades; brass-lined; steel bolsters; N/S shield; black inside; glaze-finished blades; cocobolo handle $65

S2152—ebony handle $65

S2153—bone stag handle $75

S2153¾—clip and pen blades; bone stag handle $75

S2152¾—ebony handle $65

S2151LB—*(3⅜") Jackknife;* leather punch and spear blade; brass-lined; steel bolsters; N/S shield; black inside; glaze-finished blades; cocobolo handle $85

S2153LB—bone stag handle $95

S2153EO—*(3⅜") Easy-opener Jackknife;* spear and pen blades; brass-lined; steel bolsters; N/S shield; black inside; glaze-finished blades; bone stag handle $90

C2153—*(3⅜") Jackknife;* spear and pen blades; brass-lined; steel bolsters and caps; N/S shield; black inside; glaze-finished blades; bone stag handle $90

C2151—cocobolo handle $70

C2152—ebony handle $70

C2154G—Green Pearl Pyralin handle as above except with large blade, crocus-polished one side $85

C2154—assorted celluloid handles as above except with large blade, crocus-polished one side $85

C2153½—bone stag handle as above except with pen and sheepfoot blades $90

C2151¾—*(3⅜")Jackknife;* clip and pen blades; brass-lined; steel bolsters and caps; N/S shield; black inside; glaze-finished blades; cocobolo handle $75

C2152¾—ebony handle $75

C2154¾—assorted celluloid handles $85

C2153¾—bone stag handle $95

C2154¾AP—Abalone Pearl Pyralin handle as above except with large blade, crocus-polished one side $90

C2153EO—*(3⅜") Easy-opener Jackknife;* spear and pen blades; brass-lined; steel bolsters and caps; N/S shield; black inside; glaze-finished blades; bone stag handle $95

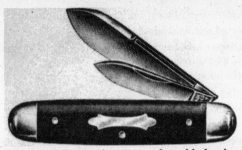

2172—(3⅝″) Equal-end Jackknife; spear and pen blades; brass-lined; N/S bolsters and shield; ebony handle $95

2171—cocobolo handle $95

2173—bone stag handle $105

2174W—ivory celluloid handle $100

2176—mother-of-pearl handle $165

2179GS—genuine stag handle $135

2173¾—clip and pen blades; bone stag handle $100

2171¾—cocobolo handle $85

2172¾—ebony handle $85

2174¾W—ivory celluloid handle $90

2172⅜—saber clip and pen blades; ebony handle $105

2193¾—(3⅝″) Equal-end Jackknife; spear and pen blades; brass-lined; N/S flat bevel bolsters and shield; bone stag handle $125

2022—(3½″) Jackknife; spear and pen blades; brass-lined; N/S Washington bolsters, flat caps, and shield; ebony handle $130

2203—bone stag handle $140

2203¾—clip and pen blades; bone stag handle $160

2213—(3½″) Jackknife; spear and pen blades; brass-lined; N/S bolsters, caps, and shield; bone stag handle $100

2211—cocobolo handle $80

2212—ebony handle $80

2214—assorted celluloid handles $110

2219GS—genuine stag handle $135

2213½—sheepfoot and pen blades; bone stag handle $120

2219½GS—genuine stag handle $160

2211¾—clip and pen blades; cocobolo handle $95

2212¾—ebony handle $95

2213¾—bone stag handle $120

SS2213—(3½″) Jackknife with stainless steel blades and springs; spear and pen blades; brass-lined; N/S bolsters, caps, and shield; bone stag handle $130

2214¾W—clip and pen blades; ivory celluloid handle $100

2214¾—assorted celluloid handles $100

2222—*(3½") Serpentine Jackknife;* spear and pen blades; brass-lined; N/S bolsters, caps, and shield; ebony handle $100

2221—cocobolo handle $100

2223—bone stag handle $120

2224GP—Golden Pearl Pyralin handle $100

2224—assorted celluloid handles $100

2226—mother-of-pearl handle $175

2223½—sheepfoot and pen blades; bone stag handle $135

2223¾—clip and pen blades; bone stag handle $120

2253—*(3¼") Jackknife;* spear and pen blades; steel-lined; steel bolsters; black-lined; glaze-finished blades; bone stag handle $75

2251—cocobolo handle $65

2252—ebony handle $65

2251 *Chain*—with chain; cocobolo handle $75

2253 *Chain*—bone stag handle $85

2252½—sheepfoot and pen blades; ebony handle $75

2253½—bone stag handle $90

2251¾—clip and pen blades; cocobolo handle $70

2253¾—bone stag handle $80

2252⅞—*(3¼") Mill Knife;* razor point and pen blades; steel-lined; steel bolsters; blade inside; glaze-finished blades; ebony handle $75

B2253—*(3¼") Jackknife;* spear and pen blades; brass-lined, steel bolsters; black inside; glaze-finished blades; bone stag handle $80

B2251—cocobolo handle $70

B2253½—sheepfoot and pen blades; bone stag handle $80

B2251¾—clip and pen blades; cocobolo handle $70

S2253EO—*(3¼") Easy-opener Boy Scout Knife* with chain; spear and pen blades; brass-lined; steel bolsters; 18″ chain; N/S shield; bone stag handle $100

2261—*(3¼") Jackknife;* spear and pen blades; brass-lined; N/S bolsters; caps, and shield; cocobolo handle $70

2262—ebony handle $70

2263—bone stag handle $90

2266—mother-of-pearl handle   *$140*

2264—assorted celluloid handles   *$85*

2263½—sheepfoot and pen blades; bone stag handle   *$90*

2263¾—clip and pen blades; bone stag handle   *$90*

2269BR—(3¼") Jackknife; spear and pen blades; solid brass composition handle   *$90*

2271—(3½") Jackknife; spear and pen blades; brass-lined; steel rat-tail bolsters; N/S shield; cocobolo handle   *$80*

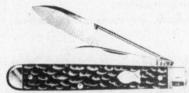

2273—(4⅛") Slim Jackknife; pen and long spear blades; brass-lined; N/S rope bolsters; N/S caps and shield; bone stag handle   *$160*

2283—(3½") Jackknife; spear and pen blades; brass-lined; N/S bolsters and shield; bone stag handle   *$90*

2283 Chain—with chain; bone stag handle   *$105*

2281—cocobolo handle   *$85*

2283¾—as above except with pen and clip blades; bone stag handle   *$90*

S2282½—(3½") Easy-opener Boy Scout Knife; sheepfoot and pen blades; brass-lined; N/S bolsters, shield, and shackle; ebony handle   *$125*

S2283½—bone stag handle   *$145*

2293—(3½") Carpenter's Knife; spear and sheepfoot blades; brass-lined; steel rat-tail bolsters; N/S shield; spear blade crocus-polished on one side; bone stag handle   *$140*

M2309GSIL—(3⅛") Senator-pattern Knife with spear and long manicure blades; thin oval N/S handle   *$45*

2311SD—(3⅝") Electrician's Knife; Sleeveboard pattern; spear and lock-back screwdriver–wire scraper blades; brass-lined; N/S bolsters and shield; cocobolo handle   *$80*

2314BSD—black celluloid handle   *$80*

2333—(3⅜") Serpentine Jackknife; spear and pen blades; brass-lined; N/S bolsters, caps, and shield; bone stag handle   *$115*

2331—cocobolo handle $100

2332—ebony handle $100

2334K—brown-lined cream Pyralin handle $100

2334—assorted celluloid handles $100

2333½—pen and sheepfoot blades; bone stag handle $115

2333¾—pen and clip blades; bone stag handle $115

2343—(3⁵⁄₁₆") Serpentine Jackknife; spear and pen blades; brass-lined; N/S bolsters and shield; bone stag handle $85

2344—assorted celluloid handles $70

2353—(3¼") Navy Knife, easy opener; regulation navy pocket blade and nail pen blades; brass-lined; N/S bolsters and shackle; bone stag handle $115

2363—(3½") Jackknife; spear blade and punch; brass-lined; steel rat-tail bolsters; N/S shield; bone stag handle $125

2364¾B—clip blade and punch; black celluloid handle $65

2364⅜B—as above except with saber clip blade $70

2392—(3½") Jackknife; spear and punch blades; brass-lined; steel bolsters; N/S shield; black inside; glaze-finished blades; ebony handle $115

2393—bone stag handle $130

2393¾—punch and clip blades; bone stag handle $130

S2393—(3½") Camper's Knife; can opener–cap lifter and spear blade; brass-lined; steel bolsters; N/S shield; bone stag handle $145

2394½B—(3⁹⁄₁₆") New England Whaler; sheepfoot and pen blades; brass-lined; rat-tail N/S bolsters; glaze-finished blade; black celluloid handle $75

1394½B—1 pen blade only $45

2423—(3⅛") Equal-end Jackknife, Slim pattern; spear and pen blades; brass-lined; N/S bolsters and shield; bone stag handle $75

2424—assorted celluloid handles $65

SS2423—(3⅛") Equal-end Jackknife, Slim pattern, with stainless steel spear and pen blades and springs; brass-lined; N/S bolsters and shield; bone stag handle $100

SS2424—assorted celluloid handles $85

SS2426—mother-of-pearl handle $140

2426—(3⅛") Equal-end Jackknife, Slim pattern; spear and pen blades; brass-lined; N/S bolsters; mother-of-pearl handle $110

2423EO—(3⅛″) Easy-opener Equal-end Jackknife, Slim pattern; spear and pen blades; brass-lined; N/S bolsters and shield; bone stag handle $80

2424—assorted celluloid handles $65

2424¾K—(3⅛″) Equal-end Jackknife, Slim pattern; clip and pen blades; brass-lined; N/S bolsters and shield; brown-lined cream Pyralin handle $65

2423¾—bone stag handle $80

2424¾J—red-white-amber striped Pyralin handle $65

2424¾—assorted celluloid handles $65

C2534M—(3¹/₁₆″) Jackknife; spear and pen blades; brass-lined; N/S bolsters, caps, and shield; Marine Pearl Pyralin handle $60

C2533—bone stag handle $75

C2534K—brown-lined cream Pyralin handle $60

C2534¾E—as above except with clip blade substituted for spear blade; black and pearl celluloid handle $60

C2534¾Q—blue and white celluloid handle $60

C2533¾SQ—(3¹/₁₆″) Jackknife; spear and pen blades; brass-lined; N/S Washington bolsters, flat caps, and shield; bone stag handle $85

2563—(3⅜″) Equal-end Jackknife; spear and pen blades; brass-lined; N/S bolsters and shield; bone stag handle $85

2564K—brown-lined cream Pyralin handle $80

2564—assorted celluloid handles $80

2566—mother-of-pearl handle $95

2563¾—(3⅜″) Equal-end Jackknife; clip and pen blades; brass-lined; N/S bolsters and shield; bone stag handle $85

SS2563—(3⅜″) Equal-end Jacknife with stainless steel blades and springs; spear and pen blades; brass-lined; N/S bolsters and shield; bone stag handle $110

SS2564—assorted celluloid handles $95

2623—(3½″) Balloon-pattern Jackknife; spear and pen blades; brass-lined; N/S bolsters and shield; bone stag handle $120

2623¾—as above except with pen and clip blades $120

2643¾—(4″) Balloon-pattern Jackknife; clip and pen blades; brass-lined; N/S bolsters, cap, and shield; bone stag handle $400

2693—(3″) Gunstock-pattern Jackknife; spear and pen blades; brass-lined; N/S bolsters, caps, and shield; bone stag handle $295

2694—assorted celluloid handles $275

2724⅜M—(2⅞") *Serpentine Jackknife;* half saber clip and pen blades; brass-lined; N/S bolsters, caps, and shield; Marine Pearl Pyralin handle $70

2723⅜—bone stag handle $75

2724⅜K—brown-lined cream Pyralin handle $70

2723—as above except with spear blade; bone stag handle $80

2723¾—as above except with clip blade; bone stag handle $80

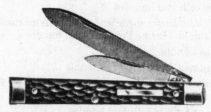

2733—(3¾") *Physician's Jackknife;* spear and pen blades; brass-lined; N/S bolsters, caps, and shield; bone stag handle $175

2813¾—(4") *Texas Jackknife;* clip and pen blades; brass-lined; N/S bolsters and shield; bone stag handle $125

2814¾—assorted celluloid handles $110

2813—spear and pen blades; bone stag handle $120

2863—(4½") *Jackknife;* spear and pen blades; brass-lined; steel bolsters and caps; N/S shield; glaze-finished blades; bone stag handle $200

2863¾—clip and pen blades $200

L2863¾—(4½") *Jackknife;* spear and pen blades; brass-lined; N/S fancy bolsters; N/S caps and shield; bone stag handle $200

2903¾—(3½") *Premium Jackknife;* clip and pen blades; brass-lined; N/S bolsters and shield; bone stag handle $90

2904¾—assorted celluloid handles $75

2903—spear and pen blades; bone stag handle $90

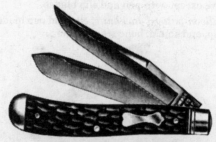

2943¾—(3⅞") *Serpentine Jackknife;* pen and half saber clip blades; brass-lined; N/S bolsters, caps, and shield; bone stag handle $185

2944¾J—amber striped Pyralin handle   *$240*

1944¾J—1-blade knife, same as above, without pen blade; glaze-finished blade   *$180*

S2943¾—(3⅞") Stockman's Knife; clip and pen blades; brass-lined; N/S bolsters, caps, and shield; bone stag handle   *$220*

1943¾—1-blade knife, same as above, without pen blade; glaze-finished blade   *$155*

2953¾—(3") Serpentine Jackknife; clip and pen blades; brass-lined; N/S bolsters, caps, and shield; bone stag handle   *$95*

2954¾M—Marine Pearl Pyralin handle   *$85*

2954¾—assorted celluloid handles   *$85*

2956¾—mother-of-pearl handle   *$110*

2953—spear and pen blades; bone stag handle   *$95*

2954—assorted celluloid handles   *$85*

2973¾—(4¼") Equal-end Jackknife; clip and pen blades; brass-lined; N/S flat bevel bolsters and shield; bone and shield; bone stag handle   *$190*

2974¾W—ivory celluloid handle   *$165*

R2973—(4¼") Equal-end Jackknife; spear and pen blades; brass-lined; round N/S bolsters and shield; bone stag handle   *$200*

R2974W—ivory celluloid handle   *$180*

7076Sha—(2⁵⁄₁₆") Sleeveboard Lobster pattern with shackle; spear and nail file blades; N/S-lined, with milled edges; mother-of-pearl handle   *$65*

7079GSilSha—satin-finish N/S handle   *$45*

7083B—(3") Senator pattern, sunk joint; spear and pen blades; N/S linings and bolsters; bone stag handle   *$45*

7086B—as above except with blades crocus-polished; mother-of-pearl handle   *$60*

7089GM—oval gunmetal handle   *$35*

SS7089GSIL—(3") Senator pattern, sunk joint, with stainless steel blades and spring; spear and pen blades; thick oval N/S handle   *$40*

7099GM Shac—(3¹⁄₁₆") Senator pattern with shackle; spear and pen blades; N/S shackle; flat gunmetal handle, beveled edges   *$35*

7099GM—as above except without shackle $35

M7099GSIL Shac—*(3¹/₁₆″)* Senator pattern with shackle; flexible manicure file and spear blades; N/S shackle; N/S handle $40

M7099GSil—as above except without N/S shackle $40

RM7099GSIL—as above except with treaded N/S handle with raised rivet heads; without shackle $40

7099GSil—as above except with small blade substituted for flexible manicure file; without shackle; satin-finish N/S handle $40

SS7099 I Shac—*(3¹/₁₆″)*Senator pattern with stainless steel blades and spring; 2 spear blades; stainless metal handle, engine-turned $35

SSF7099SI Shac—spear blade and file; smooth stainless metal handle $40

SSM7099SI Shac—as above except with carbon steel flexible manicure file substituted for stainless steel file $40

SS7099SI Shac—as above, with smooth handle not engine-turned $35

SS7099I—without shackle $35

7113—*(3⅜″)* Sleeveboard pattern; spear and pen blades; brass-lined; N/S shield; bone stag handle $65

7114—assorted celluloid handles $55

7114 Horn—horn Pyralin handle $55

S7113—glaze-finished blades as above except without shield $55

7116—*(3⅜″)* Sleeveboard pattern; spear and pen blades; brass-lined; mother-of-pearl handle $75

7118—buffalo horn handle $65

7113T—*(3⅜″)* Sleeveboard pattern; spear and pen blades; brass-lined; N/S tips and shield; bone stag handle $65

7114—assorted celluloid handles $55

7114HornT—horn Pyralin handle $55

S7113T—glaze-finished blades without shield $55

7116T—*(3⅜″)* Sleeveboard pattern; spear and pen blades; brass-lined; N/S tips, mother-of-pearl handle $75

7118T—buffalo horn handle with shield $70

7113B—*(3⅜″)* Sleeveboard pattern; spear and pen blades; brass-lined; N/S bolsters and shield; bone stag handle $65

7114HornB—horn Pyralin handle $55

7114—assorted celluloid handles $55

S7113B—glaze-finished blades; bone stag handle $55

7116B—*(3⅜″)* Sleeveboard pattern; spear and pen blades; brass-lined; N/S bolsters; mother-of-pearl handle $80

7118B—buffalo horn handle with shield $65

7114SqMB—(3⅜") Sleeveboard pattern; spear and pen blades; brass-lined; flat N/S bolsters with beveled edges; N/S shield; Marine Pearl celluloid handle   *$50*

7113SqB—bone stag handle   *$55*

SS7113T—(3⅜") Sleeveboard pattern with stainless steel blades and springs; spear and pen blades; brass-lined; N/S tips and shield; bone stag handle   *$80*

SS7114—assorted celluloid handles   *$70*

7129GSIL—(3") Corkscrew Knife; spear blade and corkscrew; cap lift formed by spring and handle; N/S handle   *$45*

7129GSIL Shac—as above except with N/S shackle   *$45*

7133—(3¼") Norfolk pattern with 1 spring; spear and pen blades; brass-lined; N/S bolsters and shield; bone stag handle   *$90*

7143T—(3⅛") Senator pattern, sunk joint; spear and pen blades; brass-lined; N/S tips and shield; bone stag handle   *$55*

7146T—as above except N/S-lined, with shield; mother-of-pearl handle   *$65*

7149GST—as above except N/S-lined, with shield; genuine stag handle   *$65*

7143B—as above except with N/S bolsters substituted for tips; bone stag handle   *$60*

7163—(3⅝") Equal-end Jackknife; 1 spring; spear and spey blades; brass-lined; N/S bolsters and shield; bone stag handle   *$105*

7164½W—(3⅝") Florist's Knife for budding, pruning, etc.; budding and sheepfoot blades; brass-lined; N/S bolsters; ivory celluloid handles *$65*

7173—(3⅝") Equal-end Jackknife with 1 spring; spear and pen blades; brass-lined; N/S bolsters and shield; bone stag handle   *$100*

7171—cocobolo handles   *$85*

7172—ebony handles   *$85*

7173¾—bone stag handles; pen and clip blades   *$95*

7174S—(3⅝") Equal-end Jackknife with 1 spring; spear and pen blades; brass-lined; N/S bolsters and shield; tortoise shell celluloid handle *$85*

7193—(3⅝") *Equal-end Jackknife,* with 1 spring; spear and pen blades; brass-lined; N/S flat bevel bolsters and shield; bone stag handle   *$125*

7233—(3⅝") *Equal-end Jackknife;* clip and spear blades; brass-lined; N/S bolsters and shield; bone stag handle   *$170*

7243T—(3⅜") Sleeveboard pattern; pen and extra-long spear blades; brass-lined; N/S tips and shield; bone stag handle   *$60*

7244HT—black-and-white Pyralin handle   *$55*

7243B—(3⅜") Sleeveboard pattern; pen and extra-long spear blades; brass-lined; N/S bolsters and shield; bone stag handle   *$60*

7243¾B—clip and pen blades; bone stag handle   *$65*

7309GSIL Shackle—(3⅛") Senator pattern with N/S shackle; spear and pen blades; thin oval N/S handles   *$40*

7309GSIL—as above except without shackle   *$40*

7309SS Shackle— as above except with shackle, blades crocus-polished; sterling silver handles   *$45*

7309GM—(3⅛") Senator pattern; spear and pen blades; flat gunmetal handle, rounded edges   *$35*

7303—(4⅛") *Budding and Pruning Knife;* pruning and spey blades; brass-lined; steel bolsters; N/S shield; glaze-finished blades; bone stag handle   *$170*

S7303—(4⅛") *Budding and Pruning Knife;* budding and pruning blades; brass-lined; steel bolsters; N/S shield; glaze-finished blade; bone stag handle   *$205*

S7309F—(4⅛") *Budding and Pruning Knife;* 2 flat-sided budding blades with bark loosener on back and a Wharncliffe pruning blade; thick brass lining; glaze-finished blades; Fibestos handle with dull finish   *$165*

RS7304W—(4⅛″) Budding and Pruning Knife; spey and pruning blades; brass-lined; glaze-finished blades; ivory celluloid handle   *$165*

S7309GSIL—(3⅛″) Lumber Rule, Senator pattern; 2″ rule and spear blade; thin oval N/S handles   *$105*

7326—(3⅜″) Sleeveboard pattern; spear and pen blades; brass-lined; N/S bolsters at one end; mother-of-pearl handle   *$85*

7324W—(4″) Florist's Knife for budding, pruning, etc.; budding and sheepfoot blades; brass-lined; N/S bolsters; ivory celluloid handle   *$75*

G7324W—(4″) Greenskeeper's Knife; spear and special weeder blades; brass-lined; N/S bolsters; glaze-finished blades; ivory celluloid handle   *$115*

G7324½W—(4″) Gardener's Knife; grafting blade flat on one side and special weeder blade; brass-lined; N/S bolsters; glaze-finished blades; ivory celluloid handle   *$105*

7344M—(3⁵⁄₁₆″) Serpentine Jackknife with 1 spring; clip and pen blades; brass-lined; N/S bolsters and shield; Marine Pearl celluloid handle   *$65*

*7343—*bone stag handle   *$75*

*7344K—*brown-lined cream Pyralin handle   *$65*

*7344—*assorted celluloid handles   *$65*

7353—(4⅛″) Marlin Spike Knife; 1 cutting blade and a marlin spike; brass-lined; N/S bolsters, caps, and shackle; cutting blade crocus-polished one side; bone stag handle   *$140*

SS7359GSil—(4⅛″) Marlin Spike Knife; large spey blade and marlin spike; N/S shackle; cutting blade crocus-polished one side; solid N/S handle   *$200*

*7359GSil—*as above except carbon steel cutting blade substituted for stainless steel   *$175*

7364¾B—(3⁹⁄₁₆″) Serpentine Knife with 1 spring; clip and pen blades; brass-lined; N/S bolsters and shield; black celluloid handle   *$60*

F7426—(3⅛″) Senator pattern; spear blade and file; brass-lined; mother-of-pearl handle   *$65*

F7423T—(3⅛″) Senator pattern; spear blade and file; brass-lined; N/S tips and shield; bone stag handle   *$55*

*F7426T—*as above except with mother-of-pearl handle (without shield)   *$65*

7429GSIL—(3⅛″) Senator pattern; spear and pen blades; solid thick oval N/S handle   *$40*

7423T—(3⅛") Senator pattern; spear and pen blades; brass-lined; N/S tips and shield; bone stag handle $55

7424—assorted celluloid handles $45

7424GPT—Golden Pearl Pyralin handle $45

M7423T—(3⅛") Senator pattern; flexible manicure file and spear blade; brass-lined; N/S tips and shield; bone stag handle $50

M7423TSha—as above except with N/S shackle $50

R7429GM—(3⅛") Ring-opening Knife, Senator pattern; spear and pen blades; thin oval gunmetal handle $45

R7429GSIL—N/S handle $45

R7429SS—as above except with blades crocus-polished; sterling silver handle $50

7426T—(3⅛") Senator pattern; spear and pen blades; brass-lined; N/S tips; mother-of-pearl handle $65

7429GST—genuine stag handle $65

7426—as above except without N/S tips; mother-of-pearl handle $65

7423B—(3⅛") Senator pattern; spear and pen blades; brass-lined; N/S bolsters and shield; bone stag handle $55

7424MB—Marine Pearl Pyralin handle $50

7424—assorted celluloid handles $50

7426B—(3⅛") Senator pattern; spear and pen blades; brass-lined; N/S bolsters; mother-of-pearl handle $70

7423¾B—(3⅛") Senator pattern; clip and pen blades; brass-lined; N/S bolsters and shield; bone stag handle $55

7423SqB—(3⅛") Senator pattern; spear and pen blades; brass-lined; flat N/S bolsters with beveled edges; N/S shield; bone stag handle $55

7424SqMB—Marine Pearl Celluloid handle $50

SS7423T—(3⅛") Senator pattern with stainless steel blades and spring; spear and pen blades; brass-lined; N/S tips and shield; bone stag handle $85

SS7424—assorted celluloid handles $70

SS7424KT—brown-lined cream Pyralin handle $70

SS7426T—(3⅛") Senator pattern with stainless steel blades and spring; spear and pen blades; brass-lined; N/S tips; mother-of-pearl handle $110

SS7426B—(3⅛") Senator pattern with stainless steel blades and spring; spear and pen blades; brass-lined; N/S bolsters; mother-of-pearl handle $115

SS7423B—bone stag handle (with shield)   *$95*

R7429GM—(3⅛") *Ring-opening Knife,* Senator pattern, spear and pen blades; flat gunmetal handle, rounded edges   *$40*

SSR7429GSIL—(3⅛") *Ring-opening Knife,* Senator pattern with stainless steel blades and spring; spear and pen blades; N/S handle   *$45*

7433—(3⅛") Senator pattern; spear and pen blades; steel-lined; black inside; glaze-finished blades; bone stag handle   *$55*

7434C—cocobolo celluloid handle   *$50*

7434G—Green Pearl Pyralin handle   *$50*

7434MB—mottled blue Pyralin handle   *$50*

7434MR—mottled red pyralin handle   *$50*

7434—assorted celluloid handles   *$50*

S7434M—(3⅛") Senator pattern; spear and pen blades; brass-lined; Marine Pearl Pyralin handle   *$40*

S7433—bone stag handle   *$55*

S7434—assorted celluloid handles   *$50*

S7434G—Green Pearl Pyralin handle   *$50*

7439GSIL—(3⅛") Senator pattern; spear and pen blades; black inside; glaze-finished blades; flat nickel gunmetal handle   *$40*

7439GM—gunmetal handle   *$40*

7479GSIL—(3⅛")Senator pattern; spear and pen blades; N/S handle with beveled edges   *$40*

7479GSIL Shackle —as above except with shackle   *$40*

7486—(3¼") Slim Senator pattern, sunk joint; spear and pen blades; N/S lined, with milled edges; mother-of-pearl handle   *$65*

7484—as above except with brass-lined assorted celluloid handles   *$50*

7483T—(3¼") Slim Senator pattern, sunk joint; spear and pen blades; brass-lined; N/S tips and shield; bone stag handle   *$50*

07484W—(3¼") *Office Knife,* Slim Senator pattern, sunk joint, spear and spey or office blade; brass-lined; ivory celluloid handle (stamped)   *$55*

SS7486—(3¼") Slim Senator pattern, sunk joint, with stainless steel blades and spring; spear and pen blades; N/S-lined, with milled edges; mother-of-pearl handle   *$90*

7494W—(3⁷⁄₁₆") Senator pattern, sunk joint; spear and pen blades; brass-lined; ivory celluloid handle   *$45*

07494W—(3⁷⁄₁₆") *Office Knife,* Senator pattern, sunk joint; spear and spey blades; brass-lined; ivory celluloid handle (stamped)   *$60*

7554¾B—*(3¼")* Serpentine Balloon pattern, clip and pen blades; brass-lined; N/S bolsters and shield; black celluloid handle $65

7563—*(3⅜") Equal-end Jackknife* with 1 spring; spear and pen blades; brass-lined; N/S bolsters and shield; bone stag handle $90

7564B—black celluloid handle $75

7564¾S—clip and pen blades; tortoise shell celluloid handle $75

7563¾—bone stag handle $80

07564W—*(3⅜") Office Knife,* equal-end pattern; spear and spey blades; brass-lined; ivory celluloid handle (stamped) $70

7573—*(3⅜") Equal-end Jackknife;* clip and spear blades; brass-lined; N/S bolsters and shield; bone stag handle $160

7604W—*(2¼")* Lobster pattern; pen and manicure blades; brass-lined; ivory celluloid handle $30

7604—assorted celluloid handles $30

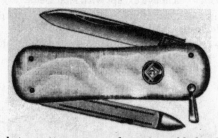

7606—*(2¼")* Lobster pattern; pen and manicure blades; N/S-lined, with milled edges; mother-of-pearl handle $45

7606 Shackle—N/S shackle; mother-of pearl handle $45

7604 Shackle—assorted celluloid handles $35

7606 Shackle Emblem—*(2¼")* Lobster pattern with emblem and shackle; pen and manicure blades; N/S-lined, with milled edges; mother-of-pearl handle $55

7609 Gold Shackle—*(2¼")* Lobster pattern with shackle; pen and manicure blades; N/S-lined; 12K gold-plate handle $55

7609SS Shackle—*(2¼")* Lobster pattern with shackle; pen and manicure blades; sterling silver handle $55

7609GSIL Shac—(2¼″) Lobster pattern with shackle; pen and manicure blades; corrugated N/S handle   *$40*

C7609SS Shac—corrugated sterling silver handle   *$45*

7609GM Shac—(2¼″) Lobster pattern with shackle, pen, and manicure blades, N/S shackle; flat gunmetal handle, rounded edges   *$40*

7609GM—as above except without shackle   *$40*

E7609GOLDSha—(2¼″) Lobster pattern with shackle, 2-blade; nickel-lined; ½₀ 12K gold-filled handle   *$55*

7623¾—(3½″) Balloon pattern; clip and pen blades; brass-lined; N/S bolsters and shield; bone stag handle   *$80*

7624¾K—brown-lined cream Pyralin handle   *$75*

7633—(3⅝″) Balloon pattern; Zulu spear and pen blades; brass-lined; N/S bolsters and shield; bone stag handle   *$75*

7653—(3″) Sunfish Lobster pattern; spear and lobster file blades; brass-lined; N/S shield; bone stag handle   *$45*

7654W—as above except with ivory celluloid handle (no shield)   *$35*

7654—as above except with assorted celluloid handles (no shield)   *$40*

7656—(3″) Sunfish Lobster pattern; spear and lobster file blades; N/S-lined; mother-of-pearl handle   *$60*

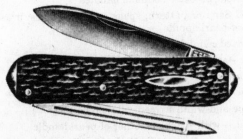

7653T—(3″) Sunfish Lobster pattern; spear and lobster file blades; brass-lined; N/S tips and shield; bone stag handle   *$45*

7654Horn T—horn celluloid handle   *$40*

7654ACT—assorted celluloid handles   *$40*

7656T Shackle—(3") Sunfish Lobster pattern with shackle; spear and lobster file blades; N/S-lined; N/S tips; mother-of-pearl handle $60

7656T—as above without shackle $50

7664M—(3¹/₁₆") Wharncliffe pattern; spear and pen blades; brass-lined; flat N/S bolsters with beveled edges; N/S shield; Marine Pearl Pyralin handle $55

7663—bone stag handle $65

R7663—(3¹/₁₆") Wharncliffe pattern; spear and blades; brass-lined; N/S bolsters and shield; bone stag handle $60

R7664E—black and pearl celluloid handle $55

R7663⅛—pen and Wharncliffe blades; bone stag handle $80

R7663¾—clip and pen blades; bone stag handle $70

R7664¾B—black celluloid handle $65

F7706—(2⅞") Senator pattern; file and pen blade; brass-lined; mother-of-pearl handle $55

F7703T—(2⅞") Senator pattern; file and pen blade; brass-lined; N/S tips and shield; bone stag handle $45

7704WT—as above except without shield; ivory celluloid handle $40

F7706T—as above except without shield; mother-of-pearl handle $55

7703—(2⅞") Senator pattern; spear and pen blades; brass-lined; N/S shield; bone stag handle $45

7706—(2⅞") Senator pattern; spear and pen blades; brass-lined; mother-of-pearl handle $60

7709GSIL—flat N/S handle $30

7706 Shackle—N/S shackle; mother-of-pearl handle $60

7709GSIL Shackle—flat N/S handle $30

7703T—(2⅞") Senator pattern; spear and pen blades; brass-lined; N/S tips and shield; bone stag handle $45

7704T—no shield; assorted celluloid handles $40

7706T—(2⅞") Senator pattern; spear and pen blades; brass-lined; N/S tips; mother-of-pearl handle $60

7704T—assorted celluloid handles $45

7704LT Shac—as above except with N/S shackle $45

7704MT—Marine Pearl Pyralin handle $45

7704MT Shac—as above except with N/S shackle $45

7704NT—blue-and-white striped celluloid handle $45

7706T Shackle—with shackle; mother-of-pearl handle $60

7704ST Shackle—tortoise shell celluloid handle $50

SS7704BT —stainless steel; black celluloid handle $45

SS7704LT—hairline pearl celluloid handle $45

SS7704LT Shac—as above except with shackle $45

SS7706T—mother-of-pearl handle $50

7703B—(2⅞") Senator pattern; spear and pen blades; brass-lined; fancy N/S bolsters and shield; bone stag handle   **$55**

7706B—no shield; mother-of-pearl handle   **$70**

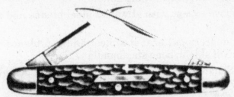

S7703B—(2⅞") Senator pattern; spear and pen blades; brass-lined; N/S bolsters and shield; bone stag handle   **$45**

S7706B—as above except without shield; mother-of-pearl handle   **$65**

M7704GT—(2⅞") Senator pattern; flexible manicure file and spear blade; brass-lined; N/S tips; green jade celluloid handle   **$40**

M7703T—as above except with shield; bone stag handle   **$45**

M7704MT—as above except with pearl celluloid handle   **$40**

M7704GT Shackle—as above except with N/S shackle; green jade celluloid handle   **$40**

M7706B—(2⅞") Senator pattern; flexible manicure file and spear blade; brass-lined; N/S bolsters; mother-of-pearl handle   **$60**

M7704NT Shac—(2⅞") Senator pattern with shackle; flexible manicure file and spear blade; brass-lined; N/S tips and shackle; blue-and-white striped celluloid handle   **$35**

M7704NT—as above except without shackle   **$35**

M7703T Shac—bone stag handle; with shield   **$45**

M7704MT Shac—Marine Pearl Pyralin handle   **$35**

M7709GOLD Shac—(2⅞") Senator pattern with shackle; flexible manicure file and spear blade; brass-lined; ½₀ 10K gold-filled handle   **$55**

M7709GOLD—as above except without shackle   **$55**

7709GOLD Shac—as above except with 2 cutting blades   **$55**

7719SS Shackle—(2⅞") Senator pattern with sterling silver shackle; spear and pen blades; thin oval sterling silver handle   **$40**

7719GSIL Shackle—N/S handle   **$35**

M7719GM—(2⅞") Senator pattern, flexible manicure file and large spear blade; oval gunmetal handle   **$35**

M7719GM Shac—as above with N/S shackle   **$35**

7743—(3") Congress pattern; sheepfoot and pen blades; steel bolsters; bone stag handle   **$70**

7744M—Marine Pearl celluloid handle   **$60**

7744K—brown-lined cream Pyralin handle   **$60**

7746—as above except with mother-of-pearl handle with N/S bolsters   **$85**

7749GS—(3") Congress pattern; sheepfoot and pen blades; brass lined; N/S bolsters; genuine stag handle $85

7753—(3½") Congress pattern; sheepfoot and pen blades; brass-lined; steel bolsters; N/S shield; bone stag handle $70

SS7753—as above except with stainless steel blades and spring; bone stag handle $90

7763—(3⅞") Congress pattern; sheepfoot and pen blades; brass-lined; steel bolsters; N/S shield; bone stag handle $85

7786—(3⁵/₁₆") Senator pattern, sunk joint; spear and pen blades; brass-lined; mother-of-pearl handle $60

7784PT—(3⁵/₁₆") Senator pattern, sunk joint; spear and pen blades; brass-lined; N/S tips and shield; Smoked Pearl celluloid handle $50

7783T—bone stag handle $55

7784MT—Marine Pearl Pyralin handle $50

7784—assorted celluloid handles $50

7786T—mother-of-pearl handle $60

7783B—(3⁵/₁₆") Senator pattern, sunk joint; spear and pen blades; brass-lined; N/S bolsters and shield; bone stag handle $55

7784B—assorted celluloid handles $50

7786B—mother-of-pearl handle $50

SS7783B—(3⁵/₁₆") Senator pattern, sunk joint, with stainless steel blades and spring; spear and pen blades; brass-lined; N/S bolsters and shield; bone stag handle $80

SS7784B —assorted celluloid handles $70

SS7786B—mother-of-pearl handle $95

7783¾B—(3⁵/₁₆") Senator pattern, sunk joint; clip and pen blades; brass-lined; N/S bolsters and shield; bone stag handle $55

7793T—(3¼") Sleeveboard Serpentine Knife with 1 spring; spear and pen blades; brass-lined; N/S tips and shield; bone stag handle $70

7794¾MT—as above except with pen and clip blades; Marine Pearl Pyralin handle $65

7793¾B—(3¼") Sleeveboard Serpentine Knife, with 1 spring; clip and pen blades; brass-lined; N/S bolsters and shield; bone stag handle $75

7803¾—(4") Sportsman's Knife; clip and 1 long clip blades; brass-lined; N/S bolsters and shield; bone stag handle $120

7813—(4") Texas Jackknife; clip and spear blades; brass-lined; N/S bolsters and shield; bone stag handle $215

7812—ebony handle $200

S7814Stg—(4") *Improved Muskrat Knife;* skinning and clip blades; brass-lined; N/S bolsters and shield; celluloid stag handle $330

S7814¾Stg—as above except with 2 slim clip blades $300

7843—(4") *Texas Jackknife;* with 1 spring; clip and spey blades; brass-lined; N/S bolsters and shield; bone stag handle $175

07894W—(3¾") *Office Knife,* equal-end pattern; spear and spey blades; brass-lined; ivory celluloid handle (stamped) $60

7894½W—(3¾") *Florist's Knife* for budding, grafting, etc.; budding and grafting blades; brass-lined; glaze-finished blades; ivory celluloid handle (stamped) $60

7903—(3½") *Premium Jackknife;* clip and spear blades; brass-lined; N/S bolsters and shield; bone stag handle $110

7904—assorted celluloid handles $100

7913—(3½") *Premium Jackknife* with 1 spring; clip and spey blades; brass-lined; N/S bolsters and shield; bone stag handle $95

7923—(3½") *Premium Jackknife* with 1 spring; clip and pen blades; brass-lined; N/S bolsters and shield; bone stag handle $70

7924G—as above except with Green Pearl Pyralin handle $65

7924—assorted celluloid handles $65

7936—(2½") Senator pattern, sunk joint; 2 pen blades; N/S-lined; mother-of-pearl handle $55

7939GSIL—N/S handle $35

7933T—as above except with N/S tips; bone stag handle $45

7936T—as above except one side crocus-polished; mother-of-pearl handle $55

7934BT—(2½") Senator pattern, sunk joint; 2 pen blades; N/S linings and tips; black celluloid handle $35

7934WT—ivory celluloid handle $35

7933T Shac—as above except with N/S shackle; assorted celluloid handles $40

7934BT Shac—as above except with black celluloid handle $40

7934WT Shac—as above except with ivory celluloid handle $40

7936T Shac—as above except with mother-of-pearl handle $65

M7936T Shac—(2½") Senator pattern, sunk joint, with N/S shackle; flexible manicure file and spear blade; N/S linings and tips, mother-of-pearl handle $60

M7933T Shac—bone stag handle $50

M7936—as above except without N/S shackle or tips; mother-of-pearl handle $50

M7936 Shac—same as above without N/S tips $55

R7973—(4¼") *Equal-end Jackknife;* large clip and spear blades; brass-lined; N/S bolsters and shield; bone stag handle $310

3053½—(3⅝″) Electrician's Knife; screwdriver–wire scraper, pen and sheepfoot blades; brass-lined; N/S bolsters, caps, and shield; bone stag handle	$200

81016Sha—(2½″) Sleeveboard Lobster pattern with shackle, spear, pen, and manicure blades; N/S-lined, with milled edges; mother-of-pearl handle	$65

C8083B—(3″) Senator pattern, sunk joint; spear, coping pen, and curly-point nail file blades; N/S linings, bolsters, and shield; bone stag handle	$85

8089GSB—(3″) Senator pattern; spear, pen, and manicure blades; N/S-lined; genuine stag handle	$85

*8083B—*bone stag handle	$75

S8083B—(3″) Scissors Knife, Senator pattern, sunk joint; pen, and spear blades and scissors; N/S linings and bolsters; bone stag handle	$80

FS8086B—(3″) Scissors Knife, Senator pattern, sunk joint; spear blade, curly-point nail file, and scissors; N/S linings and bolsters; mother-of-pearl handle	$95

8099GSIL—(3¹/₁₆″) Senator pattern; flexible manicure file, spear, and pen blades; satin-finish N/S handle	$45

81043—(4⁵/₁₆″) Premium Stock Knife; clip, spey, and sheepfoot blades; N/S linings, bolsters, and shield; bone stag handle	$300

*71043—*two-blade knife, as above except with large clip and long spey blades	$275

8103—(3⅛") Senator pattern; spear, sheepfoot, and pen blades; brass-lined; N/S bolsters and shield; bone stag handle   *$75*

8104P—Smoked Pearl celluloid handle   *$70*

8104¼LB—as above except with leather punch, spey, and spear blades; assorted celluloid handles   *$70*

8103¼LB—as above except with leather punch, spey, and spear blades; bone stag handle   *$75*

S8103—(3⅛") Equal-end Small Cattle Knife; clip, spey, and punch blades; brass-lined; N/S bolsters and shield; bone stag handle   *$75*

S8104—assorted celluloid handles   *$70*

81004⅜Stg—(3⅞") Carpenter's Knife; saber clip, small clip, and coping pen blades; brass-lined; N/S bolsters and shield; Fibestos handles   *$150*

8116—(3⅜") Sleeveboard pattern; spear, pen, and curly-point file blades; brass-lined; mother-of-pearl handle   *$110*

8114W—ivory celluloid handle   *$90*

8113T—(3⅜") Sleeveboard pattern; spear, pen, and curly-point file blades; brass-lined; N/S tips and shield; bone stag handle   *$90*

8114PT—Smoked Pearl celluloid handle   *$90*

8114ST—tortoise shell celluloid handle   *$90*

8116T—mother-of-pearl handle   *$110*

8118T—buffalo horn handle with shield   *$105*

8113B—(3⅜") Sleeveboard pattern; spear, pen, and curly-point file blades; brass-lined; N/S bolsters and shield; bone stag handle   *$100*

8114SB—tortoise shell celluloid handle   *$100*

8114PB—Smoked Pearl Celluloid handle $100

8116B—mother-of-pearl handle $135

8118B—buffalo horn handle with shield $125

8133¾—(3¼") Norfolk Cattle Knife; clip, spey, and pen blades; brass-lined; N/S bolsters and shield; bone stag handle $105

8134¾KLB—(3¼") Norfolk Cattle Knife; clip, spear, and punch blades; brass-lined; N/S bolsters and shield; brown-lined cream Pyralin handle $105

8146T—(3⅛") Senator pattern, sunk joint; spear, pen, and file blades; N/S-lined; N/S tips and shield; mother-of-pearl handle $110

8143T—as above except brass lined; bone stag handle $100

8149GST—as above except N/S-lined; genuine stag handle $110

8143B—(3⅛") Senator pattern; spear, pen, and file blades; brass-lined; N/S bolsters and shield; bone stag handle $90

8149GSB—genuine stag handle $110

SL8146B—(3⅛") Senator pattern; long spear, pen, and file blades; sunk joint, N/S-lined; N/S bolsters; mother-of-pearl handle $120

8163—(3⅝") Cattle Knife; spear, spey, and sheepfoot blades; brass-lined; N/S bolsters and shield; bone stag handle $130

8173—(3⅝") Cattle Knife; spear, sheepfoot, and pen blades; brass-lined; N/S bolsters and shield; bone stag handle $130

8172—ebony handle $110

8174GP—Golden Pearl Pyralin handle $115

8174W—ivory celluloid handle $115

8176—(3⅝") Cattle Knife; spear, sheepfoot, and pen blades, brass-lined; N/S bolsters and shield; mother-of-pearl handle $245

8179GS—genuine stag handle $200

8173¼—(3⅝") Cattle Knife; spey, sheepfoot, and pen blades; brass-lined; N/S bolsters and shield; bone stag handle $135

SS8173—(3⅝") Cattle Knife with stainless steel blades and springs; spear, sheepfoot, and pen blades; brass-lined; N/S bolsters and shield; bone stag handle $170

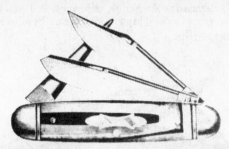

S8174¼K—(3⅝") Cattle Knife; clip, spey, and punch blades; brass-lined; N/S bolsters and shield; brown-lined cream Pyralin handle   *$175*

S8173¼—bone stag handle   *$190*

8174¾X—(3⅝") Cattle Knife; clip, sheepfoot, and pen blades; brass-lined; N/S bolsters and shield; mottled green celluloid handle   *$125*

8173¾—bone stag handle   *$125*

8174¾G—Green Pearl Pyralin handle   *$120*

8174¾W—ivory celluloid handle   *$120*

8182—(3⅝") Cattle Knife; spear, spey, and pen blades; brass-lined; N/S bolsters and shield; ebony handle   *$100*

8183—bone stag handle   *$130*

8313T—(3⅜") Sleeveboard pattern; spear and 2 pen blades; brass-lined; N/S tips and shield; bone stag handle   *$100*

8313B—as above except N/S bolsters substituted for tips   *$115*

8316B—as above except N/S bolsters substituted for tips; no shield; mother-of-pearl handle   *$165*

8323B—(4") Equal-end Knife; spear, clip, and pen blades; brass-lined; N/S bolsters and shield; bone stag handle   *$200*

8323—(3⅜") Sleeveboard pattern; spear, pen, and curly-point file blades; brass-lined; N/S bolsters at one end; N/S shield; bone stag handle   *$110*

8324S—tortoise shell celluloid handle   *$105*

8344K—(3⁵/₁₆″) Serpentine Jackknife; clip, spey, and pen blades; brass-lined; N/S bolsters and shield; brown-lined cream Pyralin handle   *$85*

8343—bone stag handle   *$95*

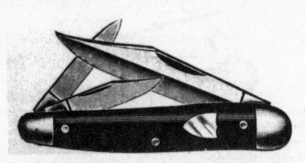

8364³/₈B—(3⁹/₁₆″) Serpentine Knife; saber clip, small clip, and pen blades; brass-lined; N/S bolsters and shield; black celluloid handle   *$115*

SC8364³/₈B—as above except with coping blade substituted for pen blade   *$115*

S8363³/₈—(3⁹/₁₆″) Carpenter's Knife, Serpentine pattern; saber clip, coping pen and regular pen blades; brass-lined; N/S bolsters and shield; bone stag handle   *$175*

S8364³/₈B—black celluloid handle   *$150*

S8363³/₈—same as above except with coping blade substituted for small clip blade; bone stag handle   *$140*

S8373—(3⁵/₈″) Cattle Knife; spear, spey, and punch blades; brass-lined; N/S bolsters and shield; bone stag handle   *$130*

S8374G—green pearl handle   *$125*

S8374—assorted celluloid handles   *$125*

S8374³/₈R—(3⁵/₈″) Cattle Knife; saber clip, spey, and leather punch blades; brass-lined; N/S bolsters and shield; red celluloid handle   *$120*

S8373³/₈—bone stag handle   *$130*

S8374³/₄K—(3⁵/₈″) Cattle Knife; clip, spey, and punch blades; brass-lined; N/S bolsters and shield; brown-lined cream Pyralin handle   *$125*

S8373³/₄—bone stag handle   *$135*

S8374³/₄—assorted celluloid handles   *$130*

8384G—(3⁵/₈″) Cattle Knife; spear, pen, and punch blades; brass-lined; N/S bolsters and shield; Green Pearl Pyralin handle   *$130*

8384GP—Golden Pearl Pyralin handle   *$130*

8384—assorted celluloid handles   *$130*

8383—bone stag handle   *$145*

8383³/₄—as above except clip blade substituted for spear pocket; bone stag handle   *$145*

M8426—(3¹/₈″) Senator pattern; long manicure file, pen, and spear blades; brass-lined; N/S shield; mother-of-pearl handle   *$85*

M8424PT—(3⅛") Senator pattern; long manicure file, pen, and spear blades; brass-lined; N/S tips and shield; Smoked Pearl celluloid handle   *$55*

M8423T—bone stag handle   *$60*

M8426T—mother-of-pearl handle   *$80*

M8423B—(3⅛") Senator pattern; long manicure file, pen, and spear blades; brass-lined; N/S bolsters and shield; bone stag handle   *$60*

M8426B—mother-of-pearl handle   *$70*

8423T—(3⅛") Senator pattern; spear, pen, and file blades; brass-lined; N/S tips and shield; bone stag handle   *$80*

8426T—mother-of-pearl handle   *$100*

8424PB—(3⅛") Senator pattern; spear, pen, and file blades; brass-lined; N/S bolsters and shield; Smoked Pearl celluloid handle   *$85*

8423B—bone stag handle   *90*

8426B—mother-of-pearl handle   *$120*

8424¾MB—(3⅛") Senator pattern; long clip, file, and pen blades; brass-lined; N/S bolsters and shield; Marine Pearl Pyralin handle   *$90*

8423¾B—bone stag handle   *$105*

L8423B—(3⅛") Senator pattern; long spear, pen, and file blades; brass-lined; N/S bolsters and shield; bone stag handle   *$90*

L8424PB—Smoked Pearl celluloid handles   *$85*

8424SqMB—(3⅛") Senator pattern; spear, pen, and file blades; brass-lined; flat N/S bolsters with beveled edges; N/S shield; Marine Pearl celluloid handle   *$75*

8443—(3⅝") Automobile and Electrician's Knife, equal-end pattern; leather punch, screwdriver–wire scraper–file and spear blade; brass-lined; N/S bolsters and shield; bone stag handle   *$165*

8456—(3⅛") Scissors Knife, Senator pattern; curly-point nail file, spear blade, and scissors; brass-lined; N/S shield; mother-of-pearl handle   *$85*

8453T—(3⅛") Scissors Knife; Senator pattern; curly-point nail file, spear blade, and scissors; brass-lined; N/S tips and shield; bone stag handle *$85*

8456T—mother-of-pearl handle   *$100*

8456B—(3⅛") Scissors Knife, Senator pattern; curly-point nail file, spear blade, and scissors; brass-lined; N/S bolsters and shield; mother-of-pearl handle   *$135*

8463—(3⅝") Automobile and Camper's Knife, equal-end pattern; screwdriver–wire scraper–file, can opener–cap lifter and spear blade; brass-lined; N/S bolsters and shield; bone stag handle   *$165*

8479GM Shac—(2¾") Sleeveboard Lobster pattern with shackle; spear, pen, and manicure blades; N/S shackle; flat gunmetal handle, beveled edges   *$40*

8479GM—as above except without shackle   *$45*

8476 Shac—(2¾") Sleeveboard Lobster pattern with shackle; spear, pen, and manicure blades; N/S linings and shackle; mother-of-pearl handle with beveled edges   *$65*

8476—as above except without shackle $65

8479GSIL Shac—(2¾") Sleeveboard Lobster pattern with shackle; spear, pen, and manicure blades; satin-finish N/S handle $40

8479GSIL—as above except without shackle $40

8554⅜B—(3¼") Serpentine Balloon pattern; saber clip, small clip, and pen blades; brass-lined; N/S bolsters and shield; black celluloid handle $120

8566—(3⅜") *Cattle Knife;* spear, sheepfoot, and pen blades; brass-lined; N/S bolsters and shield; mother-of-pearl handle $175

8563—as above except with large blade crocus-polished one side; bone stag handle $145

8564—assorted Pyralin handles $140

8563¾—as above except with clip blade substituted for spear blade; bone stag handle $140

8564¾—assorted Pyralin handles $140

8574¾AP—(3⅜") *Cattle Knife;* clip, spey, and pen blades; brass-lined; N/S bolsters and shield; Abalone Pearl Pyralin handle $110

8573¾—bone stag handle $110

8583—(3⅜") *Cattle Knife;* spear, spey, and punch blades; brass-lined; N/S bolsters and shield; bone stag handle $130

8584 Horn—horn Pyralin handle $120

8584 —assorted celluloid handles $115

8584¾GP—(3⅜") *Cattle Knife;* clip, spey, and punch blades; brass-lined; N/S bolsters and shield; Golden Pearl Pyralin handle $130

8584¾K—brown-lined cream Pyralin handle $125

8584¾—assorted celluloid handles $125

8584K—as above except with spear blade substituted for clip blade; brown-lined cream Pyralin handle $125

8584M—Marine Pearl celluloid handle $125

S8583—(3⅜") *Cattle Knife;* spear, sheepfoot, and punch blades; brass-lined; N/S bolsters and shield; bone stag handle $120

8593—(3⅜″) *Cattle Knife;* spear, pen, and punch blades; brass-lined; N/S bolsters and shield; bone stag handle $110

8594G—Green Pearl Pyralin handle $100

8594¾X—(3⅜″) *Cattle Knife;* clip, pen, and punch blades; brass-lined; N/S bolsters and shield; mottled green celluloid handle $105

8606—(2¼″) Lobster pattern; manicure and 2 pen blades; N/S-lined with milled edges; mother-of-pearl handle $60

8604—assorted celluloid handles $40

8604W *Shackle*—(2¼″) Lobster pattern with shackle; manicure and 2 pen blades; brass-lined; ivory celluloid handle $35

8604 *Shackle*—assorted celluloid handles $45

8606 *Shackle*—as above except with mother-of-pearl handle and N/S linings with milled edges $55

8606 *Shackle Emblem*—as above except with mother-of-pearl handle with emblem and N/S linings with milled edges $60

8609 *Gold Shackle*—(2¼″) Lobster pattern with shackle; nail file, spear, and pen blades; N/S-lined; 12K gold-plate handle $50

8609SS *Shackle*—(2¼″) Lobster pattern with shackle; spear, pen, and manicure blades; sterling silver handle $50

S8606 *Shac*—(2¼″) *Scissors Knife,* Lobster pattern, with shackle; flexible manicure file, pen blade, and scissors; N/S-lined, edges milled; N/S shackle; mother-of-pearl handle $70

8609GM *Shac*—(2¼″) Lobster pattern with shackle; flexible manicure file, pen, and spear blades; N/S shackle; flat gunmetal handle, rounded edges $40

8609GM—as above except without shackle $40

S8609GM *Shac*—(2¼″) *Scissors Knife,* Lobster pattern with shackle; flexible manicure file, spear blade, and scissors; N/S shackle; flat gunmetal handle, rounded edges $45

8614Y—(4″) *Slim Premium Stock Knife;* long clip, sheepfoot, and spey blades; N/S linings, bolsters, and shield; mottled horn celluloid handle $120

8613—bone stag handle $145

8614M—Marine Pearl Pyralin handle $110

8613LB—(4″) *Slim Premium Stock Knife;* long clip, spey, and punch blades; N/S linings, bolsters, and shield; bone stag handle $185

8614MLB—Marine Pearl Pyralin $170

8614YLB—mottled horn celluloid handle $170

8623¾LB—(3½″) *Balloon-pattern Cattle Knife;* clip, spey, and punch blades; brass-lined; N/S bolsters and shield; bone stag handle $125

8624¾KLB—brown-lined cream Pyralin handle $120

C8633¾—(3⅝″) Balloon pattern; clip, coping pen, and regular pen blades; brass-lined; N/S bolsters and shield; bone stag handle $145

SC8633¾—as above except small clip blade substituted for pen blade $145

8653—*(3")* Sunfish Lobster pattern; spear, pen, and manicure blades; brass-lined; N/S shield; bone stag handle $50

8654W—as above except with ivory celluloid handle (no shield) $45

8654—as above except with assorted celluloid handles (no shield) $45

8656—*(3")* Sunfish Lobster pattern; spear, pen, and manicure blades; N/S-lined, with milled edges; mother-of-pearl handle $65

8656 Emblem—with emblem; mother-of-pearl handle $80

8654SqW—*(3")* Sunfish Lobster pattern; spear, pen, and manicure blades, brass-lined; ivory celluloid handle with beveled edges $40

8654Sq—assorted celluloid handles $40

8653T—*(3")* Sunfish Lobster pattern; spear, pen, and manicure blades; brass-lined; N/S tips and shield; bone stag handle $55

8654T—assorted celluloid handles $45

8656T—*(3")* Sunfish Lobster pattern; spear, pen, and manicure blades; N/S-lined, with milled edges; N/S tips; mother-of-pearl handle $65

8656T Shackle $70

8656T Shackle Emblem—as above $75

8654MT—*(3")* Sunfish Lobster pattern; spear, pen, and manicure blades; brass-lined; N/S tips; Marine Pearl Pyralin handle $50

8654MTSha—as above except with N/S shackle $50

8666T—*(3")* Sunfish Lobster pattern; cutting-point nail file, spear, and pen blades; N/S-lined, with milled edges, N/S tips; mother-of-pearl handle $65

8666—as above except without N/S tips $55

8676—*(3")* Sleeveboard Lobster pattern; spear, pen, and manicure blades; N/S-lined, with milled edges; mother-of-pearl handle $65

8674GL Shackle—as above except with goldaleur celluloid handle, with N/S shackle $45

8676 Shackle—as above except with mother-of-pearl handle $65

8679GSil Shackle—as above except with N/S handle; N/S shackle $45

8676T Shackle—*(3")* Sleeveboard Lobster pattern with shackle; spear, pen, and manicure blades; N/S linings, milled; N/S tips; mother-of-pearl handle $75

8673T Shackle —as above except with shield; bone stag handle $60

8673T—*(3")* Sleeveboard Lobster pattern; spear, pen, and manicure blades; N/S-lined, with milled edges; N/S tips and shield; bone stag handle $50

8676T—as above except with mother-of-pearl handle (no shield) $60

8679GM Shac—(3") Sleeveboard Lobster pattern with shackle; spear, pen, and manicure blades; N/S shackle; gunmetal handle, rounded edges   *$45*

8679GM—as above except without shackle   *$45*

8686—(3") Sleeveboard Lobster pattern; spear, pen, and manicure blades; N/S-lined, with milled edges; mother-of-pearl handle   *$65*

8683—bone stag handle   *$55*

8683T—(3") Sleeveboard Lobster pattern; spear, pen, and manicure blades; N/S-lined, with milled edges; N/S tips; bone stag handle   *$55*

8704MT—(2⅞") Senator pattern; flexible manicure file, long spear, and pen blades; brass-lined; N/S tips; Marine Pearl celluloid handle *$50*

8704¾BT—(2⅞") Senator pattern; flexible manicure file, long clip, and pen blades; brass-lined; N/S tips; black celluloid handle   *$50*

8706T—as above except with N/S lining; mother-of-pearl handle   *$70*

8706B—(2⅞") Senator pattern; flexible manicure file, long spear pocket and pen blades; brass-lined; N/S bolsters; mother-of-pearl handle *$70*

8729GSIL—(2⁹⁄₁₆") Oval Lobster pattern; spear, pen, and file blades; N/S handle   *$35*

8729GSIL Shac—as above except with shackle   *$35*

SS8729I—as above except with stainless steel blades and stainless metal handle   *$35*

SS8729I Shac—as above except with shackle   *$35*

8729GM Shac—(2⁹⁄₁₆") Oval Lobster pattern with shackle; spear, pen, and nail file blades; N/S shackle; flat gunmetal handle, beveled edges   *$40*

8729GM—as above except without shackle   *$40*

8729GOLD Shac—(2⁹⁄₁₆") Oval Lobster pattern with shackle; spear, pen, and curly-point file blades; brass-lined; ¹⁄₂₀ 10K gold-filled handle *$45*

8729GOLD—as above except without shackle   *$45*

SS8729ET Shac—(2⁹⁄₁₆") Oval Lobster pattern with shackle; stainless steel blades; spear, pen, and file blades; N/S shackle; stainless metal handle, engine-turned   *$35*

8779GM—(2⅞") Scissors Knife, Lobster pattern, flexible manicure file, spear blade, and scissors; flat gunmetal handle, rounded edges   *$50*

8779GM Shac—as above except with nickel silver shackle   *$50*

8776—(2⅞") Scissors Knife; file, scissors, and spear blade; brass-lined; N/S bolsters and shield; bone stag handle   *$100*

8779GSIL—N/S handle   *$55*

8786B—(3⁵⁄₁₆") Senator pattern, sunk joint; spear, pen, and file blades; brass-lined; N/S bolsters and shield; mother-of-pearl handle *$120*

8783B—bone stag handle   *$105*

8794KT—(3¼") Sleeveboard Serpentine Knife; spear and 2 pen blades; brass-lined; N/S tips and shield; brown-lined cream Pyralin handle *$110*

8793T—bone stag handle   *$120*

8793⅛B—(3¼") Sleeveboard Serpentine Knife; Wharncliffe blade and two pen blades; brass-lined; N/S bolsters and shield; bone stag handle   *$150*

8803—(4") Premium Stock Knife; clip, sheepfoot, and spey blades; brass-lined; round-end N/S bolsters and shield; bone stag handle   *$160*

M8806—as above except with mother-of-pearl handle; fancy milled back   *$325*

SS8813—(4") Premium Stock Knife, Texas pattern, with stainless steel blades; clip, spey, and sheepfoot blades; brass-lined; N/S bolsters and shield; bone stag handle   *$250*

8813—(4") Premium Stock Knife, Texas pattern; clip, spey, and sheepfoot blades; brass-lined; N/S bolsters and shield; bone stag handle   *$180*

S08814NP—(4") Premium Stock Knife, Texas pattern with oblique bolsters; clip, sheepfoot, and spey blades; brass-lined; N/S bolsters and shield; opal celluloid handle   *$165*

8814P—(4") Premium Stock Knife, Texas pattern; clip, sheepfoot, and spey blades; brass-lined; N/S bolsters and shield; Smoked Pearl celluloid handle   *$170*

8814G—Green Pearl celluloid handle   *$170*

8814GP—Golden Pearl Pyralin handle   *$170*

8814X—mottled green celluloid handle   *$170*

8823—(4") Premium Stock Knife; clip, sheepfoot, and punch blades; brass-lined; round-end N/S bolsters and shield; bone stag handle   *$180*

8833—(4") Premium Stock Knife; clip, spey, and punch blades; brass-lined; N/S bolsters and shield; bone stag handle   *$200*

8834K—brown-lined cream Pyralin handle   *$175*

8834AP—Abalone Pearl Pyralin handle   *$175*

8834Horn—horn Pyralin handle   *$175*

08834AP—(4") Premium Stock Knife, Texas pattern with oblique bolsters; clip, spey, and punch blades; brass-lined; N/S bolsters and shield; Abalone Pearl Pyralin handle $185

08833—bone stag handle $190

08834—assorted celluloid handles $185

8853—(3⁵⁄₁₆") Serpentine Knife; clip, pen, and punch blades; brass-lined; N/S bolsters and shield; bone stag handle $105

8854K—brown-lined cream Pyralin handle $90

8853¼—(3⁵⁄₁₆") Serpentine Knife; clip, spey, and punch blades; brass-lined; N/S bolsters and shield; bone stag handle $105

8854¼K—brown-lined cream Pyralin handle $90

8854¼—assorted celluloid handles $90

8873—(4") Premium Stock Knife; clip, sheepfoot, and pen blades; brass-lined; round-end N/S bolsters and shield; bone stag handle $150

8874—assorted celluloid handles $130

8876—mother-of-pearl handle $300

08883—(4") Premium Stock Knife, Texas pattern with oblique bolsters; clip, sheepfoot, and pen blades; brass-lined; N/S bolsters and shield; bone stag handle $195

8903—(3½") Premium Stock Knife; clip, sheepfoot, and spey blades; brass-lined; N/S bolsters and shield; bone stag handle $90

8904K—brown-lined cream Pyralin handle $85

8904—assorted celluloid handles $75

8913—(3½") Premium Stock Knife; clip, spey, and punch blades; brass-lined; N/S bolsters and shield; bone stag handle $95

8914Horn—(3½") Premium Stock Knife; clip, spey, and punch blades; brass-lined; N/S bolsters and shield; horn Pyralin handle $90

8914AP—Abalone Pearl Pyralin handle $90

8914G—Green Pearl Pyralin handle $90

8914K—brown-lined cream Pyralin handle $90

8914—assorted Pyralin handles $90

8924GP—(3½") Premium Stock Knife; clip, sheepfoot, and pen blades; brass-lined; N/S bolsters and shield; Golden Pearl Pyralin handle $85

8923—bone stag handle $95

8924—assorted Pyralin handles $85

8964K—(3⁹⁄₁₆") Slim Premium Stock Knife; long clip, sheepfoot, and spey blades; brass-lined; N/S bolsters and shield; brown-lined cream Pyralin handle $120

8963—bone stag handle $130

8964GP—Golden Pearl Pyralin handle $120

8964M—Marine Pearl celluloid handle $120

8983—(3⁹/₁₆") Slim Premium Stock Knife; long clip, sheepfoot, and spey blades; brass-lined; N/S bolsters and shield; bone stag handle $140

*8984GP—*Golden Pearl Pyralin handle $120

*8984K—*brown-lined cream Pyralin handle $120

*8984M—*Marine Pearl celluloid handle $120

8984¼GP—(3⁹/₁₆") Slim Premium Stock Knife; long clip, spey, and pen blades; brass-lined; N/S bolsters and shield; Golden Pearl Pyralin handle $120

*8983¼—*bone stag handle $135

*8984¼K—*brown-lined cream Pyralin handle $120

*8984¼M—*Marine Pearl celluloid handle $125

8994M—(3⁹/₁₆") Slim Premium Stock Knife; long clip, sheepfoot, and punch blades; brass-lined; N/S bolsters and shield; Marine Pearl celluloid handle $130

*8993—*bone stag handle $140

*8994GP—*Golden Pearl Pyralin handle $125

*8994K—*brown-lined cream Pyralin handle $125

8993¼—(3⁹/₁₆") Slim Premium Stock Knife; long clip, spey, and punch blades; brass-lined; N/S bolsters and shield; bone stag handle $135

*8994¼GP—*Golden Pearl Pyralin handle $120

*8994¼K—*brown-lined cream Pyralin handle $120

*8994¼M —*Marine Pearl celluloid handle $120

9033—(3⁵/₈") Automobile Knife, equal-end pattern; auto chain hook, leather punch, screwdriver–cap lifter and spear blades; brass-lined; N/S bolsters and shield; bone stag handle $150

*9039GSIL—*solid N/S handle $120

9113B—(3⅜") Sleeveboard pattern; spear, sheepfoot, pen, and file blades; brass-lined; N/S bolsters and shield; bone stag handle $105

*9116B—*mother-of-pearl handle $135

9124M—(3¼") Champagne Knife; pen and spear blades, corkscrew, and combination champagne hook–cap lifter; N/S-lined; Marine Pearl Pyralin handle $125

9124B—black celluloid handle   *$125*

9129GSil—thick oval N/S handle   *$125*

9146T—(*3⅛″*) Senator pattern, sunk joint; spear, file, and 2 pen blades;
N/S tips and shield; mother-of-pearl handle   *$105*

9143T—as above except brass-lined; bone stag handle   *$100*

9144GLT—as above except brass-lined; goldaleur celluloid handle   *$90*

9144WT—as above except brass-lined; ivory celluloid handle   *$85*

9146—as above except N/S-lined, milled backs, without N/S tip; mother-
of-pearl handle   *$100*

9149GST—(*3⅛″*) Senator pattern, sunk joint, spear, file, and 2 pen
blades; N/S-lined; full milled backs; N/S tips and shield; genuine stag
handle   *$125*

9144WB—(*3⅛″*) Senator pattern, sunk joint; spear, file, and 2 pen blades;
brass lined; N/S bolsters and shield; ivory celluloid handle   *$75*

9143B—bone stag handle   *$85*

9173—(*3⅝″*) *Cattle Knife;* clip, spear, sheepfoot, and pen blades; brass-
lined; N/S bolsters and shield; bone stag handle   *$190*

9426—(*3⅛″*) Senator pattern; spear, file, and 2 pen blades; brass-lined;
N/S shield; mother-of-pearl handle   *$100*

9426T—(*3⅛″*) Senator pattern; spear, file, and 2 pen blades; brass-lined;
N/S tips and shield; mother-of-pearl handle   *$100*

9423T—bone stag handle   *$80*

9426B—(*3⅛″*) Senator pattern; spear, file, and 2 pen blades; brass-lined;
N/S bolsters and shield; mother-of-pearl handle   *$105*

9423B—bone stag handle   *$90*

9424PB—Smoked Pearl celluloid handle   *$85*

M9456T—(*3⅛″*) *Scissors Knife,* Senator pattern; pen and spear blades,
scissors, and long manicure file; brass-lined; N/S tips and shield; mother-
of-pearl handle   *$145*

C9463¾—(*3⅝″*) *Sportsman's Knife;* clip blade, corkscrew, can opener, and
combination screwdriver–cap lifter; N/S linings, bolsters, and shield;
bone stag handle   *$150*

SD9463—(3⅝") *Sportsman's Knife;* spear blade, can opener, leather punch, and combination screwdriver–cap lifter; N/S linings, bolsters, and shield; bone stag handle $140

9463—(3⅝") *Boy Scout Knife;* leather punch, can opener, screwdriver–cap lifter, and spear blades; brass-lined; N/S bolsters, shield, and shackle; bone stag handle $160

9464US—red-white-blue celluloid handle $190

D9463—(3⅝") *Scout Knife;* large spear blade, can opener, leather punch, and a combination screwdriver–cap lifter; N/S linings, bolsters, shield, and shackle; bone stag handle $200

M9466—(3⅝") *Boy Scout Knife;* leather punch, can opener, screwdriver–cap lifter, and spear blades; brass-lined; N/S bolsters, shield, and shackle; fancy milled edges on back of linings and centers; mother-of-pearl handle $270

S9463—(3⅝") *Boy Scout Knife* without shackle (Everybody's Companion); leather punch, can opener, screwdriver–cap lifter, and spear blades; brass-lined; N/S bolsters and shield; bone stag handle $155

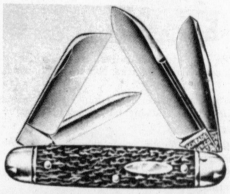

9563—(3⅜") *Cattle Knife;* spear, sheepfoot, spey, and pen blades; brass-lined; N/S bolsters and shield; bone stag handle $190

9583—(3⅜") *Cattle Knife;* spear, sheepfoot, pen, and punch blades; brass-lined; N/S bolsters and shield; bone stag handle $185

9593—(3⅜") *Junior Boy Scout Knife;* leather punch, can opener–cap lifter, screwdriver–radio wire scraper, and spear blades; brass-lined; N/S bolsters, shield, and shackle; bone stag handle $170

9594US—red-white-blue celluloid handles $205

G9594US—(3⅜") *Girl Scout Knife;* leather punch, can opener–cap lifter, screwdriver–radio wire scraper, and spear blades; brass-lined; N/S bolsters, shield, and shackle; red-white-blue celluloid handle $205

G9593—bone stag handle $200

G9594M—Marine Pearl Pyralin handle $195

G9596—as above except with crocus-polished spear blade; mother-of-pearl handle   *$265*

9606—(2¼″) Lobster pattern; spear, file, and 2 pen blades; N/S-lined, with milled edges; mother-of-pearl handle   *$65*

9604—as above except with assorted celluloid handles; brass-lined   *$45*

9604W Shackle—(2¼″) Lobster pattern with shackle; file and 3 pen blades; brass-lined; ivory celluloid handle   *$45*

9604 Shackle—assorted celluloid handles   *$45*

9606 Shackle—as above except with mother-of-pearl handle; N/S linings with milled edges   *$65*

9609 Gold Shackle—(2¼″) Lobster pattern with shackle; file and 3 pen blades; N/S-lined; 12K gold-plated handle   *$60*

9676T—(3″) Scissors Knife, Sleeveboard Lobster pattern; manicure file, pen and spear blades, and scissors; N/S lining and tips; mother-of-pearl handle   *$95*

9679SS—(3″) Scissors Knife, Sleeveboard Lobster pattern; manicure file, pen and spear blades, and scissors; solid sterling silver handle; engine-turned   *$50*

9709GST—(2⅞″) Senator pattern; flexible manicure; surgical lance blade; spear, pocket, and pen blades; N/S linings, milled; N/S tips and shield; genuine stag handle   *$80*

9704GT—without shield; Green Jade celluloid handle   *$70*

9704MT—without shield; Marine Pearl celluloid handle   *$70*

9706T—without shield; mother-of-pearl handle   *$85*

9703B—(2⅞″) Senator pattern; flexible manicure file, surgical lance blade, spear pocket and pen blade; brass-lined; N/S bolsters and shield; bone stag handle   *$65*

9706B—without shield; mother-of-pearl handle   *$85*

9736 Shac—(2⅝″) Scissors Knife, Oval Lobster pattern with shackle; manicure file, pen and spear blades, and scissors; N/S linings and shackle; mother-of-pearl handle   *$80*

9736—as above except without shackle   *$80*

9739GM Shac—(2⅝″) Scissors Knife, Lobster pattern with shackle; manicure file, pen and spear blades, and scissors; N/S shackle; oval gunmetal handle   *$55*

9739GM—as above except without shackle   *$55*

9746—(3″) Congress pattern; 2 sheepfoot and 2 pen blades; brass-lined; N/S bolsters; 1 large blade crocus-polished on one side; mother-of-pearl handle   *$145*

9743—bone stag handle   *$115*

9753—(3½″) Congress pattern; 2 sheepfoot and 2 pen blades; brass-lined; steel bolsters; N/S shield; 1 large blade crocus-polished on one side; bone stag handle   *$145*

F9753—3 blades and nail file; bone stag handle   *$140*

9763—(3⅞") Congress pattern; 2 sheepfoot and 2 pen blades; brass-lined; steel bolsters; N/S shield; 1 large blade crocus-polished on one side; bone stag handle   *$200*

9783T—(3⁵⁄₁₆") Senator pattern, sunk joint; spear, file, and 2 pen blades; brass-lined; N/S tips and shield; bone stag handle   *$85*

9786T—mother-of-pearl handle   *$100*

9783B—(3⁵⁄₁₆") Senator pattern, sunk joint; spear, file, and 2 pen blades; brass-lined; N/S bolsters and shield; bone stag handle   *$85*

9786B—mother-of-pearl handle   *$110*

9803LB—(4") Premium Stock Knife; clip, spey, pen, and punch blades; brass-lined; round-end N/S bolsters and shield; bone stag handle   *$275*

M9806—(4") Premium Stock Knife; clip, sheepfoot, spey, and pen blades; N/S-lined, with full milled back; round-end N/S bolsters and shield; mother-of-pearl handle   *$375*

M9803—as above except with clip blade crocus-polished on one side; bone stag handle, milled back   *$290*

Safety Push-Button Pocket Knives

Note. Since 1957, federal law has prohibited interstate sales or transportation of switchblade knives. Most, but not all, state and local laws prohibit possession or owning of automatic-opening knives. The collector would be well advised to understand ordinances specific to his or her location.

1404¾W—(3⅜") 1 clip blade; brass-lined; ivory celluloid handle   *$110*

1404¾K—brown-lined cream Pyralin handle   *$115*

1404¾—assorted celluloid handles   *$115*

1514J—(4") Dagger type; slim clip blade; brass-lined; N/S bolsters and caps; red-white-amber striped Pyralin handle   *$165*

1514—assorted celluloid handles   *$165*

G1514K—(4") Dagger type; slim clip blade; brass-lined; N/S bolsters with guard; N/S caps; brown-lined cream Pyralin handle   *$165*

G1514—assorted celluloid handles   *$165*

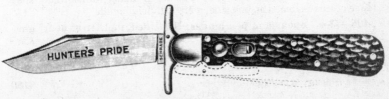

G1543¾—(4⅞") Folding guard; clip blade; steel-lined; N/S bolsters and folding guard; glaze-finished blade; bone stag handle   *$400*

G1544¾M—as above except with crocus-polished blades; Marine Pearl Pyralin handle   *$380*

G1544¾—as above except with crocus-polished blades; assorted celluloid handles   *$380*

1543¾—(4⅞") Hunting Knife; clip blade; steel-lined; steel bolsters; glaze-finished blade; bone stag handle   *$325*

B1544¾—as above except bronze linings; assorted celluloid handles   *$300*

1553¾—(4¼") Clip blade; steel-lined; steel bolsters; glaze-finished blade; bone stag handle   *$185*

1553—spear blade; bone stag handle   *$185*

1554¾M—clip blade; N/S bolsters; crocus-polished blade; Marine Pearl Pyralin handle   *$170*

1613¾—(4⅞") Saber clip blade; steel-lined; N/S bolsters; blade half crocus-polished on one side; bone stag handle   *$300*

740SSD—(3⅜") Spear and pen blades; N/S-lined; deluxe sterling silver handle   *$165*

740Gold—12K gold-plate handle   *$225*

740SSET—engine-turned sterling silver handle   *$165*

740SSS—scroll sterling silver handle   *$165*

7403—(3⅜") Spear and pen blades; brass-lined; bone stag handle   *$180*

7404Blue—(3⅜″) Spear and pen blades; brass-lined; Blue Pearl celluloid handle $155

7404—assorted celluloid handles $155

07404W—(3⅜″) Office Knife; spey and spey blades; spear and spey; brass-lined; spear blade crocus-polished on one side; ivory celluloid handle $175

N07404W—(3⅜″) Office Knife; spey and pen blades; brass-lined; spey blade crocus-polished on one side; ivory celluloid handle $175

7406—(3⅜″) Spear and pen blades; N/S-lined; mother-of-pearl handle $385

7403T—(3⅜″) Spear and pen blades; brass-lined; N/S tips; bone stag handle $180

7404T—assorted celluloid handles $160

7404K—(3⅜″) Spear and pen blades; brass-lined; brown-lined cream Pyralin handle $155

7404—assorted celluloid handles $155

7409GSil—(3⅜″) Spear and pen blades; brass-lined; N/S handle $165

7449GSil—as above except 2⅞″ long; N/S-lined; blades crocus-polished $160

7406T—(3⅜″) Spear and pen blades; N/S tips; mother-of-pearl handle $395

7404¾K—(3⅜″) Clip and pen blades; brass-lined; brown-lined cream Pyralin handle $150

7404¾E—black and pearl celluloid handle $150

7404¾—assorted celluloid handles $150

SS7404—(3⅜″) Stainless steel blades; spear and pen blades; brass-lined; handled in Marine Pearl and black-and-pearl celluloid $150

741SSS—(3⅜″) Spear and curly-point file blades; N/S-lined; scroll sterling silver handle $165

741SSD—deluxe sterling silver handle   *$165*

7413—(3⅜″) Spear and curly-point file blades; brass-lined; bone stag
handle   *$180*

7414—assorted celluloid handles   *$165*

7416—(3⅜″) Spear and curly-point file blades; N/S-lined; mother-of-pearl
handle   *$385*

7414BT—(3⅜″) Spear and curly-point file blades; brass-lined; N/S tips;
black celluloid handle   *$165*

7413T—bone stag handle   *$175*

7414ST—tortoise shell celluloid handle   *$165*

7414WT—ivory celluloid handle   *$165*

7416T—(3⅜″) Spear and curly-point file blades; N/S-lined; N/S tips;
mother-of-pearl handle   *$400*

7444E—(2⅞″) 2 pen blades; N/S-lined; black and pearl celluloid handle   *$135*

7444—assorted celluloid handles   *$135*

744SS—(2⅞″) 2 pen blades; N/S-lined; sterling silver handle   *$225*

744GG—12K green gold plate handle   *$265*

744SS Shac—as above except with sterling silver shackle   *$265*

7444STG—(2⅞″) 2 pen blades; N/S-lined; celluloid stag handle   *$170*

F7444B—black celluloid handle as above except with nail file substituted
for pen blade   *$165*

F7444S—shell celluloid handle; nail file   *$165*

F7449GSil—N/S handle; nail file   *$165*

F7444E—(2⅞″) Pen and file blades; N/S-lined; black and pearl celluloid
handle   *$135*

F744SS—sterling silver handle   *$180*

F7444 Shac—with shackle; assorted celluloid handles   *$180*

F744GG Shac—with shackle; 12K green gold plate handle   *$260*

F744SS Shac—with shackle; sterling silver handle   *$190*

F7444GG Shac—(2⅞″) Pen and file blades; N/S-lined; 12K green gold
plate handles   *$200*

F7444D Shac—black and green celluloid handle   *$190*

7503—(3¾") Spear and pen blades; brass-lined; bone stag handle   *$200*

7504—assorted celluloid handles   *$180*

7504¾G—(3¾") Clip and pen blades; brass-lined; green pearl celluloid
handle   *$180*

7503¾—bone stag handle   *$200*

7504¾—assorted celluloid handles   *$190*

7503T—(3¾") Spear and pen blades; brass-lined; N/S tips; bone stag handle   *$200*

7504T—assorted celluloid handles   *$180*

7504¾PT—(3¾") Clip and pen blades; brass-lined; N/S tips; Smoked
Pearl celluloid handle   *$180*

7503¾T—bone stag handle   *$195*

7504¾T—assorted celluloid handles   *$180*

7503B—(3¾") Spear and pen blades; brass-lined; N/S bolsters; bone stag
handle   *$230*

7504B—assorted celluloid handles   *$195*

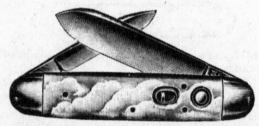

7506B—(3¾") Spear and pen blades; brass-lined; N/S bolsters; mother-of-
pearl handle   *$430*

7504¾K—(3¾") Clip and pen blades; brass-lined; brown-lined cream Pyr-
alin handle   *$175*

7504¾—assorted celluloid handles   *$165*

7506¾B—mother-of-pearl handle   *$350*

7523B—(3¾") Clip and spear blades; brass-lined; N/S bolsters; bone stag
handle   *$375*

7523¼B—as above except with clip and spey blades   *$375*

7534¾C—(3¾") Leather punch and clip blades; brass-lined; cocobolo celluloid handle   *$280*

7534C—as above except with leather punch and spear blades   *$280*

7533B—(3¾") Leather punch and spear blade; brass-lined; N/S bolsters;
bone stag handle   *$300*
7533¼B—as above except with leather punch and spey blades   *$300*
7533¾B—as above except with leather punch and clip blades   *$300*

Schrade Walden Pocketknives

C3-150—(4") Bone stag; push button; light hunting type; slim clip blade; polished on one side; brass lining; N/S bolsters and caps $225

C3-151—assorted celluloid handles $200

C3-152—(4") Celluloid of assorted colors; push-button; light hunting pattern; slim clip blade; polished on one side; N/S bolsters and caps $200

C3-153—(4⅞") Stag handle; push button; glazed-finish blade; large clip; steel linings; steel bolsters; N/S folding guard $400

C3-154—(4⅞") Stag handle; push button; large clip blade; steel linings; steel bolsters $350

C3-174—Budding Knife (6") Imported cocobolo wood handle; 1 carbon steel budding blade, 2⅛" long; 2 compression rivets $60

C3-186—Pruning Knife (4⅞") Cocobolo handle; pruning blade; steel lining; steel bolster $75

C3-234—Serpentine Jackknife (3⁵⁄₁₆") K-horn celluloid handle, 2 blades, clip and pen; large blade polished on one side; brass linings; N/S bolsters and shield $90

C3-242—Equal-end Jackknife (3⅛") Bone stag handle; slim pattern; 2 blades, spear and pen; brass lining; N/S bolsters and shield $115

C3-272—Serpentine Jackknife (2⅞") Two blades, clip and pen; large blade polished on one side; bone handles; brass lining; N/S bolsters and shield $100

C3-272Y—yellow Pyralin handle as above $85

C3-293—Stockman's Knife (3⅞") Bone stag handle, 2 blades, large half-saber clip and large spey; N/S bolsters, caps, and shields $225

C3-708—Serpentine Penknife (2¾") Bone handle, 2 blades, clip and pen; large blade polished on one side; brass lining; N/S bolsters and shield $80

C3-708 —as above with yellow Pyralin handle $70

C3-742—(3⅜") Bone stag handle, push button, 2 blades, spear and pen; brass lining $175

C3-746—(2⅞") Embossed stainless steel handle, "Executive" push button; 2 blades, pen and file; N/S lining $150

C3-750—(3¾") Celluloid handle, assorted colors, push button; 2 blades, clip and pen; large blade polished on one side $175

C3-766—(3⁴⁄₁₆") Black celluloid handle, Wharncliffe pattern; 2 blades, clip and pen; large blade polished on one side; brass lining; N/S bolsters and shield $60

C3-744—(3") Bone stag handle, Congress pattern; 2 blades, sheepfoot and pen; large blade polished on one side; brass lining; N/S bolsters $110

C3-787—Muskrat Skinning Knife (4") Bone stag handle, 2 blades, one side polished; N/S bolsters and shield; brass lining $200

C3-808—(2¾") Stag handle, Serpentine pattern; clip, sheepfoot, and pen blades; large blade polished on one side; brass lining, milled back; N/S bolsters and shield $75

C3-808Y—as above with yellow Pyralin handle $60

C3-810—(3⅛″) Bone stag handle, Senator pattern; 3 blades; spear, sheepfoot, and pen; large blade polished on one side; brass lining; N/S bolsters and shield $80

C3-820—(2¾″) Propwood handle, Serpentine pattern, 3 blades; clip, pen, and sheepfoot; large blade polished on one side; brass lining; N/S bolsters and shield $75

C3-822—*Premium Stock Knife (4″)* Texas pattern, 3 blades; clip, spey, and sheepfoot; large blade polished on one side; brass lining; N/S bolsters and shield $150

C3-825—*Westerner (3⁹/16″)* Bone stag handle, 3 stainless steel blades; slip, sheepfoot, and spey; N/S bolsters and shield; large blade polished on one side; milled back, individually boxed $150

C3-834—(3⁵/16″) Bone stag handle, Serpentine pattern, 3 blades; clip, sheepfoot, and pen; large blade polished on one side; brass lining; N/S bolsters and shield $125

C3-848—*The Cosmopolitan (2¾″)* Marine Pearl, Shadow pattern handle, handmade; 2 blades, pen and rigid nail file; N/S lining $60

C3-861—*Slim Premium Stock Knife (4″)* Bone stag handle, 3 blades; Turkish clip, sheepfoot, and spey; large blade polished on one side; N/S lining; milled back; N/S bolsters and shield $125

C3-881—(4″) Stag handle, Premium Stock Texas pattern, 3 blades; clip, spey, and sheepfoot; large blade polished on one side; brass lining; N/S bolsters and shield $200

C3-881Y—as above with yellow Pyralin handle $175

C3-890—*Premium Stock Knife (3½″)* Bone stag handle, 3 blades; clip, sheepfoot, and spey; large blade polished on one side; brass lining; N/S bolsters and shield $125

C3-900—*Field & Stream (3⅝″)* Unbreakable red handle; deeply embossed shield; 6 stainless steel blades; spear master and small clip cutting blades, can opener, screwdriver–cap lifter, punch, and corkscrew; rosette rivets; individually boxed $125

C3-906—*Spearmaster (3⁹/16″)* Red celluloid handle, 7 blades; small clip, can opener, screwdriver, cap lifter, punch, Phillips screwdriver, and beer can opener; N/S linings; embossed and shielded shackle $125

C3-951—*President (2⅞″)* Marine Pearl handle, 4 stainless steel blades; spear, pen, flexible manicure file, and lance blade; N/S linings, milled; N/S tips and shield; blades fully polished; individually boxed with purse
$95

C3-967—*Masterpiece (3″)* Mother-of-pearl handle, manicure file, pen and spear pocket blades, and scissors, all stainless; N/S linings and tips; blades fully polished; each knife packed with genuine leather purse; individually boxed $95

C3-973—(3⅛″) Bone stag handle, Congress pattern, 4 blades; 2 sheepfoot, 2 pen; brass lining, steel bolsters, N/S shield $195

C3-974—(3") Bone stag handle; Congress pattern; 2 sheepfoot and 2 pen blades; brass lining; N/S bolsters   *$175*

C3-233S—Serpentine Jackknife (3⁵/16") Stag handle, 2 blades; clip and pen; N/S bolsters and shield   *$110*

C3-233Y—as above with yellow Pyralin handle   *$95*

C3-709SHA—Esquire (3¹/16") Stainless steel engine-turned handle, 1 stainless steel spear blade and stainless flexible nail file; with shackle; large blade polished on one side; individually boxed with purse   *$50*

C3-793SHA—(2½") Solid Marine Pearl handle, Senator pattern, with shackle; 2 blades, spear and flexible nail file; large blade polished on one side; N/S lining; N/S tips and shackle   *$70*

C3-809M—Esquire (2¾") Unbreakable Marine Pearl handle, "A Country Gentleman's," handmade; 3 blades; clip, pen, and file; large blade polished on one side; N/S shield; brass lining, milled back; N/S bolsters *$45*

C3-863S—Carpenter's Knife (3⁵/8") Stag handle; 3 blades; large clip, Kon-Kay ground, coping pen, and small clip; large blade polished on one side; N/S bolsters and shield   *$135*

C3-863Y—as above with yellow Pyralin handle   *$120*

C3-896K—Slim Premium Stock Knife (3⁹/16") K-horn celluloid handle; 3 blades; clip, sheepfoot, and spey; large blade polished on one side; brass lining; N/S bolsters and shield   *$75*

C3-SS102—(4¹/16") White celluloid handle, 1 stainless steel long blade; brass lining   *$65*

C3-SS105—(5¾") White celluloid handle, 1 stainless steel long blade; brass lining   *$55*

C3-SS700—(4½") Marine Pearl handle, 2 stainless steel blades, extra long for sampling; brass lining; N/S bolsters   *$85*

115S—Barlow (3⅜") Bone stag handle; 1 blade; steel lined; steel bolsters; black inside; glaze-finished blade; 1 clip blade   *$115*

718RB—(2¾") Gentleman's Pen; Staglon   *$35*

SHAPLEIGH HARDWARE

Shapleigh Hardware Company of St. Louis, Missouri, was established in 1843 by A. F. Shapleigh. Although the company was a general line hardware distributor, it sold a number of collectible pocketknife brands produced under contract by manufacturers such as Camillus and Schrade.

Perhaps its best-known trademark was DIAMOND EDGE, a name adopted in 1864 and used until 1960. The trademark is now used by Imperial, and knives of recent manufacture should not be confused with the older Shapleigh knives, which are of much greater value. Other brands include BRIDGE CUTLERY COMPANY (1902–1931) as well as stampings of the company's name, such as SHAPLEIGH HDWE. CO. and SHAPLEIGH HDWE. CO. ST. LOUIS MO.

Shapleigh's knife line included more than six hundred patterns of quality pocketknives. The company went out of business in 1960, having been in the cutlery business for a century.

E101ST—(3") Imitation bone stag; spear and pen blades; glazed finish; iron bolsters; brass liners $50

E102ST—(3") Imitation bone stag; spear and pen blades; glazed finish; iron bolsters; brass liners $50

E103ST—(3⅛") Imitation bone stag; spear and pen blades; glazed finish; brass liners $50

E104C—(4⅞") Striped celluloid handle; nickel silver bolsters; brass liners $50

E105PC—(4⅞") Pearl celluloid handle; clip blade $50

E201C—(3¼") Celluloid handle; clip and pen blades; nickel silver shield and bolsters; brass liners $50

E202ST—as above with bone stag handle and iron bolsters $185

E205ST—(3⅜") Bone stag handle; spear pen blades; nickel silver shield; iron bolsters; brass liners $190

E206C—(3") Celluloid handle; clip and pen blades; nickel silver shield; iron bolsters; brass liners $45

E207ST—(3⅜") Bone stag handle; spear and pen blades; nickel silver shield; iron bolsters; brass liners $100

E208C—(3⅜") Celluloid handle; spear and pen blades; nickel silver shield; iron bolsters; brass liners $90

E211ST—(3¼") Bone stag handle; spear and pen blades; nickel silver shield; iron bolsters; brass liners $90

E212C—(3¼") Pearl celluloid handle; spear and pen blades; nickel silver shield; iron bolsters; brass liners $60

E217PC—(3¼") Pearl celluloid handle; large and small pen blades; nickel silver shield and bolsters; brass liners $60

E221PC—(3¼") Pearl celluloid handle; spear and pen blades; nickel silver shield and bolsters; brass liners $45

E222PC—(3¼") Pearl celluloid handle; spear and pen blades; nickel silver shield and tips; brass liners $45

1S440¾C—(5") Fancy celluloid handle; clip blade etched; nickel silver bolsters; brass liners $170

1S440¾CP—(5") Celluloid pearl handle; etched saber clip blade; nickel silver bolsters; brass liners $170

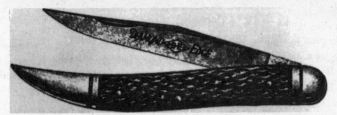

1S440¾S—(5") Bone stag handle; etched clip blade; nickel silver bolsters; brass liners   *$180*

1S441¾C—(4¾") Fancy celluloid handle; clip blade; nickel silver bolsters; brass liners   *$150*

1S442¾C—(4") Red celluloid handle; etched clip blade; nickel silver bolsters; brass liners   *$90*

1S442¾S—as above, bone stag handle   *$100*

1S443¾S—(4") Bone stag handle; etched clip blade; nickel silver bolster; brass liners   *$85*

1S445—(4⅛") Cocobolo wood handle; large maize blade; glazed and etched; steel bolsters   *$65*

1S447¾C—(4") Fancy celluloid handle; large etched saber clip blade; nickel silver bolster; brass liners   *$75*

1S448¾C—(4") Fancy celluloid handle; etched clip blade; nickel silver bolsters; brass liners   *$100*

1S449¾C—(4") Fancy celluloid handle; etched clip blade; nickel silver bolsters; brass liners   *$100*

1S621—(3⅜") Cocobolo handle; spear blade, glazed and etched; steel liners; steel bolster   *$45*

*1S621¾—*as above except with clip blade   *$45*

1S622ST—(3⅜") Bone stag handle; spear blade with glazed finish; steel bolster; steel liners   *$80*

*1S622¾ST—*as above except with clip blade   *$80*

*1S662⅝ST—*as above except with spey blade   *$75*

S14ST—(4⅞") Bone stag handle; steel liners; steel bolsters; 1 clip blade, glazed finish and etched   *$150*

S15ST—(4¼") Bone stag handle; steel liners; steel bolsters; 1 clip blade, glazed finish and etched   *$150*

S101—(4") Cocobolo wood handle; large pruning blade; glazed finish; steel bolsters; iron liners   *$60*

S103¾—(5") Bone stag handle; etched clip blade; nickel silver bolsters; brass liners   *$175*

S104—(4") Cocobolo wood handle; large maize blade; glazed finish; steel bolsters, iron liners   *$60*

*S104¾—*as above, celluloid pearl handle   *$150*

S105—(5") Bone stag handle; spear blade; glazed finish and etched; steel bolsters; iron liners   *$140*

S106¾—(5") Bone stag handle; clip blade; glazed finish and etched; steel bolsters; iron liners   *$140*

S209—(2¾") Bone stag handle; etched spear and pen blades; nickel silver shield; brass liners   *$55*

*S210—*as above, fancy celluloid handle   *$45*

S211—(2⅞") Bone stag handle; etched spear and pen blades; nickel silver shield and bolsters; brass liners   *$135*

*S212C—*as above, fancy celluloid handle   *$110*

S217¾—(3") Bone stag handle; etched clip and pen blades; nickel silver shield and bolsters; brass liners   *$70*

S218¾—(3") Fancy celluloid handle; etched clip and pen blades; nickel silver shield and bolsters; brass liners   *$60*

S231—(3") Bone stag handle; etched spear and pen blades; nickel silver bolsters; brass liners   *$60*

S232—as above, fancy celluloid handle   *$45*

S233—(3") Bone stag handle; etched spear and pen blades; nickel silver shield and bolsters; brass liners   *$50*

S234—as above, fancy celluloid handle   *$45*

S235—(3") Bone stag handle; etched spear and pen blades; nickel silver shield and bolsters; brass liners   *$60*

S236—as above, celluloid handle   *$45*

S248—(2¾") Celluloid pearl handle; spear and pen blades; nickel silver bolsters; brass liners   *$50*

S249—(2¾") Celluloid pearl handle; etched spear and pen blades; nickel silver bolsters; brass liners   *$50*

S301¼—(3¼") Bone stag handle; clip, spey, and punch blades; nickel silver shield; steel bolsters; brass liners   *$110*

S302¾—(3¼") Bone stag handle; clip, spey, and sheepfoot blades; nickel silver shield; steel bolsters; brass liners   *$130*

S303¾—(3¼") Fancy celluloid handle; clip, spey, and sheepfoot blades; nickel silver shield; steel bolsters; brass liners   *$120*

S304¼—(3⅜") Bone stag handle; spear, spey, and punch blades; nickel silver shield; steel bolsters; brass liners   *$95*

S305¼—as above, fancy celluloid handle $65

S306¾—(*3¼″*) Fancy celluloid handle; clip, spey, and sheepfoot blades; nickel silver shield; steel bolsters; brass liners $90

S307¾—(*3⅜″*) Fancy celluloid handle; clip, spey, and pen blades; nickel silver shield; steel bolsters; brass liners $90

S308¼—(*3⅞″*) Bone stag handle; clip, spey, and punch blades; nickel silver shield, bolsters, and liners $135

S309¼—(*3⅞″*) Celluloid pearl handle; clip, spey, and punch blades; nickel silver shield, bolsters, and liners $100

S310¼—(*3⅝″*) Bone stag handle; spear, spey, and punch blades; nickel silver shield, bolsters, and liners $90

S311¼—as above, celluloid handle $65

S405¼—(*3⅝″*) Bone stag handle; spear, punch, can opener, and screwdriver blades; nickel silver shield and bolsters; brass liners $120

2S2772GS—(*4½″*) Genuine stag handle; spear and pen blades; nickel silver shield and bolsters; brass liners $125

S2375C—(*3⅜″*) Fancy celluloid handle; spear and pen blades; nickel silver shield; nickel silver tips; brass liners $50

2S375S—as above, bone stag handle $60

2S375CP—(*3⅜″*) Fancy celluloid handle; spear and pen blades; nickel silver shield and bolsters; brass liners $50

2S276P—as above, pearl handle $70

2S376S—(*3⅜″*) Bone stag handle; spear and pen blades; nickel silver shield and bolsters; brass liners $50

2S377W—(*3⅜″*) Celluloid handle; large ink eraser and pen blades; brass liners $60

2S380C—(*2¾″*) Fancy celluloid handle; spear and pen blades; nickel silver shield and bolsters; brass liners $50

2S380ST—as above, bone stag handle $60

2S381—(*3⅛″*) Celluloid handle; clip and pen blades; nickel silver shield and bolsters; brass liners $40

2S305C—(*3⅞″*) Fancy celluloid handle; spear and pen blades; nickel silver shield and bolsters; brass liners $50

2S305P—as above, pearl handle $70

2S311¾C—(*3½″*) Fancy celluloid handle; clip and spey blades; nickel silver shield and bolsters; brass liners $60

2S311¾ST—as above, bone stag handle $60

2S312P—(*3″*) Pearl handle; spear and nail file blades; nickel silver shield, tips, and liners $60

2S315P—(*2½″*) Pearl handle; spear and nail file blades; nickel silver shield; brass liners $65

2S336¾C—(*3¼″*) Fancy celluloid handle; clip and pen blades; nickel silver shield and bolsters; brass liners $50

2S336¾S—as above, bone stag handle   *$65*

2S343C—*(3⅜″)* Fancy celluloid handle; spear and pen blades; nickel silver shield and bolsters; brass liners   *$60*

2S362P—*(3″)* Pearl handle; spear and flexible file blades; nickel silver shield shackle; nickel silver tips; brass liners   *$65*

2S382¾C—*(2⅞″)* Celluloid handle; large saber clip and pen blades; nickel silver shield and bolsters; brass liners   *$50*

2S382¾ST—as above, bone stag handle   *$60*

2S383¾C—*(3⅜″)* Celluloid handle; clip and pen blades; nickel silver shield and bolsters; brass liners   *$40*

2S383¾ST—as above, bone stag handle   *$45*

2S386C—*(3″)* Celluloid handle; spear and pen blades; nickel silver shield and bolsters; brass liners   *$75*

2S386ST—as above, bone stag handle   *$80*

2S404C—*(3″)* Celluloid handle; spear and pen blades; nickel silver shield and bolsters; brass liners   *$110*

2S404ST—as above, bone stag handle   *$135*

S417P—*(2¾″)* Pearl handle; spear and pen blades; nickel silver shield; brass liners   *$65*

2S432C—*(3″)* Celluloid handle; spear and pen blades; nickel silver shield; brass liners   *$125*

2S432ST—as above, bone stag handle   *$150*

2S443GS—*(3⅛")* Nickel silver handle; ring opener; spear and pen blades half polished and etched   *$40*

2S447C—*(3½")* Celluloid handle; spear and pen blades; nickel silver shield and bolsters; brass liners   *$60*

2S447ST—Bone stag handle; spear and pen blades; nickel silver shield and bolsters; brass liners   *$75*

2S447¾C—*(3½")* Celluloid handle; clip and pen blades; nickel silver shield and bolsters; brass liners   *$65*

2S447¾ST—as above, bone stag handle   *$75*

2S540C—*(3")* Celluloid handle; spear and pen blades; nickel silver shield and bolsters; brass liners   *$90*

2S450ST—as above, bone stag handle   *$95*

2S457C—*(3⅛")* Celluloid handle; spear and pen blades; glazed finish and etched; nickel silver shield; steel bolsters; brass liners   *$60*

2S457ST—as above, bone stag handle   *$100*

2S506C—*(2⅞")* Celluloid handle; spear and pen blades; nickel silver shield and bolsters; brass liners   *$50*

2S506ST—as above, bone stag handle   *$55*

2S514½ST—*(3⅓")* Bone stag handle; sheepfoot and pen blades; nickel silver shield and bolsters; brass liners   *$55*

2S520ST—*(3⅜")* Bone stag handle; spear and pen blades; nickel silver shield and bolsters; brass liners   *$60*

2S526¾ST—*(4")* Bone stag handle; clip and spear blades; nickel silver shield and bolsters; brass liners   *$180*

2S527¾C—*(4")* Celluloid handle; clip and spey blades; nickel silver shield and bolsters; brass liners   *$170*

2S427¾ST—as above, bone stag handle   *$180*

2S528C—*(3")* Celluloid handle; spear and pen blades; nickel silver shield and bolsters; brass liners   *$40*

2S528ST—as above, bone stag handle   *$50*

2S534¾C—(3¼″) Celluloid handle; clip and pen blades; nickel silver shield and bolsters; brass liners $40

2S538C—(3⅛″) Celluloid handle; clip and pen blades; nickel silver shield and bolsters; brass liners $50

2S539¾C Celluloid handle; clip and pen blades; nickel silver shield and bolsters; brass liners $50

2S542C—(3″) Celluloid handle; spear and pen blades; nickel silver shield and bolsters; brass liners $50

2S542ST—as above, bone stag handle $55

2S555P—(2¼″) Pearl handle; spear and nail file blades; brass liners $60

2S546C—(2⅞″) Celluloid handle; spear and pen blades; nickel silver shield and bolsters; brass liners $50

2S465ST—as above, bone stag handle $55

2S567C—(3⅜″) Celluloid handle; spear and pen blades; nickel silver shield and bolsters; brass liners $45

2S467CP—as above, celluloid pearl handle $45

2S467ST—as above, bone stag handle $50

2S580C—(3⅜″) Celluloid handle; spear and pen blades; nickel silver shield; steel bolsters; brass liners $50

2S580ST—as above, bone stag handle $60

2S580CEO—(3⅜″) Celluloid handle; easy opener; spear and pen blades; nickel silver shield; steel bolsters; brass liners $70

2S580SEO—as above, bone stag handle $75

2S580¾C—(3⅜″) Celluloid handle; clip and pen blades; nickel silver shield; steel bolsters; brass liners $50

2S580¾ST—as above, bone stag handle $60

2S581C—(3″) Celluloid handle; spear and pen blades; glazed finish and etched; nickel silver shield; steel bolsters; brass liners $40

2S581ST—as above, bone stag handle $55

2S586¾C—(3⅛″) Celluloid handle; clip and pen blades; nickel silver shield and bolsters; brass liners $50

2S586¾ST—as above, bone stag handle $65

2S587C—(2⅞″) Celluloid handle; spear and pen blades; nickel silver shield; brass liners $45

2S588¾C—(3⅛″) Celluloid handle; clip and pen blades; nickel silver shield and bolsters; brass liners $45

2S618C—(3⅜″) Celluloid handle; spear and pen blades; nickel silver shield and bolsters; brass liners $65

2S618S—as above, bone stag handle $85

2S623C—(3″) Celluloid handle; clip and pen blades; nickel silver shield and bolsters; brass liners $50

2S623CP—as above, celluloid pearl handle $45

2S623ST—as above, bone stag handle $60

2S623¾C—*(3")* Celluloid handle; clip and pen blades; nickel silver shield and bolsters; brass liners $50

2S6230¾CP—Celluloid pearl handle as above $60

2S623¾C—*(3½")* as above, bone stag handle $65

S264¾C—*(3½")* Celluloid handle; clip and pen blades; nickel silver shield and bolsters; brass liners $45

2S624¾ST—as above, bone stag handle $65

2S625C—*(4¼")* White celluloid handle; spear blade half-polished and etched; nickel silver shield and bolsters; brass liners $100

2S625ST—as above, bone stag handle $175

2S655¾ST—*(4¼")*Bone stag handle; clip and pen blades; nickel silver shield and bolsters; brass liners $175

2S626¾C—*(3¼")* Celluloid handle; clip and pen blades; nickel silver shield and bolsters; brass liners $50

2S626¾ST—as above, bone stag handle $65

2S627C—*(3¼")* Celluloid handle; spear and pen blades; nickel silver shield and bolsters; brass liners $50

3S20⅝ST—*(3⅞")* Bone stag handle; large spey, small clip and sheepfoot blades; nickel silver shield and bolsters; brass liners $160

3S67¼C—*(3⅜")* Celluloid handle; clip, small punch and spey blades; nickel silver shield and bolsters; brass liners $85

3S67¼ST—as above, bone stag handle $90

3S67¾C—*(3⅜")* Celluloid handle; clip, pen, and spey blades; nickel silver shield and bolsters; brass liners $85

3S67¾P—as above, pearl handle $150

3S67¾ST—as above, bone stag handle $120

3S76¾C—*(3⅜")* Celluloid handle; clip, pen, and spey blades; nickel silver shield and bolsters; brass liners $70

3S76¾ST—as above, bone stag handle $95

3S103CP—*(3½")* Pearl celluloid handle; spear, pen, and nail file blades; nickel silver shield and bolsters; brass liners $100

3S103ST—as above, bone stag handle $130

3S105P—*(3½")* Pearl handle; spear, pen, and nail file blades; nickel silver shield and bolsters; brass liners $110

3S105ST—as above, bone stag handle $90

3S109¼C—*(3⅝")* Celluloid handle; clip, spey, and punch blades; nickel silver shield and bolsters; brass liners $80

3S109¼ST—as above, bone stag handle $110

3S109¾C—*(3⅝")* Celluloid handle; clip, spey, and pen blades; nickel silver shield and bolsters; brass liners $110

3S109¾S—as above, bone stag handle $140

3S193C—(3⅜") Fancy celluloid handle; spear, pen, and nail file blades; nickel silver bolsters; brass liners $50

3S193P—as above, pearl handle $95

3S193ST—as above, bone stag handle $75

3S209C—(3¼") Fancy celluloid handle; spear and 2 pen blades; nickel silver shield and bolsters; brass liners $90

3S209P—as above, pearl handle $200

3S209ST—as above, bone stag handle $135

3S220C—(3⅛") Celluloid handle; spear and 2 pen blades; nickel silver shield and bolsters; brass liners $50

3S220ST—as above, bone stag handle $65

3S253¼C—(3¼") Celluloid handle; clip, pen, and punch blades; nickel silver shield and bolsters; brass liners $75

3S253¼ST—as above, bone stag handle $110

3S253¾C—(3¼") Celluloid handle; clip, spey, and pen blades; nickel silver shield and bolsters; brass liners $90

3S253¾P—as above, pearl handle $200

3S253¾ST—as above, bone stag handle $135

3S261P—(3") Pearl handle; 1 spear; pen and nail file blades; nickel silver liners $60

3S275C—(3⅜") Celluloid handle; spear, pen, and nail file blades; nickel silver shield and bolsters; brass liners $60

3S275P—as above, pearl handle $100

3S275ST—as above, bone stag handle $70

3S311¼C—(3½") Celluloid handle; clip, spey, and punch blades; nickel silver shield and bolsters; brass liners $100

3S311¼ST—as above, bone stag handle $125

3S311¾C—(3½") Celluloid handle; clip, pen, and spey blades; nickel silver shield and bolsters; brass liners $100

3S311¾T—as above, bone stag handle $130

3S354P—(3") Pearl handle; spear, pen, and nail file blades; nickel silver liners $60

3S355P—(3") Pearl handle; spear, pen, and long file blades; full-polished and etched; nickel silver liners $65

3S362P—(3") Pearl handle; spear, pen, and long file blades; nickel silver shield and bolsters; brass liners $85

3S374P—(3⅛") Pearl handle; spear, pen, and nail file blades; nickel silver shield and liners $60

3S375C—(3⅛") Celluloid handle; spear, pen, and file blades; nickel silver shield and bolsters; brass liners $50

3S383¾C—(3½") Celluloid handle; clip, spey, and sheepfoot blades; nickel silver shield and bolsters; brass liners $100

3S447¼ST—(4") Bone stag handle; large spey, small clip, and punch blades; nickel silver shield and bolsters; brass liners $170

3S523¼C—(4") Celluloid handle; clip, spey, and punch blades; nickel silver shield and bolsters; brass liners $110

3S523¼ST—as above, bone stag handle $140

3S523¾C—(4") Celluloid handle; clip, spey, and pen blades; nickel silver shield and bolsters; brass liners $110

3S523¾ST—as above, bone stag handle $150

3S525C—(3⅛") Celluloid handle; spear, spey, and pen blades; nickel silver shield and bolsters; brass liners $60

3S525ST—as above, bone stag handle $80

3S525¼C—(3½") Celluloid handle; spear, spey, and punch blades; nickel silver shield and bolsters; brass liners $70

3S525¼ST—as above, bone stag handle $95

3S529¾ST—(3⅞") Bone stag handle; clip and 2 spey blades; nickel silver shield; milled back and liners; nickel silver bolsters and liners $140

3S565¼C—(3½") Celluloid handle; clip, spey, and punch blades; nickel silver bolsters; brass liners $100

3S565¼ST—as above, bone stag handle $130

3S565¾C—(3⅜") Celluloid handle; clip, pen, and sheepfoot blades; nickel silver shield and bolsters; brass liners $60

3S565¾S—as above, bone stag handle $95

3S568¼C—(3½") Celluloid handle; clip, spey, and punch blades; nickel silver bolsters; brass liners $100

3S568¼ST—as above, bone stag handle $135

3S568¾C—(3½") Celluloid handle; clip, spey, and pen blades; nickel silver bolsters; brass liners $70

3S568¾ST—as above, bone stag handle $95

3S568⅝CP—(3½") Pearl celluloid handle; clip, spey, and sheepfoot blades; nickel silver shield and bolsters; brass liners $100

3S568⅝S—as above, bone stag handle $135

3S626¼S—(3¼") Celluloid handle; clip, spey, and punch blades; nickel silver shield and bolsters; brass liners $80

3S626¼S—as above, bone stag handle $100

3S565¾C Celluloid handle; clip, pen, and sheepfoot blades; nickel silver shield and bolsters; brass liners   *$60*

3S565¾S—as above, bone stag handle   *$95*

4S20¼ST—(4″) Bone stag handle; clip, spey, pen, and punch blades; nickel silver shield and bolsters; brass liners   *$160*

4S20¾ST—(4″) Bone stag handle; clip, sheepfoot, pen, and punch blades; nickel silver shield and bolsters; brass liners   *$160*

4S31P—(3″) Pearl handle; spear, 2 pen and nail file blades; full-polished and etched; nickel silver shield and liners   *$160*

4S66½ST—(3″) Bone stag handle; sheepfoot, tobacco, and 2 pen blades; glazed finish and etched; steel bolsters; brass liners   *$200*

4S214½ST—(3½″) Bone stag handle; 1 sheepfoot, 1 tobacco, and 2 pen blades; nickel silver shield; steel bolsters; brass liners   *$175*

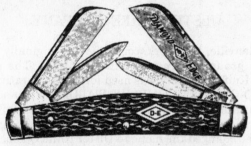

4S215½S—(3⅞″) Bone stag handle; 1 sheepfoot, 1 tobacco, and 2 pen blades; nickel silver shield and bolsters; brass liners   *$200*

4S275ST—(3⅜″) Bone stag handle; spear, sheepfoot, and pen and nail file blades; nickel silver shield and bolsters; brass liners   *$100*

4S275¼ST—(3⅜″) Bone stag handle; spear, spey, pen, punch blades; nickel silver shield and bolsters; brass liners   *$135*

4S374P—(3⅛″) Pearl handle; spear, 2 pen and nail file blades; nickel silver shield; brass liners   *$135*

4S375P—(3⅛″) Pearl handle; spear, 2 pen and nail file blades; nickel silver shield and bolsters; brass liners   *$135*

4S376P—(3⅛″) Pearl handle; spear, 2 pen and nail file blades; nickel silver shield and bolsters; brass liners   *$150*

*4S376ST—*as above, bone stag handle   *$100*

4S517S—(4⅛″) Bone stag handle; spear, punch, can opener, and screwdriver with combination cap-lifter and can-opener blades; nickel silver shield and bolsters; brass liners   *$100*

4S518S—(3⅜″) Bone stag handle; spear, punch, screwdriver, and combination can-opener and cap-lifter blades; nickel silver shield and bolsters; brass liners   *$85*

4S519CP—(2⅞″) Celluloid handle; spear, 2 pen and flexible file blades; nickel silver shield and bolsters; brass liners   *$65*

4S519S—(2⅞″) Bone stag handle; spear, 2 pen and flexible blades; nickel silver shield, bolsters, and liners   *$70*

ULSTER KNIFE COMPANY

This Ellenville, New York, company was originally formed in 1871 by a group of former Sheffield cutlers. The name Co-Operative Knife Company was used for the cooperative's knives marked CO-O. KNIFE COMPANY, WALDEN N.Y. and made by the Walden Knife Company. When the cooperative failed a half-dozen years later, its ownership was assumed by Dwight Devine & Sons, who changed the name to Ulster Knife Company. Markings used from 1876 to 1941 include ULSTER KNIFE CO. N.Y., ULSTER DWIGHT DEVINE & SONS, and ULSTER KNIFE CO. ELLENVILLE N.Y.

Ulster again changed ownership in 1941, when it was purchased by former Camillus Cutlery employee Albert Baer. Henry Baer was soon to join his brother in ownership and management of the cutlery company. That year saw the first use of the marking ULSTER USA.

Because of Ulster's wartime involvement with Imperial, a jointly owned company named Kingston Cutlery Company was formed in 1943. In 1947, Ulster joined with Imperial in forming Imperial Knife Associated Companies. Production of Schrade (purchased shortly before by the Baers of Ulster) knives was moved to the old Ulster factory in Ellenville at that time.

UNITED CUTLERY

This company was founded in 1984 by its current owners, John M. Parker, Kevin G. Pipes, Phillip S. Martin, and David K. Hall. First established as Twin Mountain Distributing Company, the

A variety of United-Boker patterns with bone handles were sold in the mid-1980s.

name was changed later that year to United Cutlery Corporation. The founders were experienced in the cutlery industry, and their combined talents have led the company in rapid development. During United's relatively short existence, an extensive product line and a number of recognized trademarks have been acquired.

In late 1985, United produced a line of knives with Boker, Germany. These knives were marked with the United/Boker trademark, using both company names. Included were seventeen standard patterns offered in a wide variety of handle materials. The United/Boker trademark for regular production knives was discontinued in 1990, and knives made during those five years will be of interest to collectors.

Knife brands that are exclusively distributed by United Cutlery throughout the United States are Kissing Crane (made in Germany), Smith & Wesson Knives (made in the United States), United/Boker (limited editions only—made in Germany), and J. A. Henckels (pocket and hunting knives only— made in Germany). After an absence from the United States for over a decade, the Henckels' line of pocket and hunting knives was reintroduced through United Cutlery in mid-1990. This brand has a 250-year history and a reputation for quality cutlery. United's licensing agreement does not include the Henckels' kitchen knife line, still marketed by the J. A. Henckels Company of Hawthorne, New York.

In addition to distribution rights of the above-listed brands, United owns the Rigid trademark for knives that were previously made in Arkansas. The Rigid line is currently being produced to United's quality specifications in Germany and in Seki, Japan.

Reproductions of popular "movie" knives have become somewhat of a specialty for United Cutlery. Through a licensing ar-

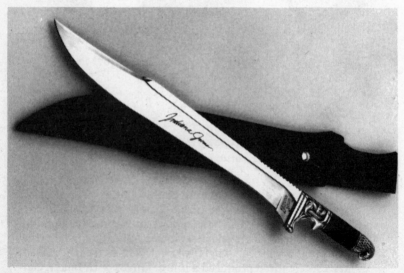

The "Indiana Jones" Kyber Bowie marketed by United Cutlery.

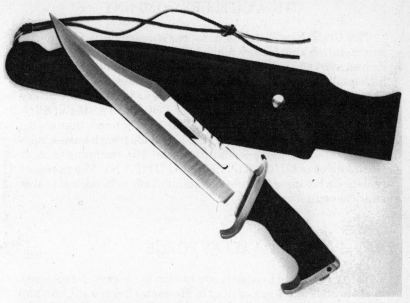

The "Rambo III," designed by Gil Hibben and marketed by United Cutlery. It was one of the best-selling knives ever issued and continues to be extremely popular with knife buyers.

rangement with knife designer and maker Gil Hibben and with Carolco Pictures, United Cutlery began marketing the "Rambo III" knife. This knife has proved to be one of the most significant introductions into the knife market in recent years, and its success led to other special knives such as those used by "Rambo" in the first two "First Blood" movies. Each is produced under full authorization of the designer and the movie producer and is an authentically detailed reproduction. More recent introductions include the "Indiana Jones" Khyber Bowie, a combination Khyber/Bowie-style knife that measures 2 feet in overall length, and the "Total Recall," a futuristic push dagger.

Recognizing that uniquely designed custom knives may be too expensive to appeal to the average collector, United began working, again with Gil Hibben, to offer these unique designs on production knives. The Silver Shadow knife was the first (excluding Rambo III items) to bear the distinctive "Designed by Gil Hibben" trademark.

UTICA CUTLERY COMPANY

This Utica, New York, company was founded in 1910 primarily as a metalworking factory named Utica Knife & Razor Company. Knives marked UTICA K & R CO. and UTK SUPREME were of high quality and are not often found in the collector market.

In 1929, the company name was changed to Utica Cutlery Company. Knife trade names such as POCKET PARD and SENECA were joined in 1937 by KUTMASTER, a name that is still used today. During World War II, Utica made trench knives, bayonets, and other items for military use. The stamping of most Utica knives is UTICA CUTLERY CO UTICA NY. The company remains in business today as a prominent manufacturer of knives and other cutlery products.

VALLEY FORGE

Valley Forge began cutlery production in Newark, New Jersey, in about 1892 and was acquired by Hermann Boker and Company in 1916. The factory made knives under the names of both Boker, USA and Valley Forge. Earliest knives were stamped VALLEY FORGE CUTLERY CO. NEWARK N.J., and knives dating from 1916 were stamped with the same name in both straight-line and curved configurations. Those made from 1916 to 1950 have the letters *VF* inside a circle on the rear tang. The company went out of business in 1950.

One of the company's most desirable knives is a bone-handled utility-type knife with a pliers that folds into the handle. Mint or excellent knives of this type are valued in the $200 to $300 range.

VAN CAMP HARDWARE

In 1876, Cortland Van Camp and David C. Bergundthal founded Van Camp Hardware & Iron Company. The Indianapolis, Indiana–based company became a major supplier of hardware, implements, and supplies within the Midwest. During the early years, the company purchased knives on contract from manufacturers such as Boker, Camillus, and Imperial. From about 1904 until 1908, Van Camp operated its own cutlery factory, Capitol Cutlery Company. The factory-made knives were stamped with both the Van Camp and Capitol markings.

Among the stampings used from 1888 until 1960 were VAN CAMP HARDWARE INDPLS, VAN CAMP INDIANAPOLIS inside a circle, VANCO INDIANAPOLIS, and VAN CAMP H. & I. MADE IN USA. Although still in the hardware wholesale business, the company no longer sells its own brand of pocketknife.

WALDEN KNIFE COMPANY

The company was first formed as the Walden Cooperative Knife Company about 1870. As strange as it may seem, the eighteen original workers were members of competitive baseball teams. Employees of New York Knife Company would play baseball during their lunch period, and Col. Tom Bradley, the company president, disapproved. A management/employee argument ensued, resulting in the employees being fired. The fired craftsmen rented some space in the Rider-Ericsson Engine Company's factory and began to make their own knives in a cooperative venture.

In 1874, the company incorporated as the Walden Knife Company and purchased a factory of its own. The company's products were of high quality, resulting in excellent sales and profits. The number of employees grew to 125 by 1881 and to nearly double that number by 1891.

The company's president persuaded George Schrade to move his Press Button Knife Company to Walden in 1893, and Walden Knife Company bought an interest in Schrade's firm. With Walden's support and Schrade's management, the firm produced well over 1 million Press Button knives within a ten-year period. In 1903, Schrade sold his patents and interest in the company to Walden Knife Company.

By 1911, the Walden Knife Company factory had been expanded, and over 600 workers were making more than 2500 different patterns of pocketknives. These knives were marketed through the E. C. Simmons Hardware Company in St. Louis, Missouri.

When George Weller, the company's principal stockholder, retired, the Simmons Company purchased his stock. With it, they gained control of the company and made Walden Knife Company the home of Keen Kutter knives. Simmons added several new buildings to the manufacturing complex, and during World War I the company operated at full capacity making large knives for the navy. At the war's end, Simmons merged with Winchester Repeating Arms Company, and Winchester assumed responsibility for knife manufacturing. The Walden Knife Company ceased to make knives in the mid-1920s. A few years later, the old Walden factory was purchased by Schrade Cutlery Company.

The Walden Knife Company made excellent-quality knives handled in bone, celluloid, pearl, and other materials popularly used at the time. Most were stamped WALDEN KNIFE CO., WALDEN, N.Y., or WALDEN KNIFE CO. MADE IN USA. Keen Kutter brand knives made by Walden and those made later by Winchester are practically indistinguishable from one another because Winchester duplicated many of the Walden Knife patterns.

WESTER BROTHERS

Knives with the stampings WESTER & BUTZ/SOLINGEN (1832–1966), JACOBY & WESTER (1891–1904), WESTER BROS./GERMANY (1904–1967), and WESTER BROS. CUTLERY CO. (1904–1967) have a common ancestry. As early as 1832, Herr Butz was making pocketknives in Solingen, Germany, and he took in an apprentice named August Wester. Wester not only became a master cutler but Butz's son-in-law as well. Together, they established the firm of Wester and Butz and made knives primarily for the European market.

In the 1880s, August Wester decided to establish a cutlery outlet in the United States in preference to paying an importer. Two of Wester's sons, Max and Charles, came to the United States and joined with a Mr. Jacoby in establishing the firm of Jacoby and Wester in New York in 1891. Knives made in Germany by Wester and Butz for the American market were marked JACOBY & WESTER on one side of the blade tang; the other side was marked with the Wester & Butz company trademark of an anchor, star, and arrow. Max and Charles Wester bought out Jacoby's interest in 1904 and changed the company name to Wester Brothers. Their knives, stamped WESTER BROS. CUTLERY CO. or WESTER BROS. NEW YORK, also used the above-described logo on the blade reverse tang. About 1915, the stamping of WESTER-STONE INC. was used on a few large jackknife patterns made for them by New England–area manufacturers.

Wester Brothers served as exclusive importers of knives and other cutlery products made by the Wester and Butz factory in Solingen, Germany. Their knives were made with handles of genuine pearl, stag, bone stag, buffalo horn, gunmetal, nickel silver, celluloid, and special alloys (used on bartender's knives).

Many of the advertising knives found in the collector market were made by Wester and Butz and imported by Wester Brothers. Those made for beer companies such as Anheuser-Busch are favorites of collectors. An excellent article, *Busch Knives by Wester,* was written by Bernard Levine and published in the July 1989 issue of *Knife World.*

WESTERN CUTLERY COMPANY

The Western Cutlery Company story and that of several other manufacturers could begin in 1864, the year that Charles W. Platts emigrated to this country from Sheffield, England. Platts was descended from a long line of knife makers, and, in turn, his descendants were to have a significant impact on a number of U.S. cutlery businesses.

Platts's first employer in this country was the American Knife Company in Reynolds Bridge, Connecticut. A few years later, he became superintendent of the factory belonging to the Northfield Knife Company in the nearby town from which the company took its name. Charles and his wife, Sarah, reared five sons, and each learned the cutlery craft at the Northfield cutlery firm. Although other sons and their descendants remained active in the cutlery industry, our focus in learning about Western will be on Harvey Nixon (H. N.) Platts.

H. N. Platts left Northfield in 1891 and moved west to Little Valley, in Cattaraugus County, New York. His experience led him to work in the blade grinding and finishing department of a new knife factory operated by Cattaraugus Cutlery Company. The company's early owners, J. B. F. Champlin and his son Tint, were joined temporarily in the business by four brothers of Mrs. Champlin (formerly Theresa Case). These Champlin brothers-in-law were W. R., Jean, John, and Andrew Case.

Working also in the Cattaraugus office was Debbie Case, who lived with her brother Russ and their father, W. R. Case. In 1892, H. H. Platts and Debbie Case were married, and within a couple of years they had become the parents of two sons, Harlow and Reginald.

Charles Platts, still a respected cutlery leader, and his other sons reentered the picture when they moved from Northfield to Little Valley in 1893 and began work with Cattaraugus. Practically every department of the Cattaraugus factory now had a Platts family member at work, and the result was almost inevitable—they decided to start their own cutlery business. In

1896, Charles Platts was joined by his five sons in forming a new company known as C. Platts & Sons Cutlery Co. in nearby Gowanda, New York, and would later move to new and larger facilities in Eldred, Pennsylvania.

In 1900, when Charles Platts died, it was H. N. who assumed leadership of the family business. In addition to managerial responsibilities, H. N. served as key salesman of Platts cutlery products. Ever expanding to new territories, his sales trips took him farther west through several states and into the midwestern plains states. More than a few of Platts's sales trips were made in the company of another cutlery salesman, brother-in-law Russ Case. Platts would sell knives on one side of the town street while Case sold on the other side, each selling knives branded with his own name.

A new company, with J. Russell Case and H. N. Platts as organizers and major stockholders, was to merge from this family and working relationship. In the early days of the business, the company sold knives branded both "Platts" and "Case," so choosing one family name seemed logical. Because Russ Case had sales responsibility and Platts oversaw manufacturing, the name Case was selected. Sometime earlier, Russ had begun a jobbing company known as W. R. Case and Son. The new company, incorporated in 1904 in Little Valley, had a similar name except that an *s* would be added to the word *Son,* thereby recognizing Platts's family membership as the W. R. Case son-in-law. Debbie Case Platts supervised the office, and summer school vacations saw the two young Platts boys working in the factory.

H. N. Platts's health began to decline due to "grinder's consumption," a disease of the lungs caused by years of work with the sandstone grinding wheels. Although the business was doing very well and the now teenage Platts sons were becoming increasingly active in the business, the father's health hinged on a move to a drier climate. In 1911, he sold his interest in the company to Russ Case and moved his family to Boulder, Colorado. But going with Platts and his family to the new home was his determination to continue his lifetime work in the cutlery industry.

A developing west proved to be fertile ground for knife sales because the cowboys, farmers, miners, and other workers needed quality cutlery to use many times every day. Platts knew the business, and he certainly had experience in starting a cutlery factory, but he also recognized the need to establish a base of business if he was to be successful in starting all over again. His connections with the eastern cutlery manufacturers were important as he sought sources of product. Before the year 1911 was over, orders were being taken and knives were arriving from the east to fill them. The new business was named Western States Cutlery and Manufacturing Company. That name was selected instead of the founder's name because "Platts" had been used as a brand for the old company mentioned earlier and had very recently been used by Platts Brothers Cutlery Co., operated by H. N. Platts's brothers. The geographical name was given to establish an identity separate from that of the Case and Platts businesses back east and the "States" extension of the name signified the company's sales territory.

Early Western States knives were manufactured by Challenge, New York Knife Company, Valley Forge, Utica, and Case Cutlery among others. Although the business was prospering and a manufacturing facility was in order, it was several years coming. World War I had begun, with shortages of materials and labor. It had also required the services of the older son, Harlow, whose aid would have been needed for factory startup. Platts's dream was realized, however, with the opening of his new factory in 1920.

In the early 1940s H. N. retired from active management of Western States Cutlery, and those responsibilities were passed on to his sons Reginald and Harlow, who continued in partnership until Reginald left the cutlery business in 1950. A new name, Western Cutlery Co., was given the business in 1953, when Harlow Platts and his son Harvey reincorporated the company. Western remained in Boulder until its 1977 relocation to nearby Longmont, Colorado.

Harvey Platts became company president and continued in that capacity until 1984, when Western was purchased by the Crossman Airgun division of Coleman Corporation, thus ending the more than one-hundred-year involvement of the Platts family in the U.S. cutlery industry.

Tang stampings on Western knives can be of some, but very little, help in determining when a knife was made. It was only in 1977 that the company began to mark knives with the year of manufacture. During the years 1911–1951, the several stampings used were

Western States Cut. & Mfg. Co. Boulder

Western States Boulder Colo.

Western States Boulder Colo. Made in USA

Westaco Boulder Colo.

Western Boulder Colo.

From 1978 the stamp Western USA has been used with a letter added beneath the USA to indicate the year. The dating system is A—1977, B—1978, etc.

The first trademark for Western was shaped like a tic-tac-toe board, as illustrated below. The trademark was discontinued when the word "States" was dropped from the company name.

WINCHESTER

When the Winchester Arms Company decided to expand into the cutlery field, shortly after World War I, they did so through acquisition. In 1919, Winchester purchased two very reputable knife manufacturers, the Eagle Knife Company of New Haven, Connecticut, and the Napanoch Knife Company of Napanoch, New York. For Winchester, these purchases were well founded in their entry into the knife market. Eagle had developed machinery and methods, such as blade blanking and automatic blade grinding, that would be important to assembly line production. Napanoch had made a very high quality knife, and the skill of Napanoch cutlers would complement the modern production methods designed by Eagle. A large percentage of the employees of the two purchased companies became employees of Winchester in the New Haven, Connecticut, factory. By combining the technology, skill, and cutlery experience so acquired, Winchester was soon able to mass-produce a high-quality knife marked with its own brand. Convinced that they were solidly entrenched within the market, Winchester adopted the motto describing their knives "As good as the gun."

In 1922, Winchester and the E. C. Simmons Hardware Company of St. Louis, Missouri, merged to form the Winchester-Simmons

Company. Winchester was to have production responsibility, and Simmons was to be responsible for marketing. At the time of the merger, Simmons owned controlling interest in the Walden Knife Company. In 1923, production of Walden knives ended, and all of Walden's equipment was moved to the Winchester site. In addition to knives marked with the Winchester trademark, the factory also made knives branded KEEN KUTTER for sale by Simmons.

The firm of Winchester-Simmons was dissolved, with Winchester retaining the manufacturing facilities and Simmons the marketing business. Until the 1930s, Winchester knives were of excellent quality. Increasing competition from manufacturers of low-priced cutlery motivated the company to begin selling dealer assortments of lesser-quality knives. (An excellent article describing these knives and the circumstances of their manufacturer was written by Bernard Levine and published in the January 1988 issue of *Knife World.*) The advent of World War II offered Winchester other manufacturing alternatives, and cutlery production ceased by early 1942.

Although a few German-made knives marked with the Winchester name appeared on the market during the late 1970s and early 1980s, these were cheap knives not authorized by the company. In the late 1980s, however, Winchester licensed the manufacture and distribution of a quality line of reproduction-type knives to Blue Grass Cutlery.

The pattern numbers used by Winchester can be used to identify knives as follows: the first digit signifies the number of blades, the second digit signifies the handle material, and the third and fourth digits signify factory pattern. Winchester used almost every common pattern, handle material, and bolster. There were two distinct lines of Winchester knives. Those of higher quality (earlier manufacture) are stamped WINCHESTER TRADEMARK MADE IN USA on each blade; the lesser-quality knives are stamped on only one blade. Although these stamping differences existed on most of Winchester's production, the collector should be aware that there are some exceptions.

Pattern	Size	Handle	Knife Type	Blades	Mint Price
H1610P	4″	Cocobola	Pruner	Pruner	$85
2H2125P	3⅜″	Cocobola	Jack	Spear	70
H1701P	3½″	Bone	Barlow	Pruner	175
2H2009P	3¾″	Celluloid	Jack	Spear & Pen	110

Pattern	Size	Handle	Knife Type	Blades	Mint Price
2H2049P	3¼″	Celluloid	Senator	Spear & Pen	$95
H2123P	3⅛″	Fiber	Jack	Spear	65
H2609	3½″	Cocobola	Barlow	Clip & Pen	225
H2615	4″	Cocobola	Pruner	Pruner & Saw	140
H2632P	3⅜″	Ebony	Stock	Clip & Pen	115
H2636P	3½″	Ebony	Jack	Spear & Pen	150
H2638P	3½″	Ebony	Serpentine Jack	Spear & Pen	195
2701P	3½″	Bone	Barlow	Spear & Pen	225
H2943P	3¼″	Stag	Sleeve-board	Spear & Pen	100
H2950P	3½″	Stag	Jack	Spear & Pen	170
H2951P	3½″	Stag	Jack	Clip & Punch	150
H2952P	3½″	Stag	Jack	Clip & Pen	165
H2953P	3½″	Stag	Jack	Spear & Pen	225
H2956P	3½″	Stag	Serpentine Jack	Spear & Pen	175
H2966P	3⅝″	Stag	Jack	Spear & Pen	200
H33050P	3⅜″	Pearl	Stock	Clip, Spey, Sheepfoot	250
H3342P	3⅜″	Pearl	Cattle	Spear, Sheepfoot, Pen	260
H3361P	3⅝″	Pearl	Cattle	Spear, Sheepfoot, Pen	260
H3646P	3⅝″	Ebony	Cattle	Spear, Sheepfoot, Punch	220
H3607P	4″	Ebony	Stock	Clip, Spey, Pen	245
H3941P	3⅜″	Stag	Stock	Clip, Spey, Sheepfoot	190

Pattern	Size	Handle	Knife Type	Blades	Mint Price
H3942P	3¾″	Stag	Cattle	Spear, Sheepfoot, Pen	$215
H3950P	3⅝″	Stag	Cattle	Clip, Sheepfoot, Pen	250
H3952P	3⅝″	Stag	Cattle	Spear, Spey, Punch	250
J3961P	4″	Stag	Stock	Clip, Spey, Punch	260
H4950P	3⅝″	Stag	Scout	Spear, Punch, Opener, Screwdriver	285
H4961P	4″	Stag	Stock	Clip, Sheepfoot, Spey, Punch	315
1050	5″	Abalone Celluloid	Toothpick	Saber Clip	315
1051	4⅜″	Red & Black Celluloid	Texas Jack	Clip	315

Pattern	Size	Handle	Knife Type	Blades	Mint Price
1060	4⅛″	Red & Black Celluloid	Texas Jack	Saber Clip	220
1201	3¼″	Nickel Silver	Jack	Sheepfoot	190
1605	3½″	Cocobola	Jack	Spear	80
1608	3½″	Cocobola	Jack	Spey	75
1610	4″	Cocobola	Pruner	Pruner	80
1611	3¼″	Cocobola	Jack	Sheepfoot	85
1613	3⅜″	Cocobola	Jack	Spey	125
1614		Cocobola	Maize Jack		85
1621		Ebony	Budding		130

Pattern	Size	Handle	Knife Type	Blades	Mint Price
1624		Cocobola	Maize Jack		$85
1632	3½″	Cocobola	Jack	Clip	85
1633	3½″	Cocobola	Pruner		85
1701	3½″	Bone	Barlow	Spear	200
1703		Bone	Barlow		275
1704		Stag	Barlow		325
1785	3½″	Bone	Barlow		165

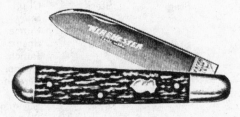

| 1905 | 4¼″ | Stag | Jack | Large Spear | 270 |

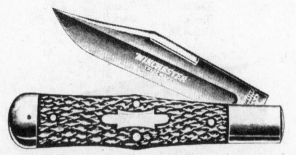

1920	5¼″	Bone	Folding Hunter	Saber Clip	1050
1921	3½″	Stag	Jack	Clip	130
1922	3⅜″	Stag	Jack	Spey	130
1923	4⅛″	Stag	Texas Jack	Clip	240
1924	4¼″	Stag	Toothpick	Clip	310
1925	3½″	Stag	Jack	Spey	300
1936	5″	Stag	Toothpick	Large Saber Clip	350

Pattern	Size	Handle	Knife Type	Blades	Mint Price
1937	3⅞″	Stag	Serpentine Jack	Saber Clip	$155
1938	3½″	Stag	Jack	Spear	130

Pattern	Size	Handle	Knife Type	Blades	Mint Price
1950	6¾″	Stag	Lockback	Clip	1250
2028	3⅜″	Shell Celluloid	Jack	Spear, Pen	155
2037	3″	Red & Black Celluloid	Jack	Spear, Pen	95
2038	3″	Pearl Celluloid	Jack	Spear, Pen	165
2039	3″	Red & Black Celluloid	Jack	Spear, Pen	95
2047		White Celluloid	Jack		225
2051	3¼″	Stag	Senator Pen	Sheepfoot, Pen	150
2052	2⅝″	Pearl Celluloid	Senator Pen	Spear, Pen	95
2053	2⅝″	Green & Red Celluloid	Senator Pen	Spear, Pen	120
2054	3¼″	Green & Black Celluloid	Senator Pen	Spear, Pen	85
2055	3¼″	Red & Black Celluloid	Senator Pen	Spear, Pen	85
2057	3⅜″	Varicolor Celluloid	Senator Pen	Spear, Pen	120
2058	3⅛″	Abalone Blue Celluloid	Senator Pen	Spear, Pen	95

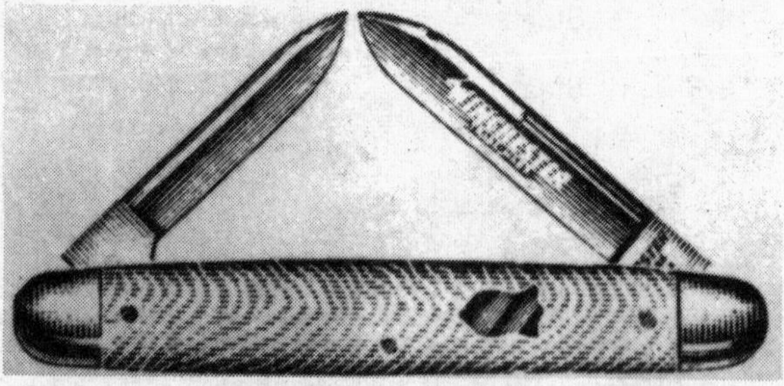

Pattern	Size	Handle	Knife Type	Blades	Mint Price

Pattern	Size	Handle	Knife Type	Blades	Mint Price
2059	3⅛″	Iridescent Celluloid	Senator Pen	Spear, Pen	$95
2067	3⅜″	Pearl Celluloid	Serpentine Pen	Spear, Pen	115
2068	3⅜″	Red & Black Celluloid	Sleeve-board	Clip, Pen	175
2069	3⅜″	Pearl Blue Celluloid	Jack	Spear, Pen	165
2070	3½″	Varicolor Celluloid	Jack	Spear, Pen	150
2078	3⅜″	Black Celluloid	Serpentine Pen	Clip, Pen	125
2079	3⅜″	White Celluloid	Office Knife	Spear, Eraser	105
2082	3⅛″	Pearl Celluloid	Sleeve-board	Spear, Pen	110
2083	3⅛″	Green Celluloid	Jack	Spear, Pen	155
2084	3¼″	Blue Celluloid	Sleeve-board	Clip, Spey	175
2085	3″	Varicolor Celluloid	Serpentine Jack	Spear, Pen	130
2086	2⅞″	Gray Celluloid	Dog Leg	Spear, Pen	130
2087	3″	Shell Celluloid	Serpentine Jack	Spear, Pen	135
2088	3⅜″	Gray Celluloid	Serpentine Pen	Spear, Pen	115
2089	3¾″	White Celluloid	Office Knife	Spear, Eraser	110
2090	3″	Silver Celluloid	Serpentine Pen	Spear, Pen	130
2094	3½″	Green & Black Celluloid	Jack	Spear, Pen	200

Pattern	Size	Handle	Knife Type	Blades	Mint Price
2098	3⅜"	Green Celluloid	Jack	Clip, Pen	$185
2099	3¾"	Shell Celluloid	Jack	Clip, Pen	200
2106	3¼"	Abalone Blue Celluloid	Jack	Spear, Punch	165
2107	2¾"	Gold Celluloid	Dog Leg	Spear, Pen	130
2109	2⅞"	Gold Celluloid	Sleeve-board	Spear, Pen	90
2110	3½"	Red & Black Celluloid	Jack	Spear, Pen	165
2111	3½"	Red & Black Celluloid	Jack	Clip, Pen	160
2112	3½"	Green & Black Celluloid	Jack	Clip, Punch	160
2113	2¾"	Celluloid	Peanut	Saber Clip, Pen	130
2114	3"	Celluloid	Serpentine Jack		135
2115	2⅞"	Pearl Celluloid	Sleeveboard Pen	Spear, Pen	150
2116	3⅜"	Celluloid	Sleeveboard Pen	Clip, Pen	95
2117	3⅛"	Black Celluloid	Serpentine Jack	Spear, Pen	175
2201	3¼"	Nickel Silver	Senator Pen	Spear, Pen	75
2202	3"	Fiber	Serpentine Jack	Spear, Pen	75
2204	3⅛"	Nickel Silver	Senator Pen	Spear, Pen	75

Pattern	Size	Handle	Knife Type	Blades	Mint Price
2205	3½″	Nickel Silver	Senator Pen	Spear, Pen	$90
2207	3⅜″	Nickel Silver	Easy Open Jack	Spear, Pen	150
2208	3⅜″	Nickel Silver	Jack	Spear, Pen	140
2215	3½″	Nickel Silver	Jack	Spear, Pen	85
2301	2¼″	Pearl	Senator Pen		85
2302	2¼″	Pearl	Senator Pen	Spear, File	85
2303	2⅝″	Pearl	Senator Pen		100

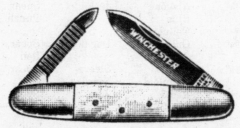

2306	2⅝″	Pearl	Senator Pen	Spear, File	95
2307	2⅞″	Pearl	Senator Pen		90
2308	2⅞″	Pearl	Senator Pen		95
2309	3″	Pearl	Senator Pen	Spear, Pen	125
2314	3″	Pearl	Serpentine Jack		95
2316	3″	Pearl	Serpentine Jack	Spear, File	155
2317	3″	Pearl	Serpentine Jack	Spear, Pen	130
2320	2⅞″	Pearl			95
2324	3″	Pearl			125
2331	3¼″	Pearl	Congress		150
2335	3¼″	Pearl	Congress		140
2337	3¼″	Pearl	Senator Pen		120

Pattern	Size	Handle	Knife Type	Blades	Mint Price
2338	3¼″	Pearl	Senator Pen	Spear, File	$160
2344	3¼″	Pearl	Senator Pen		135
2345	3¼″	Pearl	Senator Pen		100
2346	3″	Pearl	Lobster Pen	Spear, File	115
2352	3⅛″	Pearl	Jack	Spear, Pen	185

2356	3″	Pearl	Lobster Pen	Spear, File	115
2361	2⅞″	Pearl	Dog Leg	Spear, Pen	120
2363	3″	Pearl	Congress	Sheepfoot, Pen	125
2366	3⅜″	Pearl	Sleeve-board		130
2367	3″	Pearl	Sleeve-board		100
2368	3″	Pearl	Sleeve-board		100
2369	2⅝″	Pearl	Senator Pen	Spear, Pen	100
2374	2⅞″	Pearl	Senator Pen		90
2375	2⅝″	Pearl	Senator Pen	Spear, File	95
2376	3″	Pearl	Senator Pen	Spear, Pen	125
2377	2⅝″	Pearl	Senator Pen	Spear, Pen	150

Pattern	Size	Handle	Knife Type	Blades	Mint Price

Pattern	Size	Handle	Knife Type	Blades	Mint Price
2380	3¼″	Pearl	Physician's Knife	Spear, Pen	$315
2603	3½″	Cocobola	Jack	Clip, Pen	155
2604	3⅜″	Cocobola	Jack	Clip, Pen	155
2605	3⅜″	Cocobola	Jack	Spear, Pen	215
2606	3½″	Cocobola	Jack	Spear, Pen	165
2608	3½″	Cocobola	Jack	Spear, Pen	130
2610	3⅜″	Cocobola	Jack	Spey, Pen	165
2611	3″	Cocobola	Serpentine Jack	Spear, Pen	125
2612	3⅝″	Cocobola	Jack	Spear, Pen	200
2613	3⅝″	Cocobola	Jack	Spear, Pen	200
2614	3⅝″	Cocobola	Jack	Saber Clip, Pen	200
2627	3¼″	Cocobola	Jack	Spear, Pen	130

Pattern	Size	Handle	Knife Type	Blades	Mint Price
2629	3½″	Ebony	Jack	Clip, Pen	$175
2630	3⅝″	Ebony	Jack	Clip, Pen	175
2631	3¼″	Ebony	Sleeve-board	Spear, Pen	100
2632	3⅜″	Cocobola	Premium Stock		100
2633	3¼″	Ebony			115
2633	3¼″	Ebony	Premium Stock	Clip, Pen	115
2635	3½″	Cocobola	Jack	Spear, Pen	145
2636	3½″	Ebony	Jack	Spear, Pen	185

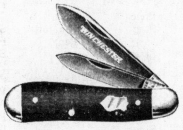

2638	3½″	Ebony	Serpentine Jack	Spear, Pen	165
2640	3¾″	Ebony	Coke Bottle		200
2641	3⅞″	Cocobola	Trapper		280
2649	3¾″	Ebony	Jack	Spear, Pen	160
2660	3½″	Ebony	Jack	Spear, Punch	160
2661	3½″	Cocobola	Jack	Spear, Pen	165
2662	3½″	Ebony	Jack	Clip, Pen	165
2665	3⅜″	Ebony	Jack	Spear, Pen	185
2666	3⅜″	Ebony	Jack		95
2681	3¾″	Ebony	Electrician		120
2690	4½″	Ebony	Texas Jack		225

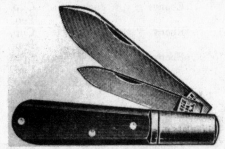

Pattern	Size	Handle	Knife Type	Blades	Mint Price
2701	3½″	Bone	Barlow		$225
2702	3½″	Bone	Barlow	Spey, Pen	265
2703	3⅓″	Bone	Jack	Clip, Pen	225
2820	3⅜″	Bone	Jack		100
2830	3¼″	Stag	Senator Pen	Spear, Pen	85
2840	2″	Stag		Spear, Pen	110
2841	3″	Stag		Spear, Pen	110
2842	3¼″	Stag	Senator Pen	Spear, Pen	130
2843	3⅜″	Stag		Spear, Pen	160
2844	3¾″	Stag	Jack	Clip, Pen	275
2845	3¾″	Stag	Jack	Clip, Pen	235
2846	3¼″	Stag	Premium Stock	Clip, Pen	130
2847	3¼″	Stag	Pen	Clip, Spey	150
2848	3½″	Stag	Jack	Clip, Pen	140
2849	3¼″	Stag	Jack	Spear, Pen	175
2850	3¾″	Stag	Jack	Saber Clip, Pen	290
2851	3″	Stag	Gunstock Jack		325
2852	3″	Stag	Serpentine Cattle		145

Pattern	*Size*	*Handle*	*Knife Type*	*Blades*	*Mint Price*
2853	3⅜″	Stag	Gunstock	Saber Clip, Pen	$200
2854	3¼″	Stag	Jack	Spear, Pen	165
2855	3¼″	Stag	Jack	Spear, Punch	165
2856	2⅞″	Stag	Dog Leg	Clip, Pen	115
2857	3⅛″	Stag	Serpentine Jack		125
2858	3″	Stag	Serpentine Jack		90
2859	2⅞″	Stag	Sleeve-board	Spear, Pen	85
2860	3¼″	Stag	Sleeve-board	Spear, Pen	155
2861	3¼″	Stag	Sleeve-board	Clip, Pen	155
2862	3⅜″	Stag	Sleeve-board	Spear, Pen	95
2863	3¼″	Stag	Congress	Sheepfoot, Pen	150
2864	3⅜″	Stag	Swell Center		180
2865	3½″	Stag	Swell Center Jack	Clip, Spear	325
2866	2⅞″	Stag	Senator Pen	Spear, Pen	85
2867	3⅜″	Stag	Senator Pen	Spear, Pen	125
2868	3¼″	Stag	Pen	Spear, Pen	130
2869	3¾″	Stag	Gunstock	Clip, Spey	230
2870	3¾″	Stag	Gunstock	Clip, Pen	185
2871	3¾″	Stag	Gunstock		215
2872	3¼″	Stag	Gunstock	Spear, Pen	200
2873	3½″	Bone	Barlow		200
2874	3½″	Stag	Jack	Clip, Punch	155
2875	3¼″	Stag	Premium Stock		145

Pattern	Size	Handle	Knife Type	Blades	Mint Price
2876	3¼″	Bone	Muskrat		$275
2878	4¼″	Stag	Texas Jack		275
2879	4½″	Stag	Sleeve-board		500
2880	4½″	Stag	Texas Jack		375
2881	4½″	Stag	Texas Jack		375
2901	3½″	Stag	Jack	Clip, Pen	160
2902	2⅝″	Stag	Pen	Spear, Pen	90

2903	3½″	Stag	Swell Center	Spear, Pen	275
2904	3⅞″	Stag	Texas Jack	Clip, Spey	400
2905	4¼″	Stag	Texas Jack	Spear, Pen	450
2906	4¼″	Stag	Slim Jack		375
2907	4¼″	Stag	Texas Jack	Clip, Pen	450
2908	3⅝″	Stag	Swell Center	Clip, Pen	180

2910	3″	Stag	Lobster Pen	Spear, File	95
2911	3½″	Stag	Jack	Spear, Pen	165

Pattern	Size	Handle	Knife Type	Blades	Mint Price
2914	3¼″	Stag	Sleeve-board	Clip, Spey	$180
2917	3″	Stag	Serpentine Jack	Spear, Pen	135
2918	3⅜″	Stag	Serpentine Pen	Spear, Pen	150
2921	3½″	Stag	Jack	Spear, Pen	285
2923	4″	Stag	Premium Stock	Clip, Spey	240
2924	3″	Stag	Congress	Sheepfoot, Pen	130
2925	3⅛″	Stag	Jack	Spear, Pen	165
2928	4″	Stag	Texas Jack	Clip, Punch	205
2930	3⅝″	Stag	Jack	Spear, Pen	205
2931	3⅜″	Stag	Jack		120
2932	3¼″	Stag	Congress	Sheepfoot, Pen	150
2933	3″	Stag	Sleeve-board	Spear, Pen	145
2934	3⅜″	Stag	Senator Pen	Spear, Pen	95

Pattern	Size	Handle	Knife Type	Blades	Mint Price
2938	3¼″	Stag	Sleeve-board	Spear, Pen	150
2940	3⅜″	Stag	Jack	Spear, Pen	210
2943	3¾″	Stag	Sleeve-board	Spear, Pen	125
2945	3¼″	Stag	Senator pen	Spear, Pen	110
2948	3⅜″	Stag	Senator Pen	Spear, Pen	115
2949	3½″	Stag	Jack	Spear, Pen	160
2950	3½″	Stag	Jack	Spear, Pen	160

Pattern	Size	Handle	Knife Type	Blades	Mint Price
2951	3½″	Stag	Jack	Clip, Punch	$155
2952	3½″	Stag	Jack	Clip, Pen	200
2954	3½″	Stag	Jack	Spear, Pen	205
2956	3½″	Stag	Serpentine Jack	Spear, Pen	160
2958	3½″	Stag	Jack	Clip, Pen	160

Pattern	Size	Handle	Knife Type	Blades	Mint Price
2959	3⅜″	Stag	Jack	Spear, Pen	215
2961	3⅜″	Stag	Jack	Spey, Pen	165
2962	2⅞″	Stag	Dog Leg	Spear, Pen	100
2963	3″	Stag	Senator Pen	Spear, Pen	125
2964	3⅝″	Stag	Jack	Spear, Pen	155
2966	3⅝″	Stag	Jack	Spear, Pen	275
2967	3⅞″	Stag	Swell Center	Spear, Clip	350
2969	3⅞″	Stag	Swell Center	Clip, Spey	285
2973	3⅝″	Stag	Jack	Clip, Pen	185
2974	3½″	Stag	Serpentine Jack	Clip, Pen	160
2976	4″	Stag	Texas Jack	Clip, Pen	200
2978	3½″	Stag	Physician	Spear, Pen	315
2980	3⅝″	Stag	Cattle	Clip, Pen	185

Pattern	Size	Handle	Knife Type	Blades	Mint Price
2981	3¼″	Stag	Pen	Spear, File	$100
2982	4″	Stag	Texas Jack	Spear, Pen	320
2983	3½″	Stag	Jack	Clip, Pen	130

Pattern	Size	Handle	Knife Type	Blades	Mint Price
2988	4″	Stag	Texas Jack	Clip, Pen	325
2990	2⅞″	Stag	Dog Leg	Clip, Pen	130
2991	3⅝″	Stag	Peanut	Spear, Clip	300
2992	3⅝″	Stag			150
2993	3⅞″	Stag	Trapper	Clip, Pen	365
2994	3⅝″	Stag	Jack	Spear, Pen	165
2995	3⅝″	Stag	Jack	Spear, Pen	210
2996	3¾″	Stag	Congress	Sheepfoot, Pen	175
2997	3⅜″	Stag	Serpentine Pen	Clip, Pen	165
2998	3½″	Stag	Jack	Spear, Pen	150
2999	3⅛″	Stag	Dog Leg Jack	Clip, Pen	210
3001	3½″	Gray Celluloid	Cattle	Spear, Spey, Punch	285
3002	3⅝″	Iridescent Celluloid	Whittler	Clip, Spey, Punch	270

Pattern	Length	Stamping	Handle		Mint Price
3003	3½″	Gold Celluloid	Premium Stock	Clip, Spear, Spey	$265
3005	3⅝″	Black Celluloid		Large Clip, Small Clip, Pen	235
3006	3⅜″	Black Celluloid	Serpentine Pen	Clip, Pen, File	200
3007	4″	Black Celluloid	Premium Stock	Clip, Sheepfoot, Spey	285
3008	3⅝″	White Celluloid	Cattle	Spear, Sheepfoot, Spey	250
3009	3⅝″	White Celluloid	Cattle	Clip, Spey, Punch	300

Pattern	Length	Stamping	Handle		Mint Price
3010	3¾″	Abalone Celluloid	Cattle	Clip, Spey, Punch	340
3014	4″	Pearl Gray Celluloid	Premium Stock	Clip, Sheepfoot, Spey	290
3015	3⅝″	Gold Celluloid		Saber Clip, Small Clip, Pen	265

Pattern	Size	Handle	Knife Type	Blades	Mint Price
3016	3⅝″	Gray Celluloid	Cattle	Clip, Spey, Punch	$315
3017	4″	Varicolor Celluloid	Premium Stock	Clip, Sheepfoot, Spey	325
3018	4″	Red & White Celluloid	Premium Stock	Clip, Sheepfoot, Spey	285
3019	3½″	Red Celluloid	Whittler	Spear, Spey, Punch	280
3020	3½″	Green & Red Celluloid	Whittler	Spear, Spey, Punch	290

Pattern	Size	Handle	Knife Type	Blades	Mint Price
3022	3¼″	Imitation Tortoise Shell	Whittler		250
3023	3⅝″	Red Celluloid	Whittler		325
3024	3⅝″	Celluloid	Whittler		325
3025	3½″	Abalone Blue Celluloid	Premium Stock	Clip, Spear, Spey	250
3026	3¼″	Iridescent Celluloid	Premium Stock	Spear, Sheepfoot, Spay	275
3027	3¼″	Red Celluoid	Premium Stock	Clip, Spey, Pen	220
3028	3¼″	Green & Black Celluloid	Premium Stock	Clip, Spey, Pen	220

Pattern	Size	Handle	Knife Type	Blades	Mint Price
3029	3¼″	Red & Black Celluloid	Premium Stock	Clip, Spey, Punch	$220
3030	3⅜″	Abalone Blue Celluloid	Senator	Clip, Spey, Pen	225
3031	3⅜″	Gray Celluloid	Senator	Spear, Pen, Punch	275
3033	3″	Gold Celluloid	Serpentine Cattle		175
3034	3″	Blue Abalone Celluloid	Serpentine Cattle		175
3035	3⅜″	Gold Celluloid		Clip, Sheepfoot, Pen	190
3036	3⅜″	Celluloid	Cattle		165
3040	3″	Celluloid	Whittler		180
3041	3″	Red & Black Celluloid	Senator	Spear, Pen, Pen	185
3042	3⅜″	Green & Black Celluloid	Senator	Spear, Pen, Pen	185
3043	3⅜″	Red & Black Celluloid	Senator	Spear, Pen, File	220
3044	3⅜″	Red & Green Celluloid	Senator	Spear, Pen, File	220
3045	3¼″	Celluloid	Whittler		165
3046	3¼″	Celluloid	Whittler		175
3047	3½″	Celluloid	Premium Stock		160
3048	4″	Celluloid	Premium Stock		200
3049	3⅝″	Imitation White Bone	Cattle		300
3331	3¼″	Pearl	Lobster Pen	Spear, Pen, File	165
3338	3″	Pearl	Sleeve-board		120

3341	3⅜″	Pearl	Cattle		$250
3345	3¼″	Pearl	Whittler		225
3347	3¼″	Pearl	Whittler		260
3348	3¼″	Pearl	Stock		175
3349	3″	Pearl	Sleeve-board		200
3350	3¼″	Pearl	Senator Whittler		235
3352	3½″	Pearl	Senator	Spear, Pen, File	265
3353	2⅝″	Pearl	Senator	Spear, Pen, File	165
3357	3¼″	Pearl	Whittler	Spear, Pen, File	275
3360	3¼″	Pearl	Bartender		225

3366	3⅜″	Pearl	Senator Whittler		295
3370	3″	Pearl	Lobster Pen	Spear, Pen, File	200
3371	3″	Pearl	Lobster Pen	Spear, Sissors, File	250

Pattern	Size	Handle	Knife Type	Blades	Mint Price
3373	2⅞″	Pearl	Senator Whittler		$175
3376	4″	Pearl	Premium Stock	Clip, Sheepfoot, Spey	275
3377	3¼″	Pearl	Sleeve-board	Spear, Pen, Pen	275
3378	3″	Pearl	Sleeve-board Whittler		210
3379	3″	Pearl	Senator Whittler		200
3380	2¾″	Pearl	Sleeve-board	Spear, Pen, File	150
3381	3⅛″	Pearl	Lobster Pen	Spear, Pen, File	185
3382	3″	Pearl	Lobster Pen	Spear, Pen, File	200
3625	3⅝″	Ebony	Cattle		150

Pattern	Size	Handle	Knife Type	Blades	Mint Price
3902	3½″	Stag	Swell Center	Clip Pen, Pen	325
3903	3¾″	Stag	Whittler	Clip, Spey, Punch	575
3904	3¾″	Stag	Whittler	Clip, Spey, Pen	650
3905	3½″	Stag	Cattle	Spear, Spey, Punch	285

Pattern	Size	Handle	Knife Type	Blades	Mint Price
3906	4″	Stag	Premium Stock	Clip, Sheepfoot, Spey	$310
3907	4″	Stag	Premium Stock	Clip, Spey, Punch	350
3908	3¾″		Balloon Whittler		275
3909	3⅜″	Stag	Senator	Clip, Spey, Pen	265
3911	3″	Stag	Senator Whittler		175
3914	2¾″	Bone	Senator Pen		125
3915	3½″	Stag	Cattle	Spear, Pen, Punch	260
3916	3½″	Stag	Premium Stock	Clip, Spey, Punch	250
3917	3½″	Stag	Premium Stock	Clip, Spear, Spey	250
3924	3″	Stag	Senator	Spear, Pen, File	225
3925	3⅝″	Stag	Balloon Whittler	Saber Clip, Clip, Pen	325
3927	3⅜″	Stag	Serpentine Pen	Spear, Pen, File	235
3928	4″	Stag	Premium Stock	Clip, Sheepfoot, Spey	300

Pattern	Size	Handle	Knife Type	Blades	Mint Price
3929	3¼″	Stag	Congress	Sheepfoot, Pen, File	290

Pattern	Size	Handle	Knife Type	Blades	Mint Price
3931	3⅛″	Stag	Sleeve-board	Spear, Pen, File	$145
3932	3⅜″	Stag	Senator	Spear, Pen, File	190
3933	3⅜″	Stag	Senator	Clip, Sheepfoot, Pen	210
3936	3⅝″	Stag	Cattle	Spear, Clip, Spey	325
3938	3⅜″	Stag	Senator	Spear, Pen, Pen	185
3939	3⅜″	Stag	Senator	Spear, Pen, Punch	275
3942	3⅜″	Stag	Cattle	Spear, Sheepfoot, Spey	265
3944	3¼″	Stag	Whittler	Spear, Pen, File	300
3948	3¾″	Stag	Gunstock	Clip, Sheepfoot, Spey	300
3949	3″	Stag	Serpentine Cattle		165

| 3950 | 3⅝″ | Stag | Cattle | Clip, Sheepfoot, Spey | 300 |
| 3951 | 3⅝″ | Stag | Cattle | Spear, Spey, Punch | 300 |

Pattern	Size	Handle	Knife Type	Blades	Mint Price
3952	3⅝″	Stag	Cattle	Clip, Sheepfoot, Pen	$300
3953	3¼″	Stag	Bartender		175
3959	4″	Stag	Serpentine Stock	Clip, Sheepfoot, Spey	300
3960	4″	Stag	Premium Stock	Clip, Sheepfoot, Pen	300
3961	4″	Stag	Premium Stock	Clip, Spey, Punch	300
3962	4″	Horn	Premium Stock	Clip, Sheepfoot, Spey	325
3963	4″	Stag	Serpentine Stock		240
3964	4″	Stag	Premium Stock		250
3965	3¼″	Stag	Premium Stock	Spear, Sheepfoot, Spey	200
3966	3¼″	Stag	Premium Stock		165
3967	3¼″	Stag	Premium Stock	Clip, Spey, Pen	220
3968	3¼″	Stag	Premium Stock	Clip, Pen, Punch	275
3969	3¼″	Stag	Whittler		250
3971	3⅝″	Stag	Swell Center	Clip, Spey, Pen	295
3972	3⅝″	Stag	Swell Center	Clip, Spey, Punch	325
3973	3½″	Stag	Cattle	Clip, Spear, Spey	265
3975	3⅜″	Stag	Cattle	Clip, Spey, Punch	275
3977	3⅜″	Stag	Cattle	Clip, Sheepfoot, Pen	200

Pattern	Size	Handle	Knife Type	Blades	Mint Price
3978	3¼″	Stag	Serpentine Stock	Clip, Sheepfoot, Pen	$160
3979	3⅝″	Stag	Cattle	Clip, Spey, Punch	290
3980	3″	Stag	Cattle	Spear, Spey, Pen	220

3991	3¼″	Stag	Sleeveboard	Spear, Pen, Pen	185
3992	3⅜″	Stag	Senator	Spear, Pen, Pen	265
3993	4″	Stag	Premium Stock	Clip, Spey, Pen	285
4001	4″	Green Celluloid	Premium Stock	Clip, Sheepfoot, Spey, Punch	425
4301	2¾″	Pearl	Lobster Pen	Spear, Pen, Sissors, File	250
4313	3″	Pearl	Senator		250
4320	3¼″	Pearl	Lobster Whittler	Spear, Pen, Pen, File	250
4340	3¼″	Pearl	Senator	Spear, Pen, Pen, File	325

Pattern	Size	Handle	Knife Type	Blades	Mint Price
4341	3¼″	Pearl	Senator	Spear, Pen, Pen, File	$325
4901	3⅜″	Bone	Utility		225
4910	4″	Stag		Clip, Sheepfoot, Spey, Punch	550
4918	3″	Stag	Congress	Sheepfoot, Pen, Sheepfoot, File	240

4920	3¼″	Stag	Lobster	Spear, Pen, Pen, File	165
4930	3¼″	Stag	Congress	Sheep foot, Pen, Pen, File	300
4931	3½″	Stag	Congress	Sheepfoot, Pen, Sheepfoot, Pen	325
4950	3¾″	Bone	Utility	Spear Punch, Can Opener, Screwdriver	260
4951	3⅝″	Stag	Utility		275

Pattern	Size	Handle	Knife Type	Blades	Mint Price
4961	4″	Stag	Premium Stock	Clip, Spey, Sheepfoot, Punch	$325
4962	4″	Stag	Premium Stock	Clip, Sheepfoot, Spey, Punch	475
4963	4″	Stag	Premium Stock		300
4975	3¼″	Stag	Bartender		215
4990	3⅝″	Stag	Utility		275
4991	3½″	Stag	Utility		250

Winchester Reproductions

New Winchester knives have been made by Blue Grass Cutlery Corporation of Manchester, Ohio, since 1987. These knives are reproductions of old Winchester knives, and their manufacture is licensed and authorized by Olin Corporation, owner of the Winchester trademark. They are made in the United States using old original dies from Winchester's factory of about a half-century ago. The knives are of high quality, most with old-style bone handles, pinned handle shields, and hand-hammered rivets. The original Winchester trademark is used for blade etching and tang stamps. The pattern number and year of manufacture are stamped on the reverse tangs.

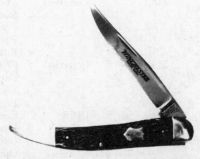

W15 1924—(4⅜″) One-blade Toothpick (or Powderhorn), Rogers bone handles; heraldic shield   *$100*

W15 3964—(3⅝″) Stockman; clip, sheepfoot, and spey blades; Rogers bone handles; heraldic shield $90

W15 1901—(3⅞″) One-blade Bow-Tie; Rogers bone handles; heraldic shield $90

W15 1987-1—(3½″) Two-blade Penknife; cast-bronze color handle; commemorates the 1873 model Winchester rifle $35

W15 2921—*(3½″) Two-blade Gunstock Jack;* spear and pen blades; Rogers bone handle; heraldic shield   *$90*

W15 2904—*(4⅛″) Trapper;* clip and spey blades; Rogers bone handles; heraldic shield   *$90*

W15 2857—*(3⅞″) Serpentine Teardrop Jack;* spear and pen blades; Rogers bone handles; heraldic shield   *$85*

W15 2967—*(3⅞″) Texas Jack;* spear and clip blades; Peach Seed bone handles; heraldic shield   *$95*

W15 3904—*(3⅝″) Whittler;* 3 backsprings; clip, spear, and spey blades; Rogers bone handles; heraldic shield   *$110*

W15 2851—(3") Gunstock Jack; spear and pen blades; Rogers bone handles; heraldic shield   *$75*

W15 1927—(5⅜") Lockback folding hunter; long clip blade; Peach Seed bone handles; propeller shield   *$100*

W15 2935—(3⅝") Wharncliffe Half Whittler; Congress pattern; Wharncliffe and pen blades; slanted pinched bolsters; Rogers bone handles; curved bar shield   *$65*

W15 2991—(3⅝") Equal End; spear and clip blades; Rogers bone handles; propeller shield   *$65*

W15 1988-1—(3") One-blade lockback; cast-bronze color handle; commemorates 1912 Winchester shotgun   *$35*

W15 2880½—(3⅞") Swell-Center Equal End; spear and clip blades; Peach Seed bone handles; balloon shield   *$65*

W15 2913½—(4¼") Moose; clip and spear blades; Peach Seed bone handles; heraldic shield   *$70*

W15 3971—(3⅝") Whittler; clip, pen, and short clip blades; Rogers bone handles; heraldic shield   *$65*

W15 2978—(3⅛") Physician's; spear and pen blades; Rogers bone handles; heraldic shield   *$60*

W15 3949—(3¾") Sowbelly Stockman; clip, sheepfoot, and spey blades; Peach Seed bone handles; heraldic shield   *$70*

W15 2904½—(3⅞") Trapper; clip and spey blades; saber-ground clip blade; Peach Seed bone handles; heraldic shield   *$70*

W15 1989-1—(3") One-blade lockback; cast-bronze color handles; commemorates Winchester 1921 shotgun   *$35*

W15 1950—(5⅜") Lockback folding hunter; clip blade; genuine stag handles; propeller shield   *$110*

GEORGE WOSTENHOLM & SON CUTLERY
COMPANY (I*XL)

The Wolstenholme family's involvement in cutlery dates back to 1745, when George Wolstenholme and his son Henry operated a small cutlery business in Stannington, England. Henry was one of the first cutlers to use springs for pocketknives and, in 1757, was granted the SPRING trademark. I*XL, the company's most famous trademark, was first used in 1787.

Henry Wolstenholme and his sons Martin and George continued the business. Upon Henry's death, George took over the business and moved it to nearby Sheffield. The name was changed at that time from Wolstenholme to Wostenholm so that it would be easier to stamp on a blade tang. In 1832, the firm moved to the Rockingham Works. Wostenholm was one of the first to concentrate cutlers in a factory, as opposed to the cottage industry that had existed earlier. His son, another George and the third Wostenholm of that name to be involved in the business, expanded the firm into the world market and became sole owner of the company.

In 1848, Wostenholm purchased the Washington Works and moved into that building, becoming a major factor in the world cutlery market. Wostenholm's primary customer became the

United States, and that market greatly influenced the patterns or types of knives made. A large percentage of the Bowie knives sold and used in the United States were marked with the famed I*XL (meaning "I excel") stamping. The location markings of the Rockingham Works and the Washington Works, coupled with markings of the English monarchs, are of great assistance in dating the manufacture of Wostenholm knives.

Among the stampings used by the company were I*XL GEORGE WOSTENHOLM & SON LTD, I*XL GEORGE WO-STENHOLM CELEBRATED, SHEFFIELD, ENGLAND, and the last named marking with "Oil the Joints" stamped on the reverse of the tang.

The firm was purchased in 1971 by Sheffield's Joseph Rodgers & Sons Cutlery to form Rodgers-Wostenholm, which was in turn sold to Imperial Knife Associated Companies in 1977. In the early 1980s a line of Schrade-I*XL knives was introduced, but although they were knives of good quality, the line was short-lived. A group of English investors purchased the firm in 1984, and U.S. distribution rights to both Rodgers and I*XL knives were sold to a new company called Rodgers-Wostenholm, USA Ltd.

PART
◁ 4 ▷

Commemorative and Limited-Edition Knives

LISTINGS OF COMMEMORATIVE AND LIMITED-EDITION KNIVES

75TH ANNIVERSARY OF AUTO AUTOMATION

Produced by Case for the Hastings Company commemorating the first auto assembly line. A pattern 41059L, the knife had never before been produced by Case. Tan composition handles engraved and filled in brown.
Collector Value   *$12*

AFRICAN SAFARI SET

500 limited-edition fixed-blade knives made for Remington Cutlery Stores; includes two stag-handled knives housed in a green leather sheath and mounted on a wall plaque.
Collector Value   *$250*

AMERICAN ARMED FORCES SERIES

Produced by United Boker in 1988. Six knives in the series, one for each branch of service plus "Vietnam Veterans" and "American Combat Veterans." Bone handles; special blade etching on both blades of each knife in the series. Display boxed.
Collector Value   *$45*

AMERICAN BICENTENNIAL SERIES

Made by Alcas Cutlery for Parker-Frost Cutlery; 1,500 sets produced. Two 5½" clasp knives, one each with wood and genuine stag handles; matching serial numbers. Blades etched with both the 1776 and 1976 U.S. flags. Housed in a walnut box.
Collector Value   *$175*

AMERICAN EAGLE BICENTENNIAL SERIES

Commemorative set of five knives honoring Patrick Henry, Nathan Hale, John Adams, Thomas Jefferson, and George Washington; 12,000 sets produced; matching serial numbers. Deluxe gift-boxed with registration papers.
Collector Value   *$150*

BERETTA

In 1984, Beretta issued a boot knife in a special limited edition of 500 serial-numbered knives. It has a 5¼″ blade and came complete with sheath and presentation case.
Collector Value   *$130*

BOKER-WISS COMMEMORATIVES

In 1971, Boker, Germany, began to produce an annual series commemorating Boker U.S.A. and Wiss anniversaries. The knives had handles of various materials, with two shields inlaid into the handles. One shield was the usual "Tree Brand" and the other was stamped "Wiss" and the issue year.

1971—15,000 produced, not serial-numbered; premium stock pattern; black composition with 2 shields.
Collector Value   *$35*

1972—20,000 non-serial-numbered knives produced; small stockman with black handles inlaid with 2 gold shields.
Collector Value   *$35*

1973—18,000 serial-numbered knives produced; four-blade Congress pattern; black handles with 2 red shields.
Collector Value   *$45*

1974—18,000 serial-numbered knives produced; 4" stock pattern with square bolsters; black handles with 2 gold shields; blades etched.
Collector Value   *$40*

1975—"The Sternwheeler" penknife pattern with simulated pearl handle; 20,000 produced; etched master blade.
Collector Value   *$40*

1976—"Heritage of Freedom" folding hunter bicentennial knife; 24,000 produced.
Collector Value   *$55*

1977—Two-blade Canoe with Cracked Ice handles; 12,000 produced.
Collector Value   *$45*

1978—Two-blade bone-handled pattern trapper, honoring the southern mountaineer; named the "Hillbilly"; 12,000 produced.
Collector Value   *$50*

1979—Lockback folding hunter with wood handles and etched blades, honoring the hardware industry; 20,000 produced.
Collector Value   *$45*

1980—"The Railroader," a stag-handled 5" folding hunter with etched blade; 8,000 produced.
Collector Value   *$70*

1980—"White Lightning"; 10,000 produced in limited edition.
Collector Value   *$45*

1981—"The Appalachian Trail," a Canoe with jigged rosewood handles; blade etching; 10,000 made.
Collector Value   *$40*

1981—"The Collector," 3-blade stockman; 10,000 produced.
Collector Value   *$45*

1982—"The Whittler"; 10,000 produced.
Collector Value   *$35*

1983—"The Farm Boy"; 8,000 produced.
Collector Value $35

1984—"Old Tom," 1-blade folding hunter; 8,200 produced.
Collector Value $25

1985—"Blackbeard"; limited edition of 4,100 produced.
Collector Value $125

1986—"The Forty-Niner," salute to gold rush; 5,000 produced.
Collector Value $40

1987—"The Constitution," 4-blade Congress pattern; 2 sheepfoot
blades, deep-etched; 8,000 produced.
Collector Value $40

1988—"The Titanic," lockback folding hunter with ivory composition handle, scrimshawed; 3,000 produced.
Collector Value $85

1989—"Spring Gobbler," 2-blade trapper with laser-engraved
oak handles; 3,000 produced.
Collector Value $45

1989—"The Graf Zeppelin," 2-blade trapper with etched blades;
black composition handles; 3,000 produced.
Collector Value $50

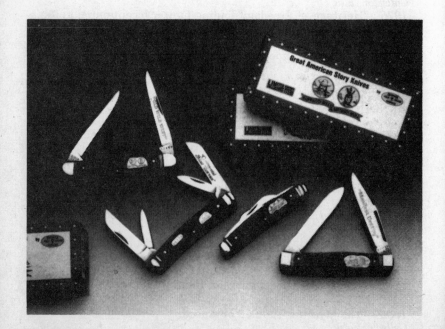

BOKER STORYTELLER SET

8,000 sets produced by Boker in 1983, consisting of a stockman, "Jesse Chisholm," with green bone handles; a 4-blade Congress, "Davy Crockett," with rosewood handles; and a trapper, "Jim Bridger," with bone handles. Redwood box.
Collector Value   *$125 set*

BOKER BONE-HANDLED SET

5,000 sets containing five different patterns made by Boker, Solingen, in 1977. Total of 25,000 knives made.
Collector Value   *$100 set*

BOKER SPIRIT OF AMERICA SERIES

Series of 24 knives introduced in 1974, with a different knife issued each 3 months until 1978. The original retail price was $12 each.

"Sweet Land of Liberty" stock knife issued May 1974.
Collector Value   *$30*

"American Eagle" stock knife issued July 1974.
Collector Value   *$25*

"The Alamo" Texas jackknife issued September 1974.
Collector Value   *$25*

"Prairie Schooner" equal-end jackknife issued December 1974.
Collector Value   *$22*

"Statue of Liberty" large stockman issued February 1975.
Collector Value   *$22*

"Dixie" Congress pattern issued April 1975.
Collector Value   *$22*

"Last Frontier" stock knife issued July 1975.
Collector Value   *$20*

"Old Wild West" trapper issued September 1975.
Collector Value   *$20*

"Rise to World Power" swell-end jackknife issued November 1975.
Collector Value   *$20*

"War to End all Wars" serpentine jackknife issued February 1976.
Collector Value   *$20*

"Dawn of the Atomic Age" stock knife issued April 1976.
Collector Value   *$25*

"200 Years of Freedom" stock knife issued July 1976.
Collector Value   *$20*

"Birth of Southern Industry" Congress pattern issued August 1976.
Collector Value   *$20*

"Westward Expansion" trapper issued October 1976.
Collector Value   *$20*

"Blazing the Trail" premium stock knife issued December 1976.
Collector Value   *$20*

"American Proclamation" Texas jackknife issued February 1977.
Collector Value   *$20*

"California Gold Rush" premium stock knife issued April 1977.
Collector Value   *$20*

"Bridging the Continent" premium stock knife issued June 1977.
Collector Value   *$20*

"Modern Fuel" jackknife issued September 1977.
Collector Value   *$20*

"Continental Mail Service" Congress knife issued November 1977.
Collector Value   *$20*

"Modern Energy" whittler issued December 1977.
Collector Value   *$20*

"On to Oklahoma" dogleg jackknife issued February 1978.
Collector Value   *$20*

"Revolution in Transportation" stockman issued April 1978.
Collector Value   *$20*

"200 Million Americans" premium stockman issued June 1978.
Collector Value   *$20*

BONNIE AND CLYDE COMMEMORATIVE

578 sets produced by Battle Axe in 1979. Bone-handled lockbacks with gold-etched blades.
Collector Value   *$95*

BUCK BICENTENNIAL

This Buck knife was a cased sheath knife with etched blade and a medallion.
Collector Value   *$225*

BUCK CUTLERY WORLD KNIFE

In 1981 Buck's custom shop issued a limited-edition Bowie exclusively for the Cutlery World retail chain. Most of the stores were allowed only one knife.
Collector Value   *$450*

BUCK FREEDOM TRAPPER

5,000-knife limited edition made by Buck. Yellow celluloid handles with American flag engraving and Buck's "Knife, Bolt and Hammer" shield; blades etched. Boxed with "Right to Bear Arms" belt buckle.
Collector Value   *$35*

BUCK GRAND SLAM SET

2,500 sets produced by Buck in 1982. Set consists of four Model 501 knives with four different wood handles. Blades etched by Aurum featuring "Sheep of the Great West." Housed in wood case with special brass belt buckle.
Collector Value   *$250*

BUCK GRIZZLY

250 made by Buck in 1983 for Smoky Mountain Knifeworks. Genuine stag handles on Model 500.
Collector Value   *$85*

BUCK REDBONE SET

500 serialized sets made by Buck Knives in 1989 for Smoky Mountain Knifeworks; includes 301 Stockman, 305 Lancer, 303 Cadet, and 309 Companion. Original "Knife, Bolt and Hammer" shield inlaid into jigged red bone handles; engraved nickel silver bolsters.

Collector Value   *$150 set*

BUCK SILVER ANNIVERSARY COMMEMORATIVE

2,500 produced by Buck to honor their 25th anniversary. Model 110 with gold-filled blade etching by Aurum.

Collector Value   *$90*

BUCK STATUE OF LIBERTY COMMEMORATIVES

Buck Knives produced two limited-edition knives in 1986 honoring the Statue of Liberty:

2,500 produced; Model 500 folders with walnut handles and etched blade, Statue of Liberty shield; with plaque.
Collector Value $95

15,000 produced in 1986; cast-pewter-handled Model 525.
Collector Value $20

BUCK YELLOWHORSE KNIVES

Knives by Buck with special channel inlay on handles blending turquoise, other stones, woods, and metals; hand-tooled bolsters. Decorative work is done individually by Navajo artisan David Yellowhorse, and no two knives are exactly alike. Knives used for these special series are Buck's Woodsman, Maverick, and Ranger. Two series produced are "Buffalo" and "Running Horse."
Collector Value $225 each

BUCK BUGLING ELKS

2,000 serial-numbered Model 110 folding hunter limited-edition knives produced by Buck; dark mahogany wood handles.
Collector Value $80

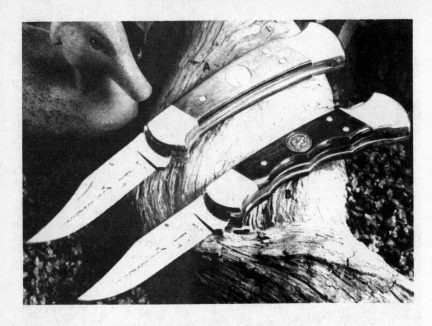

BUCK—DUCKS UNLIMITED
50TH ANNIVERSARY

Produced by Buck in the Ranger model lockback knife. Layered birch handle with brass anniversary symbol shield. Handle of U.S. knife is golden brown; Canadian knife is rich green. Blade of each has gold-filled etched design by Aurum.
Collector Value $75

BUCK GOLDEN EAGLE

1,500 serial-numbered Model 110 folding hunter limited-edition knives produced by Buck; birchwood handle.
Collector Value $85

BUCK COMMEMORATIVE BOWIE

Produced by Buck Knives to honor Hoyt Buck: a 15″ Bowie knife with gold-filled etching on blade reproducing a painting de-

picting Buck in his Kansas blacksmith shop at the turn of the century. Birchwood handle, brass guard, and rivets. Gift boxed.
Collector Value   *$275*

BUCK—THE CANOEIST

2,500 serial-numbered Model 112 limited-edition knives produced by Buck.
Collector Value   *$65*

BUFORD PUSSER COMMEMORATIVE

5,000 knives based on the R1123 Bullet pattern, honoring the "Walking Tall" sheriff. Delrin handles with a special large shield. The sharpening stick with each knife had a matching serial number.
Collector Value   *$100*

CAMILLUS WILDLIFE SERIES

Series of four knives produced by Camillus for Smoky Mountain Knifeworks. Delrin handles are inlaid with a cast-pewter wildlife engraving from originals by Sid Bell. Each knife is 4⅜" Trapper pattern with master blade etched "American Wildlife." Inlays include Charging Bear, Running Deer, Razorback Hog, and American Eagle.
Collector Value   *$40*

CASE COLLECTOR SETS

Case knives, especially Trapper patterns, have been used to market large numbers of commemorative and limited-edition knives or knife sets. W. R. Case & Sons Cutlery has been a prolific supplier of these collectibles and has marketed a large number through the company's own marketing system. In some instances, knives are made under contract by Case for distributors or dealers who are responsible for marketing them. These are usually referred to as "Factory Authorized" knives or sets. In other instances, smaller numbers of specific Case patterns are purchased and then prepared for market as limited editions by special blade etching and boxing. Because of their large number, most of the Case knives and sets have been grouped here.

Case 125th Anniversary Civil War Commemorative

Two-knife, matching serial-numbered set produced by Case. Knives are No. GR199½ "Battle of Bull Run" and No. BL199½ "Fort Sumter, 1861" with blade etching. Smooth gray and blue synthetic handles with raised-letter shield. Housed in a presentation box.

Collector Value $125 set

Case 1973 Stag Set

In 1970, concurrent with the stamping change, Case discontinued the use of stag for handles. In order to use the factory inventory of this handle material, the first Case collectors' set of assorted stag-handled knives was issued in 1973. The set consisted of 18 pocketknives and five sheath knives; 2,000 sets were produced. Knives varied in their date stamping and included U.S.A., 10 dot, 9 dot, and 8 dot. Two knives made especially for the set were the Cheetah (5111½) and the 5375.

Collector Value $2,500 set

Case 1976 Stag Set

In 1976, 700 stag-handled collector sets were issued by Case; 600 of the sets included two Cheetahs and one Bulldog; a canoe replaced one of the Cheetahs in the other 100 sets.

Collector Value $2,400 set

Case 1977 Stag Set

Set made by Case in 1977 containing 7 pocketknives and 5 sheath knives; approximately 10,000 sets were made. Several of the knives were made for the first time with stainless steel blades and were etched "Case XX Razor Edge."

Collector Value $425 set

Case 1982 World's Fair Knife

5,000 made in 1982 to commemorate the World's Fair held in Knoxville, TN; Case pattern 8220 handled in mother-of-pearl.

Collector Value $65

Case 75th Anniversary Canoe Set

5,000 matching serial-numbered sets issued in commemoration of Case's 75th year of business; consists of stag-handled Canoes with bolsters engraved and gold-plated.
Collector Value   *$325 set*

Case 75th Anniversary Set

Produced in 1980; consists of 7 stag-handled 10-dot knives, patterns 5318, 5244, 5275, 5207, 52109X, 5208, and 5235½ in wood box; bolsters engraved.
Collector Value   *$325 set*

Case 80th Anniversary Limited Edition

5,000 produced in 1985; folding hunter 5165SS, bone handle; blade is etched "W.R. Case & Sons 1905–1985 Anniversary." Wood display box.
Collector Value   *$90*

Case Alamo Bowie

3,000 produced by Case in 1985; Bowie knife with black walnut handle and nickel silver guard; blade color etched with the Alamo and Texas state outline. Serial-numbered and housed in an oak case with story of the Alamo and its heroes inside.
Collector Value   *$175*

Case Astronaut's Knife

2,494 made in 1972—the type of knife that was carried in 1965 by Maj. Virgil Grissom and Cmdr. John Young and has been carried in all NASA flights since that time. The 11″ blade is 13-gauge high-carbon stainless steel, and the handle is polypropylene, attached by round brass rods and drilled for a lanyard. Housed in a display box. Collector values vary with serial number.

Collector Value $400–$700

In the mid-1980s, Case again made a limited number of these knives and called them "the NASA knife."

Collector Value $250

Case Bicentennial Knives

Case made two different knives in 1976 to commemorate America's Bicentennial. Each was housed in a special wood box. The 5165 folding hunter with stag handles, engraved bolsters, and a deep etched blade was produced in a quantity of 10,000 pieces.

Collector Value $150

The 523-7SS stag-handled Bowie with eagle-head pommel and etched blade was produced in a quantity of 2,500 pieces.

Collector Value $285

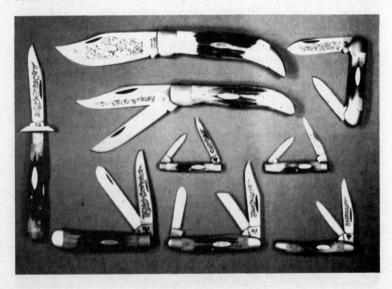

Case Blue Scroll Set

In 1978, another set was issued that contained 8 pocketknives, the 7 patterns from the 1977 set plus a Canoe. Patterns are 5347,

5254, 5111½L, 5233, 52131, 5265, 5172, and 52087 with blue scroll etching on blades, engraved bolsters. Housed in wood display box. 15,000 sets were produced.
Collector Value   *$425 set*

Case Bradford Centennial Set

Produced in 1979; consists of 6 stag-handled knives—patterns 52027, 5275, 5249, 5292, 5207, and 5318—in wood box. Bolsters engraved and blades etched "1879 Bradford Centennial 1979."
Collector Value   *$275 set*

Case Christmas Tree Set

500 serialized mint sets were produced in 1989 by Case for Smoky Mountain Knifeworks. Six knives; includes CT220SS Peanut, CT215SS Gunstock, CT225½SS Swell Center, CT1048SS Trapper, CT318SHSPSS Stockman, CT2131SS Canoe, and CT254SS Trapper. Christmas Tree celluloid handles with Case round "100 Years" shield; engraved bolsters. Housed in custom knife pack.
Collector Value   *$250 set*

In addition to the above engraved and serialized set, Case made 3,000 each of the knives without engraved bolsters and serial numbering.
Collector Value   *$25–$50, depending on pattern*

Case Family Tree Set

550 sets made by Case, consisting of 6 knives, patterns G62087, G6215, G63033, G6199½, G6225½, and G6120; green bone handles. Housed in display box that has Job Case family tree illustration on box top. Master blade of each knife is etched with the name of one of his children.
Collector Value   *$225 set*

Case/Parker Commemorative

3,000 Trapper pattern ROG6254SSD knives produced by Case in 1989. Rogers bone handle is inlaid with both a Case raised-letter shield and a Parker USA shield. Spey blade is Damascus

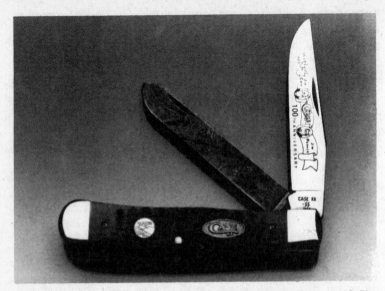

steel; clip blade is etched with likeness of Job Case and Jim Parker. Deluxe wood display case with sliding etched-marble lid.

Collector Value   *$125*

Case Tested XX Limited Edition Set

3,000 produced in 1989; raised gold letter shields; Case Tested XX etched on blades R6111½SS with red bone handle and G6111½SS green bone handle. Housed in replica of old-style Case stock box.

Collector Value   *$125 set*

Case Congress Set

2,000 sets produced by Case; includes pattern numbers 54052, 53052, and 54052 with genuine stag handles. Coffin-shaped bolsters; master blades color-etched. Housed in cherry display case.

Collector Value   *$225 set*

Case Damascus Rainbow Set

500 sets produced by Case in 1989 for Cutlery World and Smoky Mountain Knifeworks; includes 5 1-blade Trappers, patterns R6154D—red, Y6154D—yellow, G6154D—green, B6154D—

blue, and W6154D—white. Blades are 512-layer Damascus; gold-colored raised-letter shield; matching serial numbers. Wood display box with special-color rainbow set label.
Collector Value $425 set

Case First Flight Commemorative

3,000 knives produced in 1989 by Case; folding hunter No. 5265SS. Genuine stag handles; both blades photo-etched with illustrations of the Wright Brothers and their first flight at Kitty Hawk. Gold-color raised-letter Case shield and serial number stamped on bolster surrounded by a long-tail *C* logo.
Collector Value $90

Case Founders Knife

20,000 produced by Case in 1980; stag-handled 5143SSP in special wood box. Blade etched with pictures of W. R., Job, and J. Russell Case.
Collector Value $100

Case Green Bone Set

500 serial-numbered sets produced by Case in 1988, consisting of 6 knives, patterns G62087, G6215, G6120, G6199½, G6225½, and G63033. With display box.
Collector Value $275 set

In addition to the matching serial-numbered set, Case made 2,500 knives of each pattern that were not serial-numbered nor sold in sets.

Collector Value   *$30*

Case Gunboat Set

2,500 sets produced in 1985; consists of 3 Canoe-pattern knives with burnt white bone handles. Patterns are 6194SS, 6294SS, and 6394SS; blades etched with warship names. Housed in wood case.

Collector Value   *$275 set*

Case Ivory Trappers

Produced by Case in 1989, these limited-edition knives are considered transition knives designed to recognize an important period of change and progress for W. R. Case & Sons Cutlery. Handles are of mastodon ivory, and blades combine Damascus steel with modern surgical steel. Display boxes are specially made cultured marble with commemorative engraving.

500 knives were produced as "The Job Case–Jim Parker Commemorative Trappers"; 512-layer Damascus spey blade and surgical steel clip blade with illustration of Job Case and Jim Parker.

Collector Value   *$550*

200 knives were produced exclusively for Cutlery World stores as "The Cutlery World Ivory Trapper"; Damascus clip blade and etched surgical steel spey blade.

Collector Value   *$550*

Case Jack Daniels Old No. 7 Set

5,000 sets produced by Case in 1987; consists of 3 whittler knives displayed on a wood whiskey barrel plaque. Knives are a No. B6108 1-blade, a No. B6208 2-blade, and a No. B6308 3-blade. All have genuine charcoal bone handles and special tang stampings.

Collector Value   *$200 set*

Case Kentucky Bicentennial Series

30,000 each of 3 knives were produced in 1974. All knives were the Case 2137SS pattern but with a variety of handles. One knife, stamped with the pattern number G137, had green Delrin handles. A total of 35,299 of these knives were made with the Case 5-dot stamping. The serial numbers used were 0000001–00150000, 0001–9999, J0001–J9999, and the most collectible of the green handled knives, S0001–S2001.

Collector Value   *$35*

A very few of the knives were stamped and given out when Case's South Bradford plant opened in 1975. Heat-stamped into the handle were the words "Grand Opening: South Bradford Plant," and on the reverse side, "April 1975." A few of these have made their way into the collector's market and currently bring $100.

The second of the series had wood handles.

Collector Value   *$30*

The third knife of the series was stag-handled and stamped with a large serial number. Most were stamped "Case XX U.S.A.," but a rarer version of 2,000 pieces were stamped "Case XX Stainless."

Collector Value (regular version)   *$40*
Collector Value (rarer version)   *$55*

Case Moby Dick

10,000 produced in 1978; 65 pattern with whaling scene scrimshaw on smooth white bone handles; engraved bolsters. Housed in wood display box.

Collector Value   *$200*

Case Nantucket Sleigh Ride

10,000 produced in 1980; 65 pattern with sleigh ride scrimshaw on smooth white bone handles; engraved bolsters. Housed in wood display box.

Collector Value   *$175*

Case Nine Dot Set

Six stag-handled pocketknives without blade etching. Blade stamping is 9-dot "Lightning S," and knife patterns are 52027, 5235½, 5149, 5254, 52131, and Muskrat. Some of these sets have engraved bolsters and are valued higher than those with plain bolsters.

Collector Value   *$275 set*

Case Pearl Set

1,000 sets produced in 1982, consisting of 3 pearl-handled knives—patterns 8207SP SSP, 8249SSP, and 8254SSP—with file-worked backsprings. Housed in hardwood frame case.
Collector Value $575 set

Case Pure Gold Mint Set

500 serialized sets made by Case in 1989 for exclusive distribution by Smoky Mountain Knifeworks; includes patterns 3347SS, 3249SS, 31048SS, 3207SS, 3220SS, 3225SS, and 33033SS with brushed stainless steel blades. Golden celluloid handles with old-style Case logo shield; engraved nickel silver bolsters.
Collector Value $225 set

In addition to the set described above, Case made 3,000 each of the knives without engraved bolsters and serial numbering.
Collector value $17–$30 depending on pattern

Case Red Scroll Set

In 1979, 25,000 Red Scroll Sets were made, containing 7 stag-handled pocketknives, all with stainless steel blades.
Collector Value $325 set

A companion set of 4 stag-handled sheath knives was marketed in late 1979.
Collector Value $125 set

Case Redbone Mint Set

100 limited-edition serialized sets made exclusively for Smoky Mountain Knifeworks in 1987. Set includes R63052, R6205, R62109X, R6215, R6220, and R06263. Hand-engraved nickel silver bolsters, stainless steel blades, raised-letter fancy shield. Custom-made display.
Collector Value $260 set

Case Signature Knife

1,250 4-blade Congress-pattern G64088 knives produced in 1986. Special jigged green bone handles; signature of W. R. & J. Russell Case etched on both main blades. Golden, low-relief Case shield with long-tail *C* surrounding the serial number.
Collector Value $100

Case Apache and Arapaho Stags

2,000 each of the fixed-blade patterns, 5300 and 5400, were made with stag handles, pattern numbers were engraved on the blade rather than stamped; serial-numbered. Includes leather basketweave sheath.
Collector Value   *$50*

Case Stag Barlow Set

5,000 serial-numbered stag-handled Barlows, patterns 52009, 52009 RAZ, and 52009½.
Collector Value   *$165 set*

Case Stag Bowies

Three different limited-edition Bowies were produced by Case in 1985 for Smoky Mountain Knifeworks.
"Great Smoky Mountain 50th Anniversary" Bowie was limited in production to 1,000. Genuine stag-handled Bowie with deep colored blade etching; on solid cherry plaque.
Collector Value   *$165*
Mason-Dixon Series consisted of 2 stag-handled Bowies, "Confederacy" and "Union." Each was limited in production to 750 knives. Housed in deluxe gift box.
Collector Value   *$165*

Case Stag Whittler Set

In 1983, a set of 3 stag-handled whittlers—patterns 5383, 5308, and 5380—were made in a quantity of 2,500 sets. Blades are stainless steel; bolsters are engraved and gold-plated.
Collector Value   *$325 set*

Case Texas Toothpick Set

2,000 sets produced by Case; consisting of patterns 810096SS, 510094SS, and G610098SS; small pearl, medium genuine stag-, and large green bone-handled toothpicks. Each knife is serial-numbered, and master blades are color etched. Housed in a walnut display case.
Collector Value   *$200 set*

Case Texas Sesquicentennial 1836–1986

Produced by Case in 1986; green bone Texas jackknife with blades etched in two colors. Includes display box.
Collector Value   *$75*

Case Trapper Set

2,500 matching serial-number sets issued in 1983, consisting of patterns 6254, 6207, and 6249 with a long spey blade. Blades etched with picture of a trapper.
Collector Value   *$175 set*

Case U.S. Constitution Commemorative

3,000 produced in 1987 by Case; stag-handled Bowie knife with eagle-head pommel; gold-filled deep etching on the 7″ blade; tang stamp is the long-tail *C* design. Mounted on wall plaque.
Collector Value   *$190*

Case V-42 Combat Stiletto

1,500 knives made in 1984 for the American Historical Foundation. Reproduction of the famous V-42 World War II combat knife. One knife, with mirror-polished blade, was designated the American Commemorative; the other, with blued blade, was designated the Canadian Commemorative.
Collector Value   *$125*

Case—Chief Crazy Horse

5,000 produced by Case in 1981 for exclusive distribution by Davidson's Inc. Stag-handled "Kodiak" with blued blade photo-etched on both sides. Leather sheath.
Collector Value   *$325*

COAL MINER

Star Sales imported this 5½″ front lockback from Japan to honor the Coal Miners of America. The blade is etched "Coal Miners, United We Win"; 1,200 of the knives were made.
Collector Value   *$55*

COAL MINERS SERIES BY BOKER

Set of 3 knives made by Boker; medallion set into the handles. Housed in special wood box.
Collector Value   *$120 set*

COLEMAN/WESTERN TEXAS BOWIE

Fewer than 1,000 knives were made, although original plans were for 15,000. Bowie with genuine slab-cut-stag handles. Both sides of the blade feature gold and black Aurum etched scenes from Texas.
Collector Value   *$200*

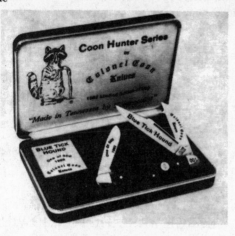

COLONEL COON BLUETICK HOUND

500 3-blade stock knives with blue jigged-bone handles produced in 1983 by Tennessee Knife Works; blade etched and serial-numbered.
Collector Value   *$80*

COLONEL COON REDBONE HOUND

500 3-blade stock knives produced by Tennessee Knife Works in 1983; red bone handles.
Collector Value   *$75*

COLONEL COON TENNESSEE RIVER PEARL

100 3-blade stock knives produced in 1983 by Tennessee Knife Works; unique pearl handles from Tennessee River mussels. All blades are deep-etched with gold filling. Hardshell display case.
Collector Value   *$150*

COLORADO FOLDING HUNTER

Folding hunter hand-assembled by Skip Bryan. Genuine stag handles with bullet shield; serial-numbered.
Collector Value   *$95*

1978 edition with white bone handles.
Collector Value   *$80*

ELVIS PRESLEY COMMEMORATIVE KNIVES

3,000 each of 2 No. 6240 trappers were produced by Case in 1989. Both clip and spey blades are etched. Each knife has the Case raised-letter shield inlaid into handle.

The "Blue Elvis" has blue jigged bone handles.
Collector Value   *$100*

The "Music Box Elvis" has white bone handles and is housed in a special wood music box display.
Collector Value   *$125*

GEORGE WASHINGTON BOWIE

600 serial-numbered large Bowie knives made by Parker Cutlery Company with the Eagle Brand stamping. Etched blade featuring George Washington, "Champion of Liberty." Pakkawood handle secured with brass rivets.
Collector Value   *$55*

GEORGE WASHINGTON VALLEY
FORGE WHITTLER

1,200 serial-numbered knives made by Robt. Klaas—Kissing Crane for J. Nielsen-Meyer. A stag-handled whittler in a pattern discontinued by Klaas prior to 1940; etched blade.
Collector Value   *$75*

GERBER MK II SURVIVAL KNIFE

5,000 knives made by Gerber Legendary Blades to commemorate the 20th anniversary of the Mark II knife; exact reproductions of the original model.
Collector Value   *$125*

JIM BOWIE'S KNIFE—FRANKLIN MINT

Sold as an authentic reproduction of Jim Bowie's knife, this unlimited-issue knife is considered an absurdity by serious knife collectors. The knife was based on one claimed by its owner to have been the knife carried by Bowie at the Alamo. There is no official documentation nor even agreement among historians that Bowie's knife has ever been found. Further, this knife is not a true copy of the knife called the "The Lost Bowie." The knife was sold by the Franklin Mint at $295. Its value would be as an oddity rather than as a collectible knife and would be well beneath the original selling price.

JOHNNY CASH COMMEMORATIVE

Commemorative Case Muskrat pattern with Honeycomb bone handles; raised-letter inlaid shield; etched blades.
Collector Value   *$100*

KISSING CRANE 150TH ANNIVERSARY KNIVES

Two knives were produced by Robt. Klaas in 1984. Each is handled in red bone and inlaid with a special anniversary shield;

blade etched in two colors. Gift boxed with registration certificate.
1,000 3-blade 4″ whittlers.
Collector Value $45
1,200 1-blade 2⅞″ Barlows.
Collector Value $22

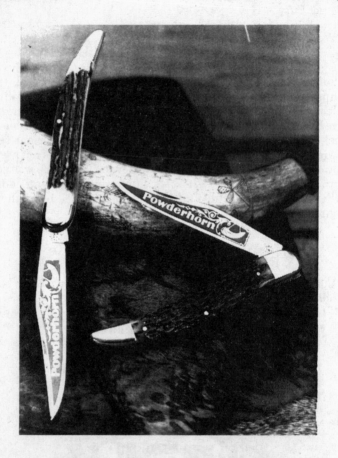

KISSING CRANE POWDERHORNS

Limited edition of 600 sets produced by Robt. Klaas. Consists
of 2 5″ Powderhorn-pattern knives, one with stag handle and one
with red bone. Each knife serial-numbered and boxed.
Collector Value $95 set

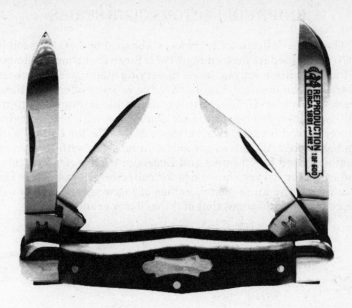

KISSING CRANE REPRODUCTION SERIES

600 each of 12 knives were made by Robt. Klaas. Each knife was a reproduction of one of the classic Kissing Crane patterns dating back nearly a century. The number preceding the description in the following list represents the year the classic pattern was used.

(1901) Two-blade stag-handled penknife	*$30*
(1893) Pearl swell-center whittler	*$40*
(1902) Stag gunstock	*$35*
(1900) Pearl Senator whittler	*$45*
(1895) Stag sheepsfoot whittler	*$35*
(1894) Stag serpentine whittler	*$35*
(1891) Stag 4-blade Congress	*$35*
(1899) Stag whittler	*$35*
(1897) Stag 4-blade Congress	*$38*
(1892) Pearl 4-blade Congress	*$50*
(1896) Pearl 3-blade whittler	*$45*
(1896) Stag 4-blade Congress	*$40*

KNIFE COLLECTORS CLUB SERIES

The Knife Collectors Club was established by A. G. Russell in 1970 and issued its first knife in 1971. Since that time, a number of limited-edition knives, made in varying quantities, have been offered to the membership. Earlier issues were offered in three grades: Premier Grade, with exquisite blade engraving and 14K-gold-engraved bolsters; Excelsior Grade, with blade etching and engraved nickel silver bolsters; and Collector Grade, with blade etching. All knives are serial-numbered, with the lowest numbers used for Premier and Excelsior grades. Descriptions and collector values shown are for collector-grade knives. Depending on the knife model, values of higher-grade issues will range from 5 to 20 times that of the collector grade.

*CM-1:*12,048 made by Schrade-Walden in 1971. Because of rejection of numbered blades at the factory, some may be found with serial numbers up to 15,000. Known as the "Kentucky Rifle," the knife is a 3-blade Stockman pattern with ivory Micarta handle and rifle shield inlay.
Collector Value $95

*CM-2:*12,000 "Grandaddy Barlow" made by Camillus in 1973. One-blade 5½" Barlow pattern has Delrin handle. Special Barlow knife shield inlay.
Collector Value $60

*CM-3:*2,650 "Luger Pistol" made in 1974 by Puma-Werk, honoring the 75th anniversary of the Luger pistol. One-blade knife with genuine stag handle; pistol on shield; blade etched "Luger 1900–1974"; 5,000 were made in three grades.
Collector Value $100

*CM-3:*350 "Luger Cartridge"; same as above except with cartridge shield.
Collector Value $145

*CM-4:*1,800 "Baby Barlow" made in 1975 by C. Bertram—Hen & Rooster. The 2½" Barlow has a genuine ivory handle; nickel silver bolsters and cartridge shield inlay.
Collector Value $235

*CM-5:*1,200 ".44 Magnum Whittler" made in 1975 by C. Bertram—Hen & Rooster. Ebony-handled 3½" whittler with cartridge shield; nickel silver liners and bolsters.
Collector Value $175

*CM-6:*2,400 "Straight Arrow" made in 1976 by C. Bertram—Hen & Rooster; 2⅞" Coffin-pattern handle with 1 saber-ground blade; India stag handle.
Collector Value $165

*CM-7:*2,800 "Long Colt" made in 1977 by C. Bertram—Hen & Rooster; 3⁷⁄₁₆" vest pocket skinner with 1 blade. Cocobolo handles with cartridge shield.
Collector Value $135

*CM-8:*2,200 ".219 Zipper" made in 1978 by C. Bertram—Hen & Rooster; 2⅞" Barlow; ebony-handled, with .219 cartridge shield.
Collector Value $135

CM-9:".300 Savage Canoe" made in 1979 by C. Bertram—Hen & Rooster; 3¼" all stainless steel Canoe pattern with nickel silver cartridge shield inlay.
Collector Value $75

*CM-10:*3,600 "20th Century Barlow" made in 1984 and marked Cattaraugus. Lockback Barlow pattern; bone-handled, with cartridge shield.
Collector Value $45

*CM-11:*3,000 "Pocket Barlow" made in 1986 and marked Cattaraugus; 2⅝" lockback Barlow pattern; bone-handled, with cartridge shield.
Collector Value $35

CM-12:"Split Bolster Jack" single blade liner-lock knife marked Cattaraugus. Bone handles with nickel silver cartridge shield.
Collector Value $35

KNIFE WORLD FIRST EDITION

2,000 made in 1982 by Cripple Creek Cutlery for Knife World Publications, issued to commemorate their 5th anniversary. Designed from a mid-1920s era Union Cut. (KA-BAR) pattern, the

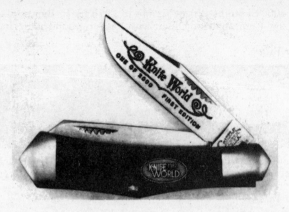

knife became known as a Dogleg Trapper. Master clip blade is etched "Knife World First Edition" and "1 of 2000." Serial numbers are stamped on the secondary spey blade; bone handles inset with special shield. 1982 issue price was $45; very low serial numbers valued up to $250.
Collector Value   *$130*

KNIFE WORLD SECOND EDITION

500 limited-edition knives made in 1987 by Cripple Creek Cutlery for Knife World Publications. Large 2-blade equal-end "cigar" jack; bone-handled; master clip blade is saber-ground and frosted etched. Issue price was $65; very low serial numbers currently valued up to $200.
Collector Value   *$100*

KNIFE WORLD AMBASSADOR'S KNIFE

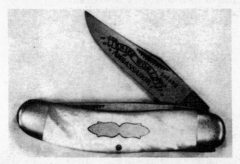

150 limited-issue knives made in 1989 by Frank Buster Cutlery Co.—Fight'n Rooster for Knife World. Sold only to lifetime subscribers (Ambassador Club members), issue price was $85. Two-blade Sowbelly pattern with copperhead-type blades; master blade is color-etched and serial-numbered; handle is mother-of-pearl with inset shield.

Collector Value   *$125*

LEGENDS OF COUNTRY MUSIC

Several knives have been issued commemorating country music stars such as Tom T. Hall and Jerry Clower. Case Razor Trappers with Rogers bone handles; blades etched with star's signature. Decorative boxes.

Collector Value   *$50*

LOU GEHRIG—THE IRON HORSE

Produced by Frost Cutlery Co. using the Case 6240 4½″ Dogleg Trapper pattern with green pick-bone handles. Special blade etching and display box.

Collector Value   *$85*

MORAN 45TH ANNIVERSARY KNIFE

A Damascus fighter patterned after Moran's ST-23 model was made by Charlton, Ltd., in 1985. Production was limited to the

number preordered that year. The knife carried the logo "W.F. Moran by Charlton, Ltd. 45th Anniversary."
Collector Value   *$800*

N.K.C.A. CLUB KNIVES

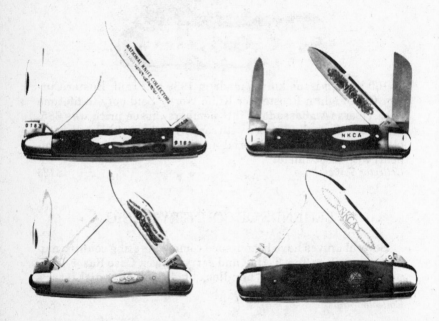

Beginning in 1975, the National Knife Collectors Association contracted for the manufacture of an annual club knife that would be available to its members. The rather remarkable value appreciation of that first knife was a motivating influence for newcomers to the knife-collecting hobby. Subsequently issued N.K.C.A. club knives have appreciated in value, some dramatically and others only slightly. Each knife has been serial-numbered, master blades have been etched, and the club's special shield has been inlaid into the handles. In 1989 and 1990, members were offered a pocketknife or a sheath knife alternative.

1975—A "Kissing Crane" 3-blade whittler made by Robt. Klaas in a limited number of 1,200; stag handles. Original cost was $12.
Collector Value   *$700*

1976—A Case 3-blade whittler made in a limited number of 3,000; white composition handle. Original cost was $15.
Collector Value   *$250*

1977—A "Kissing Crane" 3-blade Canoe made by Robt. Klaas in a limited number of 5,000; stag handles. Original cost was $17.50.
Collector Value   *$125*

1978—A 3-blade Canoe made by Rodgers-Wostenholm division of Schrade in a limited number of 6,000; green bone handles. Original cost was $18.25.
Collector Value   *$100*

1979—A 1-blade trapper made by Case in a limited number of 12,000; stag handles. Original cost was $22.
Collector Value   *$85*

1980—A "Kissing Crane" gunstock whittler made by Robt. Klaas in a limited number of 12,000; stag handles. Original cost was $21.75.
Collector Value   *$65*

1981—A 2-blade equal-end "cigar" pattern made by Queen in a limited number of 12,000; stag handle. Original cost was $24.50.
Collector Value   *$65*

1982—a 2-blade trapper made by Schrade in a limited number of 10,000; stag handles. Original cost was $24.50.
Collector Value   *$65*

1983—A 1-blade lockback folding hunter made by Case in a limited number of 7,000; green bone handles. Original cost was $45.
Collector Value   *$150*

1984—A 1-blade lockback "Hen & Rooster" made by Bertram, USA, in a limited number of 7,000; bone handles. Original cost was $38.
Collector Value   *$80*

1985—A 2-blade dogleg trapper made by Case in a limited number of 7,000; green bone handles. Original cost was $40.
Collector Value   *$75*

1986—A 1-blade lockback type made by Gerber in a limited number of 6,200; bone handles; shield is on bolster. Original cost was $39.
Collector Value   *$125*

1987—A 3-blade cattleman's knife made by Case in a limited number of 7,000; green bone handles. Original cost was $43.95.
Collector Value   *$85*

1988—A 2-blade Bullet pattern made by Camillus in a limited number of 6,500; jigged bone handles. Original cost was $41.95.
Collector Value   *$150*

1989—Folder, 2-blade modified Sunfish pattern made by Case in a limited number of 6,500; green bone handles. Original cost was $50.
Collector Value   *$50*

1989—Fixed-blade, wood-handled skinning knife made by Buck in a limited number of 1,700; Original cost was $80.
Collector Value $80

1990—Folder, 3-blade stockman made by Robt. Klaas in a limited number of 5,000; stag handle; all blades etched. Original cost was $60.
Collector Value $60

1990—Fixed-blade, stag handled Bowie made by Hen & Rooster in a limited number of 1,500. Original cost was $80.
Collector Value $80

PENNSYLVANIA TRICENTENNIAL

Serial-numbered lockback Case folder with solid pewter low-relief handles created by Shaw-Leibowitz; celebrates 300 years of Pennsylvania history. Hardshell box.
Collector Value $45

PUMA 215TH ANNIVERSARY COMMEMORATIVE

Limited edition of 1,769 knives made in 1984 to commemorate the founding of Puma-Werk in Solingen, Germany, in 1769—a handmade knife of excellent quality. Ivory handle is hand-engraved with a puma; polished blade is etched in an attractive oak leaf design. Reverse side is gold-filled etched with serial number and "Puma Germany" and the dates "1769–1984." All etching is gold-filled; brass bolsters hand-engraved; rear bolsters engraved with the words "me fecit Solingen." Handle is European stag horn.
Collector Value $500

PUMA—AFRICAN BIG FIVE COLLECTOR SET

In the early 1980s, Puma produced 300 each of 5 knives as a salute to Africa's big game animals. Blades have "zebra-striped" etching filled with gold on both sides. Handles are ivory Micarta hand-scrimshawed by well-known artists—one side features the animal; the other side, its name. Brass bolsters are elaborately hand-engraved, and the front bolster contains the Roman numeral V within an outline of Africa. Set is housed in a wood presentation box.
Collector Value $2,400 set

PUMA 4-STAR COLLECTOR SERIES

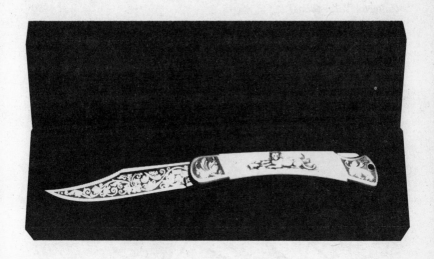

Four different Puma patterns—16-156, 16-157, 16-158, and 16-159—in a unique offering for collectors. Each knife is hand-carved and engraved on ivory Micarta handles and brass bolsters by leading artists. Backspring and blade back feature hand-worked file designs. Knives are signed with artist's name; no two are alike. Certificate of authenticity with each knife.
Collector Value (varies with knife pattern)   *$500–$1,500*

QUEEN DRAKE OIL WELL COMMEMORATIVE

3,600 made by Queen in 1972; 2-blade Barlow pattern with an oil well etched on master blade to commemorate the country's first oil well in Tidioute, PA, home of Queen Cutlery.
Collector Value   *$60*

R. KLAAS 155TH ANNIVERSARY

In 1989, Robt. Klaas produced two lockback knives to commemorate the 155th anniversary of the company; one knife with stag handle, the other with red bone. Blades of each knife are etched, and tangs are stamped with the original "R. Klaas Prussia" stamping.

Collector Value (stag)   *$60*

Collector Value (bone)   *$50*

RANDALL KNIVES 50TH ANNIVERSARY EDITION

300 knives produced in 1987 by Randall Knives to commemorate "Bo" Randall's 50 years in knife making; crown stag handles. Original cost was $375.

Collector Value   *$4,000*

REMINGTON SILVER BULLET

5,000 serial-numbered knives produced in 1988 by Remington for Smoky Mountain Knifeworks. The R4466SB is a 3¾″ 2-blade Muskrat with bone handle and a sterling silver bullet shield inlay. Housed in display box.

Collector Value   *$150*

REMINGTON CANDY STRIPE TOOTHPICK

10,000 knives made in 1988 by Remington for Smoky Mountain Knifeworks; a 5″ pattern R1615 toothpick, with Candy Stripe celluloid handle; inlaid with a unique Remington UMC shield.
Collector Value   *$50*

REMINGTON SILVER BULLET TRAPPER

5,000 serial-numbered knives produced in 1989 by Remington for Smoky Mountain Knifeworks; a 4⅜″ pattern R1128SB, the knife is a 2-blade trapper with bone handles and sterling silver bullet shield. With custom "bullet box."
Collector Value   *$135*

SCHRADE GRAND DAD'S OLD TIMER

A series of 4 knives of different patterns produced by Schrade. Grand Dad's Old Timer No. 1 is a 4″, 3-blade stock with a diamond-finish backspring.
Collector Value   *$30*

SCHRADE LIBERTY BELL, PAUL REVERE, AND MINUTEMAN SERIES

24,000 each of 3 knives made by Schrade in the early 1970s. Each is a 3⅝″ Stockman pattern; Liberty Bell and Minuteman have black composition handles; Paul Revere, red composition. Serial numbers stamped on inside of liner.
Collector Value   *$25*

SCHRADE BEAR CULT

Folding hunter lockback knife with beaded-suede leather sheath; scrimshaw-decorated imitation ivory handle; produced in 1985.
Collector Value   *$75*

SCHRADE SUNDANCE

Lockback folding hunter with decorated (scrimshaw) imitation ivory handle. Sheath is suede leather, hand-beaded. Produced in 1986.
Collector Value   *$65*

SCHRADE THUNDERBIRD

10,000 folding hunters made in 1981 as part of the scrimshaw series. Imitation ivory handles decorated with an Indian scene. Beaded sheath.
Collector Value   *$250*

SCHRADE-LOVELESS LIMITED
EDITION HUNTER

Produced by Schrade to the specifications of its designer, Bob Loveless. Blade is custom-ground high-grade steel; Delrin handle with thumb groove.
Collector Value   *$135*

SILVER ANNIVERSARY OLD TIMER

5,000 produced in 1984; bone-handled pattern 340T Stockman. Bolsters and shield are sterling silver; milled liners.
Collector Value   *$65*

SCHRADE BUFFALO BILL

A 4″ 3-blade stock knife packaged with a medallion in a satin-lined gift box.
Collector Value   *$25*

SCHRADE JIM BOWIE

18,000 serial-numbered knives made by Schrade; 4″ Stockman pattern; Delrin handle with a Bowie knife shield. Master blade tang is stamped "S.W. Cut. JBI, U.S.A." Serial number is stamped on inside liner.

Collector Value   *$30*

SCHRADE I*XL SERIES

Set consists of 5 knives honoring the combination of Schrade with I*XL. Consists of a stag-handled Canoe, a bone-handled Stockman, and 3 lockback knives with bone, stag, and Micarta handles. Housed in wood display.

Collector Value   *$275 set*

SCHRADE KACHINA

10,000 knife and sheath sets produced by Schrade as a part of their American Indian Scrimshaw Series. Knife's scrimshaw honors the Hopi Indians and the Kachina. The Kachina sheath is

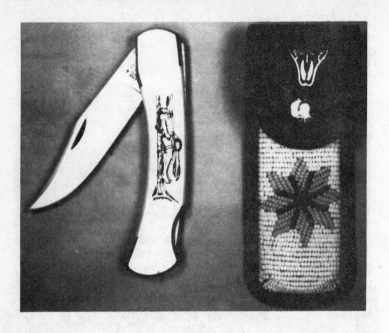

genuine leather with a suede finish, covered with a hand-sewn layer of beads in the image of a Kachina doll.

Collector Value   **$75**

SEARS 100TH ANNIVERSARY KNIFE

A 2-blade Bullet pattern with bone-stag handles inlaid with special Sears shield; both blades etched. Housed in wood display box.

Collector Value   **$50**

SECOND-CUT MINT SETS

Limited issue of 300 sets as above except with engraved bolsters and matching serial numbers; made by Case and marketed by Second Cut, Inc.

Collector Value   **$375 set**

SECOND-CUT SETS

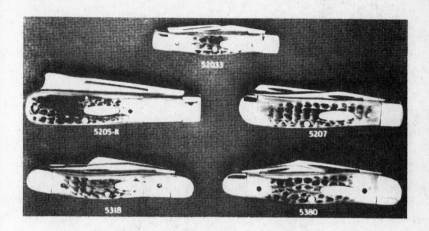

A 5-knife set marketed in 1984 by Second Cut, Inc., consisting of patterns 5220, 5254, 52131, 5383, and Muskrat. Master blades etched "Case XX Second Cut Series."

Collector Value   *$350 set*

SHAW-LEIBOWITZ BICENTENNIAL SERIES

A 10-knife set created in 1976 by the artist team of Sherill Shaw and Leonard Leibowitz. Knives of several manufacturers were used as follows:

1. "The Boston Tea Party" etched on a Rigid knife
2. "The Ride of Paul Revere" etched on a Gerber knife
3. "The Shot Heard round the World" etched on a No. P172 Case knife
4. "The Declaration of Independence" on a Westmark Western knife
5. "Washington Crossing the Delaware" etched on an Olsen Model 503 hunting knife
6. "John Paul Jones" etched on a No. 6250 Case Sunfish knife
7. "Winter at Valley Forge" on a Gerber sheath knife
8. "Patrick Henry" on a Westmark knife
9. "The Victory at Yorktown" on a Case knife

10. "Washington's Triumphant Return to New York City" on a Rigid knife

Collector Value   *$3,000–$10,000 (depending on serial number) set*

SHAW-LEIBOWITZ WILDLIFE SERIES

Shaw-Leibowitz produced a set of wildlife knives, beginning in 1974, 300 of each knife pattern. Numbers 1–15 were gold-plated and retailed for $155; numbers 16–300 retailed for $105.

1. Grizzly on a Gerber lockback
2. Raccoon on a Schrade-Walden
3. Bobcat on a Case No. 62131
4. Moose on a Case No. 5275
5. Squirrel on a Case 6380
6. Deer on a Buck Esquire
7. Big Horn Sheep on a Case 6235½
8. Eagle on a Kabar barlow
9. Elephant on Case 6250

10. Buffalo on Case P-172

Collector Value   *$2,500–$8,000 (depending on serial number) set*

SILVER COIN–AMERICAN EAGLE COMMEMORATIVE SET

5,000 coin and knife sets produced by Smoky Mountain Knifeworks in 1987; includes a 3254 Case Trapper with yellow composition handle, silkscreened with an eagle and a U.S. Mint American eagle silver dollar housed in a display box.
Collector Value   *$50*

SMITH & WESSON COLLECTORS SET

Limited edition of 1,000 sets released in 1975 by Smith & Wesson. Designed by Blackie Collins, made by Collins and his co-workers at Carolina Knife Co. Deep-etched blades. All fixed-blade knives with hardwood handles; sterling silver guards and pommels; hand-engraved escutcheons inlaid into handles.
Collector Value   *$2,000 set*

SMOKY MOUNTAIN TRAPPER SERIES

600 serial-numbered sets produced by Case in 1980 exclusively for Smoky Mountain Knifeworks to commemorate the heritage of the Great Smoky Mountains, consisting of patterns 6254, 3254, and 6254SSP; blades etched. Housed in presentation case with the Case logo.
Collector Value   *$225 set*

STAR SPANGLED BANNER COMMEMORATIVE BOWIE

A total of 2,000 stag-handled Bowie knives were produced by Case. Fully deep-etched 9½″ blades. Each knife housed in wood music box. Etching on 1,500 is black-filled and is gold-filled on the remaining 500.
Collector Value (black-filled)   *$200*
Collector Value (gold-filled)   *$250*

STATUE OF LIBERTY

1,000 each of two limited-edition trappers produced by Case for Smoky Mountain Knifeworks. Each knife has etched blades and yellow Micarta handle. Display boxed.
Collector Value   *$40*

Jigged bone handle; includes a 1 troy ounce .999 fine silver medallion.
Collector Value   *$55*

STOCK CAR LEGENDS—PAST AND PRESENT

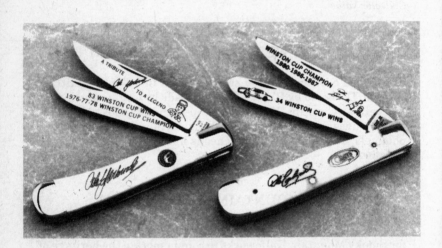

A series of commemorative knives produced by Frost Cutlery Company based on regular-production knives made by Case and other manufacturers. Each of these knives is embellished with signature blade etching. Custom display boxes and certificates of authenticity.

"Cale Yarborough"—2,000 produced; 4⅛" Case trapper with white pick-bone handles.
Collector Value   *$85*

"Dale Earnhardt"—2,000 produced; Hen & Rooster 4⅛" trapper with white smooth-bone handles.
Collector Value   *$70*

"Cale Yarborough"—2,000 produced; Hen & Rooster 4⅛" with scrimshawed white smooth-bone handles.
Collector Value   *$75*

"Dale Earnhardt"—2,000 produced; case 5¼" folding hunter with red pick-bone handles.
Collector Value   *$125*

"Lee Petty"—2,000 produced; Hen & Rooster 4⅛" trapper with full-color scrimshawed white smooth-bone handles.
Collector Value   *$75*

"Dale Earnhardt"—2,000 produced; Case 4⅛" trapper with scrimshawed white smooth-bone handles.
Collector Value   *$85*

"Lee Petty"—2,000 produced; Case trapper with scrimshaw on white smooth-bone handles.
Collector Value   *$85*

"Glenn 'Fireball' Roberts"—1,000 produced; Case 4⅛" trapper with Rogers bone handles.
Collector Value   *$85*

"Lee Petty"—500 produced; Case 5¼" folding hunter with red pick-bone handles.
Collector Value   *$125*

TEDDY ROOSEVELT

2,500 produced by Case for Smoky Mountain Knifeworks. Trapper pattern handled in bone; 24k-gold-dipped blades with deep etching.
Collector Value   *$45*

TENNESSEE HOMECOMING '86— CRIPPLE CREEK

100 knives produced in 1986. Trapper pattern with "Tennessee Homecoming '86" etched on master blade; red-white-and-blue celluloid handles.
Collector Value   *$100*

TENNESSEE HOMECOMING '86—
UNITED BOKER

Trapper pattern made by United Boker; red bone handles; master blade etched "Tennessee Homecoming '86." Included in box is a commemorative coin of .999 fine silver coin.
Collector Value   *$50*

TENNESSEE HOMECOMING '86—CASE

Case Trapper pattern with orange composition handle silk-screened with outline of the state of Tennessee. "Tennessee Homecoming '86" etched on master blade.
Collector Value   *$35*

TENNESSEE WALKING HORSE AND
KENTUCKY THOROUGHBRED

A 2-knife set of stag-handled lockback knives made by the Robert Klaas Co. (Kissing Crane) for Parker-Frost Cutlery. Three-color etching on the stainless steel blades designated them as the "Tennessee Walking Horse" or the "Kentucky Thoroughbred"; 1,000 of each were made with matching serial numbers. Housed in satin-lined display case; a walnut plaque was available as an option. This is the last limited-edition set to be marketed by Parker-Frost prior to the partnership's dissolving in 1978.
Collector Value   *$125 set*

THE COLEMAN/WESTERN COMMEMORATIVE

2,000 knives were made in 1985 to recognize the joining together of Coleman and Western. Based on Western's model 701, the knife has a stag handle and a 5½″ fully etched stainless steel blade. A hardwood presentation case with glass top, as well as a leather sheath, came with each knife. The first 250 knives were etched on both sides of the blade, one side featuring Sheldon Coleman and Harvey Platts and the other side depicting a camping scene and the new company slogan "Two Great Names, One Great Knife." The remaining 1,750 knives were etched on one side with the camping scene and slogan.

Collector Value (both sides etched)   *$250*
Collector Value (one side etched)   *$120*

THE COURTHOUSE WHITTLER SERIES

600 2-knife sets made by Frank Buster Cutlery in 1977 for Parker-Frost Cutlery. The set consists of 2 3-blade whittlers with gold-etched blades. Handles are red and blue antique celluloid. Housed in simulated alligator box.
Collector Value   *$110 set*

THE COVERED BRIDGE

Made by Alcas in a limited edition for Mrs. Dewey Ferguson; similar to the Case M1051L. Picture of a covered bridge in the handle; tang-stamped "Lavonna's Cutlery."
Collector Value   *$35*

THE GATOR SET

2,750 sets containing 2 serial-numbered Texas Toothpicks made by Case for Parker Cutlery in 1979; one handled in stag, the other in bone.
Collector Value   *$125 set*

THE GENERAL

1,200 3⅜" 3-blade knives made by Bowen Knife Company. Honors "The General," the train that participated in the Civil War's great train chase.
Collector Value   *$35*

THE GUNS THAT TAMED THE WILD WEST

3,000 sets produced in 1989 by Case; includes patterns 5215SS (3") and 5230SS (4") gunstocks with India stag handles. Gold Case raised-letter shield; master blades photo-etched.
Collector Value   *$135 set*

THE KENTUCKY DERBY

Bulldog Knives produced 4 knives honoring the 110th Kentucky Derby in 1984; serpentine stockman handles in stag, brown celluloid, marble celluloid, and green celluloid. Master blade etched "110th Run for the Roses."

Collector Value (set of 4) $275
Collector Value (individual knives) $65

THE KNIFE COLLECTOR'S TRAPPER

1,000 serial-numbered knives produced in 1989 by Case for Smoky Mountain Knifeworks. Rogers bone handle with high-relief shield. Boxed with 1 ounce pure silver medallion bearing the slogan "Knife Collectors Are Sharp People."

Collector Value $85

MAC TOOLS KNIFE

Mac Tools, Inc., contracted for the production of several limited-edition knives. The first, with 12,000 produced in 1979, was a 3-blade stock knife with antique brass cast handles commemorating the 40th anniversary of the company.

Collector Value $45

In 1979 3,600 serial-numbered Canoe pattern knives were made by George Wostenholm I*XL. Handles are white bone.

Collector Value $75

THE ORIGINAL THIRTEEN COLONY SERIES

Set of 14 knives issued beginning in March 1976, with a knife issued each month through the Bicentennial. Thirteen of the knives were issued to honor the 13 original colonies. Pewter, silver, brass, and copper handles; artwork and a diamond-finished backspring. The 14th knife—a stag-handled folding hunter with etched blade—honored the United States. Schrade Walden manufactured the 3,000 sets for Parker-Frost Cutlery.

Collector Value $300 set

CASE TEXAS SPECIAL

A Case 4165 pattern with white composition handles designed by Bill and Buck Overall of Texas to commemorate the Lone Star State. Flat-ground stainless steel etched blade with a longhorn steer, map of Texas, and the year of the Alamo battle.

Collector Value   *$85*

TRAIL OF TEARS

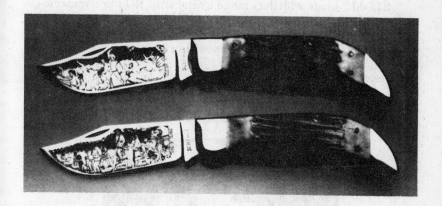

1,200 serially numbered knives made by Schrade for Parker-Frost; the fully etched blade carries an artistic representation of the Cherokee Indians' march on the Trail of Tears. Handles are thick genuine stag.

Collector Value   *$150*

CUSTER'S LAST FIGHT

1,200 serially numbered knives made by Schrade for Parker-Frost Cutlery; companion piece to the Trail of Tears, issued at the same time. Some were sold in pairs with matching serial numbers. Deep blade etching commemorating Custer's last battle; genuine stag handles.

Collector Value   *$150*

THE WHALING KNIFE

A Schrade-Loveless hunter; blade etched and handle scrimshawed by Shaw-Leibowitz. A salute to the old-time whaling industry, the etch and scrimshaw scene is both expressive and highly artistic, in keeping with the talents of the artists.
Collector Value　　　　　　　　　　　　　　　　　　*$400*

WISS WHITTLER

24,000 3-blade whittlers made by Boker in 1973 to commemorate the 125th anniversary of Wiss Cutlery. Blade is etched "Wiss Commemorative 1848–1973." Serial number stamped on the master blade tang; white composition handles with special shield. Housed in plastic box.
Collector Value　　　　　　　　　　　　　　　　　　*$28*

TOM SEAVER COMMEMORATIVE

1,200 lockback folding hunters produced in 1989 by Parker, USA. Genuine stag handles; stainless steel blade etched with Seaver signature. Includes stand to hold knife and baseball autographed by Tom Seaver.
Collector Value　　　　　　　　　　　　　　　　　　*$100*

TOMB OF THE UNKNOWN SOLDIER

1,000 produced by Case for Smoky Mountain Knifeworks. Yellow composition handles on Case trapper; both blades etched.
Collector Value   *$45*

TRIPLE CROWN SERIES

A special set of 11 knives made for Central Knife Exchange in 1980; built on the '51 pattern Case with rosewood handles. A special etch was on each knife's blade and a knife was made for each winner of the Triple Crown, the winner's name etched on the shield. Eleven sets were presented to the owners of the Triple Crown winning horses, and a set was given to Churchill Downs racetrack.
Collector Value   *$1,200 set*

VIETNAM COMMEMORATIVE SECOND EDITION

1,000 produced by Case for Smoky Mountain Knifeworks. Trapper pattern with yellow composition handle and gun-blued blades etched in gold.
Collector Value   *$60*

VIETNAM VETERANS SILVER EDITION

Commemorative knife and coin set with United/Boker trapper and 1-ounce silver coin honoring Vietnam veterans. Knife has smooth green bone handles and etched high-carbon steel blades. Gift boxed.
Collector Value   *$50*

WINCHESTER LIMITED EDITION SETS

In 1987, Blue Grass Cutlery introduced the new Winchester reproduction series, authorized by the Winchester division of Olin Corporation. To introduce the new collectible knife line, two commemorative sets were issued.

"The Scouts"—production limited to 2,500 matching serial-numbered sets. Knives are 4½" 2-blade jackknife pattern with genuine bone handles. The "Wild Bill Hickok" knife has the Winchester 1873 rifle shield. The "Buffalo Bill Cody" knife has the Winchester Horse and Rider shield.

Collector Value   *$150 set*

"Model 37 Red Letter Set"—serialized set of 5 knives; limited production of 2,000 sets. Knives are produced on the Case 042

frame and have Rogers bone handles with inlaid weapons shield of 5 different Model 37 shotguns: 12 GA, 16 GA, 20 GA, 28 GA, and 410 GA.

Collector Value   *$175 set*

WORLD WAR II VICTORY COLLECTION

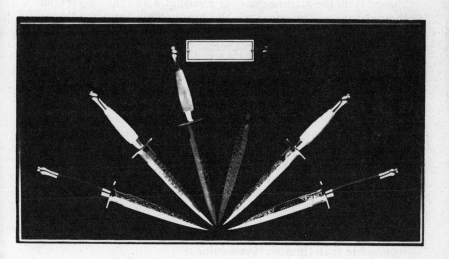

Two series of special commemorative fighting knives were produced for and marketed by the American Historical Foundation. Each knife was patterned after a variation of the famous Fairbairn-Sykes knife and is dedicated to a specific battle. The series are "War in Europe," with knives made by Wilkinson Sword, and "War in the Pacific," with knives made by H. G. Long & Co. of Sheffield, England. Each series consists of 6 knives that were available either separately or, as most were sold, in matching serial-numbered sets. Each of the knives is packaged in a velvet hard case with information about the battle it commemorates.

Collector Value (individual knives)   *$225*
Collector Value (set of 6 knives)   *$1,500*

MISCELLANEOUS CASE TRAPPER COMMEMORATIVES

During recent years the themes for commemorative knives have been limited only by the imagination, and that seems limitless. The majority of these have been based on the popular Case Trapper patterns. Most are not produced and marketed directly by the manufacturing company but rather by distributors, dealers, or individual entrepreneurs. A quantity of knives is purchased from the manufacturer or distributor and then decorated in any of several manners, such as blade etching and handle engraving, and given special boxing. The issues may or may not be limited in numbers—the limit sometimes being the number that can be sold. The proliferation of these "special" knives has largely resulted from two factors: first, the growing interest in knives as collectibles, and second, the modern technology used for attractive, high-quality blade etching and handle engraving. Some have been and will continue to be desirable collectibles; others have their greatest appeal in the themes they follow—these, too, seem to be endless.

In considering these special knives, the collector should be aware that they can usually be purchased via mail order for about one-half of their suggested retail price, and the collector values are normally within those ranges. The values of some will reach or exceed their suggested retail prices within a relatively short period. Others, however, may have more value through pride of ownership than through resale value.

Following are but a few examples of the many themes and variations of etching, engraving, and creative packaging available on the Case trapper. Retail prices are approximately $80; collector values are approximately $40.

Apache War Chief, Geronimo

Atlantic Coast ConferenceTeams

Babe Ruth

Chief Crazy Horse

Coal Miners of America "Black Gold"

Cochise, Apache War Chief

Davy Crockett

Gen. Ulysses S. Grant

Gen. Dwight D. Eisenhower

Gen. Douglas MacArthur
Gen. Robert E. Lee
George A. Custer, "Custer's Last Stand"
Iwo Jima
One Small Step—Astronaut Commemorative
Paul "Bear" Bryant
Southeastern Conference Teams
Statue of Liberty, 100th Anniversary
The Grand Ole Opry—Roy Acuff
The Titanic
U. S. Constitution—200th Anniversary

PART
◁ 5 ▷

Resources

KNIFE COLLECTORS' CLUBS

GETTING MORE INVOLVED

The term "return on investment" is usually viewed from a dollar-and-cents point of view. Although that factor certainly applies to collecting, a broader interpretation—one that costs very little money—deserves consideration. The investment of time and energy in getting more involved will surely pay dividends. One example is attendance at knife shows as discussed previously; other opportunities such as club membership and further reading are discussed in the following pages.

One of the more rewarding aspects of knife collecting is personal involvement with others who share the same or similar interests. It is likely that your own interest in knives as collectibles originated through association and friendship with another collector or would-be collector. Knife collecting clubs can and do provide excellent opportunities to further one's knowledge about knives, to enhance one's own collection, or to sell knives from a collection.

During the past two decades a large number of knife-collecting clubs have been formed in many parts of the country. Most of these clubs meet on a regular basis for fellowship, learning, and the inevitable swapping—whether of knives or information. Knife club meetings usually provide a forum and the facilities for a miniature knife show. Members bring knives for sale or trade, while others attend hoping for that rare and elusive find to add to their collection.

Although active participating membership is always more desirable, membership and remote participation is not unusual. After all, there are thousands of collectors who may not be located close enough to attend a regular meeting but who wish to enjoy the privileges of club membership; there can be many. Most clubs publish a regular newsletter reporting items of interest to members. In addition, clubs usually have their own annual club knife that is available to their membership. The majority of club knives, especially those that have been carefully selected and are truly unique, have maintained a good reputation for value and collectibility within the knife world.

Listing of Knife Collectors' Clubs

National Knife Collectors Association
American Blade Collectors Association
Canadian Knife Collectors Club
Knife Collectors Club
Antique Bowie Knife Collectors Association
Military Knife Collectors Association
Miniature Knife Collectors Association
The Knifemakers Guild
American Bladesmith Society

Regional Clubs

The addresses listed below are current as of the writing of this book. Since the officers of these nonprofit clubs change periodically, the contact address may also change. Should you be unsuccessful in contacting any club at the address listed below, current information may be obtained by contacting the regular knife publications listed elsewhere. *Knife World* publishes a listing of local clubs each month, and you may address your request for information to *Knife World,* P.O. Box 3395, Knoxville, TN 37927.

Alabama
Jackson Knife Collectors Club
Route 4, Box 215
Scottsboro, AL 35768

Wheeler Basin Knife Club
P.O. Box 346
Hartsell, AL 35640

Arizona
Arizona Knife
  Collectors Association
P.O. Box 652
Glendale, AZ 85311

California
Bay Area Knife
  Collectors Association
P.O. Box 223
Fremont, CA 94537

Southern California Blades
P.O. Box 1140
Lomita, CA 90717

Colorado
Rocky Mountain Blade Collectors
P.O. Box 115
Louisville, CO 80027

Florida
Bold City Knife Club
4652 Bankhead Avenue
Jacksonville, FL 32207

Florida Knife
  Collectors Association
3301 Delaware Avenue
Titusville, FL 32780

Fort Meyers Knife Club
P.O. Box 1274
Ft. Myers, FL 33902

Gator Cutlery Club
P.O. Box 11973
Tampa, FL 33680

Georgia
Flint River Knife Club
P.O. Box 1772
Forest Park,GA 30050

N.W. Georgia Knife Collectors
P.O. Box 116
Rockmart, GA 30153

Ocmulgee Knife Collectors Club
Route 27, Box 185
Macon, GA 31211

Peach State Cutlery Club
4561 South Main Street
Acworth, GA 30101

Three Rivers Knife Club
Route 7, Box 783
Rome, GA 30161

Illinois
American Edge
  Collectors Association
P.O. Box 2207
Hammond, IN 46323

Bunker Hill Knife Club
Route 2
Bunker Hill, IL 62014

Jefferson County Knife Club
709 Airport Road
Mt. Vernon, IL 62864

Soy Knife Collectors
P.O. Box 1752
Decatur, IL 62525

Indiana
Indiana Knife Collectors
1718 Sheffield Court
Anderson, IN 46011

Northern Indiana Knife Club
P.O. Box 6
Hobart, IN 46342

Iowa
Hawkeye Knife Collectors Club
Route 2, Box 46
Earlham, IA 50072

Kansas
Kansas Knife
  Collectors Association
1713 West 2nd
Wichita, KS 67203

Kentucky
Central Kentucky Knife Club
P.O. Box 5049
Lexington, KY 40556

Eagle Creek Knife Club
214 Seminary Street
Owenton, KY 40359

Fort City Knife Club
2200 Williams Road
Burlington, KY 41005

Kentucky Cutlery Association
P.O. Box 58012
Louisville, KY 40214

Maryland
Chesapeake Bay Knife Club
3206 Fairmount Avenue
Baltimore, MD 21224

Michigan
Great Lakes Knifecrafters
  Association
39501 Lakeshore Drive
Mt. Clemens, MI 48405

Wolverine Knife Collectors Club
1713 Anne Street
Allen Park, MI 48101

Minnesota
North Star Blade Collectors
P.O. Box 20523
Bloomington, MN 55420

Missouri
Bunker Hill Knife Club
P.O. Box 11058
Ferguson, MO 63135

Gateway Area Knife Club
P.O. Box 11775
Clayton, MO 63105

New England Area
N.E. Cutlery
    Collectors Association
P.O. Box 677
Milldale, CT 06467

North Carolina
Bechtler Mint Knife Club
P.O. Box 149
Rutherfordton, NC 28139

North Carolina Cutlery Club
113 Powell Drive
Fuquay-Varina, NC 27526

Tar Heel Cutlery Club
2730 Tudor Road
Winston-Salem, NC 27106

Ohio
Mahoning Valley Knife
    Association
1900 McLoskey Road
Columbiana, OH 44408

Western Reserve Cutlery
    Association
P.O. Box 94
Doylestown, OH 44230

Oklahoma
Antique Knife Association
12716 Burlingame Avenue
Oklahoma City, OK 73120

Sooner Knife Collectors Club
1813 SW 30th
Moore, OK 73160

Oregon
Oregon Knife
    Collectors Association
P.O. Box 2091
Cheshire, OR 97419

Pennsylvania
Allegheny Mountain Knife
    Collectors Association
P.O. Box 23
Hunker, PA 15639

Mason-Dixon Knife Club
P.O. Box 196
Quincy, PA 17247

South Carolina
Palmetto Cutlery Club
P.O. Box 1356
Greer, SC 29652

Tennessee
Colonel Coon Knife Club
P.O. Box 1676
Dyersburg, TN 38025

East Tennessee Knife Club
2515 Volunteer Parkway
Bristol, TN 37620

Fight'n Rooster Cutlery Club
P.O. Box 936
Lebanon, TN 37087

Golden Circle Knife Club
Route 1, 28 Ginger Lane
Bells, TN 38006

Hardeman County Knife Club
Route 1, Box 19-A
Hornsby, TN 38044

Memphis Knife Collectors Club
3550 Merritt Street
Memphis, TN 38128

Smokey Mountain Knife Club
P.O. Box 1176
Maryville, TN 37801

Texas
Gulf Coast Knife Club
P.O. Box 750542
Houston, TX 77275

Lone Star Knife Club
P.O. Box 8660
Waco, TX 76714

Permian Basin Knife Club
4309 Roosevelt
Midland, TX 79703

Texas Knife
  Collectors Association
P.O. Box 4754
Austin, TX 78765

Virginia
Northern Virginia Knife Club
P.O. Box 501
Falls Church, VA 22046

Old Dominion Knife Collectors
1127 Roundtree Drive
Bedford, VA 24523

Washington
North West Knife Collectors
P.O. Box 7216
Tacoma, WA 98407

West Virginia
Ohio Valley Knife Association
3707 10th Avenue
Vienna, WV 26105

Wisconsin
Badger Knife Club
7024 West Wells Street
Wauwatosa, WI 53213

BIBLIOGRAPHY

KNIFE BOOKS—OLD AND NEW

Knife collecting has not only come of age with the increasing number of collectors involved, it has also matured a great deal within the past several years. The catalyst that perhaps deserves most credit for that increasing maturity has been the amount of reference materials available to the serious collector. Whereas only a dozen or so years ago the knife collector had few places to turn for education, there are today literally dozens of books available on almost any subject within the world of knives. Surely, there is no lesson remembered quite so well as that learned in the "school of hard knocks," but there is no lesson so cheaply purchased as that learned from others. In spite of a rather limited market, there have been authors and publishers willing to share their knowledge through writing and publishing, although the pay was decidedly meager. Any collector who is at all serious about knives cannot afford to pass up the opportunities for learning offered in books and magazines.

Most books about knives and related materials are rather limited in numbers printed. Some achieve reasonably good success and are reprinted; others, although quite valuable as reference sources, are not available once the original printing is sold out. A number of the books listed below are out of print, but they may still be available from dealers or other collectors. If you find an out-of-print book from one of these sources, buying it is highly recommended. If, once you've read it, you decide that the book is not one for your own bookshelf, there are other collectors who will be pleased to obtain it from you.

RECOMMENDED FURTHER READING

A Collection of U.S. Military Knives by M. H. Cole, published by the author, Birmingham, AL.

712

A History of Cutlery in the Connecticut Valley by Martha Van Hoesen Taber, Department of History, Smith College, Northampton, MA, 1955.

A History of the John Russell Cutlery Co. by Robert L. Merriam et al., Bete Press, Greenfield, MA, 1976.

Advertising with a Sharp Edge by Ed Brady, published by the author, Traverse City, MI, 1972.

Allied Military Fighting Knives by Robert A. Buerlein, American Historical Foundation, Richmond, VA 1984.

American Handmade Knives of Today by B. R. Hughes, Pioneer Press, Union City, TN, 1972.

American Knives by Harold L. Peterson, Charles Scribner's Sons, New York, 1958.

American Made Pocketknives, Union Cutlery Co. catalog reproduced by Kabar, Cole National, Cleveland, OH, 1977.

American Premium Guide to Pocketknives by Jim Sargent, Books Americana, Florence, AL, 1986.

American Premium Guide to Pocketknives and Razors by Jim Sargent, Books Americana, Florence, AL, 1989.

An Introduction to Switchblade Knives by Ben and Lowell Meyers, American Eagle Publishing, Chicago, 1982.

Bowie Knives by William G. Keener, published by author, 1988. A reprint of Robert Abels' *Classic Bowie Knives.*

Case Brothers 1904 catalog reprinted by Bob Cargill, Lockport, IL, 1977.

Cattaraugus Cutlery Co. catalog reproduction by Dewey P. Ferguson, Fairborn, OH, 1971.

Classic Bowie Knives by Robert Abels, published by author, Ft. Lauderdale, FL, 1967.

Combat Fighting Knives by J. E. Smith, Jr., EPJ & H Enterprises, Inc., Statesboro, GA, 1987.

Custom Knifemaking: 10 Projects from a Master Craftsman by Tim McCreight, Stackpole Books, Harrisburg, PA, 1985.

E. C. Simmons & Winchester, American Reprints, St. Louis.

Encyclopedia of Old Pocketknives by Roy Ehrhardt, Heart of America Press, Kansas City, MO, 1974.

George Schrade—His Accomplishments to the Knife Industry by George M. Schrade, George Schrade Knife Co., Bridgeport, CT, 1982.

Goins Encyclopedia of Cutlery Markings by John E. Goins, Knife World Books, Knoxville, TN, 1986.

How to Make Knives by Richard Barney and Robert Loveless, American Blade Book Service, Chattanooga, TN, 1982.

I*XL Catalog—1885, catalog reprinted by Atlanta Cutlery Corporation, Decatur, GA.

I*XL Means I Excel by William R. Williamson, published by author, 1974.

Joseph Rodgers & Sons, Cutlers, an antique catalog reprinted by Adrian Van Dyk, Marietta, OH, 1974.

Kentucky Knife Traders Manual by Roy Ritchie and Ron Stewart, published by the authors, Hazard, KY, 1980.

Knife Album by Colonel Robert Mayes, published by author, P.O. Box 186, Middlesboro, KY, 1973.

Knife Digest (1st ed.) by William L. Cassidy, Knife Digest Publishing Co., Berkeley, CA, 1974.

Knife Digest (2nd ed.) by William L. Cassidy, Knife Digest Publishing Co., Berkeley, CA, 1976.

Knife Repair and Restoration by Adrian A. Harris, Tennessee Knifeworks, Columbia, TN, 1981.

Knifecraft by Sid Latham, Stackpole Books, New York, 1979.

Knifemakers, an Official Directory of the Knifemakers Guild by J. Bruce Voyles, American Blade Book Service, Chattanooga, TN, 1984.

Knifemakers of Old San Francisco by Bernard R. Levine, Badger Books, San Francisco, 1977.

Knives and the Law by James R. Nielsen, Knife World Books, Knoxville, TN, 1980.

Knives '81, Ken Warner, ed., DBI Books, Northbrook, IL, 1980.

Knives '82, Ken Warner, ed., DBI Books, Northbrook, IL, 1981.

Knives '83, Ken Warner, ed., DBI Books, Northbrook, IL, 1982.

Knives '84, Ken Warner, ed., DBI Books, Northbrook, IL, 1983.

Knives '85, Ken Warner, ed., DBI Books, Northbrook, IL, 1984.

Knives '86, Ken Warner, ed., DBI Books, Northbrook, IL, 1985.

Knives '87, Ken Warner, ed., DBI Books, Norhtbrook, IL, 1986.

Knives '88, Ken Warner, ed., DBI Books, Northbrook, IL, 1987.

Knives '89, Ken Warner, ed., DBI Books, Northbrook, IL, 1988.

Knives '90, Ken Warner, ed., DBI Books, Northbrook, IL, 1989.

Knives, Points of Interest I by Jim Weyer, published by author, Toledo, OH, 1984.

Knives, Points of Interest II by Jim Weyer, published by author, Toledo, OH, 1987.

Levine's Guide to Knives and Their Values by Bernard Levine, DBI Books, 1986.

Levine's Guide to Knives and Their Values (2nd ed.) by Bernard Levine, DBI Books, Inc., Northbrook, IL, 1989.

Light but Efficient by Albert N. Hardin, Jr., and Robert W. Hedden, published by the authors, 1973.

Marbles, Knives and Axes by Konrad F. Schreier, Jr., Beinfield Publishing, 1978.

Modern Handmade Knives by B. R. Hughes, Pioneer Press, Union City, TN, 1982.

Moran—Fire and Steel by Wayne V. Holter, published by the author, 1982.

Napanoch by Rhett C. Stidham, published by author, Belpre, OH, 1975.

New England Cutlery by Philip R. Pankiewicz, Hollytree Publications, Gilman, CT, 1986.

Pocket Cutlery, U.S. Tariff Commission, Washington, DC, 1939.

Pocketknives, Markings, Manufacturers and Dealers by John E. Goins, published by the author, Greensburg, IN, 1979.

Pocketknives, Markings of Manufacturers and Dealers (2nd ed.) by John E. Goins, Knife World Books, Knoxville, TN, 1982.

Razor Edge Book of Sharpening by John Juranitch, Warner Books, New York, 1985.

Remington 1936 catalog reprinted by American Reprints, St. Louis.

Remington C-4 catalog reprinted by J. Bruce Voyles, ca. 1974.

Remington C-5 catalog reprinted actual size, American Blade Book Service, Chattanooga, TN, 1985.

Romance of Collecting Case Knives by Dewey P. Ferguson, published by author, Fairborn, OH, 1978.

Romance of Collecting Cattaraugas, Russell, Robeson and Queen by Mrs. Dewey P. Ferguson, published by author, Fairborn, OH, 1978.

Romance of Knife Collecting, Vol. 4, by Dewey P. Ferguson and James F. Parker, Chattanooga, TN, 1976.

Russell Green River Works Cutlery by Dewey P. Ferguson, published by author, Fairborn, OH, 1972.

Scagel, the Man and His Knives by Harry McEvoy, Knife World Books, Knoxville, TN, 1985.

Schrade Pocketknives, by A. C. Russell, Knife Collector's Publishing House, Fayetteville, AR, 1971.

Straight Razor Collecting by Robert A. Doyle, Collector Books, Paducah, KY, 1980.

Sunday Knives by John Roberts, published by the author, Louisville, KY, 1979.

Survival Knives and Survival by J. E. Smith, Jr., EPJ Enterprises, Statesboro, GA, 1984.

Survival Knives and Survival (2nd ed.) by J. E. Smith, Jr., EPJ & H Enterprises, Inc., Statesboro, GA, 1985.

The Best of Knife World, Vol. 1, Knife World Books, Knoxville, TN, 1979.

The Best of Knife World, Vol. 2, Knife World Books, Knoxville, TN, 1982.

The Book of Knives by Yvan A. de Riaz, Crown Publishers, New York, 1981.

The Case Knife Story by Allen P. Swayne, Knife World Books, Knoxville, TN, 1987.

The Complete Book of Pocketknife Repair by Ben Kelley, Jr., American Blade Book Service, 1983; revised 1987.

The Gun Digest Book of Knives by B. R. Hughes and Jack Lewis, Digest Books Inc., Northfield, IL, 1973.

The Gun Digest Book of Knives (2nd ed.) by Jack Lewis and Roger Combs, DBI Books, Northfield, IL, 1982.

The Gun Digest Book of Knives (3rd ed.) by Jack Lewis and Roger Combs, DBI Books, Northfield, IL, 1988.

The Hand Forged Knife by Karl Schroen, Knife World Books, Knoxville, TN, 1984.

The Knife and Its History, Victorinox, Ibach, Switzerland, 1984.

The Knife Collection of Albert Blevins by Bernard Levine, Allon Schoener Associates, Grafton, VT, 1988.

The Knife Guide by Bernard Levine, Knife World Books, Knoxville, TN, 1981.

The Knife in Homespun America by Madison Grant, published by the author, 1984.

The Knifemakers Who Went West by Harvey Platts, Longs Peak Press, 1978.

The Official Price Guide to Collector Knives (9th ed.), by James F. Parker et al., House of Collectibles, New York, 1987.

The Old Knife Book by Tracy Tudor, published by the author, Speedway, IN, 1978.

The Pocketknife Manual by Blackie Collins, Benchmark Division, Jenkins Metal, Gastonia, NC, 1977.

The Practical Book of Knives by Ken Warner, Stoeger Publishing Co., So. Hackensack, NJ, 1976.

The Standard Knife Collector's Guide by Ron Stewart and Roy Ritchie, Collector Books, Paducah, KY, 1986.

United States Military Knives Collector's Guide by Michael W. Silvey and Gary D. Boyd, published by the authors, Sacramento, CA, 1989.

U.S. Military Knives, Bayonets, and Machetes, Book III by M. H. Cole, published by author, Birmingham, AL, 1979.

KNIFE PERIODICALS AND MAGAZINES

Knife World
P.O. Box 3395
Knoxville, TN 37927
Phone: 615-523-3339

National Knife Magazine
7201 Shallowford Road
Chattanooga, TN 37421
Phone: 615-899-9456

Knives Illustrated
2145 W. La Palma Avenue
Anaheim, CA 92801
Phone: 714-635-9040

The Blade Magazine
P.O. Box 22007
Chattanooga, TN 37422
Phone: 615-894-0339

INDEX

▽

Aerial Cutlery Company,
      201–202
African safari set, 649
Al Mar knives, 464–465
American Armed Forces series,
      649
American bicentennial series,
      649
Auctions, as source for knives,
      29–30
Automobile automation
      anniversary, 649

Baker & Hamilton, 202–203
Belknap Hardware Company,
      203–204
Benchmark knives, 204
Beretta, 650
C. Bertram, 204–205
Blade patterns, types of,
      107–109
Blade pulls, 107
Boker, 205–206
   bone-handled set, 653
   Spirit of America series,
      653–654
   Storyteller set, 653
Boker-Wiss commemoratives,
      651–652
Bonnie and Clyde
      commemorative, 655

Bowie knives, 17
   general information, 37–39
   makers of, 40–47
   markers/markings, 39–40
Buck knives, 206–208
   bicentennial, 655
   Bugling Elks, 657
   Canoeist, 659
   commemorative Bowie,
      658–659
   Cutlery World knife, 655
   Ducks Unlimited, 658
   Freedom Trapper, 655
   Golden Eagle, 658
   Grand Slam set, 655
   Grizzly, 655
   Redbone set, 656
   silver anniversary
      commemorative, 656–657
   Yellowhorse knives, 657
Buford Pusser commemorative,
      659
Bulldog knives, 208–216

Camillus Cutlery Company, 216
   wildlife series, 659
Canastota Knife Company, 217
Canton Cutlery Company, 217
Case and Sons
   collector sets, 659–670
   fixed blade knives, 232–256

Case and Sons *(continued)*
  history of company, 218–223,
    368–370
  linings on knives, 225–226
  older knives, 361–368
  pattern numbers, 226–230
  pocketknives, 256–360
  sheath knives, 230–231
  stampings, 223–224, 230–231
  Texas special, 697
  trapper commemoratives,
    702–703
  variations of stampings, 224
Cattaraugus Cutlery Company,
    370–394
Challenge Cutlery, 394–395
Clauss Cutlery Company, 395
Club swap meets, as source for
    knives, 30
Coal miner series, 670–671
Coleman/Western
    commemorative, 694
  Texas Bowie, 671
Colonel Coon knives, 395–396
  Bluetick Hound, 671
  Redbone Hound, 671
  Tennessee river pearl, 672
Colonel Knife Company,
    397–398
Colorado folding hunter, 672
Colt knives, 398–399
Commemorative knives, 16–17
  African safari set, 649
  American Armed Forces
    series, 649
  American bicentennial series,
    649
  American Eagle bicentennial
    series, 650
  automobile automation
    anniversary, 649
  Beretta, 650
  Boker bone-handled set, 653

Boker Spirit of America
    series, 653–654
Boker Storyteller set, 653
Boker-Wiss commemoratives,
    651–652
Bonnie and Clyde
    commemorative, 655
Buck, the Canoeist, 659
Buck bicentennial, 655
Buck Bugling Elks, 657
Buck commemorative Bowie,
    658–659
Buck Cutlery World knife, 655
Buck Ducks Unlimited, 658
Buck Freedom Trapper, 655
Buck Golden Eagle, 658
Buck Grand Slam set, 655
Buck Grizzly, 655
Buck Redbone set, 656
Buck silver anniversary
    commemorative, 656–657
Buck Yellowhorse knives, 657
Buford Pusser
    commemorative, 659
Case collector sets, 659–670
Case Texas special, 697
Case trapper
    commemoratives,
    702–703
Coal Miner, 670–671
Coleman/Western
    commemorative, 694
Coleman/Western Texas
    Bowie, 671
Colonel Coon Bluetick Hound,
    671
Colonel Coon Redbone Hound,
    671
Colonel Coon Tennessee river
    pearl, 672
Colorado folding hunter, 672
Country Music Legends knife,
    679

Courthouse Whittler series,
    695
Covered Bridge, 695
Custer's Last Fight, 697
Elvis Presley commemorative,
    672
Gator set, 695
general commemorative, 695
George Washington Bowie,
    672
George Washington Valley
    Forge Whittler, 672
Gerber MK II survival knife,
    673
Guns that Tamed the Wild
    West, 695
Jim Bowie's knife, 673
Johnny Cash commemorative,
    673
Kentucky Derby, 696
Kissing Crane anniversary
    knives, 673–674
Kissing Crane reproduction
    series, 675
Knife Collector's Club series,
    676–677
Knife Collector's trapper, 696
Knife World Ambassador's
    knife, 679
Knife World First Edition,
    677–678
Knife World Second Edition,
    678
Lou Gehrig knife, 679
Mac tools knife, 696
Moran 45th anniversary
    knife, 679–680
National Knife Collectors
    Association knives,
    680–682
Pennsylvania tricentennial,
    682
Puma 215th anniversary
    commemorative, 682

Puma African Big Five
    collector series, 682
Queen Drake oil well
    commemorative, 683
Randall knives, 50th
    anniversary edition, 684
Remington candy stripe
    toothpick, 685
Remington silver bullet, 684
R. Klaas 155th anniversary,
    683–684
Schrade I*XL series, 687
Schrade Bear cult, 685
Schrade Buffalo Bill, 686
Schrade Grand Dad's Old
    Timer, 685
Schrade Jim Bowie, 686–687
Schrade Kachina, 687–688
Schrade Liberty Bell/Paul
    Revere/Minuteman
    series, 685
Schrade–Loveless Limited
    Edition hunter, 686
Schrade Sundance, 686
Schrade Thunderbird, 686
Sears 100th anniversary
    knife, 688
second-cut mint sets, 688
Shaw-Liebowitz bicentennial
    series, 689–690
Shaw-Liebowitz wildlife
    series, 690
silver anniversary to Old
    Timer, 686
silver coin-American Eagle
    commemorative set, 691
Smith & Wesson collector set,
    691
Smoky Mountain trapper
    series, 691
Star Spangled Banner
    commemorative Bowie,
    691
Statue of Liberty, 692

Commemorative knives
  (continued)
  Stock Car Legends, 692–693
  Teddy Roosevelt
    commemorative, 693
  Tennessee Homecoming,
    693–694
  Thirteen Colony series, 696
  Tomb of the Unknown Soldier,
    699
  Tom Seaver commemorative,
    698
  Triple Crown series, 699
  Vietnam Veterans
    commemorative, 699
  Whaling knife, 698
  Winchester limited-edition
    sets, 699–701
  Wiss Whittler, 698
  World War II Victory
    collection, 701
Counterfeit knives, 21–26
Country Music Legends knife,
  679
Courthouse Whittler series, 695
Covered Bridge, 695
Crandall Cutlery Company, 400
Cripple Creek Cutlery, 400–403
Custer's Last Fight, 697
Custom knives, 15–16
  general information, 48–52
  makers of, 57–98

Dealers, as source for knives, 31

Eagle Pocketknife Company,
  403–404
Electric Cutlery Company, 404
Elvis Presley commemorative,
  672
Ernst Bruckman, 206
Eye Brand, 404–405

Factory knives, 13–15
Fight'n Rooster, 405–408
Flea markets, as source for
  knives, 28–29
Frost Cutlery Company, 408
Fruit knives, 18
  American, 101–102, 104–105
  English knives/forks, 102–104
  general information, 99–101

Garage/estate sales, as source
  for knives, 28
Gator set, 695
General commemorative, 695
George Ibberson & Company,
  413
George Schrade Knife Company,
  408–409
George Washington Bowie, 672
George Washington Valley Forge
  Whittler, 672
George Wostenholm & Son
  Cutlery Company,
  644–645
Gerber Legendary Blades,
  409–410
Gerber MK II survival knife,
  673
Grading knives, 194–195
Guns that Tamed the Wild West,
  695

Handle materials, 112–113
Handle shields, types of, 112
Henry Sears & Son, 412–413
Hibbard, Spencer and Bartlett,
  412
Holley Manufacturing
  Company, 411
Honk Falls Knife Company,
  411–412

Howard Cutlery Company, 412
Humason & Beckley, 410

Imperial Knife Company,
    413–414

J.A. Henckels, 410–411
Jim Bowie's knife, 673
Johnny Cash commemorative,
    673
J. Russell & Company, 529–530

Ka-Bar Cutlery Company, Inc.
    history of company, 414–415
    knives with dog's head
        shields, 417–418
    multiblade knives, 445–447
    one-blade knives, 419–423
    stampings, 417
    three-blade knives, 438–445
    two-blade knives, 423–438
Keen Kutter, 448–461
Kentucky Derby, 696
Kinfolks, Inc., 462
Kissing Crane
    anniversary knives, 673–674
    powderhorns, 674
    reproduction series, 675
Knife collecting
    clubs for, 707–714
    counterfeit knives, 21–26
    dating information, 190–191
    factors affecting values,
        193–195
    future view, 196–197
    grading knives, 194–195
    historical view, 5–8
    literature related to, 715–720
    location of manufacture, 189
    patent numbers/dates,
        191–192

patent/trademarks/steel type,
    189–190
reasons for, 9–11
restored knives 22–23
sources for
    auctions, 29–30
    club swap meets, 30
    dealers, 31
    flea markets, 28–29
    garage/estate sales, 28
    knife shows, 31–33
    mail order, 30
specialization in
    Bowie knives, antique, 17
    commemorative knives,
        16–17
    custom knives, 15–16
    factory knives, 13–15
    military knives, 17–18
    silver fruit knives, 18
    trend knives, 19–20
Knife Collectors Club series,
    676–677
Knife collector's trapper, 696
Knife shows, as source for
    knives, 31–33
Knife World
    Ambassador's knife, 679
    First Edition, 677–678
    Second Edition, 678
Knives
    historical view, 3–4
    listing of manufacturers,
        115–188
    nomenclature of 106–113

Lackawanna Cutlery Company,
    463
Landers, Frary and Clark,
    463–464
Limited-edition knives, 16–17
Lou Gehrig knife, 679

Mac tools knife, 696
Maher and Grosh, 464
Mail order, as source for knives, 30
Manufacturers
   listings of manufacturers, 155–188
   See also specific manufacturers
Marble's Arms and Manufacturing Company, 466–467
Meriden Cutlery Company, 467
Military knives, 17–18
Miller Brothers Cutlery Company, 467–468
Moran 45th anniversary knife, 679–680

Napanock Knife Company, 468–469
National Knife Collectors Association knives, 680–682
New York Knife Company, 469–470
Northfield Knife Company, 470

Pal Cutlery Company, 471
Parker Cutlery Company, 472–475
Pen knives, styles/shapes of, 111
Pennsylvania tricentennial, 682
Platts, 475–476
Pocketknives
   styles/shapes of, 110
Puma, 476–477
   African Big Five collector series, 682
   215th anniversary commemorative, 682

Queen Cutlery Company, 477–478
Queen Drake oil well commemorative, 683

Randall knives, 50th anniversary edition, 684
Remington
   bullet reproductions, 505–507
   candy stripe toothpicks, 685
   handle shields, 480
   history of company, 479–480
   listing of knives, 481–505
   pattern numbers, 480
   silver bullet, 684
   stamping, 480–481
Restoration of knives, 22–23
Robert Klaas Company, 462–463
   Klaas 155th anniversary, 683–684
Robeson Cutlery Company
   history of company, 507–508
   listing of knives, 508–528

Schatt & Morgan, 530–534
Schrade Cutlery
   Bear cult, 685
   Buffalo Bill, 686
   history of company, 535–536
   I*XL series, 687
   Grand Dad's Old Timer, 685
   Jim Bowie, 686–687
   Kachina, 687–688
   Liberty Bell/Paul Revere/ Minuteman series, 685
   listing of knives, 538–589
   numbering system of, 536
   pattern numbers, 537–538
   sundance, 686
   thunderbird, 686

Sears 100th anniversary knife,
    688
Second-cut mint sets, 688
Shapleigh Hardware, 589–602
Shaw-Liebowitz
    bicentennial series, 689–690
    wildlife series, 690
Silver coin–American Eagle
        commemorative set, 691
Smith & Wesson collector set,
    691
Smoky Mountain trapper series,
    691
Star Spangled Banner
        commemorative Bowie,
    691
Statue of Liberty, 692
Stock Car Legends, 692–693

Teddy Roosevelt
        commemorative, 693
Tennessee Homecoming,
    693–694
Thirteen Colony series, 696
Tomb of the Unknown Soldier,
    699
Tom Seaver commemorative,
    698

Trend knives, 19–20
Triple Crown series, 699

Ulster Knife Company, 602
United Cutlery, 602–605
Utica Cutlery Company, 606

Valley Forge, 606
Van Camp Hardware, 606–607
Vietnam Veterans
        commemoratives, 699

Walden Knife Company,
    607–608
Wester Brothers, 608–609
Western Cutlery Company,
    609–612
Whaling knife, 698
Winchester
    history of company, 613
    limited-edition sets, 699–701
    listing of knives, 613–640
    reproductions, 640–644
Wiss Whittler, 698
World War II Victory collection,
    701

FLEA MARKETS FOR FUN *AND* PROFIT!

Embark on a treasure hunt with *The Official® Directory to U.S. Flea Markets*, which takes us from coast to coast, covering America's best flea markets and detailing essential facts for bargain hunters, browsers, *and* dealers!

MAKE THIS BOOK A PERMANENT ADDITION TO YOUR CAR'S GLOVE COMPARTMENT!

RIGHT ON TARGET!

The Official® Price Guide to Antique and Modern Firearms is triggering sales with its detailed, informative listings!

- More than 32,000 prices for firearms manufactured from the 1600s to the 1980s.
- Complete analysis of the effect of the U.S. import regulations on the firearms market.
- Covers antique *and* modern firearms, both American and foreign.